Bourbon Spain

A History of Spain

General Editor: John Lynch

Bourbon Spain

1700–1808

John Lynch

Basil Blackwell

First published in 1989

Basil Blackwell Ltd
108 Cowley Road, Oxford, OX4 1JF, UK

Basil Blackwell Inc.
3 Cambridge Center
Cambridge, Massachusetts 02142, USA

British Library Cataloguing in Publication Data

A CIP catalogue record for this book is available from the British Library

Library of Congress Cataloging in Publication Data
Lynch, John, 1927–
  Bourbon Spain, 1700–1808/John Lynch.
     p.   cm.
  Bibliography: p.
  Includes index.
  ISBN 0-631-14576-1
  1. Spain – History – Bourbons, 1700–   I. Title.
DP192.L96   1989
946´.054–dc19
                                89-867
                                CIP

Typeset in 11 on 13 pt Garamond
by Joshua Associates Ltd., Oxford
Printed in Great Britain by
The Camelot Press Ltd., Southampton

Contents

Plates

All plates are reproduced by kind permission of the Museo del Prado, Madrid

Maps

Tables

Currency Glossary

Maravedí The basic unit of account.

Real Standard silver coin; equalled 34 maravedís. The *real de a ocho* equalled 272 maravedís.

Ducado Ducat. Originally a gold coin but by the seventeenth century a unit of account; equalled 375 maravedís.

Escudo Standard gold coin; equalled 450 maravedís.

Peso American treasure was expressed in pesos. The *peso de mina* equalled 450 maravedís. But this usage ceased in the course of the seventeenth century and the normal unit became the *peso fuerte*, or the *peso de a ocho reales*, which equalled 272 maravedís. For purposes of conversion it equalled 20 *reales de vellón*.

Vellón A copper coin.

Lliura A Catalan pound; equalled 10 reales or just under a ducat.

Abbreviations

AGI	Archivo General de Indias, Seville
AGS	Archivo General de Simancas
BAE	*Biblioteca de Autores Españoles*
BL	British Library, London
HAHR	*Hispanic American Historical Review*
JLAS	*Journal of Latin American Studies*
PRO	Public Record Office, London

Preface

Bourbon Spain, unlike the Spain of the Habsburgs, has been forgotten by British historians. Yet a century in which Spaniards increased their numbers, their output, and in some cases their wealth, a power which lost Gibraltar and colonized California, a monarchy which tolerated the Inquisition and patronized Goya, and a king who fled from a mob one year and expelled the Jesuits the next, cannot be without interest. This at any rate has been the view of Spanish historians who, seconded by their French and North American colleagues, have in the last twenty-five years transformed our knowledge of eighteenth-century Spain, especially its economic life, rural conditions, intellectual trends, and relations with America. Some of the most original results are seen in the field of regional history – that of Andalucía, Catalonia, Galicia, Castile itself – and it is hoped that this dimension is reflected in the present work. But eighteenth-century Spain was more than the sum of its regions. The Bourbons helped to make Spain a nation state, issued policy directives for the whole country, and could see, as the historian can see, that the flow of ideas did not stop at regional boundaries. So the present work has a national rather than a regional framework; this was how the Spanish Bourbons saw their country and this was the Spain which they ruled. A second concern of the author has been to readjust the chronological framework of the period and in the process to pay due attention to the earlier Bourbons, without neglecting the more familiar reign of Charles III and the crisis which followed. A third task of the historian of eighteenth-century Spain is to pick his way through a number of inherited ideas, to look critically at concepts such as 'enlightened despotism' and 'Bourbon reform', and to assess the balance between tradition and reform in the first century of Bourbon Spain.

The book acknowledges first its debt to the recent work of Spanish historians and the researches of other scholars. It draws too on contemporary narrative sources which are available in some abundance for this period. Finally, it incorporates archival material from Spain and England. The correspondence of the intendants in the Achivo General de Simancas illustrates the working of the administration and agrarian conditions in the regions. In the Public Record Office, London, British diplomatic and consular reports from Spain contain eyewitness accounts of events and intelligence on the power and wealth of Spain. It was a matter of vital interest to Britain to be accurately informed of the naval power, the war potential, and the colonial income of its rival, and it is this concern which gives the British material particular relevance.

I am grateful to Leonardo León for his expert research assistance in London. I am also pleased to record my thanks to the Archivo General de Simancas, the Public Record Office, the British Library, the Library of University College London, and the Institute of Latin American Studies. Finally, I am indebted to my daughter, Caroline, for her invaluable help in preparing the typescript for publication.

J. L.

1

The Hispanic World in 1700

The first century of Bourbon Spain was a century of growth, when Spaniards multiplied, production rose, and expectations increased beyond resources. While the monarchs spent extravagantly on palaces and pastimes in Madrid, San Ildefonso and Aranjuez, the majority of their subjects were engaged in an unequal struggle, as nobles competed for land, priests for tithes, the government for taxes, and the people for food. Modernization became a need as well as a fashion, and the conviction grew that Spain had to change to survive. Yet Bourbon Spain was the same Spain as Habsburg Spain. The new dynasty did not suddenly transform the lives of the Spaniards, improve the quality of their government, or increase the power of their country. The year 1700 was not a parting of the ways, a transition from weak to strong monarchy, from old to new empire, from depressed to buoyant economy. The decades before and after 1700 were a continuation of the unbroken course of Spanish history, merging into a middle ground of proximate solutions to permanent problems.

Were the Bourbons even an improvement on the Habsburgs? Were the new monarchs capable of breaking the mould of mediocrity in which Spanish government had long been cast? No doubt royal government suffered after 1665 from a royal weakling. The last Habsburg was a forlorn figure, infirm in mind and body, incapable of ruling personally for any length of time and, most awkward of all, of producing an heir to the throne. But Spain had councils, ministers and secretaries, and Spanish government was held together still by experienced bureaucrats, their efficiency impaired perhaps by excessive numbers, sale of office, and innate factionalism, but well capable of administering a world empire. They needed to be, for the Bourbons were not brilliant. Philip V, religious maniac one minute, sex addict the next, was in some ways even less qualified to rule than Charles II, and Spaniards had to wait half a century before their government was rescued by Charles III, a giant among Bourbon midgets.

The principal flaws in royal government were not the monarchs nor the bureaucrats but the institutions. The power of the crown was diminished by regional autonomy and aristocratic privilege, both of which prevented it from treating all its subjects as equal before the law and before the tax collector. The constitutions of Aragon, Catalonia and Valencia made these regions privileged enclaves and gave them a quasi-autonomy out of step with the rest of Spain. True, the king was able to call cortes and appoint officials, but he had to negotiate taxes and troops, the two prerequisites of sovereignty, and negotiations were never easy. These were not universal rights but the preserve of privileged elites, and the regional resistance to Castilian control was not a popular resistance but one to protect the interests of a ruling group. Spain was a cluster of ruling groups. The Basque provinces, though part of Castile, had ancient *fueros* (charter rights) which made taxation and conscription difficult. Their political identity was marked by a customs frontier which followed the course of the Ebro, an anachronism of doubtful benefit to the regional economy but valuable to the collective urge to defy Madrid. Even in Castile itself the crown did not possess absolute power. By design or default there had been a process of devolution from the centre towards local administration of taxation, military resources, and justice; in the course of the seventeenth century legal institutions under municipal control gained power at the expense of royal justice.[1] And what the cities did not acquire the aristocracy snapped up, spreading the net of seigneurial jurisdiction over the length and breadth of Spain. By the end of the seventeenth century, therefore, the large and apparently active bureaucracy in Madrid was not an instrument of absolutism or an agent of centralization but a mediator between the sovereign and his subjects, dealing with nobles, churchmen, tax-farmers, urban oligarchies and other local interests who collaborated with the crown rather than obeyed it.

Spanish statesmen were conscious of weakness at the centre. The count-duke of Olivares sought to reform the rigid constitutional structure of the monarchy in order to recover royal authority, tax the

---

[1] I. A. A. Thompson, 'The Rule of Law in Early Modern Castile', *European History Quarterly*, 14 (1984), pp. 221–34; Richard L. Kagan, *Lawsuits and Litigants in Castile 1500-1700* (Chapel Hill, NC, 1981), pp. 210–11.

regions, and tame the aristocracy, rightly seeing that by the early seventeenth century the Habsburg system was out of joint with the times. As the empire expanded, accumulated more territory, and acquired more enemies, so the costs of defence increased and reached the point when neither ordinary taxation, Indies revenue, or deficit financing were enough to keep the monarchy afloat. Meanwhile fiscal distortion not only protected the privileged, social and regional, but also harmed the economy; it concentrated capital in state loans, deterred accumulation for investment, taxed productive enterprise, and still did not produce enough to defend Spain. Olivares, therefore, strove to strengthen the crown, overcome the enemy within, the regional elites and Castilian nobles, and to integrate the whole of Spain into a centralized monarchy, providing opportunities for all in return for service from all.[2] These were radical reforms, launched at a bad time for reformers, when the king was weak, society resistant to change, and the aristocracy determined to increase their power not relinquish it.

Olivares fell, reform was abandoned, and Spain returned to its old ways. The crown rebuilt its relations with the nobility, reduced its demands for money and service, and left its powerful subjects supreme in their local fiefdoms.[3] But the monarchy could not return to pre-reform conditions. Defence problems mounted, financial requirements increased, and the twin enemies of change, the nobility and the bureaucracy, dug in their heels more firmly. The Castilian nobility were understood in the sixteenth century to have abandoned political pretensions in return for economic and social concessions, and in the knowledge that they were potentates on their own estates. This was no longer true; they now enjoyed power and privilege at the centre of the political stage and for the rest of the seventeenth century they remained high in status, wealth, and influence. Contemporaries of Philip V looked back in amazement at the late seventeenth century, when the principal magnates were accustomed to be, as a chronicler of the reign observed, 'the idols of the kingdom, despotic too, without that respect for justice and the sovereign on which peaceful government depends'.[4] Grandees, *titulos* and *caballeros*, they all jealously guarded their privileges. Spanish law treated the powerful and the weak as different species; not for nobles

[2] J. H. Elliott, *The Count-Duke of Olivares. The Statesman in an Age of Decline* (New Haven, Conn., 1986), pp. 677–8.

[3] R. A. Stradling, *Philip IV and the Government of Spain 1621-1665* (Cambridge, 1988), pp. 167–8.

[4] Vicente Bacallar y Sanna, marqués de San Felipe, *Comentarios de la guerra de España e historia de su rey Felipe V, el animoso* (*BAE*, 99, Madrid, 1957), p. 22.

the horrors of torture, the degradation of flogging, the rigours of a common prison, or service in the galleys. Exemption from taxation and immunity from the full range of the law raised them above the rest of Spaniards and gave them a head start in the competition for resources. Their own seigneurial jurisdiction made them monarchs in miniature, empowering them to appoint officials, collect taxes, and take feudal dues in areas which were not necessarily even their own estates. In the course of time they diversified their assets – estate production, seigneurial dues, rents and leases from tenants, government *juros* or annuities – and if one source of income failed another came to the rescue. They protested their poverty, but Olivares did not believe them nor did the rest of Spaniards. Even if they did fall on hard times, they could not be imprisoned for debt, their estates were secured by entail, and they obtained exemption from the tax on *juros*.[5]

Government by oligarchy was not necessarily stable government. The aristocracy were quick to notice rivals and usurpers and to defend functions which they regarded as exclusive to themselves. The *validos*, or royal favourites, of the seventeenth century, though obviously part of the nobility, were not their representatives; they were leaders of their own *clientela*, their own patronage network, monopolizing the crown and antagonizing the rest of the elite. Divided by factional and family rivalries, the aristocracy were far from being a cohesive ruling class. But they possessed an important power base, the councils, and it was here that they perpetuated their influence at the centre. The conciliar bureaucrats were products not of socially mobile groups but of wealthy landed families, and many of them knew each other from university days in the aristocratic *colegios mayores*. Graduates of these colleges, the *colegiales*, were appointed to 70 per cent of all vacancies in the council of Castile under Philip IV and Charles II, and it was they who fashioned the alliance of nobles and officials into a powerful interest group, a curb on the crown and a restraint on reformers. Conciliar government reached its peak in the reign of Charles II. As the French technocrat Jean Orry observed in 1703, 'It is the councils which rule the state and allocate all the offices, all the favours, and all the revenues of the kingdom.'[6]

The aristocracy lived for most of the year in their town houses but they derived their income from the country. Rural Spain was divided

[5] Henry Kamen, *Spain in the Later Seventeenth Century, 1665-1700* (London, 1980), pp. 226–59.

[6] Quoted by Janine Fayard, *Les membres du Conseil de Castille à l'époque moderne (1621-1746)* (Geneva/Paris, 1979), p. 171.

starkly into landlords and peasants: on the one hand, higher nobility and clergy, who monopolized ownership of land and enjoyed exemption from taxation; on the other, peasant farmers and landless labourers, who received no special protection from the state and enjoyed few other advantages in life. The most productive of these groups, the peasant smallholder, suffered the greatest burdens; they worked simply to meet their payments – to king, church, landlord, seigneurial lord, not to mention the debt collector. Agricultural communities of this kind rarely produced a surplus or a profit; all their earnings went in rent, dues and debts, an outflow that helped to destroy the peace and prosperity of rural Spain and also to depopulate it.[7]

An agrarian structure so rigid was unlikely to be greatly productive or fully commercialized. Spanish agriculture was fettered by the absence of a 'national' market and operated in small local units within the confines of regional trade.[8] Self-sufficiency is not in itself a flaw; subsistence agriculture implies a certain security. But in these enclosed communities landowners and *señores* – the *poderosos* as they were often called – were able to monopolize the limited trade in grain, holding back supplies until spring, when the peasants had consumed their own crop and were forced to buy at inflated prices, or holding back in good years to sell at a higher price in times of dearth. Such an economy, fruit of inequality, further perpetuated land concentration, seigneurial power, technical inertia, and a tendency to famine. Protected by monopoly, landowners had no stimulus to improve and compete, much less to invest in the economy. Peasants without savings, landowners without incentives, these were classical ingredients of stagnation, not only in agriculture but also in industry. Why invest in industry when peasants had nothing to spend and landowners could buy foreign imports? So Spain was left with a subsistence industry in which simple manufactures were produced by artisans for sale in local markets, while the more profitable urban markets were supplied from abroad. In the coastal regions even grain was purchased abroad, a cheaper and quicker transaction than was available in the peninsula but one which again deprived Castile of national market incentives.

The limitations of pre-industrial life were apparent all over the interior. Even Andalucía, rich in possibilities, had an agrarian economy structured upon self-sufficiency. True, its wine and oil supplied Seville,

---

[7] Kamen, *Spain in the Later Seventeenth Century*, pp. 195–204.

[8] Carla Rahn Phillips, *Ciudad Real, 1500-1750: Growth, Crisis, and Readjustment in the Spanish Economy* (Cambridge, Mass., 1979), pp. 62–4.

Madrid and America too, but by the end of the seventeenth century production had not engendered more than a limited market economy, frustrated still by latifundism and primitive transport. Agricultural output expanded only as the population grew and ploughed up more land, while marketable surpluses were generated largely through the imperatives of tithes and rents. Self-sufficiency was also characteristic of the Basque countryside. As the arms industry declined and iron production was reduced to raw materials, Bilbao became a medium of wool exports and the import of European goods for luxury consumers in Madrid. In eastern Spain, with the exception of Barcelona and its hinterland, agriculture withdrew into increased self-sufficiency, while industry and with it regional trade fell into recession. These were bleak times for Spain, and it was some decades before there were signs of remission. In the years around 1680 coastal regions began to emerge from depression as they were drawn into expanding European and American trade, and agricultural surpluses began to make their way to overseas markets. This recovery had few linkages with the Castilian interior, which remained locked in subsistence farming, its only market the consumers of Madrid; and Madrid consumed not only the products of agriculture but also its profits, sucking in rents, tithes and taxes and returning nothing in investment.[9] Yet even Castile showed signs of revival, in response not to external stimuli but to its own population growth, not as early as 1680 but in the years after 1685.[10]

Rural Spain was the heart of the economy and the harvest was its life-blood. The whole of the population from princes to peasants watched the harvest. According to its abundance or scarcity there would be profits or losses for proprietors and *señores*, plenty or poverty for the mass of the people, food or starvation for those at the bottom. Until rural Spain came out of recession there could be no talk of recovery. In the seventeenth century the three great enemies of society were plague, drought and inflation; as the preachers of the time put it, Spaniards paid the penalty for acts of God and the folly of man. The first blow was struck by the plague. In the years 1676–84 the last of three major

    [9] David R. Ringrose, *Madrid and the Spanish Economy, 1560-1850* (Berkeley/Los Angeles, Calif., 1983), pp. 312–16.
    [10] On the nature and chronology of Spain's emergence from depression see Antonio Domínguez Ortiz. 'La crisis de Castilla en 1677–1687', *Revista Portuguesa de Historia*, 10 (1962), pp. 436–51, and *Instituciones y sociedad en la España de los Austrias* (Barcelona, 1985); Henry Kamen, 'The Decline of Castile: the last crisis', *Economic History Review*, 2nd ser., 17 (1964–5), pp. 63–76, and *Spain in the Later Seventeenth Century*, pp. 67–112; José Calvo Poyato, 'La última crisis de Andalucía en el siglo XVII: 1680–1685', *Hispania*, 46, 164 (1986), pp. 519–42.

epidemics of the seventeenth century penetrated the peninsula, spreading infection from Cartagena to Murcia and Valencia, then to Málaga and throughout Andalucía, less lethal perhaps than previous plagues but devastating in its sheer duration. The effects were felt not only in mortality but in the cost to local communities; taxes were raised to pay for guards and patrols to impose quarantine; agriculture was deprived of labour, trade of goods and transport. Year after year the epidemic fed on southern Spain, dormant during the winter but returning in spring and summer to terrorize the population. In the southern Córdoba area of Andalucía 74.8 per cent of those infected died, and deaths amounted to 5.5–6.5 per cent of the population.[11] And plague was followed by an epidemic of typhus which took a further toll of life and labour in Andalucía and Castile in the years 1683–5.

In the wake of disease came agrarian crisis. This began in 1683 with a year of drought during which not a drop of rain fell in Andalucía until December and the crop was totally lost. As drought destroyed production so it damaged social relations, provoking fierce disputes over irrigation rights between rival landlords and between landlords and peasants. The combined effects of drought and plague plunged Andalucía into one of its worst ever subsistence crises in which search for food became a daily anxiety and prices soared beyond the means to pay. Oil, bread and other essentials were scarce and costly. People starved; prayers were offered; and preachers called the faithful to repentance. But when the rains came, far from bringing relief, they carried another calamity. It rained in torrents; the river Guadalquivir overflowed its banks, fields were submerged, towns and villages isolated, bridges destroyed, roads unpassable. These inundations ruined the crops of 1684, while cattle were slaughtered for short-term profit. It was only in 1685 that production recovered and life improved. By this time, however, the government had added its own share of misery. The massive 75 per cent devaluation of the currency in February 1680 reduced the value of a mark of vellon from 12 to 3 reales, a striking example of strong government in a weak reign, though not one appreciated by contemporaries; together with the partial devaluation of silver in 1686, this measure brought hitherto rampant inflation under control for the rest of the century and produced long-term benefits in monetary stability.[12] But the immediate effects were more than people could bear. In much of rural Castile and Andalucía, in towns and villages

[11] Calvo Poyato, 'La última crisis de Andalucía', p. 531.
[12] Earl J. Hamilton, *War and Prices in Spain 1651-1800* (Cambridge, Mass., 1947), pp. 20–1, 219.

throughout the country, labourers received no wages, workers were unpaid, taxes were ignored, local trade was paralysed, and people lost their savings. Spain broke out of the inflationary spiral, it is true, but the medicine almost killed the patient.

While Spain staggered from inflation to deflation, and its people were crushed by climate and contagion, there seemed little hope of 'recovery' for Castile. But Spanish society was resilient, and by 1685 the worst of the recession was over and people rose to rebuild their lives. Monetary stability began to restore confidence, epidemics to recede, and crops to grow once more. Even the weather improved and rural Spain entered the eighteenth century if not in good health at least out of danger. What were the signs of recovery?

The first indication was demographic. In spite of the plagues of 1647–52 and 1676–85, population figures began to level out and to increase from the 1660s.[13] In some sectors of the economy incipient growth now appeared. Catalans and Basques undertook a programme of industrial and commercial expansion which can be dated from the 1670s; from about 1680 new manufacturers and exporters were active in Barcelona, while Catalan agricultural production was growing and looking for markets abroad. State action was another symptom of recovery. The creation of the Committee for Trade in 1679 was important less for bringing specific projects to fruition than for evidence of state intervention in the economy and of investment in manufacturing.[14] Even Castile, in spite of the epidemics of 1676–85, achieved a rise in agrarian production. In Andalucía production levels in grain, responding unmistakably to population growth, were rising in the late seventeenth century; and production in Segovia, where output of wheat between 1640 and 1710 increased by 48 per cent and wool output quadrupled, began to reach late sixteenth-century levels.[15]

The benefits of growth, briefly and partially present before 1700, became more prolonged and more consistent in the following decades. Growth brought harder work for some, higher profits for others, and a stronger impulse to social change. After 1700 change was further accelerated by civil war which gave the central government the opportunity it needed to tame the regions and demote the aristocracy.

[13] Kamen, *Spain in the Later Seventeenth Century*, pp. 61–2.

[14] Ibid., pp. 75–81.

[15] Angel García Sanz, *Desarrollo y crisis del Antiguo Régimen en Castilla la Vieja. Economía y sociedad en tierras de Segovia, 1500-1814* (Madrid, 1977), p. 105; Kamen, *Spain in the Later Seventeenth Century*, pp. 89–90.

The proximity of the French mode of government and the vigour of its exponents in Spain enabled Philip V to strengthen the Spanish state and make it an instrument of innovation. Inheriting a trend towards recovery and encountering a new opportunity for absolutism, the crown and its servants encouraged further changes in Spanish life. The combined effect of state action and economic growth undermined the old social order. While status, precedence, and privilege certainly endured, the traditional society of estates in which nobles fought, churchmen prayed, and commoners paid taxes gave way in the course of the eighteenth century to a society of classes in which wealth rather than function determined social position and divided grandee from hidalgo, prelate from priest, proprietor from peasant, merchant from artisan. As the monarchy itself moved towards greater absolutism, so it spoke more clearly to the emerging classes, marginalizing the aristocracy, controlling the Church, and defining policy affecting merchants and manufacturers. Can we construct a chronology of these developments outside the traditional framework of dynasty and reign?

The Spanish eighteenth century was a century of demographic, agrarian, industrial and commercial growth, a period of change in political values, international power, and imperial policy. Growth began, in the years around 1685, as a recovery from the losses of the seventeenth century; it continued in a phase of moderate expansion until about 1740. The benefits of growth were unequally distributed between regions and social groups; they were more positive in the periphery than in the interior, among the higher nobility, the senior clergy, and the coastal bourgeoisie than among peasants and artisans. Population growth led to greater demand for agrarian products; aristocratic and ecclesiastical landowners thus began to profit from higher prices and respond to incentives to increase production; overseas trade expanded and returns from America increased. These trends led, in the decades after 1740, to a new phase of growth, and also to more obvious economic and fiscal distortion. The state thereupon intervened in an attempt to correct the more blatant imbalances in Spanish life, and in the period 1740–66 reformist ministers proposed a number of radical projects. But these were defeated by powerful interests and the crown stepped back, content to preside over marginal change in collaboration with privileged elites and with the support of an enlightened bureaucracy; agrarian growth was left to market forces, and the state concentrated its attention on overseas trade and colonial resources. As long as growth was assured within the prevailing framework of privilege and monopoly, the interest groups were satisfied and confrontation was avoided. This was the high season of enlightened absolutism, when a strong state guaranteed political stability, and outmoded structures were worked to the full to yield profits for landowners, income for the Church, and returns on colonial investments. If this was the Bourbon model, it lasted little over twenty years, from 1767 to 1790, during which time it produced satisfactory if unspectacular results; at least it satisfied Castilian nobles and coastal bourgeoisie.

But trends changed, obstacles emerged, and the model collapsed. From 1790 Spain was destabilized. Internally, growth could not be sustained, and as the economy went into recession it became clear that new ways of growth could only be created by abolishing privilege, liberalizing land policy, redistributing resources and enlarging the market. External shock precipitated the crisis: the French Revolution sharpened political divisions and led to foreign war; and war disrupted the colonial life-line and jeopardized American returns. The Spanish economy had boxed itself into a situation in which Castile produced grain and imported textiles, while Catalonia produced textiles and imported grain. The absence of a national market forced Spain into a permanent balance of payments deficit, which only its American income could cover. When that failed, crisis was inevitable.[16] At the same time as the economy seized up, the government was going rapidly bankrupt. The fatal and familiar mixture of economic recession and social privilege prevented full exploitation of taxable resources, and in time of war this led to crisis at the top, compounded again by loss of American revenue. A century of Bourbon promise ended in the years 1790–1808 not in fulfilment but in failure. And a century of imperial preoccupation was of no avail when American revenue was most needed.

The Spanish colonial monopoly was penetrated from early in the seventeenth century; foreigners traded in the fleets from Seville, others from island bases in the Caribbean, and yet others directly to the South Atlantic and the Pacific. In Spain itself European merchants conducted a flourishing re-export trade from Seville and Cadiz, made easier by the fraudulent practices of Spain's own merchants and more or less recognized by the authorities. The *indultos*, or fines, were meant to establish a compensation to the state for losses through fraud, and in the course of the century these came to involve the foreign merchant communities, whose activities were regarded as an acceptable risk and a

---

[16] Josep Fontana, *La quiebra de la monarquía absoluta 1814-1820 (La crisis del Antiguo régimen en España)* (Barcelona, 1971), pp. 52–3.

calculated loss. The growth of French trade to Cadiz and thereby to the Indies established a substantial breach in the monopoly and one in which the state itself connived: cloths exported from Rouen to Cadiz for re-export to America rose from a value of 6 million livres in 1676 to 12 million in 1686.[17] For fiscal reasons the state colluded with the *consulado*, or merchant guild, of Seville to keep the foreigners in the system through payment of compensation. In effect foreign and Spanish merchants in Andalucía collaborated in bribing Madrid to tolerate illegal practices in return for *donativos* of 3.5 million pesos and *indultos* of almost 6 million in fifty years (1650–1700). The process culminated in the transfer of the monopoly headquarters from Seville to Cadiz, where the opportunities for foreign intervention were greater. In this way certain privileged foreigners became part of the monopoly, enjoyed its fruits and payed its penalties.

Outside the fleets new points of entry were made from the early seventeenth century, and direct trade by foreigners soon outflanked the monopoly. From the Antilles English, Dutch, and French merchants established commercial contacts with the Spanish Caribbean and these gradually extended to the key ports of Cartagena and Portobello. Textiles from northern Europe, exported directly into Spanish colonial markets, undersold those from Spain, paying no taxes and bringing benefits to consumers and sellers alike. And this competition, directed at the very heart of the Spanish trading system, was a permanent thorn in Spain's flesh, for it was based on rival colonial possessions held by European powers. Meanwhile a direct trade to Buenos Aires was established and grew to significant levels in the second half of the seventeenth century; this was dominated by the Dutch, Portuguese, Spanish, and English, and became another sector of foreign penetration, reflecting a general expansion of European trade along the unexploited perimeters of the Spanish American economy. Trade through Buenos Aires was attracted by the silver of Potosí but did not synchronize with mining recession in Upper Peru in the years after 1650. This was an example of Atlantic trade plugging into an existing regional trade from which the provinces of the Río de la Plata earned silver in Potosí and with it the purchasing power to buy from European interlopers; and it could mean that interregional trade absorbed an increasing amount of the decreasing production of Potosí, or even that Potosí mining did not

---

[17] Albert Girard, *Le commerce français à Séville et à Cadix au temps des Habsbourgs* (Paris/Bordeaux, 1932), pp. 341–2.

decline as much as official figures indicate.[18] These are indications, too, that the monopoly was bypassed not only by foreigners but also by Americans. Intercolonial trade, for example between Peru, Mexico, and the Philippines, earned high profits for its participants and usually meant a corresponding loss for transatlantic merchants. In 1631, under pressure of the *consulado* of Seville, the crown forbad all trade between Mexico and Peru, a prohibition which endured for the rest of the century; but it was not taken seriously, and there were too many contraband outlets on the Pacific coast to permit strict control.[19]

The growth of intercolonial trade in the early seventeenth century presupposed the development of the colonial economies as producers of agricultural goods, wines, and even manufactures, all of which generated surplus for export to other colonies and established a pattern of intercolonial division of labour.[20] It also indicated the accumulation of capital, not for remittance to the metropolis but to make purchases within the colonial economies. This too eroded the monopoly, and signalled that the growth of independent economies in America was a permanent threat to Seville and one which it had to accept. Intercolonial trade was a consequence of demographic growth in the colonies, the increase of the mixed races, and the recovery of the devastated Indian populations from the middle of the seventeenth century. The Indians were now more closely integrated into the colonial economy as sellers of labour and consumers of merchandise, and they had to adjust their own production to have the means to pay tribute and fulfil their other obligations.

The growth of direct trade and the expansion of intercolonial trade implied the increasing freedom of America from monopoly control and a significant degree of colonial autonomy in economic matters. Change did not necessarily signify depression. Allowing for moderate cyclical fluctuations, the income of the Mexican treasury was sustained throughout the seventeenth century at a higher level than that of the late

[18] For the first hypothesis see Zacarías Moutoukias, *Contrabando y control colonial. El Río de la Plata y el espacio peruano en el siglo XVII* (Buenos Aires, 1988), p. 73 and the second, Enrique Tandeter, 'Buenos Aires and Potosí', paper presented at Congress, *Governare il Mondo: L'impero spagnolo dal XV al XIX secolo* (Palermo, 1988), p. 14, both references kindly supplied by the authors. On internal markets and regional integration see Carlos Sempat Assadourian, *El sistema de la economía colonial. Mercado interno, regiones y espacio económico* (Lima, 1982), pp. 72–5.

[19] Woodrow Borah, *Early Colonial Trade and Navigation between Mexico and Peru* (Berkeley/Los Angeles, Calif., 1954), pp. 124–7; María Encarnación Rodríguez Vicente, *El tribunal del consulado de Lima en la primera mitad del siglo XVII* (Madrid, 1960), pp. 244–52, 270.

[20] John Lynch, *Spain under the Habsburgs* (2nd edn, 2 vols, Oxford, 1981), II pp. 212–18, 244–8.

sixteenth century.[21] Zacatecas, which produced about one-third of Mexican silver, sustained its output beyond the time of a supposed depression. Production rose steadily from 1570 to the 1620s, and continued to increase until 1636 before falling back to levels not much lower than those registered in the 1580s and 1590s.[22] And judging by the figures of treasury income from Mexican silver, the mines were producing more at the end of the seventeenth century than at the beginning. Finally, the evidence indicates that an increasing proportion of public revenues remained in the colony and was not sent to Spain. Whereas in 1611–20 55 per cent of public revenue was sent abroad, only 21 per cent went abroad in 1691–1700. Although income of the colonial treasury increased throughout the century, the remittances to Spain fell from 10 million pesos in 1601–10 to 2.7 million in 1681–1700. The picture for Peru is less clear. Up to 1650 mining sustained its output and Potosí remained on stream; in the second half of the century output dropped, but the general trend was one of gradual recession rather than absolute collapse, and even this may have been less calamitous than supposed. The trend, moreover, punished Spain more than Peru. Whereas remittances into the Lima treasury dropped by 47 per cent compared to the previous fifty years, remittances to Castile dropped by 79 per cent.[23] The reasons were two-fold: Lima received less surplus from Upper Peru, while defence costs in the viceroyalty were climbing.

There is a presumption in favour of change rather than depression in seventeenth-century Mexico and of growing economic autonomy in Spanish America in general. There is a further hypothesis that when rising costs reduced the profits of mining and the purchasing power of silver declined, then less silver was exported and this helped to create in

[21] John J. TePaske, *La Real Hacienda de Nueva España: La Real Caja de México (1576-1816)* (Mexico, 1976); John J. TePaske and Herbert S. Klein, 'The Seventeenth-Century Crisis in New Spain: Myth or Reality?', *Past and Present*, 90 (1981), pp. 116–35. For a critical survey of the historiography and a suggested synthesis see Josep Fontana, 'Comercio colonial y crecimiento económico; revisiones e hipótesis', *La economía española al final del Antiguo Régimen. III. Comercio y colonias* (Madrid, 1982), pp. xi–xxxiv.

[22] P. J. Bakewell, *Silver Mining and Society in Colonial Mexico: Zacatecas 1546-1700* (Cambridge, 1971), p. 226.

[23] P. J. Bakewell, 'Registered Silver Production in the Potosí District, 1550–1735', *Jahrbuch für Geschichte von Staat, Wirtschaft und Gesellschaft Lateinamerikas*, 12 (1975), pp. 67–103; John J. TePaske, 'The Fiscal Structure of Upper Peru and the Financing of Empire', in Karen Spalding (ed.), *Essays in the Political, Economic and Social History of Colonial Latin America* (Newark, Del., 1982), pp. 76–80; TePaske and Klein, 'The Seventeenth-Century Crisis in New Spain', pp. 116–35; and TePaske and Klein *The Royal Treasuries of the Spanish Empire in America* (3 vols, Durham, NC, 1982), vol. I. For commentaries on use of evidence from colonial treasuries see *HAHR*, 64, 2 (1984), pp. 287–322.

America a more diversified economy.[24] There is still an element of uncertainty over mining production and over the evidence derived from tax returns. No doubt extraordinary fiscal pressure rather than economic growth can explain tax increases in the short term. But revenue expansion over a long period, comprising taxes based on production, can only take place if the economy is capable of sustaining it. The figures also indicate a change in the destination of colonial revenue. A colony without a revenue surplus for the metropolis, or with a decreasing surplus, need not be depressed but rather undergoing a degree of autonomous growth and freedom from the control of the colonial monopoly. There was a period between 1650 and 1750 when this was the case, when colonial revenue was employed on colonial administration, defence and services, and when major colonies allocated subsidies to lesser dependencies whose economies were linked to those of their sub-metropolis rather than directly to Spain. The fact that the revenues were spent in adjacent colonies rather than in their place of origin does not weaken the argument for colonial autonomy, any more than the expansion of inter-regional trade weakens it.[25] On the contrary, it is further evidence of American development.

While it may be true that the recession of silver mining and the cost of local administration and defence reduced the colonial surplus from the mid-seventeenth century, and that the colonies had reached a certain degree of self-sufficiency through investment of silver in their own economies, does it follow that the colonies were less dependent on their metropolis? In the first place, crown revenue was obviously only a fraction of the income from mining and commerce; the greatest capital resources were in private hands and their destination is more problematical. In the second place, the essential link was established by quality textiles, slaves, hardware, and paper, on all of which colonial life depended.[26] These were precisely high-cost commodities and they were supplied only from outside; so Spain continued to extract silver from Peru and Mexico in monopoly form. Many such imports, of course, were produced or distributed not by Spaniards but by foreigners, and

[24] H. and P. Chaunu, *Séville et l'Atlantique (1504-1650)* (8 vols, Paris, 1955–9), VIII, 1, 1, pp. 1128–33.

[25] Henry Kamen and J. I. Israel, 'The Seventeenth-Century Crisis in New Spain: Myth or Reality', *Past and Present*, 97 (1982), pp. 144–6, and John J. TePaske and Herbert S. Klein, 'A Rejoinder', ibid., pp. 156–61.

[26] Carlos Sempat Assadourian, 'La producción de la mercancía dinero en la formación del mercado interno colonial. El caso peruano, siglo XVI', in Enrique Florescano (ed.), *Ensayos sobre el desarrollo económico de México y América Latina, 1500-1975* (Mexico, 1979), pp. 232–5, 281–2.

profits were accordingly diverted abroad. Therefore, although Seville and later Cadiz continued to dominate the Indies trade as intermediaries, the formal metropolis no longer received exclusive benefit. If self-sufficiency was limited and dependence continued, this was not the primitive dependence of the sixteenth century but one in which the colonies had more options. We may call it a diluted dependence.

Spanish America, moreover, was not merely an Atlantic economy; it also had a strong internal market. The colonies lived by regional circulation of merchandise.[27] They produced and sold from region to region agricultural goods and some manufactures of local origin. The mining markets of Potosí and Zacatecas were important consumers, circulators and generators of growth. By the seventeenth century these colonial markets were primarily consumers of colonial products, compared to which European manufactures were relatively few.[28] The greater proportion of goods consumed before the eighteenth century – textiles, tobacco, foodstuffs – were produced by the colonies themselves. The growth of internal markets, of course, was not inconsistent with the entry of the colonies into the Atlantic economy. Spanish America had a dual economy: on the one hand, it was an internal market; on the other, it was a producer of precious metals and a consumer of European goods. These were complementary functions, and they were not under the exclusive control of the Spanish monopoly.

How did Spain respond to the shift of resources in the Atlantic world? Historiography once agreed that the Spanish American trade reached its peak at some point around 1600–20 and then receded, the victim of heavy taxation, sequestrations, and changing conditions in Spain and America. The second half of the seventeenth century was seen as the classical period of depression during which crown and commerce alike were starved of their saving silver. Official figures for treasure returns indicate a peak in 1581–1600, and from then onwards unremitting decline.[29] Trade as measured by tonnage reached its highest point in 1601–20; a downward trend began in the crisis of 1622–3 and continued

[27] Assadourian, *El sistema de la economía colonial*, pp. 85–8; Juan Carlos Garavaglia, *Mercado interno y economía colonial* (Mexico, 1983), pp. 20, 382–3.

[28] The trend towards inter-regional trade in the seventeenth century has been questioned. Was there a decline in such trade between the 1630s and 1670s, as the mining economies became depressed and the colonies suffered shortage of capital? See Murdo J. Macleod, 'Spain and America: the Atlantic trade 1492–1720', in Leslie Bethell (ed.), *The Cambridge History of Latin America, Volume I* (Cambridge, 1984), pp. 373–6.

[29] Earl J. Hamilton, *American Treasure and the Price Revolution in Spain, 1501-1650* (Cambridge, Mass., 1934), pp. 34–8.

rapidly until 1650.[30] The Spanish American trade, it was then assumed, remained depressed for the rest of the century.

The assumption is no longer valid. In the peninsula itself, as has been seen, there were signs of incipient growth in the last decades of the seventeenth century, the child and father of revival in the Atlantic economy. It is now clear that the greatest influx of precious metals in the whole century occurred precisely in the second half and was superior to the first half by more than 50 per cent.[31] It is also evident that the suppression of the burdensome *avería*, or defence tax, in 1660 inaugurated a new commercial policy and a steady recovery of the colonial trade which could be seen in the growth of exports to the Indies, the higher fleet valuations, the receipt of copious silver returns, the dramatic rise of *indultos*, and the commercial growth of Cadiz.[32] True, figures using shipping as a gauge of trade for 1650–1700 show a fall of 22 per cent of the century's total; and a 76.5 per cent loss of traffic between 1641 and 1701–10 suggests that the downward trend begun in 1620 continued and kept the Indies trade in a state of depression.[33] But official figures do not tell the whole story; while on the margin of the fleets there was much illegal shipping, within the official convoys fraudulent returns were normal occurrences.

Exports from Spain to America provide yet another guide. While the volume of exports measured in tonnage and number of ships may have been diminishing, the value of exports was increasing and pointed to a long-term upward trend in colonial trade from 1660.[34] Exports of olive oil, brandies, textiles, hardware and paper all rose substantially, with the sharpest rise from the 1670s and the most numerous commodities non-Spanish manufactured goods. The valuations of the fleets for fiscal purposes also increased, the *flotas* from 150 million maravedis in 1662 to 299 million in 1685, the *galeones* from 86 million in 1665 to 206 million

[30] Chaunu, *Séville et l'Atlantique*, VIII, 2, 2, pp. 917, 1236, 1276, 1299, 1330–45.

[31] Michel Morineau, *Incroyables gazettes et fabuleux métaux. Les retours des trésors américains d'après les gazettes hollandaises (XVIᵉ-XVIIIᵉ siècles)* (Cambridge, 1985), p. 249.

[32] Lutgardo García Fuentes, *El comercio español con América 1650-1700* (Seville, 1980), and 'En torno a la reactivación del comercio indiano en tiempo de Carlos II', *Anuario de Estudios Americanos*, 36 (1979), pp. 251–86.

[33] García Fuentes, *El comercio español con América*, pp. 164, 218; Antonio García-Baquero González, *Cádiz y el Atlántico (1717-1778)* (2 vols, Seville, 1976), I, p. 150, II, graphs 3, 4, 6, 7, 14, and the same author's 'Andalucía y los problemas de la carrera de Indias en la crisis del siglo XVII', *Coloquio de Historia de Andalucía* (1980), kindly provided by the author; for a comparison of various indices of American trade, 1651–1800, see Ringrose, *Madrid and the Spanish Economy*, pp. 223–7.

[34] García Fuentes, *El comercio español con América*, pp. 229–36, 239–326, and 'En torno a la reactivación del comercio indiano', pp. 263–6.

in 1695, further confirmation of the upward trend of exports and of the resurgence of the Indies trade. Europe was responding to sustained economic activity and consumer growth in the colonies, which were drawing in rising quantities of imports, while these in turn earned for Europe rising returns of precious metals in the period 1650–1700. These developments preceded Bourbon colonial innovation by many years and reinforce the view that *comercio libre* after 1765 reflected rather than created a long period of growth in the Atlantic economy.

The revival of the American trade was expressed in rich treasure returns. These are not easy to measure because of fraud, contraband, and direct trade, infringements which were covered to some extent by *indultos*. Official figures record that over 43 million pesos were remitted to Spain in 1659–1700, some 21 million of these for the crown.[35] But the quantities are not realistic, at least for the private sector, and the level of *indultos* would seem to imply much higher returns. Between 1684 and 1700 *indultos* rose extraordinarily over those of the previous three decades, reaching 500,000 pesos in 1684 and 1695. In 1698 the crown demanded a substantial *servicio* from the *consulado* of Seville, estimating that in that year the *almirante* of the *galeones* had illegally carried 11 million pesos and that of the *flota* 10 million.[36] But the most punitive *indulto* was that of 1692. On the departure of the *galeones* from Spain in 1690 a payment of half a million pesos had been demanded, a modest compensation for the great quantity of goods outside the register. On their return the *galeones* were threatened with an official inspection; to avoid this the *consulado* promptly offered a payment of 2.5 million pesos, which the crown accepted.

Amidst the cries of protest against the subsequent allocation of the *indulto*, which predictably favoured the main culprits, the Seville merchants and their French accomplices, it was stated by the Peruvian merchants that Peru produced each year about 6 million pesos in silver and gold; thus in five years between fleets it could have accumulated some 30 million pesos. Of these, two-thirds, or 20 million pesos, were employed in Portobello purchasing French, Genoese and English merchandise, Spanish goods being 'fewer and fewer'.[37] Silver was obviously flowing abroad through gaps in the monopoly. In fact the *galeones* of 1690 carried 36 million pesos from Peru, 27 million of which were spent in purchases in Portobello and Cartagena; the Peruvian

[35] García Fuentes, *El comercio español con América*, pp. 381–9.
[36] Ibid., p. 383.
[37] García Fuentes,'En torno a la reactivación del comercio indiano', pp. 269–70.

merchants travelling on the *galeones* therefore carried 9 million pesos. In the event, 40 million pesos were unloaded from the fleet. Figures of this magnitude are not exactly signs of depression, and on the evidence of export values and treasure returns it is reasonable to conclude that 'in the last three decades of the century the Indies trade experienced times of relative prosperity'.[38]

Treasure returns measured realistically point in the same direction.[39] These demonstrate that following a fall of treasure receipts towards 1650 – a consequence of wartime disruption of trade which held back precious metals in America – the quantities not only recovered in the second half of the century but were appreciably higher than those of the supposed peak of 1580–1620, and superior to those of the first half of the century by more than 50 per cent.[40] Moreover, the returns of precious metals during the first half of the eighteenth century, while respectable enough, were less impressive than those of the second half of the seventeenth century, except for the years around 1730. After 1750 they rose, though not continuously, and they remained thereafter at a high level, without however surpassing the old record until after 1780. Silver favoured the last Habsburg over the first Bourbon. The significance of these returns, of course, resides not only in the quantities, but in the changing conditions surrounding them, namely the presence of foreign nations in Seville and Cadiz, the distribution of profits, and the inferior position of Spain in a trade which theoretically she controlled.[41]

The period began with a torrent of treasure. The galleons of 1659 – to Santander – brought some 25 million pesos, 3.5 million of them for the crown, the best returns in one year since 1595. These were a preview of things to come, as contemporary gazettes continued to record incredible figures: 10 million pesos in 1666, 1671, 1672 and 1673; 18 million in 1682; 25 million in 1663 and 1693; 30 million in 1659, 1661, 1670, 1697; 36 million in 1686 and 1692, and 42 million in 1676. Receipts of this

[38] Ibid., p. 267.

[39] Morineau, *Incroyables gazettes et fabuleux métaux*, relies exclusively on non-official sources, that is Dutch and other European gazettes and French consular reports. These he presents as reliable, accurate and professional records, and more realistic than official statistics. It may be added that they are usually confirmed by eighteenth-century British consular reports from Cadiz.

[40] Morineau, *Incroyables gazettes et fabuleux métaux*, pp. 39, 249. There remains the question, how can increased flows of treasure be reconciled with the recession, or pause, or interlude, in American mining production in the late seventeenth century? There are three possibilities, suggested here as hypotheses: (1) recession in Potosí may be exaggerated in the official figures; (2) gold production may have compensated to some extent for decrease in silver output; (3) treasure remittances may have been drawn from accumulated resources preserved from more buoyant times.

[41] Ibid., p. 117.

magnitude easily broke the annual records of the sixteenth century; the 1595 peak of 25 million pesos was surpassed at least six times.[42] There was a difference, of course: fleets no longer crossed the Atlantic with the annual regularity of former times; mediocre years were followed by good years, and some were empty. Fluctuations were caused by international, economic and colonial factors; the plunge of 1680–4 was occasioned by European war which interrupted the rhythm of the convoys. Treasure returns, therefore, have to be grouped in quinquennia and calculations made in averages (see table 1.1).

The structure of the Spanish American trade in the last decades of the seventeenth century differed from that of the earlier period. By law one-third of cargo space was reserved for the Andalusian agricultural exports; these were almost exclusively wines and brandies, and in the period 1680–99 there was a decline of wine volume, counterbalanced by a rise in brandy shipments. The key export items, however, were not agricultural products but expensive linens, silks and woollens, which came to form the greater part of exports by value, and a high proportion of which were French. The destination of returns had also changed. Theoretically the new structure could have included Spanish merchants from other regions of Spain. But these were slow to take advantage of the breakdown of the monopoly. When the Catalans began to export from Cadiz, from about 1680, trading their wines, spirits and dried fruits against Venezuelan cacao, Cuban tobacco, and Central American

Table 1.1 American treasure returns by quinquennia in million pesos 1580-1699

1580–4	48	1620–4	50	1660–4	65
1585–9	43.2	1625–9	42.2	1665–9	61.3
1590–4	30.4	1630–4	39.8	1670–4	87
1595–9	78.4	1635–9	68.8	1675–9	84.5
1600–4	55.5	1640–4	45.2	1680–4	51.5
1605–9	51.8	1645–9	36.6	1685–9	78
1610–14	43.1	1650–4	39	1690–4	81.8
1615–19	47.4	1655–9	51.6	1695–9	65.5

Source: Michel Morineau, *Incroyables gazettes et fabuleux métaux. Les retours des trésors américains d'après les gazettes hollandaises (XVIe-XVIIIe siècles)* (Cambridge, 1985), pp. 250, 262, who revises the pre-1660 figures of Hamilton.

[42] Ibid., p. 237.

Table 1.2 Structure of Spanish American trade in 1686 in million livres

	Linens	Woollens	Silks	Garments	Wax	Hardware	Misc.	Total
France	10,004	2,740	1,440	2,359	500			17,043
Flanders	320	347		1,980	160			2,807
England	380	3,700		868	1,332			6,280
Holland	570	2,120	1,000	260	666	160	400	5,176
Hamburg	2,186					80		2,266
Genoa			5,366	1,590			375	7,331
Spain			1,200				1,200	2,400
Total	13,460	8,907	9,006	7,057	2,658	240	1,975	43,303

Source: Morineau, Incroyables gazettes et fabuleux métaux, p. 267.

cochineal, they offered little competition to Andalusian and foreign interests already established in Cadiz, and their breakthrough into the American trade had to await a later date.[43] The French were the clear leaders, followed by the Genoese, English, Dutch, Flemish, Spanish, and Germans (see table 1.2).

The figures embody Spain's Habsburg heritage, an empire invaded by rivals, an economy shorn of manufactures, a crown deprived of revenue. In the years 1660–75 the French took profits from America amounting annually to 12 millon livres tournois, the Genoese 7.5 million, the Dutch 6 million, and the English 4.5 million. In the years 1675–1700 these quantities increased: the French earned 13–14 million, the Genoese 11–12 million, the Dutch 10 million, and the English 6–7 million.[44] If the proportions received by the Seville merchants were decreasing, so were those of the crown. Around 1660 the crown returns amounted to 10–15 per cent of the total. This was more or less maintained in 1670–80, though with larger fluctuations caused by essential expenditure in America itself. Between 1680 and 1690 the royal share frequently dropped to 2–3 per cent, as taxes were lost to illicit trade and colonial revenue was pre-empted by colonial expenditure.[45] This was the permanent predicament of the Bourbons, how to realize their American assets. They spent the eighteenth century pushing up their share from 2 to 40 per cent, by taxing colonists, tightening control, and fighting off foreigners. In the process they gained a revenue and lost an empire.

---

[43] Carlos Martínez Shaw, *Cataluña en la carrera de Indias 1680-1756* (Barcelona, 1981), pp. 80-2.

[44] Morineau, *Incroyables gazettes et fabuleux métaux*, p. 302; John Everaert, 'Le commerce colonial de la "Nation Flamande" à Cadix sous Charles II', *Anuario de Estudios Americanos*, 28 (1971), pp. 139-51.

[45] Morineau, *Incroyables gazettes et fabuleux métaux*, pp. 288-9, 454.

2

The Bourbon Succession in War and Peace

The Spanish War of Succession

In 1700 Spain was a monarchy in search of a king. As Charles II, childless and near to death, desperately sought an heir for his kingdoms, states, and domains, European powers meticulously measured their rights and interests. The two major contenders were France and Austria. Both claims came through daughters of Philip IV: the first through Louis XIV's marriage to María Teresa, the second through the emperor's marriage to Margarita Teresa. Other powers too had an interest in this global expanse of territory and trade, for success to one would be danger to the rest. Therefore William III, speaking for England and Holland, insisted that Louis XIV agree to a partition treaty, dividing the inheritance between Austria and France. Partition, however, was abhorrent to Spain, to government and people alike, and on his deathbed Charles II left everything to the French candidate, Philip, duke of Anjou, second grandson of Louis XIV, exhorting him 'not to permit the slightest dismemberment or diminution of the Monarchy established by my forefathers to their greater glory'.[1]

Yet Spain was the object, not the arbiter, of these decisions. Here was an empire whose extension outstripped the means of defending it. In a predatory world Spain needed a protector as well as a successor. Only France was capable of guaranteeing the will of Charles II. Louis XIV could not resist the challenge; justice, strategy, and economics all compelled him to accept the will. But this was to break the partition treaty, and this meant war, a war for control of Spain and its world

[1] William Coxe, *Memoirs of the Kings of Spain of the House of Bourbon* (2nd edn, 5 vols, London, 1815), I, pp. 85–6.

empire.[2] Alignments were quickly established: France and Spain versus Austria and its allies, Bourbon versus Habsburg, Philip of Anjou, protégé of Louix XIV, versus the Archduke Charles, candidate of the Allies. In May 1702 the Grand Alliance – England, the Dutch Republic, and Austria – declared war on France and Spain. The anti-Bourbon cause was forged by fear that the union of France and Spain would create a super power, a trade monopoly and a protected market: so the Alliance perpetuated the basic concepts of partition. Spaniards, on the other hand, did not see themselves as subjects of a united monarchy; they wanted a king of their own, not a viceroy in disguise. Nor did they view the war as a dynastic conflict, remote from their real interests. For them it was a defence against dismemberment, against loss of territory, resources, revenues, employment and opportunities.[3]

Philip V, an unprepossessing youth of seventeen, entered Madrid on a rainy day in February 1701. His new subjects overcame their reserve and looked to him to make the Bourbon cause a Spanish one. They did not like his French entourage, but they gave the king respect and the priests called him 'vicar of God'. Philip therefore began his reign without open opposition: from some he received support, from others acceptance, from many indifference. Castile was obviously his heartland, but the regions too appeared loyal. He held a *cortes* in Barcelona in October 1701, confirming the Catalan *fueros* and receiving copious grants. While he campaigned in Italy – a measure of his security and complacency in Spain – his Savoyard queen, María Luisa, held a cortes in Zaragoza on 26 April 1702, swore to the *fueros* of Aragon, and accepted a modest grant. In the years 1700–4, therefore, Spain remained intact and in peace, and the Bourbon succession looked secure. Abroad, however, ominous signs appeared of that dismemberment which had haunted the last days of Charles II. In Italy the Austrians began to push for supremacy, while in Germany Marlborough's victory at Blenheim left the Spanish Netherlands next at risk. On both fronts it was only French arms which, until 1706, held the balance, while Spain was powerless to defend states hitherto regarded as integral parts of the monarchy. The Allies also attacked on a third front.

At sea Spain was no less vulnerable than by land, and the maritime powers soon began to penetrate its defences. Philip V had inherited

---

[2] M. A. Thomson, 'Louis XIV and the Origins of the War of the Spanish Succession', *Transactions of the Royal Historical Society*, 5th ser., 4 (1954), pp. 111–34.

[3] On the war in the peninsula see Henry Kamen, *The War of Succession in Spain 1700–15* (London, 1969), pp. 9–24.

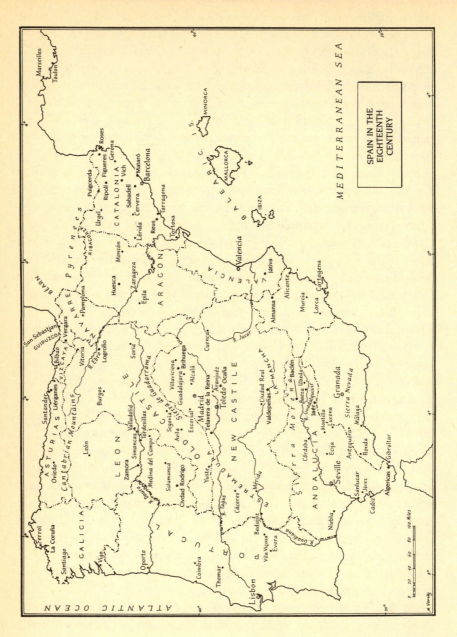

SPAIN IN THE
EIGHTEENTH
CENTURY

global commitments but only meagre naval resources. In the western Mediterranean Spain had only twenty-eight galleys, dispersed among her different possessions, in varying states of readiness, and hardly constituting a naval force. In the Atlantic she had greater sea power, but this was designed for a specific function and was fully extended in protecting trade and communications with America. In 1701 a total of twenty warships could be deployed in the Atlantic and the Caribbean, but there were no reserves and no resources for building more.[4] In the War of Succession Spain depended on French naval power for the protection of her imperial life-lines. Weakness invited aggression. An Anglo-Dutch fleet of fifty ships attacked Cadiz in August 1702, with the dual aim of raising Andalucía and commanding the Spanish end of the American trade. But the local population did not rise in their support. Unable to take Cadiz, and compromised by indiscipline among all ranks, the task force sacked Puerto de Santa María, inflicting such pillage, brutality and sacrilege that they destroyed any chance of the merchants or people of Andalucía supporting the cause of the archduke.[5] And for the rest of the war the province remained loyal to Philip.

On the way home the Allied force learnt that the Spanish treasure fleet, escorted from Mexico by a French squadron, had put into the bay of Vigo. They promptly attacked and destroyed the whole fleet, including seventeen French warships and sixteen Spanish vessels. The Spanish crown salvaged something from the disaster. In fact most of the bullion, though not the merchandise, was already unloaded. Out of a total of 13,639,230 pesos, 6,994,293 entered directly into the royal treasury. About one-third of this was sent straight to Louis XIV in payment for war services in Italy and the Netherlands, though secretly in order not to outrage Spanish opinion.[6] While Spain saved its bullion, it counted the cost in other ways. The disaster at Vigo disrupted the Spanish American trade for some years to come and confirmed the naval supremacy of the Allies, whose sailors left the scene of their triumph singing and waving branches of trees like flags, as the chronicler San Felipe records, 'and leaving Galicia desolate and horror stricken'. But perhaps the most alarming victory went to the French: 'The King lost

    [4] Ibid., p. 59.
    [5] David Francis, *The First Peninsular War 1702-1713* (London, 1975), pp. 44–52.
    [6] Kamen, *The War of Succession in Spain*, pp. 179–81, 192, and 'The Destruction of the Spanish Silver Fleet at Vigo in 1702', *Bulletin of the Institute of Historical Research*, 39 (1966), pp. 165–73; Michel Morineau, *Incroyables gazettes et fabuleux métaux. Les retours des trésors américains d'après les gazettes hollandaises (XVIᵉ-XVIIIᵉ siècles)* (Cambridge, 1985), pp. 309–11, gives 19 vessels escorted by 23 French and Spanish warships, carrying 19 million pesos.

more than anyone, not only in ships for the Indies and customs from the merchandise, but because subsequently he had to rely on French ships for the American trade, to the detriment of his interests and those of his subjects.'[7]

The war in the Atlantic entered a new stage in 1703. In that year Portugal joined England and the Alliance, bound by the Methuan treaties of 16 May and 27 December, which gave the Allies a base for future operations, an additional army in the peninsula, useful in numbers if not in quality, and conceded to England in particular valuable commercial rights. The archduke arrived in Lisbon escorted by a large allied fleet in March 1704. The intention of the Anglo-Dutch fleet was to patrol the Mediterranean coasts of Spain, hoping to make a landfall and to encourage a rebellion for the archduke. For want of alternatives, they eventually opted for Gibraltar, which was taken by surprise and by force of arms on 2 August 1704. Spain did not take the loss lightly, but the subsequent siege and its failure in 1705 only enhanced the value of Gibraltar in English eyes and confirmed Spain's naval weakness and incapacity to defend its commercial and strategic interests. English domination of the Mediterranean and the Straits was further rewarded by the capture of Minorca in September 1708. Meanwhile events in Portugal and Gibraltar were not only maritime blows; they also brought hostilities closer to the peninsula.

Spain now knew that the threat to its unity posed by the partition treaty was a reality. On three fronts, the Netherlands, Italy, and the Atlantic, long regarded as essential components of Spain's universal empire, the monarchy was in retreat and faced dismemberment, not by diplomacy, but by war. And the war aims of the Allies threatened to despoil Spain not only outside the peninsula but within Castile itself. In persuading Portugal to join them, the Allies held out the bait of specific acquisitions in Extremadura and Galicia, and also on her American frontiers in the Amazon and the Río de la Plata.[8] Militarily Portugal became one of the most vulnerable flanks of Philip V. The Bourbon government responded by affirming the territorial integrity and imperial unity of Spain. At the head of the army invading Portugal in April 1704, Philip V accused the Portuguese king of

---

[7] Vicente Bacallar y Sanna, marqués de San Felipe, *Comentarios de la guerra de España e historia de su rey Felipe V, el animoso*, ed. C. Seco Serrano (*BAE*, 99, Madrid, 1957), p. 50.

[8] San Felipe, *Comentarios*, pp. 52–3; Francis, *The First Peninsular War*, p. 75.

agreeing to divide by war the principal provinces of these kingdoms, and on the pretext of the well-being and liberty of Europe, seeks to place the Archduke Charles of Austria in possession of the whole of Spain and its dependencies, at the same time getting the archduke to cede thereby in perpetuity to Portugal the city of Badajoz, the towns of Alcántara, Alburquerque and Valencia in Extremadura, and in Galicia Bayona, Vigo, Tuy and La Guardia; and in the West Indies the whole of the eastern side of the Río de la Plata.[9]

By 1705 the phoney war was over, and the real war for the peninsula began. It began badly for Philip V. If Spain no longer had a first-class navy, nor were its military resources those of a world power. Shortage of troops, lack of arms and supplies, absence of military talent in the ruling classes, these were the more obvious deficiencies. An estimate at the beginning of the war indicated an infantry strength of 13,268 and 5,097 cavalry, most of this concentrated in Andalucía and Catalonia.[10] There was some mobilization in subsequent years, but in 1706 the total of Spanish infantry was still only 17,242. An army of this size could play only a supporting role. Even in the peninsula the main force had to come from France, and this meant that France dictated war policy. French support came in the form of generals, officers, troops, supplies, and advice on military reforms. Recruitment and organization received prompt attention. A decree of 3 March 1703 ordered the enlistment of one man out of every hundred of the population. Another decree, of 28 September 1704, abolished the *tercio*, the traditional infantry corps, and substituted the regiment; a director-general of infantry was appointed. And a royal bodyguard of four companies was created, two of the companies being non-Spanish.

France also supplied war materials, in default of local production especially in the early years of the war. None of this was pure aid. Everything had to be paid for, almost on delivery. During 1703–9, the peak years of French commitment in the peninsula, the total value of war purchases was 37,000,000 reales, an annual average of 5 per cent of the government's income.[11] In addition France sent arms into Spain to supply its own troops, who also had to be fed and kept fit for battle.

[9] Manifesto dated Plasencia, 30 April 1704, quoted by Seco Serrano in San Felipe, *Comentarios*, p. viii.

[10] Kamen, *The War of Succession in Spain*, pp. 59–60.

[11] Ibid., pp. 67–76.

Although France paid some of the overheads of her army in Spain, the major burden of all these expenses was carried by Spain. Basically it was the Spanish taxpayer and American silver which paid for the peninsular war, as well as contributing to French costs on other fronts.

This was a formidable investment and one which did not yield immediate returns. The speed of the war overtook the pace of organization and reform, and when the Allies attacked eastern Spain in 1705 there was nothing to stop them. Two positive factors were also in their favour, the Anglo-Dutch domination of the Mediterranean, and the social rebellion of the people of Valencia. The naval superiority of the Allies enabled them in August 1705 to establish a base of operations and support in Valencia, which quickly declared for the archduke, and then to move on to attack Barcelona, where the viceroy surrendered in face of the combined forces of Allied invaders and Catalan insurgents. Soon the whole of Catalonia was Habsburg territory, joined in 1706 by Majorca. Aragon was slower to commit itself, but there too the combination of external attack and internal rebellion proved fatal to the Bourbons and enabled the Allies to occupy Zaragoza in June 1706. Philip V was not inert. He made a determined effort to recapture Barcelona, but he did not have the sea power to blockade the port, the siege failed, and he was forced to withdraw in May 1706. Thus almost the whole of the crown of Aragon went over to the archduke, and Spain was engulfed in civil war.

The siege of Barcelona pinned down Bourbon forces and allowed the Allies to invade from Portugal. Louis XIV sent the duke of Berwick to strengthen the Bourbon western front, but the military balance was against him and he could not prevent the loss of Alcántara, followed by Ciudad Rodrigo and Salamanca; now there was nothing to stop the advance of the Allies on Madrid. Philip V had retreated in haste from Barcelona to Madrid only to find that the Allies were closing in from east and west. Another retreat was organized, from Madrid to Burgos, and this seemed the end of the road. The Allied army entered Madrid on 27 June and was met by a few collaborators from the nobility and bureaucracy.[12] As the Bourbon defences collapsed in Spain, the news from abroad was not encouraging: Marlborough's victory at Ramillies in May 1706 removed the Spanish Netherlands from Bourbon control, while in September the Austrian victory in Italy forced the French army to retreat across the Alps. Philip saw the Spanish empire disintegrating before his eyes, his capital lost, his armies defeated, his protector

[12] Francis, *The First Peninsular War*, pp. 222–41.

humiliated, and his policy of no dismemberment in ruins. The year 1706 was truly calamitous, the time when the new dynasty apparently lost its way and its purpose.

Adversity brought out the best in Philip V and strengthened his popular base. The failure at Barcelona and the retreat of his army into France stirred him to greater efforts, and he rejected the advice of those in his French entourage who insisted he should retire to Paris and even consult his grandfather about a peace treaty: 'He remained firm and replied that he would never return to Paris, for he was resolved to die in Spain.'[13] He hurried back to his court and government in Madrid, determined to save his throne. To counteract rumours, demonstrate his presence, and check desertions, he personally rode through the ranks, speaking to troops, reassuring the faint-hearted, and restoring morale. His support in Castile was essentially popular. It is true that the majority of the Castilian nobility were Bourbonists at heart, but their actual support was lukewarm, and the attitude of some was ambiguous. During the occupation of Madrid many grandees disappeared to their estates, to avoid collaboration or to await events but not apparently to volunteer their persons or resources in the service of Philip V:

> The Duke of Medinaceli took the road to Burgos but in very short stages. The Count of Corzana alleged that he was waiting for King Charles to arrive and therefore he did not hurry; but I do not know his intention ... Other magnates dispersed throughout New Castile, in that part abandoned by the enemy; and those people who had written to the Marquis of Minas [the Portuguese commander] did not dare see him at court.[14]

The mass of the people, however, did not hedge their bets. Philip's spirited response to the crisis of 1706 evoked a popular demonstration in his favour. In Castile, and not least in provinces and towns such as Extremadura and Salamanca which experienced occupation by the Allied forces, a new war effort was organised, troops were recruited, local forces created, arms, provisions and money found, and all in a spontaneous movement of loyalty which impressed observers.[15] These were not vague gestures or mere impressions. Without this response from the common people there would have been no recruitment and no

[13] San Felipe, *Comentarios*, p. 108; Coxe, *Memoirs of the Kings of Spain*, I, p. 379.
[14] San Felipe, *Comentarios*, pp. 115–16.
[15] Coxe, *Memoirs of the Kings of Spain*, I, pp. 386–7.

Spanish army for Philip V. No doubt there was some mobilization of resources and opinion by local authorities and above all by priests. The clergy preached a crusade, denounced heretics, condemned the compromising alliances of the archduke, and proclaimed the Catholic character of Philip's cause. In Murcia Bishop Belluga armed and led a horde of loyalists for the Bourbon cause, never doubting that this was a war of religion.[16] This too was a popular belief.

Madrid showed a particular loyalty to Philip V and maintained a passive resistance to the brief Habsburg occupation. People and priests played their part, and so apparently did other elements of the popular sectors. The chronicler San Felipe records a curious piece of history or folklore, according to which even the prostitutes helped to weaken the resolve of the Allied troops, detaining them among the enervating pleasures of Madrid, while Philip V regrouped his army at Sopetrán:

> The women of the town undertook to distract and exhaust if possible the invading army. They went in bands by night among the tents introducing disorder and disease, so that in the hospitals there were more than 6,000 sick, most of whom died. Thus even the whores showed their loyalty and devotion to the king by these wicked and abominable tricks.[17]

The enthusiasm of the people contrasted strongly with the caution of the aristocracy. Queen María Luisa, who personally inspired a new spirit of resistance, acknowledged the role of the popular sectors when she returned to Madrid: 'It has been obvious on this occasion that, after God, it is to the people that we owe the crown … We could count only on them, but thank God they count for everything!'[18] The people identified even more with the new dynasty after the birth of an heir, Luis Fernando, on 25 August 1707: 'He came just at the right time, this prince born in Castile; because now the Spaniards saw the crown confirmed in a Spanish prince, and they were more committed to supporting the rule of King Philip.'[19]

Castile saved Philip in 1707. The archduke now realized that he was in the middle of enemy territory and that his army could not hold Madrid.

---

[16] Joaquín Báguena, *El cardenal Belluga. Su vida y su obra* (Murcia, 1935), pp. 93–5.

[17] San Felipe, *Comentarios*, p. 116.

[18] María Luisa to Madame de Maintenon, 3 November 1706, in Alfred Baudrillart, *Philippe V et la cour de France* (5 vols, Paris, 1890–1900), I, p. 272.

[19] San Felipe, *Comentarios*, p. 140.

He remained in Aragon, then withdrew to Valencia in October 1706, and in March 1707 to Barcelona, his itinerary indicating varying levels of security he enjoyed in Spain. The Allied position depended upon external reinforcements and internal support. A similar combination was essential for Philip V, and in the course of 1706–7 the components of the Bourbon war machine in Spain – French military aid and new Castilian troops – were brought together by a more effective government at the centre. In June 1705 Louis XIV sent a new ambassador to Madrid, Michel-Jean Amelot, whose primary task was not diplomacy but the assembly and direction of resources for the war effort. Amelot established good relations at court, became in effect prime minister, and recruited a financial expert from France, Jean Orry, to raise the revenues on which all depended. On his arrival he found a state of military neglect, confusion and penury extraordinary in a world power; even the royal guards were queuing for free soup at convent doors. By the beginning of 1709 Philip V had 73 battalions of infantry and 135 squadrons of cavalry, all uniformed, armed and paid, still incapable of winning a war but an improvement on the phantom army of 1705. As Amelot reported to his master, 'The efforts made for the King by his generals and ministers to stir the Spaniards out of their indolence, or rather their lethargy, and to place them in a position to help and defend themselves have not frankly produced everything Your Majesty might reasonably expect. But there has certainly been a great change.'[20] Spaniards, understandably, had their reservations about Amelot. But he produced results and these were eventually seen on the battlefield. Gradually the military balance in the peninsula began to change.

The first Bourbon success came in Valencia, where the Allied army was under strength and the social rebellion unfulfilled; the retreat from Madrid had not improved morale. Meanwhile the Bourbons were closing in and attracting collaborators. In Murcia the bellicose bishop, Luis Belluga, threw his troops into a holy war and helped to recover Orihuela for Philip V. But the decisive battle was fought at Almansa on 25 April 1707, when a Franco-Spanish army of 25,000 commanded by the duke of Berwick, defeated an Allied army of 15,000 Portuguese, English, Dutch, and Germans under Lord Galway. The whole of Valencia now fell to the Bourbons, and pockets of resistance such as Játiva, inspired still by a fierce mixture of religious fervour and social defiance, were terrorized and destroyed.

[20] Amelot to Louis XIV, 2 November 1708, in Baudrillart, *Philippe V et la cour de France*, I, p. 325.

It was even necessary to attack street by street, and house by house; for these madmen defended themselves with unexampled firmness and bravery. Finally after a siege of fifteen days, and eight days possession of the town, it was carried sword in hand. Numbers of the inhabitants were slain, particularly the monks . . . To impress terror, and by a severe example, to prevent similar obstinacy, I caused the town to be razed, leaving only the principal church, and sent all the inhabitants into Castile, under a prohibition never to return to their native country.[21]

In the course of the next few months the Bourbons occupied Zaragoza and most of Aragon. Philip V now considered himself so secure in Spain that he decreed (29 June 1707) the abolition of the regional *fueros*, a measure which reinforced resistance in Catalonia but added to the abasement of Valencia and Aragon. The Archduke Charles now established his court and government in Barcelona. There he reigned securely for the next four years, but he had lost over half his subjects and lost the initiative in Spain. The Bourbons too achieved less than expected in the next two years, restrained perhaps by the subsistence crisis prevailing in Spain.

Spain suffered severe economic adversity in these years, the blows of nature compounding the burdens of war. The harvest of 1708 was poor, and as soldiers and civilians competed for supplies prices rose. Conditions were worsened by the harsh winter of 1708–9, 'the coldest year in living memory', according to San Felipe.[22] It was followed by a destructive thaw, floods, a wet spring, further crop failures leading to famine, and, in the wake of famine, epidemic disease. Few regions escaped crises of subsistence. Andalucía was badly hit by this cycle of disaster: the price of basic foodstuffs soared beyond wages and mortality rates increased. Galicia lost its crops in rain and flood. In August 1709 there was a riot in Santiago over food prices, and poor peasants died in the streets. Asturias was no better. And in Valladolid there was food rationing in 1710.[23]

The war in Spain, however, was determined not only by Spanish conditions but also by those outside the peninsula. France itself, the base

[21] Berwick, on Játiva, May 1707, quoted by Coxe, *Memoirs of the Kings of Spain*, i, pp. 412–13; see also San Felipe, *Comentarios*, p. 132.

[22] San Felipe, *Comentarios*, p. 167.

[23] Antonio Domínguez Ortiz, *Sociedad y estado en el siglo XVIII español* (Barcelona, 1981), pp. 29–32.

of the Bourbon cause, was a victim of natural and military disasters in these years. The long and cruel winter of 1708–9 left the people short of food and the government of resources. This was the background against which military glory faded. The campaign of 1708 was exceptionally long and punishing, and the defeat of Oudenarde in July 1708 was another milestone in the long retreat. The next year brought the next calamity, the battle of Malplaquet in September, which, if not an absolute defeat, caused terrible slaughter and horrified France. In 1709 the situation was so bad for the Bourbons in Italy that Pope Clement XI recognized the Archduke Charles as king of Spain. The course of events made a deep impression on Louis XIV. Marlborough's relentless campaigning, the terrible winter and the subsequent famine in France affected his will to continue the war, and in March 1709 he was ready to begin peace negotiations. The Allies demanded the abdication of Philip V without compensation and the transfer of the whole of Spain, Italy and the Indies to the archduke, hard terms, but ones which Louis believed he would have to accept, and by mid-May he was ready to impose them on Philip V. There were those in France who wanted to pull out of Spain completely, withdraw the army, remove the advisers, recall Amelot.[24] This was the severest test yet for the hallowed will of Charles II and the Bourbons' basic war aims. The protector had turned betrayer.

The integrity of the Spanish monarchy was now threatened by enemy and ally alike. The knowledge that Louis XIV was seeking peace at all costs and was ready to discard Philip and sacrifice Spain without even consulting them surprised and shocked the young king and released a torrent of anti-French feeling among his subjects. It was in these circumstances that he disavowed the policies of France and declared his Spanish sympathies:

> The crown of Spain, which God has placed on my head, I will maintain as long as a drop of blood flows in my veins. I owe this resolution to my conscience, my honour, and the love of my subjects. They, I am convinced, will never abandon me in the most adverse circumstances ... And I will never quit Spain while I have a spark of life.[25]

[24] *Historical Memoirs of the Duc de Saint-Simon*, edited and translated by Lucy Norton (3 vols, London, 1967–72), I, pp. 458–9.
[25] Philip V to Louis XIV, 17 April 1709, in Coxe, *Memoirs of the Kings of Spain*, I, p. 451; Baudrillart, *Philippe V et la cour de France*, I, p. 345.

Philip, it seemed, was now alone, Spain his only support. France was no longer the super power of Europe and Spain no longer the Bourbons' Achilles' heel. While the French king collapsed in defeatism, Philip kept his nerve and his subjects stood firm behind him. He now underwent a further process of hispanicization and looked to his Spanish supporters for government, soldiers, and resources.

Was there not an element of shadow-boxing in Franco-Spanish relations in 1709–10? Did Louis XIV definitely contemplate disengaging from Spain? How serious was Philip in declaring his independence of France? Was there really a reversal of roles? The promised change of policy, the formation of a Spanish government, the dismissal of French support staff, none of this went very deep. Separation from France was more a show of independence than a real change of direction. The French government continued to intervene; Philip still needed French military aid; he was still basically an obedient ally of the French king; and he kept Amelot in Spain as long as possible. He had shown he was extremely sensitive to any attack on his sovereignty and his inheritance. Otherwise the year 1710 was important not for a split in the Bourbon alliance but for the turning of the tide in the peninsular war.

In so far as the Bourbon cause in Spain now rested on Spanish troops, it rested on shaky foundations. As Amelot had indicated, the Spanish army was better than it had been but not as good as it needed to be. And it still had difficulty in winning battles. Meanwhile the Habsburg army had been reinforced, supplied and paid, and was ready for another campaign. It advanced through Aragon and heavily defeated the Spaniards at Zaragoza (20 August 1710). Once again Philip had to withdraw into Castile and allow the enemy to re-enact its occupation of Madrid, on this occasion accompanied by the archduke himself, aloof and impassive as ever.[26] Again the royal family went through the familiar routine of appealing to the people, and again the people responded with the conduct expected of them in these circumstances. Before leaving Madrid for Valladolid the queen appeared on the balcony of the royal palace holding Prince Luis and addressed the crowd eloquently and bravely in words which spread in the city and throughout the provinces; and when the royal family left in a second exodus from Madrid, people ran after them to show their support.[27] Certainly the Allies were met by a sullen and silent populace, and outside Madrid there was a new wave of support for Philip V. Andalucía took the lead in sending troops and

---

[26] Francis, *The First Peninsular War*, pp. 311–14.
[27] *Memoirs of the Duc de Saint-Simon*, II, pp. 94–5.

almost every province followed suit. This time the aristocracy was less equivocal, and thirty-three grandees signed a letter to Louis XIV assuring him of their loyalty to King Philip and begging for reinforcements.

Louis XIV had second thoughts, outraged by the terms proposed by the English and not entirely confident of his grandson's leadership. He sent the duke of Vendôme to command the troops in Spain and renewed the flow of French troops and supplies. Vendôme was an unstable and controversial figure but he seems to have moved the Spanish forces quickly upon the enemy, while guerrilla leaders Feliciano de Bracamonte and José Vallejo harassed them near Madrid. Spanish as well as French efforts contributed to the victory of Villaviciosa (10 December 1710), if victory it was.[28] At any rate the Allied army decided to retreat, suffered at Zaragoza another defeat, and finally left Aragon to the Bourbons. The campaigns of 1710 were decisive. They convinced the Allies that the archduke could not win an absolute victory in the peninsula, and in particular that Madrid and Castile could not be held without a large army of occupation. As the Allies lost confidence in the archduke's cause in Spain, so they had to reassess his position in Europe. The death of the Austrian emperor Joseph in April 1711, leaving the crown to his brother the archduke, opened the possibility that the Habsburgs would recreate the empire of Charles V. This was far from being an English war aim.

If Philip could not be defeated in Castile, he in turn could not overcome the Catalans without French help, or without the American treasure returns of these years.[29] Even with these resources his advance through Catalonia was unhurried, and the Habsburgs were pushed back only gradually to Barcelona and the coast. In September 1711 the archduke, now the Emperor Charles VI, left Barcelona to the regency of his queen, Isabel Cristina, who in turn left the city in March 1713. As the Catalans lost their allies, a great many lives, and finally in September 1714 the battle for Barcelona itself, the English and the Austrians sought to salvage at least the Catalan constitution, but Philip V, sensitive of his sovereignty, was determined to abolish regional rights. Short of resuming the struggle for the sake of the *fueros*, the Allies decided there was nothing they could do but withdraw from Catalonia and bring the War of Succession to a close.

---

[28] Francis, *The First Peninsular War*, p. 319.

[29] William Hodges, Madrid, 23 May 1711, Public Record Office, London, SP 94/78; Morineau, *Incroyables gazettes et fabuleux métaux*, p. 312.

The Treaty of Utrecht was signed on 11 April 1713; Spain also concluded with England the Asiento treaty on 26 March and a preliminary treaty of peace the following day. Spain fought hard at Utrecht; seeing the Allies irreversibly committed to peace, her negotiators worked to recover by diplomacy what had been lost in war. Philip was acknowledged king of Spain and the Indies. To prevent the union of France and Spain, he renewed his renunciation of the right of succession to the French throne, and declared the duke of Savoy successor to the Spanish crown on the extinction of his own issue. He yielded the Spanish Netherlands and the Spanish possessions in Italy – Naples, Milan and Sardinia – to the emperor, and Sicily to the duke of Savoy, to revert to the Spanish crown in the failure of his issue. He ceded Gibraltar and Minorca to England, granted her the *asiento de negros* (the slave-trade contract previously held by Portugal and France) together with permission to send an annual trading ship to Spanish America, and promised to restore her commerce to the same footing as under the Habsburgs. The English negotiator Lord Lexington was instructed to insist that Spain relinquish Colônia do Sacramento to the Portuguese; he confessed that he was 'entirely ignorant where it is', but by yielding to Spain on the peninsular territories claimed by Portugal under the Methuan Treaty he won Sacramento, and indirectly a valuable entrepôt for British trade.[30] After this concession, Philip V engaged never to sell or alienate to France or any other nation, any town or province in America. England won from France useful territorial concessions in America; but the Bourbons gained one of their major objectives: their candidate succeeded to the throne of Spain, and Spain retained its American empire.

The balance sheet of Utrecht was debated and denounced. In terms of the will of Charles II and the war aims of Philip V, Spain lost the War of Succession, and defeat was reflected in the Treaty of Utrecht. Two of the losses, however, were distant deadweights; it could be argued that Spain gained by shedding the Netherlands and Italy, both of which consumed rather than enhanced Spanish resources. In terms of national interest, Spain emerged from Utrecht with the peninsula intact, Gibraltar excepted, and the American empire unimpaired. But she also experienced an irreversible shift of power towards Britain, whose commercial and colonial gains tormented Spain for the rest of the century. What Spain granted by treaty, of course, she could reduce by resistance, and

---

[30] Lexington to Dartmouth, Madrid, 12 June 1713, PRO, SP 94/81.

this was her future strategy: to attack clandestine trade in Spain and America, and to undermine the conceded privileges. Utrecht remained a battlefield.

Civil War

Spaniards fought Spaniards in the War of Succession, but the frontiers of social conflict were not always clear.[31] In Spain Habsburg and Bourbon were not dynastic or ideological concepts but represented interests and aspirations. Eastern Spain, it could be said, fought Castile, but not as a separatist movement; the Catalans no less than the Castilians stood for Spanish unity and sought to impose their king on the whole of Spain. East and west were divided not only by the *fueros* or mutual prejudices but by historic experience of Habsburg rule. The reign of Charles II had been an unqualified disaster for Castile and served to alienate Castilians from the Habsburg dynasty. Recession for one was progress for another. Weak government and inertia benefited the regional kingdoms, for they thrived on neglect from the centre and saw Charles II as a benevolent devolutionist. These divisions reflected economic differences, between those who had suffered decades of depression under the Habsburgs and those who were showing signs of recovery. Eastern hostility towards the Bourbons, moreover, contained a strong element of resentment of the French and was a reaction to frontier conflicts and to French immigration and competition for opportunities.

While these factors help to explain pro-Habsburg sentiment in the eastern kingdoms from 1700, especially among the lower and middle sectors, this would not have expressed itself in armed conflict without the presence of foreign armies. Equally, foreign intervention would not have succeeded without an internal base of support; having failed to occupy Cadiz and raise Andalucía in 1702, the Allies learned to target their operations more efficiently in 1705. Thus the logic of events was external shock acting upon a revolutionary situation. Then the question posed to people was not so much why they should support Habsburg or Bourbon as why they should resist the incoming army. Once hostilities began, these fed upon themselves and expressed various conflicts, some of them long latent in the peninsula, some of them new; local rivalries set village against village, especially in the eastern borderlands; social

---

[31] Domínguez Ortiz, *Sociedad y estado en el siglo XVIII español*, p. 21.

interests divided lord from vassal, nobility from people; the Portuguese were despised in Castile and hated in Madrid; the presence of Protestants among the Allies provoked religious susceptibilities. Some people fought for a cause, others to settle an account, others to improve their condition. And, as in most civil wars, the majority of people stayed at home.

Social tensions were brought to the surface, especially in the eastern kingdoms. Castile presented a paradox. This was the heartland of the Bourbons, yet solidarity was not absolute. Castile had monopolized the machinery of government and empire in the past, so the unity and integrity of the monarchy stipulated in the will of Charles II appeared to be made for them. From 1700 Castile was fighting for its inheritance and this was identified with the Bourbon succession. In 1701 Philip V made straight for Castile, presented himself in Madrid, and showed himself to the Castilians. This was his seat of government, the base of his world empire, an inheritance prepared for Castile. Most Castilians were satisfied, but not the higher aristocracy. The grandees of Castile were guarded, even hostile, towards the Bourbons and some of them defected to the other side. They were motivated in part by pro-Habsburg political convictions, but also by ambition, personal resentment, and family loyalties. It was a serious step and carried the risk of loss of property; but many took it, especially in 1706 and 1710, when the Habsburg army reached Madrid. They could see that their hegemony was finished, their power reduced by bureaucrats, their places occupied by the French. This was the root of their alienation.[32]

The admiral of Castile, Juan Luis Enríquez de Cabrera, left Madrid with his riches, old masters, and 300 retainers, and sought exile in Portugal; from there he publicly denounced French influence in government and headed the Spanish dissidents until his death in 1705. The count of Cifuentes, a peer of Aragon with estates in Castile, defected to the archduke and became an effective guerrilla leader in his service. The count of Santa Cruz, commander of the galleys of Spain, delivered the naval base of Cartagena to the enemy in 1706. The count of Corzana, former viceroy of Catalonia and now in need of an income again, found the new regime unrewarding and defected in 1702 to the archduke, who gave him office and in 1707 made him viceroy of Valencia. The duke of Nájera, the counts of Haro, Oropesa, and Lemos all publicly espoused the archduke. The duke of Infantado vacillated and was an object of

---

[32] San Felipe, *Comentarios*, p. 32.

suspicion to the Bourbon government. So was the duke of Medinaceli, who after a career in the service of Philip V was finally arrested and imprisoned in the castle of Pamplona. Of the twelve grandees of the first class, four were disgraced for disloyalty. Though less than a third of the other grandees and titled nobility deserted, many of the rest adopted a policy of 'wait and see'.[33]

In Aragon most of the nobility supported Philip V, with the exception of the counts of Fuentes and Sástago, and a few who remained indifferent. The nobility disclaimed all responsibility for events in Aragon and denied they were ever 'in rebellion', attributing this to the lower classes.[34] There was some truth in the assertion. Grievances accumulated in the years 1701–4, when the king barely showed himself to his 380,000 Aragonese subjects, but allowed French troops to be billeted upon them, taxes to be imposed to pay for these, and the *fueros* thereby to be violated. The *fueros* in themselves, however, were not a popular cause or sufficient to inspire a rising *en masse* against Philip V. *Fueros* were for nobles and principal citizens, not for vassals and peasants.[35] It was sufficient to know that his lord was pro-Bourbon for a vassal to join the Habsburgs. The opportunity came with the advance of the Allied army, which basically owed its success in Aragon to lack of defences and absence of mass resistance. The priests in many villages supported the peasants, as did the Mendicant orders, and they were no less vociferous than the Bourbon clergy in invoking religion to justify war. In some of the towns the lower nobility and middle sectors were Habsburg, an expression of an ancient alliance against the aristocracy's control of municipal government. But in many Aragonese towns the urban patriciate kept the Bourbon flag flying and closed ranks against popular agitation. In so far as there was a rebellion in Aragon, therefore, it was a social protest that had little to do with the *fueros* and represented a desperate attempt by the oppressed to drive tyrants from their estates and seek protectors where they could.

In Valencia social protest was even closer to the surface. King, viceroy, *fueros*, these gave little cause for grievance to the 318,500 inhabitants of the kingdom, and if Philip V was neglectful he was not

[33] 'The faint-hearted feared to take a risk with the king; the miserly to lose their property; the ambitious to arrive late for the rewards; the complainers to vent their anger; the depressed to seek a better fortune', San Felipe, *Comentarios*, p. 119. See also Amelot to Louis XIV, 4 July 1706, in Baudrillart, *Philippe V et la cour de France*, I, p. 267.

[34] Kamen, *The War of Succession in Spain*, pp. 267–8.

[35] See John Lynch, *Spain under the Habsburgs* (2nd edn, 2 vols, Oxford, 1981), I, p. 358, II, pp. 54–5.

hostile. In any case his jurisdiction extended over only seventy-six towns, royal taxation was moderate, and revenue was locally consumed. The kingdom of Valencia was dominated not by its king but by its nobility and clergy. Over 300 towns were under seigneurial jurisdiction, subject to the officials, the justice, and the taxation of their lords, some of them Castilians, all of them virtual sovereigns on their estates. The Valencian peasants were victims of a system which charged them feudal dues, tithes, taxes, and seigneurial monopolies, and allowed hardly a single action in their working lives to escape the lord's control. Valencia, like Aragon, had a number of immediate grievances – hatred of the French, the indifference of Madrid, a partiality towards the Habsburgs – but the root of its resentment was social and stemmed from a seigneurial regime so absolute in its power that rebellion seemed the only way.[36] The memory of a recent rebellion, in 1693, was still fresh; in spite of its defeat there still remained, as a contemporary remarked, 'the hope and desire to gain exemption from taxes if the opportunity should again offer itself'.[37] The opportunity was better now than in 1693; the disputed succession gave the Valencians political leverage with the Habsburg pretender and this they were quick to exploit. The Habsburgs too seized their advantage and manipulated the social movement to enhance their cause and embarrass their enemies.

The Allied fleet approached the coast of Valencia in the late summer of 1705; it took Altea and put ashore two Valencian agents to organize resistance. One of these, Francisco García, was the leader of the rebellion of 1693; now he spread anew the message of liberation among the peasants, freedom from taxes and services, rejection of aristocratic dominion, division of the estates among the landless. The archduke followed up the campaign by raising some towns from seigneurial to royal jurisdiction.[38] Soon armies of peasants and urban poor assembled for the Allies. It was with their support, and virtually none from the upper and middle sectors, that the Habsburg cause triumphed in Valencia, employing a minimum of military force and pushing aside the meagre defences of the Bourbons.

As bands of peasants cast off their servitude, refused to pay dues, assaulted the lords and occupied their property, the archduke faced a dilemma, aware that support for one side would alienate the other. At

[36] Lynch, *Spain under the Habsburgs*, II, pp. 280–2; James Casey, *The Kingdom of Valencia in the Seventeenth Century* (Cambridge, 1979), pp. 76, 102–3.
[37] Quoted Kamen, *The War of Succession in Spain*, p. 276.
[38] Ibid., p. 278.

first he tried to be even handed. He ordered that people should pay their dues to the Church and for the defence of the kingdom, and as for seigneurial dues it was not in his hands to alter them without the owner's consent. But he was not unmoved and once it was clear that he had nothing to gain from the nobility he acknowledged that the people had grievances and declared his desire to redress them, 'even if it is at the expense of the powerful, the lords, and the barons, who invariably practise extortions and need restraining'.[39] In the event the military component of the anti-Bourbon alliance in Valencia collapsed, and the social revolution was left defenceless.

In Catalonia the Alliance was stronger. The Catalans had a number of options in the War of Succession but France was not one of them; the memory of the revolt of 1640–52, when France had first abandoned then dismembered Catalonia, and their subsequent resentment of the French, whether they came as immigrants or invaders, turned Catalans decisively from Louis XIV and French absolutism towards the Habsburgs and regional autonomy. The Catalan rebellion of 1705 was not spontaneous or popular in origin, but expressed the political objectives of the ruling interest group. Barcelona was the home of a cohesive urban elite, product of a merger of Barcelona's oligarchy with the traditional aristocracy, and consolidated in the revival of the Catalan economy from the 1680s.[40] This in turn generated the ambitious economic projects of the lawyer Narcís Feliu de la Penya, whose call for a reorientation of Catalan trade away from traditional Mediterranean markets towards America reflected growing involvement in colonial trade and relied basically not on Barcelona industry, still dominated by the guild regime, but upon the exportable products of the rural sector and the smaller coastal towns.

The Catalan elite saw the War of Succession as the opportunity to exploit Catalonia's position and to sell its alliance to the highest bidder. Both sides cultivated the Catalans. Louis XIV had advised his grandson to take them seriously, and Philip in fact offered them everything they wanted in the *cortes* of 1701, confirmation of privileges, a free port, tax reform, a maritime company, and direct access to the Indies trade through two annual ships 'as long as they did not infringe the rights of

[39] Instructions of Archduke Charles to the conde de la Corzana, captain-general of Valencia, 7 March 1707, in Antonio Rodríguez Villa, *Don Diego Hurtado de Mendoza y Sandoval, Conde de la Corzana (1650-1720)* (Madrid, 1907), pp. 220–2.

[40] James S. Amelang, *Honored Citizens of Barcelona: Patrician Culture and Class Relations 1490-1714* (Princeton, 1986), pp. 15, 221–2.

the commerce of Seville'. Could he fulfil this promise? Would his Castilian supporters allow him to compromise their monopoly? The Catalans had their doubts and opted for the Alliance, which gave them the protection of the Austrian army and the English fleet. In particular, the Anglo-Catalan accord corresponded to the Catalan desire to export directly to America and the English determination to break the Spanish-French monopoly of the Indies trade.[41] The war of 1705, therefore, was not a mere defence of the *fueros*, but was designed to serve the interests of the Catalan merchant elite anxious to promote Barcelona as the entrepreneurial capital of Spain, a centre of *comercio libre*, a new metropolis of colonial trade and enterprise. They did not seek the secession of Catalonia or the dismemberment of Spain; on the contrary, they fought to incorporate the Catalan model into a united Spain and one freed from the dominance of France.

The intervention of the Allies and the collaboration of the Catalan leaders soon attracted popular support. Within a month of the capture of Monjuich in September 1705 Barcelona and most of Catalonia joined the Allies. This was an agreement of equals in which the Catalans proved themselves active allies. The popular sectors among Catalonia's 400,000 people responded positively, especially at critical times. From these came the Miquelets, bands of armed peasants based on family networks and equipped with knives and short-barrelled pistols, who now transformed their local feuds into a regional cause and fought bravely, if anarchically, for the Allies. And again the priests and friars acted in solidarity.

In June 1706, when the Allied army entered Madrid, the archduke was proclaimed Charles III, and the Miquelets patrolled the streets of the capital, Catalan prospects looked good. But Castile reacted vigorously to this humiliation and repulsed the threat to its primacy. From defence it went on to the attack, and after the victory of Almansa in April 1707 Philip V was able to impose the *nueva planta* and abolish the *fueros* of Valencia and Aragon. The conflict became more brutal and more bitter; a number of border towns fell, Lérida on 14 November 1707, Tortosa on 19 July 1708. The Catalans now came face to face with French-inspired absolutism, and began to look distinctly isolated within the peninsula. But as long as the Allies opposed the presence of a Bourbon on the throne of Spain, Catalonia remained confident. In 1709 Louis XIV

---

[41] Geoffrey J. Walker, 'Algunes repercussions sobre el comerç d'Amèrica de l'aliança anglo-catalana durant la Guerra de Successió Espanyola', *2nes Jornades d'Estudis Catalano-Americans, Maig 1986* (Barcelona, 1987), pp. 69–81.

seemed on the point of capitulation. In September 1710 their king was in Madrid. But there were flaws in the alliance. Relations between Charles and the Catalan authorities were not easy. He wanted revenue, they wanted privileges; at heart Charles was no less absolutist than Philip V and found the Catalan's insistence on their rights irksome. In any case, how committed was he to Catalonia? And how committed to the archduke were the Allies? The answers to these questions became clearer in 1711. Charles left Spain to become emperor. England abandoned the war to negotiate peace. The Catalans were not forgotten, but for the English government they were not a primary war aim and Philip V knew it; he told the English ambassador, 'Peace is no less necessary to you than it is to us; you will not break with us for a trifle.'[42] The ambassador found the court 'inflexible', and was told 'the king will never grant privileges to these blackguards and scoundrels, the Catalans, for he would no longer be king if he did.'[43] The English government sent confusing signals about the *fueros*: 'In the correspondence of Bolinbroke with the plenipotenciaries at Utrecht, these privileges are described as contrary to the interests of England, and the constitution of Castile, which was tendered as an alternative, as far more valuable to subjects who intended to live in due subjection to authority.'[44] The Catalans refused to accept that the constitution of Castile was superior to their own and they rejected the terms of peace agreed on their behalf in the treaties of 1713. Isolated internationally, their own resistance reduced to Barcelona, they decided to face Bourbon power alone. Two of the three *brazos*, or estates, of Catalonia voted for war and war was declared on 10 July 1714.

The decision defied reason and set the Catalans on a suicidal course. Guerrilla resistance was quickly suppressed and the duke of Berwick concentrated his French and Spanish forces on attacking Barcelona, defended heroically on the walls, in the streets, and house by house, but finally beaten into submission on 13 September. The terms were harsh. An entire *barrio*, or district, was destroyed to construct a new fortress. Military leaders were imprisoned, exiled, and executed. The duke of Berwick assumed all military powers, José Patino was placed in charge of civil administration, agents of absolutism quickly moved in. Every vestige of Catalonia's traditional institutions was destroyed by the

[42] Coxe, *Memoirs of the Kings of Spain*, ii, pp. 137–8; Francis, *The First Peninsular War*, p. 369.

[43] Lexington to Dartmouth, Madrid, 19 March 1713, PRO, SP 94/80.

[44] Bolinbroke seems to have thought that the Catalans would be admitted to direct trade with the Indies; Coxe, *Memoirs of the Kings of Spain*, ii, p. 138.

decree of *nueva planta* (16 January 1716). The *cortes*, Generalitat, Council of One Hundred, fiscal system, monetary autonomy, all disappeared. The Catalan state suddenly ceased to exist.

The Catalan resistance of 1705–14, sustained for seven years without the support of Aragon and Valencia and for three years without solidarity from its foreign allies, was a brilliant effort of will, resources and mobilization. In spite of the wealth of Catalonia, its commercial revival of 1690–1705, and the injection of Allied money, its economy could not sustain a long war and the archduke's revenue was never equal to expenditure. Relative to Castile, the principality fought the war at a great disadvantage; Catalonia had no windfalls from the Indies, no American treasure to spend, nothing to compensate for economic recession from 1711.[45] Yet money was not the whole story of the Catalan war. The regional economy was still resilient and continued to export wine and brandy, to produce agricultural and other commodities. If prices rose, wages also held up, and the country was still capable of paying taxes and granting subsidies to the archduke.

How did the Catalan people respond to the war? Social support was not unanimous, least of all in the final stage of the struggle. The higher clergy did not give a lead, still less the upper ranks of the nobility, somewhat Castilianized and aloof from Catalan interests, as distinct from the lower nobility who identified with Catalonia and had little sympathy for the Bourbons. Equally, this was not a peasant revolt; Catalonia was not another Valencia, ripe for social revolution. Once occupied by the armies of Philip V, most villages in the west and in the mountains stayed that way, and while there was sporadic resistance to new taxes, rural Catalonia did not rise against the incoming Bourbons. The head of the Catalan movement was to be found in the urban elite of trade and production, its heart among the artisans and craftsmen of the middle sector. It was the *brazo real*, or commons, of the Catalan estates, representing the urban bourgeoisie of Barcelona, Solsona, Manresa, Sabadell, which in the cortes of July 1714 gave the vote of 78 to 43 for war. This forced a hesitant *brazo militar*, representing the nobles, to follow suit, more out of honour than conviction, while the ecclesiastical estate abstained. The middle sector of the merchants, craftsmen and artisans was the core of the resistance during the siege and they suffered heavy casualties. As for the 'people', the weavers and spinners of Barcelona, fishermen of the coast, poor artisans and workers, where did

---

[45] Ferran Soldevila, *Història de Catalunya* (3 vols, Barcelona, 1934–5), II, p. 385; Kamen, *The War of Succession in Spain*, pp. 167–93.

they stand? They certainly took part in the struggle, or were mobilized into it, but what they stood to gain or lose it is impossible to say. 'Bread, and we'll all go!', cried the women of Barcelona in response to an appeal to go to the last barricades.[46] Was it a cry of patriotism or hunger?

The defeat of 1714 was not a catastrophe. It was business as usual for the Catalans; widows and orphans carried on the work vacated by the menfolk. Post-war difficulties were gradually overcome and Catalans continued producing, selling and buying. Their sense of identity was intact and the Catalan language survived in popular if not official usage. Hallowed institutions were destroyed, but institutions are not the only expression of a people's identity. Catalonia was not a nation state, so while it had much to lose this did not include independence. In spite of severe repression, there was no resistance movement, nor even a renewal of rural banditry, and none of the ruling groups attempted to rally the masses behind a campaign for regional government. Catalonia's political inertia in the eighteenth century, however, was related not only to the loss of ancient institutions but also to the existence of compensatory factors elsewhere.

Catalan identity had been expressed not only in the *fueros* but also in the growth and ambitions of dynamic interest groups. When these were frustrated by Spanish policy they exploded.[47] The resistance to Philip V in 1705–14 was fierce and uncompromising, culminating in an heroic struggle to hold Barcelona, in which nobles, tradesmen and students fought to the end and desertion was unknown. The leadership came from the middle sector of recent economic growth and commercial expansion. What did defeat mean for them, the urban elite and petty nobility? They lost political freedom and representation in government, which hurt their self esteem. They lost the possibility of defending their own interests and of distancing themselves from a decrepit Castile. In particular, their American hopes were shattered, facing as they did a stricter application of the Cadiz-Seville monopoly. So what did the Catalans obtain from the new Bourbon state? In the short term nothing. In the medium term the possibility of economic growth, a protected market in Castile for their products, and an eventual outlet in America for their exports. The War of Succession caused the Catalans to pause rather than to halt.

---

[46] Soldevila, *Història de Catalunya*, II, p. 415.
[47] Pierre Vilar, *La Catalogne dans l'Espagne moderne* (3 vols, Paris, 1962), I, p. 676.

Ally or Satellite of France?

The War of Succession embodied for Spain another war, a peaceful but no less critical struggle for independence from France. The problem began with the king. Was Philip V 'Spanish' or 'French'? Louis XIV, presenting the new monarch to the French court at Versailles on 16 November 1700 before despatching him to Spain, turned to him and said, 'Be a good Spaniard; that is your first duty now; but never forget that you were born a Frenchman, and foster the unity between our two nations.'[48] A shy and sombre youth, aged only seventeen in 1700, Philip was indolent and taciturn unless prompted, and Louis became his prompter, making it abundantly clear that 'I am the master and I make the decisions.'[49] It was Louis who chose his wife, without even consulting him, and when the thirteen-year-old María Luisa of Savoy turned out to be a haughty, spirited and independent young woman, it was Louis who counselled the bewildered husband to stand up to her: 'The queen is the first of your subjects, in which quality, as well as in that of your wife, she is bound to obey you.'[50] Louis kept Philip and Spain under close observation during the next nine years, and he placed in the peninsula a number of agents of French control, a political agent at court, his ambassadors at the head of government, technical advisers in the administration, and, of course, numerous units of the French army.

At the Spanish court he had the princess des Ursins, French by birth, a tall, arrogant and imperious woman with a strong sense of superiority: 'She was highly ambitious', wrote Saint-Simon, 'on a noble scale far beyond her sex, and, indeed, beyond what is usual even in men, and she had a masculine longing for fame and power.'[51] She ruled the Spanish court, though only *camarera mayor*, or head of the queen's household, by making herself indispensable to the young queen, inducting her into politics, influencing the king through her, and thus establishing a kind of royal triumvirate. 'For so vast an enterprise it was vitally necessary to obtain King Louis's approval, for at the beginning at least he ruled the Spanish court no less absolutely than his own, and in this she was wholly

[48] *Memoirs of the Duc de Saint-Simon*, I, p. 139.
[49] Louis XIV to Blécourt, 3 June 1701, in Baudrillart, *Philippe V et la cour de France*, I, p. 70; Coxe, *Memoirs of the Kings of Spain*, I, p. 210.
[50] Louis XIV to Philip V, in Coxe, *Memoirs of the Kings of Spain*, I, p. 149; Baudrillart, *Philippe V et la cour de France*, I, p. 86; *Memoirs of the Duc de Saint-Simon*, I, p. 167.
[51] *Memoirs of the Duc de Saint-Simon*, I, p. 165.

successful.'[52] Thus Ursins through her royal creatures came to monopolize power from 1702 to 1704, marginalizing the Spanish ministers, excluding the grandees, and alienating even the French ambassadors. But the princess had a tendency to overreach herself and to operate outside the framework of French policy. Louis XIV was alerted and promptly recalled her to France to teach her a lesson in subordination. The lesson was short and sharp and he allowed her to return to Madrid in 1705, aware of her supreme influence over the Spanish monarchs, and convinced that he could not govern Spain without her.[53] She immediately recovered control of court patronage, throwing out her enemies and bringing in her own clients, and she re-established her domination over the queen, to such an extent that even Philip was secretly jealous of her.[54] This time, however, Louis made her share power. Her partner in the government of Spain was a new French ambassador, Michel-Jean Amelot, marquis de Gournay.

Amelot was a man skilled in the ways of administration and diplomacy, though largely ignorant of Spain. He was appointed by Louis, in April 1705, to work closely with Ursins and to become in effect the prime minister of Spain, advising Philip V, directing the administration, and providing the impetus for reform.[55] They also needed a financial expert who would supply the revenues to enable them to plan the war and govern Spain. Louis XIV supplied him, too, Jean Orry, a man 'hard of hearing but extremely shrewd, had sprung from the gutter, and had followed many different employments to gain his livelihood and advancement'.[56] Orry had served a previous term in Spain in 1702–4, when he had made himself extremely unpopular with the aristocracy through his determination to recover revenues usurped from the crown, 'a most delicate business, because the usurpers of the alcalabas were among the highest placed men in the kingdom'.[57] Now, in 1705–6, he was appointed to reorganize Spanish finances, to assemble the resources of war, and to supply ideas to the French team.

For the next five years Louis XIV governed Spain through Amelot and Ursins. The ambassador's brief was to rule Spain according to

[52] Ibid., I, pp. 218–19.

[53] San Felipe, *Comentarios*, pp. 82–5.

[54] Philip V to Louis XIV, 10 March 1705, in Baudrillart, *Philippe V et la cour de France*, I, pp. 206–7.

[55] Instructions to Amelot, 24 April 1705, in Baudrillart, *Philippe V et la cour de France*, I, p. 221; Kamen, *The War of Succession in Spain*, pp. 47–52.

[56] *Memoirs of the Duc de Saint-Simon*, I, p. 206.

[57] San Felipe, *Comentarios*, pp. 44, 52.

French principles of government and to implement a triple programme of reform: reduce the political power of the grandees; subordinate the clergy and religious orders to the state; and abolish the *fueros* of the crown of Aragon. The French took a cynical view of the Spanish aristocracy. Louis XIV advised Amelot to allow the grandees 'to preserve all the external prerogatives of their rank, and at the same time to exclude them from all matters which might increase their credit or give them a part in the government'.[58] But the grandees were not blind. First they saw that the French ambassador dominated the *despacho*, or cabinet council, and turned it into the chief policy-making body, bypassing the traditional councils, hitherto the political base of the aristocracy. Then they noticed the creation of a royal bodyguard in 1705, two of whose four companies consisted of foreign units, which in their eyes eroded the military status and privileges of the grandees.[59] Their 'national' pride was further outraged by the decision of Louis XIV, supported by Amelot and accepted by Philip, to introduce French in place of Spanish garrisons into a number of coastal towns in northern Spain. And what did the French have to show for their policies? The loss of Catalonia and the eastern kingdoms, events which prompted the council of state to compose a historic *consulta* denouncing the French-inspired methods of government and consequent war disasters, and claiming that the traditional councils 'should have cognisance of everything, to give their opinion, the decision belonging to the king of Spain'.[60] Statements of this kind did not impress the French, but they were also aware that the president of the council of Castile, the count of Montellano, worked actively to sabotage the decisions of the *despacho*, sending 'private letters and orders . . . to corregidors and judges, totally contrary to the decisions of the despacho, so that he almost always combats what the despacho (of which he is a member) has decided'.[61] In resisting the French the grandees claimed to be defending Spaniards against foreigners, traditional government against new methods, regional rights against centralization. They were also defending their class interest, as the French always maintained; Amelot crushed Aragon and Valencia and abolished their *fueros*, confident that the aristocracy could not inspire mass resistance.[62]

---

[58] Louis XIV to Amelot, 20 August 1705, in Kamen, *The War of Succession in Spain*, p. 89.
[59] Coxe, *Memoirs of the Kings of Spain*, I, p. 361.
[60] Quoted in Kamen, *The War of Succession in Spain*, p. 91.
[61] Memoir of Tessé to Chamillart, 11 April 1705, in Coxe, *Memoirs of the Kings of Spain*, I, p. 321.
[62] Ibid., I, p. 339.

Philip V had virtually nothing to say in these disputes, for he had no independent power. He was not personally strong enough at this stage of his reign to attract loyalty or encourage commitment. In the first place, he was not sure whom he could trust among the nobility, many of whom were playing a waiting game. Secondly, to win the war he needed French help. He therefore had to accept French policy, personnel, and prejudices, even if it meant alienating the grandees. This led the moderate commentator, San Felipe, to write:

> The greatest misfortune which Spain then suffered was that, although it had a saintly, just and honest king, he could not speak up, for fear of offending the French. The French sold their aid dearly, and the more interest they showed in Spain and desire for domination there, the more committed the English and Dutch became to a hard war policy, which they would not have followed so determinedly, or at all, if Spain had preserved its independence.[63]

Amelot continued to administer the affairs of Spain, directed by Louis XIV, protected by Ursins, and trusted by Philip V. While he marginalized the aristocracy, he brought into existence a new bureaucratic elite of young Spaniards, such as José Patiño and Melchor Macanaz, who were willing to serve the new king and promote Bourbon reform.[64] Yet Amelot, for all his talents, misjudged Spain and underestimated the Spaniards. After the loss of Barcelona and invasion of Castile in 1706, he believed they would accept defeat, and only a French army would rally them: 'They have neither courage nor strength, and display only weakness and cowardice ... They do as much harm as they can. Kindness and consideration will never induce them to be good subjects; only strong and firm government will succeed, and the king of Spain will never be truly king unless he can make himself feared.'[65]

In the event the Spaniards showed more stomach for war than the French, and Philip more spirit than Louis. In 1709 he rejected the French peace plan transmitted by Amelot and he was supported by his Spanish ministers. In order to push French policy through, Amelot suspended the cabinet, expelled Montellano, the leader of the Spanish

---

[63] San Felipe, *Comentarios*, p. 102.

[64] Henry Kamen, 'Melchor de Macanaz and the Foundations of Bourbon Power in Spain', *English Historical Review*, 80, 317 (1965), pp. 699–716.

[65] Amelot to Louis XIV, 5 May 1706, in Baudrillart, *Philippe V et la cour de France*, i, pp. 257–8.

opposition, and with him the duke of San Juan, minister of war. There was much indignation over these arbitrary procedures, some of it voiced in Montellano's *tertulia*, a literary salon turned political forum, where Amelot and Ursins were openly criticized. 'The Spanish magnates, who imagined that the whole weight of defending the king would fall upon the Spanish nation, openly requested that the French be expelled from the government.'[66] An elite gathering of this kind, however, was not a strong base for opposition. This was the view of the French, who were satisfied that the opposition was confined to the court and the grandees. The French could not afford to make mistakes. Their intelligence reports on Spanish morale in 1709 were vital to Louis XIV in deciding whether Spain was ready for peace or worth supporting longer. Amelot, more experienced now than in 1706, reported in January 1709 that there was not the slightest reason to suspect the loyalty of the people in general or of the lesser nobility. True, they all suffered from the war, taxes, and famine, but there were no complaints, no signs of protest or rebellion:

> These disloyal rumours spring from the discontent of those grandees, who, because they are not admitted to a share of power, murmur heavily, and complain that no regard is paid to the grandees, the nobles and people; that their customs and laws are overturned; that the authority of their councils is annihilated, that all will be lost without a change of measures.[67]

According to French analysis, if the grandees and councils now found themselves set aside, it was because of their own record of incompetence. Left to them, the government would have no resources and Philip V could not rule Spain; without reforms inspired by France and executed by the French ambassador, the Bourbon cause would be lost. The analysis was probably valid, but Spaniards criticized France not because of a new dynasty. Rather they resented French manipulation of the Spanish government, control of offices and appointments, of military decisions and commands, and of economic life; and the resentment was directed against Amelot and Ursins, not Philip V. Moreover, the validity of the French analysis depended on French success and commitment. Both were called into question during the crisis of 1709 and Philip was now obliged to draw closer to the grandees and their

[66] San Felipe, *Comentarios*, p. 169.
[67] Amelot to Louis XIV, January 1709, in Coxe, *Memoirs of the Kings of Spain*, I, p. 436.

Spanish party.[68] The defeat at Zaragoza, the advance of the archduke, and fear of losing both the war and the French alliance, made each realize that they had some interests in common in defending their country and government. The disengagement of Louis XIV in 1709 caused Philip to identify more positively with the Spanish party. In an interview with Amelot on 30 April 1709, confident of support from grandees and people alike and aware that the French might desert him, he communicated his decision to rely exclusively on Spaniards and to distance himself from his grandfather, telling the ambassador 'that he only feared he had waited too long to take the present decision, but as he had done so out of respect for his grandfather, it was not something to regret'.[69]

The declaration of independence by Philip V should not be exaggerated. He did not suddenly become a mighty king. He still needed Louis XIV, French aid, even Amelot. And the grandees did not become the saviours of Spain. They returned in strength to the cabinet, only to find that real power no longer resided there, that the king looked for advice outside their ranks, and that the principal adviser was the princess des Ursins, 'whose opinions', remarked San Felipe, 'no one opposed unless they sought their downfall'.[70] So change co-existed with continuity, and in their new role the grandees were still incompetent. They had no ideas for the mobilization of resources beyond, ironically, a further petition to Louis XIV; following the evacuation of Madrid in September 1710, thirty-two grandees signed a document invoking their loyalty to Philip V and requesting French military assistance. The only dissenting voice was that of the duke of Osuna, who thought it 'an insult to the nation to appeal for foreign aid, especially when Spain was no longer occupied by French troops'.[71] The grandees did not inspire confidence. Louis XIV renewed his military aid, though at a lower level, and from December 1710 the Spanish army had to increase its war effort. Politically, however, the country was now leaderless, for the grandees were more given to faction than to leadership and their style of government was to sit in councils uttering lofty generalizations. Philip V swallowed his pride and pleaded with his grandfather to send back Amelot, but this

[68] See above, pp. 33–5.
[69] Amelot to Louis XIV, 30 April 1709, in Baudrillart, *Philippe V et la cour de France*, I, p. 345; San Felipe, *Comentarios*, p. 175.
[70] San Felipe, *Comentarios*, p. 197.
[71] Nicolas de Jesús Belando, *Historia civil de España . . . desde el año 1700 hasta el de 1733* (3 vols, Madrid, 1740–4), I, p. 439.

was not possible, and his government was left to be rescued by Ursins and her lesser Spanish clients.

The grandees underwent from 1710 a second political defeat of their own making, as they lost credit, office and influence. Ursins survived all changes and was as powerful as ever, hated by some, cultivated by others, and feared by all. As an English observer remarked: 'She continues to be courted by everybody as before, and to be the factotum of this Court.'[72] But the court needed an administrator, if only to reorganize revenues and resources. First the king turned to one of his Flemish administrators, the count of Bergeyck, who in September 1711 was made superintendent of finances and who claimed to find nothing but 'disorder'; in his two years in Spain he generated some original ideas for naval, financial and administrative reform, but time was too short to produce results.[73] So the king asked once more for Jean Orry, who was brought back from France in 1713 to renew his collaboration with Ursins. The return of Orry signified the continuation of reform, as opposed to the traditionalism of the grandees. Did it also mean a revival of French influence? Orry told the British ambassador that it was not his object to 'capture' the Spanish court and that the interests of France and Spain were 'entirely divided'.[74] There had in fact been a shift in French relations with Spain. The disengagement of Louis XIV in 1709 meant a relative loss of power, and the balance moved further from France once negotiations for peace began at Utrecht, enabling Spain to exploit its bargaining position and recover its independence. Louis XIV was no longer the master, Spain no longer a dependency. France learned that it must proceed not by governing Spain but by diplomacy, influence, dynastic sentiment. It was a special relationship, not a political union, and it was tested in America as well as in Europe.

America: Responses and Resources

Spanish America supported the Bourbon succession. The war gave its inhabitants a golden opportunity for independent action, had they so wished, but loyalties hardly wavered. It is true that a number of interest groups had reservations. Creole merchants and consumers who had long enjoyed profitable dealings with the English and the Dutch, especially in

[72] Anon. letter, Madrid, 12 December 1712, PRO, SP 94/79.
[73] Kamen, *The War of Succession in Spain*, pp. 50–2.
[74] Burck to Delasaye, Madrid, 8 May 1713, PRO, SP 94/80.

the Caribbean, resented the idea of a Franco-Spanish monopoly. An unlikely plan was concocted by the Allies to raise Caracas, Santa Fe, Cartagena, and even Peru and Mexico. A Habsburg agent, operating from Curaçao in 1702 and working on creole sympathy on the mainland, developed contacts in Venezuela among merchants and officials, including the governor, and even managed to proclaim 'Charles III' in Caracas before he was arrested and the project suppressed.[75] Another Carlist agent was active in Mexico in the same period.[76] There were very few aliens in the colonies, but Philip V continued the practice, against the advice of the council of the Indies, of allowing foreign Jesuits and other missionaries to enter Spanish America. Some of these – Austrians and Flemings – were sympathetic towards the Habsburg cause in the Caribbean and soon established contacts with Dutch contrabandists in the region of Cumaná, Caracas, and Maracaibo, combining trade and subversion in a common cause.[77] In the Río de la Plata, on the other hand, the Jesuits were loyal and valued subjects of Philip V. In 1703, once Portugal joined the Allies, Philip V ordered the governor of Buenos Aires to take Colônia do Sacramento from Portugal, and instructed the Jesuit provincial to place mission troops at the governor's disposal. By September 1704 a force of 4,000 Indian troops was on its way accompanied by four Jesuit 'chaplains' to collaborate in a successful operation.[78]

The year 1700 meant little to the mass of Spanish Americans, and the political moment had not arrived when a conjuncture of this kind would raise thoughts of liberation. The colonial administration was solid for Philip V. In Peru the long-serving viceroy, the conde de la Monclova, adjusted without difficulty to the new regime and made an effortless about-turn from resisting the French as enemies to welcoming them as allies, because in truth they were always admitted as traders, before and after 1700.[79] Monclova served a further five years under Philip V and was a known supporter of the Bourbon cause. He was followed by the marquis of Castelldosríus, an even more ardent Bourbonist, a favourite

[75] Analola Borges, *La Casa de Austria en Venezuela durante la Guerra de Sucesión Española (1702-1715)* (Salzburg/Tenerife, 1963), pp. 92–6.

[76] Luis Navarro García, *Hispanoamérica en el siglo XVIII* (Seville, 1975), p. 20.

[77] Celestino Andrés Araúz Monfante, *El contrabando holandés en el Caribe durante la primera mitad del siglo XVIII* (2 vols, Caracas, 1984), I, pp. 135–9.

[78] Adalberto López, *The Revolt of the Comuneros, 1721-1735. A Study in the Colonial History of Paraguay* (Cambridge, Mass., 1976), p. 75.

[79] Guillermo Céspedes del Castillo and Manuel Moreyra Paz-Soldán (eds), *Colección de cartas de virreyes: Conde de la Monclova* (3 vols, Lima, 1954–5), I, p. xii, for a different view.

of Louis XIV, whose nominee he was for the office of viceroy and whose interests he faithfully served during his years in Peru from 1707 to 1710.[80] In Mexico the Habsburg viceroy, the conde de Moctezuma, was almost immediately recalled by Philip V, who was doubtful perhaps of his loyalty, but the transition was made without upheaval. The framework of colonial government remained intact. At its centre stood the *audiencias*, judicial and administrative tribunals, providing stability, continuity, and opportunities. Philip V continued the Habsburg practice of selling *audiencia* posts to locally-born creoles without regard to standards of justice or imperial control, and he allowed a flood of sales to boost his revenue in the years 1707–12.[81]

Philip V inherited Spanish America, therefore, without a crisis of succession. Once he had gained Castile as his heartland, his success in America was predictable. The monarch himself was the source of legitimacy, and of patronage, in America. Madrid was the seat of empire, Andalucía its market place. And whoever held Cadiz controlled the European end of the Indies trade. Castile had a proprietorial interest in office, trade, and all the other benefits of empire, and there was an immediate identity between king and subjects on these vital interests. Castile's special position in America was underlined in 1701 in Potosí where the authorities proclaimed 'Castile and the Indies for Philip V'.[82] The Habsburgs had none of these advantages. Barcelona had the ambition but not the instruments of colonial trade. The Allied fleet had the power to attack Spain's shipping but not the capacity to close the Atlantic routes, destroy the colonial defences, or replace the existing structure. In fact Philip V's greatest danger in Spanish America came not from his enemies but from his allies. For France saw the Indies not only as a resource for fighting the war but also as a prize for winning it.

Louis XIV did not disguise the fact that 'the main object of the present war is the Indies trade and the wealth it produces.'[83] The optimum policy for France was to gain a full and legal participation in the Spanish monopoly under its own name. In default of this it would settle for *de facto* participation with the exclusion of the English and the Dutch from (a) the re-export trade in Cadiz and (b) the interloping trade

---

[80] Geoffrey J. Walker, *Spanish Politics and Imperial Trade, 1700-1789* (London, 1979), pp. 34–48.

[81] Mark A. Burkholder and D. S. Chandler, *From Impotence to Authority. The Spanish Crown and the American Audiencias, 1687-1808* (Columbia, Missouri, 1977), pp. 32–6.

[82] Bartolomé Arzáns de Orsúa y Vela, *Historia de la Villa Imperial de Potosí*, (eds) Lewis Hanke and Gunnar Mendoza (3 vols, Providence, RI, 1965), II, p. 405.

[83] Louis XIV to Amelot, 18 February 1709, in Kamen, *The War of Succession in Spain*, p. 135.

in the Indies. This policy carried a high risk for Spain as well as for the Allies; in one way or another Louis XIV was determined to gain entry into or control of the trade of America. He opened his campaign by securing in 1701 the *asiento de negros*, which gave France the exclusive right to export slaves to Spanish America and the opportunity to export much else besides. From early in the same year Spain allowed French warships into American ports to combat Allied shipping and transport silver; they could seek supplies but not conduct trade. This was another cover for extending France's direct trade to the Indies, exploiting the breakdown of the fleet system and consequent local shortages.[84] In May 1707 Spanish merchants in Seville, who deplored these developments, estimated that since the beginning of the war thirty French ships had traded to the ports of Campeche and Vera Cruz, over eighty-six to the ports of Tierra Firme, and at the end of 1706 alone there were fifteen in Pacific waters, earning for France millions of pesos in returns. In 1707 the authorities at Vera Cruz recorded twenty-one French vessels; in the Pacific at least eighteen were identified.

The direct trade to the Pacific was new, a French initiative in an area not exploited by Spanish shipping. In 1698 the newly formed *Compagnie de la Mer du Sud* sent four vessels around Cape Horn, which returned in 1701. Between 1700 and 1721 ninety-seven French vessels called at Concepción, ninety-one at Callao, most of them preferring to enter the Pacific by Cape Horn rather than the Magellan Straits.[85] In 1714 two eyewitnesses recently returned reported 'twenty four French ships trading on that coast, and that notwithstanding all the orders that may be sent thither, it is impossible to prevent that commerce without a squadron of ships of force'.[86] The French trade to Peru owed its success to the state of the market, the prolonged absence of *galeones*, and the lengthy gap between trade fairs. When, in 1706, for the first time in over ten years a Spanish fleet brought merchandise to the Portobello fair, it found the market glutted and demand low.[87] There was an outcry from Spanish merchants, a demand that the government take action to curb its allies as well as its enemies. French trade from Saint-Malo encountered few obstacles on the Pacific coast of South America, and there

---

[84] Kamen, *The War of Succession in Spain*, pp. 143–56; Walker, *Spanish Politics and Imperial Trade*, p. 47.

[85] Carlos Daniel Malamud Rikles, *Cádiz y Saint Malo en el comercio colonial peruano (1698-1725)* (Cadiz, 1986), p. 139.

[86] Burck to Stanhope, Madrid, 5 November 1714, PRO, SP 94/82.

[87] Sergio Villalobos, 'Contrabando francés en el Pacífico, 1700–1724', *Revista de Historia de América*, 51 (1961), pp. 49–80; Walker, *Spanish Politics and Imperial Trade*, pp. 21–33.

was no lack of purchasers among Spanish and creole merchants, who in turn found willing customers in Peru and adjacent colonies. The Bourbon governments, French traders, Spanish officials, colonial merchants, and consumers, all were part of a conniving network, each group maintaining pretences while pursuing their interests. In Madrid Amelot replied to complaints by arguing that 'since the Spaniards were not themselves trading, it was more just that we should profit from it, rather than our common enemies.'[88] And in Peru Viceroy Castelldosríus, who organized in effect an alternative system of direct trade, the so-called 'Pisco Fair', proved that king, viceroy, French merchants and creole consumers could all be satisfied, and that there were profits enough for everyone, or almost everyone, if the interest groups were skilfully managed.

Direct trade to America via the *asiento*, the Pacific route, and their own warships were not the only avenues open to the French. As the senior naval partner in the Bourbon alliance, France was called upon to provide escorts for the treasure fleets returning from Mexico and Tierra Firme, as they did in 1708, 1709, and 1712. Not all of these joint operations were successful. In June 1708 an English squadron under Admiral Charles Wager inflicted severe losses on a treasure fleet sailing from Portobello to Cartagena, a disaster for Spain if not for France. Escort duty was a very profitable business, another cover for trade and treasure. While they willingly provided escorts for the *flotas* and *galeones*, the French preferred to trade directly to America on their own account rather than participate in the fleets, for which there were costs to be paid to the Spanish crown and middlemen.[89] In fact their own trade competed with the fleets and pre-empted the market.

Yet none of these concessions, or infractions, amounted to a formal entry into the Spanish monopoly, and the French had to be content with an extension of the traditional system, subject still to the resistance of the Spanish and the competition of the English. In only one case, the New Spain fleet of 1703, did French ships officially participate for their own profit.[90] Philip V could not ignore the interests of his Spanish subjects or alienate the powerful Cadiz-Seville monopolists. He had to identify with the monopoly and Louis XIV had to accept it. Nevertheless, direct trade to so many parts of the Spanish empire, on a scale not previously enjoyed by any other nation, was a considerable advance on

---

[88] Amelot to Torcy, 21 November 1707, in Kamen, *The War of Succession in Spain*, p. 149.

[89] Malamud, *Cádiz y Saint Malo*, pp. 146–7.

[90] Walker, *Spanish Politics and Imperial Trade*, p. 52.

the traditional re-export trade from Cadiz within the Spanish fleets, and for Spain was the price to be paid for its reliance on French sea power. Even in supposed defeat, in 1714, the French obtained through Orry concessions to trade with Honduras and Caracas.[91]

The transatlantic trade in its various guises yielded copious returns to France and its merchants. A French estimate of 1709 stated that in the last eight years more than 180 million livres had entered France from the Indies. This came partly in contraband trade in silver via the peninsula, partly from the direct trade with America, and not least on the French escorts themselves, escorts which Spain was already paying for in hard cash, such as the one million pesos paid to the French ambassador for the vessels escorting the two fleets of 1706. On occasion treasure returns went directly to France. In February 1707 a small fleet from Mexico decided, for security reasons, to put into Brest rather than Cadiz. It carried 7–8 million pesos in silver, 6 million of which belonged to the private sector, and goods to the value of 3 million. Louis XIV had it in mind to keep a part, while Philip V sought to dissuade him, conscious of the Francophobia already existing in Spain. He offered instead a gift of a million livres which had been brought on the king of Spain's own account. Louis graciously accepted the gift: 'You are right. It would be inadvisable to retain here the slightest amount of the money arrived from the Indies on the account of Your Majesty's subjects.'[92] In the event French rapacity overcame such scruples, and it may be doubted whether any of this money reached Spain. By fair means or foul, the French had made a breakthrough which was the envy of Europe. Not without reason did San Felipe complain: 'There was no shortage of money in France; they had more than ever, because for many years they had complete freedom of the Indies trade, something which no other nation gained.'[93]

Spain had unique experience of organizing trade with America, and this did not fail her in the War of Succession. A combination of state bureaucracy, merchant enterprise, and French naval support kept the Atlantic crossing open, and in spite of the sea power of the Allies there was no year in which the colonies were cut off from their metropolis. Regular fleet sailings were disrupted, but irregularity was already the

[91] Wishart to Bolinbroke, Cadiz, 27 April 1714, PRO, SP 94/82.

[92] Philip V to Louis XIV, 28 March, 4 April 1707, Louis XIV to Philip V, 11 April, 19 April 1707, in Baudrillart, *Philippe V et la cour de France*, I, p. 287; Kamen, *The War of Succession in Spain*, p. 183.

[93] San Felipe, *Comentarios*, p. 167.

norm before 1700. To send even five fleets, in 1706, 1708, 1710, 1712, and 1715, was a triumph of organization over discouragement. Outside the fleets warships, merchantmen and *avisos*, or dispatch boats, plied between Spain and America throughout the war, and there was traffic out and in during every year from 1701 to 1715, in all about 132 inbound vessels (see table 2.1). The returns in most years were modest, but large silver shipments were registered in 1702 (12–20 million pesos), 1707 (10 million), 1708 (20 million), 1710 (10 million), and 1713 (4–12 million).[94] American treasure helped the war effort and gave the Bourbons a financial advantage over the Habsburgs. It was not the only, or even the major, element in Philip V's annual revenue, but it was a powerful injection, available in ready money for defraying immediate needs. What were the respective treasure returns to Spain and France in the War of Succession? The precise percentage is not known, but it is probable that France gained more than Spain in the private sector, and possible that Louis XIV received more than Philip V.[95] The French initiative in the transatlantic trade after 1700 was part of a wider project for control of the economy of the whole Hispanic world, peninsular as well as American. France aimed to create a vast protected market, in which an inter-Bourbon division of labour would operate, Spain supplying the precious

Table 2.1 *American treasure returns to Spain in million pesos 1701–1720*

Quinquennia	Inbound vessels	Treasure
1701–5	61	55.1
1706–10	44	64.3
1711–15	27	46.8
1716–20	60	43.2

Not all the vessels or returns were Spanish; some belonged to the French officially participating as escorts or merchantmen. Not all the ports of return were Spanish. There were substantial French returns from direct but illegal trade. These five-yearly totals were less than before the war, but still did not amount to a 'depression'.

Source: Michel Morineau, *Incroyables gazettes et fabuleux métaux. Les retours des trésors américains d'après les gazettes hollandaises (XVIe-XVIIIe siècles)* (Cambridge, 1985), pp. 310–17.

[94] Kamen, *The War of Succession in Spain*, pp. 178–91; Morineau, *Incroyables gazettes et fabuleux métaux*, pp. 310–12.
[95] Kamen, *The War of Succession in Spain*, p. 193.

metals and raw materials with which she was endowed, France the manufactures with which she would earn bullion from the favourable trade balance. The War of Succession gave France the opportunity to promote this exercise in autarky by enabling her to exclude the enemy from the Spanish market and to gain for herself favoured fiscal treatment and even the means of discouraging manufactures in Spain.[96] The plan was not fulfilled, though France revived it later in the century. Meanwhile she successfully expanded her share of the Spanish and American market during these years. The essential leverage came from French naval power, which alone was capable of protecting Spanish trade and navigation in the Mediterranean and Atlantic.

The price of protection was paid by the Spanish merchants and the Cadiz monopolists, who saw their privileges eroded and markets invaded. Or so they claimed, blaming the French for the state of America and its trade. The French had another explanation:

> The riches of Peru and Mexico, those inexhaustible sources of wealth, are almost lost to Spain. Not only are complaints made against the French merchants for ruining the trade of Cadiz and Seville, in spite of the regulations of the French court against those who infringe the established rules, but the enormous abuses of the administration of the viceroys continue in full force. Avarice and pillage are unpunished, fortresses and garrisons are neglected; *all things seem to portend a fatal revolution*.
>
> Resolutions have to be taken to recall the two viceroys, and to fix some precise bounds to the profits of their successors, so as to give them the means of enriching themselves without departing from their duty. I acknowledge that the expedient will not suffice to restrain cupidity; yet I do not see a better, even if the choice is directed on persons most distinguished for firmness and probity. So difficult is it to find among the grandees, a mind of sufficient strength to resist the influence of example and interest.[97]

The analysis of Amelot, part of a longer criticism of the grandees, had the merit of looking beyond the immediate conjuncture. The year 1700 made no difference to Spanish America, to its institutions, its economic structure, its social organization. The Bourbon state exercised no more power, provided no better example, offered no newer policy than its

---

[96] Ibid., pp. 118–39.
[97] Amelot to Louis XIV, 1709, in Coxe, *Memoirs of the Kings of Spain*, I, p. 440.

Habsburg predecessor. The hour of reform had not yet arrived in America. Had it begun in Spain?

Bourbon State, Nation State

A monarchy intact and reformed, these ideas were not invented by the Bourbons. Charles II had ruled a Spain showing signs of revival and had died proclaiming the unity of the Spanish empire. But the Habsburgs had been incapable of overcoming two great obstacles to reform, the autonomy of the regions and the political power of the aristocracy, accustomed to being 'idols and despots of the kingdom', as San Felipe remarked.[98] A new king in himself was not a sufficient agent of change. It was the combination of a number of factors, the new dynasty, the pressure of France, the needs of war, the emergence of a bureaucratic elite, which provided the impulse for a shift in power towards the central government. The reform programme unfolded in two stages: the first, to 1714, was directed primarily to the war effort; the second was planned and executed by a series of Spanish reformers with longer-term objectives.

Philip V began by making the crown more powerful than his most powerful subjects. In confronting the aristocracy he and his advisers had no desire to undermine a social class, to destroy their privileges or reduce their estates. He demoted the grandees politically, but left them entrenched in their domains.[99] During his reign he created 200 new titles of nobility for loyalty and service, debasing the currency perhaps but also adding the weight of the crown to the prestige of nobility and producing an alternative to the grandees. Translated into institutions, the defeat of the grandees meant the elevation of the *despacho* at the expense of the councils. The reign began with the emergence of the *despacho*, or cabinet council, as the key institution at the centre, one in which the grandees were represented by only two to four members, and in which policy and administration were dominated by the French ambassador, Amelot, the effective prime minister of Spain from 1705 to 1709. The *despacho* bypassed the councils and dealt directly with regional and provincial officials, thus excluding the grandees from policy making and execution. The first victim was the council of state, which specialized in foreign affairs and was soon reduced to a nonentity.

[98] San Felipe, *Comentarios*, pp. 22, 191.
[99] Kamen, *The War of Succession in Spain*, pp. 87–94, 114–15.

Centralization then nullified other councils or diminished their personnel until only one retained its significance, the council of Castile, which
also absorbed the work of regional councils – Aragon, Flanders, and
Italy – when these became superfluous during the course of the war. The
various departments of government were now taken over by secretaries,
whose office developed out of that of secretary of *despacho*. These in
effect were ministers and their departments incipient ministries, working under a chief minister or secretary of state, an office which gradually
acquired a clearer identity once the French presence was withdrawn.[100]
Thus the centre of power moved from grandees to lesser nobles, from
councils to secretaries of state.

The priority of Bourbon government in the years after 1700 was to
mobilize resources for war. Financial reform did not involve basic
restructuring of revenue or its collection. The Bourbon state continued
to rely upon traditional revenues and to leave collection to tax farmers
and local councils operating within fixed quotas. Ordinary revenue was
still derived from the *rentas provinciales* (*alcabala*, *servicio*, and *millones*)
and the *rentas generales* (customs and monopolies). The government
increased the yield simply through greater efficiency and higher tax
levels, and also by imposing a number of extraordinary exactions, such as
forced loans, taxes on alienations of crown property and revenues, levies
on salaries, sequestrations from dissidents, revenues from vacant episcopal sees, and suspension of payments on *juros* (annuities charged on
the state). Results were positive. Ordinary revenue increased from 96.7
million reales in 1703 to 116.7 million in 1713, an increase of over 20 per
cent, extraordinary revenue from 23.6 million to 112.7 million, an
increase of over 377 per cent. Total revenue almost doubled, from 120.3
million to 229.4 million. Most of this came from Castile; even after 1707
revenue from Aragon and Valencia made little difference to central
resources. Yet under pressure of war these almost doubled between 1703
and 1713. Expenditure, of course, also soared; military costs alone
amounted to 100 million annually, a large part of which left Spain to pay
for arms and equipment from France.[101] Income only kept pace with
expenditure through loans from financiers and revenues from the Indies,
which made little contribution to ordinary expenditure but was swallowed up immediately in the costs of war and payments to France. By
1713 military and administrative costs exceeded total income by about
37 million reales.

[100] See below, pp. 99–101.
[101] Kamen, *The War of Succession in Spain*, pp. 75–6, 215, 223–31.

Tax pressure rather than tax reform was the chosen policy of the first Bourbon administration. Orry had more constructive ideas, and in 1703 he initiated a scheme to reform the entire government of Spain, its administration and its finances. He had no opportunity to implement this before 1706, when he was recalled to France, and it was 1713 before Philip V gave him another opportunity. In spite of all his claims, or fantasies, little had been done before his dismissal in 1715, and his mission in Spain remains a monument to ideas rather than achievements. A strange amalgam of ability, eccentricity, and arrogance, and perhaps inferior in talent to Amelot, Bergeyck, and the new Spanish bureaucrats, Orry was nevertheless the author of a number of specific reforms, systematic accounting methods, a separate war treasury, recovery of alienated property and taxes, which contributed to the growth of Spanish revenues and gave the government the resources to survive the war.[102]

It was the long-term aim of the central government to establish fiscal equality in Spain as between the various kingdoms, and to make the eastern regions contribute to the monarchy according to their present resources rather than their ancient privileges. The Habsburgs, too, had looked askance at regional rights but they lacked the combination of power and opportunity to destroy them. Now, in 1707, the Bourbons had both. In the eyes of Philip V and Castile the eastern regions were rebels and undeserving of their immunities. Bourbon policy contained an element of punishment, expressed in the preamble to the decree of 29 June 1707 abolishing the *fueros*: 'Considering that the kingdoms of Aragon and Valencia and all their inhabitants, by reason of the rebellion which they have raised, thus breaking the oath of allegiance they swore to me as their lawful King and Lord, have forfeited all rights, privileges, immunities and liberties which they enjoyed. . . .' The statement was of doubtful accuracy, for the aristocracy had been the objects of rebellion not its authors. But the policy embodied more than retribution. As the King explained, it also reflected 'my will to reduce all the kingdoms of Spain to obedience to the same laws, practices, customs and tribunals, each equally subject to the laws of Castile, which are so praiseworthy and acceptable throughout the world'. And finally the decree maintained that abolition of the *fueros* and subjection to the laws of Castile would bring compensating advantages to the Aragonese and Valencians, who would henceforth have access to offices and appointments in

---

[102] Domínguez Ortiz, *Sociedad y estado en el siglo XVIII español*, pp. 68–9.

Castile equal to that of Castilians in Aragon and Valencia.[103] The Nueva Planta, or New Plan, it has been aptly said, was 'a bitter but wholesome medicine',[104] a compulsory invitation to participate in a wider world.

In Valencia conquest and occupation were quickly followed by the decree of 29 June 1707 imposing the Nueva Planta. This was the first and most drastic of all the new regimes, a measure perhaps of the social division and weakness of Valencia, the absolute power of the king, and the ruthlessness of his agent, Melchor de Macanaz. Macanaz was a Salamanca-trained lawyer who had come to the attention of Amelot in the early years of the war.[105] After a period as secretary of the council of Castile, he was sent to Valencia in the wake of the army to reform finances and administration. The object was to create a new court of justice, an *audiencia*, and give one half of the seats to Castilians, a proposal which provoked the opposition of the council of Aragon. Macanaz argued that the council was now irrelevant and should be abolished with the *fueros*. This was done on 15 July, and eventually the government established a court of Chancery in Valencia in August 1707, a tribunal administering not the traditional law of Valencia but the public and civil law of Castile. Macanaz and his colleagues introduced the standard Castilian taxes, and in October he personally was put in charge of the confiscation programme, a means of profit to himself as well as revenue to the crown. Finally, Macanaz was commissioned to build a new town, San Felipe, to replace the obliterated Játiva, and this gave him the opportunity to express his ecclesiastical policy. He refused to allow the return of the religious orders or to restore any clerical property confiscated for rebellion. Excommunicated by the archbishop of Valencia and reviled by the civil authorities, Macanaz left Valencia convinced that the extension of royal power was still frustrated by the old regime of local rights, vested interests, and clerical resistance.[106] But he still enjoyed the confidence of the crown, which assigned him a similar task in Aragon.

The abolition of council and *cortes*, the transformation of the law and of legal institutions, and the replacement of traditional officials by intendants and corregidores, were applied to Aragon as well as Valencia. Here too the war effort and the future of Spain demanded centralization,

---

[103] Pedro Voltes Bou, *La Guerra de Sucesión en Valencia* (Valencia, 1964), pp. 76–8.
[104] Domínguez Ortiz, *Sociedad y estado en el siglo XVIII español*, p. 86.
[105] San Felipe, *Comentarios*, p. 145; Kamen, 'Melchor de Macanaz', p. 701.
[106] Carmen Martín Gaite, *Macanaz, otro paciente de la Inquisición* (2nd edn, Madrid, 1975), pp. 149–64.

modernization, and new personnel. When Philip V reoccupied Zaragoza he placed Macanaz in charge of reorganizing the city and province as intendant general of Aragon (February 1711). Again, Macanaz was the instrument of military-backed absolutism. An army commander, the count of Tsercaes Tilly, was appointed governor and also president of a new *audiencia*, all appeals from which were to go to the council of Castile in Madrid. Macanaz was head of finances with the duty of consulting a tribunal of the royal treasury, and in pursuit of supreme power over finance he was soon in conflict with the tribunal, with local interests, and with the military governor himself. The resistance of traditionalists, the protests of the nobility, and the temptation of royal officials to compromise, convinced Macanaz that the Bourbon regime in Aragon was at risk and that he stood alone as the instrument of pure absolutism.[107] There was some justification for his fears; nobles regained privileges, the alcabala tax was resisted. But he stood his ground and amidst another bureaucratic tumult he was supported and promoted, in 1712, to the post of *fiscal general*, or attorney general, of the council of Castile. Meanwhile Aragon had felt the weight of Bourbon reform. The province was divided into districts, each with a military governor, while municipal government was placed in a rigid Castilian mould. Larger cities were now governed by *regidores*, or aldermen, appointed by the crown from nobles only, while in smaller towns citizens had the right to nominate *regidores*, whose appointments were confirmed by the *audiencia*; the only improvement on the Castilian model was avoidance of the practice of life-term and proprietory *regidores*. Otherwise the municipality was converted into a bureaucratic agency, representing the local elite and subordinate to the crown. Between municipal and central government, the *corregidor*, another importation from Castile, replaced the traditional Aragonese officials.

Catalonia was the last but not the least of the eastern regions to succumb to the Nueva Planta.[108] The experience was the more traumatic because of its rich history, the strength of its institutions, and the emotion of its recent resistance. Yet the decree of 16 January 1716, at least in its application, proved to be more moderate and less 'Castilian'

[107] Kamen, *The War of Succession in Spain*, pp. 343–52, and 'Melchor de Macanaz', pp. 704–5; Martín, *Macanaz*, pp. 191–9.

[108] Juan Mercader Riba, 'La ordenación de Cataluña por Felipe V: La Nueva Planta', *Hispania*, 43 (1951), pp. 257–366, *Els capitans generals* (Barcelona, 1957), pp. 25–54, *Felip V i Catalunya* (Barcelona, 1968), pp. 30–55; Víctor Ferro, *El dret públic català. Les institucions a Catalunya fins al Decret de Nova Planta* (Barcelona, 1987), pp. 450–60.

than that imposed in Aragon-Valencia, and it was administered not by
Macanaz but by José Patiño who represented the more reasonable face
of Bourbon absolutism. The public law of Catalonia was now Castilian
law, but Catalan civil law and other local usages survived. The Catalan
language could not be employed in the law courts or in any official
capacity. The government of Catalonia was divided between the captain-
general and the royal *audiencia*, with the exception of financial questions
which were assigned to the intendant. In the local districts, or *comarcas*,
the ancient *vergueres* were replaced by Castilian-type *corregidores*.
Municipalities were taken out of the hands of middle-class guilds and
became the preserve of local elites, represented by twenty-four crown-
nominated *regidores* in the case of Barcelona, and varying numbers
nominated by the *audiencia* in other Catalan towns.

The two least acceptable innovations were compulsory military
service and fiscal reform. Army recruitment was resisted, and the
attempt to introduce Castilian type levies in eastern Spain provoked so
many incidents that in the end the government abandoned the idea. Tax
reform was another matter: one of the prime objects of the Nueva Planta
was to obtain an appropriate contribution from the regions towards
central resources. Castile was not considered a useful model, as its tax
structure was notoriously complex and inequitable. Instead the old
regional taxes were maintained and a new tax imposed, called the *catastro*
in Catalonia, the *única contribución* in Aragon, and the *equivalente* in
Valencia. The essential idea was to devise a simple tax which would
apply to all according to their means, though the reformers drew back
from imposing an income tax on the privileged sectors. In the case of
Catalonia, to restore the balance of revenue from the regional government to the central state, the crown first proposed a *catastro* of 1,200,000
pesos a year. This proved to be too high and was reduced to 900,000, to
be collected by a 10 per cent tax on all rural and urban properties, and an
8 per cent tax on personal incomes.[109]

The balance sheet of the Nueva Planta inevitably showed a mixture of
gains and losses. The crown of Aragon and the principality of Catalonia
ceased to exist as separate parts of the Spanish monarchy. The struggle
for a strong, central and united state had at last been won, and in the
process much of the debris of the Habsburg past was swept away, along
with some of its political values. Bourbon absolutism imposed two
principles which were alien to Catalan traditions; that royal authority

[109] Joaquín Nadal Farreras, *La introducción del Catastro en Gerona* (Barcelona, 1971), pp. 61–82.

was above the law, and that the crown was free to levy taxes. The institutional changes were less important. The council of Aragon was not a great loss; its jurisdiction passed partly to the secretaries of state, partly to the *audiencias* in Barcelona, Zaragoza and Valencia, a measure of devolution if anything. The viceroys were replaced by captains-general, indicating perhaps a militarization of power, but the difference remained to be seen. After the initial shock people accepted the new regime, if not without question at least without rebellion. Philip V acted to diminish the discontent of the local elites, recognizing that in Aragon and Valencia they had not been rebels and convinced that without them he could not rule the regions. In Valencia the seigneurial rights of the lords were expressly confirmed. In Aragon the nobles lost their jurisdiction in criminal cases but preserved their economic privileges. The lowering of interest on *censos* (mortgage loans) from 5 to 3 per cent in Castile signified a loss to the privileged classes and a gain to tenant farmers. In Aragon the nobility and clergy successfully resisted this measure until 1750.

The Bourbons and their subjects survived their ordeal by battle. The people suffered more from nature than they did from war, and the winter of 1708–9 would not be quickly forgotten. Otherwise, population growth, economic recovery and price stability all continued the positive trend begun around 1685. Philip V ruled a unitary state, its regions integrated, its dependencies reduced; no longer was the monarchy an agglomeration of component states, obsolete remnants of an imperial past. The only imperial heritage remained was one vital to the interests of Spain, the colonial empire in America. The War of Succession gave an impulse to reform. Spain acquired a modern army, greater revenues, a new central government, and a bureaucratic elite. It freed itself from two political encumbrances, the hegemony of the grandees and the presence of France, making the reform project at once modern and national. Yet a new dynasty in itself could not transform Spanish society and economy. The aristocracy were still entrenched in their estates and *señoríos* (seigneurial domains). Spain still had to prove that it could advance from a war economy to peace-time growth. And America still awaited a new policy.

3

The Government of Philip V

El Rey Animoso

Spaniards were soon disappointed in their new king, who seemed to be little improvement on Charles II and had the disadvantage of being French. Was he really committed to Spain, or more interested in the throne of France? Did he have a mind of his own? Was he even sane? Philip V's mental condition worsened as he grew older, but his curious personal behaviour had already astonished his subjects; driven by two compulsions, sex and religion, he spent his nights, and much of his days, in constant transit between his wife and his confessor, torn between desire and guilt, a comic figure easily subject to conjugal blackmail. His first bride, clever beyond her fourteen years, kept him waiting two nights to teach him an early lesson, behaviour regarded by Louis XIV as an insult to the Bourbons. Philip's absence in Italy in 1702 aggravated his sexual longings and damaged his health, until he rushed back to Spain to become in the eyes of most observers 'the slave of his wife'.[1] Yet it was a dependence which did not deeply engage his emotions. Saint-Simon records that when, in February 1714, María Luisa died of tuberculosis,

> The King of Spain was much moved, but somewhat in the royal manner. They persuaded him to go out hunting and shooting, so as to breath the fresh air. On one of these excursions, he found himself within sight of the procession that bore the queen's body

[1] Louville to Torcy, 27 May 1702, in Alfred Baudrillart, *Philippe V et la cour de France* (5 vols, Paris, 1890–1900), I, p. 109; *Historical Memoirs of the Duc de Saint-Simon*, edited and translated by Lucy Norton (3 vols, London, 1967–72), I, pp. 220–1.

to the Escorial. He gazed after it; followed it with his eyes, and went back to his hunting. Princes, are they human?[2]

Slave of his first wife, he was a child in the hands of his second. But while María Luisa was popular among Spaniards, Elizabeth Farnese was detested, and the resentment against her attached itself to Philip, who now forfeited what little credit he had in Spain. He was a ruler made to be manipulated, his only needs, as Alberoni remarked, 'a couch and a woman'.[3] But he also needed reassurance.

Philip V lacked confidence in himself, and from this stemmed his diffidence and apathy. Louis XIV admonished him, 'You have now reigned for two years and have still not spoken as a ruler, through too much mistrust in yourself.'[4] Twenty years later Saint-Simon observed his solitary, retiring and timorous character, 'fearing society, fearing even himself'.[5] And San Felipe referred to 'his suspicious nature, distrustful of everyone, even of himself and his own opinion'.[6] Two things helped to destroy Philip's identity. In France he had undergone a deliberately repressive education, to prevent his becoming a rival to his elder brother, the heir to the throne; so they broke his spirit, working on a naturally passive nature. Philip V had been trained *not* to be king. To encourage docility, his tutors instilled in him extreme piety rather than rational judgement; this was the origin of his excessive scrupulosity, and led in Spain to his daily consultations in writing with his confessor and his recurrent attempts to abdicate.[7] Once in Spain, he was kept in political tutelage by his grandfather, who expected him to be a willing instrument of French policy. When in 1703, conscious at last of Spanish opinion, Philip tried to emancipate himself from the French ambassador, Louis rebuked him like a child: 'At the very least your decisions must be taken in agreement with me; and it is little enough to insist that one of my representatives attends your cabinet.'[8] Louis XIV's agents in Spain played their part in undermining the confidence of the young

---

[2] *Memoirs of the Duc de Saint-Simon*, II, p. 319.

[3] Quoted by Teofanes Egido López, *Opinión pública y oposición al poder en la España del siglo XVIII (1713-1759)* (Valladolid, 1971), p. 112.

[4] Louis XIV to Philip V, 1 February 1703, in Baudrillart, *Philippe V et la cour de France*, I, p. 139.

[5] *Memoirs of the Duc de Saint-Simon*, III, p. 357.

[6] Vicente Bacallar y Sanna, marqués de San Felipe, *Comentarios de la guerra de España e historia de su rey Felipe V, el animoso*, ed. C. Seco Serrano (*BAE*, 99, Madrid, 1957), p. 345.

[7] *Memoirs of the Duc de Saint-Simon*, I, p. 220; Baudrillart, *Philippe V et la cour de France*, III, p. 567.

[8] Louis XIV to Philip V, 1 February 1703, in Baudrillart, *Philippe V et la cour de France*, I, p. 140.

king. They had a decisive argument, the threat of abandoning him, as Louville made insolently clear in 1703:

> 'Ah, Señor', I said, 'what will become of you if Louis XIV abandons you? Your grandees, your ladies, your dwarves, and the whole court of Savoy, would serve you for little if he withdrew his support and ceased to defend you with his numerous armies . . . You would become the most insignificant and unfortunate prince on earth'. The king was moved by this speech, and the tears flowed down his cheeks.[9]

A pathetic sight, if not a permanent one. Adversity would change Philip V and prove, in 1709, that he was more than a creature of France. But adversity could also depress him, and his second state was worse than the first.

The other side of Philip V was recurring mental illness, manifesting itself in acute melancholia and abnormal behaviour and often causing a political crisis. The first major attack occurred in 1717 when symptoms of hysteria verging on madness were reported by his minister Alberoni, and caused the king to shut himself in his room with only the queen for comfort, though even she could become an outcast if she refused his slightest whim and especially his sexual demands. He was fearful of everything, suspicious of everyone; Alberoni gained admission with difficulty but could not obtain rational decisions. Only the king's confessor was welcome from outside; tortured by scruples, Philip would send secretly for Fr Daubenton at any hour of the day or night, convinced he was on the point of dying in mortal sin. The French ambassador attributed it all to sexual addiction: 'The king is visibly wasting away through excessive use he makes of the queen. He is utterly worn out.'[10] The queen's condition was not recorded, but her husband recovered sufficiently to resume his public duties, and by 1721 Saint-Simon found him, at the age of thirty-eight, an unexpectedly aged man, with a vacuous expression, shrunken body, pronounced stoop and bow legs, his life confined to an immutable court routine of indescribable tedium, his political decisions taken for him by the queen.[11]

The king suffered a further relapse in November 1727. On this occasion the queen attempted to restrain his religious mania and restrict

---

[9] Louville to Torcy, 8 February, 1703, ibid., I, p. 143.
[10] Saint-Aignon to maréchal d'Huxelles, 20 March, 29 September 1717, ibid., II, p. 236.
[11] *Memoirs of the Duc de Saint-Simon*, III, p. 326.

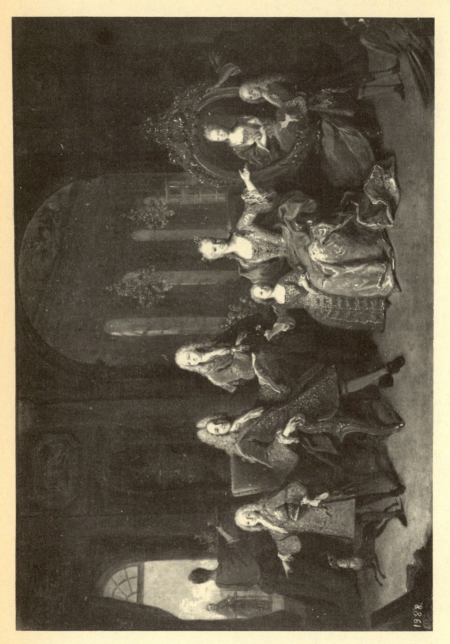

Plate 1 *The Family of Philip V*, by Jean Ranc (reproduced by kind permission of the Museo del Prado, Madrid)

him to one low mass a day and communion once a week, but was rewarded for her pains by violent abuse and beatings, emerging from these encounters covered in bruises.[12] At times the king lost all touch with reality, biting himself, screaming and singing in the night, convinced 'they' were going to imprison, or poison, or kill him. The king's illness and consequent panic of the queen persuaded them to transfer the court to Andalucía, where it remained from 1728 to 1733, most of the time in the Alcázar of Seville. It was here, in 1732, that mental instability reappeared, characterized again by religious mania, profound melancholy, prolonged silence, and violent behaviour. His son, the Prince of Asturias, was brought in to persuade him to change his sheets, cut his hair, and take an emetic, but as for public business no one could engage his interest.[13] Spain was left in these months virtually without a government, for the king refused to see ministers or sign documents, and it was rumoured that Patiño was beaten off when he attempted to obtain instructions. The British minister, Benjamin Keene, reported that 'We are now properly without any government, or even the form of it, for he has not seen either of his ministers or his confessor near twenty days past, and consequently there has been no Dispatch.'[14] In the early months of 1733 the king was still 'inactive to a degree scarce to be imagined', rejecting people and papers alike.[15] By Easter he was appearing at table shaved and dressed, but still ignoring his ministers. In May it was decided to move the court back to Castile, and there in his favourite palace, La Granja, he apparently recovered. Keene reported that he had never seen the king more lively and communicative: 'He has continued to apply to business ever since, so that the government is now upon a regular footing, and as to his health, I never saw him look more cheerful and more free of speech.'[16]

After 1733 the king's condition was more stable, but his behaviour was never continuously normal and he remained incapable of government. In the first months of 1738 he was reported to be 'disordered in his head'.[17] And in August of that year, the eve of war with England,

[12] William Coxe, *Memoirs of the Kings of Spain of the House of Bourbon* (2nd edn, 5 vols, London, 1815), III, p. 82; Baudrillart, *Philippe V et la cour de France*, III, p. 415.

[13] Keene to Newcastle, Seville, 17 October 1732, Public Record Office, London, SP 94/112; Baudrillart, *Philippe V et la cour de France*, IV, pp. 125, 150–1.

[14] Keene to Newcastle, Seville, 24 October 1732, 23 December 1732, PRO, SP 94/112.

[15] Keene to Newcastle, 17 February 1733, PRO, SP 94/116.

[16] Keene to Newcastle, Segovia, 20 July 1733, in Coxe, *Memoirs of the Kings of Spain*, III, p. 259.

[17] Keene to Newcastle, 24 February 1737, PRO, SP 94/130.

Keene wondered whether the Spanish government was capable of withstanding the strain of a deranged king and a major conflict:

> When he appears in the morning at Mass, he behaves himself as usual ... But when he retires to dinner, he sets up such frightful howlings as astonished every one at the beginning, and have obliged the confidants to clear all the apartments, as soon as he sits down to table, and as the Queen cannot be sure of his behaviour for the rest of the day, she does not fail to keep him within doors ... His behaviour at night is to hear Farinelli sing the same five Italian airs that he sung the first time he performed before him, and has continued to sing every night for near twelve months together ... The King himself imitates Farinelli sometimes air after air, and sometimes after the musick is over, and throws himself into such freaks and howlings, that all possible means are taken to prevent people from being witness to his follies.[18]

In these circumstances inertia was the least of the king's problems: 'He troubles himself with no sort of affairs, and after his appearances in publick, he applauds himself to his queen for having behaved himself, in his term, *comme un image*.'[19] Meanwhile, from the early 1730s, Philip imposed a kind of stability on the court through his eccentric timetable, which remained unchanged for the rest of the reign. Keene first observed this in 1731 when he noted that 'His Catholick Majesty seems to be trying experiments to live without sleep.'[20] Supper was taken at five o'clock in the morning with the windows closed, and the king went to bed about eight o'clock, rising at midday to have a light meal. At one o'clock he dressed and went to mass in a nearby chapel, then received visitors, and spent the evening looking out of the window, playing with his clocks, or being read to, until it was time for a musical or theatrical entertainment. After midnight, usually about two o'clock, he called his ministers to transact business, if such it could be called, until it was time to prepare for supper. And so the curious cycle was completed, as the king inverted the normal order of things and turned night into day.[21]

[18] Keene to Newcastle, Segovia, 2 August 1738, PRO, SP 94/131.

[19] Keene to Newcastle, Madrid, 9 June 1739, PRO, SP 94/153.

[20] Keene to Waldegrave, Seville, 6 April 1731, British Library, Add. MS 43, 413, f. 217 v; Keene to Newcastle, Seville, 19 August 1732, BL, Add. MS 43, 416, f. 13.

[21] Anon. document, 1746, quoted by Seco Serrano in San Felipe, *Comentarios*, pp. xxx–xxxi; Baudrillart, *Philippe V et la cour de France*, IV, pp. 73–4.

As they observed the tragicomedy of the Bourbon court, Spaniards could hardly fail to ask what they had gained from a change of dynasty. The credibility of absolute monarchy depends in part on the person of the monarch. A Spanish king was not a cipher, nor even a constitutional monarch subject to restraint. He was the source of law and legitimacy in the state, the ultimate sovereign, upon whom government depended if not to initiate policy at least not to frustrate it. Philip V was an impediment to good government and in no sense a patron of reform. The so-called Bourbon state was established in Spain in spite of the first Bourbon, to whom ministers looked in vain for initiative or innovation. The impulse to change came from a tradition stemming from the reign of Charles II; to this was added the example of France, the ideas of the time, and the ambition of a new elite.

Farnese and Alberoni

Spain's first post-war government was French in style and composition. Like most Spanish governments between 1700 and 1746 it was dominated by a woman, a sign however not of the emancipation of the queen, or her substitute, but of the weakness of the king. Philip V was abnormally dependent upon his wives, and as he waited impatiently for his second, whoever she might be, the political vacuum was filled by the princess des Ursins, who exploited the king's despondency and helplessness to monopolize him for herself and isolate him from courtiers, officials, and, of course, the people. The interregnum between one queen and the next thus became her reign, underpinned by the administrative skills of Jean Orry, her client and confidant, who became the source of ideas and the executive power of the regime. Orry was valuable to Ursins not because he was a reformer – reform did not interest her – but because he explained how she could protect herself by a French-style government, free from Spaniards and councils.[22] A ministry analogous to the one existing in France was created, consisting of an intendant general of finances and four secretaries of state.[23] Approved Spaniards were admitted to the fringes of power. José Grimaldo, a humble protégé of Philip himself, was appointed secretary of war and the Indies. But the closest collaborator of Orry was Melchor de Macanaz, an

[22] San Felipe, *Comentarios*, p. 245.
[23] *Memoirs of the Duc de Saint-Simon*, II, pp. 322–4; Coxe, *Memoirs of the Kings of Spain*, II, pp. 158–61; Baudrillart, *Philippe V et la cour de France*, I, pp. 575–6.

ultra-Bourbonist and leading Spanish exponent of state absolutism, who relentlessly attacked traditional interests from his position as fiscal general of the council of Castile.[24] The work of Orry and Macanaz in 1713–14, however, was essentially that of theoreticians who generated plans and papers, provoked bitter opposition, and in the event produced only a few results. Conciliar administration was reformed and stream-lined by the new plan of 10 November 1713, and the promotion of the *secretarías* above the councils was confirmed by the decree of 30 November 1714 which established four secretaries of state – war, navy and the Indies, state, and justice. Otherwise Orry and Macanaz were not a good combination, superior no doubt but also intolerant and unpopular. Macanaz attacked clerical power and wealth, and drew the hostility of the inquisitor general, Cardinal Giudice, Bishop Belluga of Murcia, and the Universities of Salamanca and Alcalá, a formidable opposition kept at bay only by the support of Philip V and his government. And Philip was only as strong as his current confidante.

The dictatorship of Ursins was vulnerable, for she possessed no formal power base and was threatened by the arrival of a new queen. Philip V took as his second wife Elizabeth Farnese, daughter of the deceased duke of Parma, a choice influenced not by reasons of state but by the favourable reports upon the girl fed by Julio Alberoni, the Parmesan envoy, to the person who had most influence over Philip, the princess des Ursins. Alberoni was aware that Philip 'needed only a wife and a prayer-book', and he was clever enough to emphasize his candidate's qualifications: 'She is a good girl, plump, healthy, and well fed ... and accustomed to hear of nothing but needlework and embroidery', qualities which would satisfy both the ardent Philip and the watchful Ursins.[25] The princess took the bait, only to find that she had introduced into Spain not a modest mediocrity but an imperious young woman, determined to escape from the narrow life of an Italian principality to a world stage, and from being dominated to become dominating. Soon the whole of Europe would be aware of the Spanish termagant.

The first victim of Elizabeth Farnese was Ursins herself. The two met on 22 December 1714 at Jadraque on the road to Madrid. The details of that mysterious interview were not disclosed but the outcome was

[24] Henry Kamen, 'Melchor de Macanaz and the Foundations of Bourbon Power in Spain', *English Historical Review*, 80, 317 (1965), p. 707; Carmen Martín Gaite, *Macanaz, otro paciente de la Inquisición* (2nd edn, Madrid, 1975), pp. 285–8.

[25] Coxe, *Memoirs of the Kings of Spain*, ii, pp. 170, 172–3, 175.

dramatic. Farnese summarily dismissed Ursins and sent her in the middle of the night on a winter journey to the French frontier. 'No action this century caused greater astonishment. As for the king's role, that was obscure', commented San Felipe, attributing the decision to the queen's 'ambition to command'.[26] It was a demonstration as well as a decision. The new queen was determined not to be ruled by an old woman from the past, or tolerate the presence of someone whose reputation she knew and whose control she repudiated. So she struck quickly and established her authority from the beginning. As Orry reported, 'This act is to be seen simply as the determination of the queen to take the first opportunity to exert her domination over the king.'[27] Philip's response was pitiful but predictable; he accepted the dismissal of his favourite as the price he had to pay for the favours of his wife. Alberoni was at hand to guide the transition. Convinced that the king would have no will but that of his wife 'or whatever other woman may be near him', he introduced Elizabeth Farnese to the ways of Philip V: 'I shall describe the weakness by which he may be caught, and I shall conclude by telling her the artifices by which the lady [Ursins] has contrived to be the despot.'[28] The queen employed two tactics. The first was to monopolize the king: 'The new queen and Alberoni followed her [Ursins] example, keeping King Philip entirely to themselves, and making him inaccessible to everyone else.'[29] Then the queen began to use Philip's unremitting sexual demands as a means of bargain and control: 'The king's own nature was her strongest weapon, and one which she sometimes used against him. There were nocturnal refusals arousing tempests; the king shrieked and threatened, sometimes did worse. She held firm, wept, and on occasion defended herself.'[30] Thus she combined affection and design to establish an absolute mastery over Philip.

The ascendancy of Elizabeth Farnese was a triumph of will over mind. Behind her homely appearance and slightly pock-marked face lay a powerful personality which overcame her lack of education and culture and drove her to intervene decisively in those aspects of Spanish policy of interest to her. She began with the government. The dismissal of Ursins was followed by that of her clients. Orry's mission was

---

[26] San Felipe, *Comentarios*, p. 257.

[27] Coxe, *Memoirs of the Kings of Spain*, ii, p. 185; Orry to Torcy, 31 December 1714, 5 January 1715, in Baudrillart, *Philippe V et la cour de France*, i, pp. 613, 615.

[28] Alberoni to duke of Parma, 20 October 1714, in Edward Armstrong, *Elisabeth Farnese, 'the Termagant of Spain'* (London, 1892), p. 20.

[29] *Memoirs of the Duc de Saint-Simon*, iii, p. 353.

[30] Ibid., iii, p. 359.

terminated on 7 February 1715; on the same day Macanaz was dismissed and banished, and his friend Fr Pierre Robinet was replaced as royal confessor by the Jesuit Daubenton. Cardinal Giudice, a friend of Alberoni, was restored to favour, and only Grimaldo, a favourite of Philip, survived from the previous regime. In setting the limits of French influence and the 'new' bureaucracy, Elizabeth Farnese was in a position to earn political credit with Spaniards, or at least with the traditional Spanish party. But as it became clear that the decline of the French was accompanied by the promotion of the Italians and that foreigners were still preferred to Spaniards in government and at court – even the queen's nurse, the odious Laura Pescatori, was brought from Parma – disillusion grew and Elizabeth Farnese became one of the least popular monarchs in Spanish history, universally hated, and conscious that 'the Spaniards do not love me, but equally I hate them'.[31] Spaniards hated her for her domination of the king and her contempt for national interests. She distorted Spanish foreign policy by her obsession with Italy, where she was determined to find kingdoms for her sons and a place of retirement for herself, and where Spanish armies and resources were sacrificed in purely dynastic objectives. This accounts for the vituperative language used against her in the underground press, to whom she was a 'viper', a 'sinful woman', an 'ambitious schemer', and 'la Parmesana'.

Bourbon innovation meant nothing to Farnese. She replaced the French model of government by the rule of favourites typical of the later Habsburgs. The first such *valido* was Alberoni, 'a pygmy whom fortune made a colossus'. Son of a gardener in Placentia, Alberoni rose via a Jesuit education to become a priest, a general factotum to the duke of Vendôme, and the envoy of Parma in Spain. The transition from Ursins to Farnese, from France to Italy, regarded by the English as a 'favourable conjuncture', for them, was a happy moment for Alberoni, who was quick to profit from being in the right place at the right time. 'I have found out the gentleman', wrote the English minister, 'who alone is absolute here. He has gained an entire ascendant over the queen, and, by that means, over the king, who is not a lover of business, and suffers himself to be governed by her majesty.'[32] The political situation in 1716, as analysed in terms of British interests, was propitious for Alberoni to consolidate his power:

---

[31] Ibid., III, p. 364.
[32] Bubb Dodington to Stanhope, 11 October 1715, in Coxe, *Memoirs of the Kings of Spain*, II, p. 214, 19 February 1716, PRO, SP 94/85.

We have two parties here, one Spanish and the other French. The Spaniards oppose, and create as many difficulties as they can, rather because things are not done by themselves, than from any real ill will to us. You well know that these grandees are accustomed to treat their kings like cyphers, and to do and dispose of every thing according to their fancy. This the queen will by no means permit, however the king might, which makes them raise as many obstacles as they can in the way of all business.

The French faction, from which we have the most to apprehend, and which is indeed the most active, and I believe the most powerful, because it fills the principal offices of state, has the Cardinal Giudice at its head ...

Finding his power decrease, this gentleman, by some of his party, prevailed on the king to name a committee from all the councils, at first in order to regulate some disputes with France, and now to take cognizance of all foreign affairs under the title of *Junta de dependencias extrangeras* ... I have told M. Alberoni if he does not dissolve this junta and place himself publicly at the head of affairs, Spain will be ruined ... Without the queen we should never have done anything here; and when she desists from supporting our interests, we may take our leave of Spain. I am fully persuaded she is heartily for us now, and a sworn enemy to the French.[33]

The two parties to which Dodington referred were foreign policy positions rather than different forms of government, and it was in identifying himself with the interests of the queen that the Italian favourite rose to power. Giudice was edged out, leaving Alberoni and Grimaldo as the key executives. Neither of these were ministers of state, and Alberoni did not hold a major office outside his informal *privanza*, or position of favourite. He told Dodington,

I am not yet master here; nor have the queen and myself a single person on whom we can depend. *If I did not hope to overcome the foreign spirit which reigns in these counsels, I would not remain twenty-four hours in Spain*. The queen is forced to proceed gradually; and I cannot always induce her to apply herself as much as I wish. Indeed it is difficult to engage a young lady in examining matters of trade.[34]

[33] Bubb Dodington to Stanhope, 6 July 1716, in Coxe, *Memoirs of the Kings of Spain*, ii, pp. 241–3; for a fuller version see Bubb Dodington to Stanhope, 3 June 1716, PRO, SP 94/85.

[34] Bubb Dodington to Methuen, 11 January 1717, PRO, SP 94/86.

Alberoni was promoted cardinal in 1717, but lacking a secretaryship of state he lacked the formal means of activating the bureaucracy. Even so he prompted a number of policy initiatives.

The Alberoni quinquennium (1715–19) was not exactly a stage in Bourbon reform, yet he could claim some successes. Of him Patiño said 'he turned impossibilities into mere difficulties'. He believed in the latent power of Spain, saw that it needed mobilizing by determined leadership, and lamented the inertia of the king and the indolence of the bureaucracy, including the new ministries. From the councils he expected little change, though he made a further attempt to reorganize them. While many of his collaborators were Italians, he did not deliberately exclude Spaniards. He recognized the talents of the two Patiño brothers, the marquis of Castelar, minister of war, and especially José Patiño, intendant of marine and Alberoni's right-hand man; to him, as much as to Alberoni, Spain owed the improvement of its naval and military capacity in these years. Alberoni tried to convince the monarchs that Spain should be a naval rather than a military power and was incapable of engaging in a continental war without France. He sought to activate arsenals and shipyards, and pending the construction of a national fleet he projected the purchase of ships and naval stores from Holland, Hamburg, Genoa, Russia, and the South Sea Company. Foundries were built at Pamplona; the Basque armouries were put to work; new factories were established for naval and military equipment; and recruitment of troops was stepped up, even in Catalonia and Aragon.[35] Everything depended on two basic conditions, financial improvement and trade with the Indies. To raise more revenue he imposed cuts in public expenditure, not sparing the royal household and its troops; he taxed the Church; and he increased various duties, impositions on wealthy individuals, and sale of office. He believed that trade with the Indies should be reorganized and discussed with merchants ways and means of doing so; and but for the intervention of the Italian question, an early attack would have been made on the English and French contraband trade in America.[36]

Alberoni's measures of 1717 were not part of a long-term reform programme. They were basically designed to increase state resources for immediate action and in particular to finance the expeditions to Sardinia and Sicily. No doubt he had reservations about the Sardinia expedition, which was subsidiary to the conquest of Sicily, but he certainly

[35] Coxe, *Memoirs of the Kings of Spain*, ii, pp. 287–9.
[36] Armstrong, *Farnese*, pp. 102–3.

identified with the Italian policy of the queen and was proud of the fact that he could put 300 sail, 33,000 troops, and 100 pieces of artillery at its service. In the event it was all a waste of time and money, and Spain had nothing to show for two years of frenzied effort.[37]

The king himself had little contact with government during the Alberoni years. In 1717–18 Philip was a sick man, isolated in his room and subject to strange hallucinations, a situation which simultaneously increased the power of Farnese and Alberoni and raised the hopes of the Spanish party. Alberoni watched the situation closely, seeing in the king's condition symptoms of insanity, and in the queen's tolerance of his marital demands one of the causes of the illness: 'Her indulgence is a subject for pity, because she loves him tenderly, and suffers with a courage that the greatest martyr has never shown.'[38] The king made a will, assigning a regency government to Farnese and Alberoni in the event of his death or incapacity. The opposition reacted immediately, seeing in the arrangement the continued exclusion of the grandees. The year 1718 was one of conspiracies. The first plot, French-inspired, consisted of an attempt to recruit a group of malcontents led by the duke of Veragua, the conde de Aguilar, and the conde de las Torres, who would seize power on the death of the king, oust Farnese and Alberoni, and form a junta to rule during the minority of the new king in alliance with the duke of Orleans, regent of France and hero of the grandees. In a variation of this Aguilar planned to seize the prince of Asturias and rule in his name, imprisoning the king and queen in a secure royal palace. Yet another group of nobles, the so-called *junta chica*, conspired simply to get rid of Alberoni.[39] None of these unlikely plans increased the credibility of the grandees or of French diplomacy, and for the moment Alberoni emerged unscathed. But he was becoming unpopular and – more dangerous for him – unsuccessful.

The position of Alberoni was ambiguous. If he appeared to act as a secretary of state or first minister, this was not through institutional promotion but through the mere favour of the monarchs, on whom he remained personally dependent. The administrative changes inaugurated by previous regimes – the development of ministries and intendancies – continued under Alberoni, though he was not directly responsible for them. He specialized in foreign affairs and in providing

---

[37] On Alberoni's foreign policy see below, pp. 132–3.
[38] Alberoni, 8 January 1718, in Armstrong, *Farnese*, p. 109.
[39] Coxe, *Memoirs of the Kings of Spain*, II, p. 302; Alfonso Danvila, *El reinado relámpago. Luis I y Luisa Isabel de Orléans (1707-1742)* (Madrid, 1952), pp. 106–11.

the sinews of war. In one respect he was an improvement on the French advisers, who had invariably served two masters, France as well as Spain. Alberoni served the Spanish monarchs only. Unfortunately he could not give them the success they demanded, least of all in Italy. His foreign policy, moreover, provoked England and France, led to invasions of Spain and her coasts, and ended with the Allies demanding the dismissal of Alberoni as a condition of peace. The monarchs were persuaded that he would have to go, cravenly disowned him, and on 19 December 1719 dismissed him. Alberoni had no base of power outside the royal palace; he left Spain by the Aragon road, taking with him a hoard of jewels and silver and a quantity of documents, the indispensable adjuncts of a fallen minister.

The fall of Alberoni left a power vacuum which was filled, though not completely, by José de Grimaldo, a tubby Basque who held his hands flat on his stomach as he spoke and was forced to endure the leg-pulling of Farnese. Grimaldo had started his political life as a clerk under Orry and Amelot, graduating to higher things from 1713 and now to the secretaryship of state. Under him a group of lesser ministers hispanic-ized the government, but these were not the higher aristocracy and soon became targets of grandee propaganda, no less so than previous foreigners. On the other hand the king's confessor, Fr Daubenton, who from his proximity to the king and his conscience had a considerable influence in government, collaborated closely with Grimaldo.[40] Daubenton died in August 1723 and was replaced by Fr Bermúdez, 'a Jesuit, who besides being a Spaniard has the universal character of extra-ordinary capacity, learning and piety'.[41] But if the government was stable, it was wanting in initiative and ideas, and the bureaucracy relapsed into a state of inertia. The monarchs themselves were notice-ably passive and withdrew more and more to the new palace of San Ildefonso near Segovia, not to work more conveniently but literally to retreat from decisions:

> Their Catholic Majesties remain still at St. Ildefonso, between which place and Madrid there is scarce any communication, no person being allowed to go thither from hence, upon any pretence whatsoever, and the answers to letters written from Madrid for the Indies come almost as soon back again as those for St. Ildefonso, so

---

[40] William Stanhope to Earl Stanhope, 1 July 1720, PRO, SP 94/89.
[41] William Stanhope to Lord Carteret, 9 August 1723, PRO, SP 94/92.

that during this retreat of the Court the employment of a Foreign Minister here may be almost looked upon as a sinecure.[42]

From Inertia to Abdication

Spain began the year 1724 in a state of shock. On 10 January Philip V abdicated in favour of his son, Louis. In a life of strange behaviour, this was perhaps the strangest, and Europe no less than Spain was astonished, to see the grandson of Louis XIV at the age of forty, and above all Elizabeth Farnese who was only thirty-one, renouncing power in favour of the sixteen-year-old prince of Asturias. Speculation as to the motive began immediately. The reason given by Philip himself spoke of his disillusion with the vanity of the world and his exhaustion after twenty-three years of war, sickness and tribulation:

After long and thoughtful consideration and with the agreement and consent of my dear beloved queen and wife, I have resolved to retire from the heavy burden of governing this monarchy, in order to concentrate my mind on death during the time that remains to me and to pray for my salvation in that other and more permanent kingdom.[43]

The idea had apparently first occurred to Philip in August 1719 during the war with France; it was committed to paper on 27 July 1720 as a solemn vow, renewed at least three times, and kept a secret shared only with his wife and confessor.[44] The religious motivation was not the only explanation current at the time. San Felipe, who accepted the 'purely spiritual' reasons given by Philip V, mentioned also the rumours circulating 'in the courts of northern Europe and in some in Italy that the abdication was for political and not spiritual motives, insinuating that it was to enable him to succeed to the crown of France in case of the death of Louis XV'.[45] Of course he had renounced his rights to the French succession in 1712. But did he regard as valid a renunciation made in circumstances of some constraint? And did he not always have a

[42] William Stanhope to Lord Carteret, 20 December 1723, PRO, SP 94/92.
[43] Abdication, 10 January 1724, in San Felipe, *Comentarios*, p. 351; Baudrillart, *Philippe V et la cour de France*, II, pp. 590–1; Jacinto Hidalgo, 'La abdicación de Felipe V', *Hispania*, 22, 88 (1962), pp. 559–89, esp. pp. 565–6.
[44] Baudrillart, *Philippe V et la cour de France*, I, pp. 558–64, 568.
[45] San Felipe, *Comentarios*, pp. 352–3.

predilection for France, a desire to return and rule in his native country?[46]

If the religious argument induced scepticism, the political explanation was mere conjecture. Philip V was a mentally disturbed man, whose conduct was neither stable nor consistent. His mental illness, taking the form of acute melancholia and religious scruples, led him to believe that he was incapable of ruling well. Therefore he felt obliged to withdraw and live a life of retreat in preparation for eternal life. As San Felipe remarked, 'the king suffered profound melancholy from a weakness of mind, which made it impossible for him to continue the heavy burden of governing so vast an empire.' Yet he apparently believed that the young and inexperienced Louis was capable of governing it. On 19 January at the Escorial, in an emotional scene before the whole court, Louis I was proclaimed king of Spain. On the same day he received a letter from his father, richer in pious hyperbole than practical wisdom, exhorting him to 'have always before your eyes the two Saints and Kings who are the glory of Spain and France, Saint Ferdinand and Saint Louis'.[47]

The reaction in Spain was at first one of great satisfaction. This would mean the end of French, Italian, and all foreign influence and tutelage. Spain could return to governing itself in its own interests. Louis I was the idol of the aristocracy and the Spanish party, their route to power; to the people he was young, benign, pure Spaniard, 'el bien amado'. The truth was not so idyllic but that had still to be learned. Philip of course had not consulted the 'people', even in a limited sense; he had deliberately omitted to convoke the *cortes*, an inappropriate institution in an age of absolutism. Grandees, prelates and people acquiesced in the constitutional process, or lack of it. But soon suspicions were aroused, and minds were alerted when the political details of the abdication became known. Had anything changed?

This was a spurious abdication. Philip assigned a cabinet council to Louis, 'composed of ministers whom I have judged suitable to appoint for you'.[48] These were headed by Luis de Miraval, president of the council of Castile, a former diplomat of little talent and a complete creature of Grimaldo, and Juan Bautista Orendain, another mediocrity and dependant of Grimaldo and now appointed minister of external affairs. Grimaldo himself remained with Philip as his principal adviser at

[46] *Memoirs of the Duc de Saint-Simon*, III, p. 358; Coxe, *Memoirs of the Kings of Spain*, III, pp. 50–4.

[47] San Felipe, *Comentarios*, pp. 353–4; Philip V to Louis I, 14 January 1724, in Danvila, *El reinado relámpago*, p. 211.

[48] Quoted by Hidalgo, 'La abdicación de Felipe V', p. 583.

San Ildefonso, supervising these and other appointments and controlling the new government. The boy king, tall, fair of hair and complexion, and amiable to all, was badly educated and competent only to listen to ministers, not to appoint them.[49] No one was deceived: 'The authority still resides in Mr. Grimaldo, who has found the art to retain it, by naming such persons as have almost a necessary dependence upon him.'[50] Government at a distance, this was the meaning of the abdication, and as news reached Madrid of the 'hermits of San Ildefonso' so scepticism increased. La Granja was not an austere retreat but a magnificent palace, constructed rapidly and at great expense in the years before the abdication, the site of elaborate gardens, a monument to nostalgia for France. Prayers and piety were the order of the day but these required an environment and a budget. La Granja had already cost 24 million pesos and was still growing. The abdication had stipulated an income of 600,000 escudos a year and it was rumoured that Philip had withdrawn all that remained in the royal treasury before his departure. The senior royals, already unpopular, were now suspect, their motives questioned, their behaviour deplored, while in Madrid the puppet king was an embarrassment to the Spanish party and the Spanish people alike. Was he fit for the job? Was he even interested?

Louis I understandably had other things on his mind. In the interests of amity with France he had been married in January 1722 at the age of fourteen to Luisa Isabel of Orleans, two years his junior, a wilful, ill-mannered girl, whose adolescent tantrums were signs of a sadly disturbed mind. The Spanish monarchs inspected her closely on arrival, suspecting that she was syphilitic from the sins of her father, the duke of Orleans, well known in Spain for his debauchery during the War of Succession. The French ambassador was 'inexpressibly mortified' by the king's insistence that the marriage should not be consummated for fifteen months.[51] In fact it was a year before the couple even ate together, eighteen months before they slept together, and some time after that before they succeeded in consummating the marriage.[52] The British ambassador described the court at the Escorial 'in great joy on account of the Prince of Asturias's marriage been consummated upon the 18th inst. The new married couple seemed well satisfied with each other.'[53]

[49] Danvila, *El reinado relámpago*, pp. 130–7.
[50] Keene to Walpole, 28 January 1724, PRO, SP 94/92.
[51] William Stanhope to Lord Carteret, 20 January 1722, PRO, SP 94/91.
[52] Danvila, *El reinado relámpago*, pp. 194–6.
[53] William Stanhope to Lord Carteret, 22 August 1723, PRO, SP 94/92.

Their satisfaction was short-lived. From January 1724 the rule of Louis I consisted less in governing Spain than in controlling his capricious wife who behaved not like a queen but like a disturbed abdolescent, ignoring her husband, playing with her maids, and running round the palace undressed.[54] Meanwhile Spain was governed from San Ildefonso and administered by its bureaucracy. It was a singular but brief experience. In the summer of 1724 Louis caught smallpox and died on 31 August at the age of seventeen and following eight months as king. Luisa Isabel stayed loyally at his side throughout the illness.

The abdication had provided for the succession of Ferdinand, second son of Philip and María Luisa of Savoy, if Louis died without an heir. But the reluctance of Philip to relinquish *all* sovereignty during Louis's reign, and the determination of Elizabeth Farnese to return to power left the situation in doubt. Just when it seemed that Farnese had persuaded her vacillating husband to return, they were confronted by a suddenly united opposition. One sector of opinion considered Philip incapable of ruling and opposed renewed domination by Farnese; the grandees and old Spaniards regarded the eleven-year-old Ferdinand as rightful heir and hoped to benefit from a long minority and an aristocratic regency; clerical opponents, including Jesuits of the Colegio Imperial, some of the regular clergy and a number of theologians upheld the irrevocability of a solemn vow, invoking a religious argument perhaps for a political purpose. The council of Castile gave an equivocal opinion.[55] A junta of theologians stated that Philip could not in conscience recover the throne itself but should establish a regency and a council of state. An exasperated Philip made ready to return to San Ildefonso, declaring that he would accept neither crown nor regency. At this point Elizabeth Farnese, seconded by the French ambassador, decided to call a halt; they urged Philip to stand up to the 'scoundrel theologians', and enlisted the papal nuncio to produce a piece of casuistry justifying the breaking of an oath. The council of Castile was also encouraged to reconsider its opinion, and this time concluded that the abdication was no longer valid because Ferdinand was not of an age or condition to accept the throne. Thus Philip allowed himself to be persuaded, and on 6 September 1724 signed the decree resuming the throne and sacrificing his personal welfare for the happiness of his subjects.

The return of Philip V signified the defeat of the Spanish party and its open identification as a party of opposition. It now had a policy, the

[54] Coxe, *Memoirs of the Kings of Spain*, iii, p. 70; Danvila, *El reinado relámpago*, pp. 303–12.
[55] San Felipe, *Comentarios*, p. 362.

king's lack of legitimacy, and a focus, the prince of Asturias. The young Ferdinand became the unwitting hero of the grandees and figurehead of the Spanish party, which could now call itself the *partido fernandino*. The victors were the queen and the French interest, who in rescuing Philip V had recaptured him. The key posts were the president of the council of Castile, the secretaries of state, war and finance, and the royal confessor. The queen had to control these appointments if she were to rule. So there was a purge of the administration. Councillors, theologians, priests, all those who had opposed the return of Philip or failed to follow the official line, were sent packing. Miraval was replaced as president of the council of Castile by Juan de Herrera, bishop of Sigüenza; Fr Bermúdez was replaced by Fr Robinet; Grimaldo came back as secretary of state and Orendain too joined the administration. So began the long 'second reign' of Philip V. His behaviour was no more rational than before, and he still allowed – needed – Elizabeth Farnese to rule. Farnese, however, was not much more capable of ruling than Philip himself; deficient in knowledge and judgement, she too needed a political mentor, another favourite, a second Alberoni. There was one at hand.

Johann Wilhelm, Baron Ripperdá, was another foreign adventurer, in this case Dutch, who came to Spain as a diplomat and stayed to live on his wits. Ripperdá was a confidence trickster who presented a plausible face to the world, changed his religion as often as his sovereigns, and made a career selling quick solutions. He had already made rich pickings out of Alberoni and the British embassy in Madrid. But his most distinguished victims were the Spanish monarchs. He first came to their attention as superintendent of the royal factory at Guadalajara, for which in 1718 he imported a group of Dutch artisans who produced low quality textiles at a loss; from there he was appointed to the head of all the royal factories. He saw his main chance in 1724 when a conjuncture of weak government and foreign policy impasse in the aftermath of the abdication crisis enabled him to move in on the court. In a series of memoranda, laced with projects of internal reform, reorganization of the treasury and expansion of the Indies trade, he ingratiated himself with Elizabeth Farnese. He knew her blind spot, the obsession to place her sons on thrones, and he played on this, conjuring up the possibility of obtaining the imperial crown for her eldest son Charles. No matter that Austria was a notorious enemy of Spain and had not even recognized Philip V, or that the powers of Europe might be alerted by such a union. Ripperdá sold the idea to Farnese and was sent on a confidential mission to Vienna, where he negotiated a treaty between Spain and the Empire remarkably unfavourable to Spain and provocative to the rest of Europe, and containing in the event only a very guarded promise of one of the emperor's daughters to Charles.

The Treaty of Vienna plunged Europe into turmoil for the next six years.[56] It was particularly obnoxious to Britain, and so was Ripperdá. The English ambassador in Madrid, William Stanhope, could not understand 'how a person of his infamous character could prevail upon such inveterate enemies to adjust their differences'.[57] Stanhope did not believe that the common explanation, Spanish resentment against France for breaking off the projected marriage between Louis XV and the Spanish infanta María Ana Victoria, was the true reason, for Ripperdá was sent to Vienna in November 1724, well before the suspension of the marriage in March 1725. In his view responsibility lay with the queen alone: 'The Queen had the sole direction of the late Treaty with the Emperor; it is reasonable to suppose that she would prefer the interests of her own son to those of the Prince of Asturias.'[58]

The success claimed by Ripperdá in Vienna had political implications in Spain:

This Court is at present wholly governed by the directions they receive from Ripperda (to whom it is absolutely certain the King of Spain has promised the entire direction and management of all affairs here at his return) who being a declared enemy of Grimaldo, the latter is not only without the least credit or authority here, but is even kept wholly ignorant of every thing transacting at any moment . . . Though he still keeps his place of Secretary of State, he is nevertheless wholly excluded from the management and secret of affairs; however . . . he finds the King has still some remains of kindness for him which hinders the Queen from being able to get him turned out[59]

The whole of Spanish policy suddenly turned upon the Empire: opportunism reigned, and the prime opportunist was about to claim his reward:

---

[56] On the foreign policy implications of these events see below pp. 133–4.

[57] William Stanhope to Newcastle, 11 April 1726, PRO, SP 94/92.

[58] William Stanhope to Newcastle, 22 June 1725, PRO, SP 94/93.

[59] William Stanhope to Townshend, Segovia, 22 June 1725, PRO SP 94/93.

The Spaniards have no council to assist them, nor any steady maxim to proceed upon, so that new representations from abroad change their intentions; Orendain, a verbose empty man, and the queen's confessor, a heavy stupid one, joined to Ripperda are the props of the Spanish monarchy. Marquis de Grimaldo is left at Madrid, till the king further orders, and it is certain his interest will be but inconsiderable till this court shall have had more experience of that of Vienna.[60]

When Ripperdá returned from Vienna, in December 1725, he was received with rapture by the queen and king and placed at the head of government. Stanhope found him speaking with great 'impertinence and insolence', secure in his appointment as secretary of state:

He is to the full as absolute here in all respects as the Cardinal Alberoni ever was, and although he has not the title of first minister (which is a name the King of Spain has an aversion to and could never be brought to bestow upon the Cardinal) he under that of secretary of state, without any particular department, commands all the others and the rest of the Spanish monarchy.[61]

By the beginning of January 1726 'this wildman', as Stanhope called him, had established his authority in Spain, conscious of his isolation, his utter dependence on the monarchs, and the gathering opposition. Grimaldo was confined to the affairs of Italy and Portugal; Orendain, now marquis de la Paz, to justice; and Ripperdá took over the secretaries of marine and the Indies. If the king and queen were deceived, the rest of Spain was not, and soon Spaniards began to express their outrage as the adventurer contrived 'to cancel or reduce pensions, suppress the secretaryship of the navy, force tax officials and office-holders in the Indies to give an account of their stewardship . . . and to concentrate in himself all the authority hitherto divided between various ministers. This novelty caused a lot of protest.'[62] The policy of Ripperdá was not reformist but a desperate attempt to increase revenue in order to pay large subsidies promised in the Treaty of Vienna. When it became clear that he could not deliver the Empire to Spain, could not pay the

[60] Keene to Charles Delafaye, Segovia, 5 September 1725, PRO, SP 94/93.

[61] William Stanhope to Townshend, 27 December 1725, PRO, SP 94/93.

[62] J. del Campo-Raso, *Memorias políticas y militares para servir de continuación a los Comentarios del marqués de San Felipe*, ed. C. Seco Serrano (*BAE*, 99, Madrid, 1957), p. 382.

Austrians, could not stave off the hostility of England and France, in short could not fulfil his fraudulent promises, the whole edifice collapsed.

> He finds himself (from the ruined condition of His Catholic Majesty's revenues and the total stop to all public credit from the distrust he is in with all mankind) absolutely impossibilited not only to furnish the supplies stipulated for the Emperor but even to carry on the current service in time of peace without the assistance of the Flota and Galleons, which in case of war run the risk of falling into other hands . . . He has for inveterate enemies not only all the other ministers but the whole Spanish nation, to whom he has rendered himself odious beyond imagination, and that he is by no means agreeable to the King himself, that his only support and protection is the Queen's favour.[63]

Suddenly it was all over. On the evening of 14 May the Baron Ripperdá, by now a duke and a grandee, was dismissed from all his offices with a generous pension. His greatest fear was now 'his enemies and the insults of the populace'. He sought refuge in the British embassy, claiming that his life was in danger and his enemies at his heels. The authorities ordered the street to be cordoned off and on 24 May, in spite of the protests of Stanhope, he was taken and imprisoned in the Alcázar of Segovia, from which he escaped some months later.[64]

After the excesses of Ripperdá the new government exuded solidity. The two Patiño brothers were given important ministries, the marquis of Castelar that of war and José Patiño that of the Indies and Navy; Grimaldo was retained for external affairs, but the key ministry treating with the court of Vienna was assigned to the marquis de la Paz, whose pro-imperial policy was, to many critics, an unwelcome continuity with the past and a reminder that the fall of Ripperdá did not change everything. Did it change anything? Subsidies were still being poured into Vienna, the monarchy was still fatally flawed, the queen unrepentant, the king deranged. Philip V moved through the years 1724–6 in a state of shock, not in complete control of events or of himself, and in mid-1726

[63] William Stanhope to Newcastle, 11 April 1726, PRO, SP 94/94.

[64] William Stanhope to Newcastle, 13 May, 25 May 1726, PRO, SP 94/94. Ripperdá went to England for a time, but eventually made his way to North Africa where, reputedly a convert to Islam, he led Moorish forces against Spain and was wounded in combat; he died in Tetuan in 1737 in a miserable condition; Sabins to Keene, 6 November 1737, Sir Benjamin Keene, *The Private Correspondence of Sir Benjamin Keene, KB*, ed. Sir Richard Lodge (Cambridge, 1933), p. 10.

he suffered another 'touch of madness'.[65] It was reported that the young prince of Asturias, heir to the throne, criticized openly the actions of both the king and the queen, which he described as

> destructive to his interests and those of the Spanish Monarchy and carried on by the Queen purely for the aggrandising of her own children ... as the Prince has a very good understanding but of a haughty unquiet spirit, and will be of age in two months. It is apprehended that such notions once infused into him, may put him upon thoughts of taking the government into his own hands, as in right belonging to him in virtue of his father's resignation.[66]

No doubt this was the *partido fernandino* speaking, but it indicates that twenty-five years into the new dynasty Spain still awaited a guiding hand. The abdication farce of 1724, the meteoric rise of Ripperdá, the disorientation of Spanish policy, the whole crisis of 1724–6 discredited the monarchy and weakened the government. It also brought Elizabeth Farnese to a new peak of power. In September 1726 she 'persuaded' the king to dismiss Grimaldo and Fr Bermúdez, regarded as partisans of Britain and France respectively.[67] Stanhope believed that the king could not resist her pro-imperial and anti-British policy, 'considering the violence of the Queen's temper and her present dispositions and views and the absolute power she exercises over him, of which she has just given the most signal and convincing proof by obliging him to dismiss from his service the only two persons for whom he was known to have a real affection'.[68] The episode gives a glimpse of the inner workings of Spanish government and reveals that not all Spanish ministers were cyphers, that an element of politics survived, and that the queen had to work to impose her will. At the same time, even in the 1720s, real talent as opposed to mere favouritism could come through and reach the top. Following the fall of Grimaldo, Francisco Arriaza was dismissed and in his place José Patiño, already secretary of the Indies, was appointed secretary of finance. A new phase was about to begin.

[65] William Stanhope to Newcastle, 2 July 1726, PRO, SP 94/94.
[66] Ibid.
[67] William Stanhope to Newcastle, 30 September 1726, PRO, SP 94/95.
[68] William Stanhope to Newcastle, 4 October 1726, PRO, SP 94/95.

Patiño and his Successors

The promotion of Patiño brought to an end the dominance of foreign adventurers in the government of Philip V. Patiño was a genuinely national minister, a product of Spain's own bureaucratic elite, introduced to the higher administration in the War of Succession, making his way as a servant of the new absolutism, and proving that there was a career open to talent in the Bourbon state. Before 1726 Bourbon government had not notably advanced on that of the later Habsburgs; in some ways it was inferior. The next ten years, the decade of Patiño, would show Spaniards whether the Bourbons were a boon or a burden.

Patiño was born in Spanish Milan in 1670 of a Gallician family.[69] He left the Jesuit novitiate and decided on an administrative career, receiving his first major appointment in 1711 as intendant of Extremadura. From 1713 he held a similar appointment in Catalonia, and it was Patiño who administered the new regime in post-war Catalonia, applying the Nueva Planta, introducing the *catastro*, and showing the readiness to compromise between the demands of the state and the interests of the subject which was a hallmark of all his administration. In January 1717 Alberoni appointed him intendant general of the navy, superintendent of Seville, and president of the *casa de contratación* (house of trade), whose transfer to Cadiz he formally completed. These offices were decisive for Patiño: it was in Andalucía that he showed his ability to mobilize resources and translate them into national power, and it was there that he acquired his expert knowledge of the Indies trade. He was able to appropriate a vastly increased defence budget and create almost from nothing a new Spanish navy and an army which astonished Europe. And his was the initiative behind the establishment, in 1718, of the system of intendants, key agents in the mobilizing of resources for the Bourbon state. On the fall of Ripperdá in 1726 he was appointed secretary of the Indies and navy, then of finance, as well as superintendent general of revenues. In 1731 he added the department of war to his portfolios and finally, in 1733, he was formally appointed secre-

---

[69] On Patiño see Antonio Rodríguez Villa, *Patiño y Campillo* (Madrid, 1882); Antonio Béthencourt Massieu, *Patiño y la política internacional de Felipe V* (Valladolid, 1954); Jean O. McLachlan, *Trade and Peace with Old Spain, 1667-1750* (Cambridge, 1940), pp. 146-52; Geoffrey J. Walker, *Spanish Politics and Imperial Trade, 1700-1789* (London, 1979), pp. 95-113, 159-73; Julián B. Ruiz Rivera, 'Patiño y la reforma del Consulado de Cádiz en 1729', *Temas Americanistas*, 5 (Seville, 1985), pp. 16-21.

tary of state, a function which he had been performing in fact since 1728. This was an important appointment for Patiño, for it was only there that he could cut expenditure by curbing foreign policy, and thus fulfil his naval and financial programmes. During these years his regime became a nursery of bureaucratic talent in which a number of future administrators served their apprenticeship; José de la Quintana, José del Campillo and Zenón de Somodevilla (marquis of Ensenada) all owed their promotion to Patiño and found in him their model of government.

Patiño was not an original thinker, or even a reformer. He was a conservative, pragmatic and indefatigable official who possessed superior administrative talents and wide experience. His basic idea was simple: to restore Spanish power in Europe by reviving the American trade through a strong navy, a national industry, and a fiscal policy to stimulate exports. Positive policy of this kind – naval power, military action, defence of the Indies – cost money, and the secret of Patiño's success was his ability somehow to overcome enormous financial difficulties and budget deficits. His programme was not without its critics. One of the more acute English diplomats of the time, Benjamin Keene, thought that his policy was too ideal to be realized; in particular his new commercial controls at Cadiz were simply evaded:

> But with all our grievances, I believe, the duties of half of what is introduced at Cadiz are not paid. Patiño knows it as well as the merchants, and is too rigorous in his orders to prevent this and such like abuses; and till some method be found to adjust these matters, he will be cheated, and we shall complain, just as it has been customary from the beginning of our commerce with this country.[70]

Patiño's Spanish critics were more politically motivated and comprised the grandees and the *partido fernandino*; the financial implication of a strong defence policy enabled them to appeal to tax payers and *asentistas* (financiers), but underlying their opposition was an aristocratic disdain for Patiño and his ministerial colleagues, none of whom came from the higher aristocracy, and a fear that his innovations, moderate though they were, would erode their social privileges and traditions. Opposition from the aristocracy, the *asentistas*, and the king himself, culminated in a bitter propaganda campaign reaching its peak in 1735 in

---

[70] Keene to Waldegrave, Seville, 28 March 1732, BL, Add. MS 43, 415, f 168 v.

the pages of a news-sheet *El Duende Político*, which appeared every Thursday from 8 December to 7 June of the following year and was a deliberate attempt by the aristocracy to manipulate public opinion against Patiño and his team.[71] Patiño survived only through the support of the queen, and there was a price to be paid for this, the promotion of her foreign policy. For all his interest in Spain's transatlantic trade and defences, Patiño could not disavow the dynastic interests of Elizabeth Farnese, for she was his patron.

While Patiño introduced order in Spanish government and consistency in its foreign policy, the queen was indispensable in holding the political front and in curbing the more dangerous excesses of the king. She had to watch her husband constantly for any further attempt to abdicate. In 1728, during a period of mental decline, he managed to get hold of pen and paper and send a note to the president of the council of Castile ordering him to call a meeting and announce his abdication in favour of his eldest son.[72] The president advised the queen, who recovered the note and hastened to transfer the court to Seville where the king could be more easily isolated. After this there was much rumour but little danger of abdication: 'he is in the power of the queen, at a distance from the council of Castile, and has not a person about him that dares to be the bearer of a letter to them, had he an opportunity of writing it.'[73]

These events gave heart to the Spanish party, which was further encouraged by the marriage of the prince of Asturias in January 1729. It was thought by many that Ferdinand had to sacrifice his feelings to diplomacy in marrying Barbara of Braganza, an ill-favoured bride whose greatest asset was her musical talent. But he came to be very fond of her and by 1732 he seemed to be re-enacting his father's dependence on his wife, a warning perhaps of her future influence. Politically speaking Barbara was another recruit to the *partido fernandino*, bringing with her not only a swarm of Portuguese but also a Portuguese interest which did not always coincide with the policy of Farnese. Thus, all those opposed to the Italian policy of the queen and the domestic government of Patiño – the grandees, the Spanish party, and now the *partido portugués* – joined the lobby of Prince Ferdinand. The prince himself seemed almost incidental to the politics enacted in his name, but his mere existence

---

[71] Egido, *Opinión pública y oposición al poder*, pp. 156–67.
[72] Baudrillart, *Philippe V et la cour de France*, III, p. 364.
[73] Keene to Waldegrave, Seville, 19 December 1732, BL, Add. MS 43, 416, f. 139.

caused the queen to take precautions and to exclude him from policy making:

The Prince always assists at the council of dispatches in the morning, when once the common current affairs of the kingdom are treated; but the affairs of state, and particularly those relating to the interests of the queen and her family are not produced but in his absence nor before midnight, when M. Patiño attends upon their Majesties and generally stays with them till the hour of their supper, which is about four in the morning.[74]

Yet the prince was no danger to Philip V, and his political role was less serious than he was given credit for:

As to the strong party in Spain who encourage the abdication, it is very certain there is scarce a Spaniard who does not wish for it, but it is as certain there is not one who dares to take a step towards it, if there was any possibility of putting such intentions in practice, and if I could give Your Grace the character of the adherents to the Prince of Asturias (who is too submissive to his father ever to put himself at the head of a party) the bare knowledge of them would shew that the Queen has nothing to apprehend from that quarter, for either they are already gained into her interests, or too inconsiderable to deserve her attention.[75]

So it appeared that Philip was there to stay, and that there was no chance of his abdicating or changing his way of life. It was a far from normal life; he had not had a change of clothes in nineteen months, and his extraordinary time-table placed a great strain on all who served him.[76] At Easter 1733, after months in which he refused to leave his bed, he at last appeared in public shaved and dressed, but he still refused to see ministers and expressed a particular aversion to Patiño. In May it was decided to leave Seville, and so the whole court headed north to Castile, the king looking thin and feeble, the queen fat and dull.[77] On the way the king issued, or was persuaded to issue, an order confining the prince and princess of Asturias to virtual house arrest; they were not to appear in

---

[74] Keene to Newcastle, Seville, 10 December 1730, PRO, SP 94/104.
[75] Keene to Newcastle, Seville, 23 February 1732, PRO, SP 94/111.
[76] Keene to Newcastle, Seville, 30 May 1732, PRO, SP 94/111.
[77] Keene to Newcastle, 8 May, 1733, Keene to Delafaye, 19 May 1733, PRO, SP 94/116.

public, not to receive foreign diplomats, and, in the case of Ferdinand, not even to go hunting. The order bore the hall-mark of Farnese, whose normal tendency was to over-react, and served only to increase the tenacity of the opposition and their criticisms of the queen. Yet there was little they could do outside the underground press and campaigns to move public opinion.

Policy was dictated by the queen and Patiño, and this meant priority to Italian objectives. It was not an unsuccessful policy and in 1734 resulted in the conquest of Naples and Sicily for Farnese's eldest son Charles. But it was costly and extremely unpopular in Spain, and it intensified political factionalism between Carlists and Ferdinandists, the latter arguing that Naples traditionally belonged to Spain; therefore, as Spanish arms had recovered it, so the Spanish heir, Ferdinand, should receive it. As Benjamin Keene reported:

> All sorts of people shew their disatisfaction at the disposal of the kingdom of Naples, and look upon it as an injury done to the Prince of Asturias, and to the Spanish nation with respect to their ancient right to dismembered parts of the monarchy. As to the new title of conquest now in vogue, nothing can be more just, say they, that as these conquests are made by the armies and at the expense of the crown of Spain, they should accrue to and be reunited to the crown, and not be disposed of at the pleasure of the Queen to the prejudice of the natural heir to the whole monarchy.[78]

Dissatisfaction, however, did not mean insubordination. There was not the will to create a genuine opposition or seek a power base in the country. The people were resigned, the factions elitist, and the grandees self-seeking; for Prince Ferdinand had no succession, and they hesitated to expose themselves to the displeasure of Charles, king of Naples and Sicily, who might eventually be king of Spain. The councils were traditionally the voices of constructive criticism, but they were now filled with creatures of the court. The queen was in complete ascendancy over her passive partner, and in the following years she contrived to interest him in music and other diversions to allay his melancholy, at the same time ensuring that he knew of policy only what she wanted him to know, 'which she has effectually secured by not admitting any persons to approach him with any materials which may encourage him to

---

[78] Keene to Newcastle, Madrid, 7 June 1734, PRO, SP 94/119.

oppose her ideas, when he happens to be in a disposition to interest himself in what is transacting'.[79] She concealed his true mental state, and in 1738 people were put in prison for spreading rumours that he was going to abdicate.[80]

The government of Patiño approached its end amidst clamour abroad and uncertainty at home. In 1735–6 problems pressed upon him – the Italian war and European responses, the negotiations for peace with the Emperor, ambiguity from France, trouble from the papacy, and conflict with Portugal in the Río de la Plata. Above all, he had to assemble the military and naval resources to sustain his policy and find the money to pay for them. When things went wrong, or did not go immediately right, the monarchs turned on Patiño. Queen and minister had long doctored the news given to the king; now the queen suspected that the minister was doing the same to her. Suddenly his position looked weaker: he lost his monopoly of Indies administration when the secretaryship of the Indies was assigned to the conde de Montijo; more people were gaining access to the monarchs; there was an air of change. Patiño had always remained aloof from politics, relying on his talent alone: 'Patiño has been impolitick enough not to secure himself a single friend capable to do him service . . . He has neglected all mankind, first because he thinks himself superior to all he sees here, and secondly because he knows the absolute necessity the Queen has for his service.'[81] As he struggled to satisfy the queen, he took ill in mid-September and died in 3 November 1736, working almost to the end. At the last minute the king hastened to make him a grandee and to settle a pension on his family.

Patiño was a master of bureaucratic compromise and sought a way between the demands of the crown and the needs of the country, between foreign policy and the means available. In the ultimate analysis defence spending, economic policy, the Indies trade, everything was subordinate to increasing the power of Spain and imposing it in Europe. This was his strength and his limitation. As Keene observed:

Mr Patiño founded his merit and preserved his credit by looking out for occasions to employ and gratify the natural dispositions both of King and Queen, by flattering them with sworn accounts of their power, and by his pretending to be in readiness at short warning to set fire to the four corners of the earth. Though

[79] Keene to Newcastle, Madrid, 13 December 1737, PRO, SP 94/128.
[80] Keene to Newcastle, 8 September 1738, PRO, SP 94/131.
[81] Keene to Newcastle, 23 April, 1736, PRO, SP 94/125.

sometimes, not to discover his nakedness he was obliged to find out means to inspire into them a sort of moderation.[82]

To place Patiño in a line of so-called Bourbon reformers is to misread his policy and priorities. His first object was to strengthen the state against its enemies not to employ it on behalf of its subjects, to increase Spain's profits from America not to improve the benefits America received from Spain. He redirected resources towards the central government; but he did not reorganize the economy or alter the balance of society.

The various offices which Patiño had concentrated in himself were now divided, losing force and focus, and admitting different views and interests; the navy in particular was now at risk, exposed to competition for resources from the army in Italy and from the central administration.[83] The new government seems to have been virtually nominated by Patiño, not greatly to his credit. The secretary of state, Sebastian de la Cuadra, was a man 'of very limited understanding', too weak to design a policy independent of the monarchs and too diffident to take responsibility for the slightest initiative.[84] The marquis of Torrenueva, timid and mediocre, was appointed secretary of finance and interim secretary of the navy and Indies, though his knowledge of the Indies was minimal. The rest of the government was of similar character, heirs of Patiño in policy but not in talent:

> The difference between the present system and that in the time of the late Mons. Patiño is that the cries of the public were then against the too great authority reposed in the hands of one person, and that at present it is difficult to know whether there is any delegated authority, and, if there be, in what hands it is lodged.[85]

Yet the government had enough basic cunning to seek to perpetuate itself in office through use of its own patronage, replacing Torrenueva by even more subservient clients, Francisco Iturralde for finance, and José Quintana for the navy and Indies.[86] The Queen regarded them as a group of clerks and assumed even greater control of policy. And she began to

[82] Keene to Newcastle, Escorial, 16 November 1736, PRO, SP 94/126.
[83] Keene to Newcastle, 24 September 1736, PRO, SP 94/126.
[84] Keene to Newcastle, Escorial, 16 November 1736, PRO, SP 94/126.
[85] Keene to Newcastle, Madrid, 8 July 1737, PRO, SP 95/128.
[86] Keene to Newcastle, Madrid, 9 March 1739, PRO, SP 94/133.

take advice, on financial and Italian policy, from a new administrator, a man of ideas as well as of action.

José del Campillo y Cossío was an Asturian of modest origins, left an orphan and educated with clerical help in Córdoba.[87] He entered the Bourbon bureaucracy first in the office of the intendant of Andalucía, then in 1717 that of Patiño, who promoted him to paymaster of marines in Cadiz. He acquired practical experience of the Indies trade, surviving a shipwreck off the coast of Campeche. Periods as superintendent of the shipyard at Guarnizo, as commissary-general of the army in Italy, and as intendant of Aragon widened his experience, and in 1741 he was given a number of ministries – finance, war, navy, and Indies – which made him in effect the leader of the government and the true heir of Patiño. Yet his ideas were more radical than those of Patiño; already before he reached ministerial office he was known to have independent views and a special knowledge of colonial and maritime affairs.[88] In an earlier stage of his career he was denounced to the Inquisition for reading prohibited books and for contact with heretics, accusations which he ridiculed and attributed to the envy of those whom he had overtaken in office. But he encountered more opposition than Patiño and had to fight to survive. When he was intendant of Aragon he attracted the hostility of the powerful governor of the council of Castile, Gaspar de Molina, who accused him of corrupt administration of funds. But his greatest clash was with the duke of Montemar, soldier, Spanish commander in Italy, and representative of the Spanish party, a clash which Campillo won when he secured Montemar's dismissal from his military command. Campillo was too intellectual to satisfy the aristocracy and too combative to lead a consensus government. He did not hide his ideas, and his programme for the regeneration of Spain and its American empire can be read in three major writings: *Lo que hay de mas y de menos en España* (1741), its sequel, *España despierta* (1742), and *Nuevo sistema de gobierno económico para la América* (1743).[89] These were evidence of a fertile and active mind, but they were not published in his lifetime, nor were their ideas realized by their author, whose administration was more cautious than his thinking. In any case little time was left to Campillo. He died suddenly on 11 April 1743.

Campillo was succeeded by Zenón de Somodevilla, marquis of La Ensenada, a man from the same bureaucratic stable and destined for a

[87] Rodríguez Villa, *Patiño y Campillo*, pp. 131–2.
[88] Keene to Newcastle, 5 January 1737, PRO, SP 94/127.
[89] On the Indies context of Campillo's work see below, pp. 147–9.

longer term of office, but no more capable than his predecessor of breaking the mould of royal policy. Patiño, Campillo, and Ensenada were excellent civil servants, products of political patronage no doubt but also of a new career open to talents in the higher bureaucracy. Once promoted to ministers, however, they became captives of the crown, tied to their brief, which was to provide the resources for war. Farnese's total obsession with foreign policy wasted the abilities of these ministers; in any case, it would be unhistorical to judge their govern-ment by the criteria of later times and to expect from their policy projects of structural change. Moreover, criticism of government policy did not necessarily come from more enlightened opinion. It was the traditionalist Spanish party which kept alive opposition to the queen and her Italian projects, nominally out of loyalty to Ferdinand but basically looking back to a golden age of grandee power. As a French official explained:

There are two parties: the party of the favourites, and the party of the native Spaniards. The latter consists of most of the old grandees of Spain; as they do not participate in government or its benefits, or enjoy the confidence and esteem of the queen, they wait impatiently for a change of government policy and personnel ... As for the favourites, their only influence on decisions is to agree with the way the queen happens to be thinking at any given time.[90]

The long reign came to an end on 9 July 1746. Ironically, Philip V died unaccompanied by doctor or confessor.[91] The Spanish people had few reasons to mourn his departure. Yet the reign had some positive features and under its patronage a group of ministers began the task of making Spain stronger, wealthier, and better governed.

The Agents of Absolutism

The new dynasty did not administer a miraculous cure or produce a great Bourbon reform out of thin air. Reform depended upon the impetus given by the king, the ideas and plans of ministers, and the

[90] Ministère des Affaires Etrangères, Commission des Archives, *Recueil des Instructions données aux ambassadeurs et ministres de France depuis les Traités de Westphalie jusqu'à la Révolution Française*, XII bis *Espagne* (Paris, 1899), p. 204, XXVII *Espagne* (Paris, 1960), IV, pp. 17–18.

[91] Baudrillart, *Philippe V et la cour de France*, v, pp. 441–2.

response of political opinion. Rarely were these three preconditions present simultaneously. The basic object was to reinforce the power of the state, and this involved confronting the state's competitors, particularly economic interests and the Church. But this was done within existing structures and did not imply a new ideology or an attack on traditional society. Granted these limits, three lines of policy can be identified: a reform of government; state intervention in the economy; closer control of the Church.

Habsburg government lacked a strong ministerial presence. Conciliar government was essentially government by committee, and the committees were dominated by the aristocracy. The need for change was already understood, but the advent of Philip V, the demands of war, and the influx of French absolutists gave a new impetus to reform. The higher nobility were pushed aside and replaced by ministers and bureaucrats, more efficient though not more numerous, agents of absolutism and centralization. The will of the king could be exercised either directly, the *via reservada*, or through a secretary of state, the *via de estado*. The secretary of state came to be a key figure in the Bourbon reconstruction of government, developing out of the *secretario de estado y del despacho universal* of the previous century but shedding the clerkly origins of that office and assuming a more responsible and more specialist character, expressed in the name minister which was later employed.[92] The first stage of development began in 1705 when the *secretaría* was divided into two; in the interests of efficiency and responsibility two further *secretarías* were added by decree of 30 November 1714, and the whole now comprised state, war, grace and justice, and navy and the Indies, with an inspector general of finance. After further permutations, finance became a full *secretaría* and in 1721 the basic structure of five secretarías was established and maintained more or less intact for the rest of the century.

The office of secretary was not necessarily allocated each to a separate minister, for some of the more outstanding ministers held two or more secretaryships. Campillo, for example, was appointed secretary of finance in February 1741 and in October of the same year was appointed also secretary of war and secretary of the navy and Indies; on his death in 1743 Ensenada succeeded to all these offices. But the record was held by Patiño, who accumulated the secretaryship of the navy and Indies (1726), finance (1726), war (1730), and state (1734), only justice eluding

[92] Gildas Bernard, *Le Secrétariat d'État et le Conseil Espagnol des Indes (1700-1808)* (Geneva, 1972), pp. 24–76.

him. Such concentration of power was criticized and his enemies denounced him as a minister 'without God, without law, and without judgement', wasting money on the navy, surrounding himself with incompetents and sycophants.[93] But it was a logical progression, and Patiño was regarded throughout Europe as Spain's chief minister, an office which did not exist. Yet while secretaries, or ministers, came to play an important role in government, they remained mere agents of the royal will, officials rather than politicians, administrators rather than statesmen. Patiño was a superior civil servant. Campillo had intellectual claims, but if he was more than an *arbitrista* he was less than a man of the Enlightenment.

As the secretaries grew in stature, so they became a focus of patronage as well as of policy. Each secretary had his team of officials, variously called *commis* or more characteristically *covachuelistas*, who worked in the *covachas ministeriales*, that is the 'caves' or basements of the royal palace. These were pure bureaucrats, some of them mere clerks, but as the ministries developed so they had the chance of moving up the ladder of promotion from clerk, to official, to ambassador, or even secretary of state. A secretary of state without much talent could go far with a good ministerial team, or fail if his officials were inferior. And inevitably the *covachuelistas* became politicized or factionalized, associated with the *partido* following a particular minister.

The royal preference for the *via reservada* and the advance of the secretaries of state meant to some degree the demise of the councils. Some were simply suppressed as no longer necessary, such as the councils of Aragon, Italy, and Flanders. The council of state, the right hand of the Habsburg monarchy and a preserve of the aristocracy, was simply ignored. Others, such as the council of the Indies, saw their jurisdiction curtailed and their influence diminished as they lost the struggle for supremacy with the new executive. The one exception was the council of Castile, which remained the principal agency of Spain's internal government, an incipient ministry of the interior or home office.[94] Within this council raged the debates for and against internal reform, and its meetings became a battleground of ideas as well as of personalities. The council of Castile, from 1715, was composed of a president or governor; twenty-two ministers, increased from time to

[93] *Duende Político*, quoted by Bernard, *Le Secrétariat d'État*, pp. 40-1.

[94] Janine Fayard, *Les membres du Conseil de Castille à l'époque modern (1621-1746)* (Geneva/Paris, 1979), shows that the council lost much of its independence to the crown under Philip V, with fewer *colegiales* as members.

time according to government needs; two attorneys, increased to three in 1771; and seven notaries. The president or governor was appointed directly by the king and under the Bourbons was usually a layman, as distinct from the high ecclesiastics favoured by the Habsburgs. He was present with all the council at the *consulta de viernes* held every Friday, and afterwards remained alone with the king, as did the secretaries of state, to give advice and receive orders.

The council of Castile had an exclusive social character which became more pronounced in the course of the eighteenth century as it developed into a centre of power monopolized by a group of families of middle nobility closely connected with the *colegios mayores* of the Universities of Salamanca, Valladolid and Alcalá. Many of the councillors were products of the colleges, whose admission procedures in turn favoured councillors' relatives and clients. The oath of mutual aid bound the *colegiales mayores* into a kind of masonry and was regarded as a matter of honour valid for life. Those who reached the goal of their careers – bishop or judge – continued to observe the oath and to help their own in a network of patronage and power. Meanwhile the non-collegial graduates, the *manteistas*, could not even obtain a proportion of university appointments, and these were merely the first stage on the way to higher things. In the early years of Philip V they protested. The *manteistas* of the University of Salamanca petitioned the king, claiming that out of 200 chairs filled in the last seventy years, the *colegiales mayores* had obtained 150, and their gains were even greater in government offices, in spite of the fact that their educational qualifications were inferior. Philip V made a half-hearted attempt to reform the universities, believing their mission was to 'educate youth and provide ministers for the government'.[95] He did something to aid the arts faculties and *colegios menores*, to introduce the teaching of Spanish as distinct from Roman law; he sought to reform the way chairs were filled, and in the 1720s to curb the influence of the *colegios mayores*. But, like many other projects of this reign, these measures promised more than they fulfilled, yielding too easily to interested resistance. Philip V and his ministers were far from being proponents of social or ideological change, merely of administrative reform to strengthen the power of a weakened state. But the network of councillors and *colegiales*, reinforced by other defenders of the status quo such as the Inquisition and the Jesuits, regarded any

[95] Quoted by Richard L. Kagan, *Students and Society in Early Modern Spain* (Baltimore, Md., 1974), p. 226; see also Antonio Domínguez Ortiz, *Sociedad y estado en el siglo XVIII español* (Barcelona, 1981), p. 92.

change as a danger to Spanish tradition, nationality and even religion. Macanaz was a victim of this mentality.

The reform of central government was complemented by the establishment of new links between the centre and the provinces. The model for this was the French intendant, appointed by the crown and responsible directly to it.[96] The idea can be seen in the reports of Orry in 1703, but it was 1711 before the first intendants were appointed, on the initiative of the count of Bergeyck, Philip V's chief minister. Among the first intendants were José Patiño for Extremadura and Rodrigo Caballero for Valencia, nominated to serve from 1 December; there were also nominations for Salamanca and León. The experiment was not an immediate success. In eastern Spain, in Barcelona, Valencia, and Zaragoza, where central institutions had not hitherto penetrated, the intendancies filled a gap. But in Castile they were regarded as unnecessary and were suppressed in deference to the existing *corregidores*, the traditional royal officials in major towns.[97]

Yet existing institutions did not give the central government the required responses from the regions. In 1718, with the approval of Alberoni, a new initiative was taken. José Patiño drew up the instructions for the new officials and he was the moving spirit behind their re-establishment, though the model was again French. The marquis of Compuesta, replying to an inquiry from Alberoni on the value of intendants, justified them as strong officials responsible directly to the crown and capable of taking action on a wide range of issues: 'If they are bad, the authority they are given will enable them to cheat, rob and tyrannise the people. If they are good, the King will have agents or spies informing on everything that happens in the provinces, not only concerning private individuals but the officials of public bodies.'[98] The government was convinced and on 4 July 1718 issued the *Ordenanza* for the establishment and instruction of intendants of province and army; towards the end of 1718 twenty-nine intendants were in post. As an administrative class the new officials quickly established an identity and continuity; of those appointed in 1718 no less than six had been intendants previously and others with similar experience came in later.

---

[96] Horst Pietschmann, 'Antecedentes españoles e hispanoamericanos de las intendencias', *Anuario de Estudios Americanos*, 40 (1983), pp. 359–72, emphasizes the elements of continuity in the intendant system.

[97] Henry Kamen, *The War of Succession in Spain 1700-15* (London, 1969), pp. 115–16, and 'El establecimiento de los intendentes en la administración española', *Hispania*, 24, 95 (1964), pp. 368–95, esp. pp. 368–74.

[98] Quoted by Kamen, 'El establecimiento de los intendentes', p. 374.

They had wider powers than their predecessors of 1711, possessing not only military but also administrative jurisdiction. An intendant had to reside in the provincial capital and assume the office and function of the *corregidor* of the city, except in a few places such as Barcelona, Cadiz, Mérida and Pamplona, where *corregidores* remained independent. The joint functions meant that the intendant was responsible for four areas of administration which may be listed as follows: (1) Justice: law and order; (2) Finance: collection and administration of taxes and other revenues; (3) General administration: census, inventory of natural resources, industry, agriculture, roads and bridges, public works, public health, militia, granaries, archives; (4) Military administration.

A mere recital of the duties of intendants suggests that they had too much to do. Later in the century a sceptical observer asked, 'How is it possible for an intendant of a province like Andalucía to cope with all the detail of the functions assigned to him?'[99] Moreover, in spite of the Bourbon attempt to rationalize the administration, the *corregidores* survived and continued to exercise a range of duties, mirroring in smaller divisions of the province the activities of the intendant and, like the intendant, perpetuating the Spanish tradition of confounding judicial, administrative, and economic functions in one office.[100] Here were opportunities enough for confusion of jurisdiction, and useful ammunition for opponents of the reform.

The intendants themselves proved to be exemplary officials and did their utmost to make the new system work. But they aroused opposition from vested interests in the older bureaucracy, especially from judges and law personnel, who saw their duties usurped by new officials. The most serious charges, and also the most tendentious, were mounted in 1720 by the council of Castile, true to its conservative instincts:

> They have tried their utmost to arrogate to themselves jurisdiction which Your Majesty has not granted them, seeking to persuade everyone that they have a supreme authority in their province, greater and higher than that of other magistrates and tribunals ... It would be difficult to find a single Intendant, in the whole time that they have occupied these appointments, who has personally made a visitation of his province.

[99] Antonio Rodríguez Villa (ed.), *Cartas político-económicas escritas por el conde de Campomanes el conde de Lerena* (Madrid, 1878), p. 204. These letters were wrongly attributed to Campomanes; see F. Lopez, 'León de Arroyal, auteur des "Cartas político-económicas al Conde de Lerena"', *Bulletin Hispanique*, 69 (1967), pp. 26–55.

[100] Benjamín González Alonso, *El corregidor castellano (1348-1808)* (Madrid, 1970), p. 234.

The council concluded: 'The retention of these offices is not simply useless to the public interest; the council considers it positively harmful and to the great detriment of the royal treasury.'[101]

Philip V did not immediately suppress the intendants, as requested by the council of Castile, but he introduced substantial modifications in their functions. Among other things, they were relieved of their judicial powers. He also ordered a special junta of three councillors to investigate and report on the points of criticism made by the council. The report was favourable to the government and its new officials, and rejected the council's generalizations. It found that, far from failing in their objectives, the intendants had performed well in the collection of taxes and recruitment of troops, and there was no evidence that they had sought to extend their jurisdiction beyond its proper limits.

In spite of acquittal by the junta, the intendants still had their enemies and the government its doubts. A decree of 22 February 1721 abolished the intendants in all the provinces where there were no troops; this decree was accompanied by a reform of the financial administration which deprived the intendants of all the financial powers granted by the ordinance of 1718. The effect was to make superfluous those intendants who had neither fiscal nor military duties and so they were suppressed. After 1721 it seems that there were intendants only in Barcelona, Zaragoza, Valencia, Seville, Badajoz, Salamanca, La Coruña, Pamplona and Palma de Mallorca, and from this time the formal distinction between intendant of war and intendant of province came into existence. A number of provincial intendants continued to collect their salaries, by courtesy of the government, but by decree of 19 July 1724 the intendants of province were finally extinguished in those provinces where there were no troops and for the rest of the reign there were only intendants of war.

The intendants had not had time to show their worth, and they still had defenders who regretted their passing; in 1722, from the ministry of justice, the marquis of Compuesta reacted sharply to the constant carping of the council of Castile: 'I do not know what justifies so much clamour against the intendants. They have now been established for four years, and so far I have not seen in the *secretaría* either charge or complaint, serious or trivial, against any intendant.'[102] But their enemies in the council of Castile represented powerful interests, and

---

[101] Council of Castile, Consulta, 22 November 1720, quoted by Kamen, 'El establecimiento de los intendentes', p. 377.
[102] Ibid., p. 379.

there the matter rested. The intendant system was abolished, but in nine provinces individual intendants survived and continued to exercise real functions. These of course were intendants of war and their duties were officially confined to the recruitment, provisioning and pay of troops. But they also retained in practice management of royal revenues and extensive discretionary powers, as can be seen in the case of Aragon.

Juan Antonio Díaz de Arze, intendant of Zaragoza from 1721 to 1736, was an uncompromising servant of Madrid and the political head of a province unaccustomed to rule from the central government. Behind his routine reports on taxes and troops lay a smouldering resentment among the public against what many regarded as a regime of extortion and injustice. In 1730, after ten years of his administration, a public protest was sent to the king, unsigned and containing a long list of accusations: Arze had usurped for himself the tax on coal entering Zaragoza; he had taken the entire salary of *corregidor* as well as that of intendant, without paying the tax of *media anata* (half the first year's salary) on the former; he was so weak in mind and body that he had to use a stamp for his signature; yet in spite of his advanced age he lived scandalously with low women and other men's wives; he was partial and tyrannical in the administration of justice; he cheated the treasury out of customs revenue and charged tax farmers a commission for himself.[103] No sign here of an intendant starved of activities. Arze mobilized his supporters, countered the charges, and survived, dying in office on 21 August 1736. His successor, from November 1736, was José del Campillo, whose terms of appointment specifically stated that he was authorized to act 'with the same authority and jurisdiction as your predecessors and as the other intendants of army and province, in political and economic as well as in military and financial matters'.[104] Campillo was a vigorous and talented administrator at any level; he would not accept the slightest diminution of the intendant's office or patronage, and in June 1738 insisted on the restoration of his power to appoint tax collectors in the sub-districts of the province.[105] Campillo also showed his skill in intervening between the state and the people and seeking to satisfy the interests of each. When the town of Villel petitioned for tax reduction in December 1738 after a devastating storm,

[103] AGS, Secretaría de Hacienda 536, 1730.
[104] Quoted by Kamen, 'El establecimiento de los intendentes', p. 380.
[105] AGS, Secretaría de Hacienda 536, 1738.

he accepted the facts but recommended a year's remission rather than the four years requested.[106]

There is abundant evidence, therefore, that the intendants survived the suppression of the intendant system, and came to form an elite corps of experienced officials, who moved sideways and upwards in the new bureaucracy, acquiring personal knowledge of the Spanish provinces and remaining available for further appointment when the intendant system was fully restored in 1749. This was the most convincing proof of their utility.

The Bourbon state imposed its military as well as its civil power on the regions. Habsburg-type viceroys were abolished, except in Navarre, and were replaced by captains-general, who commanded all troops in their provinces and, with the intendants, formed the front edge of the new absolutism. Each province had a military governor, but it was only the most important provinces which rated a captain-general, the highest rank in the military hierarchy. These were Aragon, Catalonia, Valencia, Mallorca, Granada, Andalucía, Canary Islands, Extremadura, Old Castile, Galicia, and from 1805 Asturias. The captain-general had civil as well as military jurisdiction, for he was also president of the *audiencia*, except in Seville and Cáceres which until 1800 retained civilian presidents. Although formally the two offices were kept distinct, in fact this represented a Bourbon tendency to militarize the administration of justice at the top. As presidents of *audiencias* military commanders secured control of law enforcement, so much so that even the council of Castile could not overturn their decisions unless the king authorized it to do so.

Bourbon absolutism left little space for representative institutions, any more than it did for conciliar bodies. The king was not only the chief executive, he was also the sole law-maker. There were certain institutions, the council of Castile and the *secretarías de estado*, which participated in the legislative process, proposing and preparing laws for royal sanction, but the *cortes* were not one of these.[107] In any case the *cortes* represented the nation in only a limited sense. Philip V abolished the *cortes* of the eastern kingdoms and left only one for the whole of Spain, with the exception of Navarre which kept its own separate assembly.

---

[106] Alcaldes, regidores y procurador síndico to crown, 13 December 1738, AGS, Secretaría de Hacienda 536.

[107] María Isabel Cabrera Bosch, 'El poder legislativo en la España del siglo XVIII', *La economía española al final del Antiguo Régimen*. Tomo IV. *Instituciones*, ed. Miguel Artola (Madrid, 1982), pp. 185–268, esp. p. 188.

Deputies now attended from Aragon as well as Castile, two from each of the thirty-six towns with right of representation. These were 'elected' in meetings of town councils, once the king had convoked the *cortes*. The deputies thus assembled had few duties and even fewer rights; they could petition, but they rarely did so successfully. Three meetings of the *cortes* were held in the eighteenth century, in 1724, 1760 and 1789. No *actas*, or minutes, of these assemblies were preserved, though their meagre proceedings are well enough known. Those convoked on 12 September 1724 were called to swear in Philip V's son Ferdinand as heir to the throne and deal with any other business put to them. The sessions were a charade. The first was held on 25 November in the convent of San Jerónimo in Madrid and the oath-taking was completed, after which there was little to do until 18 January 1725 when the *cortes* were dissolved: 'as the duties of swearing in have been concluded and there is no further need of the cortes, His Majesty has resolved that the deputies attending may return home.'[108] The *cortes* of 1760 were called to swear to Charles III's son, Carlos Antonio, as prince and heir, and lasted a mere five days.

Bourbon absolutism tolerated no alternative allegiance and no resistance. The Church too felt the force of the new state, and while its authority in faith and morals was not at issue, it was forced to concede greater demands on its resources and to take sides in the growing conflict between crown and papacy over jurisdiction, revenues and appointments. The assertion of the rights of the crown over the Church and the adoption of a distinctly 'regalist' position in Spain against the papacy were influenced by a number of factors which took the policy of Philip V beyond that of the Habsburgs. The War of Succession was itself a cause of conflict: Pope Clement XI, pressed by Austria and un-impressed by the Bourbons, recognized the archduke as king of Spain in 1709, to which Philip V replied by breaking off diplomatic relations with Rome and expelling the nuncio. Some of the Spanish hierarchy feared a schism; the majority preferred to obey the king without invoking matters of principle. Philip's victory in Spain showed the papacy that it had made a political miscalculation and relations were eventually restored. But political tension returned in the post-war period when the aggressive Italian policy of Elizabeth Farnese placed papal interests under threat and created an impression of military coercion against the pope which even the most regalist of Spanish churchmen deplored.

---

[108] Quoted ibid., p. 202.

Secular skirmishes of this kind, however, were merely a reflection of deeper conflicts between Church and state.

The attempt to exclude papal jurisdiction and taxation from Spain was not new. Bourbon regalism, however, first expressed by Philip V, adopted a more advanced position and claimed authority over all ecclesiastical institutions in Spain, including the Inquisition, an authority based on historical precedents and legal rights. In particular Philip V wanted the right to appoint to ecclesiastical benefices in Spain, two-thirds of which were in the hands of the pope; and he wanted the revenues of vacant sees and the fees charged by ecclesiastical tribunals. Melchor de Macanaz was asked to draw up a paper covering the points currently at issue between Church and state; his *proposiciones* (19 December 1713) adopted a fully regalist position, placing royal power above that of the Church in jurisdiction, and insisting that the sovereign had absolute power over temporal affairs in his own kingdom. According to Macanaz the papacy should have no rights of taxation in Spain, and there should be no appeals to Rome except through the Spanish government; ecclesiastical tribunals should be deprived of all temporal power; the crown alone had the right to appoint bishops; the Church could be taxed at the will of the state; religious orders should be reduced to their numbers under Cardinal Jiménez. The king approved and protected Macanaz against the attacks of the Inquisition and other traditionalists until the fall of the Orry government in 1715, when he was dismissed. Yet Macanaz was an orthodox Catholic, a friend of the Jesuits, an enemy of Jansenists, and a defender of the very Spanish Inquisition which prohibited his works, kept him out of Spain, and persecuted his family.[109]

There was a hint in the report of Macanaz that the Spanish Church was in need of reform. This was also the view of Rome, and it should have been possible in the 1720s for papalists and regalists to collaborate in reviewing clerical institutions, investigating religious orders, and in general improving ecclesiastical discipline. But the initiative failed because the crown was not really interested in reform, only in its power over the Church. The condition of religion was not questioned by Church or state; indeed the government authorized more fiestas and

---

[109] Kamen, 'Melchor de Macanaz', pp. 707, 709–11, 712–13. On Church-state relations under Philip V see Joaquín Báguena, *El cardenal Belluga. Su vida y su obra* (Murcia, 1935), pp. 39–50; Antonio Alvarez de Morales, *Inquisición e ilustración (1700-1834)* (Madrid, 1982), pp. 66–82; Ricardo García-Villoslada (ed.), *Historia de la iglesia en España*. Tomo IV. *La iglesia en la España de los siglos XVII y XVIII* (Madrid, 1979).

new communities, and the Inquisition continued on its way. Regalian rights, on the other hand, were a different matter. The king wanted to appoint to a majority of benefices by virtue of his *patronato real*, as in America, and to obtain maximum revenue from the Church. These were his objects in negotiating the concordat of 1737, in which king and pope agreed that the monarch had the right to appoint to benefices and vacancies, and to take revenues of vacancies previously received by the pope; that Church properties should no longer be exempt from tax; and that measures for the reform of the clergy and control of their numbers should be undertaken. But these were pious generalizations, encouraging many disputes and little action.

The reaction of the clergy to early Bourbon policy was ambiguous. While in general they supported the Bourbon succession, they were critical of particular governments and specific policies. There was an impression that they had been demoted since Habsburg times. Bourbon government was secular government and, royal confessors apart, clerics were less likely to be appointed to official posts than in the past. Regalism was a divisive issue. Many of the higher clergy were just as regalist as the secular servants of the crown, but regalism was often associated with attacks on clerical privilege, especially on the *fueros* so highly valued by the lower clergy. Reform of discipline also drew a mixed response, and the Tridentine-type measures recommended in the papal bull *Apostolici ministerii* (1723) aroused the suspicions of all sectors of the clergy. Regalists did not like accepting reform at the hands of Rome. And the lower clergy did not favour granting more power to the bishops. As for the economic position of the clergy, that was seen as constantly threatened by measures such as the concordat of 1737, for the concession of financial resources by pope to king could only be made at the expense of the Church and its priests. To many churchmen the ecclesiastical policy of Philip V seemed to be little more than a branch of his financial policy.

The Cost of Bourbon Rule

A modern and centralized government could not in itself restore the Spanish monarchy to greatness. The key to power was revenue, and unless the king of Spain could maintain his court, pay his officials, arm his troops, and replace his ships, then administrative reform was mere adornment. Absolutism depended upon resources.

Yet the tax structure of Bourbon Spain differed little from that of the Habsburgs, which in turn had grown without plan or method through the haphazard accumulation of taxes.[110] The burden fell mainly on Castile and within Castile on the common tax payer. The principal group of taxes was the so-called *rentas provinciales* paid by the people of Castile and levied on essential consumer goods. The most important of these was the *alcabala* (sales tax), followed by a group consisting of *cientos*, *tercias reales*, *millones*, *servicio ordinario y extraordinario*, *servicio de milicias*, and *cuarto fiel medidor*. The second group comprised the *rentas generales*, mainly customs and excise; these included tobacco and other state monopolies, or *estancos*, seigneurial dues, and a number of miscellaneous duties. The collection of taxes was as varied as their character; most of them were farmed out to private individuals, who sometimes sub-farmed or even mortgaged them. Nobility and clergy had a special tax status. In principle the Church was exempt but by arrangement with the papacy the crown received the *noveno* and 'three graces', that is the *subsidio*, *excusado*, and *cruzada*. The state depended heavily on ecclesiastical taxes, drawn from one of the largest concentrations of wealth in Spain, and in various ways, as has been seen, sought to expand them. Finally, there was the income from America, which had its ups and downs but showed a tendency to rise from the years around 1730 and moved more strongly upwards from 1750.

Expenditure was the recurring nightmare of every finance minister. Financial resources had a multitude of calls upon them, and in spite of the fortunate loss of the Netherlands and Italy in the War of Succession there seemed to be no fewer commitments. On the contrary, Italy now devoured more resources, for reconquest was costlier than possession; and for reasons few Spaniards could understand Philip V sometimes paid lavish subsidies to an ungrateful emperor.

If Bourbon foreign policy was expensive, so too was Bourbon domestic life. In general the Bourbons cost more than the Habsburgs. A French king, the first of a new dynasty, with a large retinue and an ambitious wife, and with the eyes of Spain and Europe upon him, was bound to increase expenditure on the court, for this was the immediate expression of his power. Inspired by sentiments of nostalgia, grandeur and pride, Philip V undertook a great building programme, a new palace in Madrid, another at San Ildefonso, extensions at Aranjuez, all of which took precedence in the queue for resources. The annual itineraries of the

---

[110] Henry Kamen, *Spain in the Later Seventeenth Century, 1665-1700* (London, 1980), pp. 357–72; Domínguez Ortiz, *Sociedad y estado en el siglo XVIII español*, pp. 70–3.

court between these various *sitios* was like the launching of major expeditions and cost a fortune in service and transport. The court employed thousands of officials and servants, not to govern Spain, but simply to look after the royal family and attend to its diversions.

Lower than the court in priority, a number of competing interests and claims clamoured for attention, led by the bureaucracy, the army, and the navy. The claims of the *secretarías*, councils, and other departments and their respective officials for salaries, increases, and pensions were always insistent, and it would need a strong minister to resist them. The army in itself had less leverage, but as an instrument of foreign policy it was vital to the plans of the monarchs and it was a large consumer of resources. Thus Elizabeth Farnese's Italian campaigns rated high in the expenditure scales, and again few ministers had the will to oppose them. This left the navy last in the queue. A Patiño might be able to salvage something for it; most ministers could not, and the true interests of empire went by default.

The priorities of the monarchs were not shared by all Spaniards. Cardinal Belluga had taken to the field for the Bourbons during the War of Succession, but he had second thoughts afterwards. He complained that consumer goods had soared in price: 'Today people are paying three times more than they did fourteen years ago.' The incorporation of *alcabalas* and other revenues to the state led to higher not lower taxes. Overseas trade had declined because of war and loss of shipping. The price of everything had gone up:

> The family which sixteen years ago managed decently on one thousand ducats, today (1721) cannot do so on two million; the result is that those who cannot maintain the same standard of living in their profession, use their positions to rob others; and those whose conscience will not allow them to do this decline and fall from their former state.

Yet the price of grain was so low that in Old Castile wheat sold at 4 reales a fanega, barley at 3, and even in Madrid the prices were only 6 and 4 respectively; consumers did not have money and farmers did not earn profits. Belluga had no doubt that the principal reason for the failure to recover after 1714 was the continuing commitment to war.[111] A second reason was the failure of the state to organize an adequate financial

---

[111] Báguena, *El cardenal Belluga*, pp. 255–61.

bureaucracy and to take the collection of taxes into the public sector, free from the fraud and extortion of financiers and tax farmers.

The Bourbon state was a high-taxing state and a high-spending state. Government income rose from some 250 million reales in 1715 to 360 million in 1745; the financial history of the reign was the struggle to keep expenditure within these limits, or more usually to find the means of exceeding them.[112] Until the early 1730s a semblance of financial order was preserved, and when pushed Spain could still find a surplus for war; this was the conclusion of an English observer:

> Their annual revenues may be calculated about sixteen millions of piastres, and the revenues of the Indies at about three millions. Of this, the King's family alone expends about seven million a year. The army on the footing of seventy thousand men cost them thirteen millions of ducats or about eight million seven hundred thousande piastres in their ordinary expenses. The remaining part of the revenues falls very short of defraying the charges of the marine, the salaries of their tribunals and ministers, etc. But although their expenses exceed their incomes by several millions, yet as they have not issued out any considerable sums from the treasury for a long time past, but what have been absolutely necessary for the payment of their troops, and as they have received very large sums by the extraordinary indultos upon the flotas and galleons, and the duties of exportation, they must in all appearance have above twenty millions of piastres by them which would have been employed carrying on a war, if the allies had agreed to one.[113]

In 1732 Spain could still maintain foreign garrisons and keep an army of 80,000 in the peninsula, and Patiño managed to pay for them with the help of large supplies from the Indies.[114] But the situation worsened in the next five years. In 1737 revenue totalled 21,100,750 escudos, plus returns from the Indies; expenditure was estimated at 34,535,296. The war ministry alone consumed more than 20 million, that is almost the whole of ordinary revenue. A special *junta de medios* was established to reform abuses, cut expenditure, and find extra means, but little was expected of it and, in spite of a valiant attempt to extract money from

---

[112] Kamen, *The War of Succession in Spain*, pp. 223, 230.
[113] Keene to Newcastle, Seville, 2 March 1731, PRO, SP 94/107.
[114] Keene to Newcastle, Seville, 23 September 1732, PRO, SP 95/112.

the higher aristocracy, little came of it.[115] Meanwhile there was no end to Italian expenditure: in addition to installing Prince Charles in Naples, there was the expense of maintaining him there and marrying him to the princess of Saxony:

> During the rejoicings the officers of the army have not received their pay for these ten months, nor the King's household for five years, and people see clearly at present that the taking so heavy and so extraordinary an indulto at Cadiz.was to defray the immense expenses that will be made both at this court and Naples and not to be applied to any other use.[116]

The imminence of financial collapse on the eve of war with England forced the monarchs to sanction yet another attempt at financial reform. On the reorganization of the government in 1739 Juan Bautista Iturralde was appointed minister of finance, a faceless man and rumoured to have made his own fortune from dealing in government revenues, but apparently knowledgeable in the ways of peculation. He attacked the excessive number of pensions on public funds in Spain and America and sought to stop the practice of pluralism among office-holders. He published a decree cutting the profits on government contracts; another suspending for two years the payment of all pensions and extraordinary salaries, hoping from this to save 2.5 million pesos a year. He proposed to pay the army on its real strength of 60,000 instead of the 100,000 normally budgeted for, thus saving 7 million ducats. These projects were the work of 'a person unknown until he was named minister, who has had more courage and resolution than ever the late Mr Patiño did, or the greatest subject now in Spain durst, pretend to put in execution'.[117] But courage was not enough in Philippine Spain. Iturralde did not have the political skill or stature to convert these short-term gains into structural reforms, and in the face of resistance from the interest groups they had no more than a temporary impact. The greatest shock in 1739 was Spain's suspension of payments, a virtual declaration of bankruptcy, which damaged its credit abroad and increased disillusion at home.

The campaigns in Italy and, from 1739, war with England drove the government to desperate and ultimately harmful remedies in the search

[115] Keene to Newcastle, 15 April 1737, 3 June 1737, PRO, SP 94/127.

[116] Keene to Newcastle, 13 January 1738, PRO, SP 94/130.

[117] On the reforms of Iturralde see Keene to Newcastle, 9 March, 30 March, 24 April, 17 August 1739, PRO, SP 94/133.

for money from a public already over-taxed. The first of these, the sale of *baldíos*, or common land belonging to the crown, was a device well known to the Habsburgs; but when, in 1738, Philip V resumed the practice *baldíos* were a diminishing resource and few Spanish peasants had the means to compete for purchase with landowners and monasteries. The alienation of the *baldíos*, therefore, was a further step towards land concentration, depriving poorer farmers, labourers, and the unemployed of access to land, without even increasing production among those who thus extended their estates. The benefit to the treasury was small: in the ten years in which the scheme was in operation it yielded only 1 million ducats.[118] The second project, in 1741, was an attempt to impose an extraordinary tax of 10 per cent on all incomes from whatever source, granting exemption to clergy, doctors, lawyers, labourers, and foreign merchants. In default of a tax office, the government gave each town a quota which it had to collect, but towns neither had the will nor the means to make an assessment based on income, so the government ended by authorizing them to collect their quotas by the age-old method of taxing commodities, thus adding to the tax burden on consumers and drawing back from the experiment of an income tax.

The tax burden within Spain was now shared more equitably between Castile and the eastern kingdom through equivalent taxation known as the *catastro* in Catalonia, the *equivalente* in Valencia and the *única contribución* in Aragon.[119] The *catastro* was designed by Patiño as a new tax of 10 per cent on all rural and urban properties and 8 per cent on personal incomes, starting from 1 January 1716.[120] Too much was expected of the Catalan economy and tax capacity, and the initial figure was set too high at 1,500,000 pesos; this was lowered to 1,200,000 in 1717 and to 900,000 in 1718, and finally settled at over 1 million. From 1724 the government was already receiving a surplus on the estimate and it appeared to be accepted without protest from tax payers. The fixed quota was maintained throughout the eighteenth century, which meant that the tax became progressively less burdensome as economic growth and population increase reduced individual payments, though later some adjustment was made. The Catalan *catastro*, however, was not a tax payer's panacea. It was an addition to, not a substitute for, the indirect regional taxes already in existence; and in exempting the nobility and

---

[118] Domínguez Ortiz, *Sociedad y estado en el siglo XVIII español*, pp. 74–5.
[119] See above, p. 65.
[120] Joaquín Nadal Farreras, *La introducción del Catastro en Gerona* (Barcelona, 1971), p. 74.

clergy it perpetuated social discrimination. Catalonia passed from a position of fiscal privilege to one of fiscal prejudice.

In half a century Bourbon government advanced only marginally on that of the later Habsburgs. Philip V was probably a greater liability than Charles II, for in addition to his personal incapacity he allowed his second wife to exercise a malign influence on policy. The machinery of government was reformed, the executive modernized, its control over all regions of Spain confirmed, and the aristocracy of privilege replaced in higher administration by an aristocracy of merit. Below the elite inefficiency and corruption thrived, and the projects of financial reform in 1737–41 served only to highlight the unreformed character of public life. And there was a further question. What difference did all this make to the power and resources of Spain?

4

Spain, Europe, and America

The Resource Base: Early Bourbon Economic Policy

The apparent eccentricity of court, government, and politics in the years 1714–46 masked a serious intent, as ministers struggled to make Spain a powerful state. Behind King Philip's follies an active administration was at work, rethinking economic and foreign policy, and developing the sinews of war. The state intervened more decisively in the economy, to direct and to consume, and it acted to protect national interests and monopolize colonial resources. To conceptualize this as 'mercantilism' would be to give early Bourbon policy a coherence it did not possess. The state was relatively weak, the heritage of the past heavy, enterprise a minority culture. Ministers worked on specific problems and looked for immediate results, to satisfy the monarchs, reward clients, or prepare for the next war. They were not conscious of a mission to propel Spain into the eighteenth century. The structure of the Spanish economy was not favourable to a rapid increase of wealth and power. No doubt the state could encourage production and promote trade, but to diversify and to develop, these were more elusive goals. In Spain, as in other traditional agrarian societies, the principal factors of production were land and labour, while capital played a minor role. The existing agrarian regime discouraged investment in agriculture, while the industrial sector was regarded as too risky, regulated and competitive to attract capital. The state could not force its subjects into productivity.

After the War of Succession better environmental conditions led to a fall in mortality rates and the Spanish population began to increase, fairly rapidly in the first half of the century (from 8.2 million in 1717 to 9.3 million in 1749), more moderately in the second half (to 11.5 million in 1797).[1] More people meant greater pressure on agricultural resources, and while there was some increase in production, this was achieved through extension of cultivation into inferior land, often by deforestation, and met the barrier of diminishing returns. As Spaniards continued to multiply, only an intensive and more productive agriculture would suffice. Meanwhile the increase of population, and therefore of demand, in conditions of diminishing supply, resulted in a rise of agricultural prices and periodic crises of subsistence. Yet property distribution did not change. More than two-thirds of cultivated land were in the hands of the nobility and the Church and thus outside the market either through entail or amortization. Except in parts of Andalucía and Castile, this land was usually farmed indirectly, through short- or long-term leases, which prevented productive investment and full exploitation. As long as no action was taken against land concentration and privilege, increase of agricultural production would continue to depend on extension into marginal lands, as later reformers such as Campomanes and Jovellanos pointed out. The agrarian sector, therefore, neither encouraged capital accumulation for investment nor created a consumer market for industry.

The early Bourbons responded to poor productivity and absence of markets not by formulating a new economic plan but by modifying the existing system. This they did in three ways.[2] First, they adjusted the institutional framework of the economy; second, they developed a public manufacturing sector; third, they revised the rules of colonial trade. In a subsequent phase of reform, from 1759, the later Bourbons responded to more radical criticism of the economy by more basic policy change. For the moment, however, the state confined itself to moderate adjustment, not so much to secure economic growth as to improve the balance of trade by encouraging Spanish exports, reducing imports and avoiding the outflow of money.

Administrative reform introduced centralization and uniformity. Decrees of 19 November 1714 and 31 August 1717 suppressed internal customs duties and transferred customs posts to the territorial frontiers of Spain, principally in the interests of freeing and encouraging trade

---

[1] Francisco Bustelo, 'Algunas reflexiones sobre la población española de principios del siglo XVIII', *Anales de Economía*, 151 (1972), pp. 89–106, and 'La población española en la segunda mitad del siglo XVIII', *Moneda y Crédito*, 123 (1972), pp. 53–104; Jordi Nadal, *La población española (siglos XVI a XX)* (Barcelona, 1973), pp. 84–105.

[2] José Rodríguez Labandeira, 'La política económica de los Borbones', *La Economía española al final del Antiguo Régimen*. Tomo IV, *Instituciones*, ed. Miguel Artola (Madrid, 1982), pp. 107–79, esp. p. 112.

between Castile, Aragon, Valencia and Catalonia. The internal customs of Jerez and Cadiz survived for reasons of revenue, and the Basque customs had to be restored in 1722 in order to tighten control. Otherwise these were necessary steps in the formation of a national market and were completed by the decree of 26 July 1757 which allowed the free circulation of national products within Spain. Export of grain was still prohibited, a facile alternative to making agriculture productive and competitive. At the first sign of a bad harvest and rising prices, the government closed the ports to grain export and authorized imports totally free of duties. The actual initiatives for imports was left to private merchants, and grain purchases by the treasury were exceptional. Meanwhile the junta of commerce, a body established in 1679 to promote trade and industry, continued to advise the central government, which was also now served by new agents of economic intelligence, the intendants; their reports from the regions gave policy-makers new information on problems of vagrancy, stock raising, irrigation, afforestation, communications, and other matters of infrastructure.

Fiscal policy remained basically unchanged. There was talk of a new single tax but plans never progressed beyond the drawing board. Thus the *rentas provinciales* continued to burden internal trade, and state monopolies still exploited the consumer. Import tariffs, except on certain commodities, did not normally exceed 15 per cent; to raise them higher might diminish trade and reduce customs revenue. Yet there was a protectionist bias in early Bourbon policy and a concern for national industries, especially textiles. The import of silk and cotton cloth from Asia was prohibited in 1718, and that of cotton and linen prints from Asia and Europe in 1728. The need to repeal these decrees in 1742, if only temporarily, indicates that traditional Spanish textiles satisfied neither public demand nor the pockets of purchasers.[3] This at any rate was the argument of Spain's French and English competitors.

Protection in itself was not enough. To stimulate national production the government began to intervene directly in the economy, creating an industrial sector financed by public funds. Royal factories were established to compete in the market with foreigners and encourage emulation among nationals. These concentrated capital and labour in one work place and were designed to amplify Spain's industrial base, hitherto confined to small artesanal establishments and a few larger

---

[3] Gonzalo Anes, *El Antiguo Régimen: los Borbones* (Madrid, 1981), pp. 236, 242–3; Rodríguez Labandeira, 'La política económica de los Borbones', pp. 164–71.

factories in Catalonia and the Basque country. Some of the new factories produced luxury articles for the court and privileged classes – tapestry at Santa Bárbara, glassware at San Ildefonso, and porcelain at Buen Retiro. The crown's most ambitious enterprise, however, was a new textile factory at Guadalajara which began operations in 1719, employing a mixture of Dutch immigrant workers and local labour, and manufacturing a product which was intended to compete directly with fine English and Dutch cloth.[4] Some progress was made: Guadalajara had 51 looms for woollen cloth and serge in 1731, 105 in 1745, 142 in 1754, and an astonishing 670 in 1784, all in one factory. Branch factories were built at Brihuega and San Fernando (1746), linen mills at León, and a silk factory at Talavera de la Reina. Yet these royal establishments, enjoying complete freedom from taxes and customs duties, a large monthly subsidy, first call on finest merino wool, and access to the most expensive foreign labour available, did not fulfil expectations. Guadalajara in particular was never profitable and its products failed to reach the quality of those of its rivals. Funding was maintained as a political decision, to demonstrate to Spain and to the world that the Bourbon state had an industrial sector, no matter what the economic cost. Privileged as they were, the royal factories had a depressive effect on other producers in central Spain and became a discouragement rather than a stimulus to private enterprise.

Yet private enterprise survived and competed for a share of the market. The village of Béjar in the province of Salamanca produced fine woollen cloth; starting in the late seventeenth century with Flemish labour, it remained small in scale but successful in operations, and by 1750 it was employing 150 looms. The textiles of Segovia and Palencia, artesanal in character, doubled their output in the period 1715–60.[5] The Valencia silk and Catalan cotton industry, using the domestic or putting-out system of production, were further and perhaps even more striking examples of industrial growth in the reign of Philip V. Outside textiles, this period saw some growth in metallurgical industries, often with state support. In Santander, Liérganes and La Cavada, where Spain's first blast furnaces developed, an armaments industry existed from the early seventeenth century. After the mid-century recession, a

---

[4] Agustín González Enciso, *Estado e industria en el siglo XVIII: la fábrica de Guadalajara* (Madrid, 1980), pp. 620, 637–53; James Clayburn La Force, Jr, *The Development of the Spanish Textile Industry, 1750-1800* (Berkeley/Los Angeles, Calif., 1965), pp. 21–2, 50.

[5] Angel García Sanz, *Desarrollo y crisis del Antiguo Régimen en Castilla la Vieja. Economía y sociedad en tierras de Segovia, 1500-1814* (Madrid, 1977), pp. 220–4.

new period of growth began under the early Bourbons, stimulated from 1716 by heavy demand from the Spanish navy for cast-iron canons.[6] Until it was expropriated by Charles III, the factory belonged to various businessmen, though heavily dependent on state contracts. Another royal munitions factory at Enguí in Navarre produced canonballs, bombs, grenades and other supplies for the army. At Ronda a tinplate factory struggled to compete throughout the eighteenth century. Initial enterprise and technology again came from abroad; in 1725 two Swiss entrepreneurs obtained permission from the government to establish the factory and they brought thirty skilled workers from Germany. Production was of good quality but constantly thwarted by obstacles. Water supply was scarce and disputed by local peasants; communications were difficult and the market was small; and when the factory decided to diversify into iron it encountered the hostility of Basque producers. The factory failed to prosper and changed ownership frequently, without any signs of profitability. At last the government took over, with no better results, and it was closed in 1780.

These examples illustrate the problems of Spanish industry. In many cases 'factories' were simply larger collections of artisans, with little change in the mode of production. There were deficiencies in technology which foreign workers could not in themselves supply. To modernize and expand production more investment was needed. It was not that capital was lacking in Spain. Interest rates were low after 1705, which indicated availability of capital, and large fortunes were made at this time in foreign and colonial trade. It would be wrong to picture Spain as expectant with industries in search of investors; on the contrary, she was living proof that accumulation could not in itself unlock the door to industrial growth.[7] The fact was that the preconditions for industrialization did not exist, either in agriculture, education, transport, or purchasing power. If capital preferred other outlets that was because the peninsula did not constitute a good consumer market for national industry and the government could not guarantee a colonial market free of foreign competition. Spaniards themselves showed much consumer resistance to the products of their own industry, and given a choice they were not normally disposed to

---

[6] José Alcalá-Zamora y Queipo de Llano, *Historia de una empresa siderúrgica: los altos hornos de Liérganes y La Cavada, 1622-1834* (Santander, 1974), pp. 223–45.

[7] Josep Fontana Lázaro, *La quiebra de la monarquía absoluta 1814-1820* (Barcelona, 1971), pp. 20–1.

buy Spanish. In any case most Spaniards were too poor to buy any manufactures, native or foreign.

There was, then, little investment in either agricultural or industrial production in the first half of the eighteenth century. The Spanish economy consisted of an under-capitalized agriculture, an equally under-capitalized industry still largely at the artisan stage, and a transport system whose bottle-necks were a further obstacle to growth. On the other hand capital *was* assembled for commercial activity and to promote overseas trade. The crown favoured all kinds of commercial companies in the period 1720–50. The mechanism of these enterprises was the same in most cases and tended to follow English and Dutch models. The public was invited to take shares; returns, but not liability, were limited to the investment; and the companies were given privileges, fiscal exemptions and monopolies over specific areas of operation or in certain products. The economist Gerónimo de Uztáriz thought they were of little benefit to Spain in the absence of exportable industrial products. But some of the companies, the *compañías de comercio y fábricas* typical of the time of Ensenada, did in fact propose to work in collaboration with local industries or even to establish factories for national exports. To demonstrate the favour of the crown, they were given the title *real* and the king sometimes had shares in them; for example, the *Real Compañía de Fábrica y Comercio de Toledo*, designed to re-establish silk manufacture; the *Compañía de Granada* and the *Compañía de San Fernando* (Seville) established to export silks to America; and the Extremadura Company, to trade with Portugal. But the most successful company, the Caracas Company, was not connected with industry at all; it dealt in cacao and other colonial products, and was followed by similar colonial companies in the middle decades of the century.[8] Yet none of these companies were agents of growth and development, and they were ignorant of the concept of limited liability as an encouragement to investment. Their existence did not imply the abolition of trade monopoly but simply a greater number of monopolists.

Catalonia emerged from the seventeenth century with better prospects of growth than Castile. These were checked but not ended by the events of 1705–14, and it became clear that the economic effects of the War of Succession were less traumatic than the political.[9] Demographic loss, material destruction and property confiscation were hard blows,

[8] See below, pp. 148–9.
[9] Pierre Vilar, *La Catalogne dans l'Espagne moderne* (3 vols, Paris, 1962), I, pp. 679–710.

and the post-war economy was far from robust; the years 1714–18 saw personal fortunes decline, prices rise and taxation increase. But these were the short-term effects of the war, prolonged no doubt by outbreaks of plague in different parts of Mediterranean Spain in 1720. After this date Catalonia entered a period of recovery and stability in 1720–6. The population rose from a post-war figure of 470,000 to 900,000 in 1787, leading to cheaper labour supply for industry and a larger labour force for agriculture.[10]

The stabilization of 1720–6 was peninsular in character and not merely regional. Now that Madrid ruled all the provinces, it did so without a rod of iron. Internal peace was the first advantage for the Catalan and other regional economies. Policy was in the hands of the new bureaucrats such as Rodrigo Caballero and Patiño, who were neither repressive by nature nor the agents of a repressive regime. Such policy as came from the centre was if anything favourable to Catalan interests. The protection of national against foreign products could only be welcome to Catalans; in the years 1717–18 the ministers of Philip V declared war on contraband and inaugurated, especially in textiles, a policy of import prohibition. Catalan industrialization, of course, did not begin with early Bourbon protectionism. The successful manufacture of printed cottons did not really gather pace until after 1740. But the 1720s saw the beginning of a more national economic policy, in the peninsula and in America, and from this Catalonia too could benefit.

The integration of the Catalan economy into that of the peninsula took place over a long period of time. But if a beginning has to be sought, the years around 1720 saw the first weak signals from the central government of the future direction of Catalonia – the suppression of internal customs, increased commercial relations between Barcelona and Cadiz, encouragement of exchange of Catalan products against Castilian grain. Gradually the Catalan economy would be compensated in the new Spain of the eighteenth century for the losses of 1714. By 1750 the Catalan model of economic growth was in place: population increase; extensive and intensive expansion of agriculture; a new impulse to traditional manufactures and the emergence of new industries employing modern modes of production; accumulation and investment of merchant capital; internal and overseas commercial expansion.[11] Such

[10] Nadal, *La población española*, pp. 96–105.
[11] Carlos Martínez Shaw, 'La Cataluña del siglo XVIII bajo el signo de la expansión', in Roberto Fernández (ed.), *España en el siglo XVIII. Homenaje a Pierre Vilar* (Barcelona, 1985), pp. 55–131, esp. pp. 67–8.

resources, projected to the whole of Spain, would have enabled the Bourbons to strengthen the sinews of war and present a new face to the world. As it was, they had to trim their defence interests and colonial policies to the means available, and in the process to find the true level of Spanish power.

The Army and Navy of Spain

The army occupied a central place in the Bourbon monarchy. Beyond its defence role, it was actually incorporated into the administrative and legal system, and the captains general and their subordinates were as much provincial governors as they were military commanders. This did not happen by chance. The Bourbons came to power in Spain by force, against the active opposition of part of the population. Philip V relied upon the army to fight for him and secure his throne, and its response to these demands earned rewards and privileges, especially for officers. Whereas in the rest of Europe the formation of a standing army implied the political demotion of the aristocracy, in Spain the growth of the army and the extension of its privileges benefited the higher nobility, who came to dominate the officer corps. The rank of colonel upwards was monopolized by the higher nobility, or *los mas calificados y titulados* as the law of 1704 described them, while the *hidalgos* and commoners could only aspire to lesser officer rank with little chance of promotion. So the army could be regarded as the vanguard of the aristocracy, not its rival, and in the course of the eighteenth century it came to dispute the front line of government with the civilian elite. The result was tension in civil-military relations leading to a crisis at the end of the century.

One of the positive achievements of the new dynasty was to rescue the army from the prostration and contempt into which it had fallen under the later Habsburgs. The change began in 1702–4 in response to the demands of war and in default of volunteers. The law of 8 November 1704 imposed selective conscription; for every hundred citizens one soldier was taken, a native of the locality, unmarried, aged 18–30, and not to be replaced by a substitute; after three years' service the conscript was demobilized and the locality drew lots for another. Recruits were mixed with veterans to form regiments of 500, later raised to 1,000.[12] Incentives were offered – access to military orders, exemption from

[12] Antonio Domínguez Ortiz, *Sociedad y etado en el siglo XVIII español* (Barcelona, 1981), p. 77.

other public duties, and the possession of the *fuero militar*, the latter a particularly valued privilege bestowing the protection of military law and other immunities. The only exempt occupations were students, various professions and offices, and certain farmers. Nobles too were exempt from conscription, on the grounds that they supplied the officer class. In fact the new army was built around the nobility, in the fond belief that they were the military estate and the traditional protectors of the realm.

The military reforms of 1702–4 were followed by others. The regiment replaced the *tercio* as the basic tactical unit, while a new system of command including brigadiers, colonels and lieutenants succeeded the Habsburg *maestres de campo* and other officers. Promotion was centralized in the crown, and the budget came from the central government. Spain soon discovered, no less than other European states, that the modern army was an extremely expensive instrument which could be maintained only by economic improvement and increase of revenue. Armies now reflected the total demographic and economic resources of a country and became in themselves a test of power. The establishment of a standing army was a great novelty for Spain and a post-war priority of Philip V. It was also a great strain on the budget and competed for revenue with other spending departments. This was not the only problem.

The army was limited by problems of recruitment as well as of revenue. The regions rejected conscription, and the attempt to apply the call-up quotas to Catalonia after the War of Succession met with protest and resistance, exposing a weakness in central control. In any case, were troops from these regions to be trusted? Catalonia was kept under surveillance after 1714 and denied the means of its own defence, even against pirates; it was allowed a local police to counter banditry, but the issue of conscription was shelved. The thirty-three regiments established by the law of 1734 were to be recruited exclusively in Castile, and the principal burden fell on the most populated region, Andalucía (fourteen regiments) and Galicia (six). The inequity, unpopularity and defects in the system of compulsory recruitment made it a last resort when all else had failed and volunteers were insufficient. Social influence and outright corruption could secure exemption from the levies of the recruiting officers, and ranks were usually filled by the underprivileged, the poor, vagrants and criminals. In practice the state tended to leave local authorities to fill a given quota; but even these resisted, and a town might send in a reduced population count or inflated numbers of exempt personnel, and end up with virtually no one fit for service.[13] The Bourbon state was less impressive in the localities than it was at the centre.

Ministers normally conceded that Spain did not have the military strength to conduct a land war alone, even in Italy. Hence the constant search for alliances; treaty support meant military support and this was essential if Spain was to remain solvent. The English ambassador calculated that from an annual revenue of 16 million pesos, plus 3 million from the Indies, the royal family expended about 7 million a year, the army (with a strength of 70,000 men) 8.7 million in ordinary expenditure, and the navy, ministries and bureaucracy competed for the rest. This was in 1731. Keene wrote: 'I have been very well informed, that even since the late recruits there is not above seventy thousand effective men comprehending about twelve thousand horse. Forty thousand, the choice of the army, are in Catalonia, about eight thousand in Andalusia, and in their several garrisons. They have likewise six regiments of marines.'[14] In 1738, when relations between Spain and England were reaching crisis point, Benjamin Keene was instructed to report on the fortifications and defences of the peninsula:

> The King of Spain has upon paper and in imagination one hundred and fifty thousand men, of which thirty thousand are militias . . . His regular troops I believe they may be computed at seventy thousand effective men, of which about nineteen battalions are employed in the garrisons of Oran and Ceuta. They have in their number of troops a larger proportion of Dragoons than any other nation whatsoever, which was an idea of Mr Patiño for the greater facility of transporting forces to such parts of the kingdom where there might be a sudden occasion for them.[15]

The modernization of the army was not achieved at every level, and the higher command structure was particularly flawed. The king's power was delegated in peacetime to regional commanders, the captains general. Apart from exercising almost viceregal political and judicial authority, these officers commanded all the army units in their provinces. Inevitably there were demarcation disputes, between captains general and inspectors in time of peace, and between captains general and army commanders in time of war. There was no general staff or

13 Ibid., p. 82.
14 Keene to Newcastle, Seville, 2 March 1731, Public Record Office, London, SP 94/107.
15 Keene to Newcastle, 26 May 1738, PRO, SP 94/130.

permanent system of higher formations. The highest formation in the Spanish army remained the regiment, and the division was unknown except as an improvised formation on the outbreak of war.

The administration of the army was also inefficient. The supreme council of war theoretically exercised the power of the king as commander-in-chief of the army; it comprised the minister of war, commanders of the infantry, cavalry and other corps of the army, and a number of officers appointed by the king. But this body was relegated to the sidelines by the Bourbon attack on conciliar government, and by the middle of the century the crown had transferred many of its administrative functions to the ministry of war, leaving only judicial business to the council. Day-to-day administration of the army was in the hands of inspectors of its various corps, who implemented the orders of the minister of war and channelled promotion lists to him. Yet the authority of the minister of war was in turn limited by the minister of finance, who controlled supply and maintenance and provided the army with money through the intendants. Authority was thus dispersed among a number of rival agencies, with resulting factionalism and confusion. The military bureaucracy became excessive, expensive, and corrupt. In the absence of firm controls regiments submitted phantom nominal rolls, and the Spanish government ended up paying for soldiers who did not exist.[16]

Spanish sea power in 1700 was negligible and shipbuilding in decline. During the War of Succession, when the naval power of England comprised a hundred sail of the line, Spain had twenty warships and depended on the French navy for the protection of its maritime routes. Yet Spain by its very nature needed a powerful navy. She was not, and did not aspire to be, a great land power. But she had to be a sea power: on that depended her national security, her trade, and her empire. No one in Spain disputed this; the only constraints were leadership and resources. At the beginning of the eighteenth century Spain had few pure warships and these were deployed according to different areas of operation; for emergencies the navy had to be reinforced with armed merchant vessels and ships bought or hired abroad, devices which were now out of date in the rest of Europe. To compete with her rivals, Spain needed new capital ships, 'of the line' as they were called, meaning that they had to be strongly constructed and carry at least forty to fifty guns for fighting, not line-abreast in hand-to-hand combat, but in line-ahead

---

[16] Keene to Newcastle, 3 March 1738, PRO, SP 94/130.

when superior fire-power would count. These requirements demanded a new administrative structure and a revival of shipbuilding.

The infrastructure of shipbuilding was not completely defunct, and in the decades following the War of Succession it underwent expansion. By 1750 *astilleros*, or shipyards, were operating in Cadiz, Ferrol, Cartagena, Mahón, Guarnizo, Pasajes, San Feliú de Guixols, Havana, Guayaquil, and Manila. Of these Cadiz, Ferrol and Cartagena were designated *arsenales*, or royal dockyards, while the rest were in the private sector though often dependent on naval contracts. An *arsenal* was part factory, part warehouse, and included a shipyard, iron furnaces, workshops, a permanent labour force, and commercial organization. Ferrol, created by Patiño and enlarged by Ensenada, was a large industrial complex and naval base, comparable to almost any dockyard in Europe. Spain also had state factories in Sada and Cadiz producing sailcloth and rigging, supplemented by private sector production in Granada, Estepa, and Cervera del Alhama.

Naval organization was modernized in this period.[17] The first significant step was the law of 14 February 1714 which suppressed 'the squadrons of the individual kingdoms with their different names' and replaced them by the *armada real*. Thus the crown began to professionalize the royal navy, and to bring naval administration and operations under unified control, independent of regional divisions and of the merchant marine. New management was brought in. Spanish ministers held a series of meetings in 1716–17 to prepare decisions on trade, colonies and the navy. One of the most important results was the appointment (28 January 1717) of José Patiño as intendant general of the navy with wide powers, almost similar to those which would later be assigned to the secretary of the navy; he held the post concurrently with the offices of president of the *casa de la contratación* and superintendent of the kingdom of Seville, and from this strong power base he was expected to produce specific results in dockyard expansion and the design and production of ships.[18] In 1726 the secretary of the navy was assigned his own department. In 1737 the admiralty was established, on the English model, and in its eleven years' existence became a useful instrument for further naval reform. This temporarily reduced the power of the secretary of the navy, until the experiment ended in 1748.

---

[17] On naval reform see José P. Merino Navarro, *La Armada española en el siglo XVIII* (Madrid, 1981), pp. 33–45; Geoffrey J. Walker, *Spanish Politics and Imperial Trade, 1700–1789* (London, 1979), pp. 94–9.

[18] C. Fernández Duro, *Armada Española* (9 vols, Madrid, 1885–1903), VI, pp. 209–10, 221–3.

It was not a coincidence that the founder of the eighteenth-century navy was a civilian; the initiative and resolution of Patiño underlined the decay of the navy's own morale. It is true that naval reform was first planned in 1712–13 and that Alberoni subsequently had pretensions as an innovator. But earlier plans had faltered, and Alberoni's idea of naval power was to assemble as many vessels as he could lay his hands on, mainly by hiring them in the open market, and to send them to sea on a spectacular mission. Patiño built on solid and permanent foundations; he constructed local dockyards and naval bases and, with the assistance of naval architect Admiral Antonio de Gastañeta, he launched a programme of modern shipbuilding. Patiño also expanded the infrastructure of naval construction by promoting supporting industries, such as mast and timber cutting centres in the Pyrenees, without prejudice to forest discipline; factories for pitch and tar in Aragon and Catalonia; rope and cordage manufacture in Galicia; and the production of canvas and rigging in Sada and Cadiz. Spain at last became virtually self-sufficient in naval stores.

The first phase of Patiño's programme, however, was sabotaged by Alberoni's Mediterranean campaign. The success of Spanish arms in Sicily in 1718 alarmed the powers, and an English squadron under Admiral Sir George Byng was sent to the Mediterranean with instructions 'to destroy their entire fleet' if necessary, though war was not declared. The Spaniards were anxious to avoid trouble, conscious perhaps of their limitations, and bore away from the English squadron down the eastern coast of Sicily; overtaken off Cape Passaro on 11 August, they did not offer a line of battle and were picked off one by one, outmanœuvred and outgunned. The Spanish fleet was virtually destroyed, its untrained crews the victim of Alberoni's premature aggression and their officers' inferior seamanship. There was no shortcut to naval power, as Patiño knew. Gastañeta produced a new shipbuilding programme from 1720, resources were assembled, and dockyards increased production. Attention was now paid to seafaring manpower. There was a new recruitment drive and changes in the law of recruitment. Steps were taken to make a naval career attractive: Spain's first naval academy, the *Academia Real de Guardías Marinas*, was established. Numerous measures were introduced to improve the training of officers and crews, to produce new naval and civilian bureaucrats, and to promote the merchant marine.[19] Gradually results were seen and,

19 Ibid., pp. 211–12.

granted the difference of enemy, the Spanish navy gave a better account of itself in the reconquest of Oran in 1732 than it had done at Cape Passaro. When Patiño took over the intendancy of the navy in 1717 'there had not even been a place where you could boil a pot of tar'; at his death in 1736 he left a fleet of thirty-four capital ships of the line, nine frigates, and sixteen lesser ships.[20]

The English were close observers of these developments, conscious that they had implications for their maritime interests in Europe and America. As Keene wrote: 'Ever since I returned to this country, I observed with the greatest concern, the progress Patiño was making towards a powerful marine ... That idea is so strong in him, that neither the subsidies paid to the emperor, nor the misery of the Spanish troops, nor the poverty of the household and tribunals can divert him from it.'[21] English intelligence kept the state of the Spanish navy under constant surveillance, noting particularly any weakness in manpower:

They have about forty ships of the line, and large frigates, but not sailors even to navigate the half of them, and their sea officers do not deserve that name. Of these ships about ten or twelve are in the Indies with the galleons at Carthagena, and azogues at Vera Cruz, and the cruizers on the coast of Caracas. There are about seven in the Mediterranean and the rest are laid up in the *puntales* at Cadiz.[22]

Four years later naval rearmament was still frustrated by manning problems and lack of trained crews:

My last advices from Ferrol [report] the Spanish ships at that port have not got half their complement of men. Those in the Bay of Cadiz are much in the same condition, and in all probability those that are lately put into commission at the Puntales will be in a worse. For the coast of Valencia and the island of Majorca from whence seamen are expected in tartanes can never furnish sailors enough to make up the deficiency for a squadron of twenty sail of large men of war, which M. Patiño told me is *what* His Master had ready.[23]

---

[20] Antonio Rodríguez Villa, *Patiño y Campillo* (Madrid, 1882), pp. 25, 187–9.
[21] Keene to Newcastle, 23 August 1728, in William Coxe, *Memoirs of the Kings of Spain of the House of Bourbon* (2nd edn, 5 vols, London, 1815), III, pp. 284–5.
[22] Keene to Newcastle, Seville, 2 March 1731, PRO, SP 94/107.
[23] Keene to Newcastle, 18 August 1735, PRO, SP 94/123.

And just as they borrowed foreign technology, so the Spaniards beckoned to British sailors:

> Captain Barnett of HMS Biddeford has represented to me according to your desire that the Spanish men of war are very assiduous in debauching our sailors from on board the merchant men of our nation into the service of Spain, and that they have a packet boat on anchor in your port [Cadiz] to serve as a receptacle and *entrepot* for such sailors.[24]

Finally, the Spanish navy was starved of money and supplies, especially after the departure of Patiño: 'They reckon they have about fifty ships, out of which I believe they can choose thirty both large and well built, but their stores houses being unfurnished, it will cost them very considerable sums before they are put into a tolerable order, and the finances are but in a bad state to succour that of the marine.'[25]

A navy is an expensive arm and its growth depends upon political decisions. Governments have to decide between conflicting claims on revenue, and a navy's case will only prevail when the maritime interest is strong enough to resist other pressure groups in society and to win the argument for resources. The navy was a primary need for a country with transatlantic trade to protect, a colonial empire to defend, and merchant interests to satisfy. But Spanish naval policy was vulnerable to rival groups and preferred priorities. The strongest pressure on revenue came from the court, the largest spender in Spain. The next favoured interest was the army, the instrument of the crown's continental policy and a source of patronage for the aristocracy. The bureaucracy was another claimant, long entrenched and difficult to resist. Amidst these contenders the navy lacked political muscle and its interests tended to be marginalized. Without a strong minister, convinced of its importance and possessed of the political will to defend it, the navy could not compete for resources with the court, the army, and the bureaucracy. In an absolute monarchy, moreover, ministers had to convince the monarchs. In the reign of Philip V this was not easy, for the monarchy was a party to the dispute and royal policy was torn between the Mediterranean and the Atlantic, between dynastic ambition and colonial interests, between the army and the navy. Patiño won some of the

---

[24] Keene to Consul Skinner, Seville, 12 November 1732, British Library, Add. MS 43, 416, f106.
[25] Keene to Newcastle, 25 March 1737, PRO, SP 94/127.

arguments, some of the time. His successors had less interest or less success.

Spain and Europe

Spanish foreign policy under the early Bourbons responded to a number of pressures. The ultimate objective was to restore a dismembered monarchy and to recover possessions lost at Utrecht, above all those in Italy. The Mediterranean was a natural priority for a power with a long Mediterranean coastline and with territory and trade in the region. Strategic objectives, however, became confused with the purely dynastic ambitions of Elizabeth Farnese, whose Italian policy did not serve Spain in any discernible way. The Mediterranean could not be the only priority. Spain also had to defend an overseas empire, the source of much of its wealth and power; the struggle for mastery in Europe would be fought in the Atlantic and beyond, not in Italian principalities. Spanish foreign policy lost its way after Utrecht and entered a period of convoluted diplomacy, distorted by false expectations and inspired by no single interest. Spain had to work within the prevailing European system of coalition politics; she did not have the resources to proceed alone. Obsession with diplomacy, otherwise inexplicable, is explained as a means of sharing the cost of war and keeping defence spending within bounds. A balance of power meant a balanced budget. For the Spanish Bourbons the obvious policy was to ally itself with France. Family sentiment apart, France was a great land power and could help Spain restore the naval balance against England. The War of Succession, however, taught the danger of excessive dependence on France, and Spain was determined to avoid satellite status and resist French pressure in America. From time to time, therefore, Spain looked to England. This was not an easy option, and usually drove Spain back to France.

War rather than peace was the normal condition of Anglo-Spanish relations in the eighteenth century, informal war or real war. For Spain Gibraltar and Minorca were losses to be redeemed, for England outposts of naval power. America in Spanish eyes was an absolute monopoly, in English an opportunity for expansion. The Spanish empire was vulnerable at various points. Portobello and Cartagena invited attack, thus exposing the rich Peru trade; Havana, a vital link in the treasure route, was always a tempting target, Central America a source of commodities and a power vacuum, the Río de la Plata an empty space and contraband route. These were the scenes of attack and counter-attack, the daily occasions of Anglo-Spanish contention. To confront Britain, however, was often to alienate Portugal, not simply because the two were allies under the Methuen Treaty but because Portugal also had expansionist aims in America. There was an element of Lusophobia in Spanish thinking, and dynastic ties such as the marriage of Barbara of Braganza to the future Ferdinand VI were mere palliatives. Portugal was perceived as part of the British sphere of influence, Lisbon as the naval base of the enemy. In America Portuguese expansion southwards from Brazil took British trade into the heart of the Río de la Plata and made Buenos Aires a new focus of Spanish imperial defence.

The first phase of Spanish foreign policy after Utrecht, from 1714 to 1727, was one of improvisation, in which policy was dictated by an Italian queen and managed by foreign adventurers. On 16 January 1716 the first son of Philip's second marriage was born, Charles of Bourbon Farnese, the future Charles III of Spain. The event reinforced Philip V's interest in Italy: he now wanted a territory for the new prince, precluded from preferment in Spain by his step-brothers, and ministers were instructed to prepare for war. To Alberoni's credit, he was not at first enthusiastic. He asked for five years' peace and he would make Philip the most powerful monarch in Europe, improve his revenue, control expenditure, revive trade, and raise an army and navy which would confound his enemies.[26] As it was he had to telescope his plans. In 1717 an expeditionary force, impressively assembled by Patiño, took Sardinia, and in 1718 a similar operation was launched against Sicily. At this point the powers reacted in defence of Utrecht and Spain was suddenly faced by the Quadruple Alliance, its navy destroyed at the battle of Cape Passaro and its army isolated in Sicily. Philip V was lucky to be offered compensation in Parma and Tuscany in exchange for signing peace with the emperor and undertaking to respect the Italian clauses of the Treaty of Utrecht. He should have cut his losses and accepted, but he continued to fight against great odds, urged on by his wife and flattered by the favourite. Alberoni conjured up a motley league of Sweden, Russia, English Jacobites, French subversives, a few Italian princes, the pope, and the Turk, none of whom was the slightest use against the Quadruple Alliance of England, France, the emperor and Savoy-Piedmont, but whose names could be recited to Philip V to strengthen his resolve.

The war was fought on various fronts, all of them the scenes of defeat.

[26] Coxe, *Memoirs of the Kings of Spain*, II, p. 206; Edward Armstrong, *Elisabeth Farnese, 'the Termagant of Spain'* (London, 1892), pp. 73–4, 102–9.

While Alberoni tried to raise Stuart supporters in Ireland and sent a small force to its doom in Scotland, an English expedition landed successfully in northern Spain and secured the surrender of Vigo and Pontevedra in 1719. While he vainly intrigued to destabilize the government of France, a French army of 20,000 invaded Guipúzcoa and took San Sebastian. In Sicily itself, after the English pre-emptive strike at Cape Passaro, it was only a matter of time before Spanish troops succumbed. Rarely has a war been so resoundingly lost, or a fall from favourite to scapegoat been so precipitate. Alberoni was denounced by public opinion as a blaspheming, fornicating priest who had not said mass for six years, and to his great indignation was dismissed from office and expelled from Spain in December 1719. The monarchs were forced into diplomacy as well as disloyalty, and after protracted negotiations (1720–4) signed the Treaty of Cambrai and returned the conquered, or half-conquered, territories to their former status.

Adventurism did not cease with Alberoni. The queen now sought the same ends by different means. She pursued an understanding with Austria in the hope of marrying her two sons, Charles and Philip, to imperial archduchesses. Her instrument was another favourite, the Baron Ripperdá, compared to whom Alberoni was a statesman.[27] The resultant Treaty of Vienna was totally disadvantageous to Spain; in return for vague promises of an Austrian marriage for Charles, the emperor obtained substantial subsidies and commercial concessions which outraged Spanish opinion and alarmed the rest of Europe. Anglo-Spanish relations thus reached a new crisis, European diplomacy adding fuel to the constantly smouldering conflict over Gibraltar, mutual seizures in the Indies, and disputes over trade in the peninsula. Britain countered the Treaty of Vienna with the Hanover alliance, and the result was a small war between Philip V and George II. By the end of March 1727, while Spanish soldiers were digging trenches around Gibraltar, the English ambassador was asked to leave Madrid. The *flota* arrived at last from the Indies, renewing Spanish hopes and reinforcing the Spanish war effort. The followers of the Old Pretender were again publicly supported, while an invasion of England was kept in suspended animation. Actual hostilities were confined to the Caribbean and Gibraltar, a colonial war in the first, an unsuccessful siege in the second; these were the real issues between Spain and England, and they lasted from January 1727 to March 1728, when Elizabeth Farnese agreed to

[27] See above, pp. 85–8.

sign the Convention of El Pardo, ending the English blockade and returning, or promising to return, Spanish seizures of English ships and assets. The alliance between Spain and Vienna thus came to an end as it became clear that there would be no marriage and no Austrian support for Spanish plans in Italy. The queen looked for another track.

The determination of Elizabeth Farnese to obtain Italian principalities and good marriages for her sons was not simply a stirring of her maternal instincts but also an insurance against the day when she would be a widow and deprived of her vicarious sovereignty. It was a calculated attempt to avoid the fate of a dowager queen by securing a haven and kingdom for her own retirement. The point seemed obvious to Benjamin Keene:

> The Queen is now sensible that the Emperor has deceived her . . . Her apprehensions now turn either upon the King's death or his abdication, which will certainly happen if not prevented by the former. These press and oblige her to take care of her family, and to procure an honourable safe retreat for herself, which she thinks cannot be effectuated without Spanish garrisons in Tuscany and Parma, and the guaranty of England and France to defend and preserve her son in the quiet possession of those Duchies.[28]

Her need for a new strategy and a new adviser coincided with the rise of José Patiñõ to a position of dominance in the administration. No more in foreign affairs than in domestic was Patiño a genius or an innovator. As a royal servant he had to accept the obligations of the queen's Italian policy and to seek the opportunity and resources to effect it; at no time does he seem to have argued against it. Did he see this policy in the wider context of Spain's Mediterranean interests, to include not only Italy but also North Africa and to prepare the way for a revival of Spanish power and the recovery of Gibraltar and Minorca? The evidence is not conclusive.[29] There was no disguising the fact that Italy was a diversion from Patiño's other priority, the Atlantic and the colonial war with Britain. Here the logic of his policy was to keep the peace with Britain while he restored Spain's naval power. His influence was seen in 1728 in ending the Austrian alliance and reaching an accommodation with the enemy. It was soon apparent that a new hand directed Spanish foreign policy, that

---

[28] Keene to Newcastle, 26 May 1729, PRO, SP 94/100.
[29] Such is the thesis of Antonio Béthencourt Massieu, *Patiño y la política internacional de Felipe V* (Valladolid, 1954), *passim*.

objectives were clearer, negotiations tougher, and sanctions harsher. His policy towards Britain, overtly correct, was hard at the centre and basically unyielding. In the Caribbean he matched aggression with aggression; to counter contraband he unleashed the *guardacostas*, a force of licensed warships; against the South Sea Company he applied the letter of the law; to British protests against the harassment of legitimate trade he replied with Spanish bureaucratic delay. Pressure of this kind could be increased or reduced as an instrument of negotiation; and it could be applied in the Atlantic to produce results in the Mediterranean.

The Spanish government wanted English and French support against the emperor to secure the succession of the two princes in Parma and Tuscany; England and France wanted the continuation of traditional commercial practices in Cadiz and America. The Treaty of Seville (9 November 1729) restored to England all her trading privileges, and in return England and France were to help Spain to introduce garrisons into Parma and Tuscany.[30] Britain welcomed the Treaty of Seville to end the colonial war. Patiño on the other hand continued the colonial war to press Britain on the Treaty; for the Italian operation was risky and expensive, and Patiño wanted English help to restrain the emperor and share the naval costs.

> M. Patiño, complaining of the expenses he had been obliged to make, which he says amounts to two million of piastres, excluding the clothing of the army and other charges which were necessary in time of peace as well as war ... asked me whether I thought we would join in any attempt with Spain in case France persisted in its inactivity.[31]

Keene was aware that his arm was being twisted. The Spanish authorities had still not restored wartime seizures; in the peninsula officials doubled their vigilance; in the Caribbean the *guardacostas* attacked licit and illicit trade alike; in all parts of the Americas Patiño applied the diplomacy of menace. The protests of Keene he rejected with the argument that as soon as Britain fulfilled its obligations in Europe, Spain would comply in America. In the course of 1730 the informal war on British trade became so critical that the Admiralty instructed Rear-Admiral Stewart to make reprisals on Spanish merchant shipping if he could not secure the return of unlawful seizures. But the South Sea Company, fearful of its

[30] Ibid., pp. 33–6.
[31] Keene to Newcastle, 17 July 1730, PRO, SP 94/103.

privileges, asked him to refrain, and he confined his attention to the Spanish *guardacostas*.[32]

Patiño played his diplomatic cards cleverly and persuaded England to move on the Italian question, if necessary without France. In April 1731 England negotiated the emperor's acceptance of Spanish intervention in the duchies, and by the Declaration of Seville (6 June 1731) agreed with Spain on implementing Charles's succession and the introduction of garrisons. In the same month English and Spanish fleets transported Charles and 6,000 Spanish troops to the duchies, and for a rare period Spain and England were not only at peace but allies. The way now seemed open for agreement on commercial and colonial issues, and this was formalized in a further Declaration (8 February 1732), signed by Patiño and Keene, and designed to end the 'state of uncertainty' in American waters. Spain solemnly undertook to make good the damage suffered unjustifiably by British commerce, to respect the 'lawful trade' of the British with their own ports and colonies, and to control the activities of the *guardacostas*, while Britain declared that it would compensate for past damage and deny the protection of its navy to those engaged in contraband.[33] These of course were well worn sentiments, and the prospects of success were not good. Terms such as 'right of search', 'proximity to the Spanish coasts', and 'origin of merchandise' remained to obscure and obstruct the practice of commerce, and negotiations in 1732–4 failed to resolve a single problem in the now tedious list of mutual grievances – codfishing rights in Newfoundland, logwood cutting in Campeche, the new colony of Georgia, and claims on maritime captures and reprisals. The failure of the South Sea Company to fulfil its obligations, and the refusal of Spanish officials in Mexico and Peru to return the assets seized from the Company's factories in the wartime *represalias* of 1718 and 1727 were ever present on this list and a constant irritant to Anglo-Spanish relations during the 1730s. Spanish delaying tactics seem not to have changed.

Spain had to defend its national interests without provoking the dominant naval power of the age. While Patiño's negotiators drove the English to distraction, he worked to protect maritime routes and improve imperial defences. He took steps, or so it seemed, to reinforce Florida against incursions from British Georgia, and he instructed the governor of Buenos Aires to prepare an offensive against Colônia do

---

[32] Richard Pares, *War and Trade in the West Indies 1739-1763* (London, 1963), p. 15.
[33] Béthencourt, *Patiño y la política internacional de Felipe V*, pp. 50–1.

Sacramento. But local officials did not seem to be aware of Patiño's concern and they continued to maintain that Florida was inadequately defended, Buenos Aires needed more troops, and Portugal traded as it willed into the Río de la Plata.[34] Patiño tended to paper over the cracks in colonial defences, and for all his diplomatic skills in confronting Britain, he could not disguise the fact that he was sailing a frigate against a ship of the line. He was convinced that Spanish and British interests in America were irreconcilable, just as Spanish and Austrian claims in Italy were still unresolved. How could he fight on two fronts? How could he match Spanish pretensions with Spanish power? Only with an ally, and conveniently one was at hand.

Europe was still fertile in family diplomacy. France wanted an ally against Austria and Russia in the impending conflict over the Polish succession and, in return for Spain's engaging Austria in another front, France was ready to make concessions. The negotiations proved that Italy still dominated Spanish policy and still remained the crucial issue. At each stage of diplomacy – the Treaty of Vienna, the Treaty of Seville, now in 1733 – the interests of Elizabeth Farnese, for good or ill, dictated the decisions of government. Philip V, obedient to her wishes, demanded that any treaty of alliance should annul all previous undertakings; this time Naples, Sicily, and the Tuscan forts should all accrue to Charles, and Patiño negotiated for nothing less. Cardinal Fleury accepted the Spanish project virtually in its entirety, and on 7 November 1733 the first Family Compact was signed at the Escorial.[35] The treaty guaranteed the future Italian possessions of Charles, and the rights of Elizabeth Farnese to the patrimonial property of the Farnese and Medici; if Spain, as a consequence of restricting British trade, were attacked by Britain, France would assist with all its forces and offer its diplomatic and if necessary military support to obtain the recovery of Gibraltar; neither side would lay down arms except by common accord and after obtaining what was agreed in Italy; France was given most favoured nation status in commerce, and the allies agreed to restore order to trade and stop English abuses, 'in the suppression of which both Spain and France are equally concerned'. The agreement was designed as a secret treaty and one which 'will be regarded from today as a Family Compact, perpetual and irrevocable, which should bind for ever the knot of closest friendship between Their Most Christian and Catholic

[34] John J. TePaske, *The Governorship of Spanish Florida 1700-1763* (Durham, NC, 1964), pp. 133–9; Enrique M. Barba, *Don Pedro de Cevallos* (Buenos Aires, 1978), pp. 35–6.

[35] Alfred Baudrillart, *Philippe V et la cour de France* (5 vols, Paris, 1890–1900), IV, pp. 199–201.

Majesties'.[36] The first Family Compact enabled each partner to exploit a particular conjuncture in Europe. For Philip V it was an opportunity to recover some of the territorial losses of Utrecht; for the queen an ideal chance to provide for her family; for Patiño a way of reconciling Spain's Atlantic and Mediterranean interests. It was also a lesson in the limitations of dynastic diplomacy.

The Spanish expedition to Naples was crowned by the victory of Britanto, and Sicily was conquered even more rapidly. Charles was proclaimed king of the Two Sicilies in 1734 and three years later the emperor recognized him as such, while recovering Parma, which remained the occasion of a future war to accommodate the other son of Farnese. The new kingdom was a viable state, overtly sovereign, but in practice a satellite of Spain. The cost to Spain was high, but this did not worry a court in which poverty and extravagance lived side by side. Yet Patiño knew the risks:

> It has already cost him about three millions of piastres since the month of October, besides the sum he has paid to the French ambassador for subsidies, which amounts at least to six hundred thousand piastres, so that it is not to be wondered at if he is extremely fearful of our sending any ships to intercept the treasure that is saved out of the Flota, on our declaring ourselves against Spain, when he imagines that the first thing that will be done in consequence of our declaration will be to stop his treasure at its source.[37]

In the event England kept out of the war and American treasure still flowed. The government was relieved in March 1734 by the arrival of a man of war, the *Incendio*, from Cartagena and Portobello carrying 3 million pesos for the trade and 1 million for the crown.[38] But the war effort devoured resources as fast as they were received. In June the *flota* arrived at Cadiz carrying 12.5 million pesos, and in August four *azogues* (mercury ships) with 3 million for the trade and almost 2 million for the crown.[39] Yet shortage of money forced Spain to negotiate with the emperor, to renounce Tuscany, and to leave the war with a strong suspicion that she had been manipulated by France.

[36] Quoted by Béthencourt, *Patiño y la política internacional de Felipe V*, p. 62.
[37] Keene to Newcastle, 17 February 1734, PRO, SP 94/119.
[38] Keene to Newcastle, 13 March 1734, PRO, SP 94/119.
[39] Keene to Newcastle, 5 July 1734, 9 August 1734, PRO, SP 94/120.

Spanish opinion in general and the merchant interest in particular were not impressed by the results of the first Family Compact. True, victories had been won in Italy. But were they victories for Spain? In the Atlantic nothing had been gained. Britain had not been lured into provoking Franco-Spanish action, and after the war the trade routes were no more secure than before. The mere presence of an English squadron in Lisbon or Gibraltar could disrupt the Indies trade, and in spite of Patiño's reform the Spanish navy on its own was still no match for the British. Patiño died in November 1736 with these and other problems pressing on him.

After Patiño Spanish foreign policy fell into the hands of wild men whose ideas outstripped their resources. This at least was Keene's opinion:

> La Quadra is more dull and stubborn than I could well conceive. He lets himself be entirely guided by Mr Casimiro Ustariz, first commis in the War Office; and these two together have so filled their heads with the grandeur of the Spanish Monarchy, the injury it received from foreigners and foreign commerce, and with notions that it has always been tricked in former negotiations and such like common places that this Court is become more untractable than in any other period of time that I have known it.[40]

But the crisis in Anglo-Spanish relations went deeper than personalities and derived basically from daily and enduring conflict in America. The Spanish government had hoped to satisfy England with some lawful share of her colonial trade through the *asiento* of 1713. But the English were difficult to satisfy and contraband continued, the newly authorized traders adding to its quantity. Spain could only counter this with the *guardacostas*, who were notoriously aggressive, harassed the trade of England with her own colonies, and made a folk hero out of Captain Jenkins. These were the origins of the diplomatic dispute which culminated in the years 1737–9, when the government so disparaged by Keene seemed to be reviving Spain's traditional claim to universal sovereignty in the Americas, its monopoly of territory as well as trade, and its right to stop and search all foreign ships. For their part English merchants were eager for new markets and anxious to increase trade by

---

[40] Keene to Newcastle, 13 January 1739, PRO, SP 94/131.

conquest in America; there were interests in the English government and in the navy ready to collaborate.[41]

The War of Jenkins' Ear, therefore, found both Spain and Britain in a mood to fight. For Britain this was a colonial war, and in July 1739 Admiral Vernon was sent to make trouble for Spain in the Caribbean. War was not actually declared until 19 October, and it lasted until 1748, during which time Spain had to defend itself against two forms of British attack, expeditions for conquest and interception of trade. Vernon captured Portobello in 1739 but failed to take Cartagena in 1741, when the Spanish defenders gave a good account of themselves. For Spain this was also a European war. The Anglo-Spanish conflict merged in the years after 1740 with the War of the Austrian Succession, in which England supported Austria, and France Bavaria, though England and France did not come to a formal rupture until 1744. The intentions of Spain were of great interest to the other powers; at stake were the balance in Europe and the trade of America. Inevitably Elizabeth Farnese used the opportunity to advance her Italian policy a stage further and gain a territory for her son Philip. Two Spanish expeditions landed in Italy in 1741 and 1742, and while Spaniards fought English invaders at Cartagena and Panama, Spanish invaders fought Austrians in northern Italy, an impressive exercise in global war but a misuse of finite resources. The tactics of Farnese were to get Spain embroiled in the general conflict and appeal to Bourbon solidarity to come to the rescue. This was the context of the second Family Compact of 25 October 1743, in which Louis XV undertook to install Philip of Bourbon in Milan, Parma, and Piacenza, to guarantee the position of Charles as king of the Two Sicilies, to support the reconquest of Gibraltar and Minorca, and to free Philip V from the commercial constraints imposed upon him in 1713.[42] The treaty contained obvious advantages for Spain and particular dangers for Britain, now threatened with a strong Bourbon block and French domination of the transatlantic trade.

The war consisted of confused operations in pursuit of incomprehensible objectives, without obvious advantage to the combatants. And when Philip V died on 9 July 1746 he seemed to have little to show for his final recourse to arms. A new reign opened new possibilities in Anglo-Spanish relations. The Spanish negotiators in 1746 included Melchor de Macanaz, one of the few Spaniards of his time who advocated a nationalist position in foreign policy, regarded a French

[41] Pares, *War and Trade in the West Indies*, pp. 10–28, 34, 62–4.
[42] Baudrillart, *Philippe V et la cour de France*, v, pp. 163–73.

alliance as prejudicial to Spain, and preferred that she stand by herself as a European power and come to terms with Britain, the strongest commercial and maritime power of the age.[43] But the negotiations failed over Gibraltar and Italy. When the European war at last ended with the Treaty of Aix-la-Chapelle in 1748, that treaty was negotiated not with Spain but with France, and Spain only reluctantly acceded. Spain wanted Milan but had to be content with Parma and Piacenza, assigned to Philip of Bourbon as an independent state. In compensation for wartime interruption, the *asiento* was restored to the South Sea Company for four years. But in the Anglo-Spanish commercial treaty of 1750 the remaining years of the *asiento* were relinquished for £100,000, opening at last a period of improved commercial relations between the two countries.[44]

Spain's performance was proof of a radical improvement in strategy and strength since 1718, and the balance sheet of war was not totally unfavourable. She had placed limits on British progress in America. True, Britain had taken many prizes and seriously dislocated the trade monopoly; but it had not succeeded in the longer aims of opening the Spanish empire by force or defeating its principal trade rival, France. Britain's failure to persuade Spain to allow direct trade to her colonies contrasted sharply with the success of France in trading through Cadiz. But perhaps the most promising result of the war for Spain was the termination of the Italian programme of Elizabeth Farnese and her final departure from power. That programme could possibly be rationalized as the recovery of a traditional sphere of influence, the revival of Spain as a Mediterranean power. Economically, however, the enterprise had consumed national resources for dynastic ends without yielding appreciable returns. The year 1748, therefore, marked the end of a policy which gave precedence to European diplomacy over imperial defence and the beginning of a new order of priorities. Spain began to recover from the age of adventurers, vain expectations, and unnecessary wars, and to settle down to the serious business of colonial rivalry.[45]

---

[43] Henry Kamen, 'Melchor de Macanaz and the Foundations of Bourbon Power in Spain', *English Historical Review*, 80, 317 (1965), pp. 699–716; María Dolores Gómez Molleda, 'El caso Macanaz en el Congreso de Breda', *Hispania*, 18 (1958), pp. 62–128, and *Gibraltar, una contienda diplomática en el reinado de Felipe V* (Madrid, 1953), pp. 237–9.

[44] Jean O. McLachlan, *Trade and Peace with Old Spain, 1667-1750* (Cambridge, 1940), p. 139.

[45] Pares, *War and Trade in the West Indies*, p. 13.

American Trade and its Defence

Spanish trade with America was organized as a monopoly. Outbound traffic left from Seville in two periodic fleets, the *flota* sailing to Veracruz, the *galeones* to Cartagena and Portobello. Only members of the *consulados*, or merchant guilds, of Seville, Mexico and Lima were allowed to participate in the trade, which at the American end was concentrated in official fairs.[46] Adam Smith described this as an 'absurd monopoly' which cancelled out many of the advantages of Spain's colonial trade.[47] Was it not unrealistic to confine trade to the rigid framework of a legal monopoly, exercised through designated ports, agencies, and fleets, and operating not only against foreigners but also against the majority of Spaniards? The answer is, not necessarily, for in the beginning the monopoly worked, and corresponded to the economic and political condition of the early modern period. Andalucía was superior to the other regions as a base for the Indies trade. Castile wanted a return on its investment; and at a time when the colonial populations were small and Spain's competitors were numerous it was in the national interest to secure the markets and resources of America by monopoly methods.

If monopoly becomes oppressive, it naturally stimulates alternatives. In the seventeenth century demographic growth in America expanded consumer demand and this, combined with more vigorous intervention by foreign merchants, made absolute monopoly unrealistic. This was appreciated in Seville, which in effect adjusted to new conditions by admitting foreigners to the Indies trade while reserving a place for itself. Thus the monopoly was modified by foreign participation in the trade from Cadiz, by contraband, by the growth of direct trade to Spanish America, and by the development of inter-colonial trade. The government itself collaborated by fining what it could not stop, and the size of *indultos* levied on inbound traffic was a measure of foreign participation. This was closely paralleled by the growing importance of Cadiz, the port most favoured by foreign merchants. Between 1679, when the dispatch of fleets from Cadiz was authorized, and 1717, when the *casa de la contratación* and *consulado* were formally transferred from Seville, Cadiz

---

[46] H. and P. Chaunu, *Séville et l'Atlantique (1504-1650)* (8 vols, Paris, 1955-9), I, pp. 70-88, 97-121, 169-75, 185-94; VIII, 1, pp. 52, 182-4. John Lynch, 'El comerç sota el monopoli sevillà', *2nes Jornades d'Estudis Catalano-Americans, Maig 1986* (Barcelona, 1987), pp. 9-30.

[47] Adam Smith, *The Wealth of Nations* (2 vols, Oxford, 1979), II, p. 609.

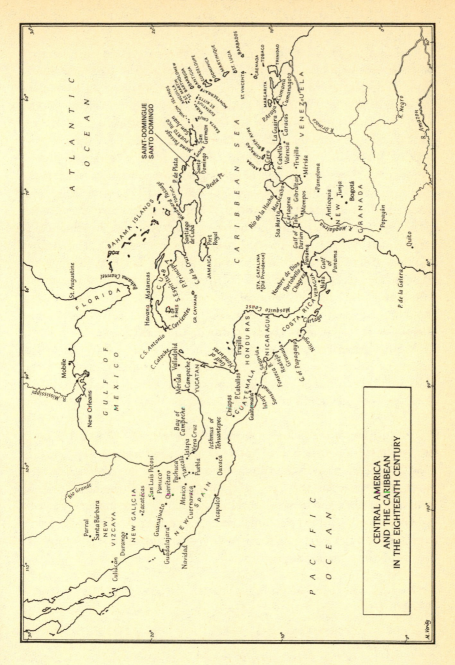

CENTRAL AMERICA
AND THE CARIBBEAN
IN THE EIGHTEENTH CENTURY

moved into first place and became the effective headquarters of the American trade.[48]

The monopoly was further eroded in the early eighteenth century when France exploited its political influence in Spain to penetrate the colonial market more directly, first in 1701 by obtaining an *asiento* for the supply of slaves to Spanish America, then from 1704 by gaining access to the Spanish Pacific for trade with Chile and Peru.[49] The *asiento* was soon lost to Britain, but French direct trade to Peru survived the War of Succession, in spite of formal undertakings to desist. French merchants pre-empted the market to such an extent that the rare trade fairs held at Portobello in these years – 1708 and 1713 – were financial disasters. In the first quarter of the eighteenth century the French extracted at least 100 million pesos from South America, and their trade represented 68 per cent of the foreign trade of Peru.[50] The second problem area was Mexico, whose trade with the Far East through the Manila galleons brought Chinese cottons and silks into direct competition with those from the peninsula. Here, however, Spain succeeded in retaining a greater share of the market. Five fleets and four pairs of *azogues* were dispatched to Mexico during the period 1699–1713. Trade with other American ports was maintained by means of register ships. Altogether there were some 132 inbound vessels from America between 1701 and 1715, proof of the survival of imperial communications during the War of Succession, but in many cases proof too of French penetration.[51]

The history of the colonial monopoly between 1714 and 1750 is a history of steady erosion, inadequate defence, and futile debate, in spite of which the Indies remained an asset to Spain. The government exerted itself to strengthen the law, without however changing the basic structure of trade and navigation.[52] First, attempts were made to exercise greater state control over colonial trade and its profits. This policy was expressed in rules excluding foreigners, insisting that all ships should be Spanish-built, and modifying the archaic tax system. Second, Spain

---

[48] Antonio Domínguez Ortiz, *Orto y ocaso de Sevilla* (Seville, 1946); Chaunu, *Séville et l'Atlantique*, VIII, 1, pp. 191, 320.

[49] Walker, *Spanish Politics and Imperial Trade*, pp. 20–33.

[50] Carlos Daniel Malamud Rikles, *Cádiz y Saint Malo en el comercio colonial peruano (1698-1725)* (Cadiz, 1986), pp. 90, 280.

[51] Michel Morineau, *Incroyables gazettes et fabuleux métaux. Les retours des trésors américains d'après les gazettes hollandaises (XVIᵉ-XVIIIᵉ siècles)* (Cambridge, 1985), pp. 310–17.

[52] Antonio García-Baquero González, *Cádiz y el Atlántico (1717-1778)* (2 vols, Seville, 1976), I, pp. 564–5.

remained firmly committed to the *pacto colonial*, whereby 80 per cent of imports from the colonies were precious metals and the rest raw materials; there was to be no industry in Spanish America except sugar mills. Third, the government acknowledged that these measures were ineffective, and that foreigners continued to dominate the Indies trade, providing 50 per cent of exports and 75 per cent of shipping. Finally, Spanish merchants continued to be mainly commission agents. In this role they could still make profits and accumulate capital, partly by exporting agricultural products, still a Spanish preserve, partly by receiving a share of the returns to foreigners on industrial exports. The crown too continued to receive an income from America, and as long as this survived, the temptation to leave well alone prevailed.

Yet colonial policy was a subject of increasing debate. Even Alberoni encouraged discussion. He himself believed that the Indies trade was the key to Spain's recovery: given five years peace and reform, Spain would be ready to confront the world. A new merchant fleet and naval units capable of capturing contrabandists were the basic requirements. In 1717 a *flota* of no less than fourteen large vessels sailed for Veracruz, carrying cargoes which Alberoni calculated would bring the crown high profits; unfortunately the market was saturated with merchandise from the English annual ship, the *Royal Prince*, a factor which Alberoni had left out of his reckoning.[53] In any case, many of the reforms of these years were the work not of Alberoni but of José Patiño.

Patiño too started from the premise that the prime object was to restore Spain as a great power; the source of power lay in trade and empire, its management in Cadiz and Madrid. It was he who, on 12 May 1717, completed the transfer of the *casa de la contratación* to Cadiz; in the same year the council of the Indies was formally stripped of any authority over the Indies trade, which was now assigned to the crown's ministers and the *casa*. His initiative was also responsible for the organization of new trading companies, experiments with register ships, ruthless campaigns against contraband, and the protection of national trade and industry, no matter what the reaction of foreign governments. As Benjamin Keene observed:

No one can be more certain than I am, that he is an enemy to all foreign commerce, and as he has more knowledge of trade and of the abuses in the customs than any minister had before him, he will

[53] Walker, *Spanish Politics and Imperial Trade*, pp. 90–1.

make us more uneasy than any has yet done. We had formerly to complain of delays and *la lenteur Espagnole*; now there is a share of malice in his resolution to reform and new model what he thinks prejudicial to Spain.[54]

Patiño was not a particularly enlightened minister of the Indies or finance. He saw the colonies as mere providers of wealth for Spain, especially for the public sector; he sought to increase trade in order to tax it, and when this failed he wanted to force the trade to pay more of the costs of defence. He was realist enough to appreciate that Cadiz merchants would also pursue their own interests, and to accept that as long as the *asiento* endured (that is to 1744) the presence of the South Sea Company would be a chink in the armour of monopoly. Meanwhile he supported the fleet system and tried to make it work. His policies had some success, but they did not constitute a grand design or a source of innovation. Not for him the ideas of Melchor de Macanaz, who in an unpublished paper written in 1719 argued that colonial administration would be improved by the establishment of intendants, that American trade should be reformed for the benefit of the whole nation, that the monopoly of Seville and Cadiz should be shared with La Coruña and Santander, and that trade should be free and open 'to all the subjects of the king'.[55]

Radical proposals of this kind were not yet common, but the terms of the debate were changing.[56] In 1724 Gerónimo de Uztáriz, administrator and theorist, published his *Theórica y práctica de comercio y de marina*, in which he advocated state intervention to develop industry and commerce on French and English models. Uztáriz seems to have believed that trade in itself would generate growth, if it were relieved of fiscal restraints, and he ignored the stronger agricultural and industrial base already existing in France and England. On the other hand he envisaged the state as creating industry as well as protecting it. He wanted to lower import and export duties on the American trade and on Spain's own production, while raising taxes on foreign imports. A national industry

---

[54] Keene to Walpole, 25 November 1731, Coxe, *Memoirs of the Kings of Spain*, III, pp. 290–1.

[55] Kamen, 'Melchor de Macanaz', pp. 713–14; on Patiño see Walker, *Spanish Politics and Imperial Trade*, pp. 159–61.

[56] Marcelo Bitar Letayf, *Economistas españoles del siglo XVIII. Sus ideas sobre la libertad del comercio con Indias* (Madrid, 1968), pp. 73–120; Andrés V. Castillo, *Spanish Mercantilism. Gerónimo de Uztáriz, Economist* (New York, 1930); Miguel Artola, 'Campillo y las reformas de Carlos III', *Revista de Indias*, 12 (1952), pp. 685–714; Robert S. Smith, 'Spanish Mercantilism: A Hardy Perennial', *Southern Economic Journal*, 38 (1971), pp. 1–11.

exporting to colonial markets in a national merchant marine was Uztáriz's ideal, the aim being to sell more, buy less, and thus retain specie. Later in the century a rather different programme was projected by José Campillo, minister of Philip V and author of *Nuevo sistema de gobierno económico para la América*, a work written in 1743 and read in government circles, though not published until 1789. Comparing the experience of rival colonial powers, Campillo underlined the opportunities that Spain was missing in America, her failure to exploit the economic and human resources of her own possessions, and her inability to assure Spanish subjects and products an adequate share in the colonial trade. He saw America not as a mere provider of precious metals but as a source of important raw materials and an unexploited market for Spanish manufactures. To raise consumption he proposed to abolish high duties and other restraints on trade. At the same time he would bring the Indians out of subsistence into the market by granting them land from which they could earn a surplus. A better administrative structure could be provided by establishing intendants in America. Finally, to open up the entire traffic between Spain and her colonies he suggested the curtailment or even abolition of the Cadiz monopoly and fleet system.

Campillo's work probably synthesized a number of ideas in vogue at the time. They were expressed in government policy, up to a point, in four directions: improvement of transatlantic communications; fiscal change; establishment of trading companies; and administrative reform. Yet neither the idea nor the regulations of the period 1700–50 were of great consequence. The theoretical works of the time, often described as masterplans of mercantilist solutions, were not distinguished for their knowledge, analysis, or judgement. Uztáriz was a useful chronicler but less convincing as an economist; behind Campillo's new ideas lurked some traditional prejudices, not least against colonial manufactures. As for the regulations, they betrayed a certain cynicism and leave the impression that they were designed to sanction existing collusion between Spanish merchants, foreign interlopers, and American importers. They were all actors in an elaborate game, each pursuing a private interest not entirely hidden from the state. Moreover, projects and policy alike ignored, if they even appreciated, developments within the colonies which had anticipated or rendered irrelevant many of the new ideas. The Indians, for example, were already part of the market; Mexican mining had already come out of recession; and the colonies were now self-sufficient in many of the products which Spanish planners were anxious to sell them.

Nevertheless, governments exist to govern, and Patiño and his colleagues did not remain idle during these years of trade adversity and relentless advice. From 1718 a new service of eight yearly *avisos*, or dispatch boats, four to Peru and four to Mexico, was found to be a useful means of improving naval communications and commercial intelligence. A measure of fiscal reform, the *Real proyecto* of 5 April 1720, was intended to stimulate greater regularity of voyages by convoyed fleets and to simplify duties.[57] The *ad valorem* duty, whose tax base was difficult to determine, was replaced by the *palmeo*, which taxed merchandise according to cubic volume; but the basic object was to increase crown revenue from the trade, and the substitution of volume for value was not well conceived. Further regulations of 1725, 1735, and 1754 were no improvement.

The most successful experiment was the development of trading companies. Organized with capital from Catalonia and the Basque provinces, these chartered companies were granted special privileges, if not a complete monopoly, in the trade of one of the more backward areas of the empire, where the Spanish presence was weak and the foreigner active. The first and most important of these ventures was the *Real Compañía Guipuzcoana de Caracas*, which by grant of 25 September 1728 was given a monopoly of trade with Venezuela.[58] The Caracas Company drove out the Dutch, took over the cacao trade, developed new commodities such as tobacco, indigo and cotton, and within twenty years turned a poverty-stricken province into an export economy producing a surplus for the metropolis. Inspired by this success further ventures were launched, the *Real Compañía de San Cristobal* in 1740 with a monopoly of trade to Cuba, and the *Real Compañía de Barcelona* in 1755 designed to expand Catalan trade to Santo Domingo, Puerto Rico and Margarita.[59] The trading companies were not a radical break with the past; basically they simply extended the monopoly principle to new privileged groups. But the four most successful ventures, the Caracas Company, the Havana Company, the San Fernando Company of Seville, and the Barcelona Company, together made an impact on the Cadiz monopoly; between 1730 and 1778 they controlled about 20 per cent of the shipping between Spain and America.[60] Whether they were good for Americans is another matter. The Caracas Company was detested in

[57] García-Baquero, *Cádiz y el Atlántico*, I, pp. 152–8, 197–208.
[58] Roland D. Hussey, *The Caracas Company, 1728-1784* (Cambridge, Mass., 1934), pp. 86–9.
[59] Martínez Shaw, 'La Cataluña del siglo XVIII', pp. 89–90.
[60] García-Baquero, *Cádiz y el Atlántico*, I, pp. 136–7.

Venezuela where it exploited its monopoly to charge high prices to consumers for imports and pay low prices to producers for exports, and where it succeeded in uniting all sectors of the population in an anti-Company rebellion in 1741; proof, if proof were needed, that the reforms of these years were narrowly conceived and looked no further than the immediate interests of the metropolis.[61]

Marginal changes of this kind could not stem the tide of foreign pressure, especially British. They did not even satisfy Spanish merchants. Within the trade itself there were deep divisions in these years. Cadiz merchants were torn between the desire to trade and the fear of exposing their returns to sequestrations and *indultos*, between official anxiety to dispatch fleets for revenue purposes and private fears concerning the state of the markets. The Spanish monopolists saw their own government as no less an enemy than the foreigners.[62] Patiño in particular was regarded by the merchants of Cadiz not as a man with solutions but as part of the problem, for with his detailed knowledge of the trade he was able to employ every trick of taxation and exaction in the crown's favour.[63] It was Patiño who raised *indultos* to 9 per cent, setting a precedent for further rises from 1737 onwards:

The Court received this week the good news of the arrival of the Flota and Azogues, consisting of thirteen ships; they bring between fourteen and fifteen millions in gold and silver, about two millions in fruits, and about four million of piastres which, to escape paying the duties, are not registered. The King's share of the Flota, and the duties arising from the rest, will amount to between three and four millions of dollars or piastres. But the commerce is under some apprehensions that the Ministers are inventing new methods to raise the indulto above the nine per cent, to which it was carried by the late Mr Patiño.[64]

The fears were justified: 'The orders for the distribution of the effects of the Flota and Azogues lately arrived in Cadiz are despatched. And by the large indulto laid upon them which in different articles amounts to between fifteen and sixteen per cent, the King, with what comes upon

[61] Francisco Morales Padrón, *Rebelión contra la Compañía de Caracas* (Seville, 1955), pp. 51–74.
[62] Keene to Newcastle, 23 June 1729, PRO, SP 94/100.
[63] W. Gayley to Townshend, Cadiz, 14 August 1729, PRO, SP 94/100.
[64] Keene to Newcastle, 2 September 1737, PRO, SP 94/128.

his own accounts, will receive in all very near six millions of dollars.'[65]
The English and French ambassadors complained and lobbied furiously,
but were answered with an even heavier *indulto*:

> Instead of the 16 per cent indulto which was demanded of the
> commerce, the orders are said to be sent to take 20 per cent. So that
> in the progress of a few years the indulto, which was thought to be
> heavy enough at 4 and 5 per cent, and was afterwards raised by Mr
> Patiño to 9 per cent, with assurances that it should remain on that
> footing and mount no higher, has at last been forced up to the sum
> above mentioned.[66]

While Spanish merchants had to share profits – and *indultos* – with
the English in Cadiz, they also had to share markets in America. By the
asiento of 1713, revised in 1716, the South Sea Company was contracted
to supply 4,800 slaves a year to Spanish America for thirty years; in
addition it was given the right to send an annual ship of 650 tons to the
trade fairs at the same time as the *galeones* and *flotas*. Of course what
Spain granted, it could also take away: subsequent administrations
mounted fierce operations against contraband in Cadiz and America,
and they did little to protect the *asiento* privileges from attack by over-
zealous local officials. Even so the opportunities for illicit trade were
manifold. The *asiento* and the annual ship were an invitation to contraband, and contraband was built into the system, partly through slave
ships and factories, partly through excess cargoes on the annual ships.
Contrary to Spanish belief, the Company's trade was not particularly
profitable; inferior operating methods and personnel, lack of research on
the labour market, the intervention of war, and other flaws added to
costs and eroded profits. The Company did not even meet its slave
quotas: in the course of nineteen years eight months of actual operations, it introduced 63,206 slaves in 538 separate voyages, an average of
almost 3,214 slaves a year.[67] Nevertheless the *asiento* had an impact on
Spanish American trade and trading patterns. During the seventeen
years between 1715 and 1732 the South Sea Company despatched seven
annual and two licensed ships carrying registered merchandise worth
approximately £2,101,487, an average of £123,617 annually (before

[65] Keene to Newcastle, 16 September 1737, PRO, SP 94/128.
[66] Keene to Newcastle, 11 November 1737, PRO, SP 94/128.
[67] Victoria G. Sorsby, 'British Trade with Spanish America under the Asiento 1713–1740', Ph.D.
Thesis, University of London, 1975, p. 277.

sale).[68] The Company probably controlled at least 25 per cent of all British exports to Spain and America, immune from the formal Spanish monopoly.

The monopoly, then, was weakened from within and without. The six *flotas* to New Spain in 1720–40 disappointed Spanish hopes of the fiscal legislation of 1720; as a further measure, the Veracruz fair was moved inland to Jalapa, a tactic which still failed to protect the market. The continued influx of imports from Manila, the increase of direct trade from various sources, and the resistance of the Mexican merchants to Spanish monopolists, all contributed to nullify Spanish policy. But the glutting of the market by the annual ship was the greatest problem and only its absence, as in 1736, could guarantee Spanish sales.

The annual ship made its presence felt in competition with the *galeones* at the Portobello fairs of 1722, 1726 and 1731, partly because its own cargo dominated the market, partly because it acted as a focus for other contrabandists, encouraging Peruvian merchants openly to spend their money on foreign goods in preference to those from Spain, and mopping up whatever purchasing capacity remained in the colonial market. The *consulado* of Cadiz complained in 1722 that contraband trade was conducted 'with greater liberty when the *galeones* are in the Indies than when they are not'.[69] After the failure of the official trade at Portobello in 1722, Patiño reacted by organizing a squadron of fighting ships to protect the coasts of the Caribbean against foreign interlopers, a measure which received some financial support from Spanish merchants. The *guardacostas*, as they were called, soon became the scourge of English shipping, lawful and unlawful alike, and their activities further embittered Anglo-Spanish relations in the years ahead.[70] At the same time a new viceroy, the marquis of Castelfuerte, relentlessly attacked contrabandists on the Peruvian coast and sought to seal the gaps in that sector. But war with England and the presence of an English squadron outside Portobello enabled the Peruvian merchants to trade as they pleased, and the fair of 1726 was another victory for the interlopers.[71] While Castelfuerte concentrated his efforts on the Pacific coast of Peru, foreigners penetrated the lines of commercial defence from other directions, in the South Atlantic from Buenos Aires to Potosí and Lima, in the Caribbean along the Magdalena to New Granada and beyond. The

[68] Ibid., p. 425.
[69] Quoted by Walker, *Spanish Politics and Imperial Trade*, p. 150.
[70] Pares, *War and Trade in the West Indies*, pp. 22–3.
[71] Walker, *Spanish Politics and Imperial Trade*, pp. 152–6.

South Sea Company seemed to be everywhere, protesting its legality but steadily siphoning off the profits of empire. At the Portobello fair of 1731 – the last of its kind – the Peruvian merchants spent half of their 9 million pesos on the 1,000 tons of merchandise supplied by the annual ship, the *Prince William*. They were compelled to accept a shipment of what they regarded as inferior and overpriced cloth from the royal factory of Guadalajara, but they could not be harassed into buying from the private Spanish merchants, many of whom found it impossible to sell their goods and faced years of bargaining in a glutted market.[72] As an alternative to further *galeones* the crown sent a number of register ships to Cartagena in 1737; where they waited impatiently for a rendezvous with Peruvian merchants in Portobello, finally arranged in 1739. This time they had to contend not with an annual ship but with six British warships under Admiral Vernon, precursors of a war which brought traditional navigation to an end.

The War of Jenkins' Ear (1739–48), in spite of diversions in Europe, was a true colonial war. It presented a double challenge to Spain in America, one to security, the other to trade. Imperial defence was not a new problem for Spain, but in this war she was faced by a new phase of British imperialism, in which annexation or perhaps liberation of Spanish colonies were envisaged as a means of creating markets for British trade. The expedition of Admiral Vernon to the Isthmus and Cartagena in 1740 was a powerful one, designed to make conquests and to assure the inhabitants that they would become British subjects with 'the privilege and right of trading directly to Great Britain'.[73] Lord Anson's expedition to the Pacific was weaker and more speculative; therefore his instructions envisaged not conquest but the possibility of rebellions against Spanish rule in Chile and Peru leading to valuable commercial agreements with Britain. Similarly the small expedition under Commodore Knowles to La Guaira and Puerto Cabello in 1743 was designed not to conquer but to free the creoles from the oppression of the Caracas Company, though Knowles's own proclamation spoke ambiguously of forming 'a new colony' composed of free Spaniards and Indians with civil, religious, and commercial rights equal to those of the British.[74] None of these expeditions, with the exception of Anson's, secured their objectives or brought the slightest benefit to Britain.

---

[72] Ibid., pp. 177–88.

[73] Quoted by Pares, *War and Trade in the West Indies*, p. 75.

[74] Charles Knowles, 1743, Archivo General de Indias, Seville, Caracas 927; reference kindly provided by Montserrat Gárate.

Spanish imperial defences remained basically intact, thinly spread perhaps but strong enough at key points to prevent the dismemberment of empire. The war demonstrated two things: that it was impossible to undermine the Spanish colonies from within by liberating creoles and Indians; and that Spain had the capacity to endure the delay of treasure returns while keeping those in America safe from attack.

The war marked the end of the old trading system. In 1740 all fleets were suspended and single ships licensed by the crown, the *registros*, henceforth supplied South America, as they did New Spain until 1757. This was the greatest innovation in two centuries of colonial trade. It began as an exceptional procedure to avoid the enemy, though it was not always successful. In 1741–5 the English took booty amounting to 15 million pesos (including that of Anson), and subsequently captured many smaller prizes; of the 118 register ships which left Cadiz during 1740–5, sixty-nine were reported lost on the round trip.[75] At the same time Spain had to share this trade with foreign ships carrying foreign merchandise; between 1740 and 1756, of the 164 *registros* which sailed to Veracruz, 119 were Spanish and forty-five neutral (most of them French).[76] But the use of single register ships was a radical break with the past, providing a more rapid and frequent service than the fleets, and attracting more traffic; in the period 1739–54 753 single vessels crossed the Atlantic, an average of forty-seven ships a year, compared to thirty ships a year in 1717–38.[77] New trade routes were developed. Some of the *registros* which sailed to Buenos Aires had the right of *internación*, which meant in practice the passage of goods across the Andes into Chile and Peru. Moreover, after 1740 ships were permitted to sail directly to Peru via Cape Horn, and in spite of the protests of the *consulado* of Lima the Portobello fair was never revived. As Spanish merchants gained new access to South American markets, so they were freed of the competition of the South Sea Company, not only during the war but afterwards. In the commercial treaty of 1750 the Company relinquished the remaining four years of the *asiento* in return for a cash settlement of £100,000.

The register ships revitalized the American trade. In spite of their provisional character, they survived the end of the war with England and were decisive for the future. Merchants profited from the greater volume of trade, the state from higher revenue. It is true that the

[75] Pares, *War and Trade in the West Indies*, p. 114.

[76] Morineau, *Incroyables gazettes et fabuleux métaux*, pp. 372, 376. In addition there were 24 *avisos*.

[77] García-Baquero, *Cádiz y el Atlántico*, i, pp. 164–74; Walker, *Spanish Politics and Imperial Trade*, pp. 211–14.

monopolists of Cadiz and Mexico and their allies in the administration restored the fleets to New Spain; defying market conditions, six *flotas* were despatched in the period 1757–76.[78] But the fleet system had lost its supremacy and could no longer compete with the *registros*. In the period 1755–78 the latter represented 79.58 per cent of the total traffic with America, while the fleets, which before 1739 had accounted for 46 per cent, now were reduced to 13.32 per cent.[79]

What trends can be observed in the American trade in the first half of the eighteenth century? The signs are contradictory, the evidence is diverse, and the difference between official and unofficial figures is not easily reconcilable. Yet some conclusions may be suggested. The story is not one of complete stagnation. While merchants complained, theorists criticized, and ministers legislated, trade and treasure survived and showed some signs of growth. From the evidence of shipping and tonnage, the American trade entered a period of modest recovery from 1709 to 1722, advanced into a more stable period of growth from 1722 to 1747, and then moved strongly upwards without further fluctuations to 1778.[80] Shipping rose by 60.3 per cent from 793 vessels in 1681–1709 to 1,271 in 1710–47; by 86 per cent to 2,365 in 1748–78; and by a total of 198.2 per cent between the first and third periods. But ships were getting bigger, and the difference in tonnage between the first and third periods was 321.6 per cent. The change from moderate to stronger growth came in the 1740s, and the vehicle of growth appears to have been the single register ships, which now virtually replaced the fleets. Tonnage figures are confirmed by treasure imports, which underwent a distinct rise from 1749, following the Anglo-Spanish war (see table 4.1).

Official figures show a 188.3 per cent increase in treasure imports, from 152.5 million pesos in 1717–38 to 439.7 million in 1749–78.[81] Totals for the royal treasury rose from 21.6 million in the first period to 38.7 million in the second; for the private sector from 130.8 million in the first period to 401 million in the second. In other words the percentage of private to royal treasure was 85.8 to 14.2 in the first period, and 91.2 to 8.8 in the second; for the whole, 89.8 per cent to 10.2 per cent. This represents a relative decline of royal income from America since the previous century, and is usually attributed to higher defence and administrative expenditure, especially in Peru. Yet the gross amount

[78] Walker, *Spanish Politics and Imperial Trade*, pp. 220–3.

[79] García-Baquero, *Cádiz y el Atlántico*, I, pp. 173–4.

[80] Ibid., I, pp. 541–56.

[81] Ibid., I, pp. 343–51.

*Table 4.1 American treasure returns by
quinquennia in million pesos 1716-1755*

Quinquennia	Unofficial estimates	Official figures
1716–20	43.2	17.6
1721–5	53.1	38.1
1726–30	76.4	36.7
1731–5	47.5	37.9
1736–40	47.1	21.9
1741–5	28.6	
1746–50	90.3	66.1
1751–5	87.5	65.8

Each of the figures in the first column is the maximum, not the minimum, estimate. Each quinquennium in the second column lacks one year's data.

Source: Michel Morineau, *Incroyables gazettes et fabuleux métaux. Les retours des trésors américains d'après les gazettes hollandaises (XVIᵉ-XVIIIᵉ siècles)* (Cambridge, 1985), pp. 317, 368, 377, 391; Antonio García-Baquero González, *Cádiz y el Atlántico (1717-1778)* (2 vols, Seville, 1976), II, pp. 250–1.

received by the crown was rising, which suggests that the real reason for the divergence was the increase in the volume of private trade, stimulated in this period by Bourbon policy. Some three-quarters of the total volume of exports were of foreign origin, while Spanish products were confined to agriculture and iron. If foreigners received the lion's share of returns, however, Spanish middlemen in Cadiz could still make large profits and many accumulated considerable fortunes from the trade with America. As for the proportion of treasure to merchandise, this conformed to the *pacto colonial*, being 77.6 to 22.46 per cent in favour of treasure imports.

The estimates obtained from unofficial sources, such as foreign gazettes and consular reports, are higher and probably more realistic than the official figures.[82] They show that treasure returns in 1721–40 were respectable but not brilliant, averaging 10.6 million pesos a year in 1721–5, rising to 15.2 million a year in 1726–30, and falling to 9.5 million in 1731–5, and 9.4 million a year in 1736–40. This compares

[82] Morineau, *Incroyables gazettes et fabuleux métaux*, p. 368.

unfavourably with the second half of the seventeenth century, particularly with the years 1685–94, when the annual average was 15 million pesos. Treasure returns in the first years of the Anglo-Spanish war were depressed by enemy action and retention of treasure for security in America, and averaged only 5.7 million a year in 1741–5. But once Spain adjusted to the colonial conflict and began to operate register ships, the accumulated treasure flowed again, averaging 18 million pesos a year in 1746–50 and 17.5 million in 1751–5, rather more from Mexico than from Tierra Firme and pointing to a recovery in Mexican mining.[83] Treasure returns remained at a high level, without however surpassing the old record until 1780.

The history of Spain's colonial trade from 1700 to 1750 was one of survival and partial revival. Participants and policy-makers looked for better results but were loath to leave the shelter of monopoly. War hastened decisions. The decade 1740–50 was the dividing line between the old trading system and the new, between tradition and change, inertia and growth.

[83] Ibid., pp. 377, 391.

5

Time of Transition 1746–1759

The New Monarchy

The wars brought little to Spain, and peace and retrenchment were the only options remaining. In the years 1746–8 Spain acquired a new king, new government and new policy, unexpected gains greeted with relief by a people more familiar with war, conscription, and adversity. At last they had a national king, born in Spain and served by Spaniards, a ruler who preferred country to dynasty, neutrality to war. These changes could not be effected in a day; it took two years to disengage from France and Italy, and Aix-la-Chapelle was not a great victory. Maritime power was still disputed, and Gibraltar remained in British hands. But the government had learned a lesson and foreign affairs no longer dominated its thinking to the exclusion of all other priorities. The new regime accepted that Spain's interests resided not in European battle-fields but in the Atlantic and beyond. Spaniards were glad to see the old age out and ready to begin a new.

Ferdinand VI, the fourth and only surviving son of the first marriage of Philip V, was not a prepossessing monarch. Like other Spanish Bourbons of the eighteenth century, he was indolent and uninvolved, full of good intentions but leaving to others their fulfilment. The new conjuncture of peace, reform and good luck placed unprecedented revenue at his disposal, some of which he allocated to needy causes, some to royal diversions. He gave impulsively to charity, as in the hot summer of 1750 when he cancelled taxes in drought-stricken Andalucía and sent subsidies to buy bread and corn;[1] and in 1755, after the Lisbon

---

[1] Keene to Castres, 4 September 1750, Sir Benjamin Keene, *The Private Correspondence of Sir Benjamin Keene, KB*, ed. Sir Richard Lodge (Cambridge, 1933), p. 251; Keene to Stone, 31 August 1750, British Library, Add. MS 43, 424, f. 201.

earthquake, when he assigned generous, though ill-received, aid to prostrate Portugal. But he could not inspire his ministers or give them leadership and unity; he was in any case poorly prepared for government; his suspicious stepmother, Elisabeth Farnese, had kept him out of public affairs, and now his solicitous wife and ministers kept public affairs from his easily disturbed mind. His personal interests lay more in play than politics. At Aranjuez large sums were expended on the miniature Tagus squadron, fifteen vessels for the King's amusement. In Madrid this was a time of court operas, balls and suppers, and also of royal patronage of the arts, when Domenico Scarlatti and the singer Farinelli made the Spanish capital a centre of musical culture and talent.

The new king behaved correctly though firmly towards Farnese and insisted that she retire to San Ildefonso, where her petty court became a focus of rumours and intrigue but not of influence. Yet while he turned his face against the past, Ferdinand curiously re-enacted many of the features of his father's life, in his abnormal sexual condition, his dependence on a dominant wife, and his frequent lapses into insanity. As Benjamin Keene tactfully put it, the king was 'excessively fond' of his wife, which gave the queen exceptional influence over her husband.[2] Stout and breathless, and sadly ill-favoured in looks, Barbara of Braganza was a notoriously avaricious woman and largely unloved in Spain. With hope abandoned of giving Ferdinand an heir and providing for the succession, she spent much of her time in a state of neurosis, torn between fear of dying and fear of destitution should the king die. But she was no Farnese, and although she had power over her husband and an eye for Portuguese interests, she did not use her position to distort Spanish policy. She strongly supported the diplomacy of neutrality and joined her husband on the path of peace. This was as much as could be expected of the new monarchs and it was enough to give Spanish government its best opportunity since 1700, free of foreign adventures and extravagances. How did the government respond?

The new administration, like the new monarchy, was 'national' in composition and character.[3] It was headed, in fact if not in form, by Cenón de Somodevilla, an able, self-confident man who affected an elegant style and lavish ways, compensating perhaps for his modest origins in Alesanco, Logroño, where he was born to an *hidalgo* family on 2 June 1701, and whence he raised himself to join the bureaucratic elite.

[2] Keene to Bedford, 25 February 1749, BL, Add. MS 43, 423, f. 40.
[3] María Dolores Gómez Molleda, 'Viejo y nuevo estilo político en la corte de Fernando VI', *Eidos*, 4 (1957), pp. 53–76.

Plate 2 *Ferdinand VI and Barbara of Braganza at Aranjuez*, by Francesco Battaglioni (reproduced by kind permission of the Museo del Prado, Madrid)

He was formed in the school of Patiño and specialized in naval administration; present at the reconquest of Oran in 1732 and on the expedition to Naples in 1733, he was rewarded for his services with the title of marquis of La Ensenada in 1736. He was promoted secretary of the admiralty in 1737 and began to work on that reconstruction of the navy which became his hallmark. The war in Italy, a deadweight for Spain, was another springboard for Ensenada, and when Campillo died, in April 1743, he was the obvious successor. On 9 May he was appointed secretary of finance, war, marine, and the Indies; in addition to the four ministries, he received the title of secretary of state and superintendent of revenues, or, as the Jesuit Padre Isla called him 'secretary of everything'.[4] Ensenada thus became the most powerful man in Spain, a model of ministerial ubiquity.

The second appointment of new for old was that of José de Carvajal y Lancaster, who in December 1746 was brought out of routine employment in the council of the Indies to replace Sebastián de la Cuadra as secretary of state; and to foreign affairs was added the offices of governor of the council of the Indies and president of the junta of commerce. Born in Cáceres in 1698, Carvajal was the son of a grandee and socially superior to Ensenada, though less ostentatious in style. A mild and diffident manner, however, masked strong opinions, stubbornly held and firmly applied.[5] Recommended by Ensenada, his appointment was supported by the duke of Huéscar, future duke of Alba, who had political ambitions of his own though these were expressed by manipulation of others rather than management of affairs. Carvajal's promotion was accompanied by that of his Jesuit friend Padre Francisco de Rávago, whom he called out of obscurity in 1747 to recommend to the king as his confessor, a choice seconded by Ensenada who regarded it as a 'national' appointment in succession to a French incumbent.[6] Rávago was not the ablest of his order and was reputedly controlled by a committee of Jesuits; but he now became in effect minister of ecclesiastical affairs and the third member of a ruling triumvirate, emerging from the shadow of Carvajal to adopt a more independent, not to say authoritarian, stance.

The new administration was a puzzle to contemporaries and to historians. Were Ensenada and Carvajal rivals for power? purveyors of

[4] Antonio Rodríguez Villa, *Don Cenón de Somodevilla, marqués de la Ensenada* (Madrid, 1878), pp. 19, 300.

[5] Keene to Bedford, 28 June 1749, BL, Add. MS 43, 423, f. 131 v.

[6] Ensenada to Huéscar, 19 April 1747, in María Dolores Gómez Molledo, 'El marqués de la Ensenada a través de su correspondencia íntima', *Eidos*, 2 (1955), pp. 48–90, esp. p. 62.

different policies? alternative guides to a single goal? Was their administration a medium of consensus or a house divided? Modern inter-
pretations have stressed balance rather than division.[7] The priority was
Spanish interests, the policy peace and neutrality. At certain points there
were differences over the means. Ensenada invoked the need for armed
strength and favoured France as a warning to England; Carvajal
proceeded by diplomacy in a world of international conflict where
English maritime power could not be ignored and might be channeled to
Spanish interests if a hard bargain were struck.[8] 'Spain for the Spaniards,
and independence in foreign affairs', this was the basic thinking of the
regime.[9] Yet beyond this minimum agreement, necessary for any
government, there were significant differences between the two
ministers and the administration did not speak with one voice.

There was obviously a power struggle and a quest for supremacy in a
government where the first place was not defined and where the over-
powering personality of Ensenada created an assumption in his favour
and a growing resentment on the part of his colleague. This was the first
unresolved question. Who was the *primus inter pares*? Secondly, disagree-
ment over foreign policy had far-reaching implications. A tendency
towards England or France was not, in the years around 1750 a trivial
difference, a mere political label. England and France were in a state of
cold war and urgently preparing for real war. Spanish naval and military
resources could make a difference to the balance between the super
powers. Each was looking for at least Spanish neutrality, preferably
alliance. In these circumstances Spanish politicians could not evade
commitment or ignore the consequences of their actions; if Ensenada
provoked England too far, especially in America, it could lead if not to
war at least to armed conflict, as Carvajal seems to have appreciated in
his preference for diplomacy. Keene believed that neutrality had its
limits:

Ensenada's scheme seems to be to fill the King's coffers to near 100
millions of dollars, to be quiet and practicable til that time, and to
form a powerful marine. This perhaps he thinks may be effected in
the 6 years, at the expiration of which the Crown being in so

[7] For an interpretation of Carvajal see María Dolores Gómez Molleda, 'El pensamiento de
Carvajal y la política internacional española del siglo XVIII', *Hispania*, 15 (1955), pp. 117–37.
[8] Gómez Molleda, 'Viejo y nuevo estilo político en la corte de Fernando VI', pp. 75–6.
[9] The words are those of Richard Pares, *War and Trade in the West Indies 1739-1763* (London,
1963), p. 523.

respectable a situation, may take new measures and, after having made an experiment of this temporary friendship, insist upon some articles which they are now sensible nothing but time and good usage will ever bring about. In this idea I believe he is joyned by Carvajal, tho' scarce in any other, and one is full of artifice as the other is free from it.[10]

In this analysis the policy of neutrality was temporary, until Spain was in a position to cast the balance in the inevitable war between England and France, with payment in kind, preferably Gibraltar and/or Minorca. Of the two ministers Carvajal was inclined to England 'though at as cheap a rate as he can', which meant demanding much and conceding little. A third area of difference lay in economic policy. Carvajal gave priority to national industry and its protection, Ensenada to the Indies trade and the crown's direct participation in it as a profit-maker. These policies tended to pull in different directions:

One of them [Carvajal], at a time that there are scarce a subject to till their ground, has attempted even during the war, to establish manufactures of all sorts, and to furnish even the Indies with the products thereof, instead of what they now take from foreign nations. The other [Ensenada] despises these attempts (pretty justly) but runs into another extreme and instead of a manufacturer would make his Master the sole banker and merchant in his country.[11]

The final source of conflict between the two statesmen was founded in personalism rather than policies and was fuelled by the determination of each to build up a political following, not of course by parties, which did not exist, but by patronage and clientage. Politics was a race to get their own clients into jobs, often in competition with the other side and at the expense of a united administration. The patronage network constituted an informal political system, enabling the leaders to build into the administration their own interest group and giving them control over policies in different ministries. But rivalry was inherent in the system, and the rivalry between Ensenada and Carvajal reached the point where an anxious monarch asked his confessor to resolve it. Francisco de Rávago relates:

[10] Keene to Newcastle, 13 August 1750, *Private Correspondence of Sir Benjamin Keene*, pp. 244–5.
[11] Keene to Holderness, 7 May 1753, BL, Add. MS 43, 429, f. 171.

I told him that this was impossible, no less with these than with anyone else, because every man wants to be the sole chief and not to share with a colleague; that His Majesty is still young and would have other ministers after these with the same fault but without the same talents; and that I would strive to prevent an actual break.[12]

But Rávago was not an honest broker. In 1749 he connived with Ensenada to oust the bishop of Oviedo, a nominee and fellow collegiate of Carvajal, from the governorship of the council of Castile and to replace him by the bishop of Barcelona, a friend of Ensenada.[13] Carvajal was not slow in promoting his own faction, whom he called the *cofradía*, but this particular manœuvre led to a bitter quarrel with Ensenada and a feeling that he was being gradually marginalized. Sterile factionalism, the elevation of patronage over policy, prevented the government from taking full advantage of the favourable conjuncture provided by the new monarchy. For the first time in fifty years Spain had a monarch who, feeble in his own reason, would yet listen to the reason of others: 'no Princes were ever more reasonable, and I may say docile.' But they did not receive clear and distinct advice: 'though we have two Ministers, we have no ministry.'[14] The lack of agreement between the two ministers and their refusal even to treat with each other were obstacles to good government. The presence of a third party, supposedly impartial but with a strong interest of his own, merely compounded the confusion.

In spite of these self-imposed flaws the new administration had talent and will enough to advance beyond the marginal changes introduced by the government of Philip V and to embark on eight years of positive action, expressed in reform at home and peace abroad. Whereas Philip V had been content to strengthen the state authority, the new regime sought to activate the state and to make it an effective instrument of change. The intervention of the central government to reform the tax structure, mobilize resources, and create an arms and shipbuilding industry was not only innovatory in itself but also implied changes in social and economic life. Moreover, far from seeking short cuts to success, the government planned for a stronger infrastructure and

[12] Rávago to Portocarrero, 25 November 1749, quoted by Rafael Olaechea, 'Política eclesiástica del gobierno de Fernando VI', *La época de Fernando VI. Ponencias leidos en el coloquio conmemorativo de los 25 años de la fundación de la Cátedra Feijóo* (Oviedo, 1981), pp. 139–225, esp. p. 148, n. 7.

[13] Keene to Castres, 15 August 1749, *Private Correspondence of Sir Benjamin Keene*, pp. 156–7; Keene to Bedford, 8 September 1749, BL, Add. MS 43, 423, f. 193 v.

[14] Keene to Castres, 13 October 1749, 23 August 1750, *Private Correspondence of Sir Benjamin Keene*, pp. 177, 247.

long-term gains. In particular it was anxious to close the technology gap that was opening between northern Europe and Spain. The collection of industrial intelligence in England and France, the grants for travel and study abroad, the acquisition of foreign experts, were all evidence of an active pursuit of technical skills for application to new projects in Spain. The organization of public works such as roads, bridges and irrigation, hitherto delegated to local authorities, was now undertaken by the central government, which was ready to employ English and French advisers and to plan larger projects beyond the scope of any individual province; such were the canal of Castile, the Guadarrama road, and the Reinosa highway, all begun under this regime, though left to others to complete. These activities gave a new role to the state and set precedents for later action. It was now that Bourbon Spain acquired an interventionist state and made a breakthrough into active government, challenging old prejudices and arousing traditionalists to denounce Ensenada as an interfering bureaucrat who was wasting a lot of public money. What in fact they were witnessing was Spain's first modernization programme, ambitious, inchoate, and incomplete, but an unmistakable example for the future.

How then, in summary, did the new regime differ from the old? First, the monarchs were open to change and gave ministers their head. Second, the interval of peace, undisturbed by adventurism, allowed government a breathing space and an opportunity to experiment. Third, the object was no longer merely to build the state but to use it, not least as a producer and consumer in the economy. Fourth, Ensenada's policy had social content, or social implications, absent in that of Patiño. For all these reasons, the year 1746 was a year of innovation for Spain, the dividing line between conservatism and change, between routine and reform.

Ensenada, Bourbon Reformer

Ensenada outlined his programme in a series of reports addressed to the king at the beginning of the reign. In 1746 his foreign policy advice was cautious. The aim was to disengage from war and establish peace, but from a position of strength, which was the only argument Britain understood: 'to leave too many gains to England could lead to the loss of the Indies.'[15] He acknowledged the difficulty of defining the correct policy

---

[15] 'Idea de lo que parece preciso en el día para la dirección de lo que corresponde a Estado y se halla pendiente', Rodríguez Villa, *Marqués de la Ensenada*, pp. 31–42.

towards England in America: 'To grant them free navigation, as they ask, is impossible without abandoning the Indies; to restrict it, as we seek to do, is no less impracticable.' The only option was to appeal to British interests, that they risked too much by war, and to negotiate a compromise over the right of search in American waters. As for Gibraltar, Spain should preserve its claim to sovereignty until it could be definitely won; meanwhile 'a studied silence would be better all round'.[16] France was a problem as well as an ally. Spain should preserve friendship, but without dependency and with alertness towards French claims in the Indies trade and territory, which they had usurped without ever legitimizing.

Further reports poured from the restless mind of Ensenada in 1747, 1748 and 1751, analysing the state of the royal treasury, assessing Spanish government and power, and advising on policy for finance, defence, the navy, and the Indies. He reserved his basic criticism for the structure of taxation and finance: 'Most of its various branches seem to have been invented by the enemies of this monarchy's welfare; as the rich contribute proportionately much less than the poor, the latter are in the depths of poverty, and our manufactures destroyed.' The two principal revenues of tobacco and customs were reduced by maladministration and corruption; the *millones* was a pernicious tax, a prime cause of impoverishment, depopulation, and decline of manufactures; the *alcabala* too weighed heavily on tax payers but especially on the poor. These taxes should be abolished and replaced by a single tax, the *catastro*, graded according to ability to pay, and levied without grace or favour. Meanwhile a number of immediate remedies were necessary. Defence costs must be cut by making peace, for by 1748 expenditure would exceed income by 6.7 million escudos, a sum which could only be reduced by revenue from the Indies, and this was a revenue which no one could guarantee.[17] There was also need for substantial savings in the royal household and palaces, not to mention the various councils and ministries, where offices multiplied to satisfy clients. For this Ensenada blamed the patronage system: 'I have noticed a universal tendency to invent jobs and other excuses to accommodate people, but not to seek the right candidates for offices which need to be filled.'[18] The object of fiscal reform, therefore, was twofold, equity between people and power

[16] Ibid., pp. 39–40.

[17] 'Representación dirigida por Ensenada a Fernando VI sobre el estado del Real Erario y sistema y método para lo futuro', Aranjuez, 18 June 1747, ibid., pp. 43–65.

[18] Ibid., p. 49.

to the state. It was this combination which gave Ensenada's reform project its originality; equity would be secured by the single tax, power by the new navy.

The navy occupied first place in Ensenada's strategic thinking and from his earliest advice to the king, in 1746, he urged its expansion 'with priority over everything', for a navy was essential to a power with an overseas empire and aspirations to respect from France and England:

> I will not claim that in a few years Your Majesty can have a navy to compete with that of England, because even if there were resources to provide it there are not enough sailors to form the crews; but I do say that Your Majesty can easily have the number of ships which, combined with those of France, are sufficient to deprive the English of their command of the sea.

He calculated that 'in eight years of peace we can construct in Spain and Havana 50 ships of the line, and prepare all the stores needed for their fitting out, provided we allocate exclusively to this object a million pesos in each of the eight years.'[19] But manpower was needed as well as money. Lack of sailors stemmed from neglect of the merchant marine through the decline of Spain's maritime trade. The process could only be reversed by paying sailors more, cultivating the merchant navy, and 'allowing all the ships and vessels sailing to America to depart from any port of Spain', a commitment to *comercio libre* twenty years before its enactment.

Ensenada was aware of the obstacles to naval growth. It tended to arouse the suspicion of rival powers and provoke an arms race. And it invariably came up against financial priorities. In 1748 he proposed fitting out six ships for operation against *los moros* and defence of the Spanish coasts, eight for the transatlantic traffic and America; at the same time he projected the construction of six ships a year in Ferrol, Cadiz, and Cartagena, three in Havana, and the extension of the Ferrol dockyard. For all this 3.8 million escudos were needed in the peninsula and 782,093 pesos in America; this may be regarded as the navy estimate, and it was about one-third that of the army. Ensenada advised the king:

> Certainly the army, the government and the royal palaces ought to have priority funding, and in that case I do not believe that the

[19] Ibid., pp. 62–3.

Spanish treasury and the income from America can cover everything; but as it is essential to establish a regular budget for the navy
and keep to that, I ask Your Majesty to indicate your royal will,
and if there is a surplus after meeting other obligations and it is
applied to the navy, then the navy could expand in accordance
with Your Majesty's wish.[20]

In other words, the first three priorities were the army, the administration and the court, with the navy coming up behind. This was the traditional formula and betrayed a certain inconsistency in Ensenada's
argument, which had begun by placing the navy at the top. It was also an
invitation to the king to preserve the mould, as seen in his annotation: 'It
is my will that, without prejudice to the other obligations of the
Monarchy, you attend to and secure the increase of the navy, taking the
necessary steps as secretly as possible.' On the other hand, by adopting a
tactful rather than a radical approach, Ensenada seems to have obtained
the flexibility and the funding he was seeking.

At the end of 1748 Ensenada was supremely positioned to implement
his programme. The peace of Aix-la-Chapelle had been signed on
18 October; he held in his hands the principal offices of state and the
favour of the monarchs; he was served by a reformed and motivated
higher bureaucracy, many of whom were his own clients. Above all, the
post-war returns of American treasure were now available in abundance,
39 million pesos in 1749, 31.3 million in 1750, a total of 90.3 million in
1746–50, and 87.5 million in 1751–5.[21] From this vantage point he began
to work his way through the list of priorities: administrative and
financial reform, the Indies trade, naval construction, army strength, and
relations with Rome.[22] The starting point was tax reform.

The need for fiscal reform had been recognized for some time and
studies of the problem had been commissioned in the reign of Philip V;
proposals had been made for a single tax, on flour and salt, which would
replace the multiplicity of existing taxes and their hordes of collectors.[23]
But the most obvious precedent was the *catastro* established by Patiño in

[20] 'Representación de Ensenada al Rey sobre fomento de la Marina', 28 May 1748, ibid.,
pp. 109–11.

[21] Michel Morineau, *Incroyables gazettes et fabuleux métaux. Les retours des trésors américains d'après
les gazettes hollandaises (XVIᵉ-XVIIIᵉ siècles)* (Cambridge, 1985), p. 391; Keene to Castres, 18 July
1749, *Private Correspondence of Sir Benjamin Keene*, pp. 150–1; see above, pp. 155–6.

[22] 'Estado de las cosas de Guerra, Marina, Indias y Hacienda, y otros asumptos', 15 November
1749, Rodríguez Villa, *Marqués de la Ensenada*, pp. 77–83.

[23] See above, pp. 110, 113–14.

Catalonia, which was a tax on income apparently acceptable to government and citizens alike. Ensenada went beyond this and planned a single tax which would not only resolve immediate problems of revenue but also effect more permanent structural change and become part of a general reform of the administration and the treasury.[24] His proposal was simple, to replace existing taxes on consumer goods and services by a single tax on income. He had to argue his case, produce facts and figures, lobby the administration and interest groups, and above all prevail upon the king to issue the necessary legislation. His tenacity and influence with the crown won the day – or seemed to – and on 10 October 1749 the king issued a royal *cédula* which decreed the abolition of the *rentas provinciales* – the *alcabalas*, *cientos*, *millones* – and their replacement by a single tax on income. The nobility as a body did not protest, though there was obvious resentment in their ranks over the threat to their privileges and fiscal immunity. The objections of the clergy were met by a papal bull which replaced the previous group of ecclesiastical contributions by a single tax. Thus the first stage of the project went ahead: the compilation of a census of persons, property and earnings of every household in Castile for 1750, a kind of national economic survey. It was preceded by a pilot survey of one province, Guadalajara, and its feasibility established; now it was extended to the whole of Castile at the cost of 40 million reales. The *catastro* of Ensenada, as it was known, was completed in 1754; copies were made, bound and sent to Madrid; officials began to make the new tax assessments, calculate the quotas, and prepare the necessary decrees. Then nothing happened. The interest groups and privileged sectors had not been idle since 1749; protests had been voiced, objections made, pressures applied. The result was that the project of a single tax was first postponed, then abandoned, leaving the *catastro* itself in the archives, a monument to Spanish bureaucracy and a prime source for the historian. The exercise was revealing in other ways.

The single tax was projected to fall on all types of income, classified according to source. Its modernity lay not in its character of a single tax – in fact only the *rentas provinciales* would be abolished, other revenues would more or less continue as they were – but in its application to all citizens, irrespective of class or estate, who would be assessed according to ability to pay. An income tax of this kind, proportionate to wealth, was a social as well as a fiscal innovation. To tax incomes rather than

[24] Dolores Mateos Dorado, 'La única contribución y el catastro de Ensenada (1749–1759)', *La epoca de Fernando VI*, pp. 227–40.

essential consumer goods and to act against privilege and exemption was to challenge some of the basic assumptions of Spanish society; if the new tax was not completely egalitarian, it was a step in that direction. In the event Ensenada's optimism was premature; the time for social change had not arrived. But not all had been lost. The single tax was part of a larger plan to reform the whole administration of taxes and revenues. It was accompanied by a further decree (11 October 1749) taking the administration of the *rentas provinciales* into the hands of the state from 1 January 1750. This de-privatization of tax collecting eliminated the tax farmers and with them a notorious source of disorder and corruption, and it proved to be a popular measure of reform, advantageous to state and tax payer alike.

The decrees of single tax and de-privatization of revenues were followed almost immediately by a third decree, designed to complete Ensenada's major project of fiscal and administrative reform. This was the *Ordenanza de Intendentes* (13 October 1749), which re-established the full intendant system after an interlude of partial suspension and provided the final link in a process of tax reform, national economic review, and improved administration.[25] The king was looking for a new start after 'forty-eight years of continual bloody wars suffered by my kingdom and subjects; hardship and deprivation caused for so long through lack of crops, commerce and manufactures; repeated conscription . . .', all of which were responsible for reducing Spain to its present state.[26] The new ordinance was based on that of 1718 and still envisaged the intendants as the regional agents of a centralized state, but it implied a closer commitment to provincial interests, a greater concern to defend the resources of the towns and villages under their jurisdiction, to protect the rural sector and promote local trade and industry. The first task of the intendants was to direct the *catastro* operations in each province, and they bore much of the responsibility and credit for the success of the inquiry, though not all were cooperative; one of its enemies, the intendant of Galicia, José de Avilés, was eventually dismissed for carrying criticism too far. Once the *catastro* was completed, they reverted to their normal fiscal functions, representing the state as tax collector and the interests of the people as tax payers. There were often petitions for tax remission, for example, from Catalonia; the intendant argued that drought and crop failures in the years 1748–51

---

[25] See above, pp. 102–6.
[26] Rodríguez Villa, *Marqués de la Ensenada*, pp. 83–4.

justified such requests, though the government of Ensenada was usually reluctant to agree.[27]

The new decree established four intendants of army in Castile – Seville, Extremadura, Zamora and Galicia – and eighteen of province. In due course the intendants of army and province became identical, though the military jurisdiction of the former gave them a somewhat higher status. The provision of resources for the army remained one of their basic tasks. But Ensenada used the intendants above all as agents of economic intelligence; he urged them to submit weekly reports of the state of agriculture, livestock, and commodity prices in their provinces, and refused to accept pleas of overwork.[28] In fact two flaws in the system emerged in the following decades, pressure of work and conflict of jurisdiction. The concentration of the four branches of finance, war, justice and administration in one office tended to stretch their resources and reduce their effectiveness. Their secretaries, who were not on the state payroll, had to correspond with numerous ministries on multiple items, in addition to tax and revenue work: 'Simply to deal with correspondence takes four days each week, leaving only three for other tasks, with no break or rest, and without counting the work pertaining to the office of corregidor.'[29] But the government was loath to assume the cost of a paid secretariat. Not all of these complaints need be taken at their face value. There was considerable absenteeism among intendants, who regularly and successfully applied for leave, ostensibly for domestic or health reasons but probably to spend time in Madrid.[30] Convinced of the declining efficiency of the intendants, the crown restored justice and administration to the *corregidores*, who traditionally exercised these functions, and left the intendants with finance and war.[31] There was tension still between the two officials and complaints from some intendants that without full jurisdiction they were unable to do their jobs effectively.[32] But it was 1802 before justice and administration were restored to them.

The *catastro* and its accompanying legislation of 1749 did not exhaust the innovative energy of Ensenada. The single tax was planned for long-term gains. But more immediately the census was costly to administer,

---

[27] Intendant of Catalonia to Ensenada, 23 October 1751, AGS, Secretaría de Hacienda 553.
[28] Intendant of Zamora to Ensenada, 22 December 1751, AGS, Secretaría de Hacienda 563.
[29] Intendant of Aragon to Squillace, 28 April 1764, AGS, Secretaría de Hacienda 542.
[30] AGS, Secretaría de Hacienda 583.
[31] AGS, Secretaría de Hacienda 590.
[32] Intendant of Palencia to Muzquiz, 3 September 1768, AGS, Secretaría de Hacienda 593.

while other government departments were clamouring for funds. Further measures were needed to yield immediate income. The success of the take-over of the *rentas provinciales* by the treasury encouraged the government to apply state control to other parts of the private sector. In 1751, impressed by the Bank of England, Ensenada established the *Giro Real* to manage the transfer of public and private funds outside Spain, to pay foreign creditors of Spanish commercial houses, meet the costs of Spanish embassies, and make other disbursements abroad. All foreign exchange operations were now placed in the hands of the treasury and earned useful savings or profits for the state until opponents of the idea prevailed and it was subsequently abandoned. Another source of income was the Church. Regalist policy had a fiscal as well as a political aim, and the concordat of 1753, for which Ensenada pushed hard, won important financial gains for the crown.[33] Finally, a series of miscellaneous reforms confirmed the impression that this government was interested not only in revenue but also in welfare. Abolition of pernicious taxes such as that on the movement of grain from one province to another, the defence of municipal funds against a predatory government, the reversal of the irresponsible order of 1738 to sell royal common lands and their restoration to the villages, these and other measures helped to improve conditions of life as well as rationalize fiscal policy.

The American trade was a prime preoccupation of Ensenada. His own instinct was to extinguish the spirit of monopoly and remove the principal restrictions on colonial commerce. There was a limit to his power against vested interests, but he gave a further impulse to the use of register ships in preference to the fleet system, and it was his policy 'to grant a licence to all those who apply for one to sail in Spanish ships'.[34] He insisted on a moderate but secure gain on private silver returns, charging 6 per cent 'hush money' for permission to extract:

> The returns of the Flota and Galleons were hitherto exported by clandestine practices: they assisted in running the silver got a premium for their risks and pains, but the government saw its laws violated and got nothing. This Gentleman (Ensenada), however, has found means and precautions to put a stop to that counterband trade; and at no less advantage to the Crown than three per cent for the extraction of funds that belong to private persons, and as far as

[33] See below, pp. 187-90.
[34] 'Estado de las cosas de Guerra, Marina, Indias y Hacienda, y otros asumptos', 15 November 1749, Rodríguez Villa, *Marqués de la Ensenada*, pp. 77-83.

six per cent for the plata he sells to the foreign merchants, allowing them a term of six months from the delivery for payment.[35]

This policy was accompanied by stricter regulation of the trade and heavier penalties against unregistered treasure. In 1749 the flota returning from Mexico carrying some 23–26 million pesos and a large quantity of cochineal and indigo was ordered to put into Ferrol, not Cadiz, to avoid the fraud that was built into Cadiz and in particular the remittance of treasure outside the register.[36] The Cadiz merchants were strongly opposed to manœuvres of this kind which caused delay and raised transport costs, as they were to other aspects of Ensenada's policy. He projected a more positive role for the state in the Indies trade, seeing it not simply as a regulating and taxing agency but as a participant. This had obvious implications for the private sector, for it interrupted the normal relations between the trade and foreign merchants and undermined the traditional position of the Spanish commission agents.[37] His method was to extend the transactions of the *Giro Real* to cover other commercial operations, such as the purchase by the state of foreign goods for re-export to the Indies and the subsequent receipt of returns, betraying a bias towards state monopoly out of tune with his advocacy of commercial freedom:

The great remittances lately made from Barcelona to Marseilles, and from thence to Lyons, as well as those from Lisbon to England, by order of this Court, I find upon enquiry are not only designed for feeding the several Banks established by order of His Catholick Majesty in most of the trading countries of Europe, but these considerable sums are to be employed in purchasing in those places at first hand, on account of the Royal Revenue, such goods and merchandizes as have usually been sent to Cadiz by commission, and brought up there in order to be embarked on Flotas and Galleons for the trade and consumption of the Spanish West Indies. By which disposition, though the Spanish Court may be a gainer in one aspect, the commerce at Cadiz, as well their own subjects as others, must be considerable losers. And a great part of

---

[35] Keene to Newcastle, 30 July 1750, BL, Add. MS 43, 424, f. 182v; Keene to Castres, 31 July 1750, *Private Correspondence of Sir Benjamin Keene*, pp. 240–1.

[36] Keene to Bedford, 21 July 1749, BL, Add. MS 43, 423, f. 146v; Morineau, *Incroyables gazettes et fabuleux métaux*, p. 385.

[37] Keene to Bedford, 10 November 1749, BL, Add. MS 43, 423, f. 266.

the trade of this country be reduced to a sort of monopoly in the hands of those who formerly were content with the indultos and taxes laid upon the exports and imports from the Spanish dominions in America.[38]

The priority given to treasure returns did not divert the government from attention to colonial administration. The demands of war had given a new impetus to sale of office in America during the decade 1740–50 and renewed entry of creoles in the colonial *audiencias*, with consequent decline of standards, dominance of local interest groups, and loss of imperial control. In an effort to restore authority, and impressed perhaps by the mordant report of Jorge Juan and Antonio de Ulloa which attributed widespread corruption in the viceroyalty of Peru to the malign influence of sale of office, the crown in 1750 called a halt to sale of *audiencia* posts and those of *corregidor*, and began the long process of recovering colonial administration from local interests.[39] On this issue the government probably spoke with one voice. But there was not always a consensus. Carvajal was governor of the council of the Indies, a body in decline; Ensenada was secretary of the Indies, an office riding high. The secretary held real power and remitted little material to the council other than lawsuits. Economic and administrative business, therefore, was in the hands of Ensenada, who dealt with America by the *via reservada*, that is through the royal signature, thus effectively cutting the council and Carvajal out of American policy making.[40]

The financial programme of Ensenada, translated into revenue figures, opened new prospects for Spanish government. He himself claimed that in the year 1750 the royal revenues underwent an annual increase of 5,117,020 escudos over those of 1742, the highest previous total, and that by the end of the same year the *giro* had gained 1,831,911 escudos. He projected an annual income to the royal treasury of 26,707,649 escudos, without counting the profits of the *giro* or the income from the Indies, which he never regarded as ordinary revenue. And he forecast that through his reforms, at the end of six years of peace, income would rise to 34 million, of which 19 million could be allocated

[38] Keene to Bedford, 6 October 1749, BL, Add. MS 43, 423, f. 223.

[39] Luis J. Ramos Gómez, *Epoca, génesis y texto de las "Noticias secretas de América"*, de Jorge Juan y Antonio de Ulloa (2 vols, Madrid, 1985), II, pp. 174, 395; Mark A. Burkholder and D. S. Chandler, *From Impotence to Authority. The Spanish Crown and the American Audiencias, 1687-1808* (Columbia, NM, 1977), pp. 89–90.

[40] Keene to Holdernesse, 30 June 1753, BL, Add. MS 43, 430, f. 27.

to the army, 6 million to the navy, and 9 million for court and government. Such a growth, from 27 to 34 millions in six years, could be achieved by establishing the single tax, by growth of population and therefore of tax payers, by greater yields from certain taxes such as tobacco and salt, and by income from the Indies which could increase from 3 to 6 million and even be raised to 12 million.[41] These figures have some validity, though they tend not to reveal that the reign began with a suspension of payment of Philip V's debts; evidence indicates that annual income from all ordinary revenues in the time of Ferdinand VI reached 360.5 million reales, compared to 211 million in 1737. At the death of Ferdinand VI the Spanish treasury had not only emerged from deficit but held a surplus of 300 million reales. Independent observers confirmed that this government had more ready cash than any previous.[42]

There were elements of welfare and equity in many of Ensenada's projects, but these did not make him a radical. He held traditional views on social hierarchy and these emerged in his Representation of 1751, where he discussed the qualifications appropriate for appointment to the higher bureaucracy. While this may be read as a plea to open the administration to a wider social group than the *colegiales*, or graduates of the elite colleges of the universities, it can also be interpreted as a conservative approach to the problem. He began by declaring that he himself had not been a *colegial mayor*, *manteista*, or *abogado*, that is in descending order the three groups professionally qualified for appointment. For him the quality of *hidalgo*, or noble, was the preferred criterion. He therefore proposed that the *colegiales* should have first place among candidates, 'for they are generally of the most noble birth, consume their property to support themselves in College, and excell in honour and integrity through their upbringing'. The *manteistas*, or non-collegiate students, should have second claim to appointments, 'for there are honourable hidalgos among them, not enough scholarships for everyone, and not enough family wealth to spend upon them'. In third place were the *abogados*, or lawyers, who also included hidalgos and honourable men among them, 'because they are so numerous that there must be some such', a curious way of admitting the existence of a few honourable *abogados*. 'All three classes ought to serve the good of the country, in which there are hierarchies and orders, and no one is bereft

---

[41] Rodríguez Villa, *Marqués de la Ensenada*, pp. 83–4, and 'Representación de 1751', ibid., pp. 115–17, 127–8.

[42] Keene to Bedford, 29 September 1749, BL, Add. MS 43, 423, f. 219.

of virtue and knowledge, although more common in those who inherit the one, and with it acquire the education to improve the other.'[43] The words of a conservative reformist.

A Navy for Peace or War

Ensenada was preoccupied with defence expenditure and sought to adjust it to resources available and international demands. He argued that Spanish foreign policy had to be geared to Spanish power; this was not sufficient to confront the army of France or the navy of Britain. These, however, were not likely to be allies against Spain, but rather each to seek Spain's alliance against the other: 'as Spain will then be seen to be moderately armed and with funds to sustain a war, she will be respected and no longer subject to the will of these two powers.'[44] Above all, Spain must not succumb to defeatism, but maintain its armed forces and avoid subordination.

To what extent was Ensenada responsible for new defence thinking? On the subject of the army he had little to offer. He aimed to increase its numbers to a strength of 100 battalions and 100 squadrons, unrealistically high for a country the size of Spain and not in fact achieved. In American defence strategy there was no sign of innovation. The victory of Cartagena in 1741, a combination of leadership, fortifications, good infantry, and inept English tactics, induced a complacency in Spanish military planning which was then prolonged by neutrality and peace with England. American revenue took precedence over expenditure on defence. The heroes of the last war were promoted to military administration and carried over the ideas of the past. The victor of Cartagena, Sebastián de Eslava, was an example; appointed captain general of Andalucía in 1749, he became a member of a series of committees used by Ensenada to plan American policy; his advocacy of a strategy of fixed fortifications of the kind that had worked at Cartagena became rigid doctrine at the expense of a basic reorganization of defence. A tiny colonial army, with small fixed battalions and inexperienced militia, reinforced in war time by Spanish troops, remained the norm, conceding

---

[43] 'Representación de 1751', Rodríguez Villa, *Marqués de la Ensenada*, pp. 110–20.

[44] 'Plano que se forma para fixar prudencialmente las obligaciones ordinarias de la Monarquía', 18 May 1752, ibid., pp. 95–6.

numerical superiority and failing to exploit the potential of creole recruitment.[45]

Ensenada concentrated his ideas and energy on the navy. In 1751 Spanish naval power consisted of 18 ships of the line and 15 lesser vessels, while England had 100 ships of the line and 180 smaller vessels. Ensenada argued that Spain needed 60 ships of the line and 65 frigates and other vessels. This of course could still not compete with the English navy, but in a defensive role it would be useful in the Atlantic and America, while in a Bourbon alliance it would be an asset to France, a threat to England, and for both reasons valuable to Spain. Whether this would make the Spanish king 'arbiter of peace and war' was another matter; in fact the argument was flawed and was shown to be so in 1762 and 1793. But the budget for the navy moved up in priority and Ensenada obtained the money it needed; in two years alone, 1752–3, 20 million pesos were spent on dockyards and shipbuilding.[46]

Ensenada inherited an infrastructure of shipbuilding from Patiño, but one which had deteriorated for want of resources. He rebuilt and extended shipbuilding capacity, particularly at Cadiz, Ferrol, and Cartagena, where he created three royal dockyards, an essential back-up for a new navy. Ferrol, designed by Cosme Alvarez on an excellent site strongly defended on its river approach from the sea, became Spain's chief dockyard, with two docks, storehouses and workshops, facilities for the construction, repair and maintenance of warships, a workforce of 6,000 men and 600 convicts, in short a major object of public investment.[47] Meanwhile Antonio de Ulloa activated Cartagena, and shipbuilding facilities at Cadiz were expanded in 1753. In America a new shipyard was established in Havana in 1723, with a numerous workforce, financial support from Mexico, and good quality timber from the Spanish Caribbean, though it depended on European supplies of cordage and rigging.[48]

Spain was only partly self-sufficient in timber and naval stores. The Spanish navy consumed some three million trees in the course of the

[45] Allan J. Kuethe, *Cuba, 1753-1815. Crown, Military, and Society* (Knoxville, Tenn., 1986), pp. 10–15.

[46] Keene to Holderness, 8 December 1753, BL, Add. MS 43, 431, f. 15 v. On the Spanish navy in the first half of the eighteenth century, including timber supplies, crews, and costs, see John Robert McNeill, *Atlantic Empires of France and Spain. Louisburg and Havana, 1700-1763* (Chapel Hill, NC, 1985), pp. 68–73.

[47] William Dalrymple, *Travels through Spain and Portugal in 1774* (London, 1777), pp. 102–3.

[48] Keene to Castres, 13 February 1750, *Private Correspondence of Sir Benjamin Keene*, p. 207; Keene to Bedford, 16 February 1750, BL, Add. MS 43, 424, f. 61 v.

eighteenth century and helped to destroy thousands of hectares of forests in the provinces of northern Spain. In the period 1700–50 the Spanish navy built some seventy ships and made only moderate demands on timber resources. In the years 1750–80 shipbuilding increased and there was greater pressure on supplies in Cantabria and Catalonia as well as Navarre. When these proved insufficient, and superior timber was needed for masts, Spain like other sea powers imported Baltic timber and to a lesser extent exploited its own American supplies of hard wood. As for naval stores, the peninsula was self-sufficient in pitch and tar, less so in hemp. Technology too had to be sought abroad. In the course of the eighteenth century the government developed a corps of naval constructors, raising their status above that of craftsmen. But Spain did not create an original naval architecture and tended to copy French designs with a bias towards large, fast ships. In 1750, on the initiative of Ensenada, a determined effort was made to recruit English designers and craftsmen and to imitate what was called 'la construcción inglesa', with its preference for strength and fire power.

The consulting engineer, Jorge Juan, recently returned from South America, was sent to England to study naval architecture, gather intelligence on the English arms industry, and hire masters and workers for the shipyards and workshops of Spain. He was also assigned many other tasks of industrial intelligence over the whole range of manufacturing and encouraged to acquire technology needed in Spain. Juan spent almost a year in England, in 1749–50, during which time he gathered material for his own treatise on naval architecture, recruited a large group of craftsmen and constructors, and despatched them more or less clandestinely to Spain along with books, training manuals and instruments. By mid-1750 three constructors, ten assistant constructors, numerous craftsmen, carpenters, riggers and interpreters, some sixty Englishmen in all, were at work in Ferrol, Cadiz, and Cartagena, helping to build Ensenada's navy.[49] Spanish labour was a bottleneck and had to be supplemented with agricultural labourers and impressed vagrants. Shipyards were well known for industrial strife and there were riots in the Ferrol dockyard in September 1754. Nevertheless, labour supply – and shipbuilding – reached its peak in the 1750s and managed to maintain itself until 1800. The quality of the products was disputed. The combination of English specialists and Spanish labour gave mixed results and there were heated arguments over the merits of English and French

---

[49] José Marino Navarro, *La Armada Española en el siglo XVIII* (Madrid, 1981), pp. 51–3.

models, rumours even that the cunning English had exported deliberate wreckers to sabotage the Spanish shipbuilding programme.[50] Meanwhile Antonio de Ulloa, colleague and collaborator of Jorge Juan, went to France on the pretext of studying mathematics but really to study the characteristics of the dockyards of Toulon, Lorient, Brest, and Rochfort, and all aspects of naval architecture. He too visited industrial centres and negotiated the transfer of technicians, artisans and specialists to Spain. Beginning in 1747, therefore, Ensenada assembled naval stores, timber, and technology. He also obtained an adequate budget. In the War of Succession England spent 40 per cent of total expenditure on the army and 35 per cent on the navy, France 57 per cent and 7 per cent respectively, though she increased naval expenditure during the rest of the century.[51] In 1753, at the peak of Ensenada's programme, Spain spent 20.4 per cent of total expenditure on the navy, a much higher figure than was normal in peace time; armed neutrality implied heavy naval costs.[52] What did Spain get for it?

At the end of the War of Jenkins' Ear Spain had only twelve ships of the line, many of them useless. Ensenada brought the Spanish navy up to forty-five ships of the line and nineteen frigates, and he was continuing the construction of a further thirty large vessels with material he had assembled in the dockyards. This was in 1754. In 1760 Spain had forty-seven ships of the line, thirty-five of them built between 1749 and 1756, and twenty-one frigates.[53] Total numbers increased to 122 in 1775, 167 in 1787, and 200 in 1795.[54] Ensenada, therefore, provided a solid base and beginning for Spanish naval power in the eighteenth century, improved the career prospects for officers, and recruited the seamen – 40,000 – without whom the navy could not grow. On his departure in 1754 well might the British ambassador heave a sigh of relief.

[50] Keene to Holderness, 27 August 1753, BL, Add. MS 43, 430, f. 68.

[51] P. G. M. Dickson, 'War Finance, 1689–1714', *The New Cambridge Modern History. Volume VI*, ed. J. S. Bromley (Cambridge, 1970), pp. 285, 299.

[52] Merino Navarro, *Armada Española en el siglo XVIII*, p. 168.

[53] Edward Clarke, *Letters concerning the Spanish Nation: Written at Madrid during the years 1760 and 1761* (London, 1763), pp. 219–22.

[54] Merino Navarro, *Armada Española en el siglo XVIII*, p. 151; on Ensenada's shipbuilding programme see also Ciriaco Pérez Bustamante, 'El reinado de Fernando VI en el reformismo español de siglo XVIII', *Revista de la Universidad de Madrid*, 3, 12 (1954), pp. 491–514, esp. pp. 506–8.

Portugal, Paraguay, and Political Change

The armed forces were the guardians of neutrality. The decade between the War of the Austrian Succession and the Seven Years War gave Spain the opportunity to reorganize and rearm, detached from the cold war between England and France. Relations with England were abnormally smooth during most of Ferdinand's reign, though areas of friction remained – logwood cutting in Honduras, fishing rights in Newfoundland, maritime clashes in the Caribbean, and always Gibraltar. Ensenada pressed hard for a basic change in commercial relations. Why should English goods entering Spain pay duties so much lower than Spanish goods entering England? Why did England claim the right of colonial monopoly for itself yet attempt to deny it to Spain? Why did the English always make the rules of the game? The new Spanish navy was intended to defend maritime routes and deter English incursions into Spain's colonial trade and territory. One of the growing points of penetration was the Río de la Plata, whence contraband trade could reach Upper Peru and siphon off silver. Here the enemy was undoubtedly England, but the English used outlets provided by their ally Portugal, particularly the enclave of Colônia do Sacramento on the eastern bank of the River Plate.

While Spain wanted to oust Portugal from Colônia, Portugal saw Ferdinand's accession and the influence of his Portuguese wife as an opportunity to advance its interests in America. Conflict thus gave way to discussion, and discussion to secret negotiations, conducted on the Spanish side by Carvajal. The result was a boundary treaty signed in Madrid on 13 January 1750.[55] Portugal surrendered Colônia and its claim to free navigation of the Río de la Plata. In exchange Spain ceded to Portugal two areas on the border of Brazil, one in Amazonia in the north, the other in the south comprising the *montaña* of Castillos Grandes up to the source of the River Ibicuí and between the east bank of the River Uruguay and the mouth of the Ibicuí. This was a controversial area for it contained seven of the thirty Guaraní missions of the Jesuits. The missionaries were ordered to leave immediately and resettle their Indians in Spanish territory; the Indians were allowed to take their personal belongings, but their villages, fields, houses, churches and other buildings became Portuguese property. This was a curious

---

[55] Guillermo Kratz, *El Tratado hispano-portugués de límites de 1750 y sus consecuencias* (Rome, 1954), pp. 23–4.

treaty for Spain to sign; in territorial terms alone it gave away too much; in human terms it was indefensible, perpetrating a great injustice on the Guaraní people. This was a prosperous and well populated region, whose seven missions housed about 30,000 Indians; in an instant they found themselves ruined and homeless. In addition, four other missions on the west bank of the Uruguay lost their communal *estancias* (landed estates), valued at 1 million pesos, for these were situated on the left bank ceded to Portugal. Carvajal was perfectly aware that this was a sensitive area; in the negotiations he had tried to save the missions for Spain, arguing that they were 'the garden of American catholicism'.[56] But Portugal insisted. Protests poured in from America, officials and churchmen alike protesting at the danger to the monarchy and the Indians. In the peninsula the treaty was severely criticized, Spaniards objecting that they lost territory, the Portuguese (seconded by their English allies) that they lost the trade of Colônia. The marquis of Pombal, in power from August 1750, while missing no opportunity to criticize the Jesuits, detested the treaty and did his best to destroy it, partly in Portugal's interests, partly in deference to the Anglo-Portuguese alliance. But the Spanish government wanted the Portuguese out of Colônia and this seemed the only way.

The Jesuit general ordered obedience and the order took steps to comply. The Paraguayan province, however, was outraged, appealed to the viceroy of Peru, wrote to Madrid, pointed to the loss of territory and souls, and pressed for a change of the boundary line. All in vain. Spain sent commissioners to execute the treaty, with threat of force against any resistance. But the debate continued. What was the moral authority of the treaty? Was it right to displace 30,000 innocent people, deprive them of their property, banish them hundreds of miles to a wilderness, their only compensation one peso each? Which had primary claim to obedience, Spanish law or moral law? There were many answers from the missionaries, some passionately critical of the treaty, others openly hostile to Spanish orders and their general's advice. A number of Jesuits wrote to Padre Rávago, declaring that as they understood it 'the expulsion and dispossession of the natives went against natural law'.[57] Letters containing hostile views were intercepted and circulated in Spain by enemies of the Jesuits, to be used as ammunition in the war of attrition now being waged against the order.

[56] Ibid., pp. 26–7.
[57] Ibid., p. 61.

Plate 3 *Marquis of La Ensenada*, by Jacopo Amiconi (reproduced by kind permission of the Museo del Prado, Madrid)

The Jesuits in Paraguay, in spite of their deep misgivings, collaborated with the authorities in applying the treaty, partly to avoid the scandal of rebellion, partly to preserve their charges from worse harm. But they could not prevent resistance by the Indians, already alienated from the Portuguese by bitter experience of slave hunters from Brazil. In 1754 Spanish and Portuguese expeditions were bloodily repulsed, but a further expedition overcame the Indians in February 1756: 1,311 were killed, 152 taken prisoner, and the rest fled to the jungle. This ended serious resistance. But the Guaraní war gave the Spanish authorities the opportunity to distort or fabricate evidence against the missionaries and eventually to incriminate the whole Jesuit order. It was a strange logic, for in practice it was the Portuguese who did most to subvert the Treaty of Madrid; they decided, on second thoughts, that they did not wish to hand over Colônia. In Naples Charles VII, the future Charles III of Spain, was also opposed to the treaty, not because it was unjust to Indians and Jesuits, but because it handed over to Portugal extensive territories valuable for Spanish trade. In due course he decided to annul the treaty, leaving everything as before. After eleven years of trouble it was brought to an end by both governments in the Treaty of Pardo (12 February 1761), which restored Jesuits and Indians to their ruined missions.

These events had political repercussions in Spain. Some believed, or wanted to believe, that the Jesuits were responsible for Indian resistance and that the day of reckoning for the order could not be long delayed. More immediately, the controversy over Paraguay imposed itself on political opinion in Madrid, polarizing positions between opponents and supporters of the treaty, between friends and enemies of the Society of Jesus, between Ensenada and his critics. The result was to destabilise the government, to isolate Carvajal still further and to associate Ensenada more closely with Rávago and the Jesuit cause. This was the background to the political crisis of 1754.

The death of Carvajal on 8 April 1754 at the age of fifty-three brought the crisis to a head. The members of his faction did not regroup around Ensenada, whom they had never trusted, but joined the ranks of the opposition. The object was to remove Ensenada; this was essential, for he was now left in a position of unrivalled power in which he could virtually monopolize patronage and impose his own view on policy, provoking a war with England whenever he wished. Ensenada, therefore, had two interests working against him, his political rivals and the English. The two came together when the duke of Huéscar, categorized by Keene as a good friend of England, was appointed temporary secretary of state.[58] At this point there was an open struggle for power between the rival factions, and Huéscar suffered from not having an alternative to Ensenada. Encouraged by the English ambassador,

---

[58] Keene to Castres, 12 April 1754, *Private Correspondence of Sir Benjamin Keene*, p. 360.

Huéscar and his associate, the count of Valparaiso, moved so quickly that already by 15 May they had persuaded the king to appoint the anglophile Ricardo Wall as secretary of state. Wall was of Irish descent, born in France in 1694; after a successful military and diplomatic career for Spain he had been appointed ambassador to England in 1748. He was a jovial extrovert, politically lightweight, but vehemently anti-Jesuit and supposedly anti-French; he therefore had the appropriate ideas to bring him to power in the conjuncture of 1754.[59] Once Wall returned to Madrid from London, everything was in place.

On 14 July Huéscar and Wall had an audience with the king and queen and, having presented their version of the resistance of the Jesuits in Paraguay and the complicity of Rávago, they were authorized to prepare a plan of action. This they now focused on Ensenada; they cited an order (a copy of which was supplied by Keene) sent by the minister to the governor of Havana to attack the British settlement in Honduras Bay, thus risking war in America while in Europe the Spanish government was talking peace; if, they argued, the king wished to control policy, maintain peace and resist France, he would have to dismiss Ensenada, who was in a position to thwart Wall and frustrate these aims.[60] The king was convinced and authorized Ensenada's arrest and dismissal. In the early hours of 21 July Ensenada's house was surrounded by troops. A group of officials and guards entered, aroused him, presented the king's orders, put him under guard in a coach, and sent him to Granada. There he had to present himself daily to the president of the chancery court. An inventory of his possessions was ordered and revealed what a leading minister could expect to accumulate in Spain: abundance of gold, diamond and silver objects, including a complete gold dinner service worth 40,000 pesos; an extensive wardrobe of luxury clothes, including numerous uniforms, suits, and 200 shirts; extensive crockery and cutlery; a major collection of pictures; six coaches and enough provisions to open a store.[61] A torrent of abuse, satires and slanders followed him into exile, but the monarchs wanted no recriminations and they resisted any suggestion of a trial. In any case, what could a trial prove?

[59] 'Don Ricardo Wall es un enemigo terrible de la Compañía de Jesús, sea por sus fines particulares o por sus antiguous prejuicios que provienen de su educación, y sin escuchar razones, desearía, si pudiese, expulsar a los jesuítas de España.' Spinola (papal nuncio) to Torrigiani, Madrid, 26 March 1759, quoted by C. Pérez Bustamante, *Correspondencia reservada e inédita del P. Francisco de Rávago, confesor de Fernando VI* (Madrid, 1943), p. 205.

[60] Keene to Robinson, 31 July 1754, BL, Add. MS 43, 432, ff. 205-20.

[61] Rodríguez Villa, *Marqués de la Ensenada*, pp. 194-5, 215-55.

There was much speculation regarding Ensenada's removal and the government allowed informal charges to circulate:

There has been no particular justification of this transaction to the public ... but what is said abroad is that Ensenada has been banished for his maladministration of all the branches committed to his charge; squandered away the public money, without any visible good to the nation and without account; and that he has dared to meddle and intrude himself into foreign negotiations, out of his own head, without the least authority of his Master.[62]

The means he adopted to prevent what he regarded as damaging to Spanish interests were thus turned against him. They may be summarized as follows: (1) He reported the secret negotiations surrounding the treaty of Madrid to the king of the Two Sicilies, the future Charles III, whose known opposition then helped to kill the treaty; (2) On his own initiative he sent instructions to the governor of Havana to take military action to evict the English logwood cutters in the Bay of Honduras;[63] (3) He opposed the anglophile party, placing himself among the pro-French faction and identifying himself with the Jesuit position in Paraguay.[64] None of these actions were stupid or dishonourable; they simply represented one side of a political conflict. Ensenada was the victim of a power struggle.

Who were the authors of the coup? They were led by the duke of Huéscar, soon to be the duke of Alba, a malicious man who hated Ensenada and Jesuits and who, it was said, would betray his own mother to further his ambitions, though, apart from an aristocratic desire to influence the monarch, these remained obscure. He was followed by the duke of Valparaiso, a nonentity with ministerial aspirations. Wall was the necessary politician, promoted to lead a new government and provide an alternative model to Ensenada. Were these the front edge of a particular opposition, representatives of an aristocratic and traditionalist minority, the so-called Spanish party? The evidence is not conclusive. Such a hypothesis omits the key role of the English ambassador, who manipulated the Spanish conspirators and worked exclusively for English interests, to counter the French bias of Ensenada, put a stop to

---

[62] Keene to Robinson, 21 September 1754, BL, Add. MS 43, 433, f. 24.
[63] Pares, *War and Trade in the West Indies*, pp. 546–50.
[64] Gómez Molleda, 'El marqués de la Ensenada', pp. 48–90.

his naval programme, and thwart his defence measures in America.[65] On Spain Benjamin Keene was the most expert Englishman of his day, not infallible in his judgements but a skilful agent in a country which he perceptively described as 'a political country'. Long residence in the peninsula, vast experience of political and commercial reporting, fluency in the language, and an easy familiarity with Spaniards, made him virtually irreplaceable, destined to end his days in his embassy. His portly figure was well known in Madrid and the royal palaces, where he was regarded as a formidable defender of British interests, a diplomat whose secret service money could open many doors in the Spanish bureaucracy and which enabled him to produce at the crucial time the evidence – Ensenada's instructions to the governor of Havana – which the conspirators needed to convince the king.[66]

Wall reported to Keene as soon as the decision was taken to activate the coup: 'The thing is done, my Dear Keene, by the grace of God, the King, Queen and my Brave Duke, and wen you will read this scrape, the mogol will bee five or six leagues of going to Granad. This news will not displease our friends in Ingland. Yours, Dear Keene, forever, Dik. At twelve oclok Saturday night.'[67] Keene rejoiced that

> an end has happily been put to the Ministry of a vain, weak, but rash man ... The King our Royal Master will have the satisfaction to find that the opposer of the public tranquility, the friend to France, the enemy to England and to his own country, has been destroyed by the same measures which he had employed to bring about his wicked intentions.[68]

He was especially satisfied that Ensenada's naval programme, directed solely against England, would be brought to an end and that further expansion would be halted by financial constraints.[69] The coup was regarded as a great personal triumph for Keene; he was awarded the red

[65] William Coxe, *Memoirs of the Kings of Spain of the House of Bourbon* (2nd edn, 5 vols, London, 1815), IV, pp. 66, 127–32, 213.

[66] See the dispatch cited in note 60. 'He had great wit, agreeableness, and an indolent good humour that was very pleasing', remarked Horace Walpole, *The Letters of Horace Walpole. Vol. IV: 1756-1760* (Oxford, 1903), p. 118.

[67] Wall to Keene, 20 July 1754, *Private Correspondence of Sir Benjamin Keene*, p. 38.

[68] Keene to Robinson, 31 July 1754, BL, Add. MS 43, 432, f. 215.

[69] Coxe, *Memoirs of the Kings of Spain*, IV, p. 146.

ribbon of the Order of the Bath by George II and was invested with it by Ferdinand VI, whose minister he had induced him to dismiss.[70]

Ensenada thus lost the struggle for power. But whereas in 1746 he had assembled his administration to carry forward a new reform programme, his successors gave no such message; their first concern was to place their own men. Ensenada's team, therefore, was dismantled; most of his right hand men in the *secretarías* were dismissed, as were other clients whom he had protected, such as Jorge Juan and Antonio de Ulloa.[71] The fall of Padre Rávago completed the purge. This was normal patronage politics, though many of his clients showed an exceptional loyalty to him during his melancholy exile in Granada. They had to defend him against a barrage of scurrility alleging womanizing, cultivation of court favourites, use of patronage and money to foment faction, the provision of extravagant amusements to flatter the monarchs, the waste of vast sums on the *catastro* and on grants for foreign study, but above all a love of novelty and change.[72] His friends refuted these charges and pointed to his policy on behalf of the national interest, especially in America; if the English embassy spent money suborning his officials and destabilizing his position, that simply confirmed his Spanish credentials. They cited too his great projects of public works, the Guadarrama highway, the road to Santander, six leagues of the canal of Castile, and the dockyards of Ferrol and Cartagena.

The contemporary debate over Ensenada's achievements is echoed in modern historiography. Did he think too little and talk too much? Were his projects realistic, his reports and representations blueprints for action? Or were they theoretical schemes beyond the scope of the Spanish state? There is a suspicion that Ensenada promised more than he fulfilled. If that is true, it is because many of his policies sought long-term change and were cut short by his opponents. His fall brought to an end the career of a true reformer, who initiated specific projects, completed some, abandoned others, and left a few to his successors. If the year 1746 is a landmark in Spanish history, it was Ensenada who made it so.[73]

[70] Keene to Castres, 30 August 1754, *Private Correspondence of Sir Benjamin Keene*, pp. 376–7.

[71] Vicente Rodríguez Casado, *La política y los políticos en el reinado de Carlos III* (Madrid, 1962), p. 61.

[72] Rodríguez Villa, *Marqués de la Ensenada*, pp. 255–62.

[73] Ensenada was brought out of exile by Charles III in 1760, but his political ambitions were finally ended when his name was associated with the *motín de Esquillache* in 1766, and he was banished again, to Medina del Campo, where he died in 1781. Ibid., pp. 286–7.

Church and State

The controversy over Paraguay and the crisis of 1754 were indicators of the passions stirred by clerical politics and the high level of state interest in the Church, an interest not so much in its welfare or personnel as in its power, independence and wealth. The Spanish crown had certain prerogatives over the Church and wanted more; this was usually presented as a defence of its rights and a remedy of grievances. The defence of the *regalías* meant the defence of the rights of the crown in ecclesiastical affairs at the expense of papal jurisdiction; the most important *regalía* was the *patronato real*, the right to present to bishoprics and major benefices. The *real patronato universal* was the highest expression of patronage, namely the right of presentation to all ecclesiastical benefices, great and small, in all the dominions of the Spanish crown. The campaign for the maximum claim began in the reign of Philip V and was brought to a conclusion by the government of Ferdinand VI. In 1746 this government had two basic objects: first, to prevent any intervention by Rome in the dominions of the Spanish crown; second, to bring the Spanish hierarchy under its control and thus complete the concentration of power in the Bourbon state, conscious that the Church was not only a rich and powerful institution but also a privileged corporation whose members enjoyed clerical immunity.

Ensenada adopted an extreme regalist position from the first years of his administration, convinced that the concordat of 1737 was worthless and urging that the time had come for a final settlement of the *patronato* issue with Rome, for this was a matter of 'religion, clerical discipline, the power of the king, the welfare of his subjects and of the royal treasury'.[74] No less regalist was the Jesuit confessor Padre Rávago, who supported the government in its claim to a universal patronage and handled the actual preparation of a new concordat. The Spanish government negotiated skilfully in Rome, counting on the cooperation of a pope, Benedict XIV, who believed in conciliation and political realism. The discussions focused on Spanish grievances against the Roman curia, which made large profits out of Spain from papal bulls, dispensations, vacant benefices, and other charges, while matrimonial dispensations alone earned a small fortune.[75] These arguments satisfied the pope, but

[74] Ibid., pp. 77–83.
[75] Rafael Olaechea, *Las relaciones hispano-romanas en la segunda mitad del siglo XVIII. La Agencia de Preces* (2 vols, Zaragoza, 1965), I, p. 76.

the cardinals needed other reasons. To compensate the curia for what it would lose in church appointments, a sum of 1.3 million pesos was agreed; together with individual gifts for pope and cardinals the Spanish government delivered to Rome in 1753 some 2.5 million pesos.[76] The money was thought to be well spent.

The concordat of 11 January 1753 conceded to the Spanish crown the right of *patronato universal*, which extended the right of presentation from that of bishops and certain other higher clerics to all canons, prebends, and benefices, except fifty-two which were reserved to the pope. This was an extraordinary increase of power for the crown and a decisive step in the subsequent bureaucratization of the Spanish Church. The state did not yet pay the salaries of clerics but it appointed them and therefore indirectly controlled their incomes, and it had in addition a new revenue from vacant benefices. The concordat of 1753 gave the Spanish crown great control over the episcopate and over the majority of the secular clergy. Ensenada, Rávago and their colleagues considered it a triumph, though in practice it did not greatly change the character of the Spanish Church. Spain was still dependent on Rome for matrimonial dispensations and other spiritual services, and still dependent on the pope for the actual making of a bishop, which left some room for conflict.

The Spanish Church was in broad agreement with the aims and results of the concordat of 1753. On other issues of the time it was divided and embroiled in the political factionalism of the age. At the working centre of Church-state relations was the royal confessor, an office monopolized from 1700 to 1755 by Jesuits, many of them French and most of them regalists; the last in this series was Padre Francisco Rávago, whose appointment in March 1747 was hailed as a victory for Spanish interests. The duties of the royal confessor were not confined to hearing the king's confession, and in the mid-eighteenth century this was probably the least of his tasks. He was not, of course, a minister, but he was part of the administration, for in practice, he exercised the function of minister of ecclesiastical affairs; he also accumulated a number of other informal offices, making him a combination of priest, theologian, political agent, ecclesiastical administrator, and adviser. Perhaps the most crucial advice he had to give concerned the selection of candidates for bishoprics and other clerical appointments, to which the king simply added his *visto bueno* or assent. This was at once a source of power and of unpopularity,

[76] Pérez Bustamante, *Correspondencia reservada e inédita del P. Francisco de Rávago*, p. 189.

for in each appointment there was only one satisfied candidate and dozens of disappointed ones, potential critics of the royal confessor and of his colleagues. Rávago's obvious delight in exercising royal power, allied to a forceful personality, provoked latent resentment against the Jesuit order which would surface a decade later. As he himself admitted, 'the royal confessional has lost us a lot of good friends and gained us false ones.'[77]

The Rávago regime was a turbulent one marked by a series of conflicts with other orders over rights and jurisdiction, with friars and priests over the opening of a Jesuit college in Vitoria, with the Dominicans over his support for the beatification of Ramon Lull, with the Augustinians over his vandalizing of a book from their library at the Escorial, and with large sections of clerical opinion over his opposition to the beatification of Juan de Palafox, an anti-Jesuit bishop of Puebla a century earlier. Most of these conflicts, trivial in themselves and hardly concerned with faith and morals, were touchstones of factional positions in Church and state, and signified a struggle for power between different orders and groups, a struggle in which Rávago appeared to use his government authority in the interests of his own religious order. Meanwhile he was not making allies in Rome. Rávago took an anti-papal stance on many doctrinal and jurisdictional issues of the time, defending the rights of the royal *patronato*, and promoting the concordat of 1753; he was convinced that the papacy was the weak link in the fight against Jansenism and risked alienating the entire Hispanic world, 'more than half the Catholic Church', while regalism was the last defence of orthodoxy.[78] He clashed repeatedly with Benedict XIV over the Augustinian theologian Enrico Noris, defended by the papacy as orthodox, denounced by the Jesuits as Jansenist. The retreat into regalism against Rome was a dangerous position for the Jesuits, for regalism could be used to attack as well as protect them, and then they would look in vain to the papacy.

The ecclesiastical policy of the second government of Ferdinand VI contained a number of distinct warnings to the Jesuits.[79] The first was the official reaction to events following the Treaty of Madrid which held the order responsible for what was called 'the Jesuit war'. The second was the introduction of the cause of Palafox, a cause which the Jesuits

---

[77] Rávago to Céspedes, 2 December 1755, in Kratz, *El Tratado hispano-portugués de límites de 1750*, p. 135, n. 34.

[78] Rávago to Portocarrero, 27 July 1750, in Pérez Bustamante, *Correspondencia reservada e inédita del P. Francisco de Rávago*, p. 260.

[79] Olaechea, 'Política eclesiástica del gobierno de Fernando VI', pp. 205–6.

rightly regarded as hopeless but which became a test of political and religious attitudes. The third was the rehabilitation of Noris and the removal of his works from the Spanish index in 1758, a measure designed as a rebuff to the Jesuits rather than a concession to the papacy. In Church, as well as in state, the years 1746–59 were a time of tension between continuity and change.

End of an Age

The first administration of Ferdinand VI fell apart in April–July 1754 with the death of Carvajal and the dismissal of Ensenada. Their successors were the authors of the coup. Huéscar did not have a permanent ministry but he was at first the *éminence grise* of the regime with bold action to his credit and effective access to the king; this did not last, however, and he subsequently adopted an olympian detachment from politics. Not so his colleagues. Ricardo Wall became secretary of state after Carvajal and on the fall of Ensenada he also acquired some policy control over American affairs. The count of Valparaiso, unqualified though he was, became minister of finance.

There was inevitably some continuity of personnel between the two administrations. The new minister of war was Sebastián de Eslava, a soldier of the old school, former viceroy of New Granada and defender of Cartagena in 1741; returning to Spain he was appointed by Ensenada to an office in the marine department, and now brought to the war ministry outmoded ideas on defence which clashed with the military reformism of the count of Aranda. In 1756–7 he rose to prominence as an active leader of the pro-French party, and in Keene's opinion perpetuated Ensenadism.[80] Disappointed in Huéscar and Eslava, the English ambassador also had his doubts about the new minister of marine and the Indies, Julián de Arriaga, a former governor of Caracas and president of the council of the Indies.[81] Arriaga was another protégé of Ensenada and friend of Rávago:

> As Arriaga has received advancement from Ensenada, I made some objections to him, when the plan was settling for the new Ministry, before Ensenada's fall, but I was answered that what he Arriaga did

[80] *Private Correspondence of Sir Benjamin Keene*, pp. 238, 489–90, 514.
[81] Gildas Bernard, *Le Secrétariat d'État et le Conseil Espagnol des Indes (1700-1808)* (Geneva, 1972), p. 51.

under Ensenada was *contre coeur*; and that if he did not do right for the future, it would be easy to remove him ... [Arriaga] has this good in him, that he is for quashing all corsarios's commissions, and employing King's ships in their stead; and has this bad, that he is a countryman of Father Ravago and is too much inclined to be governed by the Company.[82]

In short, four persons were required to fill the ministerial vacancies left by Ensenada, and the concentration of offices in a single minister came to an end, evidence perhaps of the mediocrity of the candidates, or the fear of autocracy, or the growth of specialization. Whatever the explanation, by the end of August 1754 the second government of Ferdinand VI was in place, but still incomplete. There remained a decision to make concerning an office in which continuity was not countenanced, that of royal confessor.

Rávago was linked with Ensenada; both thought alike on policy issues, not least on the Treaty of Madrid and events in Paraguay, prompting Benedict XIV to remark, 'This Jesuit and the marquis of Ensenada were almost the same person, and it is not surprising that the fall of one has caused that of the other.'[83] In addition Rávago had acquired enemies of his own in Church and state, ready to exploit his isolation once the *equipo ensenadista* had disintegrated. According to the rules of faction and the practices of patronage he had to go. For a year he clung to office, impervious to the political campaign at court and on the streets demanding the removal not only of the confessor but also of the governor of the council of Castile, Diego de Rojas, bishop of Cartagena, and that of José de Muñiz, secretary of grace and justice, both *colegiales mayores* and active in promoting their own network. At last, on 30 September 1755, ostensibly at his own request, Ferdinand VI relieved Rávago of office, though allowing him still his income and access to the monarchs. 'The Ensenadists have lost their hopes and their protector', reported Keene.[84] The Jesuits, too, felt his loss. He remained at court and, to the great irritation of government, continued to press for a more moderate application of the Treaty of Madrid. This was a controversial issue which, having helped to undermine his own position, now made

[82] Keene to Robinson, 21 September 1754, BL, Add. MS 43, 433, f. 29.
[83] Quoted by Pérez Bustamante, *Correspondencia reservada e inédita del P. Francisco de Rávago*, p. 195.
[84] Keene to Robinson, Escorial, 15 October 1755, BL, Add. MS 43, 436, f. 38; Coxe, *Memoirs of the Kings of Spain*, IV, pp. 163–4.

him a focus of opposition to the new administration. As Wall complained, 'Padre Rávago, the *colegiales mayores* and *ensenadistas* have come together, and all three do and say what they like with impunity, for in the whole ministry there is no one sufficiently ruthless to do what is sometimes politically necessary, teach the enemy a lesson.'[85] Eventually, in 1757, Rávago left court and retired to Zamora, to the great relief of the government. The new confessor was Monsignor Manuel Quintano Bonifaz, recently appointed inquisitor general, a churchman equally regalist but expected to bring an end to Jesuit influence at court.

The defeat of Ensenada was a victory for those who resented the accumulation of power by a single minister and who were themselves ambitious for office. But it was not pure factionalism: important policy issues were at stake, as the intervention of the English ambassador made clear. The new ministry was less distinguished than its predecessor and was hardly a powerhouse of ideas. But it knew what it wanted to stop. The project of a single tax, already faltering, was killed off; the *giro* too was set aside and the attempt to make an entrepreneur out of the state discontinued. In the Indies trade traditional interests were encouraged to raise their heads. The abolition of register ships, the major innovation of the 1740s, was seriously debated and the idea of restoring the discredited *galeones* and *flotas* revived; the *flotas* to New Spain in fact were restored and the monopolists enjoyed an Indian summer of official favour.[86] Finally, the navy programme and its budget were cut back, and it was decided to build no new ships.

Did this amount to a political programme representing a particular interest? Did it signify the revival of the old 'Spanish' party? There was some evidence of traditionalist thinking on government and a desire to restore the power of the councils against new ministries, especially that of the council of the Indies and even the council of state, ideas favoured by Huéscar and typical of the older aristocracy.[87] Was this an attempt to revive the power of the grandees? In the event, the ideas were too nebulous and their authors too diffident to be classified as a movement bidding for power. There was little sign of group identity in the new government, aristocratic or otherwise. Indeed there was little energy, and friends and supporters were soon disillusioned with its negative performance. Individual members lacked confidence in themselves and

[85] Wall to Portocarrero, 7 May 1756, in Pérez Bustamante, *Correspondencia reservada e inédita del P. Francisco de Rávago*, p. 324.

[86] Keene to Robinson, 9 October 1754, BL, Add. MS 43, 433, ff. 61–2; see above, p. 000.

[87] Keene to Robinson, 17 May 1754, 31 July 1754, BL, Add. MS 43, 432, f. 50, f. 220–1.

in each other; Wall was disgusted at Huéscar's indolence and Valparaiso's opportunism; they all fell short of Keene's expectations. This was a government deficient in leadership, enthusiasm and unity, while in the background the queen counselled caution and the king sank deeper in melancholy.[88] The age of ideas appeared to be at an end.

The foreign policy of the second government was incoherent and threatened the neutrality so carefully cultivated by the first. Anglo-Spanish relations deteriorated amidst mutual recrimination over conflicts in Central America and at sea, while France sought to capitalize by pressing Spain for support. Wall was soon disillusioned with the English and his attitude became one of pained benevolence: he wanted to be friends but Britain would not let him, and so he risked losing credibility at home, especially as he was foreign by birth.[89] In 1756–7, following the outbreak of war between England and France, Keene was hard put to achieve his prime objective and keep Spain neutral. But even neutrality had its problems, involving the rights of neutral shipping and their violation by English warships and privateers. These disputes brought Spain to the brink of war with Britain. Wall's anglophile reputation caused him to draw back from his former friends to preserve his credibility. Arriaga persisted in pressing colonial grievances, especially the activities of British logwood cutters in the Bay of Honduras and the return of settlers after their eviction in 1754. But the most venomously anti-British minister was Eslava, the 'old dotard' as Keene called him, in whom 'the spirit of Ensenadism' seemed to revive.[90] Eslava clamoured for war in alliance with France and at one moment seemed to have gained the support of the queen. Spain became more exacting as early setbacks, especially the loss of Minorca in 1756, reduced Britain's bargaining position. But she resisted the temptation to join France and regain Minorca and Gibraltar in favour of further neutrality, lacking confidence in her power and fearing for her independence. What naval strength Spain still possessed – seen in the ability to send twelve warships to the Indies in 1755 to defend her interests as a neutral – she owed to Ensenada.[91]

The performance of the government did not go unchallenged. There were still many who hoped for a return to Ensenada. The *partido*

---

[88] Keene to Robinson, 7 April 1755, BL, Add. MS 43, 434, f. 90.
[89] Coxe, *Memoirs of the Kings of Spain*, IV, pp. 201–2; Pares, *War and Trade in the West Indies*, pp. 550–5.
[90] Keene to Pitt, 21 April, 1757, BL, Add. MS 43, 439, f. 311.
[91] Keene to Castres, 22 May 1755, *Private Correspondence of Sir Benjamin Keene*, p. 407.

ensenadista consisted not only of adherents of the former minister but also of other factions and interests who now came together in a common purpose.[92] These included the *colegiales mayores*, the supporters of Rávago, and the wider pro-Jesuit group, all of whom would expect to benefit from a return of their patron. Support for Ensenada existed in many regions, institutions and social sectors, not excluding the nobility and the Church. It was even to be found in ministries and councils among those who survived his fall, thanks perhaps to the backlash against Britain when the details of the coup became known. Many of the *ensenadistas* were friends of the Jesuit publicist Padre Isla who kept in touch with the various networks and was the link between all three groups, *ensenadistas*, Jesuits and *colegiales*. In a system of clientage the fall of a strong and active politician like Ensenada inevitably had a ripple effect throughout the administration, and those ousted would form a reserve of opposition working or waiting for the return of better days. There was also much residual support for the reformist ideas of Ensenada which kept them alive beyond the negative interlude of 1754–9 and passed them on to a later generation.

Government and opposition alike concentrated their attention on the monarchy, which suddenly collapsed and plunged Spain into a year-long crisis. The queen died on 27 August 1758, mourned by some, villified by others and, when her will became known, deplored by all; having accumulated in Spain a fortune far in excess of her own needs, she now sent it all to Portugal to her brother and heir, Dom Pedro. The death of Queen Barbara affected the king in a different way, destroying what little sanity he retained, sending him into a permanent state of mourning and driving him to seek seclusion in the castle of Villaviciosa de Odón; there he remained month after month wandering wildly around his apartments and refusing to be washed, shaved, dressed, or fed, a danger to himself and others, and a blight on government.[93] Without the king's signature to documents, there could be no authority, no policy, no decrees, no appointments and often no pay. The disadvantages of absolutism were never more obvious. The government machine came to a stop and there it remained until Ferdinand's death on 10 August 1759 in his forty-seventh year set it in motion again. Then the succession

[92] See Olaechea, 'Política eclesiástica del gobierno de Fernando VI', pp. 194–205, who identifies this party.
[93] Bristol to Pitt, 25 September, 23 October, 13 November, 20 November, 1758, Public Record Office, London, SP 95/158.

could proceed and the country look to Charles III for relief, believing that he would make what Padre Isla called a 'happy revolution'.

Ferdinand VI occupies a special place in the history of the Spanish Bourbons. For the first time since 1700 many of the essential conditions of change appeared to be present – a compliant monarch, ministerial leadership, international peace, and a booming revenue. A strong current of reform ran through the reign, driven by the state, inspired by new ideas, and fed by rising resources. Inevitably it met a wall of resistance from vested interests, but enough impetus survived to carry it into the next reign and to form an integral part of Bourbon reformism. The reign of Ferdinand VI also contained a striking paradox: a government dedicated to the promotion of national power fell victim to a flagrant exercise in destabilization carried out by a foreign interest. There were lessons still to be learned.

6

Economy and Society

People and Prospects

There were three million more people in Spain at the end of the eighteenth century than there had been at the beginning. Population growth was continuous though not spectacular, moving upwards from 7.6 million in 1717 to 9.3 million in 1768, 10.4 million in 1787 and 10.5 million in 1797, a growth of 40 per cent, smaller than that of England, greater than that of France.[1] The rate of growth was higher in the first half of the century than the second, but there were regional variations. In northern Spain demographic growth began early, developed strongly, and slowed slightly from mid-century. In southern Spain growth was slower, but perhaps more regular, and again superior in the first half of the century; Andalucía grew by 25 per cent in 1717–52, 16 per cent in 1752–97.[2] In eastern Spain growth began later but maintained a long upward trend in Valencia and Murcia, and only in Catalonia was it checked at the end of the century.[3] By 1800 most regions of Spain had experienced a significant increase. The population of Catalonia, Valencia, and Aragon doubled in the course of the century, that of

[1] Jordi Nadal, *La población española (siglos XVI a XX)* (Barcelona, 1973), pp. 84–96, who speaks of 'el cambio de rumbo demográfico'; Francisco Bustelo, 'Algunas reflexiones sobre la población española de principios del siglo XVIII', *Anales de Economía*, 151 (1972), pp. 89–106, and 'La población española en la segunda mitad del siglo XVIII', *Moneda y Crédito*, 123 (1972), pp. 53–104. On the economy in an earlier period see above, pp. 116–23.

[2] Antonio García-Baquero González, 'Andalucía en el siglo XVIII: el perfil de un crecimiento ambiguo', in Roberto Fernández (ed.), *España en el siglo XVIII. Homenaje a Pierre Vilar* (Barcelona, 1985), p. 351.

[3] Carlos Martínez Shaw, 'La Cataluña del siglo XVIII bajo el signo de la expansión', *España en el siglo XVIII*, pp. 68–70.

Murcia tripled; Galicia increased by 36 per cent, Castile by 30 per cent, Andalucía by over 40 per cent. The pattern of population density was also changing. In contrast to the sixteenth century, the periphery experienced greater growth than the centre; and within the periphery people multiplied in the coastal zones more than in the interior, reflecting the trends of economic growth in the eighteenth century. One thing remained constant: Spain was still a rural rather than an urban society. Towards the end of the century the rural classes (farmers and labourers) comprised about 56 per cent of the active population. Only the populations of Madrid and Barcelona exceeded 100,000 inhabitants; and towns contained no more than 10 per cent of the total population of Castile.

How can we explain the population growth of the eighteenth century? Why did the population not grow more strongly than it did? What was the relative importance of economic conditions and demographic factors? In the eighteenth century, and indeed well into the nineteenth century, life expectancy in Spain did not exceed twenty-seven years; it hovered just above the level necessary if life were to continue.[4] While the birth rate was high, at forty-two per cent per 1,000, mortality rates also remained high, at 38 per cent. Infant mortality, at 25 per cent, actually worsened slightly in the second half of the century and was aggravated by the increased number of foundlings and the persistence of infanticide, features of depression rather than boom. Epidemic diseases exacted their toll, especially on the poorer sectors who were more at risk through malnutrition and immobility; smallpox, yellow fever and cholera were the leading killers, followed closely by typhus, diptheria, malaria, and tuberculosis. Spain underwent six general mortality crises in this century, in 1706–10, 1730, 1741–2, 1762–5, 1780–2, 1786–7, and another in 1804, during which agrarian crisis and epidemic disease reinforced each other to push up the death rate. The increase of population beyond resources produced two general crises – 1762–5 and 1798–9 – which were the direct result of food shortages and not of epidemic disease. But the most frequent crises were those in which hunger combined with disease to create situations of catastrophic mortality, such as in 1786–7 and 1803–5. The state offered little protection. New grain and food policies might alleviate the worst effects of crop failures,

---

[4] Vicente Pérez Moreda, *Las crisis de mortalidad en la España interior. Siglos XVI-XIX* (Madrid, 1980), pp. 453–4. There were regional differences; Galicia had greater life expectancy than Castile; see Pegerto Saavedra and Ramón Villares, 'Galicia en el antiguo régimen: la fortaleza de una sociedad tradicional', *España en el siglo XVIII*, pp. 449–50.

but they did not solve the basic problems of agricultural productivity. Preventive medicine was hardly known in Spain. Smallpox innoculation arrived late and reached only a minority; measures to control malaria, purify the water supply, and improve urban conditions had to await the nineteenth century; standards of medical training and practice were dismally low; and hospitals were places for death not for cure.

Catastrophic mortality, destructive when it occurred, played a relatively minor role in determining long-term demographic trends; these were set by ordinary mortality levels which were sufficient to restrain growth but not to prevent it.[5] If mortality did not halt demographic advance, nor did emigration, though in some regions it acted as a safety valve; in Galicia relatively low mortality was countered by high emigration – perhaps 350,000 between 1749 and 1797 – and this in turn was linked to an agrarian structure which could not support population growth.[6] Positive reasons for growth must be shared between demographic and economic factors. Earlier marriage and a higher birth rate were important determinants, but the basic preconditions were to be found in economic growth and especially agricultural expansion, which at once permitted population growth and responded to it.

Population growth was a new influence in Spanish economic and social life.[7] In the first place, there were more mouths to be fed, more people to be clothed, more families to be housed. There was greater demand for products and more labour for work. Demand for agricultural products sent up prices, especially in the second half of the century, and this favoured the producer; times were never better for landowners, the nobility and the clergy. Secondly, the growth of the rural population caused a greater demand for land and a rise in its price. Rents were increased as new leases were imposed on tenant farmers; in much of central Spain landlords had the right to raise rents if the tenant made improvements and increased production. Thirdly, the demand for manufactured goods rose and provided a new incentive for Spanish industry in the decades after 1750. These developments were not necessarily beneficial to the majority of Spaniards. It did not follow that more workers would mean more employment, or that agricultural expansion would increase domestic consumption, granted the inferior purchasing power of the mass of the people and the great inequalities in land and

---

[5] Pérez Moreda, *Las crisis de mortalidad*, p. 472.

[6] Saavedra and Villares, 'Galicia en el antiguo régimen', *España en el siglo XVIII*, p. 451.

[7] Gonzalo Anes, *Las crisis agrarias en la España moderna* (Madrid, 1970), pp. 129, 147–98, and 'La Asturias preindustrial', *España en el siglo XVIII*, p. 508–9.

income distribution. And if rising demand was met by a series of bad harvests, then disaster could follow.

Rural Spain

The greater part of productive land in Spain – more than 60 per cent in Castile – was concentrated in the hands of two privileged groups, the nobility and the clergy, locked in rigid entail and mortmain, and worked by peasants who were either tenants without security or labourers without land.[8] But rural Spain was a varied world. Conditions deteriorated progressively from north to south as the numbers of *jornaleros* increased. In northern Spain *jornaleros*, or day labourers, constituted less than 25 per cent of the active rural population; in the centre, 25–30 per cent; in the south, between 50 and 70 per cent, rising to 75 per cent in Seville, Córdoba, and Jaén. In most parts the land had to be forced into fertility against hostile climate and topography, and farming was a gamble between flood and drought.

Galicia, a province of minute plots endlessly subdivided, struggled with the dilemma of poor agriculture and a growing population, 90 per cent of whom lived in the agrarian sector. Land was monopolized by the Church – mainly monastic orders – and the nobility, and was cultivated by a mass of small producers devoid of commercial objectives; here there were no medium farmers, few *jornaleros*, and the average holdings were between 1.5 and 3 hectares.[9] Peasants held land under hereditary leases, or *foros*, binding for three generations. At the end of the lease lands returned to the owner with all improvements, and he was free to lease them anew at a higher rent. In this way the owners were able to increase their income from land in line with inflation, while peasants were subject to ever rising rents, many of them paid in kind. Many of the tenants, or *foreros*, were middle men from the minor nobility who sub-leased their *foros* to peasant farmers, the bottom line of various levels of pressure. Grievances erupted in 1724 into armed resistance, and when this was crushed peasant protest continued through litigation in a vain attempt

---

[8] Emiliano Fernández de Pinedo, 'Coyuntura y política económicas', *Historia de España*, vol. VII, *Centralismo, Ilustración y agonía del Antiguo Régimen (1715-1833)* ed. Labor (Madrid, 1800), pp. 55, 121-9.

[9] Saavedra and Villares, 'Galicia en el antiguo régimen', *España en el siglo XVIII*, pp. 452-73; on the *foro* see Pegerto Saavedra, *Economía, política y sociedad en Galicia: la provincia de Mondoñedo, 1480-1830* (Madrid, 1985), pp. 413-36; see also Jaime García-Lombardero, *La agricultura y el estancamiento económico de Galicia en la España del Antiguo Régimen* (Madrid, 1973).

to challenge, avoid or postpone the burdens of rent, dues and services to which they were subject.[10] The government of Charles III prohibited in 1763 the expulsion of tenants who paid their rent, but this was a victory for those *foreros* who lived on the revenue from sub-letting and it did nothing for the tenant farmers further down the ladder who still had to pay their rents, tithes, taxes and other dues from an agriculture not greatly productive. How then did Galicia survive? Fishing and livestock helped to keep starvation at bay. New plants, maize in the lowlands and potatoes in the interior, gave the peasants a substitute for grain and alleviation during subsistence crises. And emigration provided a safety valve. Seasonal agricultural labourers migrated to Castile and Andalucía, some 60,000 annually, setting out at the beginning of May and returning in early September with their meagre earnings of 10–12 pesos a season.[11] Others went to America, where the Galician became one of the characteristic *peninsulares* of the eighteenth century, sometimes poor, more often mobile. Meanwhile the poor peasants of Galicia, victims of privilege and monopoly, were the butt of the rest of Spain, their primitive dwellings, ragged clothes, and potato diet making them the Irish of the peninsula.

The Basque provinces of Guipúzcoa and Vizcaya had an agrarian structure distinct from the rest of Spain. The 'maize revolution' was only a partial answer to population growth and the Basques had to import foodstuffs from Castile and France, paying the deficit with iron, fish, and remittances earned in the Indies. This precarious balance depended in part on the protection afforded by the *fueros* against heavy tax demands by the central government. It also depended on the maintenance of social harmony by the discouragement of ostentatious *señores* and wealthy *cabildos* (town councils) on the one hand and of gipsies and vagrants on the other. In this sense Basque egalitarianism was a device to enable a maximum of people to live on a minimum of territory without the unemployment and begging characteristic of the rest of Spain. The *caserío*, or homestead, was a logical response to the disparity between population and resources. Land was divided into small family farms, passed from generation to generation as irreducible units, at the centre a house and grouped around it the various segments of arable, pasture and forest land. The majority of *caseros* were not owners but tenants renting

[10] Antonio Domínguez Ortiz, *Sociedad y estado en el siglo XVIII español* (Barcelona, 1981), pp. 134–7.

[11] William Dalrymple, *Travels through Spain and Portugal in 1774* (London, 1777), pp. 93, 99, who states that 30,000 also went to Portugal each year for harvest and vintage.

from an absentee landlord who often owned a number of *caseríos*. In practice the tenancy was perpetual, the rent was moderate, and the tenant could leave the farm to the son he considered most qualified for it; this avoided both short-term tenancy with its inherent insecurity and an uneconomic division of holdings into minifundia. But the Basque provinces were not immune to adversity. Population growth increased the pressure on land in the late eighteenth century and peasants were forced to extend cultivation into marginal zones, seeking mortgage loans from *señores* and convents, falling into debt, and becoming prey to foreclosure. Poverty and vagrancy raised their unaccustomed heads in the Basque country.[12]

Travellers on the long and open road from Pamplona to Madrid looked out at a large, barren country, devoid of anything green except occasional olives, oaks and cork trees. 'In themselves the villages and houses exceed in dirt and nastiness anything I had conceived', wrote an English diplomat, as he observed a region in decline, its towns decayed, industry depressed, and countryside poor.[13] This was old Castile, the northern plateau of Spain, home of powerful landlords, tyrannical stewards, farmers reduced to labourers, free peasants to short-term tenants, and scene of age-long conflict between pastoral and arable farming, the latter limited to a cereal monoculture of wheat, barley, and rye. These grains were not highly commercialized and normally farmers could not export the surplus because of prohibitive transport costs. But rural consumers were subject to alarming price fluctuations. The intendant of Guadalajara reported crisis conditions in 1764, the consequence of grain shortage, price rise, destitution and disease: 'People are dying of poverty and resulting epidemics ... I have travelled for some weeks without seeing in the villages any bread, except very poor rye and barley bread at an exorbitant price; and in every village I saw a hospital full of the sick, many of whom have died.' He attributed rural distress to excessive rents, which in his view never corresponded to the quality of the land:

Agriculture suffers in many places from the high rent which farmers have to pay. Very few farmers have their own land. Most land is owned by the church, the *señores*, and the owners of entails;

[12] Pablo Fernández Albaladejo, 'El País Vasco: algunas consideraciones sobre su más reciente historiografía', *España en el siglo XVIII*, p. 542.

[13] James Harris, First Earl of Malmesbury, *Diaries and Correspondence*, ed. Third Earl of Malmesbury (4 vols, London, 1844), I, pp. 37–8.

the ambitions of some and the needs of others have raised rents so much that farmers are perishing, and communities cannot increase, because as soon as they do the owners put up the rents on land. I have seen many villages which pay one, two or more fanegas of grain for every fanega of land, which normally ownly yields 3 to 5 fanegas. Hence the poverty of everyone and their desertion of an occupation which does not sustain them.

Moreover, rents were raised illegally beyond the ceiling price of grain:

I can say that a year of dearth finishes off a great number of farmers. It is to everyone's interest to replace them, not least that of the landowners, if they want their land cultivated; these are generally the *señores* of the villages, the cabildos, churches, colleges, chantries, and religious communities. Against the secular landlords the poor have no defence, and their rent is collected rigorously. Against the ecclesiastical landlords they have even less hope, and if they do not pay on first demand they are subject to religious censures; to free themselves from these terrible sanctions they will do anything to find payment, even if it means selling their mules or oxen; if they cannot, they become fugitives and their families are abandoned. These events are not conjecture; sadly I have seen and observed them in the villages. In my opinion the grave sanctions of the church should not be invoked in these cases and it is an abuse to do so.[14]

Depression and depopulation were the fate of many villages of Old Castile, and the region reverted almost to a subsistence economy, producing for the family, the village, the nearby market, at most the provincial capital.[15] Even Segovia, a zone of rural growth and grain surpluses, succumbed from the 1760s to population growth and a series of bad harvests, to decline into stagnation for the rest of the century.[16]

Western Old Castile, whose poor soil was more suitable for pasture than for ploughing, was the classical land of migrant sheep and empty villages.[17] Many of the great sheep proprietors lived far from their flocks.

---

[14] Intendant of Guadalajara to Squilace, 2 July 1764, AGS, Secretaría de Hacienda 588.

[15] Domínguez Ortiz, *Sociedad y estado en el siglo XVIII español*, p. 180.

[16] Angel García Sanz, *Desarrollo y crisis del Antiguo Régimen en Castilla la Vieja. Economía y sociedad en tierras de Segovia, 1500-1814* (Madrid, 1977), pp. 210–50.

[17] Joseph Townsend, *A Journey through Spain in the Years 1786 and 1787* (2nd edn, 3 vols, London, 1792), II, pp. 87–8.

The *catastro* of Ensenada showed thirty-three inhabitants of Madrid as owners of 506,000 head of sheep, among them some well known aristocrats – the duke of Infantado (36,000), the duke of Alburquerque (26,000), the duke of Béjar (18,000) – as well as numerous commoners and monasteries, in short a group of absentee sheep-owners who extracted profits from the flocks and shepherds of highland Castile and spent them elsewhere.[18] There were of course a number of resident proprietors, and below these the smaller and poorer *serranos* (hill farmers), owners of one or two hundred sheep, barely enough to provide subsistence or save them from the ranks of wage-earning shepherds and a miserable standard of living. This was the fate of most of the inhabitants of the sierras of Soría and Burgos, and of many villages of Avila, Segovia and León. The herds of migrant sheep found their winter pastures in Extremadura and La Mancha, but here too the owners of the *dehesas* (pastures) were located not in the receiving provinces but in Madrid or the cities of Old Castile, and again the profits from sheep farming were diverted from local economies and communities. In La Mancha, for example, the village of El Viso belonged to the marquis of Santa Cruz who had a palace there: 'The *posadero* informed me that numerous flocks of fine wooled sheep came here to feed annually; that Don Luis, the king's brother, and prince Maserano, have tracts of land around the town, which they let to the pastors, who arrive here from the northern parts of the kingdom with their flocks.'[19] The economy of New Castile was diverse enough to survive the attentions of the sheep interest. The region was noted for its mules, but above all for its grain and vines. All observers commented on the excellent wine of Valdepeñas, the most drinkable table wine in the whole of Spain but deprived of outlets through transport deficiencies. Extremadura, on the other hand, a province with few initial advantages, was further blighted by the double burden of absentee landlords and resident sheep.

In spite of emerging arable interests, the *Mesta*, or sheep owners' association, remained a powerful pressure group and sheep farming, far from declining, reached its peak in the eighteenth century; migrant sheep increased from 2 million in 1700 to 5 million in 1780 in response to foreign demand for merino wool and thanks to low production costs, a comparative advantage derived from the *Mesta's* privileged position in

---

[18] Domínguez Ortiz, *Sociedad y estado en el siglo XVIII español*, p. 183.
[19] Dalrymple, *Travels through Spain and Portugal in 1774*, p. 30.

Spain.[20] It was only from the 1760s, when population growth, the extension of arable land, and rising grain prices tipped the balance towards cereal production, that the sheep sector entered more difficult times. But both arable and pastoral agriculture in Castile came to the limits of their expansion in the second half of the eighteenth century; land concentration, poor rewards to farmers, the extraction of profits for spending on other activities rather than reinvestment in agriculture, all played their part in closing the door to modernization.

Andalucía, the 'agrarian problem' of Spain, where landowners exploited their estates directly by the labour of *jornaleros* or short-term lessees, was also the leading province in productivity, providing 26.6 per cent of the gross agricultural product of Castile.[21] More than half of the province was cultivated, a high percentage of land use for eighteenth-century Spain, producing grain, olives, wines, and fruits. The hills of Córdoba, the plain of Osuna, the coastal zones of Granada and Malaga, were all examples of local variety and prosperity. But the most productive part of Andalucía was Seville, the core of the region's economy. It was not a model economy. Andalucía was encumbered, even more than the rest of Spain, with a flawed agrarian structure, resistant to change and reinforced by seigneurial and political authority. The predominance of aristocratic latifundia, cultivated by a force of seasonal labourers, created a rural proletariat that lived in very precarious conditions. A total of 563 great landowners, only 0.17 per cent of the population of Andalucía, owned 13.5 per cent of land and 14.3 per cent of gross regional agricultural product.[22] A group of fifty-six proprietors, including the dukes of Medinaceli, Osuna, and Arcos, owned between them 800,000 fanegas of land, averaging 14,206 each, together with property in the *municipios*, prompting Olavide to remark, 'one of the greatest evils which we suffer is the unequal distribution of land and its concentration in the hands of a few.'[23] The *jornaleros* predominated above all in the province of Seville and western Andalucía but were also to be found in Córdoba, Jaén and Granada. They were not alone in their misery. Many small proprietors and tenants barely earned a living, victims of excessive concentration of property, high rents, and

[20] Angel García Sanz, 'El interior peninsular en el siglo XVIII: un crecimiento moderado y tradicional', *España en el siglo XVIII*, pp. 654–5.

[21] Grupo '75, *La economía del Antiguo Régimen. La 'renta nacional' de la Corona de Castilla* (Madrid, 1977), pp. 81, 85.

[22] García-Baquero, 'Andalucía en el siglo XVIII', *España en el siglo XVIII*, pp. 365–6.

[23] Antonio Miguel Bernal, 'Señoritos y jornaleros: la lucha por la tierra', *Historia de Andalucía*, VII, *La Andalucia liberal (1778-1873)* (Barcelona, 1981), pp. 272–7.

competition from pasture interests. The various domestic industries of Andalucía – textiles, silks, leather, and hardware – were desperate but limited expedients to avoid unemployment; in 1752 artisans comprised only 8.2 per cent of the active population, in 1787 12.7 per cent.[24] Land concentration did not signify efficiency. The trend of production was towards stagnation; profits moved upwards at the end of the seventeenth and the end of the eighteenth centuries, but in between they stagnated; prices were stable in the first half of the eighteenth century and rose in the period 1760–1810.[25] Andalucian agriculture produced for export, to new grain markets in Europe and traditional ones in America. As the returns went largely to the landed aristocracy, they were not likely to be invested in new enterprises or even in land improvement, but in conspicuous consumption and property accumulation.

Eastern Spain was yet another segment of Spain's agrarian mosaic. Aragon had a primitive economy, still bearing the marks of an oppressive seigneurial regime; many rural people and places were vassals of lords or prelates who appointed their officials and took their taxes. This century saw some progress and some extension of the cultivated area, but Aragon remained a poor, mountainous, semi-desert, its agriculture mainly pastoral and its arable farming confined to a few irrigated areas. Aragon was basically a sheep run and wool producer; yet there was virtually no woollen textile industry and no commerce to speak of.

Valencia by comparison, was the garden of Spain. The province underwent exceptional population growth in the eighteenth century, from 400,000 in 1712 to 825,059 in 1797, forcing the agricultural economy to respond and adjust.[26] Agriculture expanded by extending cultivation into new or marginal areas; expansion was also intensive through drainage and irrigation schemes, improved techniques and specialized crops; rice production expanded and maximized land use. Many of these changes were beyond the reach of peasant producers in the interior, and the first call on their output was family consumption, leaving little for the market. For subsistence agriculture of this kind population growth was the prime pressure. Commercial agriculture, on the other hand, responded mainly to price rises and market demand, and was to be found in the rich and populous zones of the littoral. The

[24] García-Baquero, 'Andalucía en el siglo XVIII', *España en el siglo XVIII*, p. 380; Domínguez Ortiz, *Sociedad y estado en el siglo XVIII español*, pp. 219–20.

[25] García-Baquero, 'Andalucía en el siglo XVIII', *España en el siglo XVIII*, pp. 376–84.

[26] Pedro Ruiz Torres, 'El País Valenciano en el siglo XVIII: la transformación de una sociedad agraria en la época del absolutismo', *España en el siglo XVIII*, pp. 169–87.

huertas of Alicante and Valencia, well watered and thickly planted, were scenes of vigorous production of wheat, maize, barley, citrus fruits, vines, and olives.[27] Rural society reflected new economic pressures. Population growth, a stimulus to expansion, was also responsible for keeping living standards low and many peasants, especially in the hills and mountains of the interior, lived on the margin of subsistence. Here land concentration was greater, the seigneurial regime harsher; 6 per cent of the population monopolized land, while the majority of peasants were landless *jornaleros* living on a diet of cucumbers, peppers, barley bread, and a little wine, and greatly outnumbering independent peasant proprietors.[28] Yet agricultural expansion was modifying the social structure of rural Valencia. In the littoral large landowners expanded into common land and settled *colonos* on their new holdings, granting semi-ownership and receiving payment in kind; the same model was followed by a new middle group acquiring land as an investment. But the basic system in eighteenth-century Valencia was the short-term lease; and the accumulation of lands by a few proprietors, combined with the growing number of landless peasants, inevitably led to higher rents for leases. This encouraged the urban bourgeoisie to invest in land and live off rents, with an obvious preference for commercial crops. Rural society, therefore, assumed greater diversity. At the top were the great landowners, titled nobles, the Church, and a new group from the urban middle sector investing in agriculture; in the middle a class of peasant farmers, half with small or medium properties, half with leaseholds; and at the bottom the *jornaleros*, about equal in number to the middle group.[29] If there was variety, there was also inequality: the Valencian peasant had two exploiters, seigneurial lords who took one-seventh, one-sixth or even a quarter of the total crop and a numerous group of urban *rentistas*.[30]

Catalonia provided yet a different agrarian model. The Catalan farmer rented land under a system, the *censo enfiteútico*, which gave him long-term security of tenure in return for paying a moderate quitrent and dues to the seigneurial lord. He thus had an incentive to improve and to enjoy the benefits of improvement, and belonged in effect to a rural middle class holding medium sized farms worked by the family.[31] It is not

[27] Townsend, *A Journey through Spain*, III, pp. 193–200, 268–70.
[28] Domínguez Ortiz, *Sociedad y estado en el siglo XVIII español*, p. 267.
[29] Ruiz Torres, 'El País Valenciano en el siglo XVIII', *España en el siglo XVIII*, pp. 187–203.
[30] Jean François de Bourgoing, *Modern State of Spain* (4 vols, London, 1808), III, pp. 248–51.
[31] Townsend, *A Journey through Spain*, III, pp. 328–30; on the Catalan model see Martínez Shaw, 'La Cataluña del siglo XVIII', *España en el siglo XVIII*, pp. 67–97.

surprising therefore that Catalan economic recovery began in the countryside, passing with inherent logic through a process of land extension, more intensive cultivation, crop specialization, commercialized production, and responding to rises in prices and incomes.[32] The reconquest of the soil took the form of land reclamation from dried-up river beds, the delta of the Ebro, the edges of woods and other areas of marginal land. The vine was the leading crop of agricultural extension and Mataró, Vilafranca and Tarragona its preferred sites. New land was colonized by tenants who were given long-term rent contracts by the landlord, whether king, noble or Church.[33] Intensive expansion was achieved through irrigation schemes of various kinds, new methods and fertilizers, and new crops such as maize, potatoes, and root vegetables. Progress was most apparent in the littoral districts of the Costa Brava and Tarragona, less so in the interior. From the vine a rural industry developed, *aguardiente*, cheap and easy to make and within the capacity of many farmers and artisans. The brandy was exported not only to Europe but also to America and became the leading edge of Catalonia's colonial trade. The two indicators of Catalan agrarian wealth in the eighteenth century were prices and incomes. Prices, in response to increased demand, took off upwards from 1746, fell in 1787 and then recovered; agricultural prices tripled in the eighteenth century, rising strongly in the second half.[34] Income from agriculture underwent an even greater increase than prices and quintupled in the course of the century, most noticeably in the second half, with a cyclical depression in 1782–7.[35]

Catalan agricultural growth, through specialization and commercialization, enabled large landowners, lessees of seigneurial dues, and farmers to accumulate capital, some of which was reinvested in agriculture, some in the urban economy, either commerce or industry. Yet Catalonia was not an agrarian paradise. In addition to substantial farmers there were small and poor tenant farmers and a class of *jornaleros* who had to struggle to live; and most of the rural sector was increasingly resentful of seigneurial parasitism. Arthur Young was disappointed in much that he saw between the frontier and Barcelona, poor crops and excessive waste land.[36] The central coastal zone was an important

[32] Pierre Vilar, *La Catalogne dans l'Espagne moderne* (3 vols, Paris, 1962), II, pp. 187–232.

[33] José María Torras Ribé, 'Evolución de las cláusulas de los contratos de rabassa morta en una propiedad de la comarca de Anoia', *Hispania*, 134 (1976), pp. 663–90.

[34] Vilar, *La Catalogne dans l'Espagne moderne*, II, pp. 332–418.

[35] Ibid., II, pp. 419–554.

[36] Arthur Young, *Travels during the Years 1787, 1788, and 1789* (2 vols, Dublin, 1793), I, pp. 609–18, 657.

granary for Barcelona, the second largest food consumer in Spain; but Catalonia did not feed itself, producing no more than five months' provision. Without imports from North America, Sicily and North Africa, Catalonia would run the risk of famine: 'From four hundred thousand to six hundred thousand quarters of wheat are annually imported. Canada alone sent this year about eighty thousand quarters.'[37] Barcelona, being a port, was able to obtain prompt supplies in times of dearth. The interior of the country was not so fortunate.

Spain suffered a series of agrarian crises in the eighteenth century, when harvest failure acting on a faulty structure led to food shortage, high prices and starvation. In 1753 severe drought induced famine conditions: 'We are dryed up with heat, and this is the third year we have no rain. Here is corn in private hands for the present year, but if the next resembles this, it will have more than the air of a famine. The people at Madrid have been mutinous for bread. . . .'[38] Harvests declined in the period 1764–73, in the case of wheat by more than 4 per cent and barley more than 5.5 per cent, at a time when there were no climatic catastrophes. The fact was that national grain production did not meet internal demand; grain imports exceeded exports in the period 1756–73 by 11.3 million fanegas of wheat and 1.8 million of barley. In spite of the stimulus provided by growing demand and the consequent rise of grain prices, above all in the second half of the century, agriculture did not fully respond, constrained as it was by defective structure and technique. In most of Spain production was increased by extension not improvement; agriculture grew but did not develop. Many Spaniards were perfectly aware of this and some of them wanted to change it.

Agrarian Reform

The impulse to reform can be seen in the work of the quasi-official Economic Societies which spread in the years after 1765 from the Basque country to the main towns of the rest of Spain, and whose aim

---

[37] Henry Swinburne, *Travels through Spain in the Years 1775 and 1776* (London, 1779), pp. 65–6. On heavy wheat purchases abroad in 1766 see Rochford to Conway, 17 March 1766, Public Record Office, London, SP 94/173, and in 1786–7, Consul James Duff to W. Fraser, Cadiz, August 1787, PRO, FO 72/11. Crop failure of wheat and barley in 1789 caused Spain to compete for foreign grain, especially in North Africa and Sicily; see Consul Wilkie, Cartagena, to Leeds, 4 June 1790, PRO, FO 72/16.

[38] Keene to Castres, 25 May 1753, Sir Benjamin Keene, *The Private Correspondence of Sir Benjamin Keene, KB*, ed. Sir Richard Lodge (Cambridge, 1933), p. 328.

was to encourage agriculture, commerce and industry by study and experiment.[39] Two reformists in particular focused attention on agrarian conditions, Pedro Rodríguez de Campomanes and Gaspar Melchor de Jovellanos. Campomanes denounced mortmain, short-term and insecure rentals, the price ceiling on grain, and the privileges of the *Mesta*. In 1762 he was appointed fiscal of the council of Castile with a wide commission in economic affairs. Three years later, on the evidence supplied by local officials and the strength of his own conviction, he published his *Tratado de la regalía de amortización* in which he argued that the prosperity of the state and its subjects could only be increased by attracting the peasant to the soil that he worked, and in which he advocated state intervention to modify the conditions of land distribution in the interests of society. Campomanes argued for the establishment of a *ley agraria* to give villages rights of arable agriculture over land and exclusive rights to enclose land, without the intervention of the *Mesta*, whose 'odious privileges are one of the basic causes which hinder the advance of agriculture'.[40] But he directed his sharpest attack towards the Church, insisting that a law was needed to prevent the alienation of land in mortmain without royal consent. In order to avoid the charge of novelty Campomanes used arcane historical arguments to prove that, contrary to true doctrine, the Church had departed from its primitive poverty, removing itself from the temporal power of the crown, and usurped land which rightly belonged to the laity, reducing farmers to labourers and peasants to poverty.[41] The *Tratado* was published at the expense of the crown and to a chorus of opposition from the papacy, the clergy, and the conservatives in the council of Castile. Campomanes no doubt won the battle of ideas but he was defeated by vested interests, and privilege survived in the ranks of the Church and the *Mesta*. Agrarian reform as a project was taken up again by Jovellanos in his *Informe sobre la ley agraria* (1794), a moderate but reformist document commissioned by the Madrid Economic Society and submitted to the council of Castile. Jovellanos accepted the primacy of individual interest and private wealth, from which derived public wealth, 'and only when a state has thereby made itself rich and powerful is it able to overcome

---

[39] R. J. Shafer, *The Economic Societies in the Spanish World (1763-1821)* (Syracuse, 1958), pp. 26–31, 48–57, 94–9; Gonzalo Anes Alvarez, *Economía e Ilustración en la España del siglo XVIII* (Barcelona, 1969), p. 25; Paula y Jorge Demerson and Francisco Aguilar Piñal, *Las Sociedades Económicas de Amigos del País en el siglo XVIII* (San Sebastian, 1974).

[40] Quoted by Laura Rodríguez Díaz, *Reforma e Ilustración en la España del siglo XVIII. Pedro Rodríguez de Campomanes* (Madrid, 1975), p. 116.

[41] Ibid., pp. 150–2.

nature and improve it'.[42] Liberty and private property were the bases from which Jovellanos attacked privilege – the *Mesta*, noble entail, clerical mortmain – and advocated distribution of land to peasants.

The influence of ideas, some of them inspired by the physiocrats, the policy of reformists, the pressure of population on resources, these factors for change were joined by the rise of grain prices on the international market to push Spanish agriculture into growth. Now was the time to increase production, give employment to the rural population and allocate land to those who worked it. How did the government respond? The first concern of policy makers was to find a solution to periodic subsistence crises which caused famine and provoked disorder. They began by altering the traditional bias towards the consumer in favour of the producer: the ordinance of 11 July 1765 abolished the *tasa* or price ceiling and established a free trade in grain, allowing merchants the freedom of the market, and even permitting export if prices in Spain were low enough. There was a mixed reaction. Consumers, backed by *corregidores* and intendants, complained that the abolition of the *tasa* caused a price rise and that the only beneficiaries of the law of 1765 were ecclesiastics, nobles, and other proprietors who as producers gained from the high price of grain and as consumers could afford to pay for dear bread. The town council of Madrid opposed free trade in grain and pressed for the return of the *tasa*; so did the *Mesta*, for the new grain policy favoured conversion of pasture to arable. The regional bureaucracy agreed that free trade caused price increases, that this encouraged landowners to put up rents, and that peasant farmers gained nothing. As one of these complained, this was a government of landlords: 'many of those in authority are landowners and consumers; they are not farmers.'[43] But many landlords could see the advantage of farming; attracted by the profits from grain production, they began to eject tenants from better quality land and to cultivate it themselves with the labour of *jornaleros*.

Local officials were left to pick up the pieces. They were under considerable pressure from their communities to keep down prices and transport costs. The intendant of Granada reported that in spite of his efforts,

after Easter there was a lot of murmuring and complaining about the high price of foodstuffs, which they want lowering; this was the

[42] Quoted by Anes, *Economía e Ilustración*, p. 99.
[43] Rodríguez, *Campomanes*, pp. 205–6.

message of two posters which have appeared on the door of my house. I do not take this seriously, for to overreact would only make the situation worse. But nor do I underestimate or ignore it, and I constantly seek to make sure that there is abundance of foodstuffs at a suitable price.[44]

Other intendants were caught between the demands of their own province to keep what they had and pressure from the central government to comply with the free movement of grain.[45] In Andalucía Olavide urgently sought grain supplies in 1766 and 1767, but he was refused permission to import from Sicily and had to be content with supplies from Murcia.[46] The intendant of Aragon complained that the Catalans were making heavy grain purchases in his province and farmers were tempted to take a quick profit, unmindful of the winter to come.[47]

Free trade in grain survived calamity and opposition, saved by the advocacy of Campomanes and, apparently, the support of the king. Prices, profits, and rents continued to rise, and subsistence crises occurred with sickening regularity, but the government remained convinced that only market forces would induce farmers to produce more.[48] In 1780 a nationwide drought drove up grain prices to exceptional levels, creating further profits for nobles and clergy and causing disturbances in many towns. In 1788 and again in 1790 the cycle of drought, crop failure, famine, and disease brought misery to rural Spain and food crises in Madrid and Barcelona. Now even Campomanes had doubts and advised a measure of regulation against merchants who cornered supplies and speculated in grain; but price freedom continued. The policy faced its severest test in 1803–4 when poor harvests sent prices soaring in central Spain and people died of hunger; the crisis was prolonged into 1804–5 and the agrarian economy appeared to be locked into depression. At this point, in 1804, free trade in grain was abandoned and the *tasa* restored. The policy had proved the limitations of legislation in an unreconstructed society. To release market forces without imposing agrarian reform was to further distort the balance of rural power. Free trade worked to the advantage of

---

[44] Intendant of Granada to Múzquiz, 18 April 1766, AGS, Secretaría de Hacienda 587.
[45] Intendant of Palencia to Squillace, 26 April 1764, AGS, Secretaría de Hacienda 593.
[46] Olavide to Múzquiz, 26 September 1767, 6 August 1768, AGS, Secretaría de Hacienda 545.
[47] Intendant of Aragon to crown, 13 September 1766, AGS, Secretaría de Hacienda 542.
[48] Anes, *Las crisis agrarias*, pp. 430–8.

noble and clerical landowners, increasing their income from sales and rents and creating an even more powerful agrarian interest and lobby. But it was not able to cope with the pressure of population on resources, least of all in periods of harvest failure. For this reason public and private granaries had survived alongside the free market, a fail-safe device to cushion the worst effects of famine, and a commentary on liberal legislation.

Reformers were aware that access to land was the key to agrarian reform. In 1763 the government ordered the suspension of evictions in the case of short-term leases. In April 1766 on the initiative of the intendant of Badajoz town lands there were distributed to the most needy peasants at low fixed rents; the council of Castile sanctioned this practice and ordered its extension to other towns of Extremadura, and in 1767–8 to Andalucía and La Mancha, with preference to landless labourers and farmers. In 1770 all Spanish localities were ordered to enclose and allot their town lands not then under cultivation. The object, according to the instruction of 11 April 1768, was 'to promote the common good, to encourage agriculture, and to provide industrious and landless farmers and labourers with their own land to cultivate, avoiding the harm previously caused by subletting'.[49] Whether these social and economic objectives were achieved is difficult to judge. In Segovia 72 per cent of this type of land was in fact distributed to farmers and labourers. On the other hand, the second phase of reform inaugurated by the royal provision of 26 May 1770 introduced a new element of discrimination: priority was now given to farmers with one or more yoke of oxen, for *jornaleros* lacked the means to cultivate land grants. It was obvious that without capital or credit labourers could not be expected to make barren land fruitful, and this enabled the local oligarchy to move in and monopolize municipal land.[50] The results therefore appear to have been mixed.

The failure of land reform still left the problem of feeding a growing population; in default of an agricultural revolution production could only be increased by extending the area cultivated.[51] There were a number of options available to the state: one was to encourage the ploughing of pasture; another was to sponsor projects of repopulation and internal colonization. Official policy towards the *Mesta* in the

[49] Felipa Sánchez Salazar, 'Los repartos de tierras concejiles en la España del Antiguo Régimen', *La economía española al final del Antiguo Régimen*, I, *Agricultura* (Madrid, 1982), pp. 189–258.

[50] García Sanz, 'El interior peninsular en el siglo XVIII', *España en el siglo XVIII*, pp. 660–2.

[51] Anes, *Las crisis agrarias*, pp. 165–9.

eighteenth century was more tolerant than is usually supposed.[52] There
is no evidence that in 1786 the *Mesta* lost its right of *posesión*, whereby it
could use in perpetuity and at fixed rents any land that it had once used
as pasture. The sheep and wool resources of this sector were too
important to relinquish and too closely linked to powerful social
interests to attack head on; reform measures therefore tended to be too
little and too late. The real enemy of the *Mesta* was the prevailing
economic trend: the lag of wool prices behind those of grain on the international market, the anxiety of the great landowners to profit from
higher agricultural prices, and the rise of production costs beyond wool
prices, these were the factors that, from the 1760s, helped to redress the
balance against the sheep owners in favour of agricultural interests. The
legislation of the 1790s in favour of arable farming in Extremadura and
in restraint of *Mesta* officials merely acknowledged existing conditions.[53]

The colonization of desert lands in the Sierra Morena seemed to offer
greater prospects of effective land use. In 1767 Campomanes drew up a
plan for the creation of colonies in the empty regions of royal land in the
Sierra Morena and Andalucía. Supervision of the project was assigned to
Pablo de Olavide, and after a faltering start communities of German and
Flemish Catholic immigrants, followed later by Spaniards, promoted
agriculture and industries in a hitherto barren and bandit-infested
region. The project was funded by the state and the necessary infrastructure of agrarian reform was established, from houses and furniture,
to tools, cattle and seeds; each colonist was granted 50 fanegas of land in
leasehold, for which from the tenth year he would pay the state a rent.
By 1775 the experiment was a success; out of nothing a fine town had
appeared with good roads, stone houses, and a new community of
farmers and artisans numbering more than 13,000; the land had been
made productive and was yielding abundant crops of corn; the only
problem was its remoteness and lack of integration into the Spanish
economy.[54] Sierra Morena was more than a colony. It was designed as a
model, a social experiment, to demonstrate that agrarian problems were
capable of solution by an enlightened programme untrammelled by the
Spanish past and free of latifundia, entail, and mortmain.[55] It also

[52] Nina Mikun, *La Mesta au XVIIIe Siècle: Etude d'Histoire Sociale et Economique de l'Espagne au
XVIIIe Siècle* (Budapest, 1983); Jean Paul Le Flem 'El Valle de Alcudia en el siglo XVIII', *Congreso de
Historia Rural. Siglo XV al XIX* (Madrid, 1984), pp. 235–49.

[53] García Sanz, 'El interior peninsular en el siglo XVIII', *España en el siglo XVIII*, pp. 663–6.

[54] Dalrymple, *Travels through Spain and Portugal*, pp. 24–7; Swinburne, *Travels through Spain*,
pp. 310–14.

[55] Marcelin Defourneaux, *Pablo de Olavide ou L'Afrancesado (1725-1803)* (Paris, 1959), p. 197.

showed that Spanish reformers, having looked at their society, knew what was wrong and what was needed. But it was only a small part of Spain.

Elsewhere the prospects of reform were bleak. Productivity was blocked not only by traditional farming practices but above all by the existing agrarian structure which concentrated property and power in the hands of landlords preoccupied with profits not improvements, while leaving the actual farmer without land, security, or incentives. Agrarian reform meant nothing without redistribution of rural property, and this would involve confrontation with the privileged estates. At this point reformers drew back; appalled at the enormity of the task, they engaged in a conscious compromise. Campomanes sought only to limit ecclesiastical amortization and to prevent future land accumulation by the Church. Jovellanos, aware that even this had failed, merely proposed that reform of mortmain should be undertaken by the clergy themselves, while noble entails should be prohibited in the future but not retrospectively. Moreover, these were only projects, not policies. State action was confined to freeing the grain trade and promoting a minor distribution of municipal land, the results ambiguous in both cases. Agrarian crises inevitably followed, in 1789, 1794, 1798, and 1804. The crisis of 1803–4, a culmination of population growth, crop failure, high prices, famine, and malnutrition, caused terrible mortality and showed how little the Spanish government had done to help the peasant or change the face of rural Spain. No one could accuse the policy makers of ignorance. From intendants, *corregidores*, interested parties, they were inundated with information. Rarely had Spanish leaders been so informed yet so impotent. They knew the situation but they could not change it; vested interest, tradition, opposition, royal complacency, all caused the government to retreat to a position of knowing compliance. The failure of agrarian reform meant a failure to raise the living standards of the *campesinos*. This had consequences not only for agriculture but also for industry.

Industry and Trade

Industry fascinated Spanish reformers, but it generated more ideas than capital. The encouragement of popular industry was one of the favourite themes of Campomanes. Yet he distrusted factories, and having seen the uprising of 1766 in Madrid he preferred to see urban workers dispersed rather than concentrated. His ideal of industry was one of small rural units, complementing the work of the peasant and his family and requiring little initial capital. This was not inimical to popular interests, for it offered the *campesino* an alternative security in time of unemployment.[56] To sustain popular industry Campomanes advocated an infrastructure of education and benevolence; education from the Economic Societies, investment from socially-conscious people with capital to spare. But this utopia of rural weavers and their patrons was never realized and was overtaken by other modes of manufacturing.

State policy was more pragmatic but it too owed something to contemporary ideas. There was a modest drive towards modernization. Funds were provided to experiment with new machinery and to finance technical studies abroad; schools of arts and crafts were established to improve technical education; the Economic Societies, *consulados*, royal academies and other state centres maintained special schools giving vocational courses; university reform was attempted to reduce the influence of scholasticism and create chairs in mathematics, agriculture, and political economy. But in the end Spain preferred to acquire instant technology by imitation; the easiest way was to import skill and knowledge directly, using Spanish embassies abroad as centres of talent spotting and industrial espionage. As Jovellanos observed: 'our industry is not inventive and the best it can do at present is to imitate and emulate foreign industry.'[57] Emulate but not accommodate. There was a strong tradition of protectionism in Bourbon economic policy and under the pressure of national manufacturing interests this was revived in the age of Adam Smith. A decree of 15 May 1760, departing from tradition for reasons of trade, had opened the door to all foreign cotton textiles, though subjecting them to heavy duties. Catalan manufacturers reacted sharply and the government listened. A decree of 8 July 1768 prohibited the import of foreign printed cottons. In 1770 the ban was extended to all muslins, and in 1771 to cotton velvets; unfinished articles were allowed entry subject to a duty of 15 per cent. Finally, a law of 1775 prohibited the import of foreign hardware. Protection was a sign of weakness, not of strength, appropriate perhaps to a developing economy still emerging from industrial infancy.

The standard model of Spanish industry, in towns as well as in

---

[56] Pedro Rodríguez de Campomanes, *Discurso sobre el fomento de la industria popular* (Madrid, 1774), p. 145.

[57] Gaspar de Jovellanos, 'Dictamen sobre embarque de paños extranjeros para nuestras colonias', *Obras de Jovellanos* (Madrid, 1952), ii, p. 71.

villages, was the artisan workshop; a hierarchy of masters, journeymen and apprentices worked to guild regulations which controlled the supply of labour and the quantity and quality of output. The enterprise involved little concentration of capital and labour, produced for a local or regional market, and was largely unaffected by technical change. Even so it was capable of expansion in response to population growth and greater demand, such as occurred in the second half of the eighteenth century. While some artisans worked in the subsistence sector, others in Catalonia, Valencia and the Basque country were part of a larger network operating under the putting-out system, in which capital was employed only in providing the raw material and marketing the product, not in the process of production. But in addition to this dispersed rural industry there was another side of production in factories which formed relatively large concentrations of capital and labour; some of these, principally in Castile, were state factories; others, in Catalonia, Andalucía and Galicia, belonged to private enterprise.

According to the *catastro* of Ensenada, out of nearly 200,000 people in the industrial and service sectors, more than half – 102,425 – worked in textiles; a little over one-quarter – 50,456 – in the building industry, mainly carpenters. In the remaining quarter there were two groups, metal workers – 22,777 – and seamen – 17,799.[58] Even the largest industries, textiles and metallurgy, were essentially artisan in character. Factory-type industrial production was exceptional. Many of the metal workers were blacksmiths and worked in forges, hardware workshops and other dispersed rural units. Of the 32,000 registered as working in hemp, esparto and leather 25,000 were simply cobblers and sandal makers; the rest made harnesses, bags and wine-skins; and there was no sign of saddlers and glove makers, traditional high-quality crafts in Spain. Even textiles was hardly a mass industry. Of the 70,000 registered in this sector 23,000 were employed in making clothes and accessories, most of them simply tailors. Cloth manufacture employed greater numbers: spinning 10,000, weaving 20,000, finishing and dyeing 1,200, miscellaneous 14,481. But did even these 40–50,000 producers of cloth form a 'textile industry'? They were dispersed among provinces, Jaén, Toro, Zamora, Toledo, Seville, Cuenca, Segovia, artisans working in a pre-industrial environment.

Galicia had an industrial sector of this kind, half-urban half-rural, specializing in linen production and organized on a domestic putting-

[58] Pierre Vilar, 'Structures de la société espagnole vers 1750', *Mélanges à la mémoire de Jean Sarrailh* (2 vols, Paris, 1966), ii, pp. 425–47.

out basis. Production increased in the second half of the eighteenth century, in response to demographic pressure on land, the expansion of the Castilian market, and protection against foreign imports, and the number of looms doubled between 1750 and 1800.[59] *Comercio libre* was a further stimulus and La Coruña came to export up to 500,000 yards of linen a year to the colonial market, particularly the Río de la Plata. Even so, industry was a very small sector in a predominantly agricultural province. In the two Castiles and Extremadura, around 1700, income generated by industry amounted to only 11.8 per cent of the whole, compared to agriculture, 59.4 per cent, and the service sector, 28.8 per cent.[60] In Old Castile domestic industry was a life-saving supplement to underpaid shepherds and unemployed *jornaleros*; Béjar made profits for its owners, and in various highland villages small cloth establishments experienced some prosperity with government encouragement.[61] Valladolid, Medina del Campo, and Burgos, on the other hand, were still in decline, and only Segovia survived, thanks to its woollen cloth manufactures; cloth production in Segovia doubled in the period 1715–60, to plunge thereafter into depression caused by poor regional demand during the crop failures of the 1760s.[62] The cities of New Castile, Toledo, Cuenca, Alcalá, contained no private industries of any significance and here artisans worked only at the subsistence level. Nor was Madrid an industrial centre, though it possessed the usual range of artisan activities appropriate to a capital city. Yet traditional industry proved itself capable of growth in the eighteenth century in response to enterprise and demand. The two notable examples were the Basque iron industry and the Valencian silk industry.

Iron was one of the principal earners of the Basque economy; Vizcaya produced the ore and Guipúzcoa processed it, producing also a small amount of steel. It was a primitive industry and not greatly productive, but in the first two-thirds of the eighteenth century production increased by 150 per cent and prospects for growth looked promising.[63] In the absence of any modernization of technology or organization,

[59] Domínguez Ortiz, *Sociedad y estado en el siglo XVIII español*, p. 145.

[60] Grupo, '75, *La economía del Antiguo Régimen. La 'renta nacional' de la Corona de Castilla*, p. 169.

[61] Agustín González Enciso, *Estado e industria en el siglo XVIII: la fábrica de Guadalajara* (Madrid, 1980), pp. 127–41.

[62] García Sanz, *Desarrollo y crisis*, pp. 220–4; Domínguez Ortiz, *Sociedad y estado en el siglo XVIII español*, pp. 185–6.

[63] Luis María Bilbao and Emiliano Fernández de Pinedo, 'Auge y crisis de la siderometalurgia tradicional en el País Vasco (1700–1850)', *La economía español al final del Antiguo Régimen*, II, *Manufacturas* (Madrid, 1982), pp. 133–228.

growth can only be explained by a number of other factors: strong demand abroad, both in Europe and America, the ability of the Basque producers to sell at competitive prices in the international market, the relative recovery of the internal market, and tariff protection provided by the government. As long as these conditions prevailed the Basque industry could overcome its economic inefficiency by sheer production. The industry was not concentrated in large firms but dispersed in numerous workings, about 100 ironworks in Guipúzcoa and 150 in Vizcaya. The owners were often Bilbao merchants who contracted with workers for production and marketed the product. An average-sized iron works employed two smelters, one shot-firer, and one labourer; paid by piece work, at 5 reales a quintal they could earn 30–40 reales a week each. A processing industry grew up in Vizcaya producing wheels, nails, barrel hoops; but the more specialized workshops were in Guipúzcoa, at Mondragón, Eibar, Tolosa, and Plasencia, where a number of arms factories were situated. The army and navy were important customers, while the colonies were a good market for hardware manufactures. But the industry remained technically backward and when circumstances changed – rise in production costs and loss of protection – it could no longer sustain its growth and profitability, and from the 1790s it went into recession along with the rest of the Basque economy.

The silk industry of Valencia was another example of growth within the traditional model. Valencia already exported its high quality raw silk; in the course of the eighteenth-century it began to produce the manufactured article, and while it could still not compete abroad with the French product, it began to challenge it for the domestic market. The owners of the industry were merchants of the city, who organized production by the putting-out system. By the end of the century the 800 looms of 1721 had grown to 4,000. But the success of Valencia silk was more apparent than real. The obstacles to its development were characteristic of eighteenth-century Spain.[64] First, the industry had to compete for raw material with the agro-export interest dominated by landowners, farmers and merchants; these were primarily interested in exporting raw silk not in selling to national manufacturers, who remained of secondary importance. Second, the industry lacked entrepreneurs capable of freeing it from traditional controls, so it remained

---

[64] Bourgoing, *Modern State of Spain*, III, p. 261; Vicente Martínez Santos, *Cara y cruz de la sedería valenciana (siglos XVIII-XIX)* (Valencia, 1981); Ruiz Torres, 'El País Valenciano en el siglo XVIII', *España en el siglo XVIII*, pp. 205–10.

subject to guild control and to the principles of monopoly and privilege. Third, limits to growth were set by low capital investment and the weak national market. This in turn retarded the industry's methods and machinery; production was divided among thousands of hands with little standardization. For all these reasons the Valencia silk industry failed to develop beyond a traditional artisan activity. Yet this was not a universal experience. Elsewhere in Spain and in other industries signs of modernization began to appear.

The factory system developed in both the public and the private sectors. The state had already taken the initiative in the reign of Philip V, largely for political and defence reasons. Shipbuilding and arms manufacture had been allocated a portion of the national budget, and within limits they were assured of supplies of capital and labour.[65] The tobacco industry, handsomely housed in the Royal Tobacco Factory in Seville, was an obvious candidate for the state sector because of its fiscal importance. The Almadén mercury mine was reorganized by the early Bourbons to supply the Mexican silver industry. Production increased from 1760, reaching a peak between 1800 and 1805 in response to greater treasury investment.[66] But growth was from a low base and the mine remained basically stagnant, handicapped by technical failures and the low standard of labour, most of it slaves and convicts. State enterprises of this kind, vital for security and revenue, were continued by the government of Charles III, and in some cases underwent further expansion, as did the metallurgical complex of San Juan de Alcaraz.[67] Ministers were less confident of the value of other factories, for example textiles, where the state seemed to be usurping the role of private enterprise, assuming financial risks, perpetuating monopoly, and in general providing a poor substitute for entrepreneurship. A number of these establishments were inherited from previous reigns.[68] A few produced for the luxury markets of court and aristocracy: tapestries at Santa Bárbara, glass at San Ildefonso, porcelain at Buen Retiro. Others specialized in textiles for the popular market, woollen manufactures at Guadalajara, Brihuega, and San Fernando, linen factories at León and San Ildefonso, and a silk factory at Talavera de la Reina.

[65] See above, pp. 127–8, 176–8.
[66] Rafael Dobado González, 'Salarios y condiciones de trabajo en las minas de Almadén, 1758–1839', *La economía española al final del Antiguo Régimen*, II, *Manufacturas*, pp. 337–440.
[67] Juan Helguera Quijada, *La industria metalúrgica experimental en el siglo XVIII: Las Reales Fábricas de San Juan de Alcaraz, 1772-1800* (Valladolid, 1984).
[68] See above, pp. 118–20.

In 1777, to meet the growing demand for wool serge, the government expanded Guadalajara, adding a huge serge division, and the whole plant reached its maximum size in 1784–91 with 670 looms and 24,000 workers. The royal factory for fine silks at Talavera de la Reina expanded by the 1780s to 350 looms and 863 workers. In 1788 a new royal factory was established at Avila, the royal factory for cotton textiles which by 1796 had thirteen looms and 197 workers.[69] These were all relatively large-scale establishments, possessing a high degree of vertical integration and benefiting from central funding and tax exemptions. Yet none of them were profitable; they sucked funds into a bottomless pit of over-production, over-pricing, and poor sales, and were only justified as a political and social exercise. There were a number of serious flaws in their operations. Concentrations of this size in unnecessarily elaborate buildings involved high overheads, without corresponding savings in machinery and mass production; poor management was apparently inherent in the public sector; and the weak internal market and transport bottlenecks further reduced sales and outlets. Far from being a model, the royal factories were a deterrent to private enterprise, enjoying privileged access to capital and supplies, and monopoly rights in a small domestic market.[70] Apart from the factory of Laureano Ortiz de Paz in Segovia, private enterprise in Castile did not care to challenge the royal monopoly at this level.[71]

Yet factory production in the private sector made some progress in the periphery. The ironworks established by Antonio Raimundo Ibáñez in 1788 at Sargadelos produced hardware manufactures on sufficient scale to expand, move into profitability and diversify. From 1794 Ibáñez was manufacturing arms for the state, a relationship which strengthened his hand in recruiting and controlling labour; and his experience in trade enabled him to assemble commercial capital to fund expansion. The novelty of his enterprise incurred the hostility of the nobility and clergy who in 1798 instigated a riot against the 'Jew' Ibáñez and tried to mobilize the peasantry to destroy his factory. This was an alliance of the local ruling class, defending the traditional agrarian structure against a subversive industrial enclave, and the peasantry, resentful of the labour demands of Ibáñez and his despoliation of natural resources.[72]

[69] James C. La Force, Jr., *The Development of the Spanish Textile Industry, 1750-1800* (Berkeley/Los Angeles, Calif., 1965), pp. 33–8.

[70] Ibid., pp. 44–50.

[71] García Sanz, *Desarrollo y crisis*, pp. 227–35.

[72] Saavedra and Villares, 'Galicia en el antiguo régimen', *España en el siglo XVIII*, pp. 491–3.

In Andalucía there were a number of 'modern' initiatives in which private enterprise set up factories, concentrated production and invested capital. In Seville the royal company of San Fernando began life in 1747 as a manufacturer and exporter of textiles, failed to make a profit, and slowly expired. In 1780 the Economic Society set up a hardware factory in Seville, offering shares to the public but with little response. A group of Seville entrepreneurs started a baize factory in 1779, employing 686 workers and producing strongly for a time, before fading out. Another woollen textile factory was established in Seville in 1781, taking advantage of wartime protection against English competition and employing a number of English prisoners among its 700 workers; but after 1783 it was unable to resist renewed competition. In the 1780s an English merchant, Nathan Wetherell, set up a factory in Seville producing leather goods which survived until the 1820s before being liquidated. On a smaller scale Granada had a history of similar attempts and failures, while Ronda had mixed fortunes with its tinplate factory established in 1725. Industry in Andalucía, therefore, failed to take root and develop; temporary profits could be made from a favourable opportunity such as a wartime blockade, but in the long run inadequate capital, technology and marketing would bring any enterprise to a halt.[73] Perhaps the saddest evidence revealed by these initiatives was the existence of hundreds of skilled artisans waiting for work.

Catalonia was the scene of greatest industrial activity in Spain, and this took two forms, the revival of traditional industries and the creation of new ones. The Catalan model developed from a wide economic base and was the culmination of various stages of growth. Capital was first generated in agro-export activities and was assembled in relatively small amounts from different sources – agrarian profits and rents, middle-class incomes, the earnings of richer artisans, the gains of merchants.[74] Catalonia exploited the advantages of its maritime position, overcoming the lack of a great merchant marine to dispatch its small vessels in an active coastal trade to Atlantic waters. First it exported agricultural products, wines, and spirits, then textiles. This commercial capitalism provided the impulse for industrial change, a development assisted by the existence of a skilled and specialist workforce and a reserve of labour from population growth. For some time traditional industry and new industry coexisted, but their incompatibility soon became apparent; the new industry employed women and children, moved to work sites

[73] García-Baquero, 'Andalucía en el siglo XVIII', *España en el siglo XVIII*, pp. 394–9.
[74] Vilar, *La Catalogne dans l'Espagne moderne*, III, p. 483.

outside the city, and began to free itself from the constraints of the guilds. But not from all constraints. When Pedro Colbett and Company of Puigcerdà set up a new cotton factory in 1773 the bishop of Urgel objected that he was employing French protestants and had them expelled.[75] In other respects the Catalans regarded the French as useful models and were willing to learn from the experience of others.

The Catalan economy passed through various stages of growth in the eighteenth century. In the first period, 1730–60, increase of population produced a price rise and cheaper labour supply, which encouraged accumulation of profits and a tendency to productive investment. Among textiles woollen cloth production sought to adapt itself to increasing demand, leaving the guild-dominated city in preference for a putting-out system in the countryside, and producing not only for the popular market but also for a higher-quality export trade. Minor industries such as paper, leather, and hardware also showed signs of growth. At this stage the economy was a model of proto-industrialization: it combined a commercialized agriculture with a manufacturing sector attempting to break out of the traditional corporative framework. To modernize further it needed to take the vital step to mass production, concentration of workforce, and mechanization of manufacturing. Only the cotton industry was qualified for this, producing as it did a product which was finer, cheaper, and more appropriate for printed cloth, and which would find a ready outlet in the American colonies, as the English prototype was already proving.[76] The manufacture of cotton cloth, therefore, originated as an initiative of merchant capital seeking a strong export product, and it soon became Catalonia's leading industry. The industry moved ahead into a second period of growth from the 1760s to about 1780 during which it secured protection against foreign competition, increase of raw cotton supplies from Spanish America, and the addition of a cotton-spinning sector to supply the cloth manufactures. The third phase, the 1780s, saw decisive mechanization with the introduction of the English spinning jenny and waterframe, and the first experiments with steam power. The industry benefited from *comercio libre* with America, but in the late 1780s signs of saturation in the colonial market forced Catalan producers to reorganize their manage-

[75] Bishop of Urgel to Múzquiz, 23 November 1773; R. O. to Captain General of Catalonia, 28 January 1774; AGS, Secretaría de Hacienda 546.

[76] Carlos Martínez Shaw, 'Los orígenes de la industria algodonera y el comercio colonial', in Jordi Nadal and Gabriel Tortilla (eds), *Agricultura, comercio colonial y crecimiento económico en la España contemporánea* (Barcelona, 1974), pp. 243–68.

ment and to seek alternative outlets. By now the textile industry employed by Spanish standards an unprecedented number of workers, perhaps as many as 100,000, concentrated in some 150 establishments for spinning cotton and in as many for making printed calicoes.[77] The years of war, from 1796, inaugurated a difficult period when colonial markets were virtually lost, factories closed, and workers discharged. Catalan industry was not immune from crisis, and any undue risk would frighten capital away. But a new breed of industrialists emerged who organized concentration of spinning, weaving, and printing in the same factory, introduced yet newer machines, expanded into areas where energy and labour costs were lower, and began a sales drive in the peninsular market.

The Catalan model of industrial growth was exceptional in Spain. Elsewhere most textile manufacturing was subject to guild organization or dispersed in the country, employing peasants who needed to supplement low agricultural wages, and helping to prop up the seigneurial system. Why did Spanish industry fail to modernize in the eighteenth century? Inferior technology, adverse climate, poor resource endowment, ineffective policy, transport bottlenecks, many factors no doubt played their part. But there is a prior question to pose: why did Spain not modernize its agriculture? The failure of agrarian reform denied the economy the pre-conditions of industrialization. The agrarian sector did not generate capital or raise living standards. Wheat prices stayed high and peasants remained in a state of 'chronic subconsumption'.[78] Thus the mass of the population, dependent directly or indirectly on agriculture, did not have sufficient income to consume the products of national industry; with low or inelastic demand for manufactures, they lacked a domestic market to justify expansion. Given these conditions, capital preferred other outlets, urban property, land, commerce, or jewellery. Commercial capital certainly existed, most of it from the profits of trade, but it did not play a dynamic role in the economy. Capital earned in the American trade was reinvested in property, land, and luxury in Andalucía, in trade and industry in Catalonia, reinforcing the two models already polarized by their different agrarian structures.[79] Whatever else the Indies trade did for Spain, it did not benefit the economic

[77] Townsend, *A Journey through Spain*, I, p. 143; Bourgoing, *Modern State of Spain*, III, pp. 306–11.

[78] Josep Fontana, 'Formación del mercado nacional y toma de conciencia de la burguesía', *Cambio económico y actitudes políticas en la España del siglo XIX* (Barcelona, 1973), pp. 11–53.

[79] García-Baquero, 'Andalucía en el siglo XVIII', *España en el siglo XVIII*, pp. 406–10.

structure of its home base, Andalucía; the growing profits either went abroad, or to other parts of Spain, or were invested unproductively.

Commerce was the most obvious growth sector of the eighteenth-century economy. Ministers worried about agriculture, talked about industry, but took action on trade, as seen in the activities of the junta of commerce, the creation of committees and *consulados*, and the decree of *comercio libre* of 1765 and 1778. Colonial trade was the most buoyant and provided the surplus which enabled Spain to pay for its trade deficit with northern Europe, a deficit inherent in the nature of its foreign trade which was one of primary exports against manufactured imports. The growth of Catalan commerce was an essential part of its economic growth in the eighteenth century, as it sought to conquer the Spanish, European, and American markets. Catalonia traded mainly with its own products, in its own shipping, and to its own agents stationed in the major markets. Catalan exports to foreign markets were led by agricultural products, wines, brandies, and dried fruits, and only modest amounts of manufactured goods such as silks and arms. To the American market, however, industrial exports amounted to 64 per cent, agricultural 36 per cent.[80] In 1778 Catalonia exported directly from its own ports 11 per cent of total Spanish exports to America.[81] In spite of growth, Catalonia like the rest of Spain had a deficit trade balance with Europe, which was covered by the high earnings in money returns from America. This complementarity was more difficult to maintain after 1796, when maritime war brought Spanish commercial growth in general to a halt. The provinces of the periphery were badly affected. Galicia, for example, suddenly lost its recently won colonial trade and linen outlets. It found an alternative activity in privateering: 'the golden age of Galician privateering coincided with the crisis of the Galician colonial trade.'[82]

The growth of overseas trade was not paralleled by growth in domestic trade. The Spanish economy was an archipelago, islands of local production and consumption, isolated from each other by centuries of internal tariffs, self-sufficiency, poor roads and meagre transport. Apart from a network organized to secure the supply of

[80] Vilar, *La Catalogne dans l'Espagne moderne*, III, pp. 66, 115–26, 138.

[81] Antonio García-Baquero González, 'Comercio colonial y producción industrial en Cataluña a fines del siglo XVIII', in Nadal and Tortella (eds), *Agricultura, comercio colonial y crecimiento económico*, pp. 268–94.

[82] Luis Alonso Alvarez, *Comercio colonial y crisis del Antiguo Régimen en Galicia (1778-1818)* (La Coruña, 1986), p. 221.

Madrid, there was little interregional traffic in the rest of the country beyond a limited exchange of subsistence goods, for apart from wool and wood there was no demand for raw materials for industry. Spanish transport was slow, irregular, insecure, and expensive, totally inadequate for the needs of a growing population or the development of a national market.[83] Heavy investment was needed, which implied state action to plan a national road network from general taxes and interprovincial roads from local resources. A decree of 10 June 1761 entrusted to Esquilache the execution of a new project of radial roads converging on Madrid from Andalucía, Catalonia, Galicia, and Valencia, the funding to come primarily from the salt monopoly. But whether resources were allocated in full is doubtful. When the intendant of Cuenca reported on the deplorable and dangerous condition of the road from Cuenca to Madrid he was curtly told, 'there is no money allocated to the repair of these roads at the moment.'[84] The intendant of Burgos was equally scathing about the roads in his province: 'The roads that I have seen could not be worse; it only needs a few drops of rain and they are impassable; as for the inns, they are abysmal.'[85] All eighteenth-century travellers complained of Spanish inns, filthy, inhospitable places, which provided a rough bed or the floor but no food, and welcomed the new chain of *posadas del rey* set up by the government of Charles III. Spain did not have stage coaches. It was only from 1785 that travel by post-chaise was available from Madrid to Cadiz, and by 1800 more routes were added. But the normal method of personal travel was by mule. Great hopes were held of canals, but only two advanced beyond the planning stage, one in Aragon, the other in Old Castile, and neither of them was completed in the eighteenth century.

In spite of policy initiatives, therefore, by the 1790s the transport system was still unable to meet demands upon it or to serve the needs of a growing population; transport became a major bottleneck which held back economic growth in the Castilian heartland, deterring it from developing an industry of its own, and preventing it from becoming a market for the industry of other regions. Catalonia and the other maritime provinces reached their overseas markets and sources of raw materials by sea more easily than they reached Castile by land.

---

[83] David R. Ringrose, *Transportation and Economic Stagnation in Spain, 1750-1850* (Durham, NC, 1970), pp. 135–6.

[84] Intendant of Cuenca to Múzquiz, 25 April 1769, AGS, Secretaría de Hacienda 586.

[85] Intendant of Burgos to Squillace, 8 December 1765, AGS, Secretaría de Hacienda 584.

Lords and Masters

Spain swarmed with nobles, some of them wealthy magnates, others poor labourers. Although they diminished in numbers in the second half of the century, from 800,000 in 1750 to 722,794 in 1768, 480,000 in 1787, and 403,000 in 1797, they still remained a populous species, their numbers swollen by the multiplicity of *hidalgos* in northern Spain, the traditional home of pauperized nobles. In the Montaña of Santander, according to the *catastro* of Ensenada, almost all those listed were 'of noble estate', though by occupation they were 'farmers', 'stonemasons', 'blacksmiths', and in the case of Josefa Ocharán a '*hijadalgo*, by occupation a seamstress and peddlar'.[86] These were social anachronisms, a remnant of different times. In reality the *hidalgo jornalero*, the Asturian or Basque noble labourer, the noble tenant farmer of Castile, was at the other end of the social spectrum from the grandees of Spain. In Galicia, where the clergy were the leading social group, distinguished by their superior income from land, tithes and seigneurial dues, there were few *titulados* and most of the nobility were petty *hidalgos* drawing their income from rents.[87]

Outside these provinces and above these ranks the number of nobles shrank and their property increased, moving upwards from that of medium proprietors and tenant farmers to the estates of *titulados* and grandees. The distribution of the *titulados* was exactly the reverse of the *hidalgos*. According to the census of 1797, which classified 402,059 of the population as *hidalgos*, there were only 1,323 *titulados*; of these Guipúzcoa had 14, Vizcaya 0, Asturias 15, Burgos 33, Catalonia 61, Extremadura 168, Navarre 289, Seville 100, and Madrid 289.[88] These were the real nobles, identified not by the old concept of estate but by wealth. Spain was now a society of classes.

The significance of social estate waned in the eighteenth century. The military justification of nobility was already dead even before the birth of a national army. As the crown resisted the political pretensions of the nobility, so it reduced their numbers, diminished their fiscal exemption by indirect taxation, and declared work to be compatible with nobility. The noble estate was not a closed caste. Money could open its door

[86] Vilar, 'Structures de la société espagnole vers 1750', *Mélanges à la mémoire de Jean Sarrailh*, p. 427.

[87] Saavedra and Villares, 'Galicia en el antiguo régimen', *España en el siglo XVIII*, pp. 474–6.

[88] Domínguez Ortiz, *Sociedad y estado en el siglo XVIII español*, p. 246.

without the help of blood or lineage. The *nouveaux riches* were able to move upwards, renting or buying estates, monopolizing municipal land when it came on the market, dispossessing their poorer neighbours, founding *mayorazgos* (entails), acquiring patents of nobility and joining the ranks of the local oligarchy.[89] Upward mobility of this kind destroyed the myth of a society of estates. It was wealth, above all land, that conferred social status and eased the way into local elites. Spain was basically divided between those who owned land and those who worked it, those who lived off rents and those who performed social functions. In 1797 agriculture absorbed more than 65 per cent of the active population, the service sector 22 per cent, and industry 12 per cent. Those who dominated rural Spain formed the upper sector of a class society, headed by the higher nobility and clergy who owned the best land and who between them owned more than one-half of all cultivated land. Below this were the *campesinos* (whether owners, tenants or labourers), artisans (craftsmen or apprentices), and the bourgeoisie (liberal professionals, merchants, and manufacturers). No region was exempt from the prevailing stratification. Even the Basque provinces, behind the image of an ideal society – one, equal and free – preserved a reality of social divisions, *hidalgos* and commoners, lords and vassals, wealthy and poor, the facade of equality simply a defence mechanism against the demands of the central state.

The income of the nobility came primarily from land, secured by *mayorazgos* and reinforced by *señoríos*. Entail and primogeniture were not exclusive to the nobility, but it was they who most exploited them. The institution was criticized as inequitable and inefficient, starting from the premise that it could not be subject to mortgage or long-term lease, only life-term. Thus it removed land from the market and raised its price; it constituted an obstacle to the diffusion of property and therefore to productivity. When not managed directly for the owner, noble lands were rented out to wealthy men who were in a position to rent large units; these in turn either employed labourers to farm the lands or more commonly sublet them to tenant farmers. The owner's only interest therefore was to obtain his rents, which he spent on conspicuous consumption. The lessees, enjoying only short-term leases, had no inducement to improve or invest in technical innovation, only to get the most out of the land at the least expense.

Seigneurial jurisdiction, normally obtained by royal grant or

---

[89] Richard Herr, *The Eighteenth-Century Revolution in Spain* (Princeton, NJ, 1958), pp. 107–10.

purchase, bestowed two advantages: it was a source of income and a base for social power. The economically productive *señoríos* were of two types: (1) *solariegos*, where the lord did not possess jurisdiction, simply ownership of land accompanied by certain honorific rights; (2) *mixtos*, where the proprietor of all or part of the land was also the jurisdictional lord, a characteristic combination.[90] At the beginning of the eighteenth century the greater part of Spain – Vizcaya and Guipúzcoa excepted – was subject to a seigneurial regime, thus interposing between the sovereign and the subject another, private, jurisdiction.[91] According to the census of 1797, there were 300,000 holders of seigneurial titles, or 2.8 per cent of the population; and as much as 68 per cent of the total cultivated land surface was subject to *señoríos* (51 per cent secular, 16 per cent clerical). The incidence was greatest in Galicia (over 50 per cent), Madrid, Salamanca, and Valencia (over 75 per cent), and Guadalajara (95 per cent). The pattern varied, from vast domains to deserted villages; but a number of nobles and monasteries were petty sovereigns in their *señoríos*, administering justice, controlling offices, collecting taxes, and imposing feudal-type dues and services, rents and products from land, monopolies of ovens, mills, wine and olive presses, and in general impinging directly on the lives and livelihoods of their vassals.[92] In the course of the eighteenth century the element of jurisdiction was eroded, and the real conflict between landlord and peasant was one of property, rent and dues; but both sides saw jurisdiction as a support and not merely as a symbol of power. Yet not all *señoríos* were oppressive, nor all *señoríos* heartless. Some lords, a minority no doubt, were enlightened leaders of their communities who invested in agriculture, industry, popular education, and public works. The severity of clerical *señoríos* varied. Bishops were usually mild. Monasteries were harsher and more demanding, especially in Galicia, where they charged feudal-type dues such as the right to the best head of cattle on the death of a vassal and in some cases the right to unpaid labour.[93]

In the three eastern kingdoms oaths of loyalty and homage were due from vassals to lords. Seigneurial jurisdiction was historically more severe in Aragon than in Castile and was still oppressive in the

[90] Antonio Domínguez Ortiz, *Hechos y figuras del siglo XVIII español* (Madrid, 1973), p. 6.

[91] On the previous history of *senoríos* see John Lynch, *Spain under the Habsburgs* (2nd edn, 2 vols, Oxford, 1981), I, pp. 13, 112–13, 208, 358; II, pp. 145–6, 255–6.

[92] Seigneurial administration of justice was by now confined to civil cases of first instance and minor crimes; the law was the king's law, with right of appeal to the *audiencia*.

[93] Domínguez Ortiz, *Hechos y figuras del siglo XVIII español*, pp. 1–62.

eighteenth century, especially in its fiscal administration, which exacted
exorbitant dues from vassals and their products and helped to impover-
ish many villages. In Catalonia, where *señoríos* were numerically
extensive – 778 localities of secular *señoríos*, 261 ecclesiastical, and 75
monasteries, as against only 588 royal – the exactions imposed were not
so heavy, though the fruits were enjoyed by an absentee nobility whose
lands and *señoríos* were often leased out and managed by a class of
administrators drawn from the higher peasantry or from merchants.
Valencia, on the other hand, was the whole seigneurial world in
microcosm.

In Valencia seigneurial jurisdiction continued undiminished in spite
of the revolts of 1705–7. Some 64 per cent of Valencian territory was
under *señorío*, most of it secular, and almost half the total population
were subject to its jurisdiction. Yet the great seigneurial families, the
dukes of Gandía and Segorbe, the count of Oliva, the marquis of Elche,
were not really Valencians at all but Castilians who lived in Madrid, but
each possessing tens of thousands of vassals and high feudal incomes.[94]
Another group, lesser lords with smaller incomes, derived their revenue
less from jurisdiction than from land rents. As for the *realengos*, or royal
domains, where the king was theoretically *señor*, these were hardly
different from private lordships in terms of dues and obligations. The
whole seigneurial regime in Valencia was oppressive and impoverishing,
a source of grim fascination to outside observers, a cause of enduring
grievance among its victims. The territorial lords took one-sixth or one-
eighth of all products, and any improvements or extension of cultivation
by farmers was immediately subject to new impositions. Quotas on fruit
trees, grains, and wine varied from as high as one-third to rarely less than
one-eighth; olives deteriorated because of the insufficiency of the lord's
mills.[95] Peasants could not even cut down dead trees without the lord's
permission, and then he took the trunks. Failure to observe any of these
rules would incur fines. Not content with existing practice, the lords of
Valencia staged a kind of 'feudal reaction' in the second half of the eighteenth century, when they sought to reclaim or reinforce seigneurial
rights and dues and impose yet greater fiscal obligations on their vassals.
The result was an upsurge of peasant protest which revived the tradition,
though not the scale, of the movements of 1693 and 1705–7, and was
expressed in complaints, litigation and resistance. In conjunction with
hunger riots and subsistence revolts, anti-seigneurial protest could make

[94] Ruiz Torres, 'El País Valenciano en el siglo XVIII', *España en el siglo XVIII*, pp. 233–43.
[95] Bourgoing, *Modern State of Spain*, III, pp. 248–9.

an impact in Valencia, as it did in 1766 when outrage at the price of food was canalized towards the anti-seigneurial movement by peasants who saw in feudal dues the true cause of their poverty.[96]

In most of Spain seigneurial jurisdiction lost its political implications in the eighteenth century and became a pure economic struggle between landlords and peasants, as landlords strove to increase their income from land and labour, and peasants to become proprietors. Yet *señorios* were basically incompatible with an absolutist state, and ministers regularly urged the crown to recover its lost revenues and offices. The resultant policy could hardly be called intemperate. First, the Bourbons created no new *señorios*. Then, between 1706 and 1732, they issued a series of enactments for the incorporation in the crown of specific classes of alienations. But it was not until the reign of Charles III that a serious programme of incorporation began, supported by the king, administered by the councils of finance and Castile, and starting with the recovery of *alcabalas* previously sold.[97] Even now the crown was too timid to aim for total abolition of *señorios*, as Campomanes and others advocated; instead it proceeded by partial enactments and litigation in individual cases to recover as many revenues and jurisdictions as possible. It was a weak policy, summed up in Floridablanca's *Instrucción reservada*: 'While it is not my intention to harm the lords of vassals or destroy their privileges, it is the duty of the courts and fiscals to examine carefully what they hold, and to seek to incorporate in the crown or to test all alienated jurisdictions, in accordance with existing privileges and laws.'[98] The law was slow and most of these cases took decades rather than years. It was not until 1805 that the government of Charles IV, selecting the weakest target, abolished the ecclesiastical *señorios* and incorporated their income. The structure of lay *señorio* remained intact, and its abolition had to await the *cortes* of Cadiz.

Income from land, rent, and dues more than kept pace with inflation in the second half of the eighteenth century, and the higher aristocracy enjoyed a lavish standard of living. Their conspicuous spending astonished foreigners. On journeys in the peninsula the wealthier nobility would travel in great magnificence in a train with five or six coaches, a waggon for their household effects, and a multitude of cooks, servants,

---

[96] José Miguel Palop Ramos, *Hambre y lucha antifeudal. Las crisis de subsistencias en Valencia (Siglo XVIII)* (Madrid, 1977), pp. 110–18, 136–41, 179–83.

[97] Salvador de Moxó, *La incorporación de Senorios en la España del Antiguo Régimen* (Valladolid, 1959), pp. 53–95.

[98] Quoted ibid., pp. 73–4.

and grooms.[99] Most nobles kept hundreds of servants; the top grandees many more, the maintenance of a town as well as a country house duplicating their retainers and their overheads. The Medinaceli family had a vast palace in Madrid containing offices, kitchens, an infirmary, a school for servants' children, archives, secretarial offices, stables, vaulted passages to different parts of the house, underground corridors to exit to the Prado, and sumptuous apartments on the upper floors. This great mansion covered several acres of ground and stood in three parishes, communicating by covered galleries with three churches; it housed 3,000 people, and was the centre of a nationwide domain, the outlying estates of which supplied much of the furniture, stone, wood, silks, cloth, and linen needed by the family and its retainers.[100] The dukes of Medinaceli were probably the leaders in income and property, followed closely by the dukes of Alba, Osuna, Infantado, and the count of Altamira. Nobles of this rank appeared to express their wealth and status not in artistic treasures or architectural magnificence but in the extent of their establishment and the size of its payroll.

> Their luxury is more obscure, but perhaps not the less expensive on that account. Numerous studs of mules, rich liveries which are exhibited but five or six times a year, an astonishing multitude of domestics, are the chief articles of expence among them. The management of their affairs is also expensive: they have stewards, treasurers, and offices, arranged like those of petty sovereigns. They maintain not only those who have grown old in their employment, but even the domestics of their fathers, and those belonging to the persons whose estates they inherit, and also provide for the subsistence of their whole families. The duke of Arcos, who died in 1780, maintained in this way 3,000 persons.[101]

To be a grandee, head of a great house, patron of a private welfare state, patriarch among his peoples, was almost a full-time occupation. Nobles of this station did not have to think too closely of a career. Others did, especially younger sons, or any noble in economic

[99] Keene to Castres, 11 April 1755, *Private Correspondence of Sir Benjamin Keene*, p. 403; Edward Clarke, *Letters concerning the Spanish Nation: Written at Madrid during the years 1760 and 1761* (London, 1763), p. 342.

[100] Elizabeth Vassall, Baroness Holland, *The Spanish Journal of Elizabeth Lady Holland*, ed. Earl of Ilchester (London, 1910), pp. 136, 196–7 (year 1804); see also Townsend, *A Journey through Spain*, ii, pp. 155–8.

[101] Bourgoing, *Modern State of Spain*, i, pp. 152–3.

difficulties. Many of the *titulos* had a career in the higher military; in fact they dominated the army and came to form a military elite who gained promotion rapidly through their privileged position; entrance to military colleges and military orders required noble status, and nobles more or less monopolized the rank of general. They were also favoured for certain kinds of public office, as captains general, colonial viceroys, and ambassadors. Politics were more problematical and to some extent more plebeian. The defeat of the aristocracy in the years after 1700, the abolition of the constitutions of Aragon, Catalonia, and Valencia, the downgrading of the conciliar system of government, and the reform of the *colegios mayores* in 1771, all tended to undermine the position of the magnates. If they had the perquisites of life at court, they also had its expenses and the daily reminder that the king was absolute and they were his servants. But not his most influential servants. These were drawn from a different elite, an aristocracy of office and merit.

The new men of government came from the lower nobility and even the commons, and were models of upward mobility through talent and patronage. Pedro de Lerena was the son of a publican at Valdemoro, apprenticed to a blacksmith; his first chance came with marriage to a rich widow in Cuenca, his second through meeting José Moñino, count of Floridablanca, who, once in power, helped him to become intendant of Andalucía and assistant of Seville, and, on the death of Múzquiz, secretary of finance and war. José de Gálvez came from a poor family near Malaga and earned his promotion to minister of the Indies by his own talents; his two brothers drove donkeys and were known as honest yeomen. Antonio Valdés advanced from naval officer to minister of Marine through friends and merit. Campomanes was wholly indebted to his own intelligence and ability, acknowledged by the king, recognized by the public. The most important offices of state, therefore, were occupied not by grandees but by men promoted from below; the grandees were confined to court positions, while the real task of government was left to those qualified for it.[102] They were all more or less noble, by right or aspiration, and none were the product of a 'bourgeois revolution', an impossibility in eighteenth-century Spain; but the *hidalgo* bureaucrats and ministers had very different ideas on government and policy from those of the older aristocracy.

While the nobility had lost much of their former power and significance as an estate, they still had income, social status, and influence as a

---

[102] Townsend, *A Journey through Spain*, ii, p. 269.

class. And with most to lose they of all Spaniards had the keenest sense of identity and class consciousness, the greatest urge to defend their economic and social interests. Not that the Spanish nobility was a beleaguered species in the eighteenth century. Even reformers accepted the existing social structure and justified nobility in terms of its service to the state. Campomanes thought equality 'utopian' and merely rejected 'that extreme inequality which reduces the majority of subjects to serfs'.[103] A number of writers such as León de Arroyal and Francisco Cabarrús criticized the nobility as idle and parasitic, complacent in their wealth, and indifferent to education. A few royal officials had their reservations about the provincial nobility whom they saw as useless to king and society: 'The nobility here are respectable but inert ... they ought to be encouraged to serve the king in an official or military career, to bestir themselves and not to sink into provincial obscurity.'[104] Officials worked to serve the state, not to engage in class struggle. Noble status was safe in the hands of the Bourbons. Charles III issued on 18 March 1783 a famous decree declaring that manual trades were 'honest and honourable ... nor are the arts and crafts to prejudice the enjoyment and prerogatives of *hidalguía*'.[105] Like many policy statements of this reign, it was ambiguous. It did not affirm the supremacy of economic values for social status, only their importance, and of course it accepted the superiority of *hidalguía*.

Bourgeois Precursors

In the course of the eighteenth century the higher nobility and clergy came to form an upper class. Many of the lower nobility, on the other hand, were losing income and influence and slipping out of what had become for them an archaic status. This downward mobility among the *hidalgos* was accompanied by an upward movement of merchants, urban artisans and rural farmers to coalesce in a new social class in the middle. The chronology of its formation and the stages of its existence in embryonic, incipient, and partial form until its culmination in the middle class of the nineteenth century are difficult to discern. Its composition, too, remained shadowy in the early stages. Merchant

---

[103] Quoted in Rodríguez, *Campomanes*, p. 112.
[104] Intendant of Burgos to Squillace, 8 December 1765, AGS, Secretaría de Hacienda 584.
[105] William J. Callahan, *Honor, Commerce and Industry in Eighteenth-Century Spain* (Boston, Mass., 1972), p. 52.

groups of any significance were to be found only in Cadiz and Barcelona, with smaller enclaves in Bilbao, Santander, Seville, Malaga, and Madrid. According to the census of 1797 the number of wholesale merchants was 6,824, retail 18,861. To these could be added a few entrepreneurs active in manufacturing, mainly in Catalonia. Officials numbered some 30,000, most of them in the tax service, and about 20,000 in the legal profession, including clerks and the liberal professions. The middle sectors of society, therefore, were not numerous, nor were they possessed of a strong sense of group identity or class consciousness. They were an amorphous collection, merchants, working *hidalgos*, parish priests, officials, small farmers, and members of the liberal professions, middle class in the sense that they belonged neither to the landed elite nor to the landless peasantry, many of them divided on current issues, and most of them agreed only on one, that it would be useful to acquire an estate and a title. The anxiety to escape from their class by ennoblement was understandable, for agriculture was a good investment and did not necessarily involve the abandonment of trade. But a doubt remains. Did social mobility signify the rise of the middle class or the reinforcement of aristocracy? Did not the most dynamic group in society work to profit from the existing structure rather than to change it?

The growth of the middle class corresponded to the growth of the bureaucracy and the economy in the course of the eighteenth century. The new groups, powerless to change the social structure, were capable of influencing economic policy, as seen in the corn laws of 1765, freedom of trade with the Indies in 1778, and the trend towards protectionism. But there was not a simple causal connection between economic growth and social change. In most of the cases of policy change the older privileged groups of landowners and agricultural exporters also benefited, indicating that successful pressure was the result of a coincidence of interests between the old and the new. The incipient bourgeoisie on its own was not a powerful pressure group. The Economic Societies could hardly be regarded as vehicles of middle-class ideas; they were semi-official bodies dominated by nobles of middle rank, clergy and officials, not by merchants and industrialists.[106] Nor were the universities nurseries of social change. Alcalá, Salamanca, and Valladolid experienced partial reform, in the face of considerable resistance, but they did not increase their student numbers or accom-

---

[106] Anes, *Economía e Ilustración*, pp. 11–41.

modate new social groups; by the mid-eighteenth century the universities of Castile together admitted no more than 5–6,000 students a year, less than one-third of the total in the late sixteenth century.[107]

The attributes of a new middle class were more recognizable in the periphery than in Castile. A merchant bourgeoisie with a business spirit and inspired by entrepreneurial rather than aristocratic values began to take root in Catalonia, where farmers, merchants, and artisans improved their prospects, accumulated capital, and invested in trade and industry.[108] Even the *señoríos* participated in this development, for they were often administered by lessees in the urban sector, especially in Barcelona. Bourgeois prototypes of this kind emerged clearly into the light of day in the middle decades of the century, leading families such as the Clota, Gibert, Guàrdia, Gener, and Milans, their eyes turned towards the Indies trade, their presence felt in new commercial organizations and in all sectors of the Catalan economy. Traditional values of honour, privilege, and corporatism were not extinct in Catalonia, but they were challenged by business culture, social mobility, and a preference for reason and experiment.[109] Barcelona soon acquired the educational institutions appropriate to its changing society, academies and colleges specializing in mathematics, engineering and draughtsmanship.[110]

Spain was a more complex society in 1800 than it had been a century earlier. No longer was it polarized between the two extremes of noble and peasant. Commercial growth, agricultural expansion and bureaucratic development had diversified incomes, raised expectations, and made many occupations an end in themselves. A middle class emerged, loosening the structure of traditional society, without however undermining its foundations.

The Popular Classes

The century of enlightenment, a golden age for noble and clerical landowners, and a period of opportunity for middle social groups, was a bad time for peasants and workers. Of the two the latter were the better off.

[107] Richard L. Kagan, *Students and Society in Early Modern Spain* (Baltimore, Md., 1974), pp. 200, 225.

[108] Roberto Fernández, 'La burguesía barcelonesa en el siglo XVIII: la familia Gloria', *La economía española al final del Antiguo Règimen*, II, *Manufacturas*, pp. 1–131.

[109] Martínez Shaw, 'La Cataluña del siglo XVIII', *España en el siglo XVIII*, pp. 101–4.

[110] Townsend, *A Journey through Spain*, I, pp. 116–19.

The increase of the urban population, an expanding service sector, and general economic growth all helped to improve the job prospects of the artisans and workers of the city. Urban workers lived better than the day labourers of the country. There was some upward movement of real wages which reached their highest point in the reign of Ferdinand VI. Nevertheless, taking into account the steep rise in prices from 1780–90, wages were low and even in Catalonia they lagged behind prices.[111]

The rural classes dominated the population. In central Spain – the two Castiles, Extremadura and La Mancha – peasants formed 80 per cent of the active population, the greater part of them victims of insecurity, poverty, and frequent malnutrition. North and south were at opposite extremes in the distribution of property and the proportion of *jornaleros* increased towards the south. This did not mean plenty for the north in contrast to penury in the south; rather north and south were two poles of rural misery, two modes of deprivation. In the whole of Spain, according to the census of 1797, there were 1,824,353 *campesinos*; of these 364,514 were owner farmers, or 19 per cent; 507,423 tenant farmers, 27 per cent; 805,235 day labourers, 44 per cent. Many tenants, however, had inferior leases; and many small owners were burdened with debt and ended up as tenants. La Mancha was an example of rural diversity converging into a uniform poverty: alongside a number of rich peasants who had accumulated their own land or rented from landlords, there was a more numerous class of small proprietors, many of whom slipped down to *jornalero*.[112] The popular classes, therefore, divided even in their marginality, had little sense of identity or capacity for organization. In conditions of particular oppression, in Valencia for example, a shadow of a protest movement could be observed in recurring litigation, daily resistance to seigneurial dues and sporadic violence, while in towns throughout Spain subsistence crises and food riots briefly united urban groups, poor artisans, vagrants, and immigrant peasants. Signs of disorder, but not of class conflict.

Yet in some parts of the country poverty was aggravated by the peasant's status of vassal as well as tenant. This was the case in Asturias, where deprivation was attributed to the excessive seigneurial power and exorbitant feudal dues of nobles and clerics:

---

[111] Earl J. Hamilton, *War and Prices in Spain, 1651-1800* (Cambridge, Mass., 1947), pp. 214–16; Vilar, *La Catalogne dans l'Espagne moderne*, III, pp. 419–554.

[112] Domínguez Ortiz, *Sociedad y estado en el siglo XVIII español*, p. 197.

The area [of the Montaña] is inhabited by a great many families who are so poor that even in years of plenty they have no bread, meat or wine, and consume only milk, millet, beans, chestnuts and other wild fruits. Their nakedness amounts to indecency; the same in their rooms and beds, for on the same straw and under the one blanket the parents, sons and daughters all sleep together, from which not a few offences against God result.[113]

The social structure of the countryside enclosed a crude form of domination, to which the peasant submitted through habits of obedience and docility, in the knowledge too that he was always under observation, that behind his lord stood the intendant, and behind the intendant the forces of law and order. The intendant of Burgos reported in 1765:

I am sorry to record an ingrained idleness among the people, working at nothing, lazy and wretched, wrapped in their cloaks, sunk in inertia and misfortune; but withall tranquil, obedient, and without notable vices. They have no factories, commerce, or any type of industry; yet if I am not mistaken, cloth, serge, and other woollen manufactures could easily be established . . . And by growing hemp or bringing it from La Rioja they could manufacture canvas and sail cloth and cheaply transport it to the coastal dockyards; but they would need Catalan masters to teach them.[114]

An extraordinarily obtuse report, confusing cause and effect, author and victim, and ignoring the historic conditions of rural and industrial depression in Old Castile.

Living standards of the popular sectors were kept low by permanent maldistribution of resources, aggravated in the eighteenth century by the recurrence of subsistence crises and the decline of artisan industry. Peasant conditions in Andalucía were perhaps the worst in Spain. The *jornaleros* lived on the edge of starvation, surviving with the help of work by their women and children, charity, and scavenging. At the beginning of the eighteenth century peons' wages were commonly 5 or 6 reales a day, at a time when the price of bread was 5½ reales.[115] Yet there

---

[113] Report of *visitador* Antonio José de Cepeda, *oidor* of Valladolid, on the zones of the Montaña in 1711, quoted by Domínguez Ortiz, ibid., pp. 149–50.

[114] Intendant of Burgos to Squillace, 8 December 1765, AGS, Secretaría de Hacienda 584.

[115] Dominguez Ortiz, *Sociedad y estado en el siglo XVIII español*, p. 30.

were few food riots in Andalucía; the events of 1766 in Madrid had little repercussion there, and agrarian crises were accepted with fatalist resignation, peasants finding some escape in rural industries. These of course were themselves in decline and reached their lowest point in the eighteenth century.[116] The absence of a national market and of suitable data make it difficult to determine variations of living standards and purchasing power among different occupational groups. The year following a crop failure would see grain prices rise 400 per cent, especially in the interior, adding cost to dearth in the struggle for survival.[117] In the province of Madrid in 1754 the wages of master weavers could reach 15 reales, those of journeymen 6 reales; but shepherds earned no more than 4 reales, and *jornaleros* 5. In Madrid itself living standards deteriorated in the eighteenth century, as can be seen by the decline in marriages and births and the increase in deaths and the number of foundlings.[118] As the aggregate wealth of the city increased in 1750–1800, the real wages of the low income groups lagged behind; the urban elites got wealthier, inequality in income distribution grew, and the purchasing power of the popular sectors declined. While the populations of the periphery were benefiting in the late eighteenth century from foreign and colonial trade, money wages in Madrid between 1750 and 1790 declined 30 per cent relative to the general price index. By the late 1780s urban povery was causing official anxiety, and the government began to subsidize the production of cheap *pan de pobres* (poor people's bread) at the city grain depot.[119]

Many of the poorer classes gave up the struggle and opted for vagrancy, joining the hordes of those without jobs, property or income who lived on the margin of the law and were the subject of much public debate. In the second half of the eighteenth century the *vago* was seen not as the traditional *picaro* or scoundrel but as a delinquent, and as well as the unemployed his ranks included drunks and gamblers, wife-beaters and false students. But it was also recognized that conditions could create *vagos*, and that indiscriminate charity, the *sopa boba*, agrarian and social crises, economic difficulties, all helped to swell the numbers of vagrants, not all of whom were delinquents.[120] Contemporaries probably

---

[116] Gonzalo Anes, *El Antiguo Régimen: los Borbones* (Madrid, 1981), pp. 195–203.

[117] Anes, *Economía e Ilustración*, p. 60.

[118] David R. Ringrose, *Madrid and the Spanish Economy, 1560-1850* (Berkeley/Los Angeles, Calif., 1983), p. 59.

[119] Ibid., p. 96.

[120] Rosa María Pérez Estévez, *El problema de los vagos en la España del siglo XVIII* (Madrid, 1976), pp. 56–73.

exaggerated their number – Campomanes gave a total of 160,000 – though the lists of those conscripted for military service and public works were known: 9,030 in 1759, 8,659 in 1764, lesser numbers in times of non-crisis. Most of them came from the southern half of the country, Valencia, Extremadura, and Andalucía, and mainly from rural zones where agrarian structures and crises produced an army of landless labourers and kept them in poverty and unemployment. *Campesinos* accounted for 42 per cent of vagrants, with 27 per cent from artisan and industrial occupations. Another focus was Madrid, a magnet for hungry peasants, beggars, rogues, and vagabonds, all looking for charity from court and convents or a life on the streets.[121]

For most of the eighteenth century vagrants were simply rounded up and put in the army, the navy and the dockyards. Ensenada had hundreds of them sent to hard labour in Cartagena, Cadiz and El Ferrol, where they suffered high mortality. He also rounded up some 12,000 gipsies and consigned them to prisons or dockyards amidst a storm of protest and fears that he was planning genocide.[122] Campomanes had more humane views on vagrants, the poor and the underprivileged, and he advocated that they be assigned either to work projects or to appropriate hospitals. Fom 1775 a more reformist policy was adopted and vagrants were now recruited for public works rather than the army and navy; much was made of rehabilitation, social institutions and 'honest' work. This more social approach did not appear to give successful results, so from 1785 policy reverted to conscription for the army, and vagrants were forced to remain on the alert, to pose as pilgrims, enrol as students, do anything to guard the marginalization they preferred. Some of the more docile, or less wary, were put into *hospicios* or workhouses, where they were expected to cure their idleness and produce something profitable. The state encouraged the extension of workhouses, one of which, at Cadiz, was described as a particularly successful model by the English traveller William Townsend. Housed in a large, handsome building, it trained some 850 inmates in textile work and employed them on looms, stocking frames, a spinning jenny, and other machines, giving them financial goals and incentives. Townsend had an ideological aversion to charity, generator of dependency and sloth, and challenged the bishop of Oviedo on the pernicious effect of alms-giving; the bishop

[121] Ibid., pp. 94–103, 258–9.
[122] *Private Correspondence of Sir Benjamin Keene*, pp. 180–1; Antonio Rodríguez Villa, *Don Cenón de Somodevilla, Marqués de la Ensenada* (Madrid, 1878), p. 164; Domínguez Ortiz, *Sociedad y estado en el siglo XVIII español*, pp. 292–3.

agreed but pointed out, 'it is the part of the magistrates to clear the streets of beggars; it is my duty to give alms to all that ask.'[123] On the whole vagrants preferred charity to workhouses, which were regarded as part prisons, part reformatories, and part sweat shops, and which in any case could not provide permanent employment.[124]

Conditions of life and labour at the edge of society did not go unchallenged. While social rebellion was rare, industrial protest in factories and shipyards made itself felt both among free and conscript labour. The gangs of vagrants put to work in the royal dockyards were quick to voice grievances, against long hours, harsh treatment, inadequate food and lodging, severe punishments for complainants.[125] They took their complaints to intendants, commandants, and priests, and when nothing was done they turned to more violent protest, hunger strikes, acts of arson, abortive uprisings. There was a riot in El Ferrol in September 1754 when shipyard workers' wages were delayed; they abandoned work, posted up protests and assembled outside the dockyard, whereupon payment was made the same afternoon and the leaders were arrested. The following morning many workers were taken out and pressed to explain the reasons for the walk out; when they did not respond they were placed in chains as an example to others, some were sent to African penitentiaries, and a quarter of the workforce was dismissed.[126] These were free workers. In Cartagena in 1757 convicts took the initiative in a carefully planned attempt to poison the guards and make their escape; only a last-minute disclosure by a priest thwarted the plan. A similar attempt in the dockyard of Caracca, Cadiz, in March 1765 was also revealed by a priest and stopped in its tracks. Industrial action in the dockyard of Guarnizo in April 1766 was a particular manifestation of social unrest throughout Spain in the spring of that year. In this case the grievances were the price and quality of foodstuffs, high rents, and lack of medical and religious facilities in the shipyard. The workers went on strike and threatened to march on Santander 'to prevent wheat leaving for France', thus using their industrial muscle to make a political point. The dispute rumbled on until the end of June when a settlement conceded half pay to injured workers and quarter pay to the sick, and some of the strikers were dismissed.[127] Further examples of industrial action occurred in 1782,

[123] Townsend, *A Journey through Spain*, ii, pp. 9, 374–83.
[124] Callahan, *Honor, Commerce and Industry in Eighteenth-Century Spain*, pp. 60–4.
[125] Pérez Estévez, *El problema de los vagos en la España del siglo XVIII*, pp. 259–63.
[126] José P. Merino Navarro, *La Armada Española en el siglo XVIII* (Madrid, 1981), pp. 74–5.
[127] Ibid., pp. 75–6.

1795, 1797, and 1808, usually caused by the government's financial difficulties and consequent delay in pay, and sometimes with violent results.

Strikes of shipyard workers were not unique. The textile industry also had a history of protests, walk outs and strikes, in Béjar in 1729, in Avila in 1784 and 1806, and in Guadalajara throughout the eighteenth century. Here the royal factory experienced prolonged labour unrest and frequent incidents of industrial action, not yet amounting to a labour or working class movement, but evidence that workers were capable of taking individual and collective action in pursuit of wage claims, improved conditions, and legitimate procedures. Evidence too, if more were needed, that the eighteenth century was a hard time for the popular classes.

Urban Spain

The urban life of Spain was a dichotomy between the political city of Madrid, isolated in the Castilian interior, and the commercial centres of the periphery, looking towards the Atlantic and beyond. The contrast was not necessarily to Madrid's disadvantage, for the wealth and population of Castile were significant if not dynamic. Madrid had no monumental buildings, no university, no episcopal see, and no great economic institutions. But it was the seat of government, the capital of an empire, and the largest concentration of people in the peninsula. The eighteenth century was a time of moderate though not spectacular growth. The population of Madrid increased from 11,268 in 1743 to 184,404 in 1799, moving more or less in time with economic trends and reflecting the prosperity of the 1750s, the crisis of the mid 1760s, growth and fluctuation in the years 1770–93, the sharp crisis around 1800 and then decline until 1812.[128]

Visitors enjoyed the social life of Madrid but not its environment. The surrounding landscape was desolate and melancholy, the outskirts were uniformly miserable. Whatever else affluent *madrileños* spent their money on, it was not elegant housing. But Charles III and his ministers exerted themselves to improve the city centre and visitors were soon impressed:

[128] Ringrose, *Madrid and the Spanish Economy*, pp. 27, 58–61.

It has several fine streets, but very few fine public buildings. The post-office, built by Marques de Grimaldi's direction is in bad taste, and of the worst French architecture. The custom-house, now building by Sabatini, is a good performance, and, were he not confined in space, his great talents and abilities would make it a masterpiece. The palace is an enormous pile, and, standing on the brow of a hill, appears most magnificently on the north-east of the town.[129]

Aranda made further improvements, paving and lighting the streets, and laying out the Prado as a wide public walk which separated the town from the Buen Retiro; it was now that Sabatini's Alcalá gate was planned. But the palaces of the nobility were rarely handsome and often stood within a few yards of inns, shops and shabby streets. Middle-class housing did not give the impression of a group determined to impose itself and its standards: 'The middling people live on separate floors, as at Edinburgh, which renders one common entrance to many families very dirty and disagreeable: the portals are the receptacles for every kind of filth.'[130] Hygiene in general was poor and rules for placing rubbish in public dumps and not in the streets were often ignored.

The economy of Madrid, it was often said, consisted of government and tailoring. Far from stimulating the Spanish economy, Madrid helped to deform it.[131] In the early modern period the capital's growing population and pressure on supplies diverted resources from other cities of Castile and led to their decline. Yet Madrid constituted a relatively narrow market. The concentration of income in a small political and aristocratic elite meant that Madrid consumed a lot of imported luxuries, demand for which remained inelastic. At the same time the rest of the capital's population lived near subsistence level and their demand for basic foodstuffs was also inelastic, being already irreducible. This narrow market structure was fatal to the craft industries of Castile and the manufacturing sector of Madrid, and did not even do much for agricultural producers. The result was that 'the capital transmitted economic forces into the Castilian hinterland in ways that reinforced its economic stagnation.'[132] Thus Castile was left behind when in the eighteenth century the periphery began to participate in maritime and

---

[129] Harris, *Diaries and Correspondence*, I, pp. 41–2 (writing in 1768–70).
[130] Dalrymple, *Travels through Spain and Portugal*, pp.40–1.
[131] Ringrose, *Madrid and the Spanish Economy*, pp. 85–7, 97–8, 185–92.
[132] Ibid., p. 87.

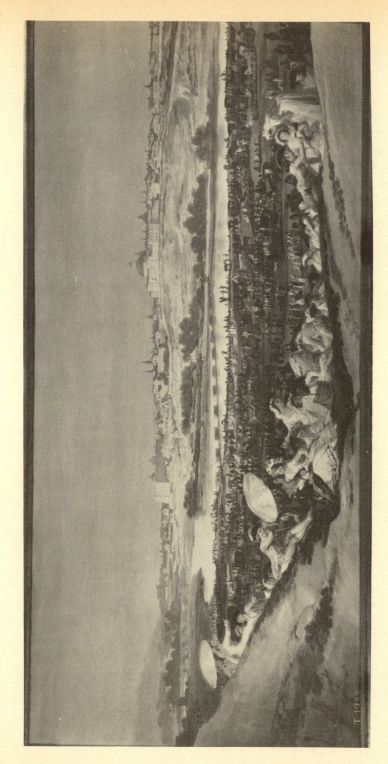

Plate 4 *The Meadow of San Isidro*, by Francisco Goya (reproduced by kind permission of the Museo del Prado, Madrid)

commercial expansion and to increase its production to meet the demands of the international market. And Madrid, the centre of so much wealth, had nothing to invest it in except land and deposits in the Five Greater Guilds. In the 1750s, therefore, the Madrid economy was dominated by political, land-owning and clerical elites, together forming 21 per cent of the active population yet receiving 67 per cent of all disposable income.[133] The mercantile and professional sectors were well below, forming 8.7 per cent of the active population and receiving 8.5 per cent of disposable income. These groups together appropriated 75 per cent of urban income. Meanwhile the artisans and other workers, forming 46 per cent of the total workforce, shared only 11 per cent of urban income. For the rest of the century income distribution in the capital moved even further against the popular sectors.

In the course of the eighteenth century Barcelona underwent not one but two forms of growth: as a commercial city it outgrew the confines of the Mediterranean and became in effect an Atlantic port; as a centre of manufacturing it developed from a traditional artisan framework to a modern industrial city. By 1805 it had 166 licensed merchants, 4 major insurance companies, 58 exchange agents and 23 consular agents, 91 factories of printed cottons concentrating large numbers of workers, canon foundries, glass works, and other factories. The model was reproduced in smaller towns of coastal Catalonia. In 1800 Barcelona had a population of 100,000 and its immediate villages were growing even faster. Another indication of change appeared in 1763–4, when agrarian crisis pushed into the city some 10,000 peasants who were almost immediately absorbed into the textile industry as factory workers and wage earners. Artisans too fell into dependence on commercial capital, either of entrepreneurs or of rich masters. A new social structure was emerging in total contrast to that of Madrid.[134] In the census of 1787 there were only 235 *hidalgos* (Madrid had 8,545) but 599 manufacturers, some of whom employed hundreds of workers and were on the way to great wealth. More developed than Madrid, Barcelona was more dynamic than Seville.

Seville was locked into the agrarian structure of Andalucía and that was immobile. True, it suffered a number of exceptional adversities in the early eighteenth century – trade damaged by the War of Succession, a cycle of crop failures and heavy mortality, loss of the American trade monopoly to Cadiz – yet it still had a number of advantages as the centre

[133] Ibid., pp. 72–4, 318.
[134] Martínez Shaw, 'La Cataluña del siglo XVIII', *España en el siglo XVIII*, pp. 97–108.

of commercial agriculture, and the seat of a regional administration which under intendants such as Olavide had its moments of enlightenment. The city had a traditional artisan sector and a number of significant factories; the royal tobacco factory, housed in a fine building, had a large work force (1,500) and a high output; private enterprise was no less persistent, though less successful. But the population remained stationary at about 85,000, with if anything a slight tendency downwards.[135] By 1800 Barcelona had taken over the position of second city of Spain.

Seville's loss was Cadiz's gain. Cadiz grew to prosperity in the eighteenth century and the years after 1778 were its golden age, when the loss of the legal monopoly of American trade only proved that it enjoyed a natural monopoly. Cadiz remained Spain's leading Atlantic port, a naval base, a centre of international commerce and capital, and a focus of European attention. It was only after 1796, during the long war with England, that the vital colonial trade of Cadiz declined and withered. Some of its 70,000 or so population was employed in artisan industry, which compensated for lack of agriculture. But Cadiz never became an industrial centre; basically it remained an entrepôt whose exports to America came from the rest of Spain and Europe. Its financial structure was dominated by foreigners, while the native bourgeoisie earned their profits as commission agents of foreign firms rather than as independent merchants and capitalists. In this sense they were more 'Hispanic' in values than the merchants of Barcelona.

Bilbao was significant for Spain but small for Europe. Its commerical function was to export wool and iron. From an average of 25,000 sacks of wool a year, exports rose to a little over 30,000 about 1780. To increase its overseas trade Bilbao would have to enter the colonial market. It had the opportunity to do this with the advent of *comercio libre* in 1778, but it preferred its traditional rights to new opportunities. The Basque customs frontier was inland on the Ebro and not on the coast; and the central government could not accept that the exempt provinces should have direct trade to America. Bilbao and Santander, therefore, were not included in the list of ports licensed to trade with America. La Coruña, on the other hand, took advantage of permission to trade with the Indies both before and after *comercio libre*, first exporting its own linen production in official mail packets, then from 1778 acting less profitably as a commission agent for Spanish and foreign exports.

<hr />

[135] García-Baquero, 'Andalucía en el siglo XVIII', *España en el siglo XVIII*, pp. 356–7.

This too was brought to an end by the onset of war in 1796, which diverted La Coruña to privateering and the slave trade.[136]

The cities reflected prevailing trends in Spanish life which they were powerless to change. Spain was an agricultural economy and its society was rural; some 65 per cent of the people and two-thirds of the gross national product were rural. The cities, pre-industrial in their own structure, varied in their capacity to impose themselves on this enduring world. Barcelona, integrating agricultural, commercial, and industrial growth, was a model of modernity. Cadiz, on the other hand, with the control of a colonial market within its grasp, failed to exploit its advantage and was content with the role of intermediary. Seville stagnated like its hinterland; Bilbao followed the Basque provinces into recession. Madrid was a special case, seat of government, centre of consumption, but a deadweight on the Spanish economy, a city of absentee landlords, rentiers and bureaucrats, sucking revenue in but investing little outside. Its rate of growth in the eighteenth century was inferior to that of London and less than half that of the 180 per cent population increase of Barcelona. In the rest of Castile Toledo, León, Avila, Segovia, and Burgos were places of inertia and routine during most of the eighteenth century, their cathedrals, convents and castles the only reminders of a great history. Such were Spain's cities, hardly the indicators of an economy on the move or a society in transition. With the possible exception of Barcelona, the cities of Spain were not places where people could escape from the hierarchical structures of the old regime or the values of the Hispanic past.

[136] Alonso Alvarez, *Comercio colonial y crisis del Antiguo Régimen en Galicia*, pp. 49–92.

7

Charles III: The Limits of Absolutism

King and Ministers

Charles III excelled by contrast, a prodigy among Bourbon misfits, a marked improvement on the past and a neglected model for the future. When he succeeded to the throne of Spain on 10 August 1759 he was forty-three, sound in mind and limb, experienced in government as duke of Parma and king of Naples, and known to be a reforming ruler with a will of his own.[1] On his arrival in Madrid in December he impressed foreign observers and his own subjects with his seriousness, ability and integrity. His personal life was exemplary and he kept a chaste loyalty to the memory of his wife Maria Amalia of Saxony who died a year after their accession, having given him thirteen children, six of whom died young. In a harsh and uncertain world he conveyed the impression of benignity and stability. Thus he was respected by his contemporaries and overrated by later historians. He was not enlightened in the eighteenth-century sense. His Catholic upbringing had been conventional and he was pious and traditional in his religious practice. He read little and had few cultural interests, and while he seems to have been aware of the world of ideas through conversation with ministers and courtiers, he was not an intellectual innovator. His interests lay elsewhere.

Even more than ruling he liked hunting, or more correctly shooting,

[1] See the classical accounts of the reign by Antonio Ferrer del Río, *Historia del reinado de Carlos III en España* (4 vols, Madrid, 1856), Manuel Danvila y Collado, *El reinado de Carlos III* (6 vols, Madrid, 1890–6), François Rousseau, *Règne de Charles III d'Espagne (1759-1788)* (2 vols, Paris, 1907), and the more recent work by Anthony H. Hull. *Charles III and the Revival of Spain* (Washington, DC, 1980).

Plate 5 *Charles III*, by Francisco Goya (reproduced by kind permission of the Museo del Prado, Madrid)

and his greatest delight was to kill driven game; this he did twice a day every day of the year except during Holy Week, a practice varied only by a grand *batida*, when he led a shooting party in the mass slaughter of deer herded down by local peasants. His physiognomy evolved with his obsession, and he came to look like a gamekeeper, more rustic than royal. Whether painted by Mengs or Goya, or described in contemporary chronicles, his appearance is unmistakable. Round shouldered, big boned, of a brown complexion, with a large prominent nose, he was usually to be seen in plain outdoor dress with a gun, followed by servants carrying provisions and dead game, such as wolves, hares, rooks, and gulls. He did not deviate in the slightest detail from his daily routine – business, shooting, dinner, more shooting, more business, and to bed at ten o'clock. Even when the Infante Xavier was dying of smallpox at Aranjuez in April 1771, the king insisted on going out on a shooting expedition; when informed that his son was dead, he replied with his usual calmness 'Well, then, since nothing can be done, we must make the best of it.'[2] The royal family moved in an unchanging itinerary around the royal *sitios*, in January to the Pardo, in April to Aranjuez, in June back to Madrid, at the end of July to San Ildefonso, in October to the Escorial, and in late November to Madrid again.[3] An expensive court, costly palaces, and wasteful routine, but royal expenditure was sacrosanct. Charles III was sensitive of his sovereignty and his ideal of government was pure absolutism, exercised when necessary by personal decisions. He was nobody's creature, he used his own judgement, and he was never dominated by ministers. Once he had made up his mind, whatever the prospects, he did not change it, any more than he changed ministers. He had a curiously fatalist submission to adversity and attributed it to the will of God, a tendency which made him ultimately complacent about the state of Spain and incapable of overcoming the obstacles to reform.

\ Charles III did not proceed beyond the established framework of law and custom. The inequalities inherent in a society divided by estate, class, and corporate privilege left him unmoved. In the 1760s an attempt was made to impose fiscal equality but it was weakly abandoned. In 1776

---

[2] Joseph Townsend, *A Journey through Spain in the Years 1786 and 1787* (2nd edn, 3 vols, London, 1792), II, p. 124.

[3] For contemporary descriptions see Conde de Fernán Núñez, *Vida de Carlos III* (2 vols, Madrid, 1898); Edward Clarke, *Letters concerning the Spanish Nation: Written at Madrid during the years 1700 and 1761* (London, 1763), pp. 323–4; James Harris, First Earl of Malmesbury, *Diaries and Correspondence*, ed. Third Earl of Malmesbury (4 vols, London, 1844), I, pp. 50–1.

he actually tightened up marriage laws to prevent unequal matches among the royal family and the grandees. He made no attempt to reduce the extensive privileges enjoyed by nobles in matters of penal law. While he was severe on individual members of the aristocracy – he banished the dukes of Arcos and Osuna from Madrid because of their affairs with actresses – he handled their class with care. His first government sought to recover from the *señoríos* vital revenues alienated in the past. The duke of Alba, drawing an income of near £8,000 a year in *alcabalas*, was offered £80,000 in compensation. When he demurred the king increased the offer to £120,000, but so unwilling was he to offend this powerful family that he allowed Alba to continue to collect the *alcabala* until the treasury had enough cash to buy him out.[4] Moral cowardice or misguided caution? Whatever the reason, the limits of Charles III's vision were predictable. His basic policy was strength not welfare: the aim was to make Spain a great power through state reform, imperial defence, and control of colonial resources. His accession was marked by the arrival of a great treasure shipment from Veracruz in August 1759 totalling 12 million pesos, most of it on the king's account.[5] This was his priority, a resource to be defended and expanded.

The test of the new king's intentions and judgement lay in ministerial appointments. To reconstruct Spain there were two possible models of government. The first would comprise men with new ideas, ready to attack traditional structures and challenge previous policies. The second would be a government of pragmatists whose priority would be to reform the state and strengthen its resources. Each approach carried risks: the first might provoke a counter-revolution, the second produce only half-measures. In fact the second option could be secured only with the help of the first, for the state could only undergo root and branch reform at the expense of privileged groups. Charles began with a bias towards the first model. When this was challenged, in 1766, he adopted a combination of the two in an administration which lasted until 1773. He then made his final choice and opted for a government of pragmatic administrators which fulfilled many of the expectations held of it but did not significantly change the face of Spain. There were various reasons for this shift. The first was the paucity of people in public life who combined enlightened ideas and administrative ability; conversely strong administrators tended to lack originality. The second reason was the dominance of foreign policy in the thinking of Charles and his ministers. The

4 De Visme to Shelburne, 17 November 1766, Public Record Office, London, SP 94/175.
5 Bristol to Pitt, 3 September 1759, PRO, SP 94/160.

war of 1762 was unpopular, costly, and a diversion from reform. Yet foreign policy and rearmament enjoyed still greater priority in the period 1776–83, and even a major war with Britain did not satisfy the government's taste for confrontation. A regime so partial to war needed stability, not experiment, on the home front and looked for immediate fiscal returns rather than long-term structural reforms.

Charles began his reign by retaining all of Ferdinand's ministers except the count of Valparaiso at finance, whom he replaced (9 December 1759) by Leopoldo di Grigorio, the marquis of Squillace, a Sicilian who had served his government in Italy and was regarded by Spaniards as an upstart. Spain therefore went to war in 1762 under a minister of state and war, Ricardo Wall, and a minister of the Indies and the navy, Julián de Arriaga, who had long been associated with a policy of peace and now had to bear the opprobrium of failure in war. As the influence of Wall and Arriaga declined, Squillace's power increased, and when Wall resigned in August 1763 Squillace added the ministry of war to his portfolios.[6] The new minister of state was the marquis of Grimaldi, another Italian, who had served under both of Charles's predecessors and who, as ambassador at Versailles, was the architect of the third Family Compact between Spain and France. He was a competent diplomat but had never had an original idea in his life. 'His chief art is conforming to the will of his superiors, and making inferiors conform to his.'[7] The ministerial reshuffle thus placed the key positions of power – finance, war and state – in the hands of Italians, whose ascendancy was further emphasized by the formation in late 1763 of a *junta de ministros*, a kind of imperial defence committee consisting of Squillace, Grimaldi, and Arriaga, and scheduled to meet every Thursday to discuss colonial and commercial policy. Charles authorized this development apparently on the initiative of Grimaldi, who wanted to keep in touch with departments other than his own, and against the will of the other two.[8] But Squillace soon realized its possibilities and, with Grimaldi, came to dominate the committee, while Arriaga, a quiet, worthy man, confused in his ideas and not highly rated either by his colleagues or by the foreign ambassadors with whom he had to deal, was gradually marginalized.[9]

    [6] Allan J. Kuethe and Lowell Blaisdell, 'The Esquilache Government and the Reforms of Charles III in Cuba', *Jahrbuch für Geschichte von Staat, Wirtschaft und Gesellschaft Lateinamerikas*, 19 (Cologne, 1982), pp. 117–36.

    [7] Harris, *Diaries and Correspondence*, I, p. 56.

    [8] Rochford to Halifax, 13 January 1764, PRO, SP 94/166, 7 May 1764, PRO, SP 94/167.

    [9] Bristol to Pitt, 31 August 1761, PRO, SP 94/164; Rochford to Halifax, 6 August 1764, PRO, SP 94/168; Allan J. Kuethe, 'Towards a Periodization of the Reforms of Charles III', in Richard L.

Charles seems not to have appreciated the political risks he was running in concentrating power in the hands of foreigners, a retrogressive move out of step with the times. Squillace in particular was vulnerable. The post-war tax increases he was obliged to introduce were not made more palatable in coming from a foreigner. At the same time he gave his uncompromising support to a number of more radical reforms stemming from the fertile mind of Campomanes in the council of Castile, the incorporation of *señorios* in the crown, the introduction of free trade in grain, the proposal to disamortize church property. Squillace was probably more interested in the fiscal than the social implications of these policies, but the fact remains that he aroused the susceptibilities of privileged interest groups at the same time as he was losing popularity in the country. Dependent exclusively on the king's support, the position of Squillace posed an interesting test for absolutism and an early trial of nerves between the king and his more powerful subjects.

Charles learned from experience, especially from the crisis of 1766, to replace his Italians by Spaniards and gradually to strengthen his government and give it a clearer identity. Manuel de Roda, lawyer, regalist and servant of absolutism, was brought in as minister of grace and justice in January 1765. He was welcomed by Grimaldi but gradually distanced himself from the Italian to move towards alliance with his countryman, the count of Aranda, for whom he was a fruitful source of ideas. Aranda himself, Aragonese, a soldier, a man of independent mind, was a rough diamond who did not mix easily in politics and retained an aristocratic arrogance towards his humbler colleagues. Yet it was these, not Aranda, who were helping to design policies. The most distinguished of the policy makers was Campomanes, son of a poor *hidalgo* family in Asturias, who had made his way up via a conventional education and law practice in Madrid to become fiscal of the council of Castile in 1762 and eventually, from 1783, its president. Intellectual, scholar, and politician, Campomanes poured forth a ceaseless stream of papers, reports, and memoranda on the problems and policies of Spain and left his mark on a wide range of legislation. Less intellectual and more political, his colleague José Moñino was equally master of his brief. Son of a notary in Murcia, he studied law at Salamanca and on the recommendation of Squillace he was appointed fiscal of the council of Castile in 1766; after a

Garner and William B. Taylor (eds), *Iberian Colonies, New World Societies: Essays in Memory of Charles Gibson* (1985), pp. 103–17.

crucial embassy in Rome he was made count of Floridablanca and he replaced Grimaldi as secretary of state in 1776, an office he retained until 1792, the ideal servant of absolutism. The important American field was left in the ineffective hands of Arriaga until his death in 1776, when José de Gálvez was appointed minister of the Indies and reactivated a programme of imperial reform which had gone cold since 1766. Gálvez, who lacked intellectual distinction, was a determined user of power and a hard-line imperialist, whose policy area gave him a lot of political influence. Finally, the administration was completed by Juan de Muniain, minister of war, and Miguel de Múzquiz, minister of finance, the first a professional soldier with administrative experience as governor of Badajoz, the second a career bureaucrat of modest origins, client and first *commis* of Squillace.

The ministers of Charles III had an identity peculiar to the reign. They came not from the aristocracy, who were politically finished, nor as is sometimes alleged from the bourgeoisie, who were not yet a recognizable force in Spain, but from a group of university-trained lawyers among the lower ranks of the nobility, who were devoted to absolute monarchy and whose minds were open to modern knowledge. Their identity can be further defined by reference to their graduate status. The majority were *manteistas*, not *colegiales*; they had begun life outside the ranks of privilege and been forced to work hard for their degrees and careers, and to demonstrate an exceptional ability to master a subject, run a department, and deal with foreigners. Once they had broken the stranglehold of the *colegiales* on government, in some cases with the help of Squillace, they tended to create their own network and perpetuate their own type. They are sometimes described as a 'team' and even 'enlightened'. Yet they were far from homogeneous. In the post-Squillace government Grimaldi, Roda, Aranda, Múzquiz, Campomanes, Floridablanca, and Gálvez were all reformists of one kind or another, but there were degrees of reform, differences over policy, divisions between factions. Aranda despised the *manteistas*, especially Campomanes whom he criticized for dominating the council, and although he was a friend of Voltaire and posed as a man of the Enlightenment, he was basically a traditionalist who favoured a return of the aristocracy to power. There was a wide spectrum of intellectual positions: at one end the freethinking Roda and secularist Campomanes, at the other the anti-Enlightenment bigot José de Gálvez. Jean François Bourgoing, who as secretary of the French embassy in Madrid had many dealings with Gálvez, recorded:

Of late, certain persons have attempted to make the Spanish literati acquainted with the philosophical history of Raynal, a work which incensed the Spanish government to such a degree that I have often seen Gálvez, minister of the Indies, burst into a violent passion at the mere mention of the author's name, regarding those who had endeavoured to introduce some surreptitious copies into the Spanish colonies in the light of criminals guilty of high treason against God and man.[10]

In spite of the Encyclopaedic influences which some of the ministers absorbed there was little ideology in their policies and no overt attack on religion. The model was Floridablanca, aware of the world, ready to learn, but quick to react.

The Enlightenment in Spain

The Spanish monarchy did not live in isolation. This was the age of absolutism, when kings everywhere sought to make themselves as powerful in practice as they were in theory, partly to overcome resistance to modernization, partly to defeat rivals for power such as the Church, and partly to survive in a world of international conflict. Some rulers attempted to reform their government and administration, and in the process they began to employ a professional bureaucracy, to improve the flow of information, and to perfect the financial machinery. To what extent were they influenced by the ideas of the time? Was the new absolutism a servant of enlightenment or convenience? The answer appears to be that philosophy was an influence but not a cause. The reform programme was informed by a spirit of empiricism and responded to needs rather than ideas. It is true that rulers invoked new theoretical justification for their position, whether it was the contractual theory of Locke, or the theory of 'legal despotism' advanced by the Physiocrats, who saw monarchy justified by its functions; these were to defend liberty and property, and if the monarchy was to do this effectively it needed strong legislative and executive powers. But on the whole it is difficult to trace a consistent pattern of Enlightenment ideas in the monarchies of the time, which continued to operate within the existing framework of authority and hierarchy.

[10] J. F. Bourgoing, *Modern State of Spain* (4 vols, London, 1808), II, p. 159.

The political ideas of the Enlightenment were far from systematic, but a number of characteristic themes can be observed.[11] Human government derived from natural rights and social contract. Among the basic rights were liberty and equality. These could be discerned by reason, and reason, as opposed to revelation and tradition, was the source of all human knowledge and action. Intellectual progress should be unhindered by religious dogma, and the Catholic Church was identified as one of the principal obstacles to progress. The object of government was the greatest happiness of the greatest number, happiness being judged to a large extent in terms of material progress. The aim was to increase wealth, though different means were envisaged, some advocating state control of the economy, others a system of *laissez-faire*. The success of the *philosophes* in propagating their ideas – and in silencing their opponents – concealed a number of flaws and inconsistencies in their view of the world. One of the blind spots of the Enlightenment was social structure and change. The Enlightenment was not essentially an instrument of revolution; it bestowed its blessing on the existing order of society, appealing to an intellectual elite and an aristocracy of merit. While it was hostile to entrenched privilege and to inequality before the law, it had little to say on economic inequalities or on the redistribution of resources within society. It was for this reason that it could appeal to absolutists. But could it appeal to Catholics? Deistic and free-thinking writings, first introduced from England, acquired a new lease of life in France in the eighteenth century. When deism emerged into the open with the writings of Voltaire and the Encyclopaedists, it was not a precise theology but a vague form of religion used as a sanction for politics and morals and as a cover against the charge of atheism. The growth of scepticism in religion and the specifically anti-Christian offensive of the *philosophes* not only represented intellectual positions; they also supported proposals to increase the power of the state over the Church and even to create a state religion which, however spurious, was regarded as necessary for public order and morals.

The literature of the French *philosophes* was known to only a small minority of educated Spaniards, a few thousand at the most, drawn from bureaucratic, academic, legal and clerical groups, most of them linked with the political establishment in Madrid and a few commercial centres

---

[11] For a comparative study, without the Spanish case, see Roy Porter and Mikulas Teich (eds), *The Enlightenment in National Context* (Cambridge, 1981); on enlightened absolutism see H. M. Scott (ed.), *Enlightened Absolutism. Reform and Reformers in later Eighteenth-Century Europe* (London, 1989).

which had contact with people, ideas and writings from abroad. There had been a faint stirring of intellectual activity in the first half of the century, reflected in the foundation of the National Library (1711), the Spanish Academy (1713), the Academy of History (1735), and other institutions which would eventually provide a research infrastructure but whose distinction and utility were not yet obvious. It was an individual precursor who showed the way. The greatest inspiration to searchers for knowledge was an obscure Benedictine monk and university teacher, Benito Jerónimo Feijóo, a writer with a mission as well as a talent – to arouse his compatriots from their torpor and persuade them to welcome new knowledge, accept change, pursue truth through reason and experience, and see innovation as a means to prosperity. In a series of encyclopaedic works he sought to bring Spain up to date in European thought. His *Teatro crítico universal* in nine volumes (1726–39) followed by the *Cartas eruditas* in five, were neither simple nor cheap but they sold briskly to a public ready for what they contained, comprehensive information on a variety of topics – philosophy, theology, science, medicine, and history – in clear and distinct language by an author who was critical without being iconoclastic, modern without abandoning Spanish values.[12] But there was a limit to what Spaniards could learn from Feijóo, a specialist in some subjects but not in all, and by the 1750s the reading public awaited new sources of knowledge.

The ideas of the Enlightenment entered Spain from the middle years of the century; they came in a trickle rather than a flood and the flow was stronger in some fields than in others, but gradually they passed the official barriers in their way and reached those with the means and the wish to know. The French *Encyclopédie*, prohibited by the Spanish Inquisition in 1759, was nevertheless available to readers who wanted it.[13] Scientific and technical knowledge was disseminated through books, visits, museums and the press, and by the 1770s and 1780s the writings of Buffon and Linnaeus were in the hands of interested readers. Economic ideas were freely discussed; mercantilist thought, much of it imported, enjoyed a new lease of life in the middle decades of the century, though the writings of the physiocrats and Adam Smith were known to only a few readers until the 1780s.[14] Political ideas were more

[12] On Feijóo see Luis Sánchez Agesta, *El pensamiento político del despotismo ilustrado* (Madrid, 1953), pp. 35–84; Julio Caro Baroja, 'Feijóo en su medio cultural', *El P. Feijoo y su siglo* (3 vols, Oviedo, 1966), I, pp. 153–86.

[13] Jean Sarrailh, *L'Espagne éclairée de la seconde moitié du XVIIIe siècle* (Paris, 1954), pp. 269–70.

[14] Robert S. Smith, 'The Wealth of Nations in Spain and Hispanic America, 1780–1830', *Journal of Political Economy*, 65 (1957), pp. 104–25.

controversial. The writings of Montesquieu, in many ways a crucial test of enlightenment, contained too many arguments for individual liberty, religious toleration and constitutional monarchy to escape the attention of the Inquisition, but in spite of its prohibition his thought still penetrated the peninsula. Rousseau had a mixed reception in Spain, as he did in most parts of Europe, and his works were greeted with outrage and condemnation, excitement and praise; but in one way or another they were all well known to the educated elite, as were those of Condillac and Raynal. Voltaire on the other hand, though certainly known, had less impact, not merely because of the Inquisition, which could be evaded, nor because of the conservative opposition, which was intellectually feeble, but because he aroused less interest among potential readers.[15]

The channels of enlightenment were themselves new creations. The universities were in the throes of reform, the conflict between tradition and modernity still unresolved, their structures too deeply rooted in the past to be ready receptacles of innovation.[16] The agencies of debate were the Economic Societies and the press, both created in the spirit of the age and both reflecting its concerns. Some seventy Economic Societies were founded in Spain between 1765 and 1820, modelled on the Basque original, protected by the patronage of Campomanes and the council of Castile, and sustained by the dual interest of their members in European ideas and Spanish conditions.[17] Although they met with some hostility from conservatives, they were by no means anti-clerical in outlook and numbered some of the clergy among their members. Their basic object was to improve agriculture, commerce and industry by study and experiment, and their interest in the Enlightenment was pragmatic rather than speculative; and socially they wanted to educate the nobility, not demote them. The press occupied a more advanced position in the struggle for change, and it was here that an element of social criticism could be observed, first in *El Pensador* (1761–7), then more insistently in *El Censor* (1781–7), edited by Luis Cañuelo, a Madrid lawyer.[18] *El Censor* did not hesitate to attack social parasites, wealthy clergy, and obscurantists whoever they were, including the Inquisition. Cañuelo anticipated events by closing the paper himself before being summoned and rebuked

[15] Richard Herr, *The Eighteenth-Century Revolution in Spain* (Princeton, NJ, 1958), pp. 42–85.
[16] On university reform see below, pp. 285–7.
[17] Sarrailh, *L'Espagne éclairée*, pp. 225–62; Robert J. Shafer, *The Economic Societies in the Spanish World (1763–1821)* (Syracuse, NY, 1958), pp. 24–8.
[18] Herr, *The Eighteenth-Century Revolution in Spain*, pp. 183–200.

by the tribunal. But other periodicals continued the trend towards press independence; *El Correo de Madrid*, established in 1786, was less radical than *El Censor* but performed a valuable role in the diffusion of European thought and current knowledge. Another vehicle of reformist tendencies was the *Semanario erudito*, founded by Antonio Valladares de Sotomayor in 1787, a periodical which published documents from Spanish history as sources of instruction and criticism, using the past to inform the present. The readership of the press was a further indicator of the composition of the intellectual elite; subscription lists confirmed the existence of a progressive minority among the aristocracy and clergy, but also that the majority of readers were *hidalgos* and commoners, specifically professional people, merchants and the bureaucracy, many of them concentrated in Madrid and Seville.

The prototype of the enlightened Spaniard was Campomanes, *hidalgo* in origin, intellectual by nature, and statesman by career. He did not disavow religion, but he was not a traditional Spanish Catholic; his faith was diluted by secularism and anti-clericalism, and his eyes were fixed firmly on this world rather than the next. He believed essentially in reason and results. His philosophy was one of utility, the greatest happiness of the greatest number, and he tended to define happiness in terms of economic progress. His economic ideas were those of free trade and market forces. Politically he was hostile to privilege: 'all privilege is odious', he said, though he did not question class divisions.[19] Nor did he question absolute monarchy; on the contrary, absolutism was his political model. He subscribed to a Hobbesian type of social contract, one which created an absolute sovereign and involved no right of revocation or resistance; he added to the argument by invoking a divine not popular origin of power. Campomanes served the Bourbon state as a theorist as well as an official. He sought to strengthen the state as an instrument of reform, placing yet greater power in the hands of the monarch to enable him to mobilize men and resources, change policy, reform institutions. The dual character of Spanish reformism, committed to royal power and open to the Enlightenment, was typified by Campomanes. So too was its pragmatism and its sense of history. But the Enlightenment was not the only source of inspiration. For

[19] Laura Rodríguez Díaz, *Reforma e Ilustración en la España del siglo XVIII. Pedro Rodríguez de Campomanes* (Madrid, 1975), pp. 45–7, 93; on Campomanes see also Felipe Alvarez Requejo, *El conde de Campomanes: su obra histórica* (Oviedo, 1954), Ricardo Krebs Wilckens, *El pensamiento histórico, político, y económico del conde de Campomanes* (Santiago, 1960), and M. Bustos Rodríguez, *El pensamiento socio-económico de Campomanes* (Madrid, 1982).

many reformers Spain's own past provided models and warnings in abundance.

The study of Spanish history entered a new phase in the eighteenth century and the first steps were taken towards the use of original research, critical methods, and wider themes. Campomanes's own writings had a strong historical dimension; he was also active in the work of the Academy and anxious to link it with developments in European historiography. Like others of his time he believed that history had a practical value, and he sought evidence from the past to justify action in the present. In his view Spain lost its way under the Habsburgs, when imperial imperatives damaged national interests and when its rulers ignored the fact that 'all states have their natural limits' and that the true greatness of a nation lies in internal stability and economic prosperity.[20] The decline of Spain began when the interests of particular groups took preference over the common good, for example the *Mesta* over agriculture, the privileges of the clergy over the welfare of society, the power of the guilds over national industry. The particular reasons for Spain's prostration he identified as the misuse of precious metals, excessive numbers of clergy, expulsion of the *moriscos*, and high taxation. This was a conventional 'liberal' view of the Spanish past, drawn from his reading of the *arbitristas*, the traditional projectors of reform schemes, and eighteenth-century authors such as Uztáriz. Such use of history ran the risk of selectivity and partiality, and in the ultimate analysis came up against the same barriers to change as those experienced by the Enlightenment. For Campomanes was unable to convince landowners, nobles and clerics of the need for reform or even of their own self-interest. Like the physiocrats, therefore, he was impelled to invoke the power of the state to impose by authoritarian means policies which should have been self-evident to the interest groups. Yet this did not invalidate his position. Campomanes was designing a political programme, not a philosophical system. As he himself said, 'Politics are not derived from general principles ... it is the consideration of actual circumstances which forms political judgement.'[21]

Pragmatism of this kind was common to most Spanish reformers. They were looking not for a new political theory but for practical answers to administrative, economic and educational problems. The spirit of reform in Charles III's government was animated primarily by the desire to increase the strength of the state and the prosperity of its

[20] Quoted by Rodríguez, *Campomanes*, p. 81.
[21] Quoted ibid., p. 91.

Plate 6 *Gaspar Melchor de Jovellanos*, by Francisco Goya (reproduced by kind permission of the Museo del Prado, Madrid)

subjects, goals which were seen as mutually dependent. The whole movement of reforming speculation has been aptly described as '*culture utilitaire et culture dirigée*', its object to promote technical skill and practical knowledge.[22] To serve this object reformers took ideas and examples from various sources, including the Enlightenment. But the Spanish elite was receptive to the Enlightenment in varying degrees. To some it was a model, to others an intellectual exercise, and to yet others a mere curiosity. In any event, it was not accepted indiscriminately. As for the mass of the people, they remained Catholic in conviction and devoted to absolute monarchy, 'more attentive to the preaching of Fray Diego de Cádiz than to ideological innovation'.[23] But Fray Diego did not have the last word.

From the 1780s the enlightened minority became more radicalized. Even before the French Revolution a new generation had graduated from the Spanish universities disillusioned with paternalist government, reform from above, and traditional values.[24] The impact of the French Revolution and the debasement of the Spanish monarchy itself sharpened political divisions. While conservatives became more conservative, progressives looked for an alternative to absolute monarchy and a submissive Church. In the process they went beyond Spanish reformism and undertook a more basic reappraisal of economic, social, and ecclesiastical institutions, challenging corporate privilege and vested interests, and projecting a new political framework. These ideas turned enlightenment into liberalism and their authors into heroes. Opportunity came in 1808.

The Riots of 1766: Politics or Poverty?

The impulse to reform came from above and at first it was too abrupt to be acceptable to the conservative elements in Spanish society. The presence of foreigners in the government and the existence of genuine grievances gave these early protests a patriotic and popular appeal. Spain's failure in the Seven Years War, a rise in the price of foodstuffs caused by inflation and a series of bad harvests, and the higher taxes demanded by Squillace to pay for Charles III's war and his own reforms

---

[22] Sarrailh, *L'Espagne éclairée*, p. 165.

[23] Antonio Domínguez Ortiz, *Sociedad y estado en el siglo XVIII español* (Barcelona, 1981), p. 494.

[24] Juan Marichal, 'From Pistoia to Cádiz: a Generation's Itinerary', in A. Owen Aldridge (ed.), *The Ibero-American Enlightenment* (University of Illinois, 1974), pp. 97–110.

provoked a resentment easily exploited by those who disliked the new direction the government was taking. There was a premonition of trouble for Squillace in mid-1765 as complaints were voiced in the streets and other politicians kept their distance.[25] In a sense he was a victim of the king's war policy and post-war rearmament:

> As the price of bread is considerably raised, there have been great clamours amongst the people of Madrid; and the day the court returned here [from the Escorial], the mob got about the Queen Mother's coach, and cried they were starving. This Her Majesty told the King the next day, when he sent for Mor. Squillace, and partly reproached him with being the cause of this disturbance; and I have been told by one who overheard the conversation, that Mor. Squillace replied, it was impossible to reconcile war with the oeconomy the finances required . . .[26]

Finally, Squillace's decree of 20 March 1766, part of a programme of urban renewal and law enforcement in Madrid, ordered the observance of an old law forbidding men to wear their broad-brimmed slouch hats and long capes on the ground that they provided camouflage for criminals, sparked off a propaganda campaign against him, not entirely spontaneous but apparently prepared by a small group of anonymous activists. The government did not take this too seriously until the evening of Sunday, 23 March, when riots broke out and agitators were observed in taverns and on the streets stirring up revolt.

Some 6,000 people gathered in the Plaza Mayor and marched on the house of Squillace; fortunately for him he was returning from the country and, while the mob was sacking his house, he took refuge in the Royal Palace. By eight o'clock that night there were 15,000 people on the streets and violence was growing; lights were smashed, windows broken, and coaches attacked. The next morning, 24 March, a mob of 20–30,000 swarmed around the Puerta del Sol. There was much political debate but this soon gave way to action as they marched on the Royal Palace and confronted the hated Walloon Guards; here they suffered their first casualties and they themselves killed ten guardsmen, dragging their mutilated bodies through the streets and burning two of them before a howling mob in an outlying slum. As tension and tempers rose, ministers and military rushed to and fro in great confusion, undecided

---

[25] Rochford to Halifax, 17 June 1765, PRO, SP 94/170.
[26] Rochford to Conway, Madrid, 9 December 1765, PRO, SP 94/172.

what to do and unable to give the king clear advice.[27] Royal spokesmen were authorized to offer reduction of food prices and freedom of dress, while troops were mobilized in the region of Madrid and priests were sent into the streets to urge calm; these were greeted derisively, 'Don't preach to us, father, we are already Christians.'[28] The offer in any case did not satisfy the rebels. They now demanded the exile of Squillace; dismissal of all foreign ministers and their replacement by Spaniards; abolition of the Walloon Guards; revocation of the dress orders; and reduction of food prices. With his advisers poised between repression and conciliation, Charles decided to conciliate. He appeared in person on the palace balcony while a friar with a crucifix in his hand read out the articles the mob insisted on, the king signifying his approval. Then, at midnight, he fled in secret to Aranjuez, taking Squillace and Grimaldi with him; once there, he went out to shoot game.

On the next day, 25 March, news that the king had fled and troop movements were being prepared infuriated the rebels, who mobilized again, seized arms, and occupied the streets. In bands of 500 or so they marched round the city, crying 'God save the king, death to Squillace.' Women too joined the mob, carrying lighted torches and the palm branches they had received at church on the previous Sunday. The troops, placing caution above courage, took refuge in Buen Retiro. Rebel emissaries were sent to Aranjuez, adding two further demands to those already presented: that the king return to Madrid, and grant a general pardon. They came back with a letter from the king which was read out on 26 March in the Plaza Mayor; he promised to fulfil what was granted but expected in turn 'due tranquility'. That night all was quiet, people returned their arms, shook hands with the soldiers, and went home as though nothing had happened. The rebels suffered twenty-one killed and forty-nine wounded; the troops lost nineteen dead.[29] It was a time to remember. For four days Madrid was without government, law and order were non-existent, the people ruled, while the Spanish Bourbons, the ultimate in absolutism, looked on bewildered. Spain had experienced the unthinkable. Europe could not believe what it heard.

What were the riots in Madrid? A mindless mob? A popular protest? A counter-revolution? A conspiracy of Jesuits? A food riot amidst a subsistence crisis?[30] It seems to have been a genuinely popular uprising,

---

[27] Rochford to Conway, Madrid, 24 March 1766, PRO, SP 94/173.
[28] Quoted by Rodríguez, *Campomanes*, p. 234.
[29] Ibid., p. 238.
[30] Constancio Eguía Ruiz, *Los jesuitas y el motín de Esquilache* (Madrid, 1947); Vicente Rodríguez

spreading out from the taverns under artisan leaders – one was a coach-maker, others were tailors – who refused to be bought off. Protest was related to the high price of bread, a consequence of poor harvests, and the liberalization of the grain trade by Campomanes. But it was manipulated by others to become a direct attack on the reform policy of the government.[31] Who, then, were the instigators of the riots? There were various candidates for the role.

According to the British ambassador, Lord Rochford, who was allowed to pass unmolested through the rebel ranks on his way to the Royal Palace and whose agents kept the movement under observation, it was an organized insurrection with specific aims:

> When one considers the great regularity with which it was con-ducted; the universal contempt the people shewed for the money that was flung to them; the very pertinent language they held, declaring that their principal object was the ruin of Monsr de Squillacci, and that the dearness of bread, and the order about hats, was only the pretext; there is not the least room to doubt, but that some of the principal Grandees, and the Heads of the Law, were at the bottom of all this affair.[32]

Rochford argued that had it been an exclusively popular insurrection then certain social groups should have been alarmed; but they were not apparently so. This was a premeditated riot, whose primary aim was to oust Squillace. The beneficiaries were the French, for they eliminated a minister who was cool towards the Family Pact and reluctant to spend money on rearmament; it would not be surprising if they were working behind the scenes. The theory is interesting – after all a British ambassador had destabilized the government of Ensenada in 1754 – but not proven. In any case, as Rochford appreciated, France would not have risked provok-ing a riot without counting on internal collaborators. Who better quali-fied for this role than Ensenada? He still had political ambitions, kept

Casado, *La política y los políticos en el reinado de Carlos III* (Madrid, 1962); J. Navarro Latorre, *Hace doscientos años. Estado actual de los problemas históricos del motín de Esquilache* (Madrid, 1966); Pierre Vilar, 'El motín de Esquilache y las crisis del Antiguo Régimen', *Revista de Occidente*, 107 (1972), pp. 200–47; Gonzalo Anes, 'Antecedentes próximos del motín contra Esquilache', *Moneda y Crédito*, 128 (1974), pp. 219–24.

[31] Laura Rodríguez, 'The Riots of 1766 in Madrid', *European Studies Review*, 3, 3 (1973), pp. 223–42, and 'The Spanish Riots of 1766', *Past and Present*, 59 (1973), pp. 117–46.

[32] Rochford to Conway, Madrid, 31 March, 5 May 1766, PRO, SP 94/173.

himself in circulation, was a favourite with the mob, and apparently in good spirits throughout the riots. Ensenada in turn could embody the hopes of another sector hostile to Squillace, the higher nobility.

The nobility as a class had not been directly hit by the reform policy, and no one suggested that their privileges were at risk. But they saw the retrieval of *señorios* announced by Campomanes in 1762 as a threat to their lands, rents and offices; and they resented the loss of political power, while upstarts and foreigners were being promoted to the highest appointments. Why should they be ruled by the likes of Squillace, Campomanes, Moñino, and Roda, men from obscure provincial backgrounds and common legal practices? The other privileged sector, the Church, had been alienated or at least alerted by jurisdictional and financial losses since 1753; it was now further outraged by Campomanes's plan to disamortize its property; and some of the clergy genuinely sympathized with popular grievances. The replacement of Squillace by Ensenada would particularly satisfy the Jesuits, who had enjoyed the favour of the former minister and were not averse to his return; and it was alleged by some that these were the hidden hands. For all these reasons it can be speculated that the riots were prepared by a group, or an alliance of groups, to call a halt to reform, warn off the government, and preserve existing privilege.

Once it had recovered its nerve, the government reacted firmly to the events of March 1766. In restrospect they were far from revolutionary and the situation soon returned to normal. But so abnormal were insurrections in eighteenth-century Spain that the government came near to panic and Charles himself retained a permanent horror of popular disturbance and kept Madrid heavily garrisoned from then onwards. His policy response combined suavity and severity. Squillace obviously had to go, but Grimaldi was kept on. The two ministries of Squillace were divided between Juan de Muniain (war) and Miguel Múzquiz (finance), both professional administrators and, to the disgust of the old nobility, hardly less parvenu than the rest of the government. So if the people had little to show from the riots the aristocracy had even less, and the new appointments were reported to create 'great jealousy among the Grandees: but they have very few men of abilities and are without union among themselves; so that all the vast ideas of some of them to reduce the royal power within bounds, and to reestablish the Cortes, is fallen to the ground'.[33] The management of internal policy was

---

[33] De Visme to Duke of Richmond, Aranjuez, 18 June 1766, PRO, SP 94/174.

now of crucial importance. On 11 April the count of Aranda was appointed president of the council of Castile with the job of restoring order, finding out who was responsible for disorder, and making sure that there was no recurrence. As an aristocrat, military, and pseudo-reformer, he was thought capable of coping with most sectors of society, and he quickly established his authority. Ensenada and his partisans were exiled from court. An army of 15–20,000 was stationed in and around Madrid. Orders were given to round up vagrants and put them in a workhouse, to prevent religious houses giving alms and encouraging idleness, to send surplus priests back to their dioceses, to repress licentious speech and writing. Aranda's programme of discipline for Madrid culminated in the reorganization of the city into eight quarters for better government and policing, and the *alcaldes* (local magistrates) were instructed in their duties. Aranda quickly restored internal security, and for all his superficial acquaintance with the Enlightenment it was the iron fist of authority rather than citizens' rights which prevailed.

The government was determined to discover the authors of the riots; and to restore its own credibility it was also determined to find a conspiracy. A special commission of enquiry was appointed under the presidency of Aranda, and Campomanes was put to work to get results. He soon decided the Jesuits were the culprits and spent the next months assembling the evidence, such as it was. His conclusions confirmed the king's own preconception against an order whom he called 'that pest' and regarded as a danger to himself and his kingdoms.[34] While the official version blamed the Jesuits, this did not end the matter; king and ministers also had to settle their account with the privileged sectors of society, about whose role they still had a lingering suspicion. The nobility, clergy, municipality, and the Five Major Guilds were all constrained to request the king to annul the concessions and return to Madrid, thus forcing them to disavow the opposition and recognize the king as the only sovereign power. The grandees and upper clergy complied with great reluctance, but in the end the matter closed, a victory for king and government. The riot was declared 'null and illicit', all concessions except the general pardon were revoked, and the court returned quietly to Madrid in December 1766.

The disturbances in Madrid spilled over into the provinces, where they took the form of food riots. There had of course been previous

[34] Rodríguez, *Campomanes*, p. 259.

crises of subsistence, in 1707, 1709, 1723, 1750, 1753, and 1763, without similar manifestations. The difference this time was the new grain policy and the successful example of Madrid. News of events in the capital spread quickly and started a chain reaction in towns like Cuenca and Zaragoza; even where the price of food was not excessive there were riots in imitation of Madrid and in the expectation that this was the way to win concessions. The poor harvest of 1765 meant that the free market in grain began in the worst possible conditions. Yet the harvest itself was not the only problem; in the winter of 1765–6 the government imported large stocks of grain and there was probably a sufficiency in most places. But the landowners used their power in local government and economy to corner grain supplies and force up prices, causing a major subsistence crisis throughout the Castiles and Andalucía, and sparking off protests against government policy and local malpractices. In Zaragoza it was the popular classes who rose, while the upper sectors supported the authorities: 'The high price of bread and the example of Madrid occasioned this rising. The instances of loyalty shewn by the principle people of Saragossa has given great satisfaction here.'[35] A number of other towns were involved – Oviedo, La Coruña, Santander, Bilbao, Barcelona, Cartagena, and Cadiz – but elsewhere it was a predominantly rural movement. The common denominator was food prices; poor people everywhere denounced profiteers and monopolists and their allies among officials and clergy, and they demanded price controls, improvement in local supplies, and punishment for the guilty. Protests were spontaneous and became violent; in Zaragoza property was attacked and the rich frightened into retaliation. But the insurgents were neither delinquents nor politically motivated; they were labourers, small peasants, and artisans, caught in the trap of poverty, unemployment, and high food prices.[36] Many local authorities recognized this. With the exception of Zaragoza, where eleven people were executed, they did not react repressively; many preferred the traditional policy of protecting the consumer against market forces; they agreed to lower food prices, and they were now on the alert to respond quickly at the first sign of shortage. By the end of April order had been restored.

The central government was more severe. Riots were an affront to royal sovereignty, a threat to public order, and a drain on government finances. This was made clear in the *auto* of 5 May 1766 which was a restatement of the basic principles of Spanish government: absolute

[35] Rochford to Conway, 14 April 1766, PRO, SP 94/173.
[36] Domínguez Ortiz, *Sociedad y estado en el siglo XVIII español*, p. 311.

monarchy and unqualified obedience. Ministers wanted to put an end to the idea that an uprising was a legitimate way of protest and pressure. The edict declared null and void all the concessions and pardons granted by the local authorities. As Campomanes explained, 'the people are persuaded that the demands on the authorities are valid, that it is in the power of the judges to concede them and then to grant pardons . . . It is necessary to remove this error from the popular mind.'[37] It was therefore decreed that (1) the *alcaldes* were to undertake an immediate investigation into the causes and authors of the riots; (2) new police measures were to be imposed; (3) vagrants and beggars were to be rounded up, the needy sent to workhouses, the rest to the army and navy. But something more constructive was needed. The provincial riots revealed a degree of opposition to the reform programme at the local level, where ineffective or corrupt officials applied not government policy but another type of despotism, what Campomanes called 'the despotism of the intendants, corregidores and town councillors'.[38] So a further reform created two new municipal officials, elected annually by the inhabitants of each parish and empowered to monitor particularly the state of food supplies and the free trade in grain.[39] But two new councillors were not enough to dilute the power of the local oligarchy. And the treasury refused either to defray the cost of lower prices or to allow the municipalities to do so; the price reductions were therefore annulled.

The crisis of 1766 brought the first phase of radical change to an end. Reform policies designed by Campomanes and backed by Squillace, inchoate though they were, alerted the nobility and clergy and drew attention to the character of the government, a coalition of foreign and Spanish politicians stronger in talent than in titles. Policy change, compounded by crop failure, provoked the popular classes too into action, as bread prices were allowed to soar and subsistence became precarious. Latent social tensions were brought to the surface in protests against local ruling classes in town and country. But in Madrid insurgency possessed a national and political character, and occurred with the acquiescence or perhaps connivance of the upper classes. There was a hard lesson here for king and ministers: Spain was going to be difficult to change, unless, of course, the crisis was a mere conspiracy.

[37] Rodríguez, *Campomanes*, pp. 292–3.
[38] Quoted ibid., p. 294.
[39] De Visme to Conway, 19 May 1766, PRO, SP 94/174; see below pp. 305–6.

Religion in Spain: Royal Church, Popular Church

The Spanish Church needed to be strong in faith and pliant in conscience to fulfil its triple allegiance, serving God, acknowledging the pope, obeying the king. The last loyalty was the most immediate. Charles III inherited a dominant position over the Church, one which had been legalized by the concordat of 1753 confirming the Spanish crown in almost universal rights of appointment, jurisdiction and revenue, and which he proceeded to consolidate and extend. The Church itself was not in a condition to resist absolutism, under which indeed it enjoyed great privilege. The combination of an assertive monarch and a compliant hierarchy reduced the Bourbon Church to a dependency unequalled in Spanish history.

In the second half of the eighteenth century there were some 150,000 ecclesiastics in Spain, 1.5 per cent of a total population of 10.5 million, and about 3,000 religious houses, which was probably more clergy than the country needed or could afford.[40] Economically the Church was a powerful institution with immense wealth in land and revenue. In the province of Castile it possessed nearly 15 per cent of land and accounted for 24 per cent of the total agricultural income, received 70 per cent of all returns on mortgage loans and owned 44 per cent of all urban property and seigneurial revenues.[41] In addition the Church had an income from tithes and even more from fees for baptism, marriages, burials, and masses. But it was as a property owner and lessor rather than a tax collector that the Church aroused criticism and drew the attention of reformers to projects of disamortization. Income from agriculture increased after 1750 with rising prices and rents; the Church was not slow to demand more from its tenants and vassals and to profit from grain shortages by cornering supplies, and it succeeded in holding its own in a time of rapid inflation.[42] Altogether church income amounted to perhaps one-fifth of all income produced by the leading sectors of the

[40] 'Demografía eclesiástica', *Diccionario de historia eclesiástica de España* (4 vols, Madrid, 1972–5), II, pp. 730–5; on the eighteenth-century Church see also Ricardo García Villoslada (ed.), *Historia de la iglesia en España*, vol. IV, *La iglesia en la Espana de los siglos XVII y XVIII* (Madrid, 1979); William J. Callahan, 'The Spanish Church', in W. J. Callahan and D. C. Higgs (eds), *Church and Society in Catholic Europe in the Eighteenth Century* (Cambridge, 1979), pp. 34–50.

[41] Pierre Vilar, 'Structures de la société espagnole vers 1750', *Mélanges à la mémoire de Jean Sarrailh* (2 vols, Paris 1966), pp. 428–9; William J. Callahan, *Church, Politics, and Society in Spain* (Cambridge, Mass., 1984), pp. 39–42.

[42] Luis Sierra Nava-Lasa, *El Cardenal Lorenzana y la Ilustración* (Madrid, 1975), pp. 90–2.

economy; moreover this was an income taken primarily from the rural sector to pay for an institution which was predominantly urban.

Church revenue had a public and social function as well as an ecclesiastical one. Much of it was siphoned off by the crown through charges on royal benefices, income from vacancies, share of tithes, and taxes on church property and personnel. Moreover the state used the Church as a reservoir of miscellaneous expenditure. The see of Toledo, in addition to supporting one archbishop, forty canons, fifty prebendaries, fifty chaplains and a total of 600 ecclesiastical personnel, also had to maintain the Infante Don Luis, pay various pensions to privileged recipients, and an annual subvention to the monks of the Escorial; further expenditure on public buildings and works in Toledo, social projects, and its own liturgy left the archbishop little out of the see's income of 9 million reales a year and justified Townsend's conclusion that 'with his vast revenue he is always poor'.[43] The crown also imposed on diocesan revenues many secular salaries, donations to hospitals, charitable foundations, and payments to such bodies as the new Economic Societies: 'There is not a bishopric in the kingdom but has somebody or other quartered upon it; and I believe the second-rate benefices are in the same predicament. Out of the rich canonries and prebends are taken the pensions of the new order of knights of Carlos tercero.'[44]

The Church was one of the largest accumulators of capital in Spain, though not an investor in the productive sectors; within the traditional pre-industrial economy, the Church was a major consumer, and many artisans and suppliers depended upon it for a living, but church capital tended to reinforce the existing structure rather than find its way into productive investment. The residual revenue of the Church was divided between buildings, liturgy, property acquisition, and artistic patrimony on the one hand, and education, health services and charity on the other. Whether the Church got its priorities right and allocated its resources with consistency is difficult to judge and impossible to quantify. Probably more was spent on buildings than on pastoral work, more on cathedral canons than on rural priests. The revenues of the bishops of Segovia doubled in the period 1721–94, but most of them were spent on buildings, a new episcopal palace, and works on the cathedral, not on

[43] Townsend, *A Journey through Spain*, I, pp. 305–6; Townsend was a Protestant clergyman who showed and received considerable toleration in Spanish religious circles.

[44] Henry Swinburne, *Travels through Spain in the Years 1775 and 1776* (London, 1779), p. 321, n. 29.

charity.[45] Education received some church funding, and local primary schools depended on this for their survival, but these schools taught only a small proportion of the total population. The religious orders were more interested in secondary than in primary education, and here the Jesuits led the way until 1767 with more than one hundred schools for local elites.[46]

The Church took its social duties seriously. It gave abundantly and comprehensively to the poor as a matter of obligation, and while it is impossible to calculate the percentage of charity to income it would appear to be increasing in the eighteenth century.[47] Charitable institutions in town and country proved its commitment to the corporal works of mercy and the convent soup was always available to feed the hungry. In addition to its normal almsgiving the Church organized special relief during times of agrarian crisis and became in effect the safety net against utter destitution. In Toledo Cardinal Lorenzana fed workers as well as employed them. In Malaga the bishop 'gives more than half his goods to feed the poor, who assemble every morning at his doors to receive each a little bit of money, and from thence disperse among the convents, where they never fail to get some bread and broth.'[48] The archbishop of Granada lived in some degree of splendour and kept a good table, but gave so much money to charity in regular pensions, crisis relief, orphan maintenance, and daily bread distribution that Townsend could 'scarcely conceive his income to equal his expenditure'.[49] The formula of bread and broth did not appeal to all; foreign observers and Spanish reformers alike criticized charity as a source of idleness and vagrancy. The enlightened argued that the Church, having enriched itself at the expense of the people, now justified its riches as necessary to assist the people, but its assistance was arbitrary and uncoordinated and worked simply because the Church had so much money. These were minority views and came from above, not below; they tended to mistake symptoms for causes and, in the case of Campomanes, to reflect his preference for the secular over the religious.

The material wealth of the Church was reinforced by its judicial privilege. The Spanish Church enjoyed an immunity from civil jurisdiction

[45] Maximiliano Barrio Gonzalo, *Estudio socioeconómico de la iglesia de Segovia en el siglo XVIII* (Segovia, 1982), pp. 273–4.

[46] Sarrailh, *L'Espagne éclairée*, pp. 45–6, 186.

[47] Callahan, *Church, Politics, and Society in Spain*, p. 49.

[48] Townsend, *A Journey through Spain*, III, p. 15.

[49] Ibid., III, pp. 57–8.

which had long since vanished in most other parts of Europe. The personal immunity of the clergy involved two basic privileges, the privilege of *fuero*, which provided exemption from judicial action, prosecution and sentencing by any but ecclesiastical judges, and the privilege of the canon, which protected the priest from any physical violence, arrest, torture and punishment. The government of Charles III promulgated legislation curtailing ecclesiastical immunity, regarding it as an unjustified exemption from the state's judicial and coercive authority and a major challenge to royal absolutism.[50] But they did not succeed in abolishing it. The same five bishops who were members of the commission investigating and recommending the expulsion of the Jesuits, also condemned a regalist work by Campomanes, not because he maintained that the popes had no jurisdiction over temporal sovereigns but because he used a supporting argument which questioned the Church's ecclesiastical immunity. Cardinal Lorenzana, who as archbishop of Mexico had organized the extremely regalist Fourth Mexican Provincial Council in 1771, became an outspoken critic of the crown's ecclesiastical policy and warned Charles III that his measures were Protestant heresies.[51]

In spite of its material strength and corporate privilege, the Church could not present a firm front to the encroachments of the state. The hierarchy – eight archbishops and fifty-two bishops – were crown appointees, and while they were usually worthy of their office most of them were convinced regalists whose *curriculae vitae* had satisfied the council of Castile. Many of them were also reformers, but even their reformism was conformist and followed the government penchant for promoting useful projects. The bishop of Málaga, José Molina Lario, spent 2 million reales on the construction of an aqueduct to the city and published a pastoral letter on the value of 'popular industry'. Bishop González Pisador established two chairs of medicine in the University of Oviedo and was a patron of Economic Societies. The archbishop of Valencia, Francisco Fabián y Fuero, defender and victim of royal absolutism, at his own expense reformed university studies in Valencia. José González Lazo, bishop of Plasencia, financed roads, bridges and mountain passes. The bishop of Cartagena, Rubín de Celis, endowed chairs in the Economic Society. The bishop of Barcelona, José Climent, established free primary schools, though he was eventually forced out of his see

---

[50] N. M. Farriss, *Crown and Clergy in Colonial Mexico 1759-1821. The Crisis of Ecclesiastical Privilege* (London, 1968), pp. 10–11, 88, 97–8.

[51] Ibid., pp. 103–4.

charged with Catalan separatism. Cardinal Francisco Antonio Lorenzana, archbishop of Toledo and primate of Spain, restored the Alcázar,
converted it into a workhouse, subsidized the silk industry, and
addressed a pastoral letter to priests on methods for instructing their
parishioners in agricultural improvement for the sake of the peasant
class 'who sustain the rest with the sweat of their brow and deserve
every praise'.[52]

Spanish bishops, however, presided over dioceses marked by extreme
inequalities of income and resources; on the one hand Toledo with its
great ecclesiastical establishment, on the other Valladolid with little
more than a history, or wealthy Seville and meagre Mondoñedo,
examples of an imbalance which affected the whole Spanish Church. The
differences of wealth, education and prospects between the higher and
lower clergy, the disparity between the high number of career benefices
and the few with cure of souls, the maldistribution of clergy between
places like Toledo and rural parishes without priests, the divisions
between the regular orders and their rivalry with the secular clergy, all
these factors combined to weaken the Spanish Church and leave it open
to attack.[53] The Church mirrored the structure of the rest of society:
bishops and higher clergy were of the elites, the lower clergy belonged to
the poor. The possibility of social mobility upwards, depending on
moral and intellectual qualities, made the Church marginally more open
than other institutions, but in most cases it conformed to the secular
career pattern: success depended on *hidalgo* origin, university education,
appointment to a canonry – these were the steps to a bishopric. Cardinal
Lorenzana showed the way; coming from a *hidalgo* family, he was
destined to the Church from childhood. He proceeded from the law
faculty at Valladolid to the College of Oviedo at Salamanca, was
appointed a canon first at Sigüenza, then in 1754 at Toledo, both
extremely wealthy cathedrals, and was then promoted to bishop of
Plasencia and archbishop of Mexico, to return to the highest appointment in the Spanish Church. Without a university education and a
canonry, a priest had no hope for promotion. A social structure of this
kind tended to produce an ignorant and negligent parish priest, and to
relegate pastoral work to the margin of the Church or to leave it to the

[52] Quoted in Domínguez Ortiz, *Sociedad y estado en el siglo XVIII español*, p. 305; see also
Townsend, *A Journey through Spain*, I, p. 305; Francesc Tort Mitjans, *El Obispo de Barcelona: Josep
Climent i Avinent, 1706-1781* (Barcelona, 1978).

[53] Juan Sáez Marín, *Datos sobre la iglesia española contemporánea (1768-1868)* (Madrid, 1975),
pp. 294–5; on Lorenzana's career see Sierra Nava-Lasa, *El Cardenal Lorenzana*, pp. 13–23, 101–8.

regular clergy, whose orders usually had an independent income and their own education system. Contemporary reformers tended to judge the Church by its social function and utility. By this criterion the rural parish priest, close to his flock and qualified to lead, was seen as potentially useful to the community, in so far as he collaborated with an enlightened programme. Canons and other clergy of cathedrals and holders of wealthy benefices were regarded as pure careerists and dismissed as social parasites. Monks, friars, and Jesuits were also unpopular with reformers like Campomanes, who dismissed the con-templative life as unproductive, despised the fundamentalist preaching of the friars, and regarded the Jesuits as a threat to the state. A British observer remarked, 'It seems to be the design of the leading men in the Council of Castile to make the condition of a monk so uneasy that few will venture to embrace it.'[54]

The religion of the people was traditional and uncompromising. Foreign observers were astonished by some of the manifestations of popular Catholicism, the constant *fiestas*, processions, flagellations, and deference to monks and priests, and some claimed to detect a lack of true religion, as distinct from popular superstitions, mechanical devo-tions, and even elite indifference:

> I was surprised to find them so much more luke-warm in their devotion than I expected ... From what little I saw, I am apt to suspect, that the people here trouble themselves with very few serious thoughts on the subject; and that, provided they can bring themselves to believe that their favourite Saint looks upon them with an eye of affection, they take it for granted ... The unconcern betrayed by the whole nation at the fall of the Jesuits, is a strong proof of their present indifference.[55]

True, a wide cultural gap divided Spanish Catholics and foreign Pro-testants, and a mutual incomprehension often distorted their views of each other. Yet historians too have sometimes presented a similar version of Spanish religion. They see an incipient 'dechristianization' of Spain in the eighteenth century and a mere survival of folk beliefs devoid of serious theological content; religion of this kind masked a basic paganism, confirmed by traditionalists and reformers alike, who pre-

[54] De Visme to Shelburne, 31 August 1767, PRO, SP 94/178.
[55] Swinburne, *Travels through Spain*, pp. 373–4.

dicted a new decline of Spain, a decline into unbelief and immorality.[56]
In this view outward observance meant little: foreigners alleged that
some priests sold certificates of yearly communion and that in Madrid
'the common prostitutes, confessing and receiving the holy sacrament in
many churches, and collecting a multitude of billets, either sell, or give
them to friends.'[57]

The evidence available indicates a high level of religious practice and
almost universal fulfilment of Easter duties.[58] Doctrinal knowledge was
less certain but most Spaniards knew the basic Catholic prayers and the
ten commandments, and the liturgy itself taught the rest, assisted by the
drama of seasonal ceremonies and the popular missions preached by
touring groups of friars and Jesuits.[59] Catechisms, manuals of doctrine,
and new devotions to the Sacred Heart and Our Lady completed the
armoury of the faith and supplied the failure of the majority of benefice
holders actually to teach Christian doctrine. But if faith was secure, what
of morals? Foreign observers were scandalized by the contrast between
rigid beliefs and lax behaviour: 'This contradiction is extremely general
in Spain, and few classes of people are exempt from it.'[60] Not even the
priests, many of whom broke their vows of celibacy. Townsend
remarked that the bishop of Oviedo, a man of high principle who was
'severe only to himself, but compassionate to others, made it a rule that
none of his curates should have children in their families . . . Beyond this
he did not think it right to be too rigid in his enquiries.'[61] As for the
faithful, most of them regarded the Church as a refuge of sinners as well
as the home of saints.

The religion of the people was expressed in various ways, vows to
Our Lady and the saints, relics and indulgences, and above all the shrines
and sacred sites of local religious life.[62] These were the scenes of cures,
miracles and visions, the holy places where prayers were said and heard,
the objects of processions and pilgrimages, part of the landscape of the
people. All testify to the popular base of the Church and the strength of
popular religiosity. Yet this was not a 'popular' religion in the sense of a

---

[56] Alfredo Martínez Albiach, *Religiosidad hispana y sociedad borbónica* (Burgos, 1969), pp. 21–4.

[57] Townsend, *A Journey through Spain*, II, p. 149; Bourgoing, *Modern State of Spain*, II, p. 275.

[58] Sáez Marín, *Datos sobre la iglesia española contemporánea*, pp. 63–8; Callahan, *Church, Politics, and Society in Spain*, pp. 52–68.

[59] Callahan, *Church, Politics, and Society in Spain*, pp. 60–5.

[60] Bourgoing, *Modern State of Spain*, II, p. 273.

[61] Townsend, *A Journey through Spain*, II, p. 150.

[62] William A. Christian, Jr, *Local Religion in Sixteenth-Century Spain* (Princeton, NJ, 1981), pp. 175–208.

non-official religion. Its characteristic practices expressed the Church's teaching on saints, indulgences, the holy souls, prayers for the dead, the veneration of relics, and wearing of medals, all of which were orthodox practices and not 'autonomous' in any discernible way. In the ultimate analysis the beliefs and practices of popular Catholicism in Spain represented no more than the people's attempt to make the abstract more concrete, to redefine the supernatural in terms of the natural environment in which they lived, and to invoke divine help against the scourges of plague, drought and famine.

The Marian devotions of the eighteenth century fused easily with previous practices which already contained a traditional cult of the Virgin Mary, Nuestra Señora de Monserrat, del Pilar, de Guadalupe. The cult of the Virgin in the eighteenth century was encouraged by the hierarchy, popularized by the missioners, and readily assimilated by the people. According to an English traveller, 'there is scarce a house in Granada that has not over its door, in large red characters, the words *Ave Maria purisima sin pecado concebida*; which is the *cri de guerre* of the Franciscan friars.'[63] And a French embassy official noticed that 'when you enter a house, unless you wish to be considered as impious, or, what is still worse, a heretic, you must begin with these words, *Ave Maria purisima*; to which you will certainly receive the answer, *sin pecado concebida*.'[64] In 1760 Charles III obtained from Clement XIII authorization that the Immaculate Mary be declared patron of Spain and the Indies, and it was normal practice for members of town councils, guilds, and other organizations to swear to be ready to defend the belief in the Immaculate Conception.

Popular religion became a target for the reformers, who criticized the cult of the saints and regarded devotees of the Virgen de Atocha and the Virgen de la Almudena as idolatrous, inciting a kind of competition in miracles and reducing religion to mere externals. There was hardly a number of *El Censor* that did not refer to the opposition between interior piety and exterior devotions, between true religion and base superstition: 'Superstition is more extensive among us than ungodliness.'[65] Roda complained bitterly to Aranda that 'superstition and ignorance rule' in Spain. And the leading reformer, Campomanes, called

[63] Swinburne, *Travels through Spain*, p. 191.

[64] Bourgoing, *Modern State of Spain*, II, p. 276; see also Joël Saugnieux, 'Ilustración católica y religiosidad popular: el culto mariano en la España del siglo XVIII', *La Epoca de Fernando VI* (Oviedo, 1981), pp. 275–95.

[65] Antonio Elorza, *La ideología liberal en la Ilustración española* (Madrid, 1970), pp. 23–36.

for an end to fiestas, processions, and almsgiving in favour of the simple Gospel, a return to primitive Christianity, and internal respect for God.[66] At this end of the spectrum politicians had to be careful not to overstep the mark in public, and they rarely did so, but their thinking revealed a rational bias against religious enthusiasm and a preference for secular values over those of religion.

Reformers were called Jansenists by their opponents, and although their Jansenism had little to do with the problems of grace and salvation, of faith and good works, posed by the early French Jansenists, it was recognizable by the way in which it criticized superstition, moral laxism, the Jesuits, religious orders and papal jurisdiction.[67] It also contained a puritanical tendency, and represented a kind of 'Irishization' of the Spanish Church. The Church itself in the period 1750–85 contained a reform movement of bishops, clergy, and faithful, whose object was to combat ignorance, expel superstition, and purify belief with the help of reason, and whose intellectual affinities lay less with Jansenists than with French Gallicans such as Bishop Bossuet and the Abbé Fleury, and contemporary Italian reformers such as the bishop of Pistoia. Leaders of the movement included bishops Climent of Barcelona, Bertrán of Salamanca, Fabián y Fuero of Valencia, and Cardinal Lorenzana; in common with Catholic reformers in Italy, France and Germany, they looked for human progress in this world as well as happiness in the next, and sought to improve agriculture and industry as well as reform their dioceses.[68] Reform went hand in hand with regalism. For religious renewal and material progress Catholic leaders looked to the state for support and in turn aligned themselves with the crown against the Jesuits and against Rome.[69] By 1790, however, the first phase of Catholic reform gave way to a second, more radical phase, in which controversial figures like Juan Antonio Llorente, canon of Valencia and official of the Inquisition, pressed more aggressively for change and turned their criticism on the religious orders, the Inquisition, and papal authority.

[66] C. C. Noel, 'Opposition to Enlightened Reform in Spain: Campomanes and the Clergy, 1765–1775', *Societas*, 3, 1 (1973), pp. 21–43.

[67] Emile Appolis, *Les jansénistes espagnols* (Bordeaux, 1966), p. 9; see also Joël Saugnieux, *Le jansénisme espagnol du XVIIIᵉ siècle: Ses composants et ses sources* (Oviedo, 1975), p. 49, and *Les jansénistes et le renouveau de la prédication dans l'Espagne de la seconde moitié du XVIIIᵉ siècle* (Lyons, 1976), *passim*, who argues for French influence and true Jansenism in such reformers as Bertrán, Climent and Jovellanos, to be seen in interest in church history, patristic studies, scripture, liturgy, ecclesiastical discipline, and concern for moral pastoral standards.

[68] Owen Chadwick, *The Popes and European Revolution* (Oxford, 1981), p. 406–17.

[69] Tort Mitjans, *El Obispo de Barcelona*, pp. 270–80; Joël Saugnieux, *Un prélat éclairé: Don Antonio Tavira y Almazán, 1737-1807* (Toulouse, 1970), pp. 50–8.

Reform, therefore, was regalist and elitist, a combination nowhere more exemplified than in the policy of Campomanes. As this lacked popular roots, he had to appeal to the state, at once the supporter and the beneficiary of religious reform. Translated into action this involved a campaign to suppress eucharistic plays, liturgical dances, flagellation, and a number of pilgrimages. The bureaucracy conducted an enquiry into the *cofradías*, or religious associations, their income and expenditure, and closed many of them on the grounds that they were mere social clubs. Public prayers for rain were prohibited because they might disturb the grain market. In October 1767 the council of Castile circulated bishops to urge them to curb abuses and superstition in their dioceses. Permission was obtained from the pope to reduce the number of feast days. Many of these 'reforms' were simply the rhetoric of rationalization and an attempt to enrol the Church in the modernizing programme; they also betrayed an unmistakable tendency to tell people what was good for them. The common people regarded the various measures with deep suspicion; it was sufficient that they were new, apparently the product of heretics, and certainly the work of the government, to condemn them in the eyes of most Spaniards.

The Church was expected to provide moral back-up for public policy, especially when it was unpopular. The government considered making smuggling a capital offence, but encountered so much opposition on the part of the clergy that legislation was never completed. Religion was then invoked in support of the treasury's campaign against revenue frauds and contraband. A theological discussion followed. Was defrauding the royal revenue a mortal sin? Some said yes, others that the government could not create new mortal sins. Floridablanca wrote to prelates urging them to come down hard on contraband. Several complied and issued stern pastoral letters. A few declined, some because they did not like taking orders on morals from the government, others because they did not regard this as an area of moral priority. Cardinal Lorenzana, of course, complied: 'it is a grave sin', he wrote, 'to defraud the king of his taxes, to smuggle prohibited goods, to receive such goods and to shelter contrabandists.'[70]

Anti-popular, reform was also anti-papal. Behind the language of enlightenment politicians like Campomanes were more interested in augmenting royal power over the Church than in inspiring a religious revival. The anti-papal content of Gallicanism and Jansenism had already

---

[70] Liston to Carmarthen, 6 February 1788, PRO, FO 72/12.

entered Spain, as has been seen. The limitation of papal power in favour of a General Council, long familiar in its Gallican form, was re-affirmed in 1763 by the bishop of Trier writing under the name of Justinius Febronius, whose work circulated in Spain and had some influence there among those who wanted to fashion a more national Spanish Church. Charles III's government was anti-papal from the beginning. A few years after his accession he showed his hand when he prohibited the publication of a papal brief condemning a French catechism by the Abbé Mésenguy which denied papal infallibility and contained 'Jansenist' views hostile to the Jesuits. When the inquisitor general published the papal prohibition he was banished from Madrid and detained in a monastery until he begged royal pardon. Moreover, by a decree of 1761 Charles III ordered that henceforth royal permission – the *exequatur* – must be given to all papal documents before they could be published in Spain, and although this decree was suspended in July 1763 it was revived in 1768, in response to the publication of the papal *Monitorio de Parma*, excommunicating the Bourbon duke of Parma.[71]

The government's obsession with royal authority and suspicion of any autonomous jurisdiction can be seen in the *Instrucción reservada* of 1787, in which Floridablanca spoke through Charles III: 'Although clergy and prelates have shown their loyalty and love to the sovereign, they are too numerous to assemble for their opinions, and in any case not a few are imbued with principles contrary to the regalian rights. For these reasons assemblies of the clergy have had to be suspended and it would be better not to revive them.'[72] Relatively few diocesan synods were held in eighteenth-century Spain and the main obstacle was government disapproval. Yet bishops gave few signs of independence. Their appointment was carefully controlled; nomination was a royal prerogative, and the Holy See rarely refused to accept a royal candidate. The government viewed bishops as a compliant establishment and the secular clergy as a branch of the administration. Many prelates resented the constant interference of the council of Castile in pastoral affairs, but only one or two had the nerve to speak up. When that happened the council pounced. The aged and austere bishop of Cuenca, Isidro Carvajal y Lancaster, criticized in a letter to the king government policy towards

[71] Marcelin Defourneaux, *L'Inquisition espagnole et les livres français au XVIIIe siècle* (Paris, 1963), pp. 62–73; C. C. Noel, 'The Clerical Confrontation with the Enlightenment in Spain', *European Studies Review*, 5, 2 (1975), pp. 103–22.

[72] 'Instrucción reservada', 8 July 1787, in Conde de Floridablanca, *Obras originales del conde de Floridablanca, y escritos referentes a su persona*, ed. A. Ferrer del Río (*BAE*, 59, Madrid, 1952), p. 214.

the Church and its immunities and denounced Campomanes's projected law of disamortization; he compared the king to Achab and the royal confessor to Squillace, and attributed all recent disasters from the fall of Havana to the rebellions of 1766 to the persecution of the Church. The government was furious, claimed to see a conspiracy of bishops, aristocrats, and higher officials against reform, linked it with the riots of 1766, and overreacted. The bishop was summoned to appear before the council of Castile and, standing, to be rebuked by Aranda. The government of Charles III was more absolute than enlightened in its dealings with the Church.

Bourbon regalism had a delayed action and the Church did not discover the full extent of its dependence until the following reign. The power of patronage, exercised by Charles III with discretion, was a different weapon in the hands of Charles IV who used it to remove Bishop Fabián y Fuero for dissent and to replace Cardinal Lorenzana by the Infante Luis de Borbón. The authority of the pope, previously resisted, was now reduced. The reform ministry of Jovellanos and Urquijo (1797–1800) decreed that matrimonial cases were to be heard not by Rome but by the bishops. The diocesan synod of Pistoia convoked by Leopold of Tuscany and chaired by Bishop Scipione de Ricca had declared that infallibility lay not in the pope but in the general council of the Church.[73] This appealed to Catholic radicals in Spain and their leader Jovellanos, and widened the gulf between those who still looked to Rome and those who supported the authority of the episcopacy. Finally, the revenue of the Church, long vulnerable to the demands of the Bourbon state, was now subject to direct attack by the government of Charles IV in its desperate struggle to avoid financial collapse. On 15 September 1798 Charles IV ordered the sale of the property of charitable institutions, the funds to be deposited in state bonds, a major breach of privilege and a hard blow to charity.[74]

The Expulsion of the Jesuits and its Aftermath

The record of the Spanish Jesuits in the eighteenth century was not an ultramontane exception to the regalist bias of the rest of the Spanish

---

[73] Chadwick, *The Popes and European Revolution*, pp. 424–8.
[74] Richard Herr, 'Hacia el derrumbe del antiguo régimen: Crisis fiscal y desamortización fiscal bajo Carlos IV', *Moneda y Crédito*, 118 (1971), pp. 37–100; William J. Callahan, 'The Origins of the Conservative Church in Spain', 1793–1823', *European Studies Review*, 10 (1980), pp. 199–223.

Church; many Jesuits, particularly the royal confessors, defended regalism as firmly as its other adherents. But the Society – some 3,000 strong in Spain – was active and articulate beyond the ordinary. While its leaders were no longer men of intellectual distinction, it produced a number of serious scholars, was successful in education and pastoral work, and in more than one sense was at the frontier of European contact with indigenous cultures.[75]

Charles III had an ingrained prejudice against Jesuits. As far as he was concerned they were an insidious and wealthy organization who had once defended regicide. They still retained their special vow of obedience to the pope and their reputation of papal agents, while their loyalty to the Spanish crown in the American colonies was also suspect.[76] An order with an international organization whose head-quarters were outside Spain was regarded as inherently incompatible with absolutism, and in seeking to implement the concordat of 1753 Charles III believed that he had to reckon with its resistance in Spain and in Rome. The role of the Jesuits in the condemnation of the Mésenguy catechism, their opposition to one of the Bourbons' favourite 'causes', the canonization of the anti-Jesuit bishop of Puebla, Juan de Palafox, and their general ubiquity in Church and state confirmed Charles III in his view that Jesuits were troublemakers and a challenge to royal power. He had the resolute support of his ministers, some of whom, such as Campomanes and Moñino, came from a class which resented the influence of the Jesuits in university education and their affiliation with the higher aristocracy.

The Jesuits also had enemies among a wider clerical and lay public. Their defence of good works as well as faith in the process of salvation and their more relaxed interpretation of Catholic moral theology brought them into conflict not only with Jansenists but also with other orders, and they had few friends among Augustinians and Dominicans. Memories of the time when they virtually monopolized the royal confessional and controlled ecclesiastical patronage and policy were still fresh and there were many clerics in Spain who bore personal grudges against the Society of Jesus.[77] Religious conflict became a code for

---

[75] Antonio Astraín, *Historia de la Compañia de Jesús en la asistencia de España* (8 vols, Madrid, 1902–25), VIII, p. 48; see also introductory study by Jorge Cejudo and Teófanes Egido to Pedro Rodríguez de Campomanes, *Dictamen fiscal de expulsión de los jesuitas de España (1766-1767)* (Madrid, 1977), pp. 5–40; Miguel Batllori, *La cultura hispano-italiana de los jesuitas expulsos. Españoles-hispanoamericanos-filipinos, 1767-1814* (Madrid, 1966).

[76] See above, pp. 179–83.

[77] See above, pp. 188–90.

political positions. To be a 'Jesuit' meant to belong to a group of *colegiales* and to disapprove of reforms introduced by *manteista* ministers; to be a 'Jansenist' was to be a supporter of *regalía*, an opponent of Rome, and a friend of heterodoxy. The Jesuits had been too successful for their own good. The controversies of the past over policy, patronage and Paraguay caught up with them and the calamity signalled in 1754 was now imminent. Rome held no hope and international precedents were against them, for the order had been expelled from Portugal in 1759 for alleged conspiracy to murder the king, and from France in 1762 after charges of financial malpractice. Therefore, although there were obvious social and economic reasons for the discontent which led to the riots of 1766, the Spanish government preferred to believe that they had been instigated by the Jesuits and their allies who wished to change the government and block further reform. This version of events was assiduously promoted by Campomanes who saw Jesuits as a political party opposed to reform and to disamortization, and Roda who never forgot his failure to gain a scholarship to a *colegio mayor*. The papacy protested that the faults of individuals did not compromise the entire order, but it soon became clear that the institution itself was at stake.[78]

A commission of inquiry was appointed, chaired by Aranda and organized by Campomanes who immediately undertook a *pesquisa secreta*. After months of investigation of witnesses and sources, both carefully selected by himself, Campomanes produced a long and detailed indictment of the Jesuits dated 31 December 1766.[79] Nothing was omitted, however obvious and however improbable: their support for Ensenada, loyalty to Rome, massive wealth, activities in America, theories on regicide, expulsion from France and Portugal, and, the last straw, their role in the riots of 1766. Who manipulated the mob? Who were the *caudillos* of the conspiracy? Campomanes had no doubt, or if he did he did not disclose it. He placed the blame squarely on the Jesuits who wanted to replace Squillace with Ensenada and Padre Eleta with a confessor of their own; and he concluded that the Jesuits, their doctrine, organization, and activities were incompatible with the security of the monarchy.[80]

---

[78] On the expulsion see Danvila y Collado, *El reinado de Carlos III*, vol. III; Eguía Ruiz, *Los jesuitas y el motín de Esquilache*, who maintains that the riots of 1766 were spontaneous; Vicente Rodríguez Casado, *La política y los políticos en el reinado de Carlos III*, who argues that the riots were planned with Jesuit connivance; Navarro Latorre, *Hace doscientos años*; Cejudo and Egido, cited above, n. 75.

[79] Campomanes, *Dictamen fiscal de expulsión de los jesuitas*, 31 December 1766.

[80] Ibid., pp. 53, 64–5, 71–2, 78, 183–4.

The report was accepted by king and council who appeared to be gripped by a collective panic and saw a Jesuit under every bed. They were a convenient culprit whose guilt whitewashed the government and relieved it of the need to confront the people and the nobility, presumably the other partners to the conspiracy. At the same time, to charge the Jesuits would also be a warning to the Jesuits' invisible army, their clients in Church and state, the graduates of the *colegios mayores* and the beneficiaries of their former patronage, all enemies of *manteista*-inspired reform. This appears to have been the thinking of Campomanes, who slipped in a hint that the Jesuits were anti-Enlightenment: 'This organization has conspired above all to extinguish interest in good studies, to weaken the royal power, and to remove enlightened people from the government', at the same time promoting ignorance, superstition and bad morals.[81] Amidst anti-Jesuit hysteria scurrilous stories were planted: the Jesuits were saying that Charles III was a bastard, offspring of adultery between Elizabeth Farnese and Cardinal Alberoni and not rightful heir to the throne; that Charles III was sleeping with the marquesa de Squillace and had turned his palace into a harem where he ruled like a Moorish despot.[82] If rumours were taken as facts and insinuations as evidence, Campomanes's own report provided the model. The charges against the Jesuits had all the violence and passion of propaganda, and showed that they were being condemned not merely or mainly for alleged intervention in the Madrid riots but for what their enemies in the government called their 'spirit of fanaticism and sedition, false doctrine and intolerable pride', and for constituting 'an open faction which disturbed the state with interests directly opposed to the public welfare'.[83] They were found guilty of provoking the riots and a royal decree of 27 February 1767 expelled them from Spain and its dominions.

The decree was kept secret for a month while the ground was prepared. Then on the night of 21 March troop movements were noticed in Madrid. About midnight a large detachment was sent to each of the six different Jesuit houses, a guard posted at each room, the occupants ordered to rise and assemble. Meanwhile every hired coach and conveyance in Madrid was commandeered, and by early morning the Jesuits were on the road to Cartagena and embarkation. These

---

[81] Ibid., p. 80.
[82] Ibid., p. 47.
[83] Consulta del consejo extraordinario, 30 April 1767, in Danvila y Collado, *El reinado de Carlos III*, III, pp. 628–33.

dramatic scenes were repeated all over Spain. The king claimed that he
had just and necessary reasons for his actions which he kept 'locked in
his soul', and public silence was imposed. In fact there was little public or
clerical reaction. The measure was supported by rival orders like the
Augustinians and they lost no time in laying their hands on Jesuit
property. The bishops were divided and some refused to bend to official
pressure to applaud the action. Nevertheless, when in 1769 the pope
asked the Spanish hierarchy for its opinion on the expulsion, forty-two
bishops approved, six opposed, and eight declined to answer.

Not content with expelling the Jesuits, the Spanish government was
also determined to suppress the order everywhere. For this it needed the
cooperation of the papacy. The Jesuits who left Spain settled in the papal
states and other parts of Europe. Pope Clement XIII, for political and
financial reasons, had not wanted them in his states, but he resisted
pressure from the Bourbon powers for their suppression. Therefore
Charles III and his allies had to work for a more amenable successor, and
the election of Cardinal Ganganelli as Clement XIV was a victory for the
anti-Jesuit powers who eventually procured a papal brief suppressing
the Society of Jesus on 21 July 1773. The principal agent working for the
Spanish government in Rome was José Moñino, assisted by Fathers
Vásquez and Boixadors, generals respectively of the Augustinians and
Dominicans. Moñino was influential even in drawing up the papal brief
and Charles III rewarded him for his efforts with the title of count of
Floridablanca. The king could not contain his satisfaction, and he
publicly told foreign ambassadors at San Ildefonso that they would see
the day 'when the necessity of that measure would be allowed by all
mankind'.[84]

There remained the question of Jesuit doctrines and Jesuit properties.
The former were proscribed and the latter sequestered. The government
sought to ensure that the property of the Jesuits was used for establishing new teaching centres, colleges of medicine, and university
residences for poor students, while Jesuit revenues were to be assigned
to hospitals and other social services. Royal decrees confined primary
education to secular teachers, made school attendance obligatory, and
regulated the chairs for universities. Not all of these projects came to
fruition and it was the state rather than society that gained from the
dissolution. Jesuit university chairs were abolished and the use of Jesuit
works of theology was prohibited. The hand of the state was felt even

[84] Grantham to Rochford, 9 September 1773, PRO, SP 94/194; on the role of the papacy see
Chadwick, *The Popes and European Revolution*, pp. 368–85.

more heavily when government censors were established at the universities to ensure the observance of the order of 1770 directed to all
recipients of degrees and university teachers not to uphold or teach any
ultramontane doctrines opposed to the regalian rights of the crown.[85]

University reform began in 1769 when the government requested the
universities to submit new academic plans. The proposals of Valladolid,
Salamanca, and Alcalá de Henares were approved in 1771, those of
Santiago in 1772, Oviedo in 1774, Granada in 1776, and Valencia in
1786.[86] The pattern of the projected reforms was to raise academic
standards; to extend general knowledge of a range of subjects; and to
place a new emphasis on science, especially applied science, to serve
agriculture, industry and trade. The plans were a mixture of tradition
and innovation, introducing minimal changes within a scholastic framework.[87] Logic and dialectic would be studied in the first year, meta-
physics in the second; in the third year future theologians would take
Aristotelian physics. In practice the sciences, and particularly medicine,
acquired more importance in the syllabus, while text books underwent
some modernization, but even these advances were contested by traditionalists.[88] In the University of Salamanca curriculum changes reflected
gains for the experimental method and the autonomy of science, and
medicine became a leading discipline; by 1808 a generation imbued with
the ideas of the Enlightenment displaced the old clerical elite in
academic government and society, before war and counter-revolution
intervened to extinguish the movement.[89] Intellectual progress was
achieved in Spain not because of university reform, which fell far short
of the country's needs, but through the efforts of individuals and the
penetration of European ideas.[90]

Medical education, too, met with obstacles. The Royal College of San
Carlos was founded in Madrid in 1787 as a school of surgery and soon

[85] Herr, *The Eighteenth-Century Revolution in Spain*, pp. 24–5; Farriss, *Crown and Clergy in Colonial Mexico*, pp. 135–6.

[86] Mariano Peset and José Luis Peset, *La universidad española (siglos XVIII y XIX). Despotismo ilustrado y revolución liberal* (Madrid, 1974), pp. 103–7.

[87] Ibid., pp. 223–4.

[88] Antonio Alvarez de Morales, *Inquisición e ilustración (1700-1834)* (Madrid, 1982), pp. 110–15; see also Francisco Aguilar Piñal, *La Universidad de Sevilla en el siglo XVIII* (Seville, 1969); Antonio Alvarez de Morales, *La 'Ilustración' y la reforma de la universidad en la España del siglo XVIII* (Madrid, 1971); Antonio Mestre, *Ilustración y reforma de la iglesia. Pensamiento político-religioso de don Gregorio Mayáns y Siscar (1699-1781)* (Valencia, 1968).

[89] George M. Addy, *The Enlightenment in the University of Salamanca* (Durham, NC, 1966), pp. 242–3.

[90] Peset, *La universidad española*, pp. 117–26.

became one of the most advanced of its kind in Europe, the result of collaboration between reformist ministers and individual initiative, and proof that pursuit of applied science and useful knowledge had more chance of success than university innovation.[91] The frustrations which the college experienced arose not from obscurantism or lack of talent but from financial constraints and the persistence of a traditional social structure. Here, as in other areas of Spanish life, reform was construed as an attack on corporate privilege and professional autonomy, as indeed it was, and it met with resistance from vested interests, that is from other sectors of the medical profession in the universities.

The second phase of post-Jesuit reform of higher education focused on the *colegios mayores*. These had gradually abandoned their original purpose to provide resident places for noble but poor students in the Universities of Salamanca, Alcalá, and Valladolid, and had become in effect preserves of rich students on their way to well paid careers in Church and state. University chairs were the first stage, though a transitory one, for they yielded at most only 10,000 reales a year, while senior posts in the *audiencias*, councils and other departments of state earned anything between 20,000 and 55,000 reales. The Jesuits played a key role in the *colegios* and the graduate network, and their protégés came to monopolize the best offices and to form a self-perpetuating elite in the universities, Church and administration.[92] All this to the detriment of the *manteistas*, the non-collegiate graduates of the universities, who could not hope to emulate the careers of the *colegiales*: 'Be he noble or plebeian, although the graduate may have spent all his days and nights and exhausted his energy in study ... if he was unable to gain entry to a *Colegio Mayor* the most that he could hope for in a civil career would be an alcalde's office or a miserable post of corregidor, or a temporary appointment in the administration.'[93] To reformers like Campomanes, Roda and Floridablanca, who also happened to be *manteistas*, the *colegios* were strongholds of privilege and long overdue for investigation. In 1771 a royal decree laid down that anyone who had received a university education in any part of Spain was now eligible to hold civil and ecclesiastical office; in future no one would be admitted to the *colegios mayores* without first proving his inability otherwise to

[91] Michael E. Burke, *The Royal College of San Carlos. Surgery and Spanish Medical Reform in the Late Eighteenth Century* (Durham, NC, 1977), pp. 83–8.
[92] Richard L. Kagan, *Students and Society in Early Modern Spain* (Baltimore, Md., 1974), pp. 145–9.
[93] Felipe Bertrán, bishop of Salamanca, quoted by L. Sala Balust, *Visitas y reforma de los colegios mayores de Salamanca en el reinado de Carlos III* (Salamanca, 1958), 394.

receive a university education; residence should be for no more than seven years. The hostile reaction from the network of *colegiales* and their families ensured that this legislation remained virtually inoperative, but in the same year the government appointed Felipe Bertrán, bishop of Salamanca, and Francisco Pérez Bayer, professor, royal tutor, and friend of the *manteistas* in the government, to investigate the functioning of the *colegios*.[94] Their enquiry, harassed all the way by *colegiales*, led to further decrees in 1777: applications for admission to places in the *colegios* were to be submitted to the council of Castile which would select the successful candidates; entrants could not remain in the *colegio* for more than eight years; the *colegios* were to be subject to the rules of the University and an annual inspection. Doubt remains whether these decrees were successful, or whether indeed they represented 'reform'. They encountered opposition, of course, and many new entrants wanted to profit from the old system, not destroy it, with the result that one set of *colegiales* was simply replaced by another. According to Cardinal Lorenzana, the *colegios mayores* still wanted 'not beggars, nor people of lowly birth, nor those tarnished by common trades, but poor and honourable nobles, and to be considered poor it is sufficient to be a third son of a grandee without an entail or an income appropriate to his status'.[95] In due course the *colegios* were in fact reformed, not by decree but by decline; changing values undermined their pre-eminence and in 1798 they were suppressed, their funds allocated to the amortization of the national debt.

The subordination of the Church to the state in Spain was completed by the curtailment of the Inquisition. Potentially this was already a royal tool, but in the eyes of the government it was compromised by its past association with the Jesuits, and it was regarded as ultramontane, obscurantist, and prone to autonomy by the reformers around Charles III. The tribunal was by no means dormant in the eighteenth century, nor did it lose its basic popularity as a defender of Spain's traditional faith.[96] But business declined. The Inquisition of Toledo heard only three or four cases a year in the late eighteenth century, compared with 200 a year in the mid-sixteenth century. Of the 4,000 cases taken to the supreme council in the eighteenth century less than 10 per cent dealt with major items of Judaism and Protestantism.[97] The death penalty was

[94] Peset, *La universidad española*, pp. 107–14.

[95] Quoted by Sala Balust, *Visitas y reforma de los colegios mayores*, p. 114.

[96] Martínez Albiach, *Religiosidad hispana y sociedad borbónica*, p. 66; Henry Kamen, *The Spanish Inquisition* (London, 1965), pp. 247–70.

[97] Bartolomé Bennassar, et al., *L'Inquisition espagnole (XVᵉ-XIXᵉ siècle)* (Paris, 1979), pp. 21–32.

carried out only in 1714, 1725, 1763, and 1781. The Inquisition's last victim, María de los Dolores López, was burnt alive as an *ilusa*, or visionary, in 1781 in Seville, claiming that she had contact with the Virgin and had released a million souls from purgatory.[98]

The council of Castile reasserted the sovereignty of the crown over the Inquisition, and Charles III began to use this sovereignty more effectively than his predecessors had done. Decrees of 1768 and 1770 regulated the procedure for censoring books; the inquisitors were advised to confine themselves to matters of faith and morals, heresy and apostacy, and to imprison only when guilt was established; no work of a Catholic author should be condemned without his being given a hearing.[99] Royal action might regulate and restrict the powers of the Inquisition but it made no attempt to remove them; it still preserved intact its traditional jurisdiction in matters spiritual, and for anyone to criticize it was like an unarmed civilian attacking a waiting army. In 1768 discussion in the council of Castile on the reform of the Inquisition brought Campomanes to its attention, when a report in which he accused it of being pro-Jesuit, pro-papal, hostile to regalian rights and arbitrary in its procedure was leaked to the tribunal. Campomanes had also written a wide-ranging criticism of papal power which aroused the opposition of the episcopal members of the council of Castile. Could he survive a dual counter-attack? Fortunately for him the king resented the Inquisition's possession of the document and was more interested in knowing the source of the leak; in effect Charles saved Campomanes from an Inquisition trial.[100] The tribunal retreated to its corner, injured but not inert.

While the Inquisition might hesitate to touch leading ministers, it could still strike at lesser men in public life, as Pablo de Olavide learned to his cost when his career as royal official, intendant of Seville and administrator of the Sierra Morena settlements was brought to a sensational end by his arrest, trial and conviction of heresy. Olavide was a reforming Catholic, not an unbeliever. He told the nobles of Seville that rather than pouring money into decorating a shrine 'it would be more devout to spend your money on developing agriculture and improving your properties, thus helping your neighbour and giving aid to the poor and destitute'.[101] He undoubtedly provoked the social and

---

[98] Ibid., p. 209.
[99] Alvarez de Morales, *Inquisición e ilustración*, pp. 102–5.
[100] Rodríguez, *Campomanes*, pp. 101–3.
[101] Marcelin Defourneaux, *Pablo de Olavide ou l'Afrancesado (1725-1803)* (Paris, 1959), pp. 293, 294–305, 309–26, 352–65.

religious establishment in Andalucía, but it was his determination to keep the Capuchins and their ways out of the Sierra Morena that led to his downfall. In 1776 he suddenly vanished into the cells of the Inquisition, sealed off from family and friends, to emerge in 1778 dressed in a penitent's cap and smock and to face formal charges of heresy; in a macabre ceremony attended by forty-six invited grandees, military, priests and monks, he was sentenced to eight years confinement in a monastery in La Mancha and confiscation of his property. Olavide escaped without great difficulty and made his way to France where after the outbreak of the Revolution 'he learned, what he could not possibly suspect fifteen years before, that there was something under the sun more formidable than the inquisition'.[102] Everyone in public life walked a tightrope, glory one day, catastrophe the next, in a world of envy, faction, and royal despotism. Macanaz, Ensenada, and others at the top knew how easy it was to be arrested and imprisoned in eighteenth-century Spain. But the case of Olavide leaves a puzzle. Why did Charles III, normally supportive of officials, and bishop Bertrán, a supposedly moderate inquisitor general, allow the case to proceed? And where were the rest of the enlightened ministers when Olavide most needed them?

In addition to inspiring terror the Inquisition could still stage a comic show. In May 1784 Ignacio Rodríguez, ex-soldier, vagrant and beggar, set up business in a church porch in Madrid selling aphrodisiacs, his female accomplices helping to boost the sales. He was arrested, tried and sentenced by the Inquisition, guardian of the nation's morals. The sentence was solemnly pronounced in the church of St Dominic in a ceremony crowded with Madrid society and thronged by nuns who thrust their way to the front; the victim was then 'whipped' through the streets of Madrid by an Inquisition familiar of noble rank in a bizarre procession through gawping crowds, 'a spectacle so inconsistent with the dawn of improvement which begins to break upon this country', thought a British observer.[103] Inconsistency was a hallmark of Charles III's government, and it was characteristic of the reign that only half-measures were applied to this anachronistic institution. In 1792 the Inquisition was mobilized by Floridablanca to censor and exclude French books, primarily for their political content, and the tribunal now underwent a revival which brought it into new conflicts with the

---

[102] Bourgoing, *Modern State of Spain*, I, pp. 563–4.
[103] Liston to Carmarthen, Madrid, 10 May 1784, PRO, FO 72/2; Townsend, *A Journey through Spain*, II, pp. 345–54; Bourgoing, *Modern State of Spain*, I, pp. 365–8.

government.[104] The minister's action was not out of line with his established view of the Inquisition. Like the rest of the government he had watched Olavide's ordeal in silence, and in his *Instrucción reservada* he wrote:

> It is important to favour and protect this Tribunal, but care has to be taken that it does not usurp the regalian rights of the Crown and that on the pretext of religion it does not disturb public order ... or depart from its proper function which is to persecute heresy, apostacy and superstition, and to enlighten the faithful in these matters with charity.[105]

For Floridablanca the Inquisition was a threat not to freedom but to absolutism.

The contrast between the government's treatment of the Jesuits, the universities and the Inquisition is a guide to the policy of Charles III. In the case of the Jesuits, where royal power was at stake, policy was conclusive: they were expelled and destroyed. In the case of the universities and the Inquisition, both embodiments of archaism, royal policy was a curious compound of a taste for reform and a bias towards tradition. By 1767 the record of the government was not one of radical change. The first policy initiative was war, a costly blunder and a self-inflicted blow to reform. The next major decision, the expulsion of the Jesuits, was a victory for absolutism but not for enlightenment; the 'research' undertaken by Campomanes was inherently flawed and the subsequent educational reform mediocre. Meanwhile, Spaniards fortunate enough to possess privileges continued to enjoy them. The legal campaign against *señoríos* was so gradualist that it was still in progress in the following century. The council of Castile failed to take up the challenge of the Church over disamortization. And the new corn laws were a recipe for disaster. The first ten years were not a new age.

---

[104] Alvarez de Morales, *Inquisición e ilustración*, pp. 148–57.
[105] 'Instrucción reservada', *Obras originales del conde de Floridablanca*, pp. 217–18.

8

The Bourbon State

Politics and Government 1766–1788

The suppression of the riots of 1766 and the expulsion of the Jesuits in the following year were a partial vindication of absolutism. The government survived the crisis, frustrated its enemies, real or imagined, and restored law and order throughout Spain. But Charles III was forced to remove his leading minister and the administration to acknowledge resistance to change. In his search for a new paladin the king chose the count of Aranda and made him in effect minister of the interior. As president of the council of Castile, Aranda became head of a department which specialized in social order and policy and was the base of the reformers in the government, Campomanes and Moñino. Aranda was already an experienced and widely travelled administrator, a soldier familiar with enlightenment, a progressive who had not abandoned Spanish and aristocratic values. Charles was acquiring, presumably by design, a tough executive and pseudo-reformer, a man who could restore order and confidence, reassure and restrain the aristocracy, and preserve a moderate commitment to change. But Aranda saw himself as more than a front man holding the ring for policy makers. He had ideas and a kind of party.

Aranda was president of the council of Castile for seven years, 1766–73. Towards the end of that time, in May 1772, the fiscals of the council, Campomanes and Moñino, complained to Charles III that the president was acting despotically, trespassing on their jurisdiction, and indirectly infringing the rights of the monarch.[1] Thus surfaced a latent conflict

---

[1] Manuel Danvila y Collado, *El reinado de Carlos III* (6 vols, Madrid, 1890–6), III, p. 452; IV, p. 269.

between the so-called Aragonese party, hostile to Bourbon concepts and centralizing officials, and the fiscals of the council, upholders of the rule of law and civil power against the excesses of Aranda and the military. The existence of these factions, whatever they stood for, was well known to contemporaries. The English ambassador, for example, writing in 1776 at the time of Grimaldi's resignation, referred to 'the personal opposition he so frequently met with from a set of men generally called the Aragonese Party'; and from Grantham's dispatches the concept was developed by the English historian William Coxe.[2] There were, of course, no parties in the modern sense, only informal groupings and factions, looking for influence but without guarantee of power. Aranda was the centre of such a group, not all of whom were actually Aragonese but who thought alike on politics.[3]

What was the particular identity of the Aragonese party? At a time when government was widely regarded in terms of patronage rather than policy the party could be defined simply as clients seeking preferment. There were a number of Aragonese in Madrid, some of them bureaucrats anxious for further promotion, others aristocrats awaiting opportunities, and all looking to Aranda as patron in chief. But patronage politics inevitably contained a few ideas. The presence of foreigners in the government caused the Aragonese – and other Spaniards too – to resent the fact that the crown preferred outsiders to natives, while the tendency to favour *manteistas*, or *golillas* as they came to be called, revived in the Aragonese their historical resentment of Bourbon opposition to their regional identity.[4] Bourbon absolutism was challenged by another concept of monarchy, one restrained by regional rights and by the nobility as an estate. Aranda saw himself as a moderator of monarchy, a bridge between king and people, and he sought aristocratic power to curb royal power. Around the Aragonese party were grouped a number of aristocrats, clerics, councillors and officials, all supporters of Aranda, not necessarily opponents of reform but hostile to the king's chosen instruments, the *golillas*, for whom they had an elitist disdain. Finally, the party responded to the thinking of the

---

[2] Grantham to Weymouth, 20 November 1776, Public Record Office, London, SP 94/102; William Coxe, *Memoirs of the Kings of Spain of the House of Bourbon* (2nd edn, 5 vols, London, 1815), v, p. 10.

[3] Rafael Olaechea, *El conde de Aranda y el 'partido aragonés'* (Zaragoza, 1969), pp. 32–3.

[4] Class distinction among graduates and careerists was expressed in terms of dress worn at the university, which in turn represented status. Non-collegiates were disparagingly called *manteistas*, after the long cape they were obliged to wear as students, or *golillas*, after their white ruffled collar.

military, many of whom were frustrated in their expectations and increasingly alienated from the civil administration. These two components, the aristocratic faction and the military malcontents, finding themselves left aside by the king and marginalized by Floridablanca, sought support in the circle of the prince of Asturias, a familiar tactic in Spanish politics.

The conflict between *golillas* and Aragonese was not a simple division between reformers and reactionaries, for Aranda and his political ally Roda might move either way according to particular issues. True, there were still nobles and *colegiales* in public life who objected strongly to reformism and expected Aranda to restrain its exponents. But these were essentially factional struggles, devoid of ideological consistency and representing tendencies, interest groups, and ministerial teams. In patronage politics of this kind those who dominated the major *secretarías* had the greatest power, and this gave ministers like Grimaldi and Floridablanca, *golillas* held in contempt by Aranda, the nobles, and the military, the edge over their rivals. They were able to fight for their own ministry or their own career from a position of strength, confident that they had the loyalty of client officials throughout the ministry. This does not mean that the administration of Charles III reflected a basic shift in the social basis of government. There were no middle-class entrants among the higher bureaucracy. They were all *hidalgos*, even if minor ones, and while the most powerful were *manteistas*, the *colegiales* were by no means absent. But this minor aristocracy was becoming an aristocracy of merit, and it held a new concept of office as a professional career, one which should have an appropriate salary and a pension on retirement.

The position of Aranda himself was ambiguous. On the one hand he had to resist the more extreme anti-reformism of many nobles and *colegiales* who did not like the favour shown by Charles III to *golillas*. On the other hand he clashed with the *golilla* ministers, if not because of their reformism then because of their control over policy, an attitude shared by Roda who in other respects should have been a *golilla*. So Aranda was not easily classified and most people, including the king, found him a difficult person to deal with. But the factions were divided if not on reform at least on a number of policy issues, and conflict was exacerbated by the Falklands crisis of 1770, when the warlike Aranda poured scorn on the diplomatic efforts of Grimaldi and gloated over his rival's failure. In the king's presence he called Grimaldi 'the most weak, indolent, sycophantic and time-serving minister with whom Spain was ever cursed'.[5] Tension within the government mounted during the next two years, and every appointment was scrutinized as evidence of factional ascendancy or decline. On the death of Muniain in January 1772 the count of Ricla, cousin of Aranda and previously placed by him in the captaincy-general of Catalonia, was appointed minister of war. But in March 1772 the appointment of Moñino, obviously a nominee of Grimaldi, to the important office of Spanish ambassador in Rome was taken as a sign that Grimaldi still commanded the royal favour and that the king listened to his advice. He was now urging Charles to replace Aranda, who as well as being an abrasive element in the government had now outlived his usefulness. Charles agreed; in April 1773 Aranda was appointed ambassador to France and in August he left for Paris. There he was flattered by the philosophers but otherwise presented an unattractive face to the world, a toothless, deaf and squinting little man, his nose stained with snuff, rough-spoken but mostly taciturn. He was replaced in the council of Castile by Ventura de Figueroa, an obscure mediocrity, whose inexplicable appointment was disturbing evidence that not all was enlightenment in the government of Charles III.

Aranda did not abandon Spanish politics, and the Aragonese party continued to function, grouped around the chamber of the prince of Asturias. Carlos had his own grievances against the king who had kept him poorly educated, confined to childish amusements, trusted with nothing, and debarred from even the appearance of doing business. The opposition found the prince and his wife Maria Luisa a receptive audience and gave the royal pair an illusion of political participation. But Grimaldi played into the hands of the opposition by further foreign policy embarrassment. Grimaldi was most successful when most inert. Initiative usually failed him, and in 1775 the failure was total. It was decided to launch a great expedition against Algiers to punish its ruler for hostilities against Spanish settlements in North Africa. The war was important to Spaniards for reasons of pride, religion, and maritime security, and the subsequent catastrophe – over 1,500 men were lost and the rest only narrowly saved – was regarded as a national scandal and disaster. The expedition was very much a project of Grimaldi and Alejandro O'Reilly, two foreigners, which revived nativist sentiment and aroused the Madrid mob to the verge of violence. 'The bulk of the people are greatly cast down, and do not scruple most openly blaming the King's confessor, who is supposed to have urged a war against the

---

[5] Coxe, *Memoirs of the Kings of Spain*, i, iv, p. 412.

infidels, and opprobriously condemning the Minister who planned and the General who has attempted to execute it.'[6] O'Reilly was henceforth known as 'general disaster', and Grimaldi was subject to a long campaign of villification. The Aragonese party, aided and abetted by the prince of Asturias, kept up its pressure on the beleagured minister who was forced to try new tactics. He persuaded the king to admit the prince to the nightly business meetings, at least when foreign affairs were discussed, in the hope apparently of gaining credit with the prince and taking the sting out of the opposition.[7] But the prince was not to be stopped, and he spoke his mind – or that of the Aragonese party – in spirited interventions in the cabinet meetings, restrained only by the king himself. It was in these circumstances that Charles III wrote to his son warning him that association with the opposition against the king's ministers would eventually rebound on him:

> It is common talk throughout the kingdom that there are two parties at Court; this can cause great harm, and more to you than to me, for you will inherit one day. If it is thought that division exists now between father and son, then there will certainly be people in the future who will suggest to your family to do exactly the same to you.[8]

The advice seemed to make little impression. The Aragonese party, manipulated by the distant Aranda, dominated by the aristocracy, and patronized by the prince of Asturias, continued to operate as an opposition, if only a destructive one. Grimaldi became aware that he was politically isolated. Ricla and Múzquiz belonged to the Aragonese, Roda was a friend of Aranda, and no one wished to be associated with policy failures stretching from the Falklands to North Africa. Grimaldi accepted the inevitable and is reported to have said to a friend in his box at the opera at Aranjuez, 'It's time for me to go.' He resigned on 7 November 1776 and was appointed ambassador to Rome. In fact he changed places with Floridablanca.

The last months of 1776 were crucial for Spain, a time of power struggle between the Aragonese party and the existing ministry, between the aristocracy and the bureaucracy, between *colegiales* and

---

[6] Grantham to Rochford, 17 July 1775, PRO, SP 94/198.

[7] Grantham to Rochford, 21 August 1775, PRO, SP 94/199; Grantham to Weymouth, 19 July 1776, PRO, SP 94/201; Coxe, *Memoirs of the Kings of Spain*, v, p. 10.

[8] Charles III to prince of Asturias, 1776, in Danvila, *El reinado de Carlos III*, iv, pp. 275–7.

golillas; the whole spectrum of political opinion and interests sought to win over the king. At stake was the nature of the Bourbon state. Was it to be a modern, centralist, bureaucratic state open to change, or was it to revert to a conciliar, aristocratic, and regionalist model, its policy an unknown quantity? The *golillas* and the bureaucracy fought back against their opponents. Grimaldi still had influence and support in his own *covachuela*, or department, at the *secretaría de estado*; from there his key official, Bernardo del Campo, mobilized opinion on behalf of Floridablanca while Grimaldi suggested his candidature to the king. As Grimaldi himself told Figueroa, 'We are going to get one of our own appointed.'⁹ Charles accepted the idea and Floridablanca took office as secretary of state in February 1777, the favourite of *golillas* and reformers.

So the way was closed to alternatives and the Aragonese party failed to gain from the resignation it had helped to engineer. One of the alternatives was José de Gálvez, whose position during the crisis was ambiguous. In February 1776 the octogenarian Arriaga died and Gálvez succeeded him as minister of the Indies. Gálvez was a man of modest origins who had taken a law degree at Alcalá de Henares and risen to become visitor general of New Spain in 1765–71 and subsequently a member of the council of the Indies. He was a *golilla* by definition but factional loyalty was never absolute, and Gálvez was not one to miss an opportunity of self-promotion; at any rate he seems to have been ready to join the Aragonese if it would secure him Grimaldi's position. This did not happen and so, more by default than design, he became a pillar of the reconstructed *golilla* government and a guide to its priorities. This was a moderate rather than a radical government; it was interested not in promoting structural reform but in raising military and naval power, expanding revenue, projecting a strong foreign policy; and it was increasingly attentive to America.

Charles III loaded work and responsibility on Floridablanca but also gave him extraordinary favour, support, and trust. The nature of the Bourbon state had now been defined. The king was satisfied that the appropriate government was in place, its policy established, its leader a man to his liking. At this point he ceased to manage personally the affairs of state and left government to Floridablanca. The minister himself claimed: 'In highest policy matters the king's confidence in me is without limits; and other ministers, seeing the king's determination to

---

⁹ Olaechea, *Aranda*, p. 110.

rely on me in everything of importance, come to consult me with astonishing frequency.'[10] From 1777, therefore, Floridablanca was all-powerful, not exactly a popular idol but a respected minister, the equal of others in Europe, and a good administrator. But he was vain, somewhat aloof, receptive to flattery, and incapable of taking criticism. His intolerance of others grew with the king's growing support for him and helped to keep alive an element of political dissent.

Aranda inevitably was hostile. As ambassador in Paris he was responsible to the new minister, a man whom he regarded as inferior in every respect, with one embassy to his credit compared to Aranda's three, and a mere legal career compared to Aranda's military record; and this was a minister blocking his access to the king. From Paris he wrote to the prince of Asturias, pouring out his resentment that one so inexperienced, qualified only in law, should be managing the affairs of Spain while his own talents were wasted in Paris, and venting his anger in terms replete with prejudice. 'Your Highness will observe the difference of birth, education, character, profession and style between these two people. And which of the two is humiliated, yet superior in understanding and judgement of affairs?'[11]

Floridablanca tended to concentrate power in his own hands and to encircle himself by a cordon of supporters. He had his own clients and creatures appointed to other ministries and so widened his sphere of influence. An example was the appointment of Lerena to war and finance on the death of Múzquiz in 1785, a client whose modest origins made him all the more dependent on his patron. Eventually he brought his own brother into the administration as governor of the council of the Indies. Upward mobility was a tactic as well as a merit, and Florida-blanca used it to the exclusion of troublesome aristocrats. Another of his tactics was to eliminate the influence of the council of state which represented traditional interests and to give authority instead to the council of ministers over which he presided. This was criticized at the time, by some on grounds of principle; as Jovellanos wrote, 'this was an encroachment by the arbitrary power of the Ministers, who cannot make or unmake the law.'[12] The Aragonese party was an opposing interest group, with a different concept of government and rival social base. It still had contact with the prince of Asturias, and he with Aranda.

[10] Floridablanca to Azara, 7 October 1777, ibid., p. 113–14.

[11] Aranda to prince of Asturias, Paris, 16 September 1781, ibid., p. 188.

[12] 'Dictamen sobre el anuncio de las Cortes', 22 June 1809, *Obras de Jovellanos*. Tomo I (*BAE*, 46, Madrid, 1963), p.96.

In 1781 the prince wrote in warm tones to his friend in the context of what he regarded as the parlous state of government and ministers: 'I would like you to prepare me a plan of what I ought to do in the event (which God forbid) of my father dying, and what people you think are most suitable to be Ministers and for other appointments ... My wife, who is with me now, asks the same of you.'[13] Aranda was pleased to be consulted, believing it to be a serious conspiracy to remove Floridablanca. In reply he sent the prince a lengthy paper on the machinery of government, mediocre in its argument and unremarkable in its conclusions; shorn of the verbiage, it placed ultimate power in the will of the monarch, seen as a theocratic figure and in the person of Charles III an 'enlightened prince', with whom, assisted by traditional councils, lay the ultimate corrective for ministerial despotism.[14] Aranda's paper had no influence in 1781 or on the accession of Charles IV in 1788. But its author maintained contact, continued to complain of ministerial despotism, and demanded meetings in Madrid with Floridablanca, the prince, and the king. 'Am I to serve the King or his Ministers?'[15] It was an old-fashioned concept of government, adroitly resisted by Floridablanca who, in the course of 1781, froze out Aranda and his ally from any entry to decision making, and continued with his own programme of modernization.

One King, One Minister, One Law

While Aranda and the aristocrats were intriguing, Floridablanca and his colleagues were governing Spain. Reform depended on agencies of government to implement it. Charles III continued the policy of absolutism and centralization begun by the earlier Bourbons, and under him the *cortes* – one *cortes* for the whole kingdom – played no more part in the national life than it had done under the earlier Bourbons. The new king had been warmly received by Barcelona on disembarking from Naples in 1759 and he had no serious problems with the Catalans, though they still reacted violently to attempts to impose military conscription. In the *cortes* of 1760, assembled to recognize Carlos as prince and heir, the deputies of Aragon, speaking for the eastern provinces, presented a paper to the king claiming to show that the

---

[13]   Prince of Asturias to Aranda, 19 March 1781, in Olaechea, *Aranda*, p. 125.
[14]   Aranda, 'Plan de gobierno para el Principe', 22 April 1781, ibid., pp. 157–82.
[15]   Aranda to prince of Asturias, Paris, 23 June 1781, ibid., pp. 183–6.

changes inaugurated by Philip V had not brought the intended results and taking a position against the Nueva Planta. Criticism of this kind did not signify a state of unrest but was primarily designed to take soundings, in case the new king might have a new policy. The most interesting petition was that reciprocity of appointments to offices should be truly effective; so far no Aragonese, Catalans or Valencians had obtained important civil or ecclesiastical appointments in Castile, while Castilians had swarmed into jobs in the east.[16] The *Memorial de Greuges*, as it was called, made little impact on the government and secured no significant change, though there was perhaps evidence in the course of the reign that subjects of the eastern provinces were appointed to the bureaucracy in greater numbers than before. The new economic groups in Catalonia played no part in the petition, nor did it represent their particular interests; they preferred to negotiate directly with the central government and on more than one occasion did so successfully. Between Madrid and the Basque provinces, on the other hand, there was continuing tension, product of the wide political, fiscal, military, and economic autonomy enjoyed by the Basques, and the corresponding aversion of the Bourbon state to all special privilege, exemption, and franchise. The state intervened where it could. There was little solidarity between the various social sectors in the Basque country, and parties with grievances or complaints frequently appealed to the central government for decisions in their favour, a tendency which gave the crown a card of entry.

The crown also sought to make itself more absolute by making itself more efficient. The conciliar system of government had already been modified by the earlier Bourbons and the councils reduced in number, jurisdiction, and political importance. The exception was the council of Castile, which was in effect a specialist department of home affairs and as such central to the work of government. This council, moreover, had greater social significance than any other department of state, both in its composition and its functions; it was from here that jurists and reformers could launch initiatives concerning agrarian policy, social order, and law enforcement, reflecting perhaps changing ideas of social needs. Finally, the council of Castile was seen by some as a possible restraint on royal power and state absolutism, servant to all and servile to none; in the reign of Charles III this was a perception rather than a reality, and he had no reason to complain of its treatment of the royal

---

[16] Enric Moreu-Rey (ed.), *El 'Memorial de Greuges' del 1760* (Barcelona, 1968).

prerogative. The key posts in the council were those of *fiscales*, law officers of the crown, who had to give advice on legislation and in some cases to prepare the *proyectos de ley* which would be discussed in full council. The fiscals had the status of ministers and attended the Friday meeting between king and council. In deference to their great work load the structure of the *fiscalía* was further rationalized in 1771 with the appointment of a third fiscal and the division of work by area into Old Castile, New Castile, and the area of the *audiencias* of Aragon, Catalonia, and Valencia.[17]

The secretaries of state, now normally called ministers, were the mainsprings of government under Charles III. He inherited five such ministries – state, war, finance, justice, and marine and the Indies. The concentration of power in the hands of a small number of men and the continual contact they maintained with the king, or increasingly with Floridablanca, gave policy an impetus and direction which was one of the characteristics of Bourbon government. Leaving administrative and judical detail to the councils, these ministers could prepare and promote policy, extend the central power to the length and breadth of Spain, and inaugurate reforms in the collection of revenue, national defence, local government, and other fields. From 1754 the *secretaría de marina e Indias* was divided into two departments, the head of which was a single minister, Julián de Arriaga, until his death in January 1776. The departments of marine and Indies were then assigned to different ministers, the first to Pedro González de Castejón, the second to José de Gálvez. On the death of Gálvez (17 June 1787) the ministry of the Indies was divided into two *secretarías*, one of grace and justice which was given to Antonio Porlier, the other of finance, war, and trade which was given to Antonio Valdés, the navy minister. This was only a temporary measure. On 25 April 1790 another royal decree abolished the ministry of the Indies and integrated its several functions into the appropriate Spanish ministry, each of which now had authority over the Indies in its own field.[18] Spanish government, therefore, reverted to five ministries: state, under Floridablanca; war, the count of Campo Alegre; navy, Valdés; finance, Lerena; and justice, Porlier. The 'reform' of 1790, in which ideas of Aranda and the hand of Floridablanca, for once coinciding, can be

---

[17] María Isobel Cabrera Bosch, 'El poder legislativo en la España del siglo XVIII (1716–1808)', *La economía española al final del Antiguo Régimen* (4 vols, Madrid, 1982), IV *Instituciones*, pp. 185–268.

[18] Decree of 8 July 1787; see Gildas Bernard, *Le secrétariat d'état et le conseil espagnol des Indes (1700-1808)* (Geneva/Paris, 1972), pp. 51, 57–8, 64–72; José Antonio Escudero, *Los orígenes del Consejo de Ministros en España* (2 vols, Madrid, 1979), I, pp. 444–52, 505–15.

discerned, was intended to centralize government still further, on the principle of one king, one law – and one powerful minister in control of all international policy. But it was a retrograde step, ending a long and proven geographical specialization in favour of a conceptual uniformity. Colonial business did not cease to be colonial because it was subsumed under a peninsula institution; it simply took its place at the end of the queue. The change was criticized by contemporary specialists, notably by José Pablo Valiente and Francisco de Requera, former members of the council of the Indies, who argued in 1809 that the internal affairs of the Indies, so distant and so different, had lost the detailed and informed attention they had received from the ministry of the Indies, while Spain's international interests in America were no longer so well appreciated or defended.[19]

Concentration of power was accompanied by greater coordination. From the early years of the reign ministers had searched for points of contact and discussion with their colleagues, and they adopted a more frequent and more systematic use of the *junta*, where ministers could meet in committee and discuss policy. At first the practice was to appoint ad hoc *juntas* for specific purposes, such as the *junta de ministros* of 1763 which met to discuss colonial reform. But gradually a *junta de estado* began to meet, to deal with peninsular as well as colonial affairs, and was found to be a useful way of resolving difficulties between departments and of devising a concerted policy. Floridablanca encouraged his ministerial colleagues to assemble more frequently and was eventually responsible, by decree of 8 July 1787, for giving permanence and some formality to this cabinet, which was to meet once a week in the secretary of state's office to discuss any and every matter of government, though without a formal agenda or rules.[20] Here was an instrument of collective responsibility and continuity long needed in Spanish government, and also the means whereby Floridablanca could know and control all. For its guidance he wrote a lengthy paper, the celebrated *Instrucción reservada*, in which he described, as though in the words of the king, the great institutions and policy issues of the Spanish state and laid down future priorities.[21] He subsequently had to defend his action

---

[19] Bernard, *Le secrétariat d'état et le conseil espagnol des Indes*, pp. 73–6; for a different interpretation, treating the change as continuity in reform, see Jacques Barbier, 'The Culmination of the Bourbon Reforms, 1787–1792', *HAHR*, 57 (1977), pp. 51–68, esp. pp. 56–7; Aranda, 'Plan de gobierno', p. 164.

[20] Bernard, *Le secrétariat d'état et le conseil espagnol des Indes*, pp. 55–7; Escudero, *Los orígenes del Consejo de Ministros en España*, I, pp. 330–52.

[21] 'Instrucción reservada', 8 July 1787, in Conde de Floridablanca, *Obras originales del conde de*

against those who decried the *Junta de Estado* as a device to guarantee his own despotic power, a perversion of the aristocratic council of state favoured by Aranda. In 1789 he wrote:

> The late king [Charles III] ordered the count of Floridablanca to compose an *instrucción reservada* for the Junta de Estado. This consisted of more than a hundred folios and covered all the confidential affairs of this great monarchy, its system of government, internal and external, in all the branches of State, Grace and Justice, War and the Indies, Navy and Finance. That great king insisted on hearing and amending by himself the said instruction, which was done in the course of three months at the cabinet meetings and with the attendance of the present king [Charles IV]. If this confidential document could be published, it would be seen whether the count has been a good or a bad servant of the crown.[22]

This may be true, but the fact remained that Charles III left government very much to Floridablanca. From 1776 royal government ceased to be personal and became ministerial, remaining so for the next sixteen years. The *Junta de Estado* lasted until the fall of Floridablanca in 1792; it was then replaced by the old council of state, in which ministers were outnumbered by outsiders, the privileged estates had a voice, and the king presided. The alternative to ministerial absolutism was not necessarily progress.

Spanish ministers were served by professional officials who staffed the ministries and departments and had a special affinity with their political chiefs, frequently dining at the same table. These were the *covachuelas*, the ministerial teams who instructed, restrained, and protected their chiefs, and kept the wheels of government moving. They were under-secretaries rather than clerks, though they would have worked their way up a recognized career structure, gaining promotion by talent as well as patronage. Floridablanca had a superior group of officials in his ministry:

> These gentlemen, having been well educated, and trained up in the various civil departments of the State, and from thence dispatched

---

Floridablanca, y escritos referentes a su persona, ed. A. Ferrer del Río (*BAE* 59, Madrid, 1952), pp. 213–72.
[22] 8 September 1789, ibid., p. 298.

into foreign countries as secretaries of the embassy, where they learn the language and acquire knowledge, they have higher claims than those who have similar employments in the other courts of Europe. When they return to Spain, considered as servants of the public, they are received into the various offices, and have each his several departments, one France and one England, another the Italian courts, where they assist in expediting business. From this office they are commonly promoted to some honourable and lucrative employment, as the reward of their long service.[23]

The ministers also had their agents in the provinces, and the most important of these were the intendants, whose introduction in 1718 and revival in 1749 transformed Spanish government.[24] The intendants were responsible for the general administration and economic progress of their provinces, as well as for military conscription and supplies, and under Charles III it was their reports that provided the local information on which the government hoped to base its policy. The office of intendant was regarded as a senior stage in a bureaucratic career but one from which an ambitious person would wish to graduate to higher things. The conditions of service were not completely satisfactory. Many complained that the salary was no more than adequate and led only to a half-pay pension; some had difficulty in paying the *media anata* and had to ask for an extension. Others sought promotion from intendant of province to intendant of army, which carried higher authority and salary, or even to combine the two; normally the treasury was unwilling to allow this and kept the appointments and the salaries separate.[25] Promotion had to be worked on. An intendant aspiring to better prospects than exile in a provincial town of New Castile had to keep himself in the government's eye, preferably in Madrid itself; this accounts for the constant applications for leave of absence to come to court.[26] The quality of intendants varied and not all were agents of enlightenment. Complaints were made against Intendant Joseph de Contamina of Barcelona who died in February 1763 'commonly believed to be over 100 years old' and so senile that his work had to be

[23] Joseph Townsend, *A Journey through Spain in the Years 1786 and 1787* (2nd edn, 3 vols, London, 1792), I, pp. 328–9; see also J. F. Bourgoing, *Modern State of Spain* (4 vols, London, 1808), I, pp. 188–9.

[24] See above, pp. 102–6, 169–70.

[25] AGS, Secretaría de Hacienda 584.

[26] Avila, 1764, 1781, AGS, Secretaría de Hacienda 583.

done by his subordinates.[27] The town of León complained against its intendant the count of Benagia, 'of advanced age and so decrepit that he cannot perform the duties of his office', and got him transferred to La Mancha.[28] The irascible and tyrannous intendant almost became a popular stereotype, such as the character Swinburne encountered in Valencia: 'The old usurer, whose figure resembles that of the bandy-legged apothecary in Hogarth's *Marriage à la mode*, received us very ungraciously, took our letter of introduction from the intendant of Catalonia and flung it on the table, without saying a word to us, or even offering us a seat.'[29] The majority of intendants, however, were conscientious officials; many came from the minor or middle aristocracy and probably represented the dull edge of the *golilla* invasion of the bureaucracy, and a few were talented and destined for higher office.

Charles III gave a new impetus to the intendant system; correspondence and reports increased, and instructions multiplied. They were urged to impose stricter collection of royal revenues, to promote public works, to foment agriculture and industry. Ministers sitting in Madrid were helpless without knowlege of actual conditions throughout Spain, and the intendants were urged to make regular visitations of their provinces and to submit annual reports.[30] In 1763–4 the intendant of Guadalajara visited 308 *pueblos*, recording in detail 'the state of each, its population, occupations, ecclesiastics, works, crops, cattle, articles of consumption, prices and price rises, rents, excise duties, government, tax distribution, salaries and taxes of officials, complaints against lords, judges and others', providing statistics, and making policy suggestions. Amidst objective descriptions of agrarian structure and oppression, his own prejudices occasionally protrude, or perhaps he was a Jansenist. He complained of heavy wine drinking and drunkenness in the province of Guadalajara, where good yields caused low prices: 'it is rare in the villages to see anyone eating nourishing food; a piece of bread with some green vegetable is their regular meal; but wine in abundance'; prohibitive taxes were called for.[31] While some were against drinking, others were opposed to entertainment. The intendant of Avila joined the bishop in refusing an application from the town council for a licence to hold a

---

[27] Tomas López to Squillace, Barcelona, 8 February 1763, AGS, Secretaría de Hacienda 555.

[28] Ayuntamiento of León to crown, 16 June 1769, AGS, Secretaría de Hacienda 589.

[29] Henry Swinburne, *Travels through Spain in the years 1775 and 1776* (London, 1779), pp. 94–5.

[30] Squillace to intendant of Barcelona, 2 January 1760, AGS, Secretaría de Hacienda 555.

[31] Intendant Ventura de Argumosa to crown, Guadalajara, 2 July 1764, AGS, Secretaría de Hacienda 588.

season of comedies in the local theatre, 'especially desirable when the Regiment of Asturias was stationed there'.[32] The intendants were the eyes and ears of the government in matters of public order and security, not least in times of agrarian crisis and worsening social conditions. In April 1766 throughout Castile they were on the alert for signs of unrest following the riots in Madrid, and the intendant of Burgos reported, 'Agitation has subsided following my speeches and my warnings to trouble makers. I continue my rounds at different hours of the night.;[33]

The intendant system eventually ran out of steam and the spirit of reform and improvement evident in the 1760s and 1770s seemed to give way in about 1790 to mere routine; instead of new projects there were more requests for leave and promotion; instead of reports, explanations as to why the royal revenues were deficient. Time was wasted in jurisdictional conflicts; in Catalonia a long history of conflict between intendant and *audiencia* culminated in the intendant conceding that his office had lost status and jurisdiction, to the detriment of royal administration.[34] The task assigned to the intendants was probably unmanageable, and there was the danger too that they would clash with the jurisdiction of the more familiar and more traditional *corregidores*, who in the smaller divisions of the provinces mirrored the activities of the intendants. In 1782 the intendant of Cuenca reported that work in two local factories had been brought to a standstill when the *corregidor*, without any consultation, had imprisoned a number of workers; the owner was indignant and the intendant helpless.[35] In general the *corregidores* were less tyrannical in the eighteenth century than they had been in the seventeenth, though they were still badly recruited. The decisive reform came in 1783 when these posts, previously granted by favour and arbitrarily revoked, were reorganized and graded according to their importance and income into three categories, thus becoming a career open to talent with a regulated system of promotion.[36]

In such a regime there was little room for municipal independence.[37] Town revenues, moreover, were too substantial to be ignored by the central government, and from 1760 they were closely supervised by a

[32] 1763, AGS, Secretaría de Hacienda 583.

[33] Intendant Bañuelos to Múzquiz, Burgos, 23 April 1766, AGS, Secretaría de Hacienda 584.

[34] 1786, AGS, Secretaría de Hacienda 559.

[35] Intendant Gaspar de Piña, Cuenca, 5 February 1782, AGS, Secretaría de Hacienda 586.

[36] Benjamín González Alonso, *El corregidor castellano (1384-1808)* (Madrid, 1970), pp. 321–8.

[37] Javier Guillamón Alvarez, *Las reformas de la administración local en el reinado de Carlos III* (Madrid, 1980), pp. 103–10.

committee of the council of Castile and its agents the intendants. The majority of town councils were dominated by the provincial nobility who had bought their way into proprietory offices. There was much at stake – control of local land policy, irrigation rights, distribution of tax burdens, perquisites of various kinds, and social prestige. Conflict between nobles and commoners over these resources disturbed the peace inside and outside council chambers, usually to the advantage of the nobles. There seemed no way of breaking the monopoly of the dominant groups over town government, except possibly by introducing new blood through a wider franchise and more frequent elections. The social unrest of 1766 in Castile, and the need to give the powerless majority some say in food and price control, added urgency to the idea. By decree of 5 May 1766 a reform devised by Campomanes was imposed, introducing into the town councils representatives of the commons elected annually 'by all the people', four in the larger towns and two in those with less than 2,000 inhabitants. Theoretically, this was one of the most striking reforms of the period, since it gave the people a place in municipal government and promised to remove the town councils from the exclusive control of the hereditary and life councillors. In practice, however, the result was quite different. Amidst the hostility of the hereditary councillors and the indifference of the people the new representatives were too weak to make their influence felt and simply aspired to join the local oligarchy by making themselves life appointees. In provinces of high social tension such as Andalucía the ruling groups could not afford to lose their grip on municipal government or to relax their vigilance against *jornalero* unrest. The reform of 1766 indicated the desire of the government to attract the collaboration of Spanish society in its own revival. It also revealed the limits of Bourbon modernization; this stopped short of the proprietory *regidores*, who continued to own, bequeath or sell their offices, to defraud the crown and the public, to practise bribery and extortion, and to perpetuate the grim subculture of Bourbon government, beyond the reach of enlightenment.

The Armed Forces

A state headed by Charles III and administered by law graduates could hardly be described as a military state. Yet the propensity of the king towards war, the presence of the military in civil administration, the growth of the armed forces and the defence budget all pointed to an unmistakable feature of the Bourbon state, that it had a strong military dimension. At the heart of Bourbon interests lay foreign and imperial policy, and from this flowed the determination to give Spain the armed forces of a world power.

As an instrument of war the Spanish army did not immediately inspire the confidence of Charles III and defeat in the Seven Years War called for a radical reappraisal. Rearmament was therefore accompanied by military reform, for which the preferred model was Prussia; impressed by the victories of Frederick the Great, Charles III sent teams of officers to study the Prussian military system and conferred rapid promotion on one of its exponents. Alejandro O'Reilly, Irish by origin, Spanish by adoption, had seen active service in two European wars and taken the opportunity to study Austrian, Prussian, and French military organization before he began to teach Prussian tactics to the Spanish army. He advanced to the rank of field marshal and was employed as a military reformer in Spain and America, establishing among other things a Military Academy at Avila for infantry, cavalry and engineers.[38] With these precedents, the Spanish army adopted a three-deep line of infantry tactics, which gave a high rate of fire power and depended upon strict discipline instilled by ruthless officers. The cavalry also followed Prussian methods of using masses of heavy cavalry to deliver death-or-glory charges, though the dragoons kept the original role of mounted infantry. Spain had good cavalry horses though not in sufficient supply. Spanish artillery, on the other hand, remained in the arms race through sheer numbers of guns, backed up by a mobile horse artillery and an artillery academy at Segovia. There were heavy arms factories at Santander, Seville, and Barcelona which increased production in this reign and, with the help of French and other foreign experts, improved the quality of Spanish guns. By 1767 the French engineer Moritz, employing Catalan workers, had caste 180 brass canon, using American metal.[39] Spain also followed the current trend towards special use of light troops to fight irregular warfare against enemy formations, giving rise to the word guerrilla. But while the organization and tactics of the Spanish army held their own by European standards, it had an inferior system of supply and logistical support, precisely those problems which the intendants of army had been created to solve.

Provisions were the first flaw. The intendants in effect gave the troops

[38] William Dalrymple, *Travels through Spain and Portugal in 1774* (London, 1777), pp. 57–8; Bibiano Torres Ramírez, *Alejandro O'Reilly en las Indias* (Seville, 1969), pp. 5–17.
[39] De Visme to Shelburne, 21 September 1767, PRO, SP 94/178.

money and expected them to buy their own supplies. A decree of 4 October 1766 raised the infantry soldier's pay, and in the 1770s they were receiving 9 shillings a month and 24 oz of bread a day; they had a good uniform, four months' paid leave for the harvest, and little reason to desert. But the army did not have its own supplies or supply system, depending for food and transport on purchasing off the land. The Spanish army, therefore, was not designed to fight a major war. Protected by the Family Compact, Spain had few military commitments: coastal defence against the British, periodic blockades of Gibraltar, an occasional swipe at Moors and Portuguese, and reinforcement of garrisons in America. These tasks were within its competence, they did not strain the treasury, and they kept the army out of the sights of civilian politicians. But any extraordinary demand on military resources could easily cause the supply system to seize up, as it did in O'Reilly's expedition to Algiers in 1775, when a minor operation became a major catastrophe.

The second problem was recruitment of troops. Military service was unpopular and the government was sensitive to resistance from conscripts, preferring instead to recruit volunteers and foreigners. By the end of the reign the Spanish army contained eight foreign regiments, three Flemish, two Italian, and three Irish; in addition there were six battalions of Walloon Guards, and four infantry regiments recruited by contract from the Catholic cantons of Switzerland. These foreign recruits, however, were in many cases deserters from their own regiments, a poor advertisement for the military profession and a deterrent to volunteers in Spain itself. William Dalrymple, a British officer travelling in Spain in 1774, reported of a brigade of cavalry he saw in La Mancha that it had few young men among the troops (though the horses were good), no great discipline, and was very 'rusticated' from being stationed always in La Mancha.[40] Young volunteers in fact did not come forward in sufficient numbers to fill the ranks and there was no alternative to conscription.

Conscription was universally detested and therefore had to be minimal and equitable. This meant that the government had to reduce exemptions and end regional immunity. Quotas were kept small, confined to the infantry, and of the 6,000 troops needed each year only 3,000 were to comprise conscripts. New regulations were introduced in November 1770. Every year a quota of conscripts was to be allocated to

---

[40] Dalrymple, *Travels through Spain and Portugal*, pp. 31–2, 65.

each province, applicable to all unmarried men aged seventeen to thirty-six, selected by *sorteo*, or ballot, to serve for eight years. Results were poor.[41] People bribed magistrates, used influence, hid, fled, or got married, anything rather than join the army, which was perceived, rightly or wrongly, as the worst life in Spain. The system was far from equitable: large sectors of the population still had exempt occupations – *hidalgos*, bureaucrats, the professions, skilled workers. So many were the claims to exemption that the poorer and weaker social groups were conscripted, and the result was an infantry composed not of the dregs of society, as is sometimes said, but of *campesinos* without the means of escape.[42] As for regional privilege, this too was an affront to equity, an issue which the government evaded. Conscription always met with resistance in the Basque provinces, Navarre, and Catalonia. In March 1773 the authorities sought to apply the law and stop exemptions. But there was silent resistance in Vizcaya. And in Barcelona there were disturbances; 2,000 artisans rioted in confrontation with the military authorities. Local leaders advised objectors to accept conscription for the moment and they would negotiate with the central government; but many Catalans did not trust the government and melted away or left for a visit to France. A further edict, in May 1774, warned against riots and sought to enforce the quotas in Catalonia.[43] But the government never really grasped this nettle.

Almost the entire weight of the *sorteo*, therefore, had to be borne by the rural provinces of Castile, León, Asturias, Galicia, and Andalucía, that is precisely those provinces which were already liable for service in the militia, a corps distinct from the regular army and numbering some 23,000 part-time and ill-trained soldiers. The *sorteo*, moreover, was supplemented by the *leva*, or levy, a device by which magistrates were empowered to impress into the army convicted criminals, beggars, and vagrants, the latter term designed to trap those fleeing from the *sorteo* and theoretically solve the problem of poverty and unemployment. So the *sorteo* remained unpopular, evaded often with the connivance of priests, landlords, and anyone else who wished to retain his labour supply. After 1776 it was abandoned and the state relied on the diminishing number of foreign recruits and Spanish volunteers, accepting the inevitability of a shortfall. The nominal size of the army varied

---

[41] Ibid., p. 67.

[42] As was appreciated by Dalrymple, ibid., p. 63.

[43] Grantham to Rochford, 17 May 1773, PRO, SP 94/193; Grantham to Rochford, 9 May 1774, PRO, SP 94/195.

between 70,000 and 80,000, but the effective figure rarely reached this. In 1764 it was 40,000 and hovered around that total in peace time. In 1788 there were forty-four infantry regiments of which thirty-five were national and the rest Italian, Flemish and Swiss. Theoretically, therefore, Spain had an army of 60,000, with 11,500 cavalry, but throughout the 1770s and 1780s the real size was no more than 30,000. A great war effort could raise this, as it did in 1792, to 80,000,[44] but this meant that if Spain had to mobilize rapidly for a major war the army would be swamped by a mass of raw recruits.

Deficient in organization and recruitment, the Spanish army was also badly led. The officer corps was not a cohesive body but divided by social origins and career prospects. There was an influx of foreign military under the Bourbons and in 1792 they accounted for no fewer than seventy-seven of Spain's 327 generals.[45] The majority became assimilated into the Spanish nobility but their presence left a residual resentment. The Spanish nobility themselves enjoyed privileged access to the officer corps and were regarded by the crown as its natural leaders. Only nobles could become officer cadets. In the infantry and cavalry, however, while two-thirds of the officers came from this source, the rest could be promoted from the ranks; this concession later included *hidalgos*, sons of officers in some regiments, and qualified sergeants. Nevertheless, *hidalgos* and commoners tended to stay at the bottom, while the upper ranks were dominated by the higher nobility who often moved straight to the top through wealth and influence at court. The bias against less privileged officers was exacerbated by the lag of military salaries behind inflation, especially in the period 1780–98; officers salaries remained fixed at the 1768 level until 1791, when they were raised by an average of 16.5 per cent; five years later the severe financial difficulties of Charles IV's government forced it to reduce officers' salaries by some 21 per cent. Thus the officer corps remained divided between a privileged minority drawn from the upper nobility with influence at court and good promotion prospects, and a mass of lower officers living a life of boredom and poverty with little prospect of promotion. The army was top heavy in general staff officers, who increased from forty-seven lieutenant generals in 1788 to 132 in 1796, and deficient in well educated and trained subaltern officers; and this in spite of the efforts of the military academies at Santa María (previously

---

[44] Bourgoing, *Modern State of Spain*, ii, pp. 69–74.

[45] Charles J. Esdaile, 'The Spanish Army, 1788–1814', Ph.D. thesis, University of Lancaster, 1985, p. 49.

Avila) for infantry, Ocaña for cavalry, and Segovia for artillery. Conditions were against improvement:

> Let us add, as an apology for the Spanish officers, that the life they lead is such as to benumb all their faculties. Most of their garrison towns are lonely places without resources either in respect of instruction or genteel amusements. Deprived entirely of furloughs, they seldom obtain leave to attend to their affairs ... the obscure and monotonous life they lead, without any manoeuvres on a great scale, and without any reviews, at length deadens all activity ... It has moreover the inconvenience of making the service little attractive, and keeping from it those to whom a small fortune and a good education present other resources.[46]

The army was resented by the majority of Spaniards. Unattractive though it was in many ways, it did possess one advantage, the *fuero militar*, a corporate privilege which set it apart from the rest of society and was comparable to the *fuero eclesiástico* enjoyed by clerics. The military privilege conferred on officers, men, and their families the right to be tried in civil and criminal cases by military jurisdiction, exemption from civil courts and from certain taxation.[47] Corporate privilege of this kind was characteristic of Spanish society; to an army which was unpopular with tax payers, householders, bread rioters, bandits, smugglers, in short with most of civil society, it provided a certain compensation.

Spanish military capacity was seen at its worst and its best in this reign. The expedition to Algiers in 1775 was a model of military incompetence. It was extremely expensive in preparation, yet the actual pay of the troops was long overdue. The assembly of 20,000 men and forty vessels took an inordinate length of time, yet the army command totally neglected to inform itself of the strength of the enemy and the configuration of the Algerian coast. The Algerians on the other hand were ready for the Spaniards, for whom everything went wrong. The place of landing was ill chosen; the whole army disembarked at once and simply plunged inland where they were an easy target for an enemy they could not see; there was no reserve plan. They received a severe mauling, lost 5,000 dead and wounded, and reembarked ignominiously for

[46] Bourgoing, *Modern State of Spain*, ii, pp. 75–6.
[47] Lyle N. McAlister, *The "Fuero Militar" in New Spain, 1764-1800* (Gainesvill, Fla., 1953), pp. 5–8.

Spain.[48] 'We left on the field of battle one thousand three hundred men, and brought off three thousand desperately wounded.'[49] On his return to Spain O'Reilly had the effrontery to blame his defeat on the alleged cowardice of the troops. Officers in Cadiz and Barcelona mutinied in protest, but Charles III refused to dismiss his commander-in-chief outright and merely sent him to Andalucía as captain general, where he remained until Floridablanca forced him out in 1785. Yet within six years of the Algiers disaster a Spanish army from Cuba, its main component European, crowned a successful campaign against the British with the capture of Pensacola, overcoming far greater planning, logistic and military difficulties than had ever presented themselves in the Mediterranean.[50] For imperial operations of this kind the navy was a vital link and naval power an essential preparation.

Charles III inherited a relatively strong navy from his predecessors, most of it built in the rearmament programme of Ensenada. At that time the model had been the English navy, but England was not a favourite of Charles III, least of all after the defeats of 1761–2, and in the post-war years he turned to France for technical aid. Choiseul sent François Gautier, a young but experienced naval constructor, who met some opposition in Spain but was strongly backed by the French embassy and apparently by the king. First he went to Ferrol and laid down three ships of the line.[51] In 1766 he was at work at Guarnizo where he directed the construction of six ships in the yards of Manuel de Zubiría on contract from the Spanish navy. These were finished in 1767 and six more ordered.[52] Gautier scorned both Spanish and English naval design and introduced the French system, that is bigger and faster ships but so top heavy that the Spanish navy found them difficult to sail in bad weather. Gautier modified the design successfully to meet Spanish needs, though he never satisfied the 'English' school led by Jorge Juan. In 1769 he was appointed superintendent of warship construction with a high salary and remained in Spain for the next two decades; most of the Spanish ships on service in the American War of Independence were built by Gautier.[53] In Cartagena the crown contracted with Italian ship builders:

[48] Dalrymple, *Travels through Spain and Portugal*, pp. 177–8.

[49] 'Journal of the Spanish Expedition against Algiers, in 1775', in Swinburne, *Travels through Spain*, p. 42.

[50] Allan J. Kuethe, *Cuba, 1753-1815. Crown, Military, and Society* (Knoxville, Tenn., 1986), p. 78.

[51] De Visme to Halifax, 13 May 1764, PRO, SP 94/170.

[52] De Visme to Shelburne, 10 August 1767, PRO, SP 94/178.

[53] Dalrymple, *Travels through Spain and Portugal*, p. 103; José P. Merino Navarro, *La Armada Española en el siglo XVIII* (Madrid, 1981), pp. 55–7.

A contract was lately made with some Genoese builders for six ships of the line of seventy guns, three of them of eighty, if the king of Spain should require it, to be finished two in a year at the price of 120,000 piastres, or £20,000 each, to be built in the King's yard under the eye and direction of Mr Bryant an English constructor hired by Jorge Juan in 1749. It is not conceived how the contractors can afford the hulls so cheap, as little of the timber is brought from the Genoese territory, and much from the coast of Italy in the Adreatick, some even from Dalmatia.[54]

The Spanish shipbuilding programme continued strongly in the 1770s and in 1778 the yards at Ferrol were busy building ships of the line and frigates. In the 1780s Havana was active too, launching two ships of the line in 1788–9.[55]

Spain was not completely self-sufficient in naval stores. The navy had left its mark on the forests of the peninsula. The intendant of La Mancha, under pressure to provide timber for the navy, was unable to do so in the quantities required because of a long period of deforestation unaccompanied by new planting; only unsuitable supplies were left.[56] By the 1790s Andalucian white oak was exhausted and Cadiz had to purchase timber from Italy or use cedars from Cuba. Cartagena used white oak from Catalonia but supply was subject to transport bottlenecks. Ferrol obtained its timber from the mountains of Burgos, Navarre and Asturias, as did Guarnizo.[57] But for masts all these yards depended on imports from northern Europe and Russia, though Spain was not the only naval power in this situation. In 1785 timber imports cost Spain 8.5 million reales. In hemp and copper (American), on the other hand, she was almost self-sufficient.[58]

The navy and its construction had come to represent a large-scale business operation, employing thousands of personnel and spending large sums of money. This placed greater strains on planning, management and organization, and these too had to be modernized. In 1770 a corps of naval engineers was established, inspired by Gautier and supported by Castejón, and the new personnel, now called 'ingenieros',

---

[54] Rochford to Halifax, 8 July 1764, PRO, SP 94/167.

[55] Grantham to Weymouth, 10 December 1778, PRO, SP 94/206; Eden to Carmarthen, 18 September 1788, PRO, FO 72/13.

[56] Juan de Piña to Squillace, San Clemente, 16 March 1766, AGS, Secretaría de Hacienda 591.

[57] Intendant of Burgos to Múzquiz, 27 July 1766, AGS, Secretaría de Hacienda 584.

[58] Bourgoing, *Modern State of Spain*, ii, pp. 122–4.

were made responsible for a wide range of building functions from ports to ships. Supplies and maintenance were another headache for the administration, and on the efficiency of those responsible depended not only the economic use of resources but the operational efficiency of a squadron at sea. On the initiative of Castejón an *ordenanza de pertrechos* was prepared in 1772, creating an inspector general of ordnance and a subinspector in each dockyard. But the question remained as to whether the navy should be administered by naval officers or civilian bureaucrats. This was a long-standing problem, in Spain as in other countries, and in 1776 it was resolved in favour of the naval officers. The *ordenanza de arsenales* relegated intendants and other officials to a secondary role and placed real power over planning, personnel, and supplies in the hands of the officer corps, operating through a series of juntas dominated by officers. Whether this was progress was debatable, given the quality of Spanish naval officers; inferior as administrators, they were not much better as seamen.

In the course of the eighteenth century the Spanish navy acquired a professional officer corps, recruited and trained for the job rather than taken from the merchant navy or privateers. Unfortunately the naval education they received was second-rate, comprising too many academic subjects and not enough special training in sailing and fighting. Spain won no great naval victories and fought few distinguished battles in this century. On the contrary she suffered a number of painful disasters at sea, and these were caused not by inferior ships or faint hearts but by inadequate officers who seemed to be quite incapable of finding and engaging the enemy, or even avoiding him effectively. In the reigns of Charles III and Charles IV many Spanish admirals were simply incompetent and often an embarrassment to their allies. The French complained of the poor standard of Spanish naval officers and the inappropriateness of their tactics in the years around 1780 when the two countries were at war with Britain. The English too, during their brief alliance with Spain in 1793–5, found it impossible to work with the Spanish navy or even to persuade it to go to sea; and Nelson subsequently remarked that England had nothing to fear from Spain as an enemy if its navy was no better than it had been as an ally. The Spanish navy had great experience of colonial wars and in American waters, though even here its navigation was regarded as inferior to the English. The defence of transatlantic commerce was also a special task which the navy performed with adroitness and, to the relief of the Spanish treasury, with success. For its triple role, in the Mediterranean, the

Atlantic, and America, the Spanish navy had the ships but not always the seamen. Shortage of sailors was chronic and irremediable because of the neglect of the merchant navy. By 1800 Spain had only 500 or so merchant vessels, most of them Catalan and Basque. The nominal total of registered seamen rose from 50,000 in 1761 to 65,000 in 1794, but these figures represented needs rather than recruits and the real strength was probably 25,000.

Yet the Spanish navy was not neglected by the state and it competed successfully for resources with the rest of the public sector. The number of ships of the line placed it second to England in terms of growth, though admittedly the number of ships listed bore little relation to their effectiveness at sea or revealed the often parlous state of manning and supplies. The British embassy in Madrid watched and recorded its growth carefully, and the British government was concerned enough to protest to Spain that it was fuelling an arms race. The sheer size of the Spanish navy commanded respect (see table 8.1); allied to that of France

Table 8.1 The Spanish navy: number of ships
1760-1804

	Ships of line (112 to 58 guns)	Frigates	Misc.
1760	40	10	
1761	49	21	16
1763	37	30	
1765	25		
1767	32 ·		
1769	32		
1770	51	22	29
1772	56	25	37
1774	64	26	37
1777	65	16	20
1778	67	32	
1783	67	32	
1787	67		
1792	80	14	
1804	65		

Source: Public Record Office, London, SP 94/161, 164, 166, 172, 181, 191, 204; J. F. Bourgoing, *Modern State of Spain* (4 vols, London, 1808), II, pp. 110–12.

it looked positively menacing. The cost of course was crippling and the time came when further growth was beyond Spain's means. Meanwhile, the struggle for empire forced Spain to preserve its guard against England and where possible to take the initiative; this made naval power a priority, otherwise colonial life-lines would be cut at sea. The navy was the guardian as well as the spender of revenue. Expenditure on the navy increased in years of crisis, war, perceived danger, or simply rearmament (see table 8.2). Until 1796 Spain struggled to maintain its naval strength within the limits of possibilities; after that irreversible decline overtook the Spanish navy during the long years when Spain was a satellite of France and at war with England.

The Spanish navy was a valuable asset, to be exhibited, protected, and if necessary withdrawn from view. Its peacetime role was to transport treasure, patrol sea lanes, and look menacing. War brought greater discretion. In Spanish strategic thinking the navy was best used by *not* going to sea. A curious paradox emerged. The larger the navy became, the less mobile it was; the more guns it carried, the less they were fired. During the war with France in 1793–5 the navy achieved its maximum size and its minimum activity, being slow to leave port and then loath to engage the enemy. There was reason behind this reluctance. The Spanish government valued the navy so highly that it could not bring itself to use it; it had cost too much to risk in war; and the time came when losses could not be replaced. Ministers were impressed not only by the skill of the enemy but even more by the incompetence of their own officers. It was a vicious circle. The navy was too expensive and too badly led to expose to battle, a policy which perpetuated inexperience. Still, a ship in port was better than a ship sunk. The navy was kept intact for its deter-

Table 8.2 Spanish naval expenditure as percentage of total expenditure

1753	20.4	1790	20.7
1760	6.8	1795	8.3
1762	11.2	1797	7.9
1770	21.7	1800	9.2
1774	12.1	1805	4.4
1782	20.0	1807	0.4
1785	27.8		

Source: José P. Merino Navarro, *La Armada Española en el siglo XVIII* (Madrid, 1981), p. 168.

rent effect; it kept the enemy guessing. As such it was a useful sanction of Spanish foreign policy, if not the arm of an imperial power.

Family Compact, Familiar Conflict

Reform, rearmament, recovery abroad – this was the ideal order of Spanish policy and one with a logic of its own. Charles III began his reign by reversing the process and seeking a short-cut to strength and security. The temptation to strike an early blow at Britain was strong and the opportunity at hand. The Anglo-French colonial conflict, then at its height, was a spur and a threat to Spain. If France was ousted from Canada, that would increase British power in the Americas and have implications for Spain. Anglo-Spanish relations were no better than normal and the issues between the two powers remained unchanged: Spain's affinity with France, the Newfoundland fishery, logwood cutting in Honduras, breaches of Spain's neutrality by the English navy, they all had a familiar ring and seemed impervious to diplomatic solution. Charles decided there was no alternative to war to preserve a colonial balance of power; the object and the means remained the hallmark of his foreign policy. He was fortified in his decision by a timely influx of colonial revenue, and the characteristic interplay of the *equilibrio americano* and American treasure made an early appearance.

> Two ships have lately arrived at Cadiz with very extraordinary rich cargoes from the West Indies, so that all the wealth that was expected from Spanish America is now safe in Old Spain; perhaps this circumstance has raised the language of the Catholick King's Ministers ... I have long observed the jealousy of Spain at the British conquests and am now convinced that the consciousness of this country's naval inferiority has occasioned the soothing declarations so repeatedly made of a desire to maintain harmony and friendship with England.[59]

Charles III believed that alliance with France would supplement Spain's naval power and give him the protection of a large land force. He

[59] Bristol to Egremont, Escorial, 2 November 1761, PRO, SP 94/164. The treasure shipments of 1761 amounted to 16 million pesos; see Michel Morineau, *Incroyables gazettes et fabuleux métaux. Les retours des trésors américains d'après les gazettes hollandaises (XVIᵉ-XVIIIᵉ)* (Cambridge, 1985), pp. 401–2.

therefore entered the third Family Compact (15 August 1761) which
created an offensive and defensive alliance between the two Bourbon
powers and took Spain into the colonial conflict when Britain reacted by
declaring war in January 1762. The French alliance has been defended as
a 'natural' alliance, 'the only logical formula for Spain's foreign policy,
given the circumstances of the world'.[60] Was it not in fact a mistake, the
progenitor of future mistakes, which did not serve the interests of Spain
and did not preserve the balance in America? Charles III made three
miscalculations in 1762. He entered the war at the worst possible time
when it was already turning in England's favour; he underrated
England's war potential; and he entered a colonial conflict with
inadequate naval resources.[61] The English war machine was now in full
working order and equal to the combined forces of both France and
Spain. Havana and Manila fell more easily than should have been
possible in a closed empire. The best prospect for Spain was the war in
the peninsula. Had she been able to take out Portugal and capture
Lisbon she could have deprived Britain of a naval base, a commercial
outlet, and a foothold in the Brazil trade. But the Spanish army was
incapable of such a task, and Spain had to be content with Colônia do
Sacramento, a small victory in the Río de la Plata. The war was a lesson
in relative power. By the Peace of Paris (9 February 1763) not only had
Spain to tolerate British logwood cutters in Honduras and renounce any
rights to the Newfoundland fishery but she also had to return Colônia to
Portugal and cede Florida and all Spanish territory in North America
east of the Mississippi to Britain. The latter returned her conquests,
Havana and Manila, while from France Spain procured Louisiana – and a
new frontier to defend against her rival.

If Spain was defeated, she was not crushed, and the Bourbon allies
worked to strengthen the alliance and its resources. Wall was succeeded
by the pro-French Grimaldi, and he and Choiseul concerted to establish
a joint defence policy.[62] French technical advisers were seconded to
Spanish dockyards and arms establishments; France pushed hard to

---

[60] Vicente Palacio Atard, *El tercer Pacto de Familia* (Madrid, 1945), p. 289.

[61] Richard Pares, *War and Trade in the West Indies 1739-1763* (London, 1963), pp. 590–5.

[62] Rochford to Halifax, 24 January 1764, PRO, SP 94/167. On Franco-Spanish defence and
colonial policy as concerted by Choiseul, see Coxe, *Memoirs of the Kings of Spain*, IV, pp. 313–31,
375–7; Arthur Scott Aiton, 'Spanish Colonial Reorganization under the Family Compact', *HAHR*,
12 (1932), pp. 269–80; A. Christelow, 'French Interest in the Spanish Empire during the Ministry of
the Duc de Choiseul, 1759–1771', *HAHR*, 21 (1941), pp. 515–37; John Lynch, *Spanish Colonial
Administration, 1782-1810. The Intendant System in the Viceroyalty of the Río de la Plata* (London,
1958), pp. 15–19.

develop a Bourbon economic bloc in Europe and America in which she would supply the manufactured goods and Spain the primary produce; Spain strove to avoid underdevelopment; and Charles III prepared for another round with Britain. In 1767 there were twenty issues, disputes and incidents between Spain and England on the English ambassador's desk in Madrid, and of these the Manila ransom and the Falkland Islands were causing particular irritation.[63] In 1770, on the instruction of Arriaga, a Spanish expedition from Buenos Aires dislodged the English settlement at Port Egmont and occupied West Falkland.[64] Spain was not really ready for war. Politically it would not be popular, least of all on so marginal an issue as the Falklands; militarily, the infantry was in poor shape and although the navy had been restored and expanded since 1763 it was chronically short of seamen; financially, Spain did not have the resources to fight a war without American treasure, whose receipt would be at risk from British attack. For all these reasons the British concluded, 'far from a design to break with us they fear nothing so much as our breaking with them.'[65] At this point the Family Compact failed Spain; she appealed to her French ally, was rebuffed, and found herself powerless. After a prolonged war of nerves, Spain gave in and satisfied Britain, disavowing the expedition to Port Egmont and restoring the status quo. Another false move, another defeat. But again, Spain picked herself up, went back into training, and prepared for the next fight.

The revolt of Britain's North American colonies in 1775 removed the danger of British expansion southwards at the expense of the Spanish empire and gave Spain an opportunity to recover her losses. Profiting from her rival's preoccupation and the consequent isolation of Portugal, she sent an expedition of 20 naval vessels, 96 transports and over 9,000 troops from Cadiz, which in 1777 occupied the island of Santa Catalina off the coast of Brazil, and captured the Portuguese outpost of Colônia.[66] The War of American Independence, however, was not an easy field for intervention.[67] Charles III was caught between the desire to embarrass his colonial rival, which accounts for his undercover aid to the rebels

[63] Located in PRO, SP 94/177.
[64] Julius Goebel, *The Struggle for the Falkland Islands* (Newhaven, Conn., 1982), pp. 271–83; see also Octavio Gil Munilla, *Malvinas. El conflicto anglo-español de 1770* (Seville, 1948).
[65] Harris to Weymouth, 4 October 1770, PRO, SP 94/185.
[66] Consul Hardy to Weymouth, Cadiz, 5 November 1776, PRO, SP 94/202; Octavio Gil Munilla, *El Río de la Plata en la política internacional* (Seville, 1948), pp. 305–7.
[67] Mario Rodríguez, *La Revolución Americana de 1776 y el mundo hispánico* (Madrid, 1976), pp. 77–115; Peggy K. Liss, *Atlantic Empires. The Network of Trade and Revolution, 1713-1826* (Baltimore, Md., 1983), pp. 127–46.

from 1776, and fear for his own American possessions, which accounts for his ambivalent attitude towards independence. Floridablanca told the English ambassador, 'such an event as Independence of America would be the worst example to other colonies, and make the Americans the worst neighbours, in every respect, that the Spanish colonies could have.'[68] But this did not prevent Spain selling arms, colluding with North American privateers, and, in the course of 1777, actively recruiting and assembling army units, preparing the navy, and increasing its warships in American bases.[69] In 1778 France took the decision that Spain was contemplating, and now Spain herself prepared for war, under cover of proposing mediation.[70] In February 1779 Gálvez despatched the Regiment of Navarre to Havana, bringing the Spanish forces in Cuba to the full crisis strength of four regiments, and by July the colonial authorities knew that war was to be declared.[71]

Spain's war aims in America were to expel the British from the Gulf of Mexico and the shores of the Mississippi, and to wipe out their settlements in Central America. The Florida campaign of 1780–1 demonstrated Spain's capacity as a colonial power, given the right conjuncture. During the early phases of the war the colonial authorities had to rely on local resources, and it was the army of Cuba which captured Mobile. The Army of Operations from Spain itself, delayed and depleted by its service in the siege of Gibraltar, the ravages of disease, and a hurricane in the Gulf of Mexico, joined the campaign at a later stage, and it was a combined force of Spanish and Cuban units which Bernardo de Gálvez led to Pensacola, forcing the British to surrender on 10 May 1781, and proving in the process that Spain could recruit, train, assemble, transport, and land in enemy territory diverse units from both sides of the Atlantic, join them in a combined army of 7,437 men and, having defeated the forces of nature, defeat the resident British.

Charles III, therefore, attempted to solve the dilemma of taking an imperial power into an anti-colonial war by pursuing exclusively Spanish interests without allying directly with the United States and without recognizing American independence. Before entering the conflict the Spanish government had signed a secret treaty with France

[68] Grantham to Weymouth, 26 May 1777, PRO, SP 94/203.

[69] Grantham to Weymouth, 7 October 1776, PRO, SP 94/202; see also various reports, Grantham to Weymouth, 1777, PRO, SP 94/203, 204.

[70] In justifying mediation to the British ambassador, arch-imperialist Floridablanca actually spoke of 'liberty' of subjects, though these presumably did not include Spanish subjects; Grantham to Weymouth, 22 April 1779, PRO, SP 94/208.

[71] Kuethe, *Cuba, 1753-1815*, pp. 97–8; on the Florida campaign see pp. 103–12.

(Aranjuez, 12 April 1779) from which Spain secured specific concessions in return for joining her ally in the war. France promised to help in the recovery of Minorca, Mobile, Pensacola, the bay of Honduras, and the coast of Campeche, and to conclude no peace that did not return Gibraltar to Spain. Gibraltar was central to Spanish war aims, and this meant defeating Britain in Europe as well as in America. The Spanish planners designed a dual strategy, an invasion of England and a siege of Gibraltar. A Franco-Spanish fleet and invasion force was deployed in the English Channel but was thwarted less by the enemy than by sickness and disease among crew and troops.[72] Attention was then focused on Gibraltar and a great siege was mounted, crude in concept and inept in execution. An army of 30,000 and 190 guns laid siege by land on a garrison of 7,000, while a Franco-Spanish fleet blockaded the port. The land forces suffered heavy casualties, yet made little impression on the defences, and in successive years, 1780, 1781, 1782, the British navy outmanœuvred the blockading fleet and brought relief to the garrison. Gibraltar continued to elude Spain. On the other hand a successful expedition to Minorca recovered the island in February 1782 and enabled Spain to end the war with something to show in Europe as well as in America. By the Peace of Versailles (3 September 1783) she regained Florida and Minorca, but restored the Bahamas to Britain and gave the English certain rights in Honduras.

Spain fought the war of 1779–83 with moderate success; she regained lost ground and restored her imperial credentials. Within a few years, however, in a traditional area of Spanish influence she appeared to lose her way. Morocco and Algeria posed difficult problems; they constantly pinned down the Spanish army and navy, not because they had powerful armed forces but because they were maintained in effect by powers who wished to trade in the Mediterranean without being molested by Barbary pirates and bought exemption in various ways including the supply of arms. Spanish relations with Morocco were improved from 1766 and envoys were exchanged; this was an area of some economic interest to Spain and a useful source of grain for Andalucía in times of dearth. The Algerians were more recalcitrant, though in 1780 they had a navy of no more than fifteen small vessels. Free from the war with England, Spain decided in 1784 to bring matters to a head and reassembled an expedition which had been previously destined for an attack on Jamaica. A fleet of seventy sail was sent against the negligible

[72] A. Temple Patterson, *The Other Armada. The Franco-Spanish Attempts to Invade Britain in 1779* (Manchester 1960), pp. 160–8, 204–12.

naval forces of the Algerians and for eight successive days Algiers was bombarded, before the Spaniards withdrew with nothing to show for the loss of 400 troops, and convinced that Algerian resistance was stiffened by French aid.[73] Another expedition in 1785 met with no more success and Spain decided to negotiate. Floridablanca had boasted that Spain would teach Europe how to treat these barbarians and would give an example to those powers which were mistaken tributaries to them. But he himself was now forced to deal with the Algerians and he bought peace at a price of 14 million reales, not one of the more glorious episodes of his foreign policy and a prelude to further retreat. Spain subsequently decided that possession of Oran was a source of friction rather than profit; on 26 February 1792 its 6,500 Spanish personnel were evacuated and the once famous conquest of Cardinal Jiménez was relinquished.

The balance sheet of Charles III's foreign policy showed an accumulation of gains and losses which are difficult to correlate; in many respects the account was not closed until the following reign, and then the balance would be seen to be unmistakably adverse. Decisions were taken within a closed circle of advisers dominated by Floridablanca and answerable only to the king. Public opinion played no part; even important interest groups, such as merchants, had little influence in the absence of a legitimate or an active opposition. It is true that English foreign policy did not always benefit from party politics and change of ministries; but ministers had to defend their decisions before parliament, the opposition, even the mob. In Spain there were no such constraints.[74] Absolutism worked when decisions were correct and needed prompt action; otherwise it perpetuated misjudgement. The first misjudgement was the Family Compact, which was built into Spanish policy in spite of its evident failure to serve Spanish interests. It had failed Spain in 1762 and 1770, though over the Falklands crisis French judgement was arguably better than Spanish. In 1778 France entered the War of American Independence without consulting Spain; and whatever Spain gained in 1783 owed little to her ally. The strength of Spanish policy was its link with imperial defence. The expedition to the Río de la Plata in

[73] Liston to Carmarthen, 2 August 1784, PRO, FO 72/3; on relations with Morocco see Vicente Rodríguez Casado, *Política marroquí de Carlos III* (Madrid, 1946).

[74] Floridablanca argued to the British ambassador that he too had an opposition to contend with: 'Our Ministry ought to remember that though he had not literally a House of Lords and Commons to satisfy, and a professed opposition to encounter, yet he had also a species of Parliament, a publick, and a discontented Party to manage, and that it was not in his power to do in every respect what his inclination might dictate.' A new concept of absolutism. Liston to Carmarthen, 16 April 1787, PRO, FO 72/10.

1776 not only captured Colônia and gave Spain undisputed dominion over the region, it also led directly to the creation of the viceroyalty of the Río de la Plata in 1778 and the reorientation of Spanish imperial strategy in South America. At the northern extremity of the empire the recovery of Florida was part of an integrated plan to strengthen defences, which included further colonization along the Pacific coast and the creation of the Interior Provinces of New Spain in 1776.[75] At a time when British territory in the Americas was contracting, the Spanish empire appeared to enter an expansive phase. The same year, 1778, which saw the Declaration of Independence in North America, saw the creation of a new viceroyalty in South America. While the British were losing Florida, Spanish religious and military expeditions were consolidating their occupation of Upper California. Charles III could be forgiven for believing that the *equilibrio americano* had not only been restored but was moving in Spain's favour.

There was a price to pay. Economically the war of 1779–83 was harmful to Spain and punishing to the mass of its people who bore the brunt of shortages and high prices. The effects of the free trade regulations of 1778 were delayed and the Spanish export trade was hit. Three years of fighting seriously strained Spain's fiscal resources.[76] The government was even deprived, temporarily, of its income from America, for the Bourbon alliance did nothing to alter the naval balance against Spain or prevent Britain from cutting the trade routes. The balance of power, as distinct from territory, was moving inexorably away from Spain; it was precisely in the post-war years that Britain entered a decisive stage of industrial and commercial expansion and opened the gap still further between her economic and naval power and that of Spain. In these conditions there was an air of fantasy in the strategic thinking of king and ministers in the years after 1783. Charles III, Floridablanca, and Gálvez regarded the war as incomplete and envisaged a further round to finish the colonial war and settle the account once and for all. The sticking points were trade inequality, Gibraltar, and the Mosquito Shore, and from time to time Floridablanca exploded in rage at the British ambassador over what he regarded as British duplicity but what was in truth Spanish impotence:

[75] Lynch, *Spanish Colonial Administration*, pp. 20–1, 40–3; Gil Munilla, *El Río de la Plata en la política internacional*, pp. 305–7, 376; Bernardo de Gálvez, *Instructions for Governing the Interior Provinces of New Spain, 1786*, ed. Donald E. Worcester (Berkeley, Calif., 1951), pp. 1–24.

[76] Jacques A. Barbier and Herbert S. Klein, 'Revolutionary Wars and Public Finances: the Madrid Treasury, 1784–1807', *Journal of Economic History*, 41 (1981), pp. 315–39, esp. pp. 331–2, 339.

He plainly saw it was impossible we should continue friends: that the time must soon come when we should be violent and implacable enemies; that if the event confirmed his suspicions that Britain was deceiving Spain over the evacuation of the Mosquito Shore he would proclaim our disingenuity to all the Courts of Europe: that the cause of Spain must be considered as the common cause of every nation, and that, at all events, it was better to die with arms in their hands than to lead a life of meanness and disgrace.[77]

The Price of War

The Bourbon state was a militant state, if not a military one. Charles III regarded war as an instrument of policy, not simply a last line of defence. He began his reign with resources which falsely raised his expectations. In 1759 he had a total revenue of 488.8 million reales and expenditure of 322 million, giving him a surplus of 166.8 million. In December 1761 there was a favourable balance of 227 million reales, though this included recent American returns.[78] He even allocated 50 million reales to pay owners of credits from the time of Philip V and promised to maintain such payments at 10 million reales a year. This stable financial position was soon fully extended and, like others before him, he learned that any extraordinary demand went beyond the resources of the Bourbon state; it was impossible to increase ordinary revenue, and the economy did not have the capacity to respond quickly to demands for new revenues in times of crisis.[79] The reason for financial stagnation was the rigidity of the fiscal structure which was based almost exclusively on taxes on consumer goods and excise duties.

The government of Charles III was aware of the problem and of the solution proposed by Ensenada. In January 1760 the crown initiated a new round of *consultas*, discussions and reports, and the single tax

[77] Liston to Carmarthen, 20 April 1785, PRO, FO 72/5; on Spanish strategic thinking at this time see 'Instrucción reservada', *Obras originales del conde de Floridablanca*, pp. 263, 264–6, where Floridablanca spares England the final solution: 'we are not proposing a total destruction of English power.'

[78] Bristol to Pitt, 11 February 1760, Bristol to Egremont, 6 December 1761, PRO, SP 94/161, 164.

[79] 'On balance, Spain was a prosperous but limited fiscal entity in the late eighteenth century. The strains of war quickly destroyed its fiscal prosperity, and eventually its economy as well' Barbier and Klein, 'Revolutionary Wars and Public Finances', p. 331.

project was restored to the political agenda. The actual establishment of a single tax, however, was delayed by other political priorities and then killed off by the hostility of vested interests and their bureaucratic spokesmen. True, a number of towns and villages also objected to their particular quotas, and public opinion in general was not sufficiently aroused to revive the impetus lost in 1757. But the basic obstacle was the resistance of privileged groups to a single tax based on income. This was explained later by Floridablanca, speaking through the king:

> I have done all I can to implement the plan of a single tax proposed in the previous reign and continued in this, and after immense expenditure, juntas of experts, scrutiny of the tax rules, all printed and circulated, there have been so many thousands of appeals and objections that they have intimidated and frightened off the 'office of single tax', and it has been impossible to proceed further.[80]

Expenditure in 1778 totalled 454.5 million reales, of which the army and navy took 72 per cent, the court 11 per cent, and the central administration the remainder.[81] This was more or less the traditional allocation, but the court remained expensive. Much of Charles III's expenditure on public works did not benefit the public at all but was concentrated on the royal palace and other *sitios*. The royal palace in Madrid was completed in 1764 and henceforth occupied as a residence; extensions were made to the Pardo and Aranjuez, and new towns were built at Aranjuez, the Escorial and San Ildefonso; roads were constructed from Madrid to all the *sitios*. Shooting was a very expensive sport; as a way of life it was exorbitant. Apart from his own retinue the king employed hundreds of hands from Madrid to beat the country and drive the wild boar, deer and hares into the sights of the royal guns, while a very large annual sum was distributed to the proprietors of land in the vicinity of the royal palaces to indemnify them for damage to crops.[82]

An expenditure of 454.5 million reales was a normal peace time estimate. The annual average revenue in the period 1784–9 totalled 466.9

---

[80] 'Instrucción reservada', *Obras originales del conde de Floridablanca*, p. 254.

[81] Antonio Domínguez Ortiz, *Sociedad y estado en el siglo XVIII español* (Barcelona, 1981), p. 306, n. 9. Jacques Barbier and Herbert S. Klein, 'Las prioridades de un monarca ilustrado: el gasto público bajo el reinado de Carlos III', *Revista de Historia Económica*, 3, 3 (1985), pp. 473–95, show that in the period 1760–88 the greater part of the budget went to defence, and the army and navy received 60 per cent of total expenditure; while the army allocation was relatively stable, naval expenditure grew in response to the growing needs of imperial defence.

[82] Swinburne, *Travels through Spain*, p. 335.

million reales, not so divergent.[83] In the meantime, however, a major war had intervened, and the bills had still to be paid. American treasure was a decisive component of total income, accounting for about one-quarter of ordinary revenue.[84] Whether it arrived or not depended on whether Spain was at peace or war with Britain. War meant blockade, and the non-arrival of American income would force the Spanish government to adopt other financial expedients either in the form of new taxes or by the issue of paper money with consequent inflation. In 1775 Campomanes could still boast that Spain, unlike other European countries, was free from the inflation caused by paper money. But Spain soon had to issue it. The war with Britain from 1779 raised expenditure to over 700 million reales; it also interrupted the flow of American treasure. When an increase in taxes (on tobacco among other things) failed to supply money for war, *vales reales*, or royal bonds, were issued; these had a double function, first as interest-bearing loans yielding 4 per cent a year, second as paper money useful for larger payments. The device served to defray the cost of war and then to finance infrastructure projects such as the canals of Aragon and Castile. But the number of *vales* increased beyond reason and soon depreciated. To restore royal credit a French-born financier, Francisco Cabarrús, was authorized in June 1782 to found the first national bank of Spain, the Banco de San Carlos, with the task of redeeming the bonds. Peace with Britain was followed by the arrival of the accumulated treasure from America and the bank began to retire the bonds which now recovered their value and retained it for the rest of the decade.

The peace of 1783 brought a brief period of relative prosperity, perhaps twelve years at the most, when foreign trade was released once more and the economy could respond to the post-war consumer demand at home and in the colonies. The effects of freer trade and the moderate industrial growth were now being felt and Spain began to enjoy some of the fruits of her empire which had long been the preserve of her commercial rivals in northern Europe. In the post-war years there were large quantities of specie in private hands which could have been lured into the treasury had the government inspired confidence; but the mediocre finance ministers of the time did nothing to reassure the public, and private accumulation found other outlets or remained at home.

---

[83] Coxe, *Memoirs of the Kings of Spain*, v, p. 385.

[84] Josep Fontana, 'La crisis colonial en la crisis del antiguo régimen español', in Alberto Flores Galindo (ed.), *Independencia y revolución (1780-1840)* (2 vols, Lima, 1987), I, p. 19.

The high spending of Charles III's government could not simply be cancelled or reversed. It was now built into the system; the expensive things he had created and the high-cost policy he had inaugurated were there to stay, inherited by the next regime and then enlarged by its own particular profligacy. The war of 1779–83 was the first of a series of crises which kept the state in a condition of semi-permanent indebtedness beyond its capacity to resolve. The constant issue of royal bonds between 1780 and 1799 enabled the government to live in a debtor's paradise but merely postponed the day of reckoning. In spite of the efforts of the Banco de San Carlos to maintain the quotation of the bonds, depreciation was inevitable and reached almost 50 per cent in the course of the 1790s. Charles III left his successor an unreformed tax system and an example of financial expediency which signalled the eventual collapse of the Bourbon state.

The foreign policy of Charles III, based on expensive rearmament and culminating by choice in a second war with Britain, was an inherent impediment to reform and destroyed any chance of structural change. Money spent on war could not be allocated to agrarian, social, or infrastructural projects. An active foreign policy and a programme of internal reform were incompatible. The priorities were obvious: power came before welfare. Even after 1783 a renewal of the colonial war was contemplated and the colonies examined for yet more resources to pay for it. Spain had reached a peak of power, if not in the highest range, but in the process it remained an unreconstructed society and economy. The crown continued to seek the support of nobles and clergy, to respect inherited or acquired privileges, to protect noble estates and church property, to allow *mayorazgos* to reach their maximum extension and Spain to look like one vast immobile entail, to pay very high salaries to top officials, in short to preserve the Spain of hierarchy and class, of corporate privilege and rural oligarchy. Spain was given an illusion of reform and presented with a parody of a modern state.

The government of Charles III was dominated by lawyers. Many of the so-called reform documents of the reign were legal papers written by officials who were more concerned with royal rights than radical change. Floridablanca was the archetypal lawyer whose mentality had not changed in his ascent to power. In the last decade of the reign Charles III was no longer served by a 'team'; he reverted to the Bourbons' traditional reliance on one adviser. The death of José de Gálvez in June 1787 removed the only other minister of stature and left the influence of Floridablanca greater than ever. Floridablanca was more than the king's right hand; he was his guide, mentor, and policy maker. He developed an aura of his own, aloof, seldom seen, difficult to meet, but omnipresent in government. In these years he rained decrees upon Spaniards, curbing disorder, reducing the number of animals in coaches, restricting bull fights, anything to improve the behaviour of his countrymen, in the vain belief that legal enactments alone would make a difference. But no one doubted that he was in control, author and agent of absolutism.

The last years of the reign were not happy ones for Spain. Epidemic disease, compounded by poor crops and food shortages, killed many people in 1785–7, and the government had to spend heavily on emergency imports of foreign grain.[85] Shadows fell across the court too. The government lost Roda in 1783, Múzquiz in 1785, and Gálvez in 1787. In October 1786 the king suffered a 'fainting fit' lasting about half an hour, and after another two in the following July there was unease about his health. From 1 July 1787 the prince of Asturias was brought into meetings between the king and ministers in all departments of government.[86] Disease imposed a kind of equality between the highest and the humblest. On 2 November 1788 the Infanta Mariana Victoria died of smallpox after a difficult confinement, and the baby succumbed soon afterwards. The disease struck again on 23 November and claimed the husband, the Infante Gabriel; thus within the space of a month Charles lost a son and entire family in whom he had great hopes. He returned to Madrid from the Escorial at the end of November, nursing a cold. On 6 December, after hunting, he felt unwell and was confined to bed with a fever. He received the last sacraments and died on 14 December 1788.

[85] Consul James Duff to William Fraser, Cadiz, August 1787, PRO, FO 72/11.

[86] That is, not only in foreign policy, as previously. Liston to Carmarthen, Madrid, 16 July 1787, PRO, FO 72/11.

9

Spain and America

Government by Compromise

The imperial state appeared to rest on firm foundations of bureaucracy, tribunals, and laws, designed to endure and tested by time. But there were features of American government which disturbed the Bourbons. Institutions did not function automatically by issuing laws and receiving obedience. The normal instinct of colonial subjects was to question, evade or modify laws, and only as a last resort to obey them. Colonial government, moreover, operated at a great distance from Spain, among people divided by competing interests and in societies which absorbed officials rather than confronted them.

The politics of governing were just as important as the administrative process. Officials had to negotiate obedience. Political manœuvre was not alien to their office. They themselves had negotiated their appointment in Madrid, and viceroys and *corregidores* behaved with some degree of independence, not necessarily agreeing with every law they had to apply. Viceroys and other higher officials were part of a tripartite power structure in America, where Spanish rule rested on a balance of interest groups – the administration, the Church and the local elites. The administration possessed political though little military power, and derived its authority from the sovereignty of the king and bureaucratic imperatives; its principal duty was to collect and remit revenue. The bureaucracy was only partly professionalized. Some officials derived their income from fees charged to the public for services; others from entrepreneurial activities; others from salaries. All more or less participated in the economy and supplemented their earnings. The crown had long sought to isolate the colonial bureaucracy from local ties and pressures, yet in all cases – viceroy, *audiencia*, *corregidor* – this was an unattainable ideal. So too was its desire for a united bureaucracy presenting a single front to the American world; officials were divided by ideas and interests, and the power of the crown reached its American subjects in a fragmented form.

Secular sovereignty was reinforced by the Church, whose religious mission was backed by moral and material power as well as by law. The Church was compliant but not subservient and did not identify completely with the state; in any case it too had particular interests, economic, social, and ecclesiastical, often linked with those of secular groups, and sometimes a cause of division within its own ranks. The Church added to faction rather than appeased it. But the greatest economic power lay with the local elites, property owners in town and country, comprising a minority of *peninsulares* and a greater proportion of creoles. It was their stake in the local economy which introduced an element of politics into relations between the bureaucracy and the people, and forced officials to bargain and compromise. For the growth and development of Spanish America inevitably created interest groups, all of whom in one way or another were competing for resources and labour. The starting point was the conquest itself, which the crown had left to the private sector, thereby giving the first settlers a bargaining device for securing privileges, especially access to Indian labour. Since then vested interests in land, mining, and commerce had consolidated the local elites, who forged enduring ties of kinship and alliance with the colonial bureaucracy, with the viceregal entourage and the judges of the *audiencia*, and who developed a distinct sense of local identity within the administrative boundaries of the empire.[1] The bureaucracy was thus drawn into a network of interests linking officials, *peninsulares*, and creoles, and forming a series of local oligarchies throughout Spanish America.

The colonial bureaucracy was under constant pressure to modify the law in favour of local interest groups. Officials in Upper Peru accepted that the *mita* should be delivered to mine owners not in the form of Indian conscripts but in silver as an alternative income to mining. In the

---

[1] José F. de la Peña, *Oligarquía y propiedad en Nueva España 1550-1624* (Mexico, 1983); J. H. Elliott, 'Spain and America in the Sixteenth and Seventeenth Centuries', in Leslie Bethell (ed.), *The Cambridge History of Latin America. Volume I* (Cambridge, 1984), pp. 314–19; and the chapters by Morse, Bakewell and Florescano in *The Cambridge History of Latin America. Volume II* (Cambridge, 1984); Murdo J. MacLeod, *Spanish Central America. A Socioeconomic History, 1520-1720* (Berkeley/ Los Angeles, Calif., 1973), pp. 313, 350, 383–4.

course of the seventeenth century the Potosí *mita* was thus transformed into a money tax for the benefit not of the crown but of the mine owners. While the crown theoretically had the power to abolish the *mita*, it was reluctant to exercise it out of fear that the whole mining economy might collapse and that reform might provoke resistance and rebellion.[2] Compromise of this kind involved many layers of colonial society. The imperial government tried to control the whole bureaucracy, viceroys to direct distant officials; these were making deals with local elites, while government and viceroys manœuvred to stay in the picture. At many points along this line of command royal authority could be weakened by connivance, corruption, or intimidation. The mine owners were not the only pressure group in colonial society. Elsewhere in Peru there were linked elites of landed, merchant, municipal, and bureaucratic personnel, against which the government in Madrid might well feel a certain helplessness. A viceroy would not normally impose a new tax, no matter how urgent, without consulting local interests, if only because he needed their collaboration in collecting it. In 1741 the viceroy of Peru, faced with the need for extraordinary expenditure on naval defence during the war with England, consulted the *cabildo* of Lima and obtained a new tax on local products but at levels which represented a compromise between the demands of the crown and the interests of the tax payers.[3] In the last decades of the eighteenth century new waves of immigration to Peru reshaped the local ruling class into one dominated by recently arrived *peninsulares* who quickly came to control commerce, forge links with the bureaucracy, acquire titles of nobility, and constitute for Spain a loyal support but also a demanding one.[4]

This version of the colonial compact, characteristic of Habsburg and early Bourbon government, was repeated throughout Spanish America. In Mexico the nobility – about fifty families in the eighteenth century – combined a number of roles and offices.[5] One group made its fortune in overseas trade, invested profits in mines and plantations, and acted primarily in the export sector. Others concentrated on mining and on

[2] Jeffrey A. Cole, *The Potosí Mita 1573-1700. Compulsory Indian Labor in the Andes* (Stanford, Calif., 1985), pp. 44, 123–30, 132.

[3] José A. Manso de Velasco, *Relación y documentos de gobierno del virrey del Perú, José A. Manso de Velasco, conde de Superunda (1745-1761)*, ed. Alfredo Moreno Cebrían (Madrid, 1983), pp. 285–6.

[4] Alberto Flores Galindo, *Aristocracia y plebe, Lima 1760-1830* (Lima, 1984), pp. 52–7.

[5] Doris M. Ladd, *The Mexican Nobility at Independence 1780-1826* (Austin, Texas, 1976), pp. 46–52, 317–19.

agriculture producing for the mining industry. They all preferred to co-opt the imperial bureaucracy by marriage and interest rather than confront it in protest and resistance. In Central America owners of *obrajes* persuaded crown, *audiencia*, and local officials to connive at the illegal employment of Indians in indigo dye works, and all the dominant interests were satisfied by a carefully adjusted system of fines and bribes.[6] In Chile too the bureaucracy was sucked into the local interest groups by marriage, kinship, economic activities, and corruption, and bureaucratic rivalries between governor, *audiencia*, and *cabildo* simply reflected factional struggles within colonial society.[7]

Spanish government in America was not as strong as it appeared. Ministers and councillors of the Indies were on the other side of the Atlantic; officials had to live relatively unprotected among the people they administered; the crown required revenue. Needs were weaknesses, and these gave Spanish Americans the essential leverage to deal with the imperial government instead of merely obeying it. The result was that government proceeded not by absolute commands and unqualified obedience but by negotiation and bargain. Spain had come to lower its expectations. The metropolis looked for collaborating elites, the colonies for conniving officials.

Colonial Consensus

The vulnerability of government, the power of local interests, led to a system of bureaucratic adjustment. The process has been described as an informal understanding between the crown and its American subjects, an 'unwritten constitution' which produced 'a workable compromise between what the central authorities ideally wanted and what local conditions and pressures would realistically tolerate'.[8] The argument perhaps needs further refinement, especially the suggestion that there was a pact between monarch and subjects, and that the procedure was one of 'bureaucratic decentralization'. In the first place, the informal compromise was not a transfer of power from an imperial metropolis to a developing colony. The government in Spain was always a party to decisions, both in administrative and in economic policy; it was the

---

[6] MacLeod, *Spanish Central America*, pp. 187–90.

[7] Jacques A. Barbier, *Reform and Politics in Bourbon Chile, 1755-1796* (Ottawa, 1980), pp. 5–10.

[8] John Leddy Phelan, *The People and the King. The Comunero Revolution in Colombia, 1781* (Madison, Wis., 1978), pp. xviii, 7, 30, 82–4.

crown which sold colonial offices in Madrid, and it was the royal officials in Seville who colluded with merchants in breaking the laws of trade. The true contrast was not between centralism and devolution but between the degrees of power that the metropolis was prepared to exercise at any given time. The imperial state embraced both the metropolitan government and the administration in the colonies, but until about 1750 it was a consensus state, not an absolutist state. This was the difference between Habsburg and Bourbon government in America. In the second place, for all the links between colonial officials and local interests, these never became completely identified. The ceaseless complaints and appeals against officials to the council of the Indies are evidence enough that there was always a distinction between the crown's representatives and the crown's subjects. Yet if some of the concepts of 'bureaucratic decentralization' need qualification, the situation it describes was well known to contemporaries: the colonial bureaucracy came to adopt a mediating role between crown and subjects which may be called a colonial consensus.

The consensus took various forms, though not of course a written or legislative form. It could be seen first in the growing participation of creoles in the colonial bureaucracy. Americans wanted office for a number of reasons, as a career, an investment for the family, an opportunity to accumulate capital, or as a means of influencing policy in their own regions and to their own advantage. They wanted not only equality of opportunity with *peninsulares*, or a majority of appointments; they wanted them above all in their own districts and to the exclusion of creoles from other regions. From the 1630s there was an opportunity to obtain offices, if not by right then by purchase or in *beneficio*; the crown began to sell treasury offices in 1633, *corregimientos* in 1678, judgeships in the *audiencias* in 1687, and by 1700 even the office of viceroy.[9] Creoles took advantage of the opportunity, with obvious effects: purchase of office gave the encumbent a certain bureaucratic independence, and it tended to bypass the state of isolation which the crown sought for its colonial bureaucracy. The sale of fiscal offices from 1633 to 1750 diluted royal authority. In Peru treasury officials came to act as mediators between the financial demands of the crown and the resistance of tax payers. Local citizens came to dominate the treasury, with the result that crown control diminished, local interests prevailed,

---

[9] Alfredo Moreno Cebrián, 'Venta y beneficios de los corregimientos peruanos', *Revista de Indias*, 36, 143–4 (1976), pp. 213–46; Fernando Muro, 'El "beneficio" de oficios públicos en Indias', *Anuario de Estudios Americanos*, 35 (1978), pp. 1–67.

and remissions of revenue to Spain declined.[10] In return for a quick profit, sale of office incurred a long-term loss.

The second agent of compromise was the *corregidor*. Many of these officials, from 1678, bought their office in Spain, thus incurring a debt which was then increased by the cost of travelling to America. They derived their income not from a salary but from entrepreneurship, trading with the Indians under their jurisdiction, advancing them capital and credit, supplying equipment and goods, and exercising an economic monopoly in their districts.[11] Their financial backers, merchant specula- tors in the colonies, guaranteed a salary and expenses to ingoing officials, who with the connivance of caciques then forced the Indians to accept advances of cash and equipment in order to produce an export crop or simply to consume surplus commodities. This was the notorious *repartimiento de comercio*, and by it the different interest groups were satisfied. The Indians were forced into producing and consuming; merchants gained an export crop; royal officials received an income; and the crown saved money on salaries. Yet all this was illegal and involved the imperial authorities at every level in a process of lawbreaking, a '*mal necesario*' as one viceroy described it, justified by the need to give the Indians an economic stimulus. And official connivance reached the point of attempting to revise the system, or at least to regulate the quota and the prices of the *reparto*, 'in order above all to bring relief to the Indians and to give the *corregidores* a moderate income'.[12] The interest of historians in this process has focused mainly on its meaning for Indian society and its role in Indian rebellion. But it has a further significance as a crucial detail in the diminution of imperial authority and control. A *corregidor* whose quasi-independent financial and administrative status had to be recognized by a viceroy was not an ideal instrument of colonial government.

A third agency of bureaucratic compromise was the *audiencia*. Americans began to regard their own *audiencia* districts as *patrias* and to claim that, in addition to their intellectual, academic and economic qualifications, they had a legal right to hold offices within their homelands. During the period 1687–1750 the financial needs of the

[10] Kenneth J. Andrien, 'The Sale of Fiscal Offices and the Decline of Royal Authority in the Viceroyalty of Peru, 1633–1700', *HAHR*, 62, 1 (1982), pp. 49–71; see the same author's *Crisis and Decline: the Viceroyalty of Peru in the Seventeenth Century* (Alberquerque, NM, 1985).

[11] Alfredo Moreno Cebrián, *El corregidor de indios y la economía peruana en el siglo XVIII* (Madrid, 1977), pp. 108–10.

[12] Manso de Velasco, *Relación de gobierno*, pp. 291–3.

crown, usually for defence expenditure, caused it to extend the practice of sale of office to American *audiencias*, and creoles now began to buy their way into office at the highest level. By 1750 Peruvians dominated their home *audiencia* of Lima; local appointments also dominated the *audiencias* of Chile, Charcas, and Quito. In this way money payments and local influence came to prevail over the independent administration of justice. In the years 1687–1750, out of a total of 311 *audiencia* appointees in America, 138 or 44 per cent were creoles compared with 157 *peninsulares*. Of the 138 creoles, forty-four were natives of the districts in which they served, and fifty-seven were from other parts of the Americas; almost three-quarters of the 138 American appointees bought their appointments.[13] Sale of office implied that discrimination against creoles still prevailed. While 103 (75 per cent) of the Americans who obtained *audiencia* appointments had to pay for them, only thirteen of the 157 Spaniards (8 per cent) had to do so. But in this way the creoles advanced. By the 1760s the majority of judges in the *audiencias* of Lima, Santiago, and Mexico were creoles. This was a shift of power within the empire and had implications for imperial government. The dilution of royal authority, the indifference towards standards of competence and honesty, the inertia in the face of local influence and creole wealth, and the emergence of local ruling classes and linked interest groups, went beyond consensus government and signified an abdication of imperial control. Most of the creole *oidores* (judges) were tied by kinship or interest to the landowning elite; the *audiencia* became a reserve of the rich and powerful families of their region, and sale of office helped to create a kind of creole representation in government.

Audiencias, *corregidores*, treasury officials, all played their part in establishing a colonial compromise, reducing the power of the metropolis and increasing the participation of Americans. Finally, the viceroys themselves became part of this informal system. The theory was that only a son of a distinguished and powerful family among the higher aristocracy could exercise sufficient authority and inspire the necessary respect in Mexico, Peru, and, from 1739, New Granada. This gave viceroys a certain leverage and most of them went to their viceroyalties with expectations of making a fortune. They were, of course, exclusively *peninsulares*, but once in America they were not totally amenable to metropolitan control; to profit from their office meant to collaborate

[13] Mark A. Burkholder and D. S. Chandler, *From Impotence to Authority. The Spanish Crown and the American Audiencias, 1687-1808* (Columbia, Mo., 1977), p. 145.

with local interests, and unless they badly overstepped the mark they had little to fear from the *residencia* at the end of their term. Viceroys, like *corregidores*, were appointed in Spain; their formal instructions and informal understanding were prepared in Spain. The metropolis and the colonial bureaucracy were all part of the consensus, and viceroys would continue to enrich themselves, while the metropolis hoped they would also do their duty.

This was the empire inherited by Charles III, an empire which had reached a stage of development somewhere between dependence and autonomy, no longer a recent conquest but not yet a nation, hitherto docile but still needing a skilful hand. For all his interest in America, for all his expert advisers, the king seems not to have been aware of the requirements of colonial societies. His only concern was that they did not meet his revenue needs or conform to his international interests. The first priority was to reassert imperial control, remind Americans of their status, and raise the level of taxation. None of these policies was appropriate to the time or the place; nor did they stop at the colonial elites. While these had grown in power against the bureaucracy, so they had increased their exploitation of the Indians, encroaching on their lands and appropriating their labour in haciendas, plantations, mines, and *obrajes*. Traditionally the crown and *audiencias* had been, at least in theory, protectors of the Indians against local oppressors and corrupt officials. Now, as the crown prepared to increase its demands on the elites, so it increased its fiscal pressure on the Indians. All sectors were under pressure, the king from his enemies, the elites from the king, and the Indians from everyone. America was about to experience a second colonization.

The Imperial State

Bourbon government emerged from imperial inertia and began to apply its authority; the time had come to restore its control of American resources and defend them against foreign rivals. The change of dynasty in itself made no difference to Spanish America and creole society had little reason to regret the years after 1700; sale of office was never more buoyant than in the first half of the eighteenth century.[14] Policy change depended on the stimulus and support of the king, the ideas and

---

[14] See above, pp. 52–4, 173.

initiatives of ministers, and the response of political opinion. Rarely were these three preconditions present simultaneously. In the decades from 1750, however, they came together and produced a new colonial programme embracing the whole range of political, military, and economic relations between Spain and America, with policy peaks in 1765 and from 1776. In that year José de Gálvez became minister of the Indies, following over ten years' experience of colonial problems. One of his priorities was to reduce creole participation in American government, a personal as well as a political preference. His bias was fed by his own officials. In Peru visitor general José Antonio de Areche villified Americans as people who 'have been in a state of great liberty, doing what they pleased, either by force or by buying justice'; they criticized the government 'not as the people of London and other civilised people might criticize their government while respecting its authority in general, but as opponents bitter at being governed by Europeans whom they deeply hate', an attitude which could be checked only by applying uniformity of institutions and laws between America and Spain and by governing Americans by Spanish intendants.[15] And from Upper Peru Intendant Francisco de Viedma confirmed the minister's viewpoint:

> For appointments here natives of the country are not suitable, because they are extremely difficult to dissuade from the customary ways ingrained in them even in contravention of the laws; they lack that mode of thinking, at once pure, sincere and impartial, prevalent in Spain, and even Spaniards who live for some time in these parts come to acquire the same or worse customs. How can we possibly appoint to the office of subdelegate people who do not even know who their fathers are?[16]

The advance of the Bourbon state, the end of compromise government and creole participation, and the reduction of links between bureaucrats and local families were regarded by the Spanish authorities as necessary steps towards control and revival. Sale of higher office was officially ended in 1750, and from then on a concerted effort was made to reduce the presence of Americans in Church and state. José Antonio de San Alberto, archbishop of La Plata, steadfastly opposed the appointment of Americans to high positions in the Church, or even as parish

---

[15] Areche to Gálvez, 22 December 1780, Archivo General de Indias, Seville, Audiencia de Buenos Aires 354.

[16] Viedma to Gálvez, Cochabamba, 3 November 1784, AGI, Aud. de Buenos Aires 140.

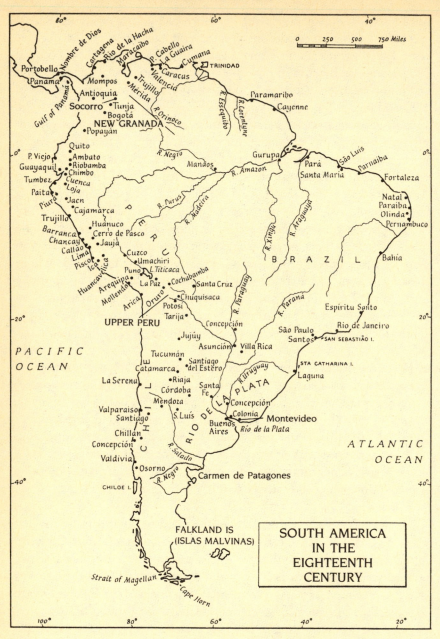

SOUTH AMERICA
IN THE
EIGHTEENTH
CENTURY

priests, 'because they are superficial people and hostile to everything Spanish'.[17] As views of this kind became more prevalent, so higher appointments in the Church were gradually restored to European Spaniards. The administration, too, closed its ranks to creoles. At a time when the American population was growing, the number of graduates multiplying, the bureaucracy itself expanding, it was *peninsulares* who were preferred for appointments. From 1764 new officials, the intendants, began to replace *corregidores*; by 1808 no American, much less a local candidate, had obtained a permanent appointment as intendant in the Río de la Plata or Peru, and there were few in Mexico.[18] In Upper Peru Ignacio Flores, a native of Quito and temporary intendant of La Plata, was hounded by the viceroy and the *audiencia* as a creole, a man who appointed creoles to subdelegacies and armed creole militias, thus 'putting arms in the hands of those whose motives are not to be trusted'.[19] Other sectors of the bureaucracy were recolonized by Spaniards. A growing number of senior financial officials, and even some minor ones, were appointed from the peninsula, 'one of ours' as the Spanish used to say.[20] In the army creole officers were replaced by Spaniards on retirement. The object of the new policy was to de-Americanize the government of America, and in this it was successful. Sale of *audiencia* offices was ended, the creole share of places reduced, and the appointment of creoles in their own districts virtually stopped. In the period 1751–1808, of the 266 appointments in American *audiencias* only sixty-two (23 per cent) went to creoles, compared with 200 (75 per cent) to *peninsulares*. In 1808 of the ninety-nine men in the colonial tribunals only six creoles had appointments in their own districts and nineteen outside their districts.[21] The bureaucracy of Buenos Aires was dominated by *peninsulares*; in the period 1776–1810 they held 64 per cent of appointments, *porteños* (natives of Buenos Aires) 29 per cent, and other Americans 7 per cent.[22]

[17] San Alberto to Gálvez, Potosí, 15 January 1787, in Viceroy Loreto to crown, 1 April 1787, AGI, Aud. de Charcas 578.

[18] John Lynch, *Spanish Colonial Administration, 1782-1810. The Intendant System in the Viceroyalty of the Río de la Plata* (London, 1958), pp. 290–301; J. R. Fisher, *Government and Society in Colonial Peru. The Intendant System 1784-1814* (London, 1970), pp. 239–50; D. A. Brading, *Miners and Merchants in Bourbon Mexico 1763-1810* (Cambridge, 1971), p. 64.

[19] Libro de autos reservados, 31 August 1785, AGI, Aud. de Buenos Aires 70.

[20] Scarlett O'Phelan Godoy, *Rebellions and Revolts in Eighteenth Century Peru and Upper Peru* (Cologne, 1985), p. 180.

[21] Burkholder and Chandler, *From Impotence to Authority*, pp. 115–35.

[22] Susan Migden Socolow, *The Bureaucrats of Buenos Aires, 1769-1810: Amor al Real Servicio* (Durham, 1987), p. 132.

There was indeed, after 1750, a 'Spanish reaction' in America. Was the new bureaucracy an improvement on the old? The results were not uniform throughout the Americas. There were still examples of local marriages and local influence, of nepotism, inefficiency, and even corruption.[23] When Viceroy Amat returned from Peru in 1777 it was said in Spain that he had amassed 5 million pesos in fifteen years.[24] Everywhere new institutions clashed with the old and Spanish divisiveness asserted itself. In Mexico, where much was at stake, the crown closely monitored the new administration. In Chile, where resources were less obvious, the bureaucracy remained a captive of the local elite and the crown appeared unconcerned. In Buenos Aires, where pre-viceregal government and society were weak, the new bureaucracy grew up in isolation from local pressure but also, in the crisis of 1810, from local support.[25] In general the crown acquired a more professional administration, less dependent on local interests, and a keener instrument of imperial control. But the cost was high. Frustration among Americans mounted as their claims were ignored and their expectations denied, and the new policy further disturbed the balance of interests on which colonial government rested.

The Hispanicization of American government was set in motion during the period 1750–65. Then there was a pause. For ten years, 1766–76, there was little basic input into American policy and the government appeared to return to its old inertia. This is a pointer perhaps to its priorities. It was satisfied that the major components of empire were now in place: revenue was flowing in, commerce was growing steadily, and Spaniards were displacing creoles. And all these results were achieved within the traditional structure without involving radical change. This was not resumed until 1776 and only reached fruition in 1782–6, that is some twenty-three years after the accession of Charles III. In the meantime there had been much talk about America; ministers met, circulated papers, discussed projects, waited for each other's opinions, alerted traditionalists, and did anything rather than take a decision. Yet when the decisions were eventually assembled, they contained a certain logic. A harder administration, free from rivals, and backed by the military, would force larger tax returns from America, whose growing economy would take the strain.

---

[23] Linda K. Salvucci, 'Costumbres viejas "hombres nuevos": José de Gálvez y la burocracia fiscal novohispana, 1754–1800', *Historia Mexicana*, 33 (1983), pp. 224–64.

[24] Grantham to Weymouth, 17 April 1777, PRO, SP 94/203.

[25] Barbier, *Reform and Politics in Bourbon Chile*, pp. 75, 190–4; Brading, *Miners and Merchants in Bourbon Mexico*, pp. 63–90; Socolow, *The Bureaucrats of Buenos Aires*, pp. 262–4.

The government of Charles III overhauled imperial government, centralized the mechanism of control, and modernized the bureaucracy. New units of administration were created, the viceroyalty of the Río de la Plata in 1776, the captaincy general of Venezuela in 1777 and of Chile in 1778. New officials, the intendants, were appointed, to Caracas in 1776, the Río de la Plata in 1782, Peru in 1784, Mexico, Guatemala, and Chile in 1786. These were partly administrative and fiscal devices; they also implied closer control of the local elites. For the intendants replaced *alcaldes mayores* and *corregidores*, officials who had long been adept at reconciling different interests, and brought to an end the system of *repartos*, in which local merchants had a stake. The new legislation introduced paid officials; and it guaranteed the Indians the right to trade and work as they wished, a measure which Areche justified in Peru on the grounds that 'we are now fortunate to be in an age which favours free trade' in preference to 'private monopoly'.[26] Economic liberalism did not work in colonial America. Local interests, peninsular and creole alike, found the new policy inhibiting and they resented the unwonted intervention of the metropolis. The abolition of *repartimiento* threatened not only merchants and landowners but also the Indians themselves, unaccustomed to using money in a free market and dependent on credit for livestock and merchandise. The interest groups took the law into their own hands. In Mexico and Peru the *repartos* reappeared, as the landowners sought to retain their grip on labour and the merchants to re-establish old consumer markets. Thus Bourbon policy was sabotaged within the colonies themselves; the old consensus between government and governed no longer functioned.[27]

As the Bourbons strengthened the state, so they weakened the Church. In 1767 they expelled the Jesuits from America, some 2,500 in all, the majority of them Americans, who were thus removed from their homelands as well as their missions.[28] The expulsion was an attack on the semi-independence of the Jesuits and an assertion of imperial control. For the Jesuits possessed a great franchise in America, and in Paraguay a fortified enclave. Not everyone believed the reports of the 'Jesuit war' in Paraguay, perhaps not even the king himself; but it was a convenient

[26] Areche to Viceroy Guirior, 18 June 1779, AGI, Indiferente General 1713.

[27] Stanley J. Stein, 'Bureaucracy and Business in the Spanish Empire, 1759–1804: Failure of a Bourbon Reform in Mexico and Peru', *HAHR*, 61, 1 (1981), pp. 2–28.

[28] Miguel Batllori, *El Abate Viscardo. Historia y mito de la intervención de los Jesuítas en la indepedencia de Hispanoamérica* (Caracas, 1953); Merle E. Simmons, *Los escritos de Juan Pablo Viscardo y Guzmán* (Caracas, 1983); A. F. Pradeau, *La expulsión de los Jesuítas de las Provincias de Sonora, Ostimuri y Sinaloa en 1767* (Mexico, 1959). See above, pp. 179–82, 281–4.

story and an additional argument. Their long-term assets were more important; ownership of haciendas and other property gave them independent economic power which was enhanced by successful entrepreneurial activities. The Jesuits were a predictable target for an absolutist government. So was the rest of the colonial Church, an institution which possessed two assets – corporate privilege and great wealth – regarded with particularly jealousy by the Bourbon state. Its wealth was measured not only in terms of tithes, real estate and liens on property, but also by its enormous capital, amassed through donations of the faithful, capital which made the Church the largest spender and lender in Spanish America.[29] In America, no less than in Spain, ministers viewed the Church as a rival as well as an ally, one which needed to be brought into line. They sought to bring the clergy under the jurisdiction of the secular courts, and in the process they increasingly curtailed clerical immunity.[30] And once the Church's defences were breached, the next target was its property. Not all of these plans were successful, but they were sufficient to alert the clergy and further to disturb the political balance on which colonial rule rested.

The new absolutism also had a military dimension, and here too the results were ambiguous. Spain had never maintained a large military presence in America. In the first half of the eighteenth century the garrisons of the strategic ports were reorganized into a series of fixed battalions, first in Havana in 1719, followed by Cartagena in 1736, Santo Domingo in 1738, Veracruz in 1740, and Panama and San Juan in 1741. The idea was that Spanish battalions would reinforce the permanent garrisons during wartime. But the defeat and occupation of Havana in 1762 forced Spain to rethink her defence policy. The conde de Ricla was sent to Cuba in 1763 as captain general and governor, accompanied by Field Marshal O'Reilly. Between them they reorganized the regular forces of the island and expanded the militia. To pay for this programme taxes were increased (the *alcabala* from 2 to 6 per cent); an intendant was appointed to administer them; and they were made more palatable by a measure of freer trade.[31] In the years 1763–5, therefore, Cuba became a prototype of the new empire: a military base, an intendancy, a tax

---

[29] Arnold J. Bauer, 'The Church in the Economy of Spanish America: Censos and Depósitos in the Eighteenth and Nineteenth Centuries', *HAHR*, 63, 4 (1983), pp. 707–33.

[30] N. M. Farriss, *Crown and Clergy in Colonial Mexico 1759-1821. The Crisis of Ecclesiastical Privilege* (London, 1968), pp. 149–96.

[31] Allan J. Kuethe, *Cuba, 1753-1815. Crown, Military and Society* (Knoxville, Tenn., 1986), pp. 33–75.

source, and an export economy. Gradually the Cuban model was extended to other parts of the empire, and in the process Spain had to overcome its prejudice against creoles in deference to pressing defence needs. The metropolis had neither the money nor the manpower to despatch regularly large forces of Spanish troops to America; the Americanization of the colonial army thus became inevitable and irreversible. Creole officers of the army in America totalled 34 per cent in 1740, 33 per cent in 1760 and 60 per cent in 1800; creole troops formed 68 per cent in 1740–59, 80 per cent in 1780–1800.[32] The point at which creoles overtook Spaniards were the years around 1780; by 1788 fifty-one of the eighty-seven officers of the Fixed Infantry Regiment of Havana were creoles.[33] Spanish ministers, not least Gálvez, were reluctant to arm colonials, but this was the price of a high-cost defence policy, reliance on creole contributions to war loans, sale of army commissions, and shortage of peninsular reinforcements. In 1786, to cut manpower and transport costs, it was decided to suspend the practice of employing Spanish battalions for turns of duty in America.

The army of America was perforce supplemented by colonial militias. The new Cuban model was extended to New Spain and in the 1770s to New Granada, Peru and Quito, thus placing the burden of defence squarely on colonial economies and personnel.[34] To encourage recruits, militia members were admitted to the *fuero militar*, a status which gave creoles, and to some extent even mixed races, the privileges and immunities already enjoyed by the Spanish military, in particular the protection of military law and a degree of fiscal exemption. Nevertheless, there were some misgivings over committing imperial defence, especially internal security, to a colonial militia officered by creoles. In Peru Spain employed regular army units officered by *peninsulares* to crush the revolt of Tupac Amaru and subsequently took steps to de-Americanize the officer corps. In Mexico Viceroy Revillagigedo considered it a folly to give weapons to Indians, negroes and other castes, and he doubted the loyalty of creole officers. Military policy remained partial to *peninsulares*, even if it was no longer a realistic position. Defence costs limited

[32] Juan Marchena Fernández, *Oficiales y soldados en el ejército de América* (Seville, 1983), pp. 112–13, 300–1.

[33] Kuethe, *Cuba, 1753-1815*, pp. 126–7; Marchena, *Oficiales y soldados en el ejército de América*, pp. 95–120.

[34] Allan J. Kuethe, *Military Reform and Society in New Granada, 1773-1808* (Gainesville, Fla., 1978), pp. 63–78, 90–1; Leon G. Campbell, *The Military and Society in Colonial Peru 1750-1810* (Philadelphia, 1978), pp. 74–7, 173–7; Christon I. Archer, *The Army in Bourbon Mexico, 1760-1810* (Albuquerque, NM, 1977), pp. 8–31, 191–222.

the size of the military establishment; Americanization was regarded as an acceptable risk; and the new imperialism was never based on massive militarization. This was not a fortress empire. For internal security at least Spanish colonial government depended on the legitimacy of the crown and the strength of the new bureaucracy. Spain's second empire was administered by Spaniards, defended and financed by Americans.

The tax payers of empire were creoles, mestizos, and Indians; they were also expected to subsidize Spain. Charles III summarized his basic aim in America in simple terms, 'To bring my royal revenues to their proper level'.[35] Viceroy Revillagigedo was equally frank: the imperative was 'that the Indies yield more utility to the crown'.[36] These were very traditional aims, now made more urgent not simply by the resurgence of colonial war but by the rigid fiscal structure in Spain itself and the failure to reform it in the years 1750–65. From the 1750s great efforts were made to increase imperial revenue, by raising tax rates, taking them into state administration, and extending royal monopolies. The latter were imposed on more commodities, including tobacco, spirits, gunpowder, salt, and other consumer goods. Monopoly control over tobacco was gradually extended throughout America, to Peru in 1752, Chile and the Río de la Plata in 1753, Venezuela, Guatemala, Costa Rica, and New Granada in 1778. All these yielded high returns, though the highest of all were in Mexico, where the monopoly was established in 1764 and where protesting planters, manufacturers, and consumers met the hard edge of Bourbon bureaucracy in its most uncompromising mood. By controlling cultivation, manipulating planters, and establishing royal factories monopoly officials gave an object lesson in the new administration and earned large profits for the state. Total profits in Mexico in 1765–95 equalled 69.4 million pesos, of which 44.7 million (64 per cent) were remitted to Spain.[37]

The colonial government assumed direct administration of taxes traditionally farmed out to private contractors. The hated sales tax, the *alcabala*, continued to burden all transactions, and now its level was raised from 2 to 4, to 6 per cent, while its collection was more rigorously enforced. A number of completely new taxes were created, such as those

---

[35] *Cédula*, 15 August 1776, incorporating Upper Peru into the viceroyalty of the Río de la Plata, in Octavio Gil Munilla, *El Río de la Plata en la política internacional. Génesis del virreinato* (Seville, 1949), pp. 428–32.

[36] Ibid., p. 101.

[37] Susan Deans-Smith, 'The Money Plant: The Royal Tobacco Monopoly of New Spain, 1765–1821', in Nils Jacobsen and Hans-Jürgen Puhle (eds), *The Economies of Mexico and Peru during the Late Colonial Period, 1760-1810* (Berlin, 1986), pp. 361–87.

in Peru on coca, *aguardiente*, and grains.[38] In addition to the complaints of all consumers, particular economic interests had particular grievances. The mining sectors in Mexico and Peru paid substantial sums in the royal fifth or tenth, war taxes on silver, duties on refining and coining, fees on state-controlled supplies of mercury and gunpowder, not to mention defence loans and other extraordinary contributions. Yet Spain valued mining and favoured its interests. From 1776 the state played its part in reducing production costs, halving the price of mercury and gunpowder, exempting mining equipment and raw materials from *alcabalas*, extending credit facilities, and in general improving the infrastructure of the industry. Other sectors were not so privileged. Agricultural interests had various grievances against Bourbon policy. Ranchers deplored the many taxes on marketing animals and the *alcabalas* on all animal sales and purchases; sugar and spirits producers complained of high duties; and consumers in all sectors resented the taxes on goods in daily use.[39] Revenue from Mexico increased enormously in 1750–1810, as the state imposed unprecedented levels of taxation and monopoly. The thirty years after 1780 yielded an increase of 155 per cent in *alcabala* revenue over the thirty years before, an increase not derived from economic growth but from pure fiscal extortion.[40] Bourbon policy culminated in the Consolidation decree of 26 December 1804 which ordered the sequestration of charitable funds in America and their remission to Spain. As applied to Mexico this arbitrary expedient forced the Church to remove its money from Mexican creditors to the state and to accept a reduced return. It also attacked the entire propertied class in the colony who suddenly had to redeem the capital value of their church loans and encumbrances. Tax burdens did not necessarily make revolutionaries of their victims, but they engendered a climate of resentment and a desire to return to the time of compromise or, more ominously, to advance to a greater autonomy.

Resistance to imperial taxation took the Bourbon planners by surprise. In Mexico the *visita* of José de Gálvez (1765–71) drew a fierce response from various sectors of the population. Attempts to cut mining costs by reducing miners' customary rights led to violent riots at Real

---

[38] O'Phelan, *Rebellions and Revolts in Eighteenth Century Peru and Upper Peru*, pp. 164–5.

[39] For a further example of *alcabala* severity see W. Kendall Brown, *Bourbons and Brandy: Imperial Reform in Eighteenth-Century Arequipa* (Albuquerque, NM, 1986).

[40] Juan Carlos Garavaglia and Juan Carlos Grosso, 'Estado borbónico y presión fiscal en la Nueva España, 1750–1821', in Antonio Annino and others (eds), *America Latina: Dallo Stato Coloniale allo Stato Nazione (1750-1940)* (2 vols, Milan, 1987), I, pp. 78–97.

del Monte and Guanajuato in 1766–7, adding fuel to the tension caused by tax pressure, the tobacco monopoly and the expulsion of the Jesuits.[41] Gálvez personally directed the subsequent repression, and left in his wake a high level of conflict and protest in towns, villages, and mining communities in reaction to the new threats from the Bourbon state.[42] Soon he spread his net more widely. In 1776 he was appointed minister of the Indies and immediately instituted *visitas* of Peru and New Granada. In New Granada the ruthless procedure of the regent and visitor general, Juan Francisco Gutiérrez de Piñeres, contrasted harshly with the traditional process of bargain and compromise. He increased the *alcabala* to 4 per cent, took it out of farm into direct administration and revived an obsolete tax for naval defence. He also reorganized the tobacco and spirits monopolies, increasing the price to the consumer and, in the case of tobacco, restricting production to high quality areas. These burdens fell on a stagnant economy, poor population, and, above all, numerous small farmers. After a series of protests and disturbances, outright rebellion erupted in March 1781 centred on Socorro and San Gil; the rebels refused to pay taxes, attacked government warehouses, drove out the Spanish authorities and, in the name of the *común*, proclaimed a group of leaders.[43] Soon the movement spilled over into Andean Venezuela.

The rebellion of the *comuneros* was essentially a creole and mestizo movement. In Peru Bourbon tax changes reduced the living standards of a wider sector of the population and drew into temporary association a number of different protests, creole, mestizo, and Indian.[44] In the course of 1780 urban creoles expressed their opposition to internal customs, increased sales taxes and other forms of fiscal pressure, and soon they were joined by poorer creoles and mestizos, resentful of the extension of tribute status to themselves. Creole riots were overtaken by Indian rebellion, and as this spread from Cuzco across southern Peru into the altiplano of Upper Peru it became clear that Bourbon government had made a great miscalculation. The Indians of Peru were burdened by two particular charges, the tribute and the *mita*, to both of which they had

[41] Brading, *Miners and Merchants in Bourbon Mexico*, pp. 146–9, 276–7.

[42] These were 'spontaneous, short-lived armed outbursts by members of a single community in reaction to threats from outside'; William B. Taylor, *Drinking, Homicide and Rebellion in Colonial Mexican Villages* (Stanford, Calif., 1979), pp. 115–16, 124, 146.

[43] Phelan, *The People and the King*, pp. 179–80; Anthony McFarlane, 'Civil Disorders and Popular Protests in Late Colonial New Granada', *HAHR*, 64, 1 (1984), pp. 17–54, esp. pp. 18–19, 53–4; Carlos E. Muñoz Oraá, *Los comuneros de Venezuela* (Merida, 1971), pp. 81–98.

[44] O'Phelan, *Rebellions and Revolts in Eighteenth Century Peru and Upper Peru*, pp. 278–9.

adjusted their economies. The *reparto* came as an additional charge, at which point fiscal pressure caused many Indians to avoid tribute payment by passing as mestizos. In the years around 1780, however, new census counts expanded the range of tribute payers and caught more Indians and mestizos in the tax net. Finally, these traditional Indian grievances were aggravated by two new forms of exploitation, the brain-child of Charles III's government. The *alcabala* was raised to 4 per cent in 1772 and to 6 per cent in 1776, and it was extended to products hitherto tax-free; at the same time internal customs posts were established to ensure collection. Each stage of Bourbon policy was calculated yet ill-informed, and Gálvez and his agents could not escape the accusation that they directly provoked the rebellion of Tupac Amaru; in particular the *alcabala* expedients, weighing heavily on Indian producers and traders, served to alienate the middle groups of Indian society and to nurture a rebel leadership.[45]

The imperial state was given a severe shock before it recovered its nerve and restored order. The rebellions of 1780–1 represented a classical sequence of Bourbon innovation, colonial resistance, and renewed absolutism. The work of rooting out creoles from important offices continued. Adjustments were made to tax demands but the pressure was maintained. Indians were relieved of a few burdens but not released from tributary status. *Corregidores* were replaced by intendants but these brought new demands. Meanwhile the *visitas* had not persuaded the colonies to contribute to the costs of the war of 1779–83, while the counter-insurgency operations had still to be paid for. Yet the experience did not demoralize Gálvez or deprive him of the king's favour, and he continued to work for a tighter administration and higher revenue.

What was the American income of Spain? It consisted of two components, revenue raised within America and taxes levied on the American trade. Peace with Britain in 1748 and reduction of military expenditure enabled Ferdinand VI to improve the flow of American revenue to Spain, maintain it at a high level throughout the 1750s, and leave a surplus of 6.1 million pesos to Charles III.[46] American revenue could be used either for peace or for war. The government of Ferdinand VI used it to improve American government and ended sale of office in 1750. Charles III had other priorities; he spent the surplus left by

[45] Ibid., pp. 161–73, 232.
[46] Jacques A. Barbier, 'Towards a New Chronology for Bourbon Colonialism: The *Depositaria de Indias* of Cadiz, 1722–1789', *Ibero-Amerikanisches Archiv*, 6 (1980), pp. 335–53.

Ferdinand on war with Britain. Nevertheless, colonial revenues mounted as Gálvez continued to modernize financial organization and eventually to extend the intendant system. But the cost of imperial defence and of the growing bureaucracy meant that much of the royal income never left America, and large debts remained in New Granada, Peru, Chile, and probably other colonial treasuries, with the result that remissions to Spain may well have declined below the levels reached in the final years of Ferdinand VI.[47] The Bourbons, of course, did not expect to receive surplus remissions from all parts of America. They did not exploit Central America for revenue purposes but kept fiscal wealth in the colony by investment in improved bureaucracy and defence, thus making it a more effective unit of a larger empire.[48] New Granada, even with its mining sector, also appeared to be exempt from remitting public sector surpluses, in spite of the efforts of Gutiérrez de Piñeres. At any rate none were sent in the period 1760–90; the New Granadan treasury was subsidized by transfers from Quito and Lima, and it was not until 1790–6 that the first remittances to Spain were made.[49]

Spain looked to the mining economies to provide the greatest revenue, but even here there was disappointment. Peru was not a uniformly successful provider. Remissions from Upper Peru to Lima between 1700 and 1770 dropped to 20 million pesos, from the 200 million of 1561–1700, the result of lower levels of mining production and rising local expenditure. By 1770 there were virtually no surplus revenues from Upper Peru to Lima; they were now sent east to Buenos Aires for defence expenditure. In the period 1674–1770 Buenos Aires received subsidies totalling 11 million pesos, but these were boosted with the establishment of the viceroyalty of the Río de la Plata in 1776 and the improvement of revenue administration in Upper Peru. The subsidy sent from Upper Peru to the Río de la Plata reached almost 12.5 million pesos in 1771–80, rising to 13 million in the next ten years, and

[47] Barbier, 'Towards a New Chronology for Bourbon Colonialism', pp. 336–44, and the same author's 'Venezuelan *Libranzas*, 1788–1807: From Economic Nostrum to Fiscal Imperative', *The Americas*, 37 (1981), pp. 457–78, esp. pp. 460–1; Juan Marchena Fernández, 'La financiación militar en Indias: Introducción a su estudio', *Anuario de Estudios Americanos*, 36 (1979), pp. 93–110, estimates that 80 per cent of the expenditures of the treasuries of Mexico and Peru, the traditional source of *situados*, were on defence; for New Granada see Kuethe, *Military Reform and Society in New Granada*, pp. 114, 144–6.

[48] Miles L. Wortman, *Government and Society in Central America, 1680-1840* (New York, 1982), pp. 31, 107, 131.

[49] Anthony McFarlane, 'The Transition from Colonialism in Colombia, 1819–1876', in Christopher Abel and Colin M. Lewis (eds), *Latin America, Economic Imperialism and the State* (London, 1985), pp. 101–24, esp. pp. 105–6, 122, n. 15.

to 16.5 million in the next. In this way Buenos Aires came to replace
Lima as the recipient of Upper Peruvian treasury surpluses.[50] In the
periods 1791–5 and 1796–1800, 72.55 per cent and 71.69 per cent of the
income of the Buenos Aires treasury came from transfers from Potosí.
And in these years Buenos Aires remitted to Spain approximately one-
third of the sums received from Potosí. In 1801–5 and 1806–10 Potosí
was incapable of maintaining these levels of transfer and they declined
to 32.87 per cent and 29.63 per cent; remittances to Spain first rose but
then declined from 1806, the year of the British invasions.[51] In 1791–
1805 Buenos Aires sent 8.6 million pesos to Spain. Remittances from
Peru to Spain, on the other hand, declined in the eighteenth century.
Between 1701 and 1750 only 4.5 million pesos were sent to Spain, an
average of less than 100,000 pesos a year. For the last half of the
eighteenth century defence expenditure comprised the greatest single
drain on the Lima treasury, amounting to more than 55 million pesos
and 40 per cent of total income. Peruvian revenue was now spent on
defence and administration in Peru and neighbouring colonies, and such
surpluses as reached Spain from Upper Peru were channelled through
Buenos Aires.[52]

Mexico was the last reservoir. There royal income rose from 3 million
pesos in 1712 to 14.7 million net a year by the end of the century. Of this
4.5 million was appropriated for local administration and defence, while
a further 4 million subsidized other colonies in the Caribbean and the
Philippines. The remaining 6 million pesos went as pure profit to the
treasury in Madrid.[53] But the question remains, what did American
income mean for Spain? In good years it might represent at least 20 per
cent of Spanish treasury income. This dwindled to 5 per cent or zero in
times of war with Britain, especially in the years 1797–1802 and 1805–8,
though even then the crown received a colonial revenue indirectly by
selling bills of exchange and licences for neutrals – and sometimes for the

[50] John J. TePaske, 'The Fiscal Structure of Upper Peru and the Financing of Empire', in Karen
Spalding (ed.), *Essays in the Political, Economic and Social History of Colonial Latin America* (Newark,
NJ, 1982), pp. 69–94, esp. pp. 77–8.

[51] Enrique Tandeter, 'Buenos Aires and Potosí' (Palermo, 1988), paper kindly facilitated by the
author, pp. 25–7.

[52] TePaske, 'The Fiscal Structure of Upper Peru', pp. 79–80; see John J. TePaske and Herbert S.
Klein, *The Royal Treasuries of the Spanish Empire in America* (3 vols, Durham, NC, 1982), I,
pp. 340–65.

[53] Alexander von Humboldt, *Ensayo político sobre el reino de la Nueva España*, ed. Juan A. Ortega y
Medina (Mexico, 1966), pp. 386–7, 425, 540–52; Brading, *Miners and Merchants in Bourbon Mexico*,
pp. 29–30, 129–46; D. A. Brading, 'Facts and Figments in Bourbon Mexico', *Bulletin of Latin
American Research*, 4, 1 (1985), pp. 61–4.

enemy – to trade with the Spanish colonies.[54] American income made a difference to Spain, the difference between fifty years of relative solvency and power before 1797 and ten years of deficit and crisis afterwards.

To raise his American revenues to their proper level Charles III had looked to José de Gálvez, whose programme of de-Americanization, bureaucratic adjustment, and fiscal pressure left its imprint on Spanish America for many years to come. He first came to public notoriety during his visit to Mexico where he suffered mental illness or, as some said, bouts of insanity. Even his normal behaviour alerted those around him, and many contemporaries found him personally aggressive, ill-tempered, and intolerant, a bigot in the age of Enlightenment. The British thought he was anti-British, the French that he was anti-French. He seems in fact to have been a Spanish nationalist, equally hostile to Robertson and Raynal. Though personally incorrupt, he used his patronage unstintingly in favour of his family and friends, and there were few parts of the Spanish empire where a Gálvez relative or client was not to be found in the bureaucracy or the army. In the 1790s Spaniards were still debating whether he had done more harm than good to the Spanish colonies, and many people, in Spain as well as in America, blamed him personally for the rebellions of 1780–1. 'And at what time did he choose to sour the minds of the Spanish colonies? The same in which the English colonies shook off the yoke of Great Britain, for grievances perhaps not so heavy.'[55] But Gálvez believed that the correct formula for colonies was to maximize revenues and minimize dissent, and the men to do it were Spanish intendants.

The Second Empire

The economic policy of Spain in America followed the same pattern as political development and showed a similar contrast between the periods before and after 1750, between compromise and control,

[54] Jacques A. Barbier, 'Peninsular Finance and Colonial Trade: the Dilemma of Charles IV's Spain', *JLAS*, 12 (1980), pp. 21–37; Josep Fontana, 'La crisis colonial en la crisis del antiguo régimen español', in Alberto Flores Galindo (ed.), *Independencia y revolución (1780-1840)* (2 vols, Lima, 1987), I, pp. 17–35, esp. p. 19, calculates that the colonies contributed 25 per cent of the ordinary revenue of the Spanish government.

[55] J. F. Bourgoing, *Modern State of Spain* (4 vols, London, 1808), II, pp. 181–4, an appraisal of Gálvez by a French diplomat who was secretary of the French embassy in Madrid, 1777–85, and returned as chargé d'affaires in 1792–3.

between a relaxed and a rigid monopoly. The growth of direct trade enabled America to bypass the Spanish monopoly and deal directly with the trading nations of the world, supplementing the foreign imports already obtained via Cadiz. America, moreover, had developed a strong internal market, producing agricultural products and manufactured goods, and selling them from region to region.[56] Peru achieved a high degree of self-sufficiency and regional integration in the seventeenth century; in 1603 Potosí took only 9.5 per cent of its consumption from non-American sources, a proportion which grew but slowly in the next 150 years.[57] The growth of the internal market and the expansion of inter-American trade were signs of a growing freedom from monopoly control and a significant degree of colonial autonomy. And what the colonies did not produce for themselves they could obtain from foreigners. The Seville monopolists adjusted to new conditions by admitting foreigners to the Indies trade while reserving a place for themselves. Foreigners too profited from the expansion of American trade after 1660, and it was they who supplied most of the manufactured goods and siphoned off profits in treasure.

Treasure returns moved ahead strongly under the last Habsburg and if anything were more impressive than those under the first Bourbons, except for the years around 1730.[58] After 1750 treasure returns rose, though not continuously, and they remained thereafter at a high level, without however surpassing the old record until after 1780. Not all of these returns were profits for Spain. Foreign nations were now dominant in Cadiz and relegated Spain to an inferior position in a trade which theoretically she controlled.[59] There is, however, another way of looking at this inferiority. Colonial returns were the means by which Spain balanced her trade with the rest of Europe and by which the Spanish imperial economy imported what it did not produce, paying the difference in what it did produce, precious metals. This structure could not be changed by commercial reform alone. To change it Spain would

[56] See above, pp. 10–12, 14–15, 142–4.

[57] Carlos Sempat Assadourian, *El sistema de la economía colonial. Mercado interno, regiones y espacio económico* (Lima, 1982), pp. 112, 278–93, and the author's 'La producción de la mercancía dinero en la formación del mercado interno colonial. El caso del espacio peruano, siglo XVI', in Enrique Florescano (ed.), *Ensayos sobre el desarrollo económico de México y América Latina (1500-1975)* (Mexico, 1979), p. 233.

[58] Michel Morineau, *Incroyables gazettes et fabuleux métaux. Les retours des trésors américains d'après les gazettes hollandaises (XVIe-XVIIIe siècles)* (Cambridge, 1985), pp. 39, 249–50; Antonio García-Baquero, *Cádiz y el Atlántico (1717-1778)* (2 vols, Seville, 1976), I, p. 150.

[59] Morineau, *Incroyables gazettes et fabuleux métaux*, p. 117.

have to industrialize, and this was not a realistic option. Meanwhile, granted that Spain was an agricultural economy, her commercial and colonial system in the age of compromise made sense.

But Bourbon man did not like it. He identified two enemies of Spanish interests: American manufacturers and foreign merchants. No matter how enlightened they were, Spanish planners from Campillo to Campomanes wanted the extinction of American manufacturing; then, if the other gap were closed, Spain would have a true monopoly, a captive market. So economic consensus gave way to controls, autonomy to dependence, in a process which paralleled the chronology of political change. The Indies were treated as purely colonies, their role to produce exclusively for the metropolis. Bourbon planners had been seeking to re-monopolize the transatlantic trade since the efforts of Patiño in the 1720s, while merchants and consumers in America, in collusion with foreign interlopers, clung to the old ways of direct trade. Now, about 1760, a number of factors – a new king, defeat by England, need of revenue, and hope of economic development – came together to produce a new impetus and a new policy. A technical commission on colonial commerce was organized in the summer of 1764 and issued its findings in February 1765. The Cadiz monopoly, the use of fleets, the limitations on the numbers of licensed ships, the high duties on exports and imports, and the antiquated method of taxation on volume of goods without reference to value, all were condemned and their replacement by a more rational policy advocated. Action soon followed. A decree of 16 October 1765 opened the Spanish islands of the Caribbean to trade with eight additional Spanish ports, and *comercio libre* was born. The decree of 1765 provided the model for the gradual extension of free trade beyond the Caribbean, to Louisiana in 1768, and Yucatan and Campeche in 1770. Early in 1778 decrees extended the system to Chile, Peru and the Río de la Plata. Finally, on 12 October 1778, a *reglamento* establishing 'a free and protected trade' and consolidating all the previous concessions dismantled the traditional framework of colonial trade; it lowered tariffs, ended the monopoly of Cadiz and Seville, opened free communications between the major ports of the peninsula and Spanish America, and heralded a new phase of the *pacto colonial*.[60]

The freedom of trade announced in 1778, however, was a limited

[60] Eduardo Arcila Farías, *El siglo ilustrado en América. Reformas económicas del siglo XVIII en Nueva España* (Caracas, 1955), pp. 94–117; C. H. Haring, *The Spanish Empire in America* (New York, 1963), pp. 341–2; J. Muñoz Pérez, 'La publicación del reglamento del comercio libre de Indias', *Anuario de Estudios Americanos*, 4 (1947), pp. 615–64.

freedom. It abolished the monopoly of Cadiz but reaffirmed the monopoly of Spain; it opened Spanish America to all Spaniards but closed it more firmly to the rest of the world. The colonies were given more avenues into the Spanish market but denied access to the world market. They were flooded with imports from Spain but protected more closely against foreign interlopers. *Comercio libre*, moreover, was not for everyone even in the Hispanic world. Venezuela was excluded until 1788 because the Caracas Company was powerful there; Mexico was excluded until 1789 in case its booming economy drew off trade from poorer colonies. Finally, free trade was by no means free of taxes; 3 per cent was charged on Spanish goods, 7 per cent on foreign, and the charge was now *ad valorem*.[61] Free trade, in fact, was designed to make the colonial monopoly more effective, to relax controls among Spaniards but tighten them against foreigners, to encourage competition between national products and lower their price against foreign goods. The idea was to prime the colonial economy and make it ripe for plucking. If trade followed the flag, the tax collector was close behind the trader. To what extent, then, did *comercio libre* benefit Spain?

The ports of the peninsula did not suddenly compete for the American trade. There was some regional adjustment but not sufficient to reduce the primacy of Cadiz. Andalucía in general and Cadiz in particular continued to enjoy a natural advantage of trade and navigation with America, firmly rooted in history and geography. Cadiz still dominated the trade, now with the benefit of more outlets in America. Its exports moved strongly ahead and in the period 1778–96 they accounted for 76 per cent of all Spanish exports to America. This was the golden age of the Cadiz trade. Catalan exports also flourished, though some way behind those of Cadiz, accounting for about 10 per cent of the total. Catalan interest in America had helped to prepare the way for *comercio libre*. In the late seventeenth and early eighteenth centuries Catalan agents in Cadiz sold their regional goods to Andalucian shippers; then, from the 1730s, Catalan merchants shipped their goods directly in the fleets, trading on their own account though within the Cadiz monopoly.[62] Next, the Catalan merchant marine began to participate in the Indies trade; between 1740 and 1743 the first Catalan ships sailed from Cadiz, to be followed in 1745 by a Catalan vessel with a local cargo sailing from Barcelona and calling at Cadiz only to complete

[61] *Reglamento para el comercio libre, 1778*, eds Bibiano Torres Ramírez and Javier Ortiz de la Tabla (Seville, 1979), article 17.

[62] Carlos Martínez Shaw, *Cataluña en la carrera de Indias 1680-1756* (Barcelona, 1981), pp. 72–148.

the administrative formalities. Commercial ventures of this type were repeated in the following years, which also saw the use of Catalan ships by Cadiz exporters. In America itself Catalan agents were now stationed in a number of ports, representing the interests of their principals in Barcelona. The foundation of the Royal Company of Barcelona in 1755–6, privileged to trade with Santo Domingo, Puerto Rico, Margarita, and subsequently Cumaná, did not fulfil its expectations; in the following thirty years it organized forty trading expeditions, all of them modest affairs and undercapitalized, and its chief merit was to preserve the Catalan presence in American waters.[63] *Comercio libre* made the Company superfluous; now Catalan merchants, ports, and shipping had direct access to America without the interposition of Cadiz.

Comercio libre was not an unmixed blessing for the Catalan economy, or for the regions in general. Modern historiography has seen it as an essentially fiscal measure, subordinating everything to tax increase; it failed to raise the interest of the Spanish regions in the American trade beyond its previous level; and the authorization to export foreign goods 'finished' in Spain on equal terms as national simply encouraged the massive import of foreign goods for re-export.[64] Nevertheless, *comercio libre* was important for Catalonia; it stimulated an increase in the volume of its colonial trade and this included its own production, not merely foreign re-exports; and the American trade became the most dynamic sector of Catalan commerce in the second half of the eighteenth century.[65] The leading export was *aguardiente* (31 per cent) followed by printed linens and calicoes, silks, wines and dried fruits, miscellaneous textiles and paper. Industrial products accounted for 64 per cent of Catalan exports to America, agricultural 36 per cent.[66] While Barcelona came well behind Cadiz in its share of the American market,

[63] José M. Oliva Melgar, 'El fracàs del comerç privilegiat', in Josep M. Delgado and others, *El comerç entre Catalunya i Amèrica (segles XVIII i XIX)* (Barcelona, 1986), pp. 37–63.

[64] Josep María Delgado Ribas, 'El impacto de las crisis coloniales en la economía catalana (1787–1807)', *La economía española al final del Antiguo Régimen. III. Comercio y colonias* (Madrid, 1982), pp. 99–169, and the same author's 'El miratge del lliure comerç', *El comerç entre Catalunya i Amèrica*, pp. 65–80.

[65] Josep María Delgado Ribas, 'Els catalans i el lliure comerç', *El comerç entre Catalunya i Amèrica*, pp. 81–93.

[66] Pierre Vilar, *La Catalogne dans l'Espagne moderne* (3 vols, Paris, 1962), III, pp. 66–138; Antonio García-Baquero, *Comercio colonial y guerras revolucionarias* (Seville, 1972), pp. 68–74, and the same author's 'Comercio colonial y producción industrial en Cataluña a fines del siglo XVIII', in Jordi Nadal and Gabriel Tortella (eds), *Agricultura, comercio colonial y crecimiento económico en la España contemporánea* (Barcelona, 1974), pp. 268–94.

three-quarters of its exports were national products, compared with one-quarter in the case of Cadiz; Barcelona was an outlet for Catalan products, and Cadiz an intermediary between Europe and America.[67] The volume of Catalan colonial trade increased with the general increase of Spanish colonial trade: from 8 million reales in 1778 to 31 million in 1788, to 56 million in 1792.[68] Yet Barcelona never depended on the American market to the same extent as Cadiz. For its textiles, brandies, and wines Barcelona also had markets in Europe, in Spain, and in its own interior, which enabled the port to survive the collapse of American trade in the period 1797–1808.

Galicia, on the other hand, was not in a position to emulate Catalonia. Protected from 1764 to 1778 by the privilege of sending packet boats to Havana and Montevideo, La Coruña was able to participate in the monopoly and consign cargoes of which 44 per cent were its own linen products made for the popular market. Under *comercio libre*, however, it had to compete with other Spanish ports for the Río de la Plata trade and do so in high quality products; thus it came to be a commission port for foreign and Spanish exports, and its American trade declined in the decades after 1778. Recession turned into collapse in 1796 when war with Britain cut the trade routes, and once Galicia lost its American trade it had no other markets to turn to. At this point the commercial sector cut its losses and invested the returns from colonial trade in land purchase.[69] Land remained the traditional haven in a storm, an ironic twist to *comercio libre*. As for the other ports of the peninsula, free trade provided a useful outlet for the industrial products of their hinterlands, but these did not respond in a way that would affect industrial growth.[70] What, then, did free trade mean for the Spanish economy as a whole?

The period 1748–78 was one of steady growth for the Indies trade, and apart from a slight depression in 1771–5 exports and imports moved upwards, reflecting perhaps a period of growth in all sectors of the Mexican economy and an increase of silver production.[71] Trade was no

---

[67] García-Baquero, 'Comercio colonial y producción industrial', pp. 278–86.

[68] Delgado, 'El miratge del lliure comerç', pp. 75–7.

[69] Luis Alonso Alvarez, *Comercio colonial y crisis del Antiguo Régimen en Galicia (1778-1818)* (La Coruña, 1986), pp. 163–206, 256.

[70] John Fisher, *Commercial Relations between Spain and Spanish America in the Era of Free Trade, 1778-1796* (Liverpool, 1985), pp. 50–3.

[71] García-Baquero, *Cádiz y el Atlántico*, I, pp. 540–56; John J. TePaske, 'General Tendencies and Secular Trends in the Economies of Mexico and Peru, 1750–1810: The View from the *Cajas* of Mexico and Lima', in Jacobsen and Puhle (eds), *The Economies of Mexico and Peru during the Late Colonial Period*, pp. 316–39.

longer confined to the fleet system but moved in a variety of ways. The New Spain *flota* survived, it is true, and sailed in 1760, 1765, 1768, 1772, and 1776, but this constituted only a limited portion of total trade. From 1765 free trade ships sailed to the Caribbean and Central America, and even to Mexico between *flotas*, and these provided a more dynamic service. South America was served by a growing number of register ships, quicker and more responsive to the market than the fleets. And various privileged companies traded to special areas. Thus Spain rediscovered the routes, regions, and markets of its own empire and reconstituted the imperial economy. The introduction of full *comercio libre* in 1778 released a greater flow of trade. The average annual value of exports from Spain to America in the years 1782–96 was 400 per cent higher than in 1778, and there seems little doubt that the metropolis profited from the receipt of greater colonial surpluses, public and private, and from better export opportunities for Spanish goods.[72] The object of *comercio libre*, however, was not simply to increase colonial trade but to change its structure, specifically to substitute Spanish manufactures for foreign re-exports, and Spanish nationals for foreign merchants. Here success was more elusive.

In spite of the formal exclusion of foreigners from colonial trade, Spain still relied on the more advanced economies of western Europe for goods and shipping, and even for permission to keep the routes open. The British did not at this stage fear *comercio libre*: 'I should think this will be of an advantage likewise to us, as there will certainly be a greater call for our goods by the Spanish merchants here, now they have a free liberty of exporting them without a licence.'[73] According to British commercial intelligence, the *flota* of 1772 carried 19.7 million pesos worth of exports, of which Spanish products accounted for only 12.6 per cent, French 36.6 per cent, and British 15 per cent.[74] The conclusion appeared obvious: 'All the attempts to exclude foreign traders from the market are absurd, and have hitherto proved unsuccessful.'[75] In 1778 foreign products – led by linen cloth, woollens, and silks – amounted to 62 per cent of registered exports to America, and they were also ahead in 1784, 1785, and 1787. Thereafter the share of national goods improved

---

[72] Fisher, *Commercial Relations between Spain and Spanish America*, 45–9; TePaske, 'General Tendencies', p. 330, suggests for this period even greater growth in the Mexican economy (especially mining and tax yields), now joined by some growth in Peruvian mining.

[73] Rochford to Conway, Escorial, 28 October 1765, Public Record Office, SP 94/172.

[74] Enclosure in Pro-consul Dalrymple to Rochford, Cadiz, 17 March 1772, PRO, SP 94/189.

[75] Grantham to Rochford, 16 December 1772, PRO, SP 94/191.

and in the whole period 1782–96 they averaged 52 per cent. But these were predominantly agricultural goods. National industry did not respond to the colonial market, Spain did not become a developed metropolis, and the Spanish economy, far from complementing colonial production, competed with it. In Cadiz itself foreigners were still dominant. In the 1750s foreigners were taking 80 per cent of profits. While most of them earned over 1,000 pesos a year, the income of more than half the Spaniards did not exceed 500 a year; the richest Spaniards earned 6,000, while there were four French merchants who earned 35–40,000.[76] There were a number of Spaniards in Cadiz who made great fortunes in the second half of the eighteenth century, but the foreign fortunes were greater. The dependence of the Spanish economy on northern Europe, however, had to be seen in a wider context. There was, it is true, an adverse balance of trade with Europe, amounting in the period 1787–92 to an annual average deficit of 20 million pesos, half of it representing the import of goods for re-export to America. The favourable balance of trade with America, however, not only cancelled this deficit but also yielded an overall trading surplus of 9 million pesos a year.[77]

America supplied Spain with an annual average of 15.2 million pesos in public and private treasure returns in the period 1756–78 (see table 9.1). The most meagre quinquennium was 1761–5 with an annual average of 13.5 million, the most generous 1766–70 with 17.2 million.[78]

Table 9.1 American treasure returns by quinquennia in million pesos 1756-1778

Quinquennia	Total	Annual average
1756–60	76.4	15.2
1761–5	67.9	13.5
1766–70	86.3	17.2
1771–5	76.1	15.2
1776–8	44.5	14.8

Source: Michel Morineau, Incroyables gazettes et fabuleux métaux. Les retours des trésors américains d'après les gazettes hollandaises (XVIe-XVIIIe siècles) (Cambridge, 1985), pp. 417–19.

[76] Morineau, Incroyables gazettes et fabuleux métaux, p. 541.
[77] Fisher, Commercial Relations between Spain and Spanish America, pp. 60–1.
[78] Morineau, Incroyables gazettes et fabuleux métaux, p. 416.

Mexico contributed the greater share, 56 per cent compared with Tierra Firme's 43.3 per cent. The *flota* returning in March 1774 brought 22.3 million pesos, of which 3.2 million were for the king.[79] The share to the crown varied between a minimum of 0.6 per cent in 1767 and a maximum of 23.4 per cent in 1761. The general trend of the period was inferior to that of the immediately preceding decade, which had yielded an annual average of 17 million pesos, and the first phase of *comercio libre* did not bring a strong upsurge of trade and returns. This had to await the years after 1778.

These were the peak years of the American trade, and the results were seen in treasure returns (see table 9.2). The war of 1779–83 did not cause a complete stoppage; Franco-Spanish convoys in 1780–2 got through and landed some millions of pesos. But major production was retained in America until the security of peace. Then in 1784 began the 'avalanche', 46 million pesos, in a post-war quinquennium (1781–5) which was 'the most brilliant in the whole history of the Spanish Atlantic'.[80] There was another wartime gap in 1796–1801, and this too was followed by release of accumulated treasure, giving the four years 1801–4 an annual average of 29.9 million, even better than the 22.8 million of 1781–5. But the American trade was not made by exceptional years alone. The more normal ten-year period 1786–95 yielded an annual average of 25.6 million pesos, which can be compared with the previous eighteenth-century record of 19.9 million in 1766–70, and the

Table 9.2 *American treasure returns by quinquennia in million pesos 1779-1805*

Quinquennia	Total	Annual average
1776–80	59.5	11.6
1781–5	114.0	22.8
1786–90	135.1	27.0
1791–5	120.9	25.9
1796–1800	49.5	9.9
1801–4	119.8	29.9

Source: Morineau, *Incroyables gazettes et fabuleux métaux*, pp. 438–40.

[79] Enclosure in Consul Hardy to Rochford, Cadiz, 22 March 1774, PRO, SP 94/195.
[80] Morineau, *Incroyables gazettes et fabuleux métaux*, pp. 437–8.

corresponding decades of previous centuries: 14.5 million in 1686–95, and 9.7 million in 1586–97. Mexico continued to provide the superior share, in 1781–5 62 per cent compared with 38 per cent from Tierra Firme. The share of the crown cannot be easily separated from that of the private sector, but in the post-war period from 1783 the trend of royal returns was rising, no doubt reflecting the Mexican contribution. In 1793 the share to the crown from Mexico was 27 per cent, in 1795 61 per cent, and in 1802–4 40 per cent.[81] According to British consular sources, which closely monitored treasure returns because of their importance for Spain's subsidies to France, the total amount of American treasure entering Spain from October 1801 to August 1804 was 107,308,152 pesos, of which 37,528,068 (35 per cent) belonged to the crown.[82]

While Spain profited from America, how did America respond to Spain in the age of free trade? The results were contradictory, a temporary revival but denial of long-term development. The natural trade routes to America were opened up and export opportunities expanded. During 1782–96 the average annual value of American exports to Spain was more than ten times greater than that of 1778.[83] Mexico accounted for 36 per cent of these, followed by the Caribbean (23 per cent), Peru (14 per cent), the Río de la Plata (12 per cent), and Venezuela (10 per cent). Treasure exports, at 56 per cent, continued to dominate the trade, and of these about one-quarter were crown revenues.[84] But agricultural exports, tobacco, cacao, sugar, cochineal, indigo, and hides, accounted for 44 per cent. This indicates that hitherto marginal regions – the Río de la Plata and Venezuela – and neglected products – agropastoral goods – were now brought into the mainstream of the export economy. In the Río de la Plata a combination of *comercio libre*, the ban imposed on the export of unminted bullion to Peru, and the region's new strategic role in the South Atlantic led to an increase in population and turned Buenos Aires into a growing consumer market for imported products, an important point of distribution to other markets, and an earner of silver for transatlantic trade. This perhaps was the clearest example of what could be achieved by royal will and government policy acting on hitherto inert economy, though at a heavy cost to Upper Peru which was forced to subsidize the new imperial role of

[81] Ibid., pp. 448–54.
[82] J. B. Duff, Cadiz, 30 August 1804, PRO, FO 72/53.
[83] Fisher, *Commercial Relations between Spain and Spanish America*, p. 61.
[84] Ibid., p. 67.

Buenos Aires. Cuba too was a success story; the output of Cuban sugar tripled by 1791 at an annual growth of over 4 per cent and producers were able to take advantage of the difficulties of rival sugar colonies.[85] Cuba's plantation economy became so profitable that sugar joined silver as the prop of the imperial economy and Cuba joined Mexico as the leading supplier of colonial products to Spain.[86] Mexico itself, at first protected from *comercio libre*, then responded to it; a new commercial class was born, and immigrants from Spain came to compete with the old monopolists and to penetrate most sectors of the economy.

The chronology of colonial revival in the eighteenth century, therefore, bore some relation to *comercio libre*. But not an exclusive one. Spanish America was subject in this period to a dual process: the impact of new Spanish policy, and the pressure of changing conditions in America. New policy was expressed in *comercio libre* but also included strategic priorities. Changing conditions took the form of population growth, a mining boom, agricultural expansion, and the development of the internal market, not all of which responded to imperial imperatives. Economic growth in Mexico originated in 1690–1730 and had its roots in demographic increase. Mexico and Peru both experienced real though not spectacular growth in the period 1770–95, followed by stagnation and perhaps slight decline in the years 1795–1810, when isolation from Spain was not entirely balanced by trade with alternative markets, and when a period of price rises began. Whatever the immediate impact of *comercio libre*, Americans soon learned that it had built-in limitations for their economies, that they were still subject to monopoly, still deprived of market options, still dependent on Spanish-controlled imports, and still sufferers from discriminatory duties or even outright prohibitions in favour of Spanish goods. The new impulse to Spanish trade soon led to the saturation of these limited markets, and in the 1780s the problem of the colonies was to earn enough to pay for increasing imports. Bankruptcies were frequent, local industry declined, even agricultural products like wine and brandy were subject to competition from imports, and precious metals flowed out in this unequal struggle.

The role of America remained to consume, to mine, and to cultivate plantations. In this sense *comercio libre* was another instrument of

---

[85] Kuethe, *Cuba, 1753-1815*, pp. 73, 132–6.

[86] Stanley J. Stein, 'Caribbean Counterpoint: Veracruz vs. Havana. War and Neutral Trade, 1797–1799', in J. Chase (ed.), *Géographie du capital marchand aux Amériques, 1760-1860* (Paris, 1987), pp. 21–44, esp. p. 21.

recolonization, a return to a primitive idea of colonies and a crude division of labour, after a long period when consensus had allowed a measure of more autonomous growth. This does not mean that European products displaced American products in the colonial markets. European imports, it is true, increased in the eighteenth century, helped by the greater purchasing power of Spanish America from precious metals, sugar, cacao, and hides.[87] The penetration of European products was most noticeable in 'new' areas of development such as the Río de la Plata and New Granada. But this was a slow and partial process; in the case of Potosí the European share of the market grew from 9.5 per cent to only 24 per cent between 1603 and 1793.[88] European imports to the urban markets of Mexico and Peru in the years 1786–92 did not reach 25 per cent of total transactions and in most cases were well behind internal products.[89] Qualitatively, of course, European products enjoyed a greater advantage than these figures suggest. The influx of manufactured goods damaged local industries such as the textiles of Tlaxcala, Cochabamba, and north-west Río de la Plata, while Cuyo felt the effects of European wine imports. The evidence perhaps is not comprehensive. The textile industry of Querétaro suffered from problems within the regional economy rather than from *comercio libre*; and elsewhere other forms of textile production sometimes developed to take the place of early victims of competition.[90] But there were many indications that industrial enterprise throughout South America was disrupted by *comercio libre*. Exports from Guayaquil, a traditional source of textiles for many parts of the Americas, declined from 440 bales in 1768 to 157 in 1788.[91] From this time the textile industry of Quito remained in depression, displaced in Peruvian and other markets by cheaper imports from Europe. The decline of Quito's textiles was reported complacently by Archbishop Antonio Caballero y Góngora, viceroy of New Granada (1782–9), when he observed that agriculture and mining were 'the appropriate functions of colonies', while industry

---

[87] García-Baquero, *Cádiz y el Atlántico*, II, pp. 260–1; Fisher, *Commercial Relations between Spain and Spanish America*, pp. 60–4.

[88] Assadourian, 'La producción de la mercancía dinero en la formación del mercado interno colonial', p. 233.

[89] Garavaglia and Grosso, 'Estado borbónico y presión fiscal en la Nueva España', in Annino (ed.), *America Latina: Dallo Stato Coloniale allo Stato Nazione*, I, p. 95, n. 13.

[90] Fisher, *Comercial Relations between Spain and Spanish America*, p. 81; John C. Super, *La vida en Querétaro durante la colonia 1531-1810* (Mexico, 1983), pp. 98–107.

[91] Michael T. Hamerly, *Historia social y económica de la antigua provincia de Guayaquil, 1763-1842* (Guayaquil, 1973), pp. 57–85.

simply produced 'manufactures which ought to be imported from the metropolis'.[92]

The fact that Spanish industry could not adequately supply the colonial markets did not move the minds of the planners. There was, after all, a small industrial sector in Spain, determined to retain its captive market; to supplement national production Spanish merchants could still make profits from re-exporting the products of foreign suppliers; and to maintain dependency was regarded as more important than to appease colonials. It was an axiom of Spanish imperial thinking that economic dependence was a precondition of political allegiance, and that growth of manufacturers in the colonies would encourage self-sufficiency and autonomy. Imperial definitions of this kind led officials into a fanatical logic. The advice given by the count of Revillagigedo in 1794 to his successor as viceroy of Mexico has become notorious: 'It should not be forgotten that this is a colony which must depend on its mother country, Spain, and must yield her some benefit because of the protection it receives ... dependence would cease once European manufactures and products were not needed here'.[93] Viceroy Francisco Gil de Taboada reported that the decline of manufactures in Peru and neighbouring colonies was due not to the abolition of *repartimiento* but to higher imports and lower prices under free trade, to the great benefit of the state.[94] He suggested it would be a good idea to diminish local manufactures still further in such a way 'without the people noticing', for Peru was only useful to the metropolis as a mining economy:

These remote dominions are bound to the ruling country by specific ties; each need satisfied without its help is another link broken, and when few are left they will not stand the pressure ... The government must not lose sight for a moment of the damage which is bound to be done by the factories which have been established and survive here for want of European manufactures; only a highly protected trade will suffice to destroy them.[95]

[92] 'Relación del estado del Nuevo Reino de Granada' (1789), José Manuel Pérez Ayala, *Antonio Caballero y Góngora, virrey y arzobispo de Santa Fe 1723-1796* (Bogotá, 1951), pp. 360–1.

[93] Quoted in Catalina Sierra, *El nacimiento de México* (Mexico, 1960), p. 132.

[94] Gil de Taboada to Antonio Valdés, 20 July 1790, Comisión Nacional del Sesquicentenario de la Independencia del Perú, *Colección documental de la independencia del Perú* (30 vols, Lima, 1971-2), tomo XXII, 1, p. 10.

[95] Gil de Taboada to Pedro Lerena, 5 May 1791, ibid., pp. 23–4.

An echo of the *reglamento* of 1778 which had called for '*un comercio libre y protegido*', protected against Americans as well as against foreigners. Spanish manufacturers were constantly on the alert for any infringement of this formula. The textile workshops of Mexico and Puebla were productive enough to alarm Catalan manufacturers; they frequently complained of the effect of colonial competition on their exports, and sought from the crown 'the strictest orders for the immediate destruction of the textile factories established in those colonies'.[96]

The imperial government did not exist to arbitrate between Spain and America. Urged by officials and lobbied by manufacturers, its response was predictable. A royal decree of 28 November 1800 prohibiting the establishment of manufactures in the colonies was followed by another of 30 October 1801 'concerning the excessive establishment there of factories and machinery in opposition to those which flourish in Spain and which are intended to supply primarily our Americas'. The government explained that it could not allow the extension of industries even during wartime, for these diverted labour from the essential tasks of mining gold and silver and producing colonial commodities. Officials were instructed to ascertain the number of factories in their districts and 'to effect their destruction by the most convenient means they can devise, even if it involves taking them over by the royal treasury on the pretext of making them productive'.[97] Statements of this kind were the clearest expression of recolonization and the end of consensus. But times were changing, and from 1796 to 1802, when war with Britain isolated the colonies from the metropolis and gave their own industries an involuntary protection, local textile manufacturers emerged to renew operations, and from 1804 further war gave further opportunities.

Economic policy, transatlantic trade, and treasure returns, all told the same story: the second Spanish empire was a working empire, whose mines, plantations and ranches yielded profits to their owners and surpluses to Spain. In the course of the eighteenth century Mexican silver production rose continuously from 5 million pesos in 1702, to 18 million in the boom of the 1770s, and a peak of 27 million in 1804. By this time Mexico produced 67 per cent of all American silver, a position which had been achieved by a conjunction of circumstances – rich bonanzas, improved technology, restructuring of ownership, lowering of production costs by tax concessions – in a colony whose population

---

[96] García-Baquero, *Comercio colonial y guerras revolucionarias*, p. 83.
[97] Ibid., pp. 93–4.

growth in the early eighteenth century generated economic expansion in later decades. Mining soaked up investment. From the 1780s the industry received large injections of merchant capital, a by-product of *comercio libre*. New merchants entered colonial trade with less capital but more enterprise. As competition lowered profits, the old monopolists began to withdraw from the transatlantic trade and to seek more profitable investments in agriculture and mining, with results advantageous to the economy and themselves.[98] Mexico was exceptionally successful, but South America too was built on mining risks and no one scorned silver. Lower Peru increased its silver output in the late eighteenth century, a modest boom compared with that of Mexico but vital for the colony's overseas trade. Registered silver rose from 246 marks in 1777 to a peak of 637,000 marks in 1799, maintaining a high level until 1812; during this period superior draining techniques, diversion of capital from Potosí, a supply of free labour and the support of the mining tribunal, all contributed to higher output.[99] In Upper Peru mining had long been synonymous with crisis. But silver production at Potosí began to recover from the beginning of the eighteenth century, registered higher official output figures from 1736, and maintained a regular upward trend until the 1790s. From 1740 to 1790 the amount of silver exported from Potosí doubled. Here too the action of the Bourbon state was positive, if interested, and mining benefited from concessions to entrepreneurs and the establishment of the Banco de San Carlos as a source of credit. But the basic reason for increased output was the greater exploitation of the *mitayos*, the Indian conscripts, whose production quotas were doubled in these fifty years and who were forced to work longer for the same wages, supplementing their own labour with that of their wives and families.[100] For them the second empire was indeed a working empire.

The Bourbons did nothing to modernize agriculture in America, any more than they did in Spain. They taxed it as a source of revenue, either directly or by monopoly, but they were looking for immediate returns

[98] Brading, *Miners and Merchants in Bourbon Mexico*, p. 152.

[99] A mark was worth 8 pesos 4 reales; John Fisher, *Minas y mineros en el Perú colonial 1776-1824* (Lima, 1977), pp. 213–27.

[100] Enrique Tandeter, 'La rente comme rapport de production et comme rapport de distribution. Le cas de l'industrie minière de Potosí 1750-1826', Doctoral Thesis, Ecole des Hautes Etudes en Sciences Sociales (Paris, 1980), pp. 1–5, and the same author's 'Forced and Free Labour in Late Colonial Potosí', *Past and Present*, 93 (1981), pp. 98–136; on the price context of mining in Upper Peru see Enrique Tandeter and Nathan Wachtel, *Precios y producción agraria. Potosí y Charcas en el siglo XVIII* (Buenos Aires, 1983), pp. 89–90.

not long-term benefits; restructuring therefore was not an option.[101] Peninsular profitmakers and royal tax officials were regarded as parasites in the agrarian sector. Creole landowners sought greater outlets than Spain would allow. In Venezuela the great proprietors, producers of cacao, indigo, tobacco, coffee, cotton, and hides were permanently frustrated by Spanish control of the import-export trade. Even after *comercio libre* ended the monopoly of the Caracas Company the new breed of merchants, whether they were Spaniards or Spanish-orientated Venezuelans, exerted a renewed stranglehold on the Venezuelan economy, paying low for exports and charging high for imports. Venezuelan landowners and consumers demanded more trade with foreigners, denounced Spanish merchants as 'oppressors', rejected the assumption that commerce existed 'solely for the benefit of the metropolis', and campaigned against what they called in 1797 'the spirit of monopoly under which this province groans'.[102] The Río de la Plata was another target for Spanish merchants who soon dominated the trade of Buenos Aires, sometimes in collusion with local agents. But in the 1790s local merchants challenged the monopolists and began to compete in exports, capital, and shipping, and to demand access to the international markets. Here too the new colonization met the limits of American passivity.

Bureaucrats, merchants, and migrants, these were the agents of the second empire. The promotion of migration to the colonies was not part of an official programme to repopulate America, though it synchronized with renewed imperialism and strengthened the Spanish presence. Emigrants were attracted across the Atlantic by market forces and new opportunities in the colonial bureaucracy, at a time when the government did not disguise its preference for *peninsulares*, and when Spanish firms would rather employ family networks than unknown creoles. Galicians, Asturians, and Basques were the typical emigrants from Bourbon Spain, pushed out by the pressure of population on land and employment and seeking in America a fortune, a wife, and a family. This was a traditional justification of empire, one made more credible in an

---

[101] Eric Van Young, 'The Age of Paradox: Mexican Agriculture at the End of the Colonial Period, 1750–1810', in Jacobsen and Puhle (eds), *The Economies of Mexico and Peru during the Late Colonial Period*, pp. 64–90, esp. pp. 66–8; for further evidence see the same author's *Hacienda and Market in Eighteenth-Century Mexico: the Rural Economy of the Guadalajara Region, 1675–1820* (Berkeley, Calif., 1981).

[102] E. Arcila Farías, *Economía colonial de Venezuela* (Mexico, 1946), pp. 368–9; on the Río de la Plata see Susan Migden Socolow, *The Merchants of Buenos Aires 1778-1810* (Cambridge, 1978), pp. 124–35.

age of mining boom, flourishing trade and greater social mobility than could be found in Spain. The emigrants quickly integrated into colonial society and soon it became difficult to distinguish Spanish fathers and husbands from creole wives and children, though many creoles who were passed by these newcomers on the road to riches were resentful and this too was a sign of the times. Such was Mexico. In Peru a renewed flow of immigration in the second half of the eighteenth century reshaped the ruling class and gave it a strong complexion of northern Spain; 70 per cent of immigrants arriving in 1787–1814 were northerners and 46 per cent were Basques.[103] They wasted no time in moving into the commercial life of Lima and soon they dominated the Atlantic and Pacific trades and, in collusion with Spanish officials, established their control over the internal market. As they were all first or second generation *peninsulares*, they left no room at the top for creole competition or even resentment; rather it was they who absorbed the eligible Peruvians. Thus the Lima elite came to be characterized by solidarity against the popular sectors and loyalty towards Spain.

All over America Spain relied upon the *peninsulares* to renew the ties of empire among a population whom it did not entirely trust. Yet it is doubtful if the Spanish government even knew how many of its own people were in America. According to Alexander von Humboldt, Spanish America contained in 1800 a total population of 16.9 million; there were 3.2 million whites, and of these only 150,000 *peninsulares*. In fact the true number of *peninsulares* was lower than this, nearer to 30,000 and not more than 40,000. Even in Mexico, the area of greatest immigration, there were only about 14,000 *peninsulares* in a total population of 6 million, of whom 1 million were whites.[104] This was the human frontier of the Spanish world, a fragile frontier and one soon to be broken.

From Revival to Recession

The government of Charles III replaced consensus by absolutism, and in the process refashioned the fiscal, economic and administrative machinery of empire. These policies remained in place until about 1792.

[103] Flores Galindo, *Aristocracia y plebe*, pp. 78–96.
[104] Humboldt, *Ensayo político*, pp. 36–40; Romeo Flores Caballero, *La contrarrevolución en la independencia. Los españoles en la vida política, social y económica de México (1804-1838)* (Mexico, 1969), pp. 15–23; Brading, *Miners and Merchants in Bourbon Mexico*, pp. 14–15, 30, 105–6.

After that year political change and international war led to the adoption of a new colonial policy consisting of short-term extortion and structural atrophy. Now there was no pretence; colonies were for exploiting, or in the words of a senior official, 'countries from which we seek to squeeze the juice'.[105] The pickings should have been rich but, in one of the great ironies of Spanish history, the climax of the silver age and the peak of the transatlantic trade coincided with the destruction of Spain's maritime power and the closure of her imperial routes. From 1796 Spanish rulers and merchants were helpless spectators as the fruits of empire were diverted into the hands of foreigners, neutrals at best, enemies at worst. The imperial power of Spain and the defence of America were put to their final test during the long war with Britain from 1796. In April 1797, following victory over the Spanish at Cape St Vincent, Admiral Nelson stationed a British squadron outside the port of Cadiz and imposed a total blockade, while the British navy blockaded Spanish American ports and attacked Spanish shipping at sea. The result was commercial collapse. In 1796 171 ships entered Cadiz from America with cargoes worth 53.6 million pesos; in 1797 only nine ships got through, with cargoes worth no more than 500,000 pesos.[106] Imports into Veracruz from Spain dropped from 6.5 million pesos in 1796 to 520,000 pesos in 1797; exports from 7.3 million pesos to 238,000; and the prices of many European goods rose by 100 per cent.[107]

The colonies suffered shortages of consumer goods and vital materials and pressed for access to foreign suppliers. The merchants of Cadiz insisted on preserving the monopoly. As the Spanish government considered the dilemma, its hand was forced. In March 1797 Spanish officials in Cuba, impressed by the colony's demands for slaves and food supplies, took the initiative and opened Havana to North American and other neutral shipping.[108] Spain was therefore obliged to allow the same for all Spanish America or risk losing control and revenue. As an emergency measure a decree of 18 November 1797 allowed a legal and heavily taxed trade with Spanish America in neutral vessels or, in the official words, 'in national or foreign vessels from the ports of the

[105] Jorge Escobedo, visitor general of Peru, intendant of Lima and councillor of the Indies, quoted by Barbier, 'Peninsular Finance and Colonial Trade', p. 33.

[106] Fisher, *Commercial Relations between Spain and Spanish America*, p. 64.

[107] Javier Ortiz de la Tabla, *Comercio exterior de Veracruz 1778-1821. Crisis de dependencia* (Seville, 1978), pp. 225–40.

[108] Jacques A. Barbier, 'Silver, North American penetration and the Spanish imperial economy, 1760–1800', in Jacques A. Barbier and Allan J. Kuethe (eds), *The North American Role in the Spanish Imperial Economy 1760-1819* (Manchester 1984), pp. 10–11.

neutral powers of from those of Spain, with obligation to return to the latter.'[109] For the next eighteen months neutral shipping from Europe and America was authorized to enter Spanish colonial ports from which they had previously been barred; it was a radical departure from Spanish practice and a measure of the commercial and financial crisis of these years.[110] Neutrals became virtually the only carriers, the one life-line linking the Spanish colonies to markets and supplies. The results were as revealing as the previous stoppage. Under neutral trade imports into Veracruz rose from 1.7 million pesos in 1798 to 5.5 million in 1799, exports from 2.2 million to 6.3 million.[111]

These were grudging concessions. The Spanish government tried to persuade itself that cheap foreign goods would kill off colonial manufactures and leave the way clear for Spanish exports when peace returned.[112] But basically it feared that its control was slipping away, that neutrals were merely a front for the trade and industry of the enemy, that Spain was left with all the burdens and none of the benefits of empire. Meanwhile the merchants of Cadiz and Barcelona lobbied strongly against neutral trade, and in spite of colonial protests the permit was revoked on 20 April 1799. The result was to damage Spain's credibility still further, for the revocation was ignored. Colonies such as Cuba, Venezuela and Guatemala continued to deal with neutrals, and North American shipping still traded into Veracruz, Cartagena, and Buenos Aires. Spanish vessels could find no way to break through the British blockade; of the twenty-two ships which left Cadiz in the twelve months after the order of April 1799 only three reached their destination. So it was the neutrals who saved the colonial trade and the neutrals who profited. Their presence also benefited the colonies, providing multiple sources of imports and renewed demand for exports. The Spanish government repeated the prohibition on neutral trade by decree of 18 July 1800, but by now no one was listening, even in Spain. War dictated compliance. North American vessels picked up cargoes in Havana and La Guaira, 'landed' them in the United States and re-shipped them to Spain, to Cadiz if they could get through the blockade, otherwise to ports in northern Spain. This was regarded by the British navy as 'indisputably the greatest channel through which our enemies

---

[109] Sergio Villalobos R., *El comercio y la crisis colonial* (Santiago, 1968), p. 115.
[110] 'Support of the vales was a primary, if not *the* primary consideration in authorizing neutral trade', Stein, 'Caribbean Counterpoint', p. 41.
[111] Ortiz de la Tabla, *Comercio exterior de Veracruz*, p. 315.
[112] Barbier, 'Peninsular Finance and Colonial Trade', p. 28.

get home an immensity of the produce of their West India planta-tions'.[113] In the course of 1801 special permission was given to Cuba and Venezuela to trade with neutrals. And to retain a place for itself Spain was reduced to selling licences to various European and North American companies, and to individual Spaniards, to trade with Veracruz, Havana, Venezuela, and the Río de la Plata; many of their cargoes were British manufactures, sailing with British as well as Spanish licences, making returns in gold, silver, or colonial produce to Spain, or neutral ports, or even to England.[114]

The Spanish monopoly perished in the period 1797–1801 and the colonies receded from their role in the restored empire. In 1801 Cadiz colonial exports were down 49 per cent on 1799 and imports 63.2 per cent. Meanwhile the trade of the United States with the Spanish colonies was booming, exports rising from 1.3 million dollars in 1795 to 8.4 million in 1801, and imports from 1.7 million to 12.7 million.[115] The peace of Amiens in 1802, it is true, enabled Spain to renew communica-tions with America; there was a surge of trade in 1802–4 and Cadiz recovered many of its markets, though 54 per cent of its exports to America were foreign goods.[116] But it was impossible to revive the old monopoly: the colonies had now established active trading links with foreigners, especially with the United States, and the renewal of war with Britain merely confirmed that they could survive without Spain.

Spain now lost the last shreds of its sea power. On 5 October 1804, anticipating formal war, British frigates intercepted a large treasure shipment from Callao and Buenos Aires, sank one Spanish vessel and captured three others carrying 4.7 million pesos, of which 1.3 million were for the crown.[117] In the following year at Trafalgar catastrophe was complete and Spain entered unknown territory, an imperial power without a fleet, colonies without a metropolis. Imports of colonial products and precious metals slumped, and in 1805 Cadiz exports went down by 85 per cent on those of 1804.[118] Once more other powers, not least the enemy, moved in to supplant Spain. Excluded from Europe by Napoleon's continental system, Britain sought alternative markets and

---

[113] Capt. R. G. Keats to Earl St Vincent, *Boadicia*, off Ferrol, 7 July 1800, PRO, FO 72/46.

[114] Barbier, 'Peninsular Finance and Colonial Trade', pp. 30–1; see also 'Papers relative to a negotiation with the Court of Spain for a partial commercial intercourse between His Majesty's dominions and those of His Catholic Majesty, London, May 1801', PRO, FO 72/46.

[115] García-Baquero, *Comercio colonial y guerras revolucionarias*, pp. 131, 156–7.

[116] Ibid., p. 164.

[117] Morineau, *Incroyables gazettes et fabuleux métaux*, p. 437.

[118] García-Baquero, *Comercio colonial y guerras revolucionarias*, p. 177.

the sinews of war in Spanish America, causing a colonial official to lament that 'the English take out of our possessions the money which gives them the power to destroy us.'[119] The only antidote to contraband was neutral trade. In 1805 such a trade was again authorized, this time without obligation of returning to Spain. Neutral shipping now dominated the trade of Veracruz, contributing 60.5 per cent of total imports in 1807 and 95.1 per cent of exports (over 80 per cent silver). In 1806 not a single vessel from Spain entered Havana, and the Cuban trade was conducted by neutrals, foreign colonies, and other Spanish colonies. In 1807 the metropolis received not one shipment of treasure and to all appearances had disappeared from the Atlantic.[120]

If America could survive without Spain, it was not so obvious that Spain could survive without America. The effect of the colonial wars on the metropolis was that of a national disaster. Agriculture was hit by the loss of vital markets; the textile industry suffered closures and unemployment. Producers and consumers alike felt the shortage of colonial products, while the non-arrival of precious metals hurt the state as well as merchants. The crown had to seek new sources of income: from 1799 it tried to impose economies on the administration and demanded an annual contribution of 300 million reales; new issues of state bonds were launched, higher taxes demanded, and finally the desperate expedient of the *consolidación* was decreed. For a state which had geared its budget to receipt of an American revenue this was the ultimate disaster. The future of Spain as a colonial power was now in doubt, its own model of empire undone. If the economic monopoly was lost beyond recovery, how long could political control endure? It was a question which Spaniards themselves had often asked.

The Bourbon Model

The transition from consensus to control was partial and protracted. The machinery of Bourbon absolutism was not in place nor was the mobilization of colonial resources yielding positive results until 1782–5, thirty years after the initial purge of the bureaucracy, and twenty years after the first measure of free trade. Full *comercio libre* was delayed by the war of 1779–83, but to expand trade and to go to war with Britain

---

[119] Antonio de Narváez, Cartagena, 30 June 1805, in Sergio Elías Ortiz (ed.), *Escritos de dos economistas coloniales* (Bogotá, 1965), p. 112.

[120] García-Baquero, *Comercio colonial y guerras revolucionarias*, pp. 182–3.

were both deliberate decisions of the Spanish government, which seems to have closed its eyes to the inherent contradiction. Imperial revival then lasted some fifteen years, during which America was treated as a pure colony, to be possessed, primed, and plundered. The heyday of empire was immediately followed, in 1797, by war-induced recession and a prolonged crisis from which Spain emerged without an empire.

Fifteen years of restored imperialism is hardly sufficient to provide a comparison with a century of colonial consensus. But the new model was not obviously superior to the old. The transition from the Habsburg to the Bourbon empire was not of course a transition from inertia to activity, from loss to profit. Negotiation and compromise were methods born of experience and proved by results, achieving a balance between the demands of the crown and the claims of the colonists, between imperial authority and American interests. These methods of government kept the peace and, except in Paraguay in 1721–35, avoided confrontation between local elites and colonial officials; they favoured in fact a kind of American participation, if not in government at least in administration. At the same time they did not deprive Spain of the profits of empire; it is now clear that the age of depression was in fact an age of abundance, and that treasure receipts had never been greater. No doubt these had to be shared with foreigners, but that too was part of the consensus and not in itself harmful to the imperial economy of the time. The collaboration of local elites and the maintenance of treasure returns were obtained at a price, and this was ultimately paid by the Indians and other labouring groups, whose work made mines, haciendas, and plantations productive. These were the victims of the age of consensus. But they were not doubly victimized, as they were under the restored empire, when the crown added new tax demands to the labour burdens already imposed by local interest groups.

The Habsburg system withstood one of Spain's greatest crises, the War of Succession in 1700–14. Spanish America, like Castile, supported the Bourbon succession. The war gave its inhabitants a unique opportunity for independent action, not in a nationalist sense, but in the possibility of making a choice, as Spain itself did. But loyalties hardly wavered and there was no sign that compromise government had compromised allegiance. It is true that a number of interest groups had reservations and feared that traditional ways were at risk. Merchants and consumers in America who had long enjoyed profitable dealings with the English and the Dutch, especially in the Caribbean, resented the idea of a Franco-Spanish monopoly. But the year 1700 meant little to the mass of Spanish Americans, and the political moment had not arrived when circumstances of this kind would raise thoughts of liberation. The colonial administration was solid for Philip V, if for no other reason than that he represented political legitimacy. Even in Mexico, where there were signs, if only weak, of a Habsburg opposition, the transition to a Bourbon-nominated viceroy was uneventful.[121] On the economic front a combination of bureaucratic expertise, merchant enterprise, and French naval support kept the Atlantic open, and in spite of the sea power of the Allies there was no year in which the colonies were cut off from their metropolis. In short, the framework of colonial government remained intact; the consensus system stood the test of war; and the crisis of succession receded.[122]

A century later the situation was very different. It would, of course, be unhistorical to compare too closely the response of Spanish America to the War of Succession and its response to the Napoleonic wars. The passage of a hundred years had basically changed the political, economic and ideological context and introduced a number of causal factors unknown in 1700. Nevertheless, one of the factors operating in Spanish America from 1808 was the previous alienation of American interest groups by the new mode of government imposed from the 1750s. In changing the political rules, Charles III and his advisers ignored history. It was impossible to restore the pre-consensus relationship intact. The intervening period of compromise government and local participation had left a historical deposit which could not be effaced. Consensus, or the memory of it, was now part of the political structure of Spanish America. Events had moved on since the seventeenth century; local oligarchies no longer functioned in the same way as their ancestors; colonial society was now locked into the royal administration. In the process interest groups became more exploitative and saw themselves as part of the imperial elite with a right to share in the gains of empire. Their own demands on Indian labour were not really compatible with the crown's new charges on Indian tax payers in the decades after 1750. There was now competition between exploiters. Spanish America in the late eighteenth century was the scene of irreconcilables. On the American side entrenched interests and expectations of preferment; on the Spanish greater fiscal demands and fewer political concessions. A clash appeared to be inevitable.

    [121] Luis Navarro García, 'El cambio de dinastía en Nueva España', *Anuario de Estudios Americanos*, 36 (1979), pp. 111–68.
    [122] See above, pp. 52–4.

The advance of the Bourbon state, the curb on American participation, and the mounting taxation did not go unchallenged. Resistance to government innovation and abuse of power found expression in protest and rebellion, culminating in revolts in Peru, New Granada, and Venezuela in 1780–1, when the drive for war revenue was at its fiercest. These were not so much popular movements as coalitions of social groups – creoles, mestizos, Indians – which the creoles first led and then, alarmed by violence from below, abandoned. The rebels appealed not to a past Utopia but to a recent reality, when absolutism and tax oppression were unknown. They sent a signal to Spain, demonstrating that the traditional formula of protest, 'Long live the king, down with bad government', was finished, destroyed by the Bourbons themselves whose concept of empire joined king and government in a unitary state. The difference between the old empire and the new was not a simple difference between concord and conflict. Even after the civil wars of the sixteenth century the Spanish bureaucracy had to live with opposition, violence, and assassination. But large-scale rebellions were characteristic of the second empire, not the first, and they were a response to absolutism by those who had known consensus.

Colonial history invariably involves problems of nomenclature. Modernization means different things to rulers and ruled. To colonial societies modernization was likely to signify greater autonomy, not the advance of the imperial state; in these terms the policy of the Bourbons was retrogressive. To the metropolis modernization was personified in a Spanish intendant, a professional bureaucrat, a generator of resources, a collector of revenue. From this standpoint, too, there is a question mark over Bourbon policy. If the new imperialism was politically flawed, did it make economic sense? The policy of compromise which had allowed Spaniards and foreigners to break the rules of trade and navigation responded to two conditions, or weaknesses, long endemic in Spain – lack of a national industry to supply the colonial market, and lack of a navy to defend it. The new policy of *comercio libre* would equally depend for its success on these essentials. Spanish planners seem to have believed that both national industry and maritime power would develop at the same time as, or perhaps as a result of '*comercio libre*.[123] But this did not happen, and the preconditions for the new policy were absent. The result was that in time of peace Spain lost a large part of the colonial

[123] 'Solo un comercio libre y protegedo entre Españoles Europeos, y Americanos, puede restablecer en mis dominios la agricultura, la industria, y la población a su antiguo vigor ...', *Reglamento para el comercio libre, 1778*, p. 1.

market to foreign manufactures, and in time of war was excluded from almost the whole market by foreign sea power. There remained the mining boom, a testament to state planning, but even more to business acumen, and above all to *mitayos* and mine-workers. Here the state could impede as well as promote; from 1796, when war with Britain cut the supply of mercury from Spain, miners suffered heavy lossess. In general the Bourbon state was the heir rather than the creator of colonial wealth.

10

Charles IV and the Crisis of Bourbon Spain

Continuity and Change

The Spain inherited by Charles IV gave few intimations of instability. Spanish imperial power had never been greater. American trade was free and protected, revenues were high, defences secure. In the peninsula agricultural exports from Andalucía, Catalonia and even Castile were earning profits for producers and income for Spain. Public works, the construction industry, textile factories, these and other enterprises were material signs of progress and prosperity. While ministers, architects and planners worked to improve the face of Bourbon Spain, bureaucrats in Madrid, shippers in Cadiz, merchants in Barcelona, all could face the future with confidence in their country and reliance on its resources. Yet the confidence was misplaced and Spaniards were deceived. The decades after 1788 marked the ebb tide of Spanish history, and the eighteenth century went out not in a glow of achievement but a mood of anxiety.

The new king inherited problems as well as power. The reign of Charles III had ended with its two policy objectives – the modernization and aggrandizement of Spain – still unfulfilled. In the following years both were further undermined, the first by the entry of French revolutionary ideas, the second by the invasion of French armies. These extraordinary shocks would have tested any regime. Now they had to be met in worsening economic conditions and by a government unequal to the task. The moderate prosperity experienced in the middle decades of the century was drawing to a close, as population growth, agrarian expansion, and industrial output reached a plateau and began to recede, and the country collapsed into a series of subsistence crises worse than any before. Budget deficits originating in the war of 1779–83 returned to haunt every succeeding administration, to expose the rigid fiscal system and reveal its inability to meet any exceptional demand. The rapid deterioration of Spain in these years was not due primarily to inferior government but was inherent in economic and social conditions, and derived from events beyond the full control of monarchs and ministers. But challenge demands response and government implies responsibility.

At the heart of the old regime was absolute monarchy. Absolutism needed a monarch, not necessarily a great or even a good monarch but a working monarch who could assess advice and reach decisions. The monarch in turn needed a first minister who had worked his way up through the administration and was credible at home and abroad. At this critical juncture Spanish government reverted to a *roi fainéant*, a domineering queen, and an old-fashioned *valido*. Charles IV brought little to the monarchy except a sense of duty and this was nullified by inertia. Badly educated and deprived of experience in government, he was more interested in hunting, carpentry, and collecting clocks than in affairs of state, and at the age of 40 he was still out of touch with the world around him. The weak and vacant benevolence depicted by Goya was also characteristic of his political attitudes, and Godoy recalled how each night the king would ask him, 'What have my subjects been doing today?'[1] He never grew to maturity, remaining infantile in knowledge and judgement, unable to distinguish between supporters and scoundrels. He was not incapable of political decisions, and the notion that 'he effectively abdicated power and placed it in the hands of his wife' was a mistaken one.[2] But María Luisa was invariably at his side when he saw ministers, and the failure of his government to command confidence was due in no small part to the political influence of his strong-willed wife, who was more intelligent, alert, and ambitious than her husband, and who seemed to go out of her way to alienate his subjects.

María Luisa of Parma was a source of scandal in Spain and speculation abroad. Not all of it was justified. Assigned a specific role in the royal family, to produce an heir to the throne and a host of reserves, she had spirit enough to rebel against the conventions of the court but not the discretion to avert suspicion. Observers noted that she dominated her husband from the earliest years of their marriage, a common enough Bourbon experience, but in addition was invariably frank and friendly,

---

[1] Príncipe de la Paz, *Memorias* (*BAE*, 88–9, 2 vols, Madrid, 1956), i, p. 409.
[2] Andrés Muriel, *Historia de Carlos IV* (*BAE*, 114–15, 2 vols, Madrid, 1959), i, p. 136.

especially in male society.[3] Her voluptuous appearance survived almost annual confinements, while her penetrating eyes and imperious carriage announced a woman of character. But it was not a character liked by Spaniards, who believed that she took lovers even before she met Manuel Godoy and was not averse to them thereafter. The subject is popular, the evidence exiguous, but whether the allegations were true or false she did not go out of her way to dispel them or to assuage the adverse publicity. On the contrary, she introduced to court the most controversial of her favourites and made him an ally in government. It was a risky course at a time when monarchy was on trial in France, as the liberal Alcalá Galiano pointed out: 'What was happening in Spain, with the excesses of the queen, the weakness and negligence of the king, and the arrogance of the favourite, showed that royal authority through its own action could become tarnished, diminished and weakened, and inflict more damage on itself than any caused by violent opposition or even outright rebellion.'[4]

Charles IV began his reign by continuing the policy and the ministers he inherited. He retained Floridablanca as first secretary of state, and his government appeared ready to revive the policies of earlier reformers. The *cortes* met under the presidency of Campomanes in September 1789 with an agenda more significant than that of previous Bourbon *cortes*. After recognizing Ferdinand, prince of Asturias, as heir to the throne, the seventy-four procurators were asked to repeal the Salic law of succession introduced by Philip V and designed to exclude females, a request inspired by concern for Spanish traditions, to which they assented without discussion. Proposals to prevent the accumulation of property in entail and the foundation of new entails, and to halt the abandonment of agricultural land occasioned rather more discussion and some difference of opinion; but if these reforms were received without enthusiasm, equally they were not opposed. The *cortes*, of course, did not represent public opinion; in fact their deliberations were held in secret. These proposals were an exercise in royal, not parliamentary, legislation and they emanated from the king, advised by Floridablanca. In the event times were not propitious for assemblies; the recent history of the estates general in France was a disturbing precedent for any monarch. After a few weeks the Spanish *cortes* were brought to a close and no action was taken on the proposals for agrarian change. This

---

[3] James Harris, First Earl of Malmesbury, *Diaries and Correspondence*, ed. Third Earl of Malmesbury (4 vols, London, 1844), I, pp. 53–4.

[4] Antonio Alcalá Galiano, *Memorias* (*Obras escogidas*, BAE, 83–4, 2 vols, Madrid, 1955), I, p. 266.

was the first blow to political continuity and to the programme of Floridablanca. The second was in foreign policy. During 1790 a territorial dispute over Nootka Sound on the Pacific coast of North America brought Spain and Britain to the verge of war, but Floridablanca preferred to negotiate with the traditional enemy rather than invoke the support of revolutionary France. Outside events were already casting their shadow over Spain.

Floridablanca brought to the service of Charles IV the same qualities and limitations he had displayed in serving Charles III, efficiency, seriousness and command of his brief, and there was no one in public life to approach him in status or ability. But he did not suffer opposition and he treated other ministers as subordinates. He was accused of ministerial despotism by his opponents, those remnants from the previous reign who were grouped around the count of Aranda, recently retired as ambassador to France, and who expressed the hostility of aristocrats and military towards *golillas* and bureaucrats. Floridablanca, therefore, had constantly to look over his shoulder towards Aranda and the generals. But his greatest anxiety concerned events in France. The outbreak of the French Revolution horrified Floridablanca and thenceforth conditioned all his policy. This was not a volte-face. Floridablanca was a servant of absolutism; he had always been a conservative rather than a radical reformer, a believer in order as well as progress, and his reaction to the French Revolution was a natural one for a Spanish minister. His political views had no place for disobedience to legitimate authority, and in a letter to Fernán Nuñez, the Spanish ambassador in Paris, he declared his anxiety at events in France: 'It is said that the century of enlightenment has taught man his rights. But it has deprived him of true happiness and contentment and of his personal and family security. In Spain we do not want so much enlightenment nor its consequences – insolence in deeds, words and writings against legitimate powers.'[5]

Revolution and Counter-revolution

Floridablanca decided that at all costs Spain must be preserved from contagion, and he quickly took steps to keep Spaniards ignorant of events in France. Decrees multiplied, many of them duplicating each other in an effort to fill every loophole. In October 1789 he increased the

[5] Quoted by Cayetano Alcázar Molina, 'Ideas políticas de Floridablanca', *Revista de Estudios Políticos*, 53 (1955), p. 53.

number of troops on the Pyrenees frontier. By a rigid press censorship he sought to suppress news from France.[6] To check the entry of French newspapers he ordered in September 1789 stricter vigilance in the ports and on the border, and in December he authorized the post office to inspect and seize suspect packets. An edict of the Inquisition in December 1789 prohibited the introduction of publications from France relative to the Revolution on the grounds that such works sought 'to establish a system of independence of all lawful authority', and to disseminate 'the productions of a new race of philosophers, men of corrupt mind', whose object was 'to build on the ruins of religion and monarchy that imaginery liberty which they wrongly suppose to be granted to all men by nature'.[7] A decree of 1 January forbade the entry or publication of any foreign newspapers or material referring to the revolution in France. On the 6 August 1790 the government prohibited the entry into Spain and export to America of jackets with the name 'liberty' on them, and all goods carrying illustrations of disturbances in France. Another decree of 25 May 1791 prohibited the export from Spain to America of pocket watches and snuff boxes bearing illustrations of a woman in white holding a flag and inscribed *libertad americana*.

When revolutionary literature continued to enter Spain in 1791 Floridablanca mobilized the Inquisition more directly in his service and its officials were stationed at the customs posts to check material from France. He reinforced the cordon of troops on the frontier, and inside Spain he set spies to work to discover subversive talk, especially among the upper classes. On 24 February 1791 a royal edict ordered the suspension of all private Spanish periodicals, and only the official press with its heavily censored news was allowed to continue. In this way fear of propaganda caused the government to suppress political speculation in Spain itself and to encourage the Inquisition to proceed with more vigour against exponents of enlightenment, thus initiating a campaign which severely restricted freedom of thought and eventually, in 1794, affected university teaching. The reaction was also seen in changes in the personnel of the government. In 1790 Cabarrús was denounced to the Inquisition and imprisoned. His friend Jovellanos was banished to write a report on coal mines in Asturias. Campomanes, who contrasted, somewhat theoretically, the necessary abolition of feudalism in France

---

[6] Richard Herr, *The Eighteenth-Century Revolution in Spain*, (Princeton, NJ, 1958), pp. 42–85.
[7] Merry to Leeds, 17 December 1789, Public Record Office, FO 72/15.

with the irrelevance of such measures to Spain, found himself relieved of the presidency of the council of Castile in 1791.[8]

The object of this campaign was to preserve Spain from subversion. But the danger was imaginary. It is true that news from France coincided with great discontent in Spain as the country faced a major economic crisis in 1789, the result of harvest failure in 1788; shortage of grain and the high price of bread caused riots in numerous towns of Old Castile and other regions in early 1789, while Galicia was the scene of violent tax protests in the winter of 1790–1. Agitation was serious enough to cause the government to intervene in the grain market in order to forestall any linkage between economic and political unrest, and to increase the pay of the household guards.[9] But these were traditional bread riots and lacked ideological content. Spain was not fertile ground for revolutionary literature, much less for the French propaganda campaign which was unleashed in these years.[10] The existence of a few encyclopaedists and even of some admiration for the French constitution of 1791 in government and intellectual circles was unrepresentative of the mass of the Spanish people who knew little about events in France and showed even less concern.

For Charles IV, however, the French Revolution was a threat to the Bourbons as well as to Spain. His overriding concern was first to save the throne of his cousin Louix XVI, and then simply to save his life. This was one of the reasons why he kept Floridablanca in office, relying on his experience in diplomacy and his known support for the traditional alliance between Spain and France. But Floridablanca pursued a hard line towards France, not only sealing the frontier but also taking a position on political developments within that country, as though the leadership of the Bourbons in Europe had devolved, 'by a kind of hereditary right', to the Spanish branch of the house of Bourbon.[11] The French government reacted angrily, and it soon became clear that Floridablanca's policy was not only out of touch with the real situation in France but was also endangering the monarchy there. So the policy had to be changed and to signal the change a new minister was appointed. Floridablanca was dismissed on 28 February 1792, victim not

[8] Laura Rodríguez Díaz, *Reforma e Ilustración en la España del siglo XVIII. Pedro Rodríguez de Campomanes* (Madrid, 1975).

[9] Fitzherbert to Leeds, 7 April 1791, 14 April 1791, PRO, FO 72/21. The British embassy concluded that 'the most profound tranquility continues to prevail here, and throughout the country'. Fitzherbert to Leeds, 21 April 1791, PRO, FO 72/21.

[10] Carlos Corona, *Revolución y reacción en el reinado de Carlos IV* (Madrid, 1957), pp. 247–52.

[11] Lord St Helens (Fitzherbert) to Grenville, 22 September 1791, PRO, FO 72/22.

of the *partido aragonés*, nor of the queen's resentment of his censorious-ness, but of his intransigence towards France; in particular Spain's refusal to recognize Louis XVI's oath to the French constitution as valid was thought to place the French royal family in peril.[12] Charles IV, therefore, sacrificed his minister for the sake of his relations. Florida-blanca was at first allowed to retire to his native Murcia; but on 11 July he was surprised at dawn in his house at Hellín by troops who gave him time only to dress; he was then escorted to the fortress of Pamplona where he was confined until April 1794 under investigation for abuse of power and malversation of funds. This was the work of his old enemy, Aranda, still burning with twenty years' resentment, while his freedom he owed to Godoy.

Floridablanca was replaced as first secretary of state by Aranda, another stalwart from the previous reign, another expert on France. The new minister set about reversing his predecessor's policies. The *junta de estado* was abolished and its place taken by a council of state. This was a traditional institution presided over by the king and containing not only ministers but representatives of the privileged classes and was primarily a means of reintroducing the higher aristocracy to the fringes of government; but only to the fringes, for little of consequence was submitted to the restored council.[13] Aranda also relaxed the official Spanish attitude to the French Revolution and moderated the stringent press laws with which the government had sought to protect itself. He argued that hostility towards France was counter-productive, lacked any military sanction, and deprived Spain of diplomatic leverage against Britain. But he failed in his prime task of saving the French monarchy and his indulgent attitude towards the French Revolution irritated the Spanish monarchs, especially when it gained nothing in return. Aranda's position thus became precarious; the queen and Godoy monopolized government patronage and increasingly marginalized the struggling minister. The appeasers were shown to be powerless to halt the course of events in France. The deposition of Louis XVI and the imprisonment of the French royal family in August 1792, together with the military victories of the new republic and its policy of revolutionary expansion, caused Spain to close its ranks once more and the king to try another

---

[12] Muriel, *Historia de Carlos IV*, I, pp. 90–4; Cayetano Alcázar, 'España en 1792: Floridablanca, su derrumbamiento del gobierno y sus procesos de responsabilidad política', *Revista de Estudios Políticos*, 71 (1953), pp. 93–115.

[13] Muriel, *Historia de Carlos IV*, I, pp. 95–6; José Antonio Escudero, *Los orígenes del Consejo de Ministros en España* (2 vols, Madrid, 1979), I, pp. 583–600.

way. He dismissed Aranda on 15 November, and thus finally liquidated the policies and the policy makers of Charles III, in favour of a new regime of his own.

Aranda was replaced by Manuel Godoy, whose rapid rise to power was widely reputed to be due solely to the favour of the queen. But there was more to his appointment than palace intrigue. The British view was that the monarchs had long been grooming Godoy for office, and the failure of appeasement at a time when counter-revolution was in the ascendant gave them the opportunity to appoint him.[14] The fact was that the political system and the politicians of Charles III had been tried and found wanting; neither Floridablanca nor Aranda could deliver the results that Charles IV sought. The time had come to leave the past and seek advisers outside the traditional groupings of *golillas* and *militares*, whose outmoded rivalries destabilized government and encouraged France. The appointment of Godoy, therefore, can be seen as an alternative, a third way. Beyond this, of course, there remained further questions. Why Godoy? And was he qualified? These were the questions Spaniards were asking.

·Godoy, Instant Statesman

Godoy wrote, or dictated, his *Memorias* in exile in Paris, forty years after these events, partly as a record, partly a justification. The version he there gave of his rise to power, though inconsistent with some of the facts, was not entirely contrived. According to this, the monarchs chose Godoy for his very insignificance, in order through him to direct their own policy without restriction.

> It was not my fault, nor my ambition, that Charles IV should decide to have a man whom he could trust as his own creature, whose personal interest would be his own, whose fortune would depend on his own, whose advice and judgement, free from previous links and influences, would be a means to his success and safety in the fearful times then prevailing in Europe. With this idea, entirely his own, he lavished favours on me, endowed me with a settlement from his own funds, raised me to the rank of grandee, linked me with his family, and joined my future to his own.[15]

[14] Jackson to Grenville, 16 November 1792, 4 December 1792, PRO, FO 72/25.
[15] Príncipe de la Paz, *Memorias*, I, p. 54.

Events, not liaisons, dictated the rise of Godoy; events had created a new world which demanded a new policy and a new person, not identified with the past.[16] In particular he was able to launch a new policy towards France: after sixty years of family compact he took Spain to war with its traditional ally, responding to the national mood in a way which Floridablanca and Aranda could not have done without disavowing their past policies.

Godoy was born in Badajoz on 12 May 1767 to a family of provincial nobility of moderate means. His education was no more than adequate, but noble status facilitated his entry to the household guards and this in turn brought him to the notice of the royal family in September 1788 when he was thrown from his horse during escort duty at San Ildefonso. María Luisa saw the accident from her coach and was immediately impressed by the young man of twenty-one, with a fine figure and a cool nerve, who picked himself up and remounted without fuss. A few days later he was summoned to the apartments of the princess of Asturias, who introduced him to her husband and, on no further evidence, launched him on his astonishing career. His new friends, now monarchs from December 1788, introduced him to court life and politics, secured him accelerated promotion in the guards, showered him with honours, titles, and riches, admitted him to the council of state, and appointed him first secretary of state in 1792 at the age of twenty-five.[17] Godoy himself, as he implies in his *Memorias*, appeared to be the passive spectator of these events, but he adapted quickly to the role, assisted by his vanity, immaturity, and insensitivity, and soon he was behaving as one born to distinction. Godoy was no fool, but his mind had few resources and he relied on a crude capacity for assimilation; foreign ambassadors noticed that he held his own in negotiation only by refusing to discuss anything other than his prepared brief.[18] Otherwise he impressed by his good nature and freedom from malice; and if power corrupted, it did not brutalize. When Aranda derided him for his youth, he retorted that he could overcome inexperience by hard work: 'It is true that I am only 26; but I work fourteen hours a day, something which few have done; I sleep four hours and, apart from eating, never stop attending to business.'[19] Youth in itself, of course, was not a disqualification; William Pitt had become prime minister at the age of twenty-four.

---

[16] Carlos Seco Serrano, *Godoy, el hombre y el político* (Madrid, 1978), pp. 29–32.
[17] Corona, *Revolución y reacción*, pp. 269–72; Seco Serrano, *Godoy*, pp. 44–7.
[18] Jackson to Grenville, 4 December 1792, PRO, FO 72/25.
[19] Muriel, *Historia de Carlos IV*, I, p. 204.

Plate 7 *The Family of Charles IV*, by Francisco Goya (reproduced by kind permission of the Museo del Prado, Madrid)

Observers queried rather the lack of political education and experience, the hint of the adventurer and the favourite in Godoy, which threatened to take Spanish government backwards and cast a cloud of suspicion over the new regime. But what was the alternative? Absolutism bred bureaucrats, not politicians. The famous 'team' of Charles III had left no successors, only a long list of mediocrities and a rapid turnover of failures: Gardoqui, Valdés, Varela, Lángara, Campo Alange, Alvarez, Acuña, Llaguno, Caballero, Cevallos, and others equally unmemorable. Godoy was the one living figure in a generation of shadows.

Godoy had no recognizable power base. He was lucky in that his initiation into government and his policy of war with France coincided with an upsurge of Spanish nationalism, and he benefited from popularity with the clergy and the people. He was also the focus of hopeful attention from a group of young intellectuals, Forner, Moratín, Meléndez Valdés, as a possible friend of enlightenment, or at least an improvement on Floridablanca and Aranda.[20] His favour with the royals and control of patronage filled his lobby with *pretendientes* (petitioners or suitors) and gave him a shifting *clientela*, many of them women. 'He gives audiences to women of all descriptions – you meet Princesses, Duchesses, titles and no titles all huddled together in the anteroom lighted with a single lamp.'[21] 'His antichamber is crowded with all that is great and distinguished and beautiful in the kingdom', reported Lady Holland, and she too observed that clients entrusted their cause to the prettiest female of their family, so there was always a queue of these for private audience with the *valido*.[22] But he did not have a social base or a political following and it was the Spanish bureaucracy which enabled him to govern the country and conduct its foreign relations. It was a mutual interest in resolving financial problems that brought Godoy and the bureaucracy together in a number of radical projects for raising revenue, often at the expense of the Church. Otherwise Godoy's only basis of support was his friendship with the king and queen.

The monarchs were unstinting in their favour. They made Godoy a grandee of Spain, the duke of Alcudia, the prince of the Peace; they awarded him with honours and decorations, *comendador mayor* of Santiago, grand order of Charles III, order of the golden fleece; they appointed him field marshal, *generalísimo*, and *almirante*. They gave him

[20] Corona, *Revolución y reacción*, pp. 274–7.
[21] Bute to Grenville, Aranjuez, 26 June 1795, PRO, FO 72/37.
[22] Lady Holland, 24 November 1803, Elizabeth Vassall, Baroness Holland, *The Spanish Journal of Elizabeth Lady Holland*, ed. Earl of Ilchester (London, 1910), p. 118.

wealth to match. In August 1789 the crown ordered the creation of a
fictitious debt of 266,667 reales to provide an annuity for Godoy, who
subsequently, in 1797, transferred it to his mistress, Josefa Tudó.[23] In
1792 he received 'a very large grant of crown lands, producing an annual
income of at least ten thousand pounds sterling ... This instance of
profusion in favour of so obnoxious a person, has naturally occasioned
discontent ...'[24] So the titles accumulated, the honours multiplied, the
wealth increased. Yet this was not indiscriminate favouritism; there was
purpose in this prodigality. The monarchs made Godoy; in the absence
of a suitable first minister they created one, moulding him to their liking,
giving him the titles, wealth, and estates that such a person needed at the
time. The criteria may have been superficial, but they were calculated,
designed to create a model minister, an instant statesman. It is not
surprising that they became protective, even possessive, towards their
creature; he was their hope for the future and they had invested much in
him. They even planned his marriage, making it clear that only the best
was eligible. He seems to have fallen in love about 1796 with Josefa
'Pepita' Tudó, daughter of a modest Cadiz family. The royals had higher
things in mind for him, marriage to one of their own, thus giving him a
further qualification. Godoy allowed himself to be led by the head rather
than the heart and married María Teresa de Borbón, cousin of the king.
But he continued to associate with Pepita Tudó, receiving her into his
home, obtaining for her a title of countess, having two children by her,
and converting her into a kind of official mistress.

With one mistress at home, another – reputedly – in the royal palace,
and women swarming in his ante-room, Godoy was not a model
Spaniard, and in the eyes of most Spaniards not a model statesman. As
the historian Muriel observed, it was the element of sexual influence in
his appointment which caused the greatest outrage: 'What grieved
Spaniards was the origin of the favour shown to Manuel Godoy; it was
due exclusively to the queen's passion.'[25] There was, of course, no actual
proof. Lady Holland made extensive enquiries during her visit to Spain
in 1803–4 and had to conclude: 'It is impossible with truth to ascertain,
what are the ties between him and the Queen. He neglects, has insulted
her, and possessed himself of the King's confidence, independent of her
influence; and yet whenever he is badly pressed by unpopularity or by

[23] Jacques A. Barbier and Herbert S. Klein, 'Revolutionary Wars and Public Finances: the Madrid Treasury, 1784–1807', *Journal of Economic History*, 41 (1981), pp. 331–2.

[24] St Helens to Grenville, 19 April 1792, PRO, FO 72/23.

[25] Muriel, *Historia de Carlos IV*, I, p. 141.

French interference, she supports him effectually . . .'[26] If the queen was
his lover in the years after 1788, this relationship lasted only until his
marriage in 1797, and was followed by a close friendship; he remained
with her during exile, was present at her death bed in Rome, and she
named him her sole heir 'for the many great losses' he had suffered in the
royal service.[27] The king shared in this curious 'Trinity on earth' as she
called it, and both believed that Godoy was a political genius, the saviour
of Spain, their ultimate hope. 'You know I have told you', the queen
wrote to him, 'that I want all the letters and decisions to be composed by
you, because you speak with such force, justice, and propriety, so that
the king is respected and this poor kingdom is not disparaged by
everyone, including its own people.'[28] Her letters to Godoy over ten
years reveal the thoughts not of a lover but of two politically bewildered
monarchs who rely on their minister to see them through the surrounding turmoil: 'Dear Manuel, take no risks and look after yourself, for
there are evil scoundrels about; may you continue always as up to now,
for we have no greater friend than you and no one as loyal and close as
you. María Luisa.'[29]

As loyalty was all, ideas were not really important. Godoy obviously
adhered to conservative political values, with occasional deference to
reformed absolutism, and he saw himself as holding a balance between
extreme monarchy and liberal revolution. His political ideas, however,
like most of his opinions, had an imitative quality: 'If he does not follow
his own ideas, he adopts those of other people with a great facility, and
delivers these with so much clearness and comprehension that it may
soon become more agreeable to do business with him than with more
refined politicians.'[30] He aroused the criticism of conservative clerics and
was reported to the Inquisition for atheism and immorality.[31] But
whatever his behaviour, his beliefs were orthodox enough and free
moreover of that extreme regalism characteristic of the Bourbons. He
was not aggressively anti-papal, if only because he wanted the financial
cooperation of the pope; and, in spite of the king's opposition, he was
instrumental in 1797 in allowing ex-Jesuits to return to their country

[26] Lady Holland, 24 November 1803, *Spanish Journal*, p. 118.
[27] Francisco Martí, *El proceso de El Escorial* (Pamplona, 1965), p. 56.
[28] María Luisa to Godoy, Aranjuez, 25 June 1803, San Ildefonso, 14 August 1806, in Seco
Serrano, *Godoy*, pp. 88, 97.
[29] Quoted by Corona, *Revolución y reacción*, pp. 283–5; see also Carlos Pereyra (ed.), *Cartas
confidenciales de la reina María Luisa y de don Manuel Godoy* (Madrid, 1935).
[30] Jackson to Grenville, 1 January 1793, PRO, FO 72/26.
[31] Muriel, *Historia de Carlos IV*, I, pp. 301–2.

and families. Clerical opposition to Godoy could often be traced to his fiscal policy and to his apparent sympathy towards freedom of thought.[32] He himself claimed that in spite of the revolutionary dangers of the time he sought to keep doors open to modern study and that his rule was never oppressive: 'I harmed no one, not even my own enemies. No victims of mine were shut up in fortresses or castles; there were no prisoners of the state. Even the cells of the Inquisition were empty. Peace reigned in all parts. Wherever a Spaniard wept, I did my best to dry his tears.'[33] This was not entirely true, and intellectuals such as Jovellanos were bitterly disappointed in their hopes. But even the radical Blanco White acknowledge what he called 'the general mildness of Godoy's administration'; and the evidence indicates that he was not a monster of ideological reaction.[34] What, then, was Godoy? A pragmatist? An opportunist? A parody of a prime minister? He was all these things; his regime was a series of ad hoc policies, some of which might appear reactionary, some progressive, the only unity the constant search for money.

Search for money dominated Godoy's American policy. He was shrewd enough to detect the flaw in the policy of Charles III and Gálvez, and to appreciate that their basic mistake lay in trying to put the clock back and deprive Americans of gains already secured: 'It was not feasible to turn back, even though it might have been convenient to do so. People endure with patience the lack of benefits they have not yet enjoyed; but granted that they have acquired them as of right and enjoyed the taste, they are not going to agree to have them taken away.'[35] His own colonial policy involved no structural change, simply higher and higher levels of taxation, culminating in the controversial Consolidation.

Spain between Allies and Enemies

Godoy was expected to deal firmly with France, but his attempt to save the life of Louis XVI without involving Spain in war with her neighbour failed. The Convention resented Spanish interference and rejected it with contempt. Godoy in turn rejected the French demands – mutual

[32] Herr, *The Eighteenth-Century Revolution in Spain*, pp. 348–75.
[33] Príncipe de la Paz, *Memorias*, I, pp. 190–1, 284.
[34] J. M. Blanco White, *Letters from Spain* (2nd edn, London, 1825), p. 316.
[35] Príncipe de la Paz, *Memorias*, I, p. 416.

disarmament except that France was to keep troops near Bayonne – and France declared war on 7 March 1793, encouraged by the weakness of Spain's defences and the disorder of its government. In accepting the inevitability of war Godoy had the Spanish people behind him. Yet the important factor was not what Spain wanted but what France wanted and that too was war, a war to remove another Bourbon from his throne and to carry the revolution to the Spanish people.

The Spanish people, however, did not want the Revolution, and the war of 1793–5 produced one of the most spontaneous war efforts in Spanish history. Priests preached it from their pulpits. Fray Diego de Cádiz hailed it as a 'war of religion'. Gifts of money poured into the government. The rush of volunteers came faster than the government could arm them. The Spanish people's traditional passion for their religion and their monarchy reasserted itself and they rejected the Revolution and all its implications with a militant fervour that caused a revolutionary agent writing at the beginning of 1793 to declare, 'The religious fanaticism of the Spaniards is higher than ever ... The people regard the war as a war of religion.'[36] To the surprise of the Revolutionaries a Spanish army invaded Roussillon in April, a premature success to be sure, but during the rest of 1793 the French army of the Eastern Pyrenees was occupied in repulsing the Spanish invasion.

Revolutionary expansion and imperial ambition made France a difficult neighbour and posed unprecedented problems for Spain. For sixty years the Family Compact had given Spain the appearance of a great power. Whether this was in her best interests was a matter of debate. It could be argued that Spain gained little from the French alliance; it simply tempted her to take short cuts to international power and influence, hoping in 1761 and 1779 to ride to success on the French war machine. A policy of neutrality, even armed neutrality, might have been a better option, enabling her to strengthen her resources while France and Britain exhausted theirs. In 1789–92 the Spanish government had no mind for a French alliance and remained determinedly neutral, even though this meant retreating before Britain over Nootka Sound; neutrality was adopted through aversion to the new France, but especially in Spain's own interests. This was a brief interlude of sanity in Spanish foreign policy, the kind advocated earlier in the century by Macanaz and now – it was claimed – by Floridablanca. The French Revolution destroyed the basis of the old system and brought the

---

[36] P. Vidal, *Histoire de la Révolution française dans le département des Pyrénées-Orientales* (2 vols, Perpignan, 1885), II, pp. 100–1.

Family Compact to an abrupt end. Even so, Spain found it difficult to relinquish familiar ties; by the late eighteenth century the French alliance had become a habit of mind, and it was Bourbon doctrine that war with France across the Pyrenees was too dangerous and too costly to contemplate. Now it was a reality and Spain urgently needed a new ally, even one who was normally the enemy.

Godoy was converted to the idea of an English alliance by the end of December 1792.[37] The execution of the French monarchs on 21 January 1793 convinced him and his masters that there was no other way for Spain and by March the alliance was in place. Relations were uneasy from the beginning. British strategic thinking saw Spain primarily as a naval ally who could put enough frigates to sea to protect her own commerce against France and send a fleet into the Mediterranean to act jointly with a British force and win superiority there.[38] But Godoy would not contemplate sending a Spanish squadron to blockade Toulon until a British squadron arrived, and no argument would move him. The British became impatient at his inability to think and act for himself and the ambassador reported 'his utter unfitness to conduct the affairs of a great country at a crisis like the present'.[39] But Godoy was still learning his job, was not yet in full control of his colleagues, and was not completely confident in the Spanish navy. The real problem was the conviction held by the navy minister Valdés and many other Spaniards that Britain's true aim was to get Spain and France to destroy each other's navies and so to remain undisputable mistress of the seas. The ambassador concluded that the Spaniards were 'infinitely more intractable and difficult to deal with as friends than as enemies'.[40] For their part Spaniards suspected that the British were no different as allies than as enemies. When the two navies did eventually collaborate in taking Toulon in August 1793, Admiral Hood was tactless enough to claim it for Britain alone, a needless provocation, for the French retook it in December.

For the rest of the war the Spanish navy was reluctant to venture beyond coastal patrols or even to leave port and risk defeat, damage and sickness. In the course of 1794 Admiral Lángara refused to relieve the British squadron in the Mediterranean or to engage in direct action with the enemy, and effectively kept his twenty-three ships of the line and

[37] Jackson to Grenville, 1 January 1793, PRO, FO 72/26.
[38] Grenville to St Helens, 8 February 1793, PRO, FO 72/26.
[39] St Helens to Grenville, 10 April 1793, PRO, FO 72/26.
[40] St Helens to Grenville, 29 May 1793, PRO, FO 72/27.

seven frigates out of the range of enemy guns. The other Spanish squadron on the northern coast was equally inert. Spanish naval policy, it is true, was subject to various pressures. After decades of deference to France the navy lacked experience of taking the initiative and attacking the enemy in time of war; it therefore kept to its accustomed role of convoying treasure fleets, protecting merchantmen, patrolling coasts, and otherwise avoiding operations. Meanwhile the suspicion lingered that Britain was trying to push the Spanish navy into action in order to have it eliminated for the future. This made Spain the more determined to come out of the war with its navy intact, a more valuable asset than one stricken by fighting. In 1795 Britain urged Spain to collaborate more closely: the French conquest of Holland and acquisition of extensive naval stores made it more vital than ever to maintain Anglo-Spanish naval superiority; without it Spain could not win the war.[41] British conquests and naval victories in the West Indies and Europe, culminating in Admiral Hotham's victory over the French squadron in the Mediterranean in March 1795, compared glaringly with Spanish naval paralysis, and was the subject of much anti-government comment in Spain.[42] The result was that Spain came out of the war with its navy relatively intact, an important consideration for an imperial power; of a total force of eighty-six ships of the line, forty-five were in commission and ready for sea. But it had not covered itself in glory, and the disposition of many of its officers towards the government was equivocal.

Spain was no more successful by land. This was a war for God, king and country. But the truth was that the Spanish army was not ready for any war. There was no preparation for mobilization, and most regiments were below strength, totalling no more than 56,000 men; volunteers increased this number and, when enthusiasm waned, conscripts added a few more. Yet the Spanish forces were always inferior to the enemy in effective numbers. When the French struck back in Roussillon in April–May 1794 they had 40,000 men against 12,000 on the Catalan front; in October 1794 the French had 50,000 men in Navarre and Guipúzcoa, the Spaniards only 23,000 to defend Pamplona. The Spanish supply system was inadequate to start with and rapidly deteriorated. Troops were badly fed and clothed and in the later stages of the war short of arms; they could not have kept the field but for the supplies convoyed to them by the British navy. Finally, poor generalship helped to lose the war for Spain. The military talents of the higher command fell far short

[41] Grenville to Jackson, 13 February 1795, PRO, FO 72/36.
[42] Jackson to Grenville, 1 April 1795, PRO, FO 72/37.

of what was required and reflected badly on the Spanish aristocracy; on the Roussillon front the generals were unbelievably inert; elsewhere they were simply incompetent. Godoy himself was found wanting, a decorative soldier masquerading as a war minister.

The campaign itself was ineptly fought and the leaders failed to match the prodigious war effort of the Spanish people. The war began with Spanish forces dispersed along the frontier in a thin line. The offensive in Roussillon under the impetuous Ricardos was not strong enough in depth and came to a halt in a fruitless blockade operation. This allowed the French to recover and hit back from April 1794. The Spaniards were repulsed across the Pyrenees and soon a large part of northern Catalonia was in French hands. Madrid was not confident of Catalan allegiance; influenced by past prejudice and overimpressed by republican subversion, the government was reluctant to arm the principality and held back arms and troops in 1793. But the Catalans rose to oppose the enemy troops and defend their homeland. When French victories in November 1794 led to the capitulation of the fortress of Figueres without a shot in its defence and then to the loss of Gerona, defence committees were set up in Barcelona. The Catalans tended to bargain with the government for tax relief against military service and they could not completely overcome their ancient antipathy to Madrid. But in spite of political caution or demagogy, the Catalans voted in January 1795 to raise and pay 20,000 more troops.[43] There were no signs of independence. The French sought to win friends among the Catalans by awakening their resentment of Castilian rule; but the war in fact revived a primitive hatred not of Castilians but of the French, and the patriotism incited by priests and press, together with the pillaging of the French army, nullified republican propaganda. When peace was signed in July 1795 it was the Catalan peasants as well as Spanish troops who were on the offensive in the eastern Pyrenees.

The same was true in the Basque provinces. In July 1794 the French broke into Guipúzcoa and forced San Sebastian to surrender. The governing body of Guipúzcoa, abusing the extensive *fueros* of the Basque provinces, negotiated a separate peace with France.[44] In Madrid these events were thought to be the result of treason by a populace imbued with autonomy and seduced by revolutionary ideas, but in fact

---

[43] Jackson to Grenville, 4 February 1795, PRO, FO 72/36; Ll. M. de Puig i Oliver, 'L'impacte de la Revolució Francesa', in A. Balcells (ed.), *Història de Catalunya*, v (Barcelona, 1978), pp. 103–17.

[44] Described as 'the principal magistrates' of Guipúzcoa in Jackson to Grenville, 13 August 1794, PRO, FO 72/34.

there was no more danger of defection here than in Catalonia. The small group of Basques who dealt with the French were unrepresentative *ilustrados*, men of the Enlightenment. The mass of the people were traditionalists who, led by their priests, rose against the republican invaders and rejected their gratuitous anti-clericalism. Vizcaya armed spontaneously to protect its frontiers; the Guipúzcoans repudiated the treason of their leaders; in Navarre peasants volunteered for military service; all fought loyally for Spain, though Spain left them largely unarmed. The combination of local volunteers and army reinforcements prevented a total collapse of the Spanish front. In mid-1795 Navarre and Catalonia were fighting back vigorously, an unequal struggle perhaps but one which raises the suspicion that the Spanish government sued for peace prematurely.

Attacked by France and divided by *ilustrados*, Spain was also failed by its own ruling class. The high command belonged to the *grupo arandista*, whom Godoy had left in place to avoid trouble. Ricardos was recalled to Madrid; O'Reilly died before he could reach the army; and command was seized in a coup by the conde de la Unión, a young and inexperienced general who combined aristocratic arrogance and incompetence in equal measure. With such commanders, what hope had the popular resistance? By April 1795 the Spanish war effort appeared to have broken, recruits were hard to find, and in Castile at least there appeared to be no will to win. In July the French army pressed forward in Navarre and took Vitoria. At this point Godoy and his colleagues lost their nerve and decided to cut their losses. The peace of Basle brought the war to a conclusion on 22 July 1795; this restored to Spain all the territory lost in the peninsula, and Spain ceded to France the colony of Santo Domingo. It was an acceptable peace, if a unilateral one, and was celebrated at court with illuminations, receptions and the granting of honours. Godoy was rewarded with the title of Principe de la Paz, the 'Prince Duke', a title greater even than that of Olivares.

The events of 1793–5 revealed Spain's utter unpreparedness for total war. Sixty years of the Family Compact had made it inconceivable in Spanish military thinking to fight France; the army therefore was not equipped for this kind of war or this kind of enemy, an eighteenth-century army against a nation in arms, a dynastic cause against a revolutionary struggle. In March 1794 some of these points were made by Aranda in a confrontation with Godoy in the council of state. Aranda argued that the war with France was unjust, impolitic, beyond Spain's resources, and risky to the monarchy, and that it was not in Spain's interest to support the house of Bourbon. The French were fighting for liberty and independence, unlike the Spanish army; their cause was superior to that of Spain.[45] Godoy rejected the argument and appealed to the king to take action against its author. Aranda was immediately dismissed from the council and exiled to Jaén, an abrupt end to an ambiguous career. But Godoy did not provide alternative principles or inspire Spain in a great cause. His identity with the popular nationalism and religion of 1793–5 did not convince all Spaniards, who saw only his rapid rise to power and his inexperience. The war left liberals too in a dilemma, unable to accept the tarnished government of Godoy yet disillusioned with the French Revolution.

Godoy justified the peace of Basle on three grounds: economic difficulties, shortage of recruits, and lack of money. The argument was one of the many ironies of these years. The Spanish economy was always in difficulties. The army was stronger on the eve of peace than it had been at any time during the war. And within a few years Spain was paying France a financial subsidy. For France did not go away after 1795. The British were convinced that peace would be followed by a spurious neutrality in which Spain favoured France, then by alliance with France and war with Britain.[46] This is precisely what happened. Godoy signed the treaty of San Ildefonso with France (18 August 1796), an offensive and defensive alliance against Britain, but also in many respects a capitulation of Spain to France. Spain was to put at the disposal of France an army of 18,000 infantry and 6,000 cavalry, and a fleet of fifteen ships of the line and six frigates. This was a valuable asset to France and gave her a naval power to which she could not aspire on her own. As Edmund Burke observed, Spain became 'the fist of the regicide'. On 5 October 1796 Spain declared war on Britain.

The renewed alliance with France was a catastrophe for Spain. It was defended then – and now – on the grounds that there was no alternative. The principal priority was resistance to Britain, the arch enemy of the Spanish empire; as Spain could not overcome Britain alone, it was necessary to revive the French alliance, which was thus justified in terms of national and imperial interests. There are obvious flaws in the argument. In the first place, Britain did not suddenly cease to be a threat to Spain's overseas interests by making her an enemy instead of an ally. On the contrary, she became an even greater threat, and one which

---

[45] Príncipe de la Paz, *Memorias*, I, pp. 66–82; Muriel, *Historia de Carlos IV*, I, pp. 198–217; Seco Serrano, *Godoy*, pp. 56–61.

[46] Bute to Grenville, 10 September 1795, PRO, FO 72/38.

Franco-Spanish naval power was insufficient to deter. Spain suffered a double blow in February 1797, a decisive naval defeat at Cape St Vincent and in America the loss of Trinidad, disasters which the alliance had been created to avoid. Worse was to come. The British blockade of Cadiz and attack on Spanish shipping effectively severed Spain from her colonies, disrupted trade, and retarded colonial revenue. The war with Britain became one of the most damaging in the history of the Spanish empire.[47] In the second place, the alliance did nothing for the Spanish navy. In fact the obligation to make a fleet available to France was one of the reasons for the final decline of Spanish sea power. There was little point now in building a national navy, as it was virtually commandeered by France under the Treaty of San Ildefonso, a treaty far more specific than the Family Compact had ever been. This deterrent, together with financial cuts, brought to an end almost all activity in Spanish dockyards. Finally, the treaty had the effect of making Spain a satellite of France, her only function to meet greater and more frequent demands from an insatiable ally. Dependence was aggravated by Godoy's own position. There was an element of personal interest in Godoy's alliance with France. For him the treaty of 1796 was a means of assuring his political survival; to remain in office, against enemies waiting to destroy him, meant cultivating foreign friends who would have an interest in maintaining him in power to secure the policy he could deliver. Godoy therefore dealt with the Directory and Napoleon from a position of personal as well as national weakness.

Foreign policy was the Achilles' heel of Godoy's regime. Foreign policy weakened Spain, destabilized the government, divided Spaniard from Spaniard, and encouraged rulers to place personal and factional interests before those of the nation. Above all, foreign policy was ruinously expensive. The years 1793–1808 were years of almost uninterrupted warfare, which stretched financial resources to breaking point and became one of the components of the Spanish crisis.

Reform and Reaction

As Godoy grew in the royal favour, contemplated his rising income, reviewed his estates, counted his titles and medals, discarded the latest threatening letters, and prepared each morning for the fourteen-hour

---

[47] See above, pp. 367–70.

day ahead, he must have asked himself from time to time, How does Spain work? The mechanism started with agriculture. Peasants toiled to subsist and pay their taxes, the privileged to accumulate rents and spend their profits. But after this, how did the economy function? How did Spain pay for its imports? Where did American treasure fit in, and what happened when it stopped? Who paid the army, the navy, the administration and, above all, the court? By 1795 he had learned many of the answers to these questions and believed he could improve on some of them. To mitigate the inferiority inherent in Spain's position after 1796 and redress the balance against France, he grasped at reform, or at least that compromise reformism inherited from Charles III, inspired at the beginning by what Blanco White called 'vague wishes of doing good'.[48]

He began with economic policy, advised no doubt by bureaucrats familiar with previous policy directives. Legislation was published in January 1793 to reduce the monopoly of the guilds in the silk industry and to open it to new forms of labour; this was followed by other measures designed to make the guilds obsolete. Agriculture too engaged the attention of the government. A decree of 24 May 1793, referring back specifically to the edict of 1770 urging distribution of common lands to peasants, ordered that municipal commons in the province of Extremadura be divided by the town councils and distributed to individuals to enclose and farm as they saw fit; in ten years they could earn possession in return for a small rent. This represented a new attempt to overcome the opposition of the rural oligarchy to the plan of Charles III for extending land under cultivation, rendered more urgent by the wartime rise in grain prices, and was consonant with Godoy's support of Jovellanos' *Ley agraria*. A few months after the end of the French war, the government took further steps to diminish economic privilege, abolishing the tax that discriminated between commoners and nobles, the *servicio ordinario y extraordinario*, collected in the provinces of Castile from non-noble farmers. The decision was taken, the decree stated, to promote agriculture and to reward the poorest and most numerous class of people for their loyal service in the war.[49] At the same time Charles IV obtained from the pope permission to end the privilege of exemption from tithes enjoyed by a number of individuals and religious institutions, the proceeds to be used in support of needy priests; they were also to be used to increase royal revenue, for the crown received two-ninths of the tithes of the Church. 'Few actions as

---

[48] Blanco White, *Letters from Spain*, p. 304.
[49] Príncipe de la Paz, *Memorias*, I, p. 175.

just as this', wrote Godoy, 'met greater opposition or caused more displeasure among the upper privileged classes.'[50]

Assistance to national manufactures and small farmers were the policies first marked out by Campomanes and now taken up by Godoy. A decree of 20 December 1796 ended price regulation on all cloths and other manufactures produced in the kingdom. Prices would depend on the market, and the state would intervene only to punish fraud. The government also took steps to extend the work of the Economic Societies and to use rural parish priests to disseminate modern knowledge of farming and manufacture, in a way long advocated by the ministers of Charles III. A letter from Godoy to the bishops of Spain on 24 November 1796 signalled a new start to this policy, announcing the forthcoming publication of a weekly periodical for parish priests that would describe new methods of farming and manufacture. Only in this way, he argued, could the *luces* be spread from the cities to the countryside, because 'in Spain those who till do not read and those who read do not till.'[51] The first number of the periodical, the *Semanario de agricultura y artes dirigido a los párrocos*, appeared on 5 January 1797 and was published without interruption until the French invasion of 1808, carrying translations from contemporary foreign writers, including Arthur Young and Jeremy Bentham, as well as articles by Spaniards.[52] In other ways too Godoy responded to the Enlightenment. Jovellanos owed the creation of his favourite project, the Real Instituto Asturiano in Gijón in 1792, an institute specializing in mathematics, navigation, and mineralogy, to the protection and sympathy of Godoy.[53] And it was Godoy who made possible, in 1795, the publication of Jovellanos' most important work, the *Informe de ley agraria*.

These were the policies which in retrospect Godoy outlined and recommended as his 'programme' in 1798, when he was out of office and anxious to retain the attention of the monarchs:

The agricultural policy which I began should be continued. Military academies and colleges should be established, to restrain unruliness and make soldiers. Factories should be established once

[50] Ibid., i, p. 179.

[51] Ibid., i, p. 205.

[52] F. Díaz Rodríguez, *Prensa agraria en la España de la Ilustración. El Semanario de Agricultura y Artes dirigido a los párrocos (1797-1808)* (Madrid, 1980).

[53] Príncipe de la Paz, *Memorias*, i, pp. 233–4; Herr, *The Eighteenth-Century Revolution in Spain*, pp. 354–5.

more, and then trade will be activated; we do not need anything from abroad and everything they bring us is harmful. The clergy should be reduced to what is appropriate for their function. Class distinctions should be preserved and social hierarchies maintained.[54]

He had evidently picked up a smattering of knowledge from Spanish writers and his own officials, but his basic ideas were crude and his policy derivative. Was he a modernizer and reformist, in the tradition of the previous regime? In the first place, as has been seen, the economic policy of Charles III was 'modern' only in a limited sense and had only a marginal effect on the basic structures of Spanish life. Godoy too adhered to these structures. He was appointed to fulfil the role of the king; as Alcalá Galiano remarked, Godoy was 'the true monarch, and he regarded himself as such'.[55] He was therefore bound to be an absolutist and his reformism to remain within the framework of absolutism. In the second place, the Godoy phase of modernization was too brief to be significant, except as a sign of intentions; for it was soon overtaken by wartime conditions which effectively destroyed any chance of basic change. Third, the most radical projects of Godoy – or of the bureaucracy – derived not so much from reformist objectives as from revenue needs. Thus his conflict with the Basques over *fueros*, and with the clergy over property and taxes, were not so much attacks on privileges in themselves as attempts to remove obstacles to revenue-raising and aspects of the desperate search for income in time of war. When revenue priorities were placed at risk, or when the opposition of traditionalists was too strong, as in the case of military reform, Godoy stepped back and his initiatives came to nothing.

Finally, Godoy's reform programme was flawed by his own venality. Even by the standards of the time his regime was remarkable for its nepotism, and his own family was the first beneficiary of his position. He made his father president of the council of finance. In the army Godoy's brothers Luis and Diego, both members of the household guards, and his uncles José and Juan Alvarez, all became lieutenant generals. His brother-in-law, the marquis of Branciforte, former viceroy of Mexico, was made a captain general with a seat on the council of war. He created many more higher officers than the army needed, simply to exercise patronage, thus encouraging waste and incompetence which in

[54] Quoted by Corona, *Revolución y reacción*, p. 289.
[55] Alcalá Galiano, *Memorias*, I, pp. 317–321.

another capacity it was his duty to eliminate. In the Church he promoted many clerics from his own region of Extremadura with the intention of creating client bishops to counter his clerical critics. He was always followed by a crowd of sycophants and kept his cronies in tow, especially if they had 'a handsome wife or blooming daughter'.[56] The luxury and ostentation of his life did not go well with reformism or reassure his political contemporaries. He was still handicapped by lack of a support base and the persistence of opposition. He was of course opposed by revolutionary extremists such as those revealed in the conspiracy of San Blas in February 1795, when Juan Picornell and his colleagues planned to establish a French-style government and were so easily discovered and dispersed that it was not thought necessary to execute them.[57] Republicanism of this kind was an eccentric fringe of politics. But there was a hard, if small, core of liberals, more radical than the *ilustrados* of Charles III's reign, many of whom had become disillusioned with what they saw in France, and less adventurist than Picornell. The new liberals were more open to French influence and propaganda, and without being republican many of them believed in the sovereignty of the people and the need for a constitution. The measures of repression imposed by Floridablanca were ineffective and did nothing to protect the government of Godoy. It was relatively easy and cheap to acquire French books. 'It was no longer necessary to go in search of them in the capital or main cities. Such quantities were imported from France that sellers went out to offer them in smaller towns and at moderate prices.'[58] According to Godoy himself, sympathizers with the new ideas were to be found among younger lawyers, professors, students, and even members of the upper classes who embraced them from fashion or conviction. Godoy in effect was attempting to claim the middle ground of reform. But while he was being outflanked by radicals, so he was under attack by the conservative opposition grouped around the marquis of Caballero, a second-rate politician but one who had access to the king.

Late in 1797 Godoy reconstructed his government. He decided on one more attempt to win political support among mainstream reformists and reinforced his administration with leading figures of Charles III's reign whom Floridablanca had banished. In November Cabarrús was named ambassador to France. On his advice Godoy recalled Jovellanos

[56] Blanco White, *Letters from Spain*, pp. 323–4.
[57] Herr, *The Eighteenth-Century Revolution in Spain*, pp. 325–7.
[58] Muriel, *Historia de Carlos IV*, I, p. 269.

from Asturias to become secretary of grace and justice, with jurisdiction over ecclesiastical affairs. Jovellanos was reluctant to join the government of Godoy, and first impressions were not reassuring. He found the state of the court in 1797 depressing; invited to lunch by Godoy, he was shocked to see 'on his right side the princess; on his left side Pepita Tudó', a scene which in the eyes of Jovellanos and his like belittled the statesman and his office.[59] He accepted the appointment with misgivings, regarding a *privanza* of this kind as an anachronism. He was joined, also on the recommendation of Cabarrús, by a young official with a reputation for expertise in state finances, Francisco de Saavedra, who was appointed secretary of finance. Finally, Godoy promoted to first place, under himself, in the ministry of foreign affairs Mariano Luis de Urquijo, translator of Voltaire whom Aranda had protected against the Inquisition in 1792. If ever there was an 'enlightened' ministry in Spain, this was it. Four months later, on 28 March 1798, Godoy himself resigned, ostensibly at his own request, and Saavedra was named first secretary in his place, retaining also the ministry of finance. Godoy was subject to a number of pressures at this time, opposition from conservative courtiers led by Caballero, disagreements with Jovellanos and Saavedra, and the temporary petulance of the queen. These were critical days for the royal finances, which faced a deficit of 800 million reales at the beginning of 1798 and were one of the reasons for government changes.[60] But the immediate occasion of Godoy's retirement, as for previous changes among Charles IV's first ministers, was pressure from France. The Directory suspected that their client was backtracking on the alliance, and in particular resented his intrigues with French royalists and émigrés.[61] So they pressed for the dismissal of Cabarrús and Godoy, whose departure indicated abject fear of France in the Spanish court rather than loss of favour by the *valido*.

While Godoy aroused the opposition of traditionalists, his political initiative of 1797–8 left genuine liberals in power. The government of the *ilustrados* was short-lived but it lasted long enough to open a number of ideological scars and to undermine political stability. The ecclesiastical policy of Charles IV contained elements of continuity but also of change.[62] Charles III had already secured crown control over patronage. Now it was used less responsibly. Godoy did not disguise his promotion

[59] Gaspar Melchor de Jovellanos, *Diarios*, *Obras, IV* (*BAE*, 86, Madrid, 1956), p. 11.
[60] Barbier and Klein, 'Revolutionary Wars and Public Finances', p. 333.
[61] Príncipe de la Paz, *Memorias*, I, pp. 248–52; Muriel, *Historia de Carlos IV*, II, pp. 36–9.
[62] On the ecclesiastical policy of the regime see above, pp. 277, 280.

of clients, especially from his native Extremadura; and any prelate raising a critical voice, no matter how pastoral his record, was quickly removed. State control over the Church was not new but, either by design or default, Godoy took it to new lengths, encouraged no doubt by a bureaucracy imbued with regalism.[63] The results could be seen in two directions. First, opposition to papal jurisdiction culminated in the policy of the liberal government of 1797–1800, which ordered marriage cases to be decided in Spain not Rome. This sharpened the division within the Church between those who feared a schism with Rome and those who favoured an extension of episcopal authority and what Jovellanos called 'the restoration to the bishops of the rights they have lost'.[64] Second, a combination of rising defence expenditure and an unyielding tax system brought the day of reckoning near and forced the state to look desperately to the Church for relief. Churchmen were already worried by some of the ideas now in vogue: in 1795 Jovellanos published, with the support of Godoy, his *Informe de ley agraria*, a discussion paper openly hostile to the Church's accumulation of property in mortmain, and an example of the way in which liberal ideas and state interests could come together in active liaison. By decree of 19 September 1798 the reformist government ordered the sale of the property of charitable institutions at public auction; the funds realized were to be deposited in the *vales* redemption fund in return for annual interest at 3 per cent.

Aggressive regalism and radical financial demands disturbed the Church and brought to the surface latent conflict between traditionalists and reformers. The radical cleric, hitherto a rare specimen in Spain, now made his appearance. Juan Antonio Llorente, secretary general of the Inquisition, Bishops Antonio Tavira, Agustín Abad y Lasierra, and the latter's brother Manuel, inquisitor general in 1792, these and others emerged to influence opinion and policy and to publicize works endorsing ecclesiastical reform, while in the universities a new generation of teachers and students disavowed scholasticism and embraced the ideas of Pistoia. The division could be seen within the Inquisition itself, between individual officials of liberal tendencies and those of no compromise; the latter enjoyed a new lease of life after 1791 hunting liberals, Jansenists, French propagandists, and other subversives.

---

[63] William J. Callahan, *Church, Politics, and Society in Spain, 1750-1874* (Cambridge, Mass., 1984), pp. 73–85.

[64] Jovellanos, 'Representación a Carlos IV sobre lo que era el Tribunal de la Inquisición' (1798), *Obras*, V (*BAE*, Madrid, 1956), pp. 333–4.

There was a religious backlash in the 1790s fuelled by the upsurge of revolution and the onset of disaster. As Spain endured successive blows of war, invasion, harvest losses, epidemic disease, and always mal-administration, preachers came into their own, denouncing immorality, corruption, libertinism, and impiety as the great sins of the age, reproaching Spaniards for their faithlessness, and warning of the national apocalypse to come. Spain could be saved only by returning to the true religion, not the religion of the Enlightenment, but the faith and morals found in the Catholic Church.[65]

Traditionalists turned their anger on reformers within the Church itself.[66] The papal bull of 1794 condemning the propositions of the synod of Pistoia was welcomed by some but opposed by others; opponents had their allies in the council of Castile who detained the bull and prevented its publication in Spain. The issue simmered throughout the 1790s and formed the background to a number of incidents between Church and state, as liberals invoked regalist principles in their cause and conservatives defended the institutions and privileges of the traditional Church. The conflict came to a head during the liberal interregnum of 1797–1800, when Urquijo lost no opportunity of provoking clericals and resisting the papacy. Eventually Godoy threw his weight on the side of tradition and the bull was published in 1801, regarded as a great victory against Jansenism by the majority of the Spanish Church and a setback for the radical cause. It was also a setback for consensus. Between 1790 and 1808 the Spanish Church lost the balance imposed on it by Charles III and became subject to acute pressures and divisions, as it too was drawn into the crisis of the old regime.

The first victim of the conservative reaction was Jovellanos. He was dismissed on 24 August 1798 and returned to Asturias, to be replaced in the ministry of grace and justice by Caballero, a leading conservative and clerical. Godoy denied personal responsibility for the dismissal of Jovellanos and his subsequent imprisonment, for which he blamed Caballero.[67] The fact was the monarchs were part of the reaction and they did not like the government with which Godoy had saddled them. Simultaneously Saavedra retired through ill health, though also under a cloud of financial failure, and Urquijo moved up to the office of first secretary of state to begin a political rivalry with Caballero which

[65] Alfredo Martínez Albiach, *Religiosidad hispana y sociedad borbónica* (Burgos, 1969), pp. 53–6.
[66] Herr, *The Eighteenth-Century Revolution in Spain*, pp. 400–30.
[67] Príncipe de la Paz, *Memorias*, I, pp. 258–9.

mirrored that between papalists and regalists, conservatives and progressives. Urquijo lasted two years, presiding with unwarranted confidence over a failing economy, financial crisis, controversy with Rome, and dissension with France, and acquiring a reputation at court as a dangerous innovator. But it was Napoleon's decision which counted and when he indicated that Urquijo was too independent, he was dismissed in December 1800 and, like others before him, sent to prison.[68]

The monarchs now turned back to Godoy. He claimed in his memoirs that Charles IV offered to reappoint him as first secretary of state but he refused to return to that office lest the public conclude that his resignation in 1798 had been a mark of royal disapproval.[69] The years out of office had modified his political position. His reform policies had failed to win the middle ground, and the over-exposure of liberalism in 1797–1800 had polarized positions. Godoy in future adopted a more cautious policy. Although he did not become first secretary – the office went to a relation, Pedro Cevallos – he was if anything more powerful than before. He returned not as minister but as head of government with extraordinary powers, below the monarchs but above the ministers.[70] He was reappointed not only to end two years of misgovernment but also to undertake a military task. Just as he had been dismissed to please France, so one of his first duties on returning was to do something for Napoleon. In 1800 Napoleon began to press Spain to help him subjugate Britain's ally Portugal, another awkward requirement of the Franco-Spanish alliance. Godoy was appointed commander-in-chief and took the field in May 1801 with 60,000 men. The Portuguese capitulated after only three weeks in a war which the Franco-Spanish agreement admitted was 'more important for France than for Spain' and which Spaniards derisively termed 'the War of the Oranges'.[71] A small war, but one which won Godoy further accolades from his royal friends and a hero's welcome at court. He was promoted to the unprecedented rank of Generalísimo and subsequently to Admiral, with the style of *Alteza Serenísima*.

While war and its consequences preoccupied the Spanish government, it was drawing to a close outside the peninsula. Peace between Britain, France, and Spain was concluded at Amiens on 27 March 1802. Spain gained nothing from the French alliance, not even the protection of her empire, and was forced to purchase the restitution of some of the

[68] Muriel, *Historia de Carlos IV*, II, pp. 211–16.
[69] Príncipe de la Paz, *Memorias*, I, pp. 313–14.
[70] Seco Serrano, *Godoy*, p. 120.
[71] Pereyra, *Cartas confidenciales*, p. 388–9.

French losses by the cessation of Trinidad to Britain. Only from Portugal did Spain make a small gain, in the form of Olivenza. Otherwise war simply exposed Spain's military inferiority and exerted its malign influence on her independence, economy, and expenditure.

Enlightened reform was now forgotten in the preoccupation with military modernization. Yet little was accomplished. Attempts to improve officer training through the establishment of military academies were thwarted by cash shortage and ingrained prejudice. Conservative opposition prevented Godoy from introducing new French tactics, and the army's supply system continued to be neglected. Godoy created too many generals and not enough troops. His appointment of numerous higher officers simply to satisfy his favourites was an expensive and corrupt form of patronage. Meanwhile he failed to solve the problem of recruitment. Regulations retaining but restructuring the traditional *sorteo*, reducing exemptions and extending it to the regions, were politically difficult and made worse by Godoy's attempt to derive recruitment from the provincial militia. This meant extending the militia system to the regions and implied a form of conscription among communities which claimed exemption; and it was resisted in 1801 by open rebellion in Valencia and in 1804 by severe rioting in Vizcaya, where the *corregidor* was lucky to escape with his life.[72] Godoy was forced to step back from confrontation with the military and the masses, and the army remained unreformed to face further trials.

The second government of Godoy was a prolonged trial of strength with enemies at home and abroad. Spanish 'neutrality' in 1802-4 was in fact servility to France, allowing her bases, facilities, and transfer of troops to Portugal. When the British ambassador protested at such submission to French demands, Godoy asked, 'How can we refuse?' It was suggested to him that he could concert with Great Britain, but this he refused to consider.[73] He was also warned against spending money on a navy just to give it to France: 'For that matter said he we have no money at all to spend.'[74] Finally, once Britain renewed the war with France, in May 1803, he was warned that treasure shipments were now at risk. 'Great Britain would never allow that the treasure of South America should remain as a reservoir to be drawn upon by Spain and Portugal in favour of France.'[75] Godoy's dilemma was acute but he never

[72] Lady Holland, 25 August 1804, *Spanish Journal*, pp. 167–8.
[73] Frere to Hawkesbury, 3 June 1803, PRO, FO 72/48.
[74] Frere to Hawkesbury, 4 April 1803, PRO, FO 72/48.
[75] Frere to Hawkesbury, 27 December 1803, PRO, FO 72/50.

wavered in his choice, or fear, of France. This enabled Napoleon to exploit his neighbour's timidity and to force Spain to purchase the right to remain neutral through payment of a subsidy of 6 million livres a month to France. To make these payments the Spanish government raised a loan in France at 10 per cent:

> The subsidy paid by this country to France has been regularly acquitted up to the month of May, at the rate of 800,000 dollars per month. A new expedient has since been hit upon for enabling the French government to avail itself of the resources of Spain to an extent which will not be limited by those difficulties which must sooner or later have put a stop to the extraction of specie. A loan of 5 millions of dollars has been negotiated at Paris in favour of this Government, or more properly speaking in favour of that of France, as it is not to be imagined that any part of it will ever find its way into this Country, or be applied to any other purpose than that of the payment of the stipulated tribute.[76]

The Spanish government had manœuvred itself into the weakest of positions. Peninsular defences had not improved since 1793; colonial trade was threatened by Britain; and treasure receipts were drained by France. Napoleon was unwilling to exchange a useful tributary for a burdensome ally; Britain was preparing to force the issue; and Spain had lost the means of deciding its own fate. In October 1804 a British squadron intercepted four Spanish frigates fifty-eight days from the Río de la Plata bound for Cadiz carrying 4.7 million pesos, 1.3 of them for the crown; three were taken and the fourth blew up.[77] On 12 December Spain declared war on Britain, entered a maritime alliance with France on 4 January 1805, and ten months later suffered disaster at Trafalgar.

Godoy still lacked a firm political base and his freedom of action was restricted by his utter dependence on the monarchs. Royal favour became more crucial as opposition gathered strength. Another generation of 'Aragonese', aristocrats and militarists, outraged by the fall of Aranda and rise of Godoy, grouped themselves around the heir to the throne in much the same way as their predecessors had done under Charles III, and formed a *partido fernandista* to legitimate their

---

[76] Frere to Harrowby, 5 July 1804, PRO, FO 72/52.

[77] Michel Morineau, *Incroyables gazettes et fabuleux métaux. Les retours des trésors américains d'après les gazettes hollandaises (XVIᵉ-XVIIIᵉ siècles)* (Cambridge, 1985), p. 437; for an account of this action see Capt. Hammond to Marsden, HMS *Lively*, Spithead, 17 October 1804, PRO, FO 72/53.

opposition to the favourite.[78] The new Aragonese party acted as a focus for the politically discontented and dispossessed, the dukes of Infantado, San Carlos, Sotomayor, the counts of Orgaz, Oñate, and Altamira, and the marquis of Caballero, now minister of war; with these were associated officers in the higher ranks of the army, and conservative clerics alienated by Godoy's attack on their property. Unlike Godoy, the *partido fernandista* had an identifiable social base; it also had the active patronage of the heir to the throne and with that some popularity of a demagogic kind.

The prince of Asturias was a distinct danger to Godoy, who feared a future with Ferdinand as king and the *partido fernandista* in power. María Luisa faced the same prospect; both she and Godoy depended on the life of Charles IV, an awareness which drew them closer together in premonition of the perils ahead. The hostility of Ferdinand, a young man who only knew how 'to resent and to fear', was an amalgam of rancour towards his mother, hatred of the favourite and his special relation with his parents, and a suspicion that he was being excluded from the succession, the whole stirred up by his tutor, canon Juan de Escoiquiz, encouraged by the *fernandistas*, and sharpened by his brief marriage to María Antonia of Naples.[79] In the years 1801–7 Ferdinand became more embittered and more ambitious, seeing Godoy now as a personal enemy allied to his mother, and convinced that they were seeking to rearrange the succession to bypass him in favour of one of the younger *infantes* and even to elevate Godoy to regent.[80] Godoy had already begun to think of his future. One of the reasons for his deference to Napoleon was to secure an ally and an insurance outside Spain. In the course of 1806–7 events concentrated his mind more urgently, and he began to consider the possibility of a principality for himself in a French-ruled Portugal. The idea found expression in the Treaty of Fontainebleau, signed on 27 October 1807 by the Spanish king and the French emperor and designed to secure the conquest of Portugal by France and Spain and so complete the continental blockade against Britain. By this treaty French troops could enter Spain in transit to Portugal. That country would be divided into three parts, one of which, the principality of the Algarve, would be assigned to Godoy.

---

[78] Corona, *Revolución y reacción*, pp. 328–30.

[79] 'El príncipe Fernando no aprendió nunca a amar, sino a recelar y a temer' Príncipe de la Paz, *Memorias*, I, p. 257.

[80] Manuel Izquierdo Hernández, *Antecedentes y comienzos del reinado de Fernando VII* (Madrid, 1963), pp. 166–73; Martí, *El proceso de El Escorial*, pp. 93–115.

He was taking high risks. His French friends could at any time switch sides and adopt an alternative client. In 1807 Napoleon no longer believed that Godoy had a future either in Spain or as prince of the Algarve. So he also cultivated the opposition, the *fernandistas*, taking Ferdinand under his 'protection'. The prince of Asturias responded to Napoleon's overtures and on 16 October 1807 wrote to the emperor in obsequious terms asking for a bride from his family. For an heir to the throne to intrigue with a foreign power was criminal conduct, as Napoleon himself observed. And Ferdinand compounded this political solecism by patronizing a campaign of obscene libels against his mother and Godoy.[81]

While the two factions competed for Napoleon's favour, they ended by convincing him that neither was reliable and only direct intervention would serve his interests. Spanish government was first destabilized from within, then destroyed from without. To pre-empt the alleged regency plans of Godoy, the opposition prepared a decree signed by Ferdinand as king of Castile, the date left blank, to take effect on the death of Charles IV; as king, Ferdinand appointed the duke of Infantado captain general and commander of the armed forces.[82] Godoy penetrated the conspiracy, identified himself as its intended victim, and with María Luisa disclosed it to Charles IV as a plot against the king's life. On 29 October the prince of Asturias was arrested at the Escorial and his papers confiscated. On the following day Charles IV announced that his son had confessed to a plot to dethrone him and on 5 November published Ferdinand's confession: 'My Dear Father, I have committed an offence, I have failed you as king and father; but I have repented . . . and I have denounced the guilty persons.'[83] These were the duke of Infantado and a group of noble malcontents, who were arrested and tried; the council of Castile resisted Godoy's attempt to put the prince of Asturias on trial, and in the event serious charges were not proved against any of the accused, and the trial of the Escorial ended with Godoy banishing them from court. The conspiracy, like many of the incidents of this time, was a tragi-comedy, stage-managed by Godoy, ill rehearsed by the *fernandistas*, and watched by a public bemused at the spectacle of royal government at war with itself in the middle of a great foreign war. As the two factions nursed their self-inflicted wounds, Godoy and the monarchs enjoyed another breathing space, Ferdinand

[81] Martí, *El proceso de El Escorial*, p. 262; Seco Serrano, *Godoy*, pp. 179–80.

[82] Martí, *El proceso de El Escorial*, pp. 167–9.

[83] Ibid., p. 253.

acquired a pseudo popularity, and the nobles prepared a further bid for power. All sides, apparently, were resolved to rule or to ruin Spain.

The Crisis of the Old Regime

The crisis of the old regime was a total crisis embracing the whole of Spain and all its people – state and Church, army and navy, economy and society, the interior and the regions, and eventually the overseas empire. The government of Charles IV aggravated the crisis but did not create it. The roots of political instability lay in the Bourbon past. The growth of absolutism and the expansion of the central state under Charles III had already created tension, drawing a hostile response not only from liberals but also from traditionalists. Tradition was represented by regional and aristocratic interests, the former seen in resistance to conscription, the latter in opposition to ministers and bureaucrats. Privileged sectors perceived themselves as ignored by the absolute state, and they denounced ministerial despotism and the authority of a chief minister over the rest as an erosion of aristocratic rights, whether the minister were Floridablanca or Godoy, and whether his master were Charles III or Charles IV.

While traditionalists deplored absolutism for its innovation, reformists expressed a different disillusion. They saw the Bourbon state abandon early reforms and go into reverse. At the death of Charles III it was clear that all the most discredited institutions of Bourbon Spain were still alive; the *Mesta*, the Inquisition, oligarchic town councils, seigneurial jurisdiction, entails, corporate *fueros*, the whole panoply of privilege was still in place, a fatal inheritance for an inferior king in a time of adversity. The sharp edge of absolutism had been applied only against the Jesuits; and before the Inquisition was unleashed in 1791, it had already been allowed its head against Olavide in 1778. What then was the crucial difference between the reigns of Charles III and Charles IV? Not between a reforming and a reactionary government, but between a strong and a weak government, between one which commanded respect if not support and one which commanded neither respect nor support.

The problems underlying Bourbon government persisted into a time of worsening economic conditions. These were manifested first in demographic adversity.[84] The great epidemics at the end of Charles III's

---

[84] Jordi Nadal, *La población española (siglos XVI a XX)* (3rd edn, Barcelona, 1973), pp. 131–42.

reign, against a background of poor harvests, marked the end of the moderate population growth of the eighteenth century. Growth was now slower and interrupted by further epidemics in the south of Spain. In 1800 yellow fever struck Cadiz and killed about 13 per cent of its 79,000 inhabitants; from there it spread to Seville and Triana, with losses of 19 per cent of the population; in the same epidemic Jerez lost one-third of its people.[85] In 1804 Andalucía was visited by another scourge, cholera, which ravaged the urban populations and had repercussions too in Cartagena and Alicante. The ally of epidemics was malnutrition, and this was related to living standards in town and country.

Rural Spain was divided between an oligarchy of great proprietors and their local satellites on the one hand and a mass of peasants on the other; between great estates undercultivated, undercapitalized, and used primarily as sources of rent, and subsistence agriculture practised by peasants who had no surplus to sell but worked simply to meet their ordinary rent and tax burdens and to pay in addition the dues and tithes demanded by the seigneurial system. The great proprietors exploited their monopoly of land and of grain to force up rents and prices, thus completing the cycle of control and extortion. Rural Spain, therefore, suffered not only from the climate, or the soil, or communications, but from neglect of resources.[86] With underemployment in towns and under-cultivation in the country, it was not land or labour that was lacking. As Jovellanos asked: 'Why in our towns are there so many hands without land, and in the country so much land without hands? If one could only bring them all together, then all, people and land, would be better off.'[87] There was little evidence of any increase in large-scale farming or intensive techniques, only of the extension of traditional farming into less fertile land. Consequently the sale of large quantities of produce at Madrid did little to improve rural resources and purchasing power or to rescue the interior from stagnation. Most of the rewards from the supply trades ended up in the pockets of absentee landlords, tax officials, tithe collectors and entrepreneurs, most of them resident in Madrid. So taxes and rents flowed to the capital, which returned little to rural society.[88]

[85] 'Report from Spain', Gregory to Grenville, 23 October 1800, PRO, FO 72/46.

[86] Josep Fontana Lázaro, *La quiebra de la monarquía absoluta, 1814-1820* (Barcelona, 1971), pp. 48–52, and the same author's 'Formación del mercado nacional y toma de conciencia de la burguesía', *Cambio económico y actitudes políticas en la España del siglo XIX* (Barcelona, 1973), pp. 32–7.

[87] Jovellanos, *Diarios, Obras, III* (*BAE*, 85, Madrid, 1956), p. 291.

[88] David R. Ringrose, *Madrid and the Spanish Economy, 1560-1850* (Berkeley and Los Angeles, Calif., 1983), pp. 316–24.

Even in Catalonia, Spain's model economy, the growth characteristic of the period 1730–90 came to a halt in 1793 when Spain entered a period of twenty years war. In 1793 Catalonia became one of the principal theatres of war, and war, if not the cause of recession, was the blow which shattered Catalan commerce and confidence. The crisis in Catalonia had its origins before 1793 and was caused by saturation of colonial markets for printed cottons, markets which were also targets for English competition. The crisis of 1787, therefore, came at a time of rising production, peace and prosperity; but when stocks in America remained unsold it became necessary to curb production and dismiss workers. Worse was to come: the war with England from 1796 to 1808 paralyzed trade with America and caused serious problems for Catalonia, closure of markets, cut-back in production, unemployment, and in the longer term withdrawal of the commercial bourgeoisie from many economic activities in which they had previously risked their capital.[89] The number of vessels leaving Catalan ports dropped from 105 in 1804 to 1 in 1807.[90] Meanwhile agricultural conditions also worsened amidst wartime shortages, crop failures, and price rises, erupting in full crises of subsistence in 1799 and 1802; and in Catalonia too war and epidemics reduced population growth in the years 1793–1812. The crisis demonstrated to Catalans the limits of enlightened absolutism and the eighteenth-century model, as their economic world collapsed and prosperity receded.

Agrarian conditions in Spain became more critical during the reign of Charles IV, and food supplies more difficult through war-induced inflation.[91] The reign began with a year of food deficiency caused by the severe drought of 1787 and the catastrophic crop of 1788. As usual it was the urban poor who suffered most. In Barcelona there were bread riots in February 1789; in Zamora the hungry and unemployed begged in the streets. In the whole of the Castiles food was scarce and expensive; landowners held back grain to force up prices and merchants emptied the countryside to feed Madrid. The government attempted to alleviate shortages by reorganizing the public granaries, where supplies could be held from years of abundance. Other measures were less convincing, such as the edict in November 1789 commanding all Spaniards and foreigners whose work did not require them to reside in Madrid to quit

---

[89] Josep Maria Fradera, *Indústria i mercat. Les bases comercials de la indústria catalana moderna (1814-1845)* (Barcelona, 1987), pp. 15–26.

[90] Fontana, *Cambio económico y actitudes políticas*, p. 44.

[91] Gonzalo Anes, *La crisis agrarias en la España moderna* (Madrid, 1970), pp. 401–22, 432.

the capital immediately and retire to their respective regions under penalty of 50 ducats. The law was not seriously applied, except perhaps against the French.[92]

But all measures failed in the face of the disastrous harvest of 1803–4, the culmination of a series of bad years and the ultimate expression of a flawed economy. The government took action to stimulate local authorities, to assign welfare funds to the rural poor, to provide work for the unemployed; and it allocated funds from charitable foundations to purchase seed for poor peasants. Yet these initiatives brought little relief to the thousands of victims of starvation, malnutrition and disease in Castile and Andalucía. In Segovia a rapid and unprecedented rise in the price of wheat drew a cry of despair from the deputies of the commons in October 1804; 'In these circumstances', it asked the council of Castile, 'who will be able to subsist? If the rich, the well-off, and the poor spend the principal part of their livelihood on bread, at what price will the *jornalero* obtain any, whose only means is his daily work?'[93] The crisis of 1804 proved conclusively that the basic lack of integration between the interior and the coastal markets was never overcome in the eighteenth century. While wheat prices rose 100 per cent over those of 1799 in the eastern and northern coastal towns, they soared by more than 350 per cent in Old Castile and Extremadura.[94] At the same time absence of a national market deterred Castile from growing a surplus for sale in the periphery and forced the latter to import supplies from abroad.[95]

Inflation added to the problems of the old regime and widened still further the divisions in Spanish society. Inflation was a variable threat, carrying less terror for a landlord than for a labourer, for a producer than for a peon. In rural Spain inflation combined with crop fluctuations and property differences to depress the living standards of the majority of peasants at a time when the privileged sectors could protect their position by raising rents and dues. In the towns industrial workers compared badly with masters and owners who could pass on price rises to the consumer. A journeyman carpenter in the royal palace of Madrid earned 344 maravedis in 1737 and only 365 in 1800; in the same period the wages of a journeyman mason rose from 365 to 405, of a mason's

---

[92] Merry to Leeds, 30 November, 31 December 1789, PRO, FO 72/15, who observed that there were only seven British subjects in Madrid.

[93] Quoted by Anes, *Las crisis agrarias*, p. 409.

[94] Ibid., p. 495.

[95] Fontana, *Cambio económico y actitudes políticas*, p. 23.

labourer from 198 to 286, and of an unskilled labourer from 144 to 173.[96] Price rises were much greater; between 1771–80 and 1796–1800 prices went up from a base of 100 to an index number of 153.2 in New Castile, to 161.1 in Old Castile, 169.1 in Andalucía, and 160.1 in Valencia.[97] Between 1741–5 and 1796–1800 real incomes fell from a base of 100 to 71.7 in Valencia, and to 59 in New Castile.[98] Disadvantaged by the population rise, labourers in New Castile and Valencia lost about three-tenths of their real incomes in 1751–90, and workers in New Castile lost a further tenth in the next decade. The increase of commodity prices by almost 100 per cent in the second half of the eighteenth century while wages were rising less than 20 per cent raised business profits but eroded living standards; accumulation and growth were obtained at a price.

The effect of inflation on the urban upper classes, many of whom derived income from the rural sector, was not especially harmful, and many profited from the crisis. The lag of wages behind prices enabled businessmen, in Catalonia for example, to save and invest. The higher clergy were protected by property and privilege from the ravages of price rises, and in general ecclesiastical incomes kept pace with prices, as did those of all who derived wealth from land. If, in 1793 and other years of war, the Church made large donations to the state, it was an indication of its wealth as well as its patriotism. The servants of the state on the other hand, and all who depended on fixed salaries, were less protected from inflation. Even so, they were not starving. An administrative career was becoming more professionalized; Charles III had raised salaries and paid them regularly, and higher officials were among the chief beneficiaries of the Bourbon state, enjoying large incomes and often more than one appointment.

Social divisions became deeper, stratification more rigid, as the crisis worsened; and in the thinking of most Spaniards social interest took precedence over ideological position. If it is true that 'two Spains' emerged in these years, they were not primarily conservative and liberal Spains but upper class and lower class Spains, and they were expressed in privilege on the one hand and discrimination on the other. Spaniards were not cold-hearted, and disaster excited pity; but they were trapped in the structures of the old regime. When the great reservoir of Lorca in south-east Spain collapsed in 1802, the poor people of the area suffered terrible losses to life and livelihood in the subsequent flood. A public

---

[96] Earl J. Hamilton, *War and Prices in Spain, 1651-1800* (Cambridge, Mass., 1947), pp. 268–71.
[97] Ibid., p. 157.
[98] Ibid., pp. 214–15, 220.

subscription was started and a relief fund established; large sums were subscribed, but two years later the money still remained in Madrid, undistributed among those who were most in need. Yet damages were promptly paid to many proprietors.[99] It did not surprise foreign observers that, in default of redress, social unrest came to be expressed in protest and violence. Food shortages in Madrid in 1803 unleashed a wave of discontent and riot which reached a new level of social antagonism:

> Great failures throughout the Peninsula in corn crops, especially about Seville and in Portugal. Yesterday there were only 4,000 fanegas of wheat in Madrid, and but for a fortunate supply this morning, a ferment would have taken place in the town. Bread is exorbitantly dear; many bakers' shops have been assaulted. Within these 10 days the streets are infested by robbers, who rob, insult, and even strip those they fall upon. In consequence of this numerous patrols on horseback go about the streets soon after the *Angelus*.

The authorities intervened on behalf of law and order:

> Many bakers' shops have been assaulted. A man endeavoured to force the door of the Chief of the Council's house. The streets are infested with numerous bands of robbers; two days ago an order was issued that any person upon applying to the *Corps de gardes* might obtain an escort. Cavalry patrols are in every street. Above 20 gentlemen have been plundered, some even to their shirts; many severely wounded.[100]

Areas sensitive to oppression in the past erupted once more, as did Valencia in 1801. Climatic adversity, crop failures and price rises battered Valencia as much as Castile in the years after 1788. The price of wheat rose to reach a peak in 1795 and remained high thereafter. The successive wars with France and Britain caused further damage to the economy, and by 1800 the silk industry was in the grip of severe depression. Subsistence crises and industrial depression were aggravated by extortionate tax demands by the central government and provoked violence in the city in August and September 1801. Urban fury was

---

[99] Lady Holland, *Spanish Journal*, pp. 42–4.
[100] Lady Holland, 5 September, 13 September 1803, *Spanish Journal*, pp. 85–6, 90–1.

directed at the new system of conscription for the militia imposed by Godoy, while peasant protest focused on the traditional burden of feudal dues, particularly dues payable in produce.[101] As unemployment and vagrancy merged into delinquency and banditry, Valencia showed all the signs of a society in crisis.

Social divisions among Spaniards had political implications and weakened the national will. There was no consensus on behalf of resistance to France or in support of the country's independence, and the government was inhibited by its awareness of social conflict and lack of popular support.

> To do that [resist French demands] with success and glory so much must be renounced on the part of the Court that to hope it is in vain. Besides, the influence which must necessarily be given to the people to excite them to repel the enemy, by letting them have something worth defending, would to this corrupt Minister be infinitely more alarming than ever seeing the enemy lodged in all the forts and garrisons of the kingdom. The expenses of the Court is exactly one-third of the revenue. . . .[102]

Budget priorities lay at the heart of the problem.

The tax structure of the old regime was designed for an ideal state, unencumbered at home, at peace abroad. The onset of famine, plague, and war, any extraordinary emergency, immediately strained resources and the budget dropped into deficit. Three wars in succession, against France in 1793–5, Britain in 1796–1802 and again in 1804–8, cost more than taxes provided, even when these were increased and supplemented; and however hard the treasury tried, it could never keep up with inflation. The average income of the treasury general in Madrid rose from 642 million reales in 1792 to 1,438 in 1795, and remained around 1 million until 1807, an increase achieved mainly through deficit financing, European borrowing, and colonial revenues.[103] Rather than reorganize the tax structure and challenge fiscal privilege, the government preferred to borrow its way out of trouble by successive issues of

[101] José Miguel Palop Ramos, *Hambre y lucha antifeudal. Las crisis de subsistencias en Valencia (siglo XVIII)* (Madrid, 1977), pp. 219–22; Ruiz Torres, 'El País Valenciano en el siglo XVIII', in Roberto Fernández (ed.) *España en el siglo XVIII. Homenaje a Pierre Vilar* (Barcelona, 1985), pp. 247–8.

[102] Lady Holland, 21 September 1803, *Spanish Journal*, p. 97.

[103] Jacques A. Barbier, 'Peninsular Finance and Colonial Trade: the Dilemma of Charles IV's Spain', *JLAS*, 12 (1980), p. 23.

state bonds, the infamous *vales reales*, and so unleashed a monster it could not control. Massive issues of *vales* in 1794–5 and 1799–1800 caused them to depreciate in value and they were being discounted at 25 per cent by 1798, 43 per cent by 1799, 47 per cent by 1803, and 63 per cent in 1808.

The two largest items of the budget were the court and defence. Undeterred by national needs, the royal household continued to absorb large amounts of money in lavish expenditure on palaces, patronage, entertainments, and journeys to the *sitios*, accompanied by arbitrary commandeering of mules, provisions, and quarterings.[104] Defence expenditure began to surge upwards in the war with France in 1793–5; between 1780–2 and 1794–5 military spending tripled the public debt.[105] The state of the treasury in 1797 was critical: international tension forced the government to increase defence allocations, and these in turn depended on the uninterrupted flow of American trade and revenue. Colonial revenue and taxes on colonial trade provided at least 20 per cent of total receipts of Madrid's treasury general in the period 1784– 1805, constituting the 'single, largest ultimate sources of Madrid's income'.[106] The war against Britain, however, immediately placed these sources at risk, for the British navy cut the colonial trade routes and threatened remittances of treasure. Colonial-related input to Madrid's central treasury fell, contributing to the overall decrease of 38 per cent in the treasury's receipts in 1797 from the twelve-year peak of 1795.[107] How could Spain maintain colonial trade, however indirectly, and secure colonial revenue, however eroded? Spanish bureaucrats thought long and hard, gritted their teeth, and turned their backs on three centuries of monopoly. In November 1797 they issued authorization for a neutral trade with America, renewed it in 1801 and again in 1804.[108] But it was not enough.

The war continued, commitments increased, debts mounted. Further expedients were tried. From 1799 the government attempted to impose economies on the administration and demanded of it an annual contribution of 300 million reales; new issues of *vales* were launched, higher import taxes demanded, and still income could not meet

---

[104] Lady Holland, 26 July 1804, *Spanish Journal*, p. 158.

[105] Stanley J. Stein, 'Caribbean Counterpoint: Veracruz vs. Havana. War and Neutral Trade, 1797–1799', in J. Chase (ed.), *Géographie du capital marchand aux Amériques, 1760-1860* (Paris, 1987), p. 25.

[106] Barbier and Klein, 'Revolutionary Wars and Public Finances', p. 328.

[107] Ibid., pp. 328–38.

[108] Barbier, 'Peninsular Finance and Colonial Trade', pp. 31, 36; see above pp. 367–70.

expenditure.[109] It was in this nightmare, when bureaucrats chased an ever-elusive solvency, not for solvency itself but simply to raise further credit, that they took one more despairing decision. Could a government which challenged the colonial monopoly draw back from confrontation with another hallowed interest, the Church itself? In 1798 it decided to lay hands on the Church's property. The Spanish Church was a wealthy institution: its lands alone produced one-quarter of the income generated by agriculture, while its total wealth amounted to between one-sixth and one-fifth of total income in Castile.[110] By decree of 19 September 1798 the government ordered the sale of 'all the real property belonging to hospitals, poor houses, orphanages', other charitable institutions and certain pious foundations; the funds realized were to be deposited in the *vales* redemption fund in return for annual interest at 3 per cent.[111] The measure was designed not for reasons of reform or redistribution but simply to relieve the treasury, defray the mounting debt, and raise public credit, debased by the depreciation of *vales*. In fact the proceeds were not treated as revenue but used to sustain royal credit and with it the crown's capacity to borrow yet more money; it was for this reason that they were assigned to the consolidation fund.[112] To limit the political damage, it was the funds dedicated to social services which were singled out for attack. Between 1798 and 1808 estates to the value of 1,600 million reales, amounting to between one-sixth and one-seventh of ecclesiastical property, were sold, although in some regions such as Andalucía the proportion was higher. The greater part of these lands was acquired not by small farmers but by rich and powerful purchasers, most of them already landowners. For the sake of a partial palliative financial planners worsened the imbalance in the agrarian structure and dealt a heedless blow to the class most dependent upon the welfare services of the Church.

The papacy was curiously complaisant towards Spanish demands, affected perhaps by its own crisis of these years, and on 6 October 1800

[109] Josep Fontana, *Hacienda y estado en la crisis final del antiguo régimen español: 1823-1833* (Madrid, 1973), pp. 37–43.

[110] Pierre Vilar, 'Structures de la société espagnole vers 1750', *Mélanges à la mémoire de Jean Sarrailh* (2 vols, Paris, 1966), ii, pp. 425–47.

[111] Fontana, *La quiebra de la monarquía absoluta*, pp. 152–3; Richard Herr, 'Hacia el derrumbe del Antiguo Régimen: crisis fiscal y desamortización bajo Carlos IV', *Moneda y Crédito*, 118 (1971), pp. 37–100, esp. p. 47.

[112] 'In effect, the old choice between borrowing and attacking privilege vanished, for it had become necessary to attack privilege in order to borrow' Barbier and Klein, 'Revolutionary Wars and Public Finances', p. 333.

Pius VII further conceded an extraordinary *noveno* (ninth) on the tithes, which produced 31 million reales for the government. The Spanish clergy, on the other hand, were outraged. They branded Godoy as a dangerous revolutionary and condemned his government as a despoiler which took their rents and lands and left them in a state of destitution.[113] Worse was to come. On 30 August 1800 a royal decree created the *Caja de consolidación de vales reales*, and demanded of religious houses half of those estates originally granted them by the crown, or half a year's products of each. On 15 October 1805 a more ominous decree, again with the authorization of Pius VII and with very few exemptions, ordered the sale of ecclesiastical estates up to a value of 6.4 million reales a year, which, capitalized at 3 per cent, would give a sale value of 215 millions. 'A good sum, but not one likely to solve a problem as large as that of the Spanish public debt, in view of the fact that the issues of *vales reales* amounted to some 2,000 million reales.'[114] As disamortization failed to deliver the required amounts, the government turned – inevitably – to one more expedient: to meet the costs of war and the French subsidy, the *noveno* and, more significantly, disamortization were extended to the colonies from December 1804, securing further income but at great political cost.

Ordinary taxation, American revenue, disamortization, extension of disamortization to the colonies, one expedient after another had been tried and still the Spanish state teetered on the verge of bankruptcy. On 21 February 1807 the government of Godoy did the unthinkable and published a papal brief authorizing the king of Spain to sell one-seventh of all ecclesiastical property. At the same time the seizure of episcopal *señorios* was decreed, and it was now clear that nothing was immune, neither privilege nor property. The operation was too large and too controversial to take effect before the old regime collapsed upon itself. But disamortization had been launched, not by the liberals but by the Catholic king, not for ideology but for money. The money was an illusion, but it cost Godoy the support of many priests.

The partial expropriation of church property fell far short of covering the government deficit; expenditure was now double the revenue, reaching in 1808 a total public debt of 7,000 million reales, the equivalent of ten years' income. Why then did the government not demand from other classes what it demanded from the clergy? The economy was depressed, it is true, but there was a large untaxed reserve

---

[113] Fontana, *La quiebra de la monarquía absoluta*, pp. 151–8.
[114] Ibid., p. 156.

among the privileged classes. Why was this ignored? The reason was that the government could not escape its own origins; it was not strong enough or independent enough of prevailing society to challenge the basic structures of the old regime. Austerity was alien to the Spanish court, which continued to move around its costly palaces in timeless ritual and even – at Aranjuez – to construct more. The aristocracy was asked for nothing; the government took part of the *diezmos*, but did not lay its hands on seigneurial dues. The propertied classes complained of even a moderate tax on inheritance. The Church was singled out because, in social terms, it was the weakest sector of privilege and unlikely to cause a revolt. Once the barrier had been passed, once the first church properties had been appropriated, disamortization was there to stay. The Church was thus the great loser from the collapse of the old regime and the transition to the new, while the other privileged classes managed to escape relatively unscathed. The Spanish monarchy, conscious of its support bases, was more calculating than Catholic. The irony was not lost on the Church and its supporters: 'The King, they say, makes the Revolution in Spain, the people in France.'[115]

The flaws in the Spanish economy and the tensions in Spanish society were brought to the surface in conspiracy, riot and rebellion; undermined from within, the government was destabilized from without, and Godoy was caught between his enemies, the *partido fernandista* on one side, Napoleon on the other. In the course of 1804–8 Napoleon's policy towards Spain moved from intervention, to dismemberment, to deposition of the Bourbons. By March he believed there were two options, and at the same time as he was negotiating with the Bourbons the cession of the left bank of the Ebro, he was secretly preparing their dethronement. In Spain itself it did not need great insight to see that the French armies were there not to guard the route to Portugal but to occupy the whole peninsula. Godoy was also aware that the French were dispersing Spanish troops in Portugal against his orders to concentrate. In these circumstances it was reasonable to take defensive action against Napoleon and he decided therefore to transfer the court to Aranjuez as a prelude to moving to Andalucía and America. The government was now in disarray. The majority of ministers disagreed with the plans of Godoy; the council of Castile rejected his orders; and the opposition put it about that he planned to seclude the royal family to save his own skin. What did the king intend to do? Godoy was probably right when he said,

---

[115] Lady Holland, *Spanish Journal*, p. 44.

'Charles IV himself did not know.'[116] The opposition, on the other hand, was well prepared.

On the night of 17 March 1808 there was a riot at Aranjuez by a mob of soldiers, peasants, and palace workers. Godoy, whose home had been heavily guarded for years, was suddenly left unprotected; he went into hiding inside a rolled-up carpet in an attic of his house, emerging on 19 March hungry and thirsty to face arrest and maltreatment by the mob. Prince Ferdinand was now making decisions and meting out pardon and punishment.[117] He pardoned Godoy and saved him from the rebels, and when thanked and asked if he were now king he replied, 'No, I am not king yet, but I soon will be.'[118] The fallen favourite was confined to harsh imprisonment and did not see his royal friends again until they all met in France. In Aranjuez there was a new riot, demanding the abdication of Charles IV. Abandoned by his ministers and courtiers and in a state of some shock, Charles abdicated in favour of his son and heir. In Madrid meanwhile the houses of Godoy and his family and friends were attacked and the mob ran riot; a proclamation of the new king restored order, but not before Miguel Cayetano Soler, minister of finance, had been assassinated.[119] On 23 March General Murat entered Madrid at the head of the French forces. On the next day Ferdinand VII, the 'desired one', made a triumphal entry, believing that the French had come to save and sustain him.

Charles IV had been forced to abdicate. But by whom? The *motín de Aranjuez* was not a 'popular' rebellion. It was headed by the prince of Asturias and his partisans, organized by the grandees and titled nobility, implemented by the army and the mob, and activated at the grass roots by the radical count of Montijo improbably disguised as a labourer. The monarchs were convinced that Ferdinand was the author both of the conspiracy of the Escorial and the revolt of Aranjuez, his object to remove Godoy and destroy the king. As the queen subsequently said: 'My son Ferdinand was the head of the conspiracy. The troops were won over by him: it was he who had a light placed in a window of his room to signal the start of the uprising.'[120] But it was not simply a *golpe de estado* to replace one ruler by another. The council of Castile, which was itself a partner to the conspiracy, refused to accept Godoy's orders

[116] Príncipe de la Paz, *Memorias*, II, p. 311.
[117] Francisco Martí Gilabert, *El motín de Aranjuez* (Pamplona, 1972), pp. 174–80.
[118] Príncipe de la Paz, *Memorias*, II, p. 322.
[119] Martí, *El motín de Aranjuez*, pp. 81, 204.
[120] Quoted by Corona, *Revolución y reacción*, p. 365.

and instead proposed changes in the system of government, the convocation of an extraordinary junta of '*vasallos instruidos*'. In other words, the revolt was planned not simply to remove Godoy but to change absolute monarchy into something more constitutional, simultaneously establishing a new monarch and ensuring an aristocratic government as against one of favourites and bureaucrats.

If prince and council were in the movement, so too was the army. The revolt would not have succeeded without the support of the army, 10,000 strong, which Godoy had summoned from Madrid to Aranjuez.[121] The military were opposed to Godoy and all he stood for, and the troops at Aranjuez were won over to the coup without difficulty. This was not a 'liberal' army, any more than the revolt was a precursor of liberal government. The army was dominated by grandees and titled nobles and was linked to the *fernandista* faction. If Aranjuez was a military coup, this meant that it was an aristocratic coup; it had a specific social base among the higher nobility who were determined to remove Godoy and hoped to manipulate an alternative government under Ferdinand VII. The events of March 1808 therefore were an aristocratic reaction.[122] They were also a clerical reaction, supported by elements in the Church who resented Godoy's treatment of ecclesiastical property. Finally, and superficially, the revolt was supported by the *ilustrados*, who had long since lost hope in Godoy and who had nothing to lose, and perhaps something to gain, from the French. One of the first acts of Ferdinand VII was to absolve all those punished for the Escorial conspiracy; to end the exile of the great and the good, Jovellanos, Cabarrús, Urquijo, and others; and to revoke a number of orders of Godoy, such as the sale of church property. These measures were designed to placate vested interests and give an impression of reform totally out of character with Ferdinand and in the event short-lived.

There were no winners at Aranjuez. Godoy was lucky to escape with his life and spent the rest of it in exile. Charles IV and María Luisa abdicated and were sent to France. The *fernandistas* found that they had miscalculated and Napoleon had sent his troops not to rid them of Godoy but to rob them of Ferdinand. He too was sent to France and at Bayonne on 10 May, amidst mutual recriminations, the Spanish Bourbons were forced to abdicate in favour of the emperor's candidate, his brother Joseph Bonaparte. But Napoleon did not win either. At first the Spanish people blamed Godoy for everything. They soon discovered

---

121 Martí, *El motín de Aranjuez*, pp. 140–2.
122 Ibid., pp. 446–50.

that things were not so simple and that Spain had many problems, some of its own making, some from across the Pyrenees. They rose against the French, joined the British, and re-enacted with greater confidence, stronger interests, and eventually more success, the alliance of 1793. These singular events carried a novel message: the monarchy was not inviolate, the form of government not immutable. A bitter struggle between reaction and reform still lay ahead. But the revolt of Aranjuez, for all its limitations, left an indelible mark on Bourbon Spain, signifying the end of one age and the beginning of another.

Few Spaniards regretted the passing of the eighteenth century and few emerged from it without pain. The fifteen years between 1793 and 1808 had been years of disaster and disillusion, during which the old regime embarked on a course of self destruction quickened by external shock. Bourbon monarchy, which Charles III had brought to a peak of proficiency to restore the economy and the power of Spain, collapsed in 1804–8 in a turmoil of agrarian crisis and foreign invasion, unable either to feed or defend its people.

Bibliographical Essay

General

The standard guide to the sources and older literature is Benito Sánchez Alonso, *Fuentes de la historia española e hispanoamericana* (3rd edn, 3 vols, Madrid, 1952), which can be supplemented by the periodical, though not regular, *Indice histórico español* (Barcelona, 1953–), and the bibliographical section of the journal *Hispania*.

There are two distinguished general works on eighteenth-century Spain, each of which contributes to, as well as synthesizes, modern research: Antonio Domínguez Ortiz, *Sociedad y estado en el siglo XVIII español* (Barcelona, 1981), to which should be added the same author's *Hechos y figuras del siglo XVIII español* (Madrid, 1973); and Gonzalo Anes, *El Antiguo Régimen: los Borbones* (Historia de España Alfaguara, 5th edn, Madrid, 1981), to which may be added Gonzalo Anes and others, *España a finales del siglo XVIII* (Tarragona, 1982). W. H. Hargreaves-Mawdsley, *Eighteenth-Century Spain 1700-1788* (London, 1979) is a political and diplomatic narrative, while Philippe Loupès, *L'Espagne de 1780 à 1802* (Paris, 1985), is a general work on the later period, though the reader will find the first two chapters of Raymond Carr, *Spain 1808-1939* (Oxford, 1966) a far more perceptive introduction to the old regime. The eighteenth century is covered by a number of general histories of Spain. Among older works of this kind, that by F. Soldevila, *Historia de España* (2nd edn, 8 vols, Barcelona, 1961–4), volumes v and vi, is still worth consulting. Manuel Tuñón de Lara (ed.), *Historia de España. VII. Centralismo, Ilustración y agonía del Antiguo Régimen (1715-1833)* (ed. Labor, Madrid, 1980), and C. E. Corona Baratech and J. A. Armillas Vicente (eds), *La España de las reformas: hastal el final del reinado de Carlos*

IV in *Historia general de España y América*, Tomo x, vol. 2 (ed. Rialp, Madrid, 1984), are modern works of reference and interpretation. *Mélanges à la mémoire de Jean Sarrailh* (2 vols, Paris, 1966) is a mixture of the useful and the highly specialized.

Regional history has been one of the most fruitful fields of new research in recent decades, and this too is reflected in a number of general works. Among the leaders is Antonio Domínguez Ortiz (ed.), *Historia de Andalucía* (2nd edn, 8 vols, Barcelona, 1984), vols vi and vii of which cover the period 1621–1860; and Antonio Domínguez Ortiz and Francisco Aguilar Piñal, *El Barroco y la Ilustración. Historia de Sevilla: IV*, ed. Francisco Morales Padrón (Seville, 1976). *Historia de la región murciana* (Murcia, 1981), vol. vi is useful for the eighteenth century. Catalonia is rich in such works. J. Nadal Farreras (ed.), *Història de Catalunya*, iv (Barcelona, 1978); A Balcells (ed.), *Història dels Països Catalans*, iii (Barcelona, 1980); and *Actes del Primer Congrés d'Història Moderna de Catalunya* (Barcelona, 1984). The State of the art in the regional history of the eighteenth century is impressively presented in Roberto Fernández (ed.), *España en el siglo XVIII. Homenaje a Pierre Vilar* (Barcelona, 1985), a boon to specialists and students alike.

In welcoming the new, let us not forget the old. The English scholar William Coxe, *Memoirs of the Kings of Spain of the House of Bourbon* (2nd edn, 5 vols, London, 1815) was one of the first historians in Europe to study the eighteenth-century Bourbons, in a work combining robust ideas and original sources.

Economy and Society

The study of economic and social life benefits from a number of narrative sources by contemporary observers, some of which are minor classics of travel literature. In chronological order, Edward Clarke, *Letters concerning the Spanish Nation: Written at Madrid during the years 1760 and 1761* (London, 1763), whose declared hope was to give his reader 'a fresh proof of the happiness which he enjoys in being born a Briton' (p. vi); Antonio Ponz, *Viaje de España* (Madrid, 1773–83); William Dalrymple, *Travels through Spain and Portugal in 1774* (London, 1777); Henry Swinburne, *Travels through Spain in the Years 1775 and 1776* (London, 1779), Joseph Townsend, *A Journey through Spain in the Years 1786 and 1787* (2nd edn, 3 vols, London, 1792), a work of rare observation and research; Arthur Young, *Travels during the Years 1787,*

1788, and 1789 (2 vols, Dublin, 1793), volume I of which is interesting for Catalonia; Jean François Bourgoing, *Tableau de l'Espagne moderne* (4th edn, 3 vols, Paris, 1807), translated as *Modern State of Spain* (4 vols, London, 1808), by a French diplomat well placed to observe; Robert Southey, *Letters written during a Journey in Spain and a Short Residence in Portugal* (3rd edn, 2 vols, London, 1808); Elizabeth Vassall, Baroness Holland, *The Spanish Journal of Elizabeth Lady Holland*, edited by the Earl of Ilchester (London, 1910).

Economic history is perhaps the field which shows most results from the resurgence of research on the eighteenth century in recent decades. Again, there are a number of useful general works, pioneered by Jaime Vicens Vives (ed.), *Historia social y económica de España y América* (2nd edn, 5 vols, Barcelona, 1971), of which see especially Juan Mercader Riba and Antonio Domínguez Ortiz, 'La época del despotismo ilustrado', iv, pp. 1–257. Particular themes and specialist research in the fields of agriculture, manufactures, commerce and colonies, and institutions are well represented in *La Economía española al final del Antiguo Régimen* (4 vols, Madrid, 1982). Jordi Nadal and Gabriel Tortella (eds), *Agricultura, comercio colonial y crecimiento económico en la España contemporánea* (Barcelona, 1974) is a collection of significant and original conference papers. Amidst so much that is new there is still a place for G. N. Desdevises du Dézert, *L'Espagne de l'ancien régime: La société. Les institutions. La richesse et la civilization* (3 vols, Paris, 1897–1904), revised as articles in *Revue Hispanique*, 64 (1925), pp. 225–656; 70 (1927), pp. 1–556; 73 (1928), pp. 1–488.

Regional history has come to maturity with the study of regional economies. Pierre Vilar, *La Catalogne dans l'Espagne moderne* (3 vols, Paris, 1962) for long stood alone but also encouraged by its example. Galicia is now better known thanks to the works of Jaime García-Lombardero, *La agricultura y el estancamiento económico de Galicia en la España del Antiguo Régimen* (Madrid, 1973), and·Pegerto Saavedra, *Economía, política y sociedad en Galicia: la Provincia de Mondoñedo, 1480-1830* (Madrid, 1985). Castile too has much to show. Two works of research and interpretation lead the way: Angel García Sanz, *Desarrollo y crisis del Antiguo Régimen en Castilla la Vieja. Economía y sociedad en tierras de Segovia, 1500-1814* (Madrid, 1977), and Carla Rahn Phillips, *Ciudad Real, 1500-1750: Growth, Crisis, and Readjustment in the Spanish Economy* (Cambridge, Mass., 1979). These have recently been joined by a worthy companion: Alberto Marcos Martín, *Economía, sociedad, pobreza en Castilla: Palencia, 1500-1814* (2 vols, Palencia, 1985). A useful exercise in assessing the 'national income' of Castile is performed by Grupo '75, *La economía del Antiguo Régimen. La "renta nacional" de la Corona de Castilla* (Madrid, 1977).

Population study can begin with Jordi Nadal, *La población española (siglos XVI a XX)* (3rd edn, Barcelona, 1973), and for further analysis of the eighteenth-century censuses continue with Francisco Bustelo, 'Algunas reflexiones sobre la población española de principios del siglo XVIII', *Anales de economía*, 151 (1972), pp. 89–106, and 'La población española en la segunda mitad del siglo XVIII', *Moneda y Crédito*, 123 (1972), pp. 53–104. Vicente Pérez Moreda, *Las crisis de mortalidad en la España interior. Siglos XVI-XIX* (Madrid, 1980) is essential reading for the effects of epidemics and subsistence crises. Examples of regional demography may be found in Josep Iglesias, *El cens del compte de Floridablanca, 1787 (Part de Catalunya)* (2 vols, Barcelona, 1969–70); Antonio Meijide Pardo, *La emigración gallega intrapeninsular en el siglo XVIII* (Madrid, 1960); Mercedes Mauleon, *La población de Bilbao en el siglo XVIII* (Valladolid, 1961).

Agrarian history was transformed with the appearance of Gonzalo Anes, *Las crisis agrarias en la España moderna* (Madrid, 1970), a subject placed in a wider context by the same author's *Economía e Ilustración en la España del siglo XVIII* (Barcelona, 1969). It is also a central feature of the regional studies cited above. On the *Mesta* see Nina Mikun, *La Mesta au XVIIIᵉ Siècle: Etude d'Histoire Sociale et Economique de l'Espagne au XVIIIᵉ Siècle* (Budapest, 1983), and Jean Paul Le Flem, 'El Valle de Alcudia en el siglo XVIII', *Congreso de Historia Rural. Siglo XV al XIX* (Madrid, 1984), pp. 235–49. Bartolomé Clavero, *Mayorazgo. Propiedad feudal en Castilla 1369-1836* (Madrid, 1974) contains chapters on the eighteenth-century attack on entail.

Industry still lacks a framework and has to be studied in a number of dispersed items. James C. La Force Jr, *The Development of the Spanish Textile Industry, 1750-1800* (Berkeley/Los Angeles, Calif., 1965) also glances back at the first half of the century. Agustín González Enciso, *Estado e industria en el siglo XVIII: la fábrica de Guadalajara* (Madrid, 1980) sets the state sector in a wider context than the title implies. The Valencia silk industry has its modern historian in Vicente Martínez Santos, *Cara y cruz de la sedería valenciana (Siglos XVIII-XIX)* (Valencia, 1981). The Catalan cotton industry can be studied in the work of Vilar and that of Nadal and Tortella (eds), mentioned above. On the metallurgical industry see José Alcalá-Zamora y Queipo de Llano, *Historia de una empresa siderúrgica española: Los altos hornos de Liérganes y La Cavada,*

1622-1834 (Santander, 1974), and Juan Helguera Quijada, *La industria metalúrgica experimental en el siglo XVIII: Las Reales Fábricas de San Juan de Alcaraz, 1772-1800* (Valladolid, 1984). For the industrial and other sectors of the Basque economy see E. Fernández de Pinedo, *Crecimento económico y transformaciones sociales del país vasco* (Madrid, 1974).

Trade can be studied in Vilar, and Anes, *Economía e Ilustración*, cited above. Jean O. McLachlan, *Trade and Peace with Old Spain, 1667-1750* (Cambridge, 1940), is important for Anglo-Spanish trade in the earlier part of the century. On the interaction of colonial trade and a regional economy see the interesting and original work of Luis Alonso Alvarez, *Comercio colonial y crisis del Antiguo Régimen en Galicia (1778-1818)* (La Coruña, 1986). David R. Ringrose, *Transportation and Economic Stagnation in Spain, 1750-1850* (Durham, NC, 1970), throws light on the transport bottleneck to trade and the national market, while S. Madrazo, *El sistema de comunicaciones en España, 1750-1850* (2 vols, Madrid, 1984), brings further evidence to the same subject. For acute analysis of the absence of a national market see Josep Fontana, *Cambio económico y actitudes políticas en la España del siglo XIX* (Barcelona, 1973).

The starting point for a study of Spanish society in the eighteenth century is the *catastro* of Ensenada, total figures of which are published by Antonio Matilla Tascón, *La única contribución y el catastro de La Ensenada* (Madrid, 1947); this has been acutely analysed by Pierre Vilar, 'Structures de la société espagnole vers 1750', *Mélanges à la mémoire de Jean Sarrailh*, ii, pp. 425–47. Social structure is comprehensively covered by Domínguez Ortiz, *Sociedad y estado*, who also clarifies seigneurial jurisdiction in *Hechos y figuras*, pp. 1–62. For a particular case study of seigneurial jurisdiction see Departamento de Historia Moderna y Contemporánea, Universidad Autónoma de Madrid, *La economía del Antiguo Régimen. El señorío de Buitrago* (Madrid, 1973). The social consequences of *señorío* in Valencia are considered by José Miguel Palop Ramos, *Hambre y lucha antifeudal. Las crisis de subsistencias en Valencia (siglo XVIII)* (Madrid, 1977). Salvador Moxó, *La incorporación de señoríos en la España del Antiguo Régimen* (Valladolid, 1959) and *La disolución del régimen señorial en España* (Madrid, 1965) outlines the crown's attempts to reclaim *señoríos*.

María Angeles Durán, 'Notas para el estudio de la estructura social de España en el siglo XVIII', in Rosa María Capel Martínez (ed.), *Mujer y sociedad en España 1700-1975* (Madrid, 1982), pp. 15–46, is a useful introduction to social structure. There is as yet little bibliography devoted specifically to the bourgeoisie and the popular sectors, but relevant material can be read in William J. Callahan, *Honor, Commerce and Industry in Eighteenth-Century Spain* (Boston, Mass., 1972) on attitudes to trade and industry; Richard L. Kagan, *Students and Society in Early Modern Spain* (Baltimore, Md, 1974) on social divisions among graduates; and the chapter by Roberto Fernández on the Gloria family of Barcelona in *La Economía española al final del Antiguo Régimen*, II, pp. 1–131. Prices and wages in an age of inflation are measured by Earl J. Hamilton, *War and Prices in Spain, 1651-1800* (Cambridge, Mass., 1947). On vagrancy see the interesting study by Rosa María Pérez Estévez, *El problema de los vagos en la España del siglo XVIII* (Madrid, 1976). Much can be learned about economic and social structure by a reading of David R. Ringrose, *Madrid and the Spanish Economy, 1560-1850* (Berkeley/Los Angeles, Calif., 1983), a study of city-country interaction. Jesús Maiso González and Rosa María Blasco Martínez, *Las estructuras de Zaragoza en el primer tercio del siglo XVIII* (Zaragoza, 1984) dissect the early eighteenth-century society of Zaragoza, 'capital of Aragon'.

The Early Bourbons

Vicente Bacallar y Sanna, marqués de San Felipe, *Comentarios de la guerra de España e historia de su rey Felipe V, el animoso*, ed. C. Seco Serrano (*BAE*, 99, Madrid, 1957) is the principal contemporary narrative source for the period of the war of succession and its aftermath, and can be supplemented by J. del Campo-Raso, *Memorias políticas y militares para servir de continuación a los Comentarios del marqués de San Felipe*, in the same volume. N. de Jesús Belando, *Historia civil de España, sucesos de la guerra y Tratados de paz desde el año mil setecientos hasta el de mil setecientos treinta y tres* (3 vols, Madrid, 1740–4), is a 'Spanish' point of view, hostile to foreigners and to Jesuits. The *Mémoires* of Saint-Simon are a rich source of information on politics and personalities, always interesting though not always reliable; there is a convenient English edition, *Historical Memoirs of the Duc de Saint-Simon*, edited and translated by Lucy Norton (3 vols, London, 1967–72). José del Campillo y Cossío had a lively pen as well as policy: *Lo que hay de más y de menos en España*, ed. Antonio Elorza (Madrid, 1969), and *Nuevo sistema de gobierno económico para la América* (Madrid, 1789). Alfred Baudrillart, *Philippe V et la cour de France* (5 vols, Paris, 1890–1900) is a classic history of the reign of Philip V, whose extensive quotations from the archives make it a source as well as a narrative.

The emergence of Spain from the depression of the seventeenth century can be studied in Henry Kamen, *Spain in the Later Seventeenth Century, 1665-1700* (London, 1980); the same author has also written the best, indeed virtually the only, comprehensive history of the war of succession, *The War of Succession in Spain 1700-15* (London, 1969). David Francis, *The First Peninsular War 1702-1713* (London, 1975) is a good military narrative with emphasis on British participation. The introductory study by Carlos Seco Serrano to San Felipe, *Comentarios*, provides a useful framework and discussion of significant themes. On the war in the south-east see Antonio Rodríguez Villa, *Don Diego Hurtado de Mendoza y Sandoval, conde de la Corzana (1650-1720)* (Madrid, 1907); Joaquín Báguena, *El cardenal Belluga. Su vida y su obra* (Murcia, 1935); Pedro Voltes Bou, *El Archiduque Carlos, rey de los catalanes* (Barcelona, 1953). The war in Catalonia has a large bibliography, of which the following are the key items: Juan Mercader Riba, 'La ordenación de Cataluña por Felipe V: La Nueva Planta', *Hispania*, 43 (1951), pp. 257-366, *Els capitans generals* (Barcelona, 1957), and *Felip V i Catalunya* (Barcelona, 1968); Víctor Ferro, *El dret públic català. Les institucions a Catalunya fins al Decret de Nova Planta* (Barcelona, 1987). On the Nueva Planta see also Joaquín Nadal Farreras, *La introducción del Catastro en Gerona* (Barcelona, 1971). The work of Ferran Soldevila, *Història de Catalunya* (3 vols, Barcelona, 1934–5), vol. II, is a fruitful source of data and judgement on the events of this period. On propaganda during the war of succession see María Teresa Pérez Picazo, *La publicística española en la Guerra de Sucesión* (2 vols, Madrid, 1966).

The political history of the time is only partially covered as yet. Edward Armstrong, *Elisabeth Farnese 'The Termagant of Spain'* (London, 1892) is still useful. On the political opposition there is a more modern study, Teofanes Egido López, *Opinión pública y oposición al poder en la España del siglo XVIII (1713-1759)* (Valladolid, 1971); see the same author's *Prensa clandestina española del siglo XVIII: "El Duende Crítico"* (Valladolid, 1968). The brief life and reign of Luis I is the subject of Alfonso Danvila, *El reinado relámpago. Luis I y Luisa Isabel de Orléans (1707-1742)* (Madrid, 1952). Melchor de Macanaz receives an interesting political biography from Carmen Martín Gaite, *Macanaz, otro paciente de la Inquisición* (2nd edn, Madrid, 1975). José Patiño has attracted interest, though there are still gaps in knowledge of his life and policy. The following deal with particular aspects: Antonio Rodríguez Villa, *Patiño y Campillo. Reseña histórico-biográfica de estos dos ministros de Felipe V* (Madrid, 1882); Antonio Béthencourt Massieu, *Patiño en la política internacional de Felipe V* (Valladolid, 1954); Julián B. Ruiz Rivera, 'Patiño y la reforma del Consulado de Cádiz en 1729', *Temas Americanistas*, 5 (1985), pp. 16–21. Andrés V. Castillo, *Spanish Mercantilism. Gerónimo de Uztáriz, Economist* (New York, 1930), gives a useful account of his subject. On Campillo there is less: see Miguel Artola, 'Campillo y las reformas de Carlos III', *Revista de Indias*, 115–18 (1969), pp. 685–714, and José Martínez Cardós, 'Don José del Campillo y Cossío', *Revista de Indias*, 119–22 (1970), pp. 525–42.

The formation of early Bourbon government has been studied by Henry Kamen in 'El establecimiento de los Intendentes en la administración española', *Hispania*, 24, 95 (1964), pp. 368–95, and 'Melchor de Macanaz and the Foundations of Bourbon Power in Spain', *English Historical Review*, 80, 317 (1965), pp. 699–716. José Antonio Escudero, *Los secretarios de Estado y del Despacho, 1474-1724* (4 vols, Madrid, 1969) is useful for the transition from Habsburg to Bourbon government, while the same author's *Los orígenes del Consejo de Ministros en España* (2 vols, Madrid, 1979), ranges widely over the administrative history of the eighteenth century. Janine Fayard, *Les membres du Conseil de Castille à l'époque modern (1621-1746)* (Geneva/Paris, 1979) and the same author's 'La tentative de réforme du Conseil de Castille sous le regne de Philippe V (1713–1717)', *Mélanges de la Casa de Velázquez*, 2 (1966), ppl. 259–81, indicate the social structure and political role of a key council. Gildas Bernard, *Le secrétariat d'état et le conseil espagnol des Indes (1700-1808)* (Geneva/Paris, 1972) places Indies administration in its central context. Benjamín González Alonso, *El corregidor castellano (1348-1808)* (Madrid, 1970) describes the development of an important local office. On the navy José P. Merino Navarro, *La Armada Española en el siglo XVIII* (Madrid, 1981) is a useful though not always consistent source of information, and can be supplemented by the classic C. Fernández Duro, *Armada española* (9 vols, Madrid, 1885–1903). John Robert McNeill, *Atlantic Empires of France and Spain. Louisburg and Havana, 1700-1763* (Chapel Hill, NC, 1985) places naval history in a wider context.

On the international dimension of Spanish interests see Peggy K. Liss, *Atlantic Empires. The Network of Trade and Revolution, 1713-1826* (Baltimore, Md., 1983). The foreign policy of Philip V and Farnese can be studied in Béthencourt, cited above, and José María Jover Zamora, *Política mediterránea y política atlántica en la España de Feijóo* (Oviedo, 1956). Colonial war is superbly treated by Richard Pares, *War and Trade in the West Indies 1739-1763* (Oxford, 1936 , new impression, London,

1963), who illuminates Spanish as well as English policy. On the Gibraltar factor see María Dolores Gómez Molleda, *Gibraltar. Una contienda diplomática en el reinado de Felipe V* (Madrid, 1953). On the colonial policy of the early Bourbons Geoffrey J. Walker, *Spanish Politics and Imperial Trade, 1700-1789* (London, 1979) is indispensable, and the older work of Roland D. Hussey, *The Caracas Company 1728-1784* (Cambridge, Mass., 1934) is still of value; see also Vicente de Amezuga Aresti, *Hombres de la Compañía Guipuzcoana* (Caracas, 1963).

For the study of Ferdinand VI's reign we have useful sources in Francisco de Rávago, *Correspondencia reservada e inédita del P. Francisco de Rávago, confesor de Fernando VI*, ed. C. Pérez Bustamante (Madrid, 1943); and Sir Benjamin Keene, *The Private Correspondence of Sir Benjamin Keene, KB*, ed. Sir Richard Lodge (Cambridge, 1933), a shrewd commentary on life and politics at court by the English ambassador. Antonio Rodríguez Villa, *Don Cenón de Somodevilla, marqués de La Ensenada* (Madrid, 1878) publishes basic policy documents as well as narrating the political life of Ensenada. *La Epoca de Fernando VI. Ponencias leidos en el coloquio conmemorativo de los 25 años de la fundación de la Cátedra Feijóo* (Oviedo, 1981), is a useful collection of papers, of which those by Olaechea, Mateos Dorado, and Saugnieux may be mentioned. The interaction of international, imperial and religious interests are well studied by Guillermo Kratz, *El Tratado hispano-portugués de límites de 1750 y sus consecuencias* (Rome, 1954). The American policy of Ensenada is described by Lucio Mijares Pérez, 'Programa político para América del marqués de La Ensenada', *Revista de Historia de América*, 81 (1976), pp. 82–130. On relations between Spain and Rome see Rafael Olaechea, *Las relaciones hispano-romanas en la segunda mitad del XVIII. La Agencia de Preces* (2 vols, Zaragoza, 1965).

Charles III and the Bourbon State

The reign of Charles III was soon identified as the peak of Bourbon Spain and became a focus of historiography. Older historians retain their value as sources of information and documentation: Conde de Fernán Núñez, *Vida de Carlos III*, eds. A. Morel-Fatio and A. Paz y Melia (2 vols, Madrid, 1898); Antonio Ferrer del Río, *Historia del reinado de Carlos III en España* (4 vols, Madrid, 1856); Manuel Danvila y Collado, *El reinado de Carlos III* (6 vols, Madrid, 1890–6); François Rousseau, *Règne de Charles III d'Espagne (1759-1788)* (2 vols, Paris, 1907). Anthony H. Hull,

Charles III and the Revival of Spain (Washington, DC, 1980) is the latest in this tradition, adding new data and bibliography. A number of sources have been published, of which the works of Campomanes, Floridablanca, and Jovellanos are indispensable and reasonably accessible. Pedro Rodríguez de Campomanes, *Dictamen fiscal de expulsión de los Jesuitas de España (1766-1767)*, eds Jorge Cejudo and Teófanes Egido (Madrid, 1977), and *Discurso sobre la educación popular*, ed. F. Aguilar Piñal (Madrid, 1978) are good examples of the writings of the leading *ilustrado*, to which can be added his *Epistolario. Tomo I (1747-1777)*, eds Miguel Aviles Fernández and Jorge Cejudo López (Madrid, 1983), and *Cartas entre Campomanes y Jovellanos*, ed. Ramón Jordan de Urries (Madrid, 1975); the *Cartas político-económicas*, ed. A. Rodríguez Villa (Madrid, 1878) were wrongly attributed to Campomanes and have now been identified as written by León de Arroyal (*Cartas político-económicas*, ed. José Caso González (Madrid, 1971)). Conde de Floridablanca, *Obras originales del conde de Floridablanca, y escritos referentes a su persona*, ed. A. Ferrer del Río (*BAE*, 59, Madrid, 1952) contains among other things the '*Instrucción reservada*' for the *Junta de Estado*. There are various editions of works by Jovellanos, of which the following is the most convenient: Gaspar Melchor de Jovellanos, *Obras de Jovellanos*, Tomos ii, iii, iv, v (*BAE*, 50, 85, 86, 87, Madrid, 1952, 1956).

The political history of the reign can be studied in Vicente Rodríguez Casado, *La política y los políticos en el reinado de Carlos III* (Madrid, 1962), as an example of past controversies. There are a number of interesting works on Campomanes: Felipe Alvarez Requejo, *El Conde de Campomanes: su obra histórica* (Oviedo, 1954); Ricardo Krebs Wilckens, *El pensamiento histórico, político, y económico del Conde de Campomanes* (Santiago, 1960); M. Bustos Rodríguez, *El pensamiento socio-económico de Campomanes* (Madrid, 1982); and Laura Rodríguez Díaz, *Reforma e Ilustración en la España del siglo XVIII. Pedro Rodríguez de Campomanes* (Madrid, 1975), important for the history of the time as well as for Campomanes. The *motín de Esquilache* has a large bibliography, from which the following may be selected: Constancio Eguía Ruiz, *Los jesuítas y el motín de Esquilache* (Madrid, 1947); J. Navarro Latorre, *Hace doscientos años. Estado actual de los problemas históricas del motín de Esquilache* (Madrid, 1966); Pierre Vilar, 'El motín de Esquilache y la crisis del Antiguo Régimen', *Revista de Occidente* 107 (1972), pp. 200–47; Gonzalo Anes, 'Antecedentes próximos del motín contra Esquilache', *Moneda y Crédito*, 128 (1974), pp. 219–24; Laura Rodríguez, 'The Spanish Riots of 1766', *Past and Present*, 59 (1973), pp. 117–46, and 'The

Riots of 1766 in Madrid', *European Studies Review*, 3, 3 (1973), pp. 223–42. Rafael Olaechea, *El conde de Aranda y el "partido aragonés"* (Zaragoza, 1969) identifies the political 'opposition'; for further work on Aranda see José A. Ferrer Benimeli, *El Conde de Aranda y el partido aragonés* (Zaragoza, 1969). Cayetano Alcázar Molina, *El Conde de Floridablanca. Su vida y su obra* Murcia, 1934), deals with the first phase of Floridablanca's career, as fiscal of the council of Castile; see also *El testamento político del conde de Floridablanca* (Madrid, 1962), documents introduced by Antonio Rumeu de Armas. María Rosa Saurín de la Iglesia, *Reforma y reacción en la Galicia del siglo XVIII (1764-1798)* (La Coruña, 1983) studies the impact of the regime at a regional level.

Institutions are studied by a number of authors, including Bernard, cited above; Escudero, *Los orígenes del Consejo de Ministros en España*; Jacques Barbier, 'The Culmination of the Bourbon Reforms, 1787–1792', *HAHR*, 57 (1977), pp. 51–68; Javier Guillamón Alvarez, *La reformas de la administración local en el reinado de Carlos III* (Madrid, 1980), and 'Disposiciones sobre policía de pobres: establecimiento de diputaciones de barrio en el reinado de Carles III', *Cuadernos de Historia Moderna y Contemporánea* 1 (1980), pp. 31–50. Aspects of military policy are clarified by Bibiano Torres Ramírez, *Alejandro O'Reilly en las Indias* (Seville, 1969).

The foreign policy of the reign begins with the third Family Compact: Vicente Palacio Atard, *El tercer Pacto de Familia* (Madrid, 1945). Octavio Gil Munilla, *Malvinas. El conflicto anglo-español de 1770* (Seville, 1948) and *El Río de la Plata en la política internacional. Génesis del virreinato* (Seville, 1949), cover a number of imperial and international issues, while Allan J. Kuethe, *Cuba, 1753-1815. Crown, Military, and Society* (Knoxville, Tenn., 1986), clarifies the American dimension of the war of 1779–83. On Campomanes's thinking on foreign policy issues see María Victoria López-Cordón Cortejo, 'Relaciones internacionales y crisis revolucionaria en el pensamiento de Campomanes', *Cuadernos de Historia Moderna y Contemporánea*, 1 (1980), pp. 51–82. Jacques Barbier and Herbert S. Klein, 'Las prioridades de un monarca ilustrado: el gasto público bajo el reinado de Carlos III', *Revista de historia económica*, 3, 3 (1985), pp. 473–95, provide a valuable service in estimating the defence budget.

Relations with the Church were one of the prime preoccupations of the Bourbons, not least of Charles III. On the eighteenth-century Church see Ricardo García Villoslada (ed.), *Historia de la iglesia en España*. vol. IV, *La iglesia en la España de los siglos XVII y XVIII* (Madrid,

1979), for a general account, and for the clerical population 'Demografía eclesiástica', *Diccionario de historia eclesiástica de España* (4 vols, Madrid, 1972–5), II, pp. 730–5; further data may be drawn from Juan Sáez Marín, *Datos sobre la iglesia española contemporánea (1768-1868)* (Madrid, 1975). William J. Callahan, *Church, Politics, and Society in Spain, 1750-1874* (Cambridge, Mass., 1984) is authoritative on all aspects of the subject, to which his chapter, 'The Spanish Church', in W. J. Callahan and D. C. Higgs (eds), *Church and Society in Catholic Europe in the Eighteenth Century* (Cambridge, 1979), may regarded as an introduction. Christian Hermann, *L'Eglise d'Espagne sous le patronage royal (1476-1834)* (Madrid, 1988) studies anew Church-state relations under the royal patronage, including ecclesiastical, political, financial and career aspects. Church property and its implications are assessed in Maximiliano Barrio González, *Estudio socioeconómico de la iglesia de Segovia en el siglo XVIII* (Segovia, 1982). N. M. Farris, *Crown and Clergy in Colonial Mexico 1759-1821. The Crisis of Ecclesiastical Privilege* (London, 1968) throws light on clerical privilege in the peninsula as well as in Mexico. State interest in the education of priests and other themes are studied in Francisco Martín Hernández and José Martín Hernández, *Los seminarios españoles en la época de la Ilustración* (Madrid, 1973). There are a number of case studies of Bourbon churchmen, of which the following may be cited: Luis Sierra Nava-Lasa, *El Cardenal Lorenzana y la Ilustración* (Madrid, 1975); Francesc Tort Mitjans, *El Obispo de Barcelona: Josep Climent i Avinent, 1706-1781* (Barcelona, 1978); Joël Saugnieux, *Un prélat éclairé: Don Antonio Tavira y Almazán (1737-1807)* (Toulouse, 1970). Religion at the popular level is perceptively studied by William A. Christian, Jr, *Local Religion in Sixteenth-Century Spain* (Princeton, NJ, 1981), a model for later periods, and by Alfredo Martínez Albiach, *Religiosidad hispana y sociedad borbónica* (Burgos, 1969). On Spanish jansenism the student may begin with Emile Appolis, *Les jansénistes espagnols* (Bordeaux, 1966) and María G. Tomsich, *El jansenismo en España* (Madrid, 1972), and supplement these with the various works by Joël Saugnieux, *Le jansénisme espagnol du XVIIIᵉ siècle: Ses composantes et ses sources* (Oviedo, 1975), *Les jansénistes et le renouveau de la prédication dans l'Espagne de la seconde moitié du XVIIIᵉ siècle* (Lyons, 1976), and Joël Saugnieux (ed.), *Foi et lumières dans l'Espagne du XVIIIᵉ siècle* (Paris, 1985). On the European context of Spanish religious history, Owen Chadwick, *The Popes and European Revolution* (Oxford, 1981) is a reliable guide. The Jesuits have their historian in Antonio Astraín, *Historia de la Compañía de Jesús en la Asistencia de España* (8 vols, Madrid, 1902–25) of which vol. VII is relevant for the eighteenth century. The report by Campomanes, *Dictamen fiscal*, cited above, gives a partial view of the role of the Jesuits in the political life of Spain; the editors provide a useful introduction.

The Enlightenment in Spain

Richard Herr, *The Eighteenth-Century Revolution in Spain* (Princeton, NJ, 1958) is a comprehensive and scholarly study of the Enlightenment in Spain, placing it firmly in its political, religious and economic context. Jean Sarrailh, *L'Espagne éclairée de la seconde moitié du XVIIIᵉ siècle* (Paris, 1954) is a modern classic, a rich source of facts and ideas. Spanish political thought of the period is interpreted by Luis Sánchez Agesta, *El pensamiento político del despotismo ilustrado* (Madrid, 1953). Ramón Otero Pedrayo, *El padre Feijóo. Su vida, doctrina e influencia* (Orense, 1972) introduces Feijóo and his world, which can be further studied in Universidad de Oviedo, *El P. Feijóo y su siglo* (3 vols, Oviedo, 1966), a collection of conference papers. On the clerical Enlightenment, Antonio Mestre, *Ilustración y reforma de la Iglesia. Pensamiento político-religioso de don Gregorio Mayáns y Siscar (1699-1781)* (Valencia, 1968) contributes an interesting case study; see also the works of Saugnieux cited above. The radicalization of the Spanish Enlightenment is briefly discussed by Juan Marichal, 'From Pistoia to Cádiz: a Generation's Itinerary', in A. Owen Aldridge (ed.), *The Ibero-American Enlightenment* (University of Illinois, 1974), pp. 97–110, and in greater detail by Antonio Elorza, *La ideología liberal en la Ilustración española* (Madrid, 1970); see also the latter's *Pan y toros y otros papeles sediciosos de fines del siglo XVIII* (Madrid, 1971). Jovellanos can be approached through John H. R. Polt, *Gaspar Melchor de Jovellanos* (New York, 1971), and Cabarrús through José Antonio Maravall, 'Cabarrús y las ideas de reforma política y social en el siglo XVIII', *Revista de Occidente*, 6 (1968), pp. 273–300. On the press, one of the channels of Enlightenment, see Paul-J. Guinard, *La presse espagnole de 1737 a 1791* (Paris, 1973).

The Economic Societies have a substantial bibliography, beginning with Robert J. Shafer, *The Economic Societies in the Spanish World (1763-1821)* (Syracuse, NY, 1958), and continuing with Paula and Jorge Demerson and Francisco Aguilar Piñal, *Las Sociedades Económicas de Amigos del País en el siglo XVIII* (San Sebastian, 1974), a guide to research; Jorge Demerson, *La Real Sociedad económica de Valladolid (1784-1808)* (Valladolid, 1969), and *La Real Sociedad económica de amigos del país de*

Avila (1786-1857) (Avila, 1968); Paula and Jorge Demerson, 'La Sociedad Económica de amigos del país de Ciudad Rodrigo', *Cuadernos de Historia Moderna y Contemporánea*, 3 (1982), pp. 35–59; Lucienne Domergue, *Jovellanos et la Société Economique des Amis du Pays de Madrid (1778-1795)* (Toulouse, 1971). The economic thought of the period can also be studied in the works on Campomanes cited above, and in Robert S. Smith, '*The Wealth of Nations* in Spain and Hispanic America, 1780–1830', *Journal of Political Economy*, 65 (1957), pp. 104–25. The reception of Adam Smith in Spain is also one of the subjects of Javier Lasarte, *Economía y hacienda al final del Antiguo Régimen. Dos estudios* (Madrid, 1976). Ernest Lluch, *El pensamiento económico en Catalunya (1700-1840)* (Barcelona, 1973) studies the origins of protectionism in Catalan economic thought. The campaign to diffuse knowledge of modern agriculture is the subject of F. Díaz Rodríguez, *Prensa agraria en la España de la Ilustración. El Semanario de Agricultura y Artes dirigido a los párrocos (1797-1808)* (Madrid, 1980). Agrarian reform and other features of the Enlightenment occupy both the subject and the biographer in Marcelin Defourneaux, *Pablo de Olavide ou l'Afrancesado (1725-1803)* (Paris, 1959); on Olavide see also Francisco Aguilar Piñal, *La Sevilla de Olavide 1767-1778* (Seville, 1966).

Study of the Enlightenment in the universities can begin with Mariano Peset and José Luis Peset, *La Universidad Española (siglos XVIII y XIX)* (Madrid, 1974), and for individual universities continue with George M. Addy, *The Enlightenment in the University of Salamanca* (Durham, NC, 1966); Sondalio Rodríguez Domínguez, *Renacimiento universitario salmantino a finales del siglo XVIII. Ideología liberal del Dr. Ramón de Salas y Cortés* (Salamanca, 1979); Francisco Aguilar Piñal, *La Universidad de Sevilla en el siglo XVIII* (Seville, 1969). Luis Sala Balust, *Visitas y reforma de los colegios mayores de Salamanca en el reinado de Carlos III* (Salamanca, 1958) studies the indeterminate reform of the *colegios mayores*, and Antonio Alvarez de Morales, *La 'Ilustración' y la reforma de la universidad en la España del siglo XVIII* (Madrid, 1971) adds further detail on university reform. On medical reform see Michael E. Burke, *The Royal College of San Carlos. Surgery and Spanish Medical Reform in the Late Eighteenth Century* (Durham, NC, 1977).

The opposition to the Enlightenment was part intellectual, part repressive. On the former see Javier Herrero, *Los orígenes del pensamiento reaccionario español* (Madrid, 1971). The Inquisition in the eighteenth century has been investigated in Bartolomé Bennassar and others, *L'Inquisition espagnole (XVᵉ-XIXᵉ siècles)* (Paris, 1979), and by Antonio

Alvarez de Morales, *Inquisición e Ilustración (1700-1834)* (Madrid, 1982). The Inquisition's role in censorship is also the subject of Marcelin Defourneaux, *L'Inquisition espagnole et les livres français au XVIIIᵉ siècle* (Paris, 1963), a theme which is further explored by Lucienne Domergue, *Censure et lumières dans l'Espagne de Charles III* (Paris, 1983). C. C. Noel, 'The Clerical Confrontation with the Enlightenment in Spain', *European Studies Review*, 5, 2 (1975), pp. 103-22, deals with the ecclesiastical opposition.

Charles IV and the Crisis of the Old Regime

There are two accessible narrative sources for the period 1788-1808: Andrés Muriel, *Historia de Carlos IV* (*BAE*, 114-15, 2 vols, Madrid, 1959), and Príncipe de la Paz, *Memorias* (*BAE*, 88-9, 2 vols, Madrid, 1956), to each of which there is a useful introduction by Carlos Seco Serrano. To these may be added the works of Jovellanos cited above and the *Memorias* of Antonio Alcalá Galiano, in *Obras escogidas* (*BAE*, 83-4, 2 vols, Madrid, 1955). J. M. Blanco White, *Letters from Spain* (2nd edn, London, 1825) is entertaining as well as informative on the Spain of Godoy, as is Lady Holland, *Spanish Journal*, cited above. Carlos Pereyra (ed.), *Cartas confidenciales de la reina María Luisa y de don Manuel Godoy* (Madrid, 1935), throws some, though not startling, light on the queen and Godoy.

The political history of the reign can be approached through Carlos Corona, *Revolución y reacción en el reinado de Carlos IV* (Madrid, 1957). On Godoy Carlos Seco Serrano, *Godoy, el hombre y el político* (Madrid, 1978) displaces the older Jacques Chastenet, *Godoy, Master of Spain, 1792-1808* (London, 1953). The role of the prince of Asturias is described by Manuel Izquierdo Hernández, *Antecedentes y comienzos del reinado de Fernando VII* (Madrid, 1963). Francisco Martí, *El proceso de El Escorial* (Pamplona, 1965) gives a detailed account of the background and development of the Escorial conspiracy, and does the same for the *motín de Aranjuez*: Francisco Marti Gilabert, *El motín de Aranjuez* (Pamplona, 1972). For a structural framework see Miguel Artola, *Los orígenes de la España contemporánea* (2 vols, Madrid, 1959). On relations with France see André Fugier, *Napoléon et l'Espagne, 1799-1808* (2 vols, Paris, 1930).

The financial crisis is analysed by Josep Fontana, *La quiebra de la monarquía absoluta 1814-1820* (Barcelona, 1971), a key work in modern historiography, and in the same author's *Hacienda y estado en la crisis final del Antiguo Régimen español: 1823-1833* (Madrid, 1973); his *Cambio económico y actitudes políticas en la España del siglo XIX* (Barcelona, 1973) includes 'Formación del mercado nacional y toma de conciencia de la burguesía', pp. 11–53. Special aspects of the crisis are the subject of important articles by Richard Herr, 'Hacia el derrumbe del Antiguo Régimen: crisis fiscal y desamortización bajo Carlos IV', *Moneda y Crédito*, 118 (1971), pp. 37–100; Jacques Barbier, 'Peninsular Finance and Colonial Trade; the Dilemma of Charles IV's Spain', *JLAS*, 12 (1980), pp. 21–37; Jacques A. Barbier and Herbert S. Klein, 'Revolutionary Wars and Public Finances: the Madrid Treasury, 1784–1807', *Journal of Economic History*, 41 (1981), pp. 315–39; and Stanley J. Stein, 'Caribbean Counterpoint: Veracruz vs. Havana. War and Neutral Trade, 1797–1799', in J. Chase (ed.), *Géographie du capital marchand aux Amériques, 1760-1860* (Paris, 1987).

Spain and America

A basic bibliography will be found in Charles C. Griffin (ed.), *Latin America. A Guide to the Historical Literature* (Austin, Texas, 1971), and Francisco Morales Padrón (ed.), *Bibliografía básica sobre historia de América* (Seville, 1975). These can be supplemented by two periodical guides, *Handbook of Latin American Studies* (Gainesville, University of Florida Press), and *Historiografía y Bibliografía Americanistas* (Escuela de Estudios Hispanoamericanos, Seville).

Among general works, a number of recent examples may be mentioned: Leslie Bethell (ed.), *The Cambridge History of Latin America*, vols I and II (Cambridge, 1984); Luis Navarro García (ed.), *América en el siglo XVIII. Los primeros Borbones*, in *Historia general de España y América*, Tomo XI, vol. 1 (ed. Rialp, Madrid, 1983); Guillermo Céspedes del Castillo, *América Hispánica (1492-1898)*, in Manuel Tuñón de Lara (ed.), *Historia de España*, vol. VI (ed. Labor, Barcelona, 1983); and Tulio Halperín Donghi, *Reforma y disolución de los imperios ibéricos 1750-1850*, in Nicolás Sánchez-Albornoz (ed.), *Historia de América Latina*, III (Madrid, 1985). Nils Jacobsen and Hans-Jürgen Puhle (eds), *The Economies of Mexico and Peru during the Late Colonial Period, 1760-1810* (Berlin, 1986), is a combination of new research and state of the art.

The colonial economy has been studied in various contexts. Spanish thinking on colonial trade is the subject of Marcelo Bitar Letayf, *Economistas españoles del siglo XVIII. Sus ideas sobre la libertad del comercio con Indias* (Madrid, 1968). The internal market has been opened up by Carlos Sempat Assadourian, 'La producción de la mercancía dinero en la formación del mercado interno colonial. El caso del espacio peruano, siglo XVI', in Enrique Florescano (ed.), *Ensayos sobre el desarrollo económico de México y América Latina, 1500-1975* (Mexico, 1979) and *El sistema de la economía colonial. Mercado interno, regiones y espacio económico* (Lima, 1982); and by Juan Carlos Garavaglia, *Mercado interno y economía colonial* (Mexico, 1983). The transatlantic trade is the subject of basic new research: Lutgardo García Fuentes, *El comercio español con América, 1650-1700* (Seville, 1980), and 'En torno a la reactivación del comercio indiano en tiempos de Carlos II', *Anuario de Estudios Americanos*, 36 (1979), pp. 251–86; Antonio García-Baquero, *Cádiz y el Atlántico (1717-1778)* (2 vols, Seville, 1976); Carlos Daniel Malamud Rikles, *Cádiz y Saint Malo en el comercio colonial peruano (1698-1725)* (Cadiz, 1986); and Geoffrey J. Walker, *Spanish Politics and Imperial Trade, 1700-1789*, cited above. Between them these works provide a new history of the American trade up to the establishment of *comercio libre*. John Fisher, *Commercial Relations between Spain and Spanish America in the Era of Free Trade, 1778-1796* (Liverpool, 1985) takes up the story at that point and gives a precise measurement of trade under *comercio libre*, while its fate during the Anglo-Spanish wars is treated by Antonio García-Baquero, *Comercio colonial y guerras revolucionarias* (Seville, 1972), and Javier Ortiz de la Tabla Ducasse, *Comercio exterior de Veracruz 1778-1821* (Seville, 1978); on this subject see also the references to Barbier and Klein and to Stein under *Charles IV and the Crisis of the Old Regime*. The role of colonial trade in Spanish economic development is discussed in Nadal and Tortella (eds), *Agricultura, comercio colonial y crecimiento económica*, cited above. Jacques A. Barbier and Allan J. Kuethe (eds), *The North American Role in the Spanish Imperial Economy 1760-1819* (Manchester, 1984) deals with United States trade with Spanish America in the late colonial and early independence periods. Catalan trade with America has now been clarified thanks to the works of Carlos Martínez Shaw, *Cataluña en la carrera de Indias 1680-1756* (Barcelona, 1981), and Josep M. Delgado and others, *El comerć entre Catalunya i Amèrica (segles XVIII i XIX)* (Barcelona, 1986). On public and private income from America pride of place goes to Michel Morineau, *Incroyables gazettes et fabuleux métaux. Les retours des trésors américains d'après les gazettes hollandaises (XVIᵉ-XVIIIᵉ siècles)* (Cambridge, 1985), who has re-written the history of treasure returns.

Economic conditions in Spanish America can now be studied with the help of basic new research. The mining sector and its position in the socio-economic structure of Mexico are established by D. A. Brading, *Miners and Merchants in Bourbon Mexico 1763-1810* (Cambridge, 1971). Mining in Peru and Upper Peru are placed on the map of history by J. R. Fisher, *Silver Mines and Silver Miners in Colonial Peru, 1776-1824* (Liverpool, 1977), and Rose Marie Buechler, *The Mining Society of Potosí, 1776-1810* (Syracuse, NY, 1981). Enrique Tandeter, 'Forced and Free Labour in late Colonial Potosí', *Past and Present*, 93 (1981), pp. 98–136, demonstrates the importance of *mita* labour to the survival of Potosí production. Enrique Tandeter and Nathan Wachtel, *Precios y producción agraria. Potosí y Charcas en el siglo XVIII* (Buenos Aires, 1983) establish a price series for the eighteenth century and relate it to the economy of Upper Peru. Enrique Florescano, *Precios del maiz y crisis agrícolas en México (1708-1810)* (Mexico, 1969) examines rising maize prices, agrarian crisis and rural misery. For regional studies of the agrarian sector see D. A. Brading, *Haciendas and Ranchos in the Mexican Bajío: León 1700-1860* (Cambridge, 1978); Eric Van Young, *Hacienda and Market in Eighteenth-Century Mexico. The Rural Economy of Guadalajara, 1675-1820* (Berkeley and Los Angeles, Calif., 1981). Humberto Tandrón, *El real consulado de Caracas y el comercio exterior de Venezuela* (Caracas, 1976) illustrates the tension between colonial producers and Spanish merchants, while problems of another export economy and its hinterland are studied by Michael T. Hamerly, *Historia social y económica de la antigua provincia de Guayaquil, 1763-1842* (Guayaquil, 1973). Susan Migden Socolow, *The Merchants of Buenos Aires 1778-1810. Family and Commerce* (Cambridge, 1978) analyses the formation and interests of the *porteño* merchant group.

Imperial reorganization and American responses can be studied in Mark A. Burkholder and D. S. Chandler, *From Impotence to Authority. The Spanish Crown and the American Audiencias 1687-1808* (Columbia, Mo., 1977), which measures creole office-holding, and in John Lynch, *Spanish Colonial Administration, 1782-1810. The Intendant System in the Viceroyalty of the Río de la Plata* (London, 1958), Luis Navarro García, *Intendencias en Indias* (Seville, 1959), J. R. Fisher, *Government and Society in Colonial Peru. The Intendant System 1784-1814* (London, 1970), Brading, *Miners and Merchants*, cited above, Reinhard Liehr, *Ayuntamiento y oligarquía en Puebla, 1787-1810* (2 vols, Mexico, 1976), and Jacques A. Barbier, *Reform and Politics in Bourbon Chile, 1755-1796* (Ottawa, 1980), which establish the main lines of innovation. The attempt to abolish *repartimientos* is dealt with in Brian R. Hamnett,

Politics and Trade in Southern Mexico 1750-1821 (Cambridge, 1971), and in Stanley J. Stein, 'Bureaucracy and Business in the Spanish Empire, 1759–1804: Failure of a Bourbon Reform in Mexico and Peru', *HAHR*, 61, 1 (1981), pp. 2–28. Juan Marchena Fernández, *Oficiales y soldados en el ejército de América* (Seville, 1983) shows the 'Americanization' of the Spanish army in America, while military changes are precisely defined by Christon I. Archer, *The Army in Bourbon Mexico 1760-1810* (Albuquerque, NM, 1977), Leon G. Campbell, *The Military and Society in Colonial Peru 1750-1810* (Philadelphia, Pa., 1978), and Allan J. Kuethe, *Military Reform and Society in New Granada, 1773-1808* (Gainesville, Fla., 1978); in *Cuba, 1753-1815. Crown, Military, and Society* (Knoxville, Tenn., 1986) Allan J. Kuethe shows that concessions to local interests are the price paid for collaboration. The colonial bureaucracy is now subject to closer scrutiny than hitherto in Susan Migden Socolow, *The Bureaucrats of Buenos Aires, 1769-1810: Amor al Real Servicio* (Durham, NC, 1987). Clerical immunity and its erosion by the Bourbons are studied by Farris, *Crown and Clergy*, cited above, while the economic role of the Church is clarified by Arnold J. Bauer, 'The Church in the Economy of Spanish America: *Censos* and *Depósitos* in the Eighteenth and Nineteenth Centuries', *HAHR*, 63, 4 (1983), pp. 707–33; religious trends in Mexico are now identified by D. A. Brading, 'Tridentine Catholicism and Enlightened Despotism in Bourbon Mexico', *JLAS*, 15, 1 (1983), pp. 1–22.

Colonial finance and fiscal pressure are explored in their various aspects by D. A. Brading, 'Facts and Figments in Bourbon Mexico', *Bulletin of Latin American Research*, 4, 1 (1985), pp. 61–4; in the works of Barbier, and Barbier and Klein, cited above, as well as in Jacques A. Barbier, 'Towards a New Chronology of Bourbon Colonialism: The *Depositaria de Indias* of Cadiz, 1722–1789', *Ibero-Amerikanisches Archiv*, 6 (1980), pp. 335–53, and 'Venezuelan *Libranzas*, 1788–1807: From Economic Nostrum to Fiscal Imperative', *The Americas*, 37 (1981), pp. 457–78; and Josep Fontana, 'La crisis colonial en la crisis del antiguo régimen español', in Alberto Flores Galindo (ed.), *Independencia y revolución (1780-1840)* (2 vols, Lima, 1987), I, pp. 17–35. Further evidence of tax severity is available in W. Kendall Brown, *Bourbons and Brandy: Imperial Reform in Eighteenth-Century Arequipa* (Albuquerque, NM, 1986), and of fiscal pressure in Mexico in Juan Carlos Garavaglia and Juan Carlos Grosso, 'Estado borbónico y presión fiscal en la Nueva España, 1750–1821', in Antonio Annino and others (eds), *America Latina: Dallo Stato Coloniale allo Stato Nazione (1750-1940)* (2 vols, Milan,

1987), I, pp. 78–97. Statistics from which fiscal trends may be constructed are compiled by John J. TePaske and Herbert S. Klein, *The Royal Treasuries of the Spanish Empire in America* (3 vols, Durham, NC, 1982); see John J. TePaske, 'The Fiscal Structure of Upper Peru and the Financing of Empire', in Karen Spalding (ed.), *Essays in the Political, Economic and Social History of Colonial Latin America* (Newark, Del., 1982).

The reaction to taxation and other burdens has been studied in a number of works on the rebellions of the eighteenth century. Joseph Perez, *Los movimientos precursores de la emancipación en Hispanoamérica* (Madrid, 1977), identifies the major movements. Segundo Moreno Yáñez, *Sublevaciones indígenas en la Audiencia de Quito, desde comienzos del siglo XVIII hasta finales de la colonia* (Bonn, 1976), describes Indian protest in the region of Quito against a background of agrarian structure. Gilma Mora de Tovar, *Aguardiente y conflictos sociales en la Nueva Granada durante el siglo XVIII* (Bogotá, 1988) demonstrates popular protest against the *aguardiente* monopoly in New Granada. Anthony McFarlane, 'Civil Disorders and Popular Protests in Late Colonial New Granada', *HAHR*, 64, 1 (1984), pp. 17–54, interprets the numerous examples of popular protests, hitherto overshadowed by the *comunero* movement. On the latter see John Leddy Phelan, *The People and the King. The Comunero Revolution in Colombia, 1781* (Madison, Wis., 1978); Carlos E. Muñoz Oraá, *Los comuneros de Venezuela* (Mérida, 1971). Scarlett O'Phelan Godoy, *Rebellions and Revolts in Eighteenth Century Peru and Upper Peru* (Cologne, 1985) places the eighteenth-century protest movements in the colonial economic and fiscal structure and explores their culmination in the great rebellion of Tupac Amaru.

The study of social structure, which now tends to emphasize economic interests, social perceptions and political groupings rather than simply creole-peninsular conflict, can begin with David A. Brading, 'Government and Elite in Late Colonial Mexico', *HAHR*, 53, 3 (1973), pp. 389–414, and continue with Doris M. Ladd, *The Mexican Nobility at Independence 1780-1826* (Austin, Texas, 1976). Venezuelan structures are explained by Germán Carrera Damas, *La crisis de la sociedad colonial venezolana* (Caracas, 1976), and Miguel Izard, *El miedo a la revolución. La lucha por la libertad en Venezuela (1777-1830)* (Madrid, 1979). Alberto Flores Galindo, *Aristocracia y plebe, Lima 1760-1830* (Lima, 1984) studies the formation of a new ruling elite in Peru.

The influence of ideas has a large bibliography, to which a useful introduction is provided by José Carlos Chiaramonte (ed.), *Pensamiento de la Ilustración. Economía y sociedad iberoamericanas en el siglo XVIII* (Caracas, 1979), who gives a selection of primary texts, prefaced by a survey of the state of the art. The scientific expeditions can be identified in María de los Angeles Calatayud Arinero, *Catálogo de las expediciones y viajes científicos españoles a América y Filipinas (siglos XVIII y XIX)* (Madrid, 1984), and studied in Iris H. W. Engstrand, *Spanish Scientists in the New World: the Eighteenth-Century Expeditions* (Seattle, Wash., 1981). Groupe Interdisciplinaire de Recherche et de Documentation sur l'Amérique Latine, *L'Amérique espagnole à l'époque des lumières. Tradition-Innovation-Représentations* (Paris, 1987), a collection of conference papers, employs the term 'enlightenment' in a general sense and includes contributions on economic and social, as well as intellectual life.

Index

Abad y Lasierra, Agustín, bishop, 401
Abad y Lasierra, Manuel, inquisitor, 401
Academia de la Historia, Real, 256, 259
Acuña, Pedro de, 385
agriculture, 5, 199–205, 236–8, 409; agrarian
crises, 7, 117, 197, 208, 210, 211, 214, 236,
237, 263–4, 267, 375, 380, 410–11, 421;
agrarian policy, 114, 117, 118, 208–14, 377,
396–7; in America, 345, 364–5
Aix-la-Chapelle, peace of (1748), 157, 167
Alba, duke of, 160, 182–5, 190, 192–3, 231, 250
Alberoni, Julio: and Farnese, 75–6, 283; foreign
policy, 132–3; government, 77–80, 102, 128,
145; and Philip V, 68, 69
Alburquerque, duke of, 203
alcabala: in Spain, 61, 110, 111, 165, 168, 230,
250; in America, 342, 344–5, 346, 347
Alcalá Galiano, Antonio, 377, 398
Alcalá de Henares, 217; university of, 74, 101,
234–5, 285, 286
Algiers, 294–5, 308, 311–12, 321–2
Alicante, 409
Almadén, mercury mine, 219
Almansa, battle of, 31, 42
Altamira, counts of, 231, 406
Alvarez, Juan Manuel, uncle of Godoy, 385
Amat y Junient, Manuel de, viceroy of Peru,
340
Amelot, Michel-Jean, 31, 34, 47–51, 56, 59, 60,
62
America: army of, 342–4; autonomy, 13–15;
Bourbon succession, 52–4, 59–60, 336,
371–2; bureaucracy, 329–32; Church, 341–2;
colonial consensus, 332–6, 370–1; financial
offices, 333–4; Godoy and, 388;
immigration, 200, 365–6; inter-colonial
trade, 12, 351; rebellions, 345–7, 373; reform
of government, 336–41, 370–4; revenue,
344–5, 347–50; trade and navigation, 10–12,
15–16, 25–6, 142–54, 171–3, 192, 223–4,
351–60, 367–70, 375; treasure, 15, 17–19,
57–8, 110, 112, 138, 149–50, 154–6, 167,
172–3, 317, 324, 326, 351, 357–9, 369, 370,
404, 405, 415
Andalucía: American trade, 142, 223–4, 353;
economy and society, 5–6, 204–5, 211, 212,
221, 225, 237–8, 239, 313, 375, 412;
institutions, 106, 124, 306, 312; population,
196–7, 409; subsistence crises, 7, 32, 157,
238, 267, 411
Anson, Lord, 152
Aragon: economy, 205, 225; *fueros*, 2, 23, 39,
42, 48; intendant, 105, 211; Nueva Planta,
62, 63–4, 106, 299; *señorío*, 228–9; War of
Succession, 28, 32, 34–5, 39
Aragonese party, 292–7, 381, 405–6
Aranda, count of: ambassador to France,
294–5, 297–8, 300, 378; military reforms,
190; president of council of Castile, 242,
252, 253, 266, 280, 291–8; secretary of state,
381–2, 400; subsequent career, 383, 385,
393–4
Aranjuez: royal palace, 110, 158, 249, 263, 325,
418; *motín de Aranjuez*, 418–21
Arcos, duke of, 204, 250
Areche, José Antonio de, 337, 341
aristocracy, 2, 3–4, 38–41, 48, 50, 51–2, 60–1,
66, 192–3; and army, 123–4, 232, 310–11,
392, 393; under Charles IV, 381; and
Enlightenment, 258; land, 199–205, 211–12,
226–7, 230–3, 250, 306,
opposition, 84–5, 91–2, 184, 292–3, 405–6,
408; and riots of 1766, 265–6, 267–8; and
revolt of Aranjuez, 419–20; *señorío*, 227–30;
status and income, 226–7, 230–3, 250, 306,
418
army: under early Bourbons, 123–6, 175–6;
under later Bourbons, 292–3, 306–12, 382,
404, 420; in War of Succession, 27, 31; in

L